Expository Sermons on Revelation

Expository Sermons on Revelation

FIVE VOLUMES COMPLETE AND UNABRIDGED
IN ONE

VOLUME 1—REVELATION 1:1-19

by
W. A. CRISWELL, Ph.D.

ZONDERVAN
PUBLISHING HOUSE   OF THE ZONDERVAN CORPORATION
GRAND RAPIDS, MICHIGAN 49506

DEDICATION

To Dr. F. Leon Ware, God's beloved physician and faithful deacon,
whose philanthropy has made possible the distribution of these sermons
on the Revelation to untold thousands.

FOREWORD

These are sermons, not lectures. They were preached extemporaneously, not written out and read. They were delivered without notes, a way I have sought to preach throughout the years of my ministry. They were tape recorded as they were delivered and from these tapes they were reduced to writing, through secretarial help provided by Dr. F. Leon Ware. They have been corrected, grammatically, for publication, but outside of these necessary emendations, they are published exactly as they were delivered. I write these things because there is a vast, vast difference between a sermon preached in the heat and the fury of the burning pulpit hour, and a sermon written out in the calm, cool leisure of the pastor's study. The closing appeal is not included in the sermons, but each one was so closed and each one was blessed of God with a reward of many souls. A praying people gave them power and unction from heaven.

This series of sermons on the Revelation, closing seventeen years of preaching through the Bible, is being prepared and delivered now. Following this first published volume, we hope next year to publish the second, and so to continue until all the sermons on the Apocalypse have been printed. Our deepest gratitude is expressed to Mr. Pat Zondervan for his interest and for his encouragement in this endeavor. May the effort bless many, many lives. I could pray that other pastors and teachers will take the material and use it for the glory of our living Lord.

As with my previous books, Mrs. B. B. Binford has generously given of her time in reading the manuscript and in offering invaluable suggestions. And as with my other books, Mrs. Bailey Forester has faithfully typed the sermons and has prepared them for publication. Thank you both for a kindness that has helped me immeasurably.

And now may God bless the eyes that look upon these pages. We possess the perfect assurance that victory belongeth to the Lord. The down-look and the out-look may be dark, but the up-look is bright with the glory of the coming of the Eternal Christ, whom John saw on the Isle of Patmos and whom Charles Wesley by faith saw in his song:

> . . . . with clouds descending
> Once for favored sinners slain;
> Thousand thousand saints attending
> Swell the triumph of His train.
> Alleluia, Alleluia!
> God appears on earth to reign.
>
> Every eye shall now behold Him,
> Robed in splendor's majesty;
> Those who set at naught and sold Him,
> Pierced and nailed Him to the tree,
> Deeply wailing, deeply wailing,
> Shall the true Messiah appear.
>
> Now the Saviour, long expected,
> See, in solemn pomp appear.
> All who have not Him rejected
> Now shall meet Him in the air.
> Alleluia, Alleluia!
> See the day of God appear.
>
> Yea, amen, let all adore Thee,
> High on thine eternal throne:
> Saviour, take the power and glory
> Claim the kingdom for Thine own:
> Oh, come quickly, oh, come quickly,
> Everlasting God, come down.

— W. A. CRISWELL

Pastor's Study
First Baptist Church
Dallas, Texas

TABLE OF CONTENTS

Expository Sermons on Revelation

Volume 1—Revelation 1:1-19

THE VISION OF THE APOCALYPSE

The Revelation of Jesus Christ, which God gave unto him, to show unto his servants things which must shortly come to pass; and he sent and signified it by his angel unto his servant John. — Revelation 1:1

After fifteen years of preaching through the Bible, beginning at the first verse of the first chapter of Genesis, we have now come to the last and the climactic book, the Revelation of Jesus Christ. This is the Apocalypse, the unveiling, the uncovering, the manifestation, the presentation of Jesus Christ. We shall be preaching a long time through this book; at least two years, maybe longer. It is a book in which all things in the Bible find an echo and a reverberation. It delineates the consummation of the age. It is the great goal toward which all of the plans and purposes of God in history reach. It touches things in heaven, things in earth, and things under the earth. It speaks of Christ and of angels and of demons; of war in heaven and Armageddon on earth; of the judgments of God and the pouring out of the bowls and vials of wrath; of the sounding of the trumpets and the breaking of the seals. It speaks of the new heaven and the new earth. It announces the destruction of the grave and of death and of hell and of all the enemies of Christ. No other book in the Bible has such circumference and height and depth as does the Apocalypse of Jesus Christ. It describes the great consummation of the age, and we are in that plan and that program and that

13

unfolding now. We are involved in it. It is a part of our life and ultimately a part of our destiny. When we read the book of Revelation, we read about ourselves. When we scan the vistas of the ages in this book, we are looking at the destiny of our own souls. It is not something far off; the time is at hand. It concerns us.

This message is taken from the first three words of the book, "Apokalupsis Iesou Christou." "The Apocalypse, the Revelation, the unveiling, the presentation of Jesus, the Christ." That word "Apokalupsis" is compounded from a verb and a preposition. "Apo" means "away from." "Kalupto" means "to cover, to hide." "Apokalupsis," therefore, means "to take away the covering," "to unveil," "to reveal." It is a word used in classical Greek. Herodotus uses it to refer to the uncovering of the head. Plato uses it in a request, "Apokalupto . . . Reveal unto me the power of rhetoric." Plutarch uses it referring to uncovering of error. The only time it is used religiously is in this book of the Bible, and it has here that same distinctive meaning. "Apokalupsis Iesou Christou" is the unveiling, the uncovering, the presentation in majesty and in glory of our Lord Jesus Christ.

"Apokalupsis Iesou Christou" is an objective genitive: the Apokalupsis, the Revelation, of Jesus Christ. There are two kinds of genitives, a subjective genitive and an objective genitive. To illustrate a subjective genitive, one could refer to "the words of Jesus Christ." They are *His* words; He spoke them; they belong to Him. They are the words of Jesus, and therefore a subjective genitive. To illustrate an objective genitive, one could refer to "the death of Jesus Christ." He experienced mortality — death. It is thus with this phrase, "The Revelation of Jesus Christ." It is Christ who experiences the unveiling, the manifestation. It is our Lord who is uncovered and presented in all of His glory and majesty.

THE UNVEILING OF CHRIST

The only "Apokalupsis" of our Lord that we read in the Bible is the appearing or the manifestation of our Saviour. For example, in I Corinthians 1:7 it says: "Waiting for *the Apokalupsis Iesou Christou.*" We see here the exact sentence structure and the exact words, "Waiting for the coming of our Lord Jesus Christ." No one mistakes these words. The "Apokalupsis" of our Lord is the unveiling of our Saviour; "waiting for *the Apokalupsis,*" the presentation, the appearance, the coming of our Lord Jesus Christ. Another instance of those same words (in the English translation it does not appear, but the identical words are used in the Greek) is in II Thessalonians 1:7, 10a, "And to you who are troubled rest with us, when the Lord Jesus shall be revealed from heaven with his mighty angels, . . . When he shall come to be glorified in his saints, and to be admired in all them that believe." Those are the same words again, the "Apokalupsis Iesou Christou." "When he shall come," equals "when he shall be revealed from heaven. . . ." The "Apokalupsis Iesou Christou" is the Revelation of Jesus Christ in His glorious coming and appearance. Another instance of the phrase is found in I Peter 1:7, "That the trial of your faith, being much more precious than of gold that perisheth, though it be tried with fire, might be found unto praise and honor and glory at the appearing of Jesus Christ." There are those same words again, "at the *Apokalupsis Iesou Christou,*" "at the appearing of Jesus Christ." No one doubts the meaning of those words. They refer to the great unveiling and the presentation of our Lord from glory. I cite one other example in Galatians 1:12. Paul writes: "For I neither received it of man, neither was I taught it, but by the revelation of Jesus Christ." There are those words again, "Apokalupsis Iesou Christou." At first appearance it might seem that this is a revelation concerning our Lord, a communication about our Lord, but immediately in the verses that follow, Paul writes what he means. He describes the appearance of Jesus to him on the Damascus road and he calls that appearance an "Apokalupsis Iesou Christou," the Revelation, the Apocalypse, of Jesus Christ. Paul saw the Lord Himself in glory, above the brightness of the sun, when he met Him and saw Him face to face on the Damascus road.

So, when we come to the title of the Book, we come to the key of its content. The Apocalypse of Jesus Christ is not a communicative message about Him, concerning Him, but it is the actual presentation of our Lord Himself. This is the uncovering, the unveiling, the manifestation of the incomparably glorious Son of God, Himself. When we read the Revelation, the Apocalypse, we see, before the time, those judgments and appearances that someday our very eyes shall look upon.

The title of the Book, the Revelation of Jesus Christ, is the summation of its contents. It is the same as the text and the theme of the Book found in the seventh verse of this first chapter, "Behold, he cometh with clouds; and every eye shall see him, . . ." This is the Revelation, the appearance, the manifestation of the Son of God with clouds of glory, in great majesty and power.

The first time our Lord came into this world, He came in the veil of our flesh. His deity was covered over with His manhood. His Godhead was hidden by His humanity. Just once in a while did His deity shine through, as on the Mount of Transfiguration, or as in His miraculous works. But most of the time the glory, the majesty, the deity, the wonder and the marvel of the Son of God, the second person of the Holy Trinity, were veiled. These attributes were covered over in flesh, in our humanity. He was born in a stable. He grew up in poverty. He knew what it was to hunger and to thirst. He was buffeted and beaten and bruised. He was crucified and raised up as a felon before the scoffing

gaze of the whole earth. The last time that this world saw
Jesus was when it saw Him hanging in shame, misery and
anguish upon the cross. He later appeared to a few of His
believing disciples, but the last time that this unbelieving
world ever saw Jesus was when it saw Him die as a malefactor, as a criminal, crucified on a Roman cross. That was
a part of the plan of God, a part of the immeasurable, illimitable grace and love of our Lord. "By His stripes we are
healed."

But then is that all the world is ever to see of our Saviour
— dying in shame on a cross? No! It is also a part of the
plan of God that some day this unbelieving, this blaspheming, this godless world shall see the Son of God in His full
character, in glory, in majesty, in the full-orbed wonder and
marvel of His Godhead. Then all men shall look upon Him
as He really is. They shall see Him holding in His hands
the title-deed to the Universe, holding in His hands the
authority of all creation in the universe above us, in the
universe around us, and in the universe beneath us; holding
this world and its destiny in His pierced and loving hands.

THE REWARD GIVEN FROM GOD

Notice the words of the text, "which God gave unto
him." God has in covenant made a promise to our Lord
Jesus because of His acceptance of the mediatorial office of
atonement. Because Christ humbled Himself, because He
poured out His life unto death, because He became flesh
and blood and suffered for the sins of the world, God has
given Him a great reward. Look at the text: "The Apokalupsis, the Revelation, the unveiling of Jesus Christ which
God gave unto Him." Because our Lord humbled Himself
and suffered for our sins, God in covenant has declared that
He will exalt our Saviour above all principalities, above all
powers, above all authorities. In His Son's pierced and suffering hands God has promised that He will place the des-

tiny of this universe, both now and in the ages that are to come. This Apocalypse, this unveiling is something that God has given to Jesus Christ by way of an infinitely precious and marvelous reward. A part of that reward, an earnest of that glory, we can see when God raised our Saviour from among the dead, when He received Him up into glory. But that is just a part, it is just an earnest. The fulness and the glory of that reward are to be seen in the pages of the Revelation. This is what God has given to His Son, our Saviour, the Lord Jesus — this glorious appearing in wonder, in majesty and in glory.

This can be likened to the kind of recognition that the Roman Senate voted to a great military hero, like Pompey or Julius Caesar or Titus. When he had finished his great commission and had come back to the eternal city, there the hero was honored in glory for a Roman triumph. It was a reward to the military genius for what he had wrought for the Roman Empire. In like manner, on a spiritual level, the Lord God in covenant shall exalt Jesus Christ. Because Jesus has done this, has suffered for our sins, humbled Himself and bowed and died for our iniquities, God has promised that Jesus Christ shall be exalted, raised high and lifted up. How meaningful this passage from Philippians 2:6-10, "Jesus Christ, who, being in the form of God, thought it not robbery to be equal with God: but made himself of no reputation, and took upon him the form of a servant, and was made in the likeness of men: and being found in fashion as a man, he humbled himself, and became obedient unto death, even the death of the cross"! Down and down and down until He was buried in the heart of the earth. "Wherefore God also hath highly exalted him, and given him a name which is above every name: that at the name of Jesus every knee should bow, of things in heaven, . . . of things in earth [every blaspheming man shall bow] . . . and things under the earth [the devil and his angels and the

demons shall surrender their power in His presence] . . .
And that every tongue should confess that Jesus Christ is
Lord, to the glory of God the Father." And the day of that
bowing, the day of that confessing, the day of that exaltation, we find in the pages of the "Apokalupsis Iesou Christou," the day of the Revelation, the uncovering, the presentation of Jesus Christ in His glory.

THE SYMBOLS OF THE BOOK

And now, let us look at this word, "signified." Let us pronounce it as it is spelled, *sign*-ified. The angel referred
to in the passage in a way we cannot understand was the
intermediary between the senses of John and those great
Apocalypses of the future. The angel was able to pass
before the eyes and in the presence and hearing of John the
apostle these things that are yet to come. John saw them;
they were signified; they were *sign*-ified. John saw them
by signs and symbols. How that was done, I say, we cannot understand. It is the same kind of thing that Satan did
for Jesus when he took our Lord up on a high mountain
and showed Him all the kingdoms of the world and the
glory of them, in a moment, in the twinkling of an eye. How
Satan could do that I cannot understand, but it is the same
kind of thing that the angel did for John here. He caused
to pass before John's eyes, where the apostle could see it,
all of these things that are to come in the future years and
generations and ages that are to follow. "And he sent and
sign-ified it by his angel unto his servant John."

The symbols in that *"sign*-ified" Apocalypse represent
many different things. For example, the book symbolizes
and portrays things seen and unseen, things corporeal and
incorporeal, things of this world and things of the world
that is yet to come. It portrays angels and demons and
powers and principalities in the heavenlies. It also portrays
agents and nations and potentates here below. Sometimes

these symbols are of persons. In the first chapter of the book of the Revelation we see Jesus as a Judge. In the description John says that out of His mouth went a sharp, two-edged sword. No man ever wielded a two-edged sword out of his mouth. It is a symbol of something. The antichrist is symbolized as a beast. Sometimes the symbols are of things, as the meaning of the city of Babylon. Sometimes the symbols are of great political or religious movements, as the scarlet woman, in chapter 17, symbolizing the development in history of the Roman religion. All of these symbols have a great meaning. Many times they are explained. For example, in the last verse of the first chapter, "the seven stars are the seven angels of the seven churches" and "the seven candlesticks which thou sawest are the seven churches."

Where they are not explained, usually we can find their meaning in the apocalyptic and in the prophetic words of the Old Testament. Though he never quotes from the Old Testament directly, John reflects the prophetic language and visions of the books of the Old Testament. When we see the symbols and the signs and the pictures in the Revelation, we can go back to the Old Testament and find their meaning. For example, in the fifth chapter of the book of the Revelation and the sixth verse, he says: "And I beheld . . . in the midst of the elders, stood a Lamb as it had been slain." The Greek word for "slain," "sphizo," is the word used of the sacrificial knife. John saw a lamb, as it had been, slain in the sacrifice. When I go back to the Old Testament, I read there of the lamb of the sacrifice. The writer is talking about the atoning Christ. The sign and symbol of our dear Saviour is the sacrificial Lamb.

An example of the use of other symbols can be found in the fourth chapter of the book. Look at the third verse: "And he that sat was to look upon like a jasper and a sardine stone. . . ." The jasper is our diamond and the sardine stone is our ruby. ". . . And there was a rainbow round about the throne, in sight like unto an emerald." The diamond represents holiness and purity and crystal clearness. The ruby, with its red bloodstain, represents atonement. The rainbow represents our covenant-keeping God. The emerald is green, the color of living things, referring to our living hope. Further on in the passage, in verse 4 and in verses 6-9, "the four beasts" are presented. They are the cherubim of Ezekiel. And thus the symbolism continues through the whole Revelation. We can usually find in the Scriptures the meaning of the words and what we cannot understand we shall await in glorious anticipation until that full and final and consummating day when God will make it plain.

So we begin, and may the Lord bless us and lead us in the way.

Sermon 2

FOR THE TIME IS AT HAND

> The Revelation of Jesus Christ, which God gave unto him, to show unto his servants things which must shortly come to pass; and he sent and signified it by his angel unto his servant John: who bare record of the word of God, and of the testimony of Jesus Christ, and of all things that he saw. Blessed is he that readeth, and they that hear the words of this prophecy, and keep those things which are written therein: for the time is at hand. — Revelation 1:1-3

In this introductory word to the vast Apocalypse there are two indications of time. The first verse mentions "the things which must shortly come to pass." The third verse says, "Blessed is he that readeth, and they that hear [God blesses the lector that reads, and God blesses the people who listen and who treasure up these things which are written] . . . for the time is at hand." Now what do those words mean, and what is the reference here as to the fulfillment of this great, extended prophecy of twenty-two chapters, "things which must shortly come to pass" and "for the time is at hand"? In answering that question — when these things are to come to pass, and when this prophecy is to be fulfilled — you can group almost every presentation, persuasion, idea, and theory under about four headings. No matter what, how or when one may write, when he seeks to interpret the Book of Revelation, he may be placed in one of four general groups, concerning the time when these things are to come to pass.

22

The Preterist Interpretation

The First Group. There is and has been through the years a great group of interpreters who think that all of these things spoken of in the book of the Revelation have been fulfilled centuries ago. They are called Preterists. The word "preterist" is taken from a Latin word, "praeter," meaning "past." So the Preterists are those who look upon the Revelation as having already been fulfilled in the years and generations that are past.

They, in turn, are usually classified under two headings. First, the Neronian group. They are those who believe that all of these prophecies were fulfilled in the days of the Roman Caesar Nero, who reigned from A.D. 54 to 68, and under whose reign Simon Peter and the Apostle Paul and others of whom we do not know were martyred. Nero was the first one who largely persecuted the Church. He did it because when Rome burned, he needed a culprit upon whom to lay the blame. He accused these new Christians of having done it. The angry mobs burned the followers of Christ as torches on the streets at night, while Nero furiously drove his chariot through the boulevards of the city. All of these things are familiar to you.

The second group of Preterists, who believe that the Revelation was fulfilled in the ages past, are Domitianists. They believe that the Apocalypse was written in the days of the Roman Caesar Domitian, who reigned from A.D. 81 to 96, and that the book was fulfilled in his time. They say that the two beasts in Revelation 13 are first, Nero, and second, Domitian. Those are the two emperors who, in the first Christian century, largely persecuted the Christian Church.

The people who hold the Preterist view, that all of the Revelation was fulfilled in the days past, are mostly Roman Catholic interpreters. The reason that they do so is this: In the seventeenth chapter of the book of the Revelation, there is a harlot called the great whore. She is described as a scarlet woman. She is interpreted by the author of the Revelation as being a false system of religion, the seat of which is on a city built on seven hills and whose spiritual, mystery name is Babylon. There is no doubt that the seventeenth chapter of the book of the Revelation, in describing the great whore, refers to a system of religion that is an affront to God and whose seat is on a city that is built on seven hills. Now the city that has been known in antiquity and through history as being built on seven hills is the city of Rome. In other words, the seventeenth chapter of the book of the Revelation (as we shall see when we come to it) plainly describes Roman religion. In order to obviate that plain interpretation, Roman Catholic theologians invented the Preterist interpretation of the Revelation, saying that all of these prophecies were fulfilled in the days of Nero or in the days of Domitian, or within the first few centuries thereafter, and that it has nothing at all to do with things that are yet to come. What they do to the book of the Revelation is this: They make it a literary curiosity and that is all. It has no meaning for us; it has no message for today. They make it a strange document, written in an apocalyptic language that was in conventional use in the days when the Jewish people wrote this kind of literature. According to the Preterist view of the Revelation, maybe it had a message for those who lived in the days of Nero or Domitian, but it has no message for us today. It is just like any other relic of antiquity: a thing to be looked at, to be classified, to be put in a museum somewhere, to be given a number and to be forgotten. Such is the first one of these interpretations, the Preterist.

The Historically Continuous Interpretation

The Second Group. There is a large number of interpreters of the Revelation who look upon these prophecies as being historically continuous. That is, they believe that the Revelation is a panorama of the history of the Church and the history of the world from the apostolic days until the consummation of the age. They see the history of the world pre-written in all of these symbols and signs and apocalyptic visions. They see the rise of the Papacy, the corruption of the Church, the invasion of the Saracens, the great Reformation, the struggle with the Papacy and all the stories of humanity and of the nations of the world until the Lord shall come again.

The men who largely espoused this continuous historical interpretation of the book are the great Reformers — the Reformation men. They saw in the Revelation the rise of the Papacy, and they saw in the destruction of Babylon the destruction of the Papacy. In the first beast that arose out of the sea, in the thirteenth chapter of the book of the Revelation, they saw the political power by which the Roman Church was sustained; and in the second beast in Revelation 13 they saw that ecclesiastical tyranny itself. So in interpreting the book of the Revelation, the Reformers saw in it the story of humanity, and they identified different things in the book as being great historical incidents and events.

Dr. Joseph Angus, in writing on this historical theory, said: "It would be wrong to ridicule the mistakes and contradictions of the interpreters whose solemn pursuit was that of truth, in their calculations of times and seasons and their interpretations of apocalyptic symbols. But, in the fact that authorities of such reputation as Bengel, Wordsworth, Elliott and others are at hopeless variance, this system breaks down. Where one interpreter (Elliott) sees in the sixth seal a reference to Constantine, another (Faber) sees allusion to the first French revolution. Where one sees in the star fallen from heaven a good angel (Bengel), another (Elliott) discerns Mohammed. The scorpion-locusts that have power for five months mean to Mede one hundred and fifty years of the domination of the Saracens, but to Vitringa they mean the Goths, and to Scherzer the Jesuits. All this seems to be arbitrary and hazardous in the extreme." And with that judgment I agree. When you seek to make the book of the Revelation a panorama of prewritten history, and you seek to identify in the book all of the great historical events that have happened, you are going to fall into hopeless contradiction. No man can solve this successfully, and I do not think the historical interpretation of the book can be defended. Though there are able interpreters who present it ingeniously and make it sound very plausible in many ways, I do not think that the historical interpretation is of God.

THE SPIRITUALIZING SCHOOL OF INTERPRETATION

Now, *the third great group* of interpreters. There are many who are spiritualizers; they are sometimes called Idealists. They interpret the book of the Revelation as being not a representation of actual things and events that are past or that are going to come to pass, but as being a symbol and metaphor of the great struggle between good and evil. What they believe is that the book of the Revelation contains not a prophecy or a record of events or occurrences or happenings but the great moral implications that lie back of the events and happenings that go on in this world. Here are depicted, according to them, a struggle between the forces of good and the forces of evil and the ultimate triumph of that which is good.

Of all of the theories and interpretations of the book of the Revelation, I like this one the least. To begin with, I do not like spiritualizing the Bible. I think we ought to accept the Book for what it says and for what it means, and deliver its message, whether we understand it or not, whether we are able to see it all or not. If God says it, I believe it and that settles it. To take the Word of God and spiritualize it means to empty it of all its content. It can be made to mean just what anyone in any particular time might want to make it mean. That prince of preachers, Charles Haddon Spurgeon, was keen and witty. There once came to him a critic who wanted to catch Spurgeon in his words. This man went up to the great preacher with an open Bible in his hand, and pointing to a difficult passage, said, "Here now, tell me what that means." Spurgeon, with a twinkle in his eye, said, "Why, sir, I can tell you exactly what that means. It means exactly what it says." That is a fine, and to me, a brilliant answer. What do these things mean? They mean what they say. If God did not mean what He said, why did He not say what He meant? I do not like spiritualizing the Word of God. I think the man of God ought to stand in the pulpit with the open Book and tell the people what God has said. This is the word that is written, and this is the thing that God has revealed.

Before discussing the fourth group, let us recapitulate. We have spoken of the Preterists, those who believe that everything in the Revelation was fulfilled centuries ago, that it had a meaning to the people to whom it was written, but that it has no meaning to us today. They assume that the ancients had a key to the book, but that we have lost the key and do not have any idea what it means. Then we have spoken of the Historicists, with their continuous historical theory, interpreters who make of the Revelation a blueprint of history through the coming ages. Then we have spoken of a third group, the spiritualizers, the Idealists, those who look upon the book as having no meaning at all in time or in history, but who see in it merely a symbolic panorama of the conflict between good and evil. They view it just as an allegory.

THE FUTURIST SCHOOL OF INTERPRETATION

Now we come to *the fourth group,* and I belong to this fourth school. Here, to me, is the meaning of the Revelation. Members of this group are called Futurists; that is, they believe that, beginning at the fourth chapter of the book of the Revelation, an apocalypse of the consummation of the ages is described. Here is a description of the coming of our Lord and a presentation of Jesus as the ruler of the world. In these chapters, we look upon Him when He comes in power and great glory. We see Him establish His Kingdom in the earth. We behold Him binding Satan with an iron chain. In this interpretation, we follow in the Revelation the things that lead up to that great, final consummation, the establishment of the kingdom of our Lord in the earth. And finally we have a record of the new heaven and the new earth and the new Jerusalem and our eternal home with God. This is why I believe this is the true interpretation of the Revelation of God.

First, most of the things that are written in the book of the Revelation have never been fulfilled. They are still to be seen, they are still to come to pass. For example, there has never been in the story of history or of humanity such terrors and such judgments as you find recorded in the book of the Revelation. There has never been anything known to compare to the terrible judgments depicted in the Apocalypse. Even the destruction of Jerusalem, with all its blood and its horror, is nothing compared to the great worldwide judgments that are to fall upon the human family and the human race in this great Apocalypse written by John.

Another thing: The Revelation speaks of resurrections that are yet to come to pass. God's people are going to be raised from the dead. They are going to be given a part in the Kingdom of Jesus. God's saints are going to be with Him at the Marriage Supper of the Lamb. The wicked dead are going to stand at the White Throne Judgment of God to be judged according to their works and to be sent into eternal perdition to suffer for those things evil that they have done in the earth.

Go out to any cemetery and see if the dead have been raised. They are still in their graves. When I go to California, I visit the grave of my father. There his body lies in the dust of the ground, but this book says that some day our beloved dead are going to be raised to live in the sight of our Lord and to reign with Him forever and ever. But my father still sleeps in the dust of the ground. These things are in the future. They have not come to pass. There is not any new heaven, there is not any new earth, and there is not any new Jerusalem.

To my amazement, I have listened to interpreters who tell me that we are in the millennium now. My soul, my soul, if this is the millennium with all of the death and misery and heartache and tears and sufferings and war and fear and terror that we know in this present world, and if this is the binding of Satan, then words do not mean what they say, and God is not God, and there is no hope for us now or ever. To me, these great things are yet to come.

Our dead are going to be raised, but they are not raised yet. We are going to live in His sight, but we are still under this bondage and sentence of death. God is going to give us a new home, a new body and a new life which our very eyes shall see. We shall look upon it ourselves, yes, as Job cried, "And though after my skin worms destroy this body, yet in my flesh shall I see God: Whom I shall see for myself, and mine eyes shall behold, and not another . . ." (Job 19:26-27). These eyes shall look upon our Lord and these hands shall some day touch Him. All of these things are future.

The prophetic utterances in the Revelation correspond to those in the rest of the Bible. The book of the Revelation says that before the consummating day of our Lord there are to be unprecedented trials and troubles and tribulations. All the other Scriptures avow the same thing. In fact, the Scriptures say that those very trials and troubles precipitate the intervention of God. For example, our Lord Himself says, "For then shall be great tribulation, such as was not since the beginning of the world to this time, no, nor ever shall be. And except those days should be shortened, there should no flesh be saved." He also says: "Immediately after the tribulation of those days shall the sun be darkened, and the moon shall not give her light, and the stars shall fall from heaven, and the powers of the heavens shall be shaken: And then shall appear the sign of the Son of man in heaven: and then shall all the tribes of the earth mourn, and they shall see the Son of man coming in the clouds of heaven with power and great glory." That is what Jesus said in Matthew 24. That is exactly what is written in the Revelation.

Take again another typical instance. In the second chapter of the second Thessalonian letter: "Let no man deceive you by any means: for that day shall not come, except there come a falling away first, and that man of sin be revealed, the son of perdition; who opposeth and exalteth himself above all that is called God, or that is worshiped; so that he as God sitteth in the temple of God, shewing himself that he is God. Remember ye not, that, when I was yet with you, I told you these things? . . . For the mystery of iniquity doth already work." Paul says that we are in this consummation now, only there is someone or something that hinders, that restrains; but someday that restraint will be taken away, and then shall that evil one be revealed whose coming is after the working of Satan, with Satan's power and signs and lying wonders and deceitfulness. This same prediction is a part of the Revelation. The apocryphal matter found elsewhere in the Word of God is found in detail, revealed in the Revelation. II Timothy 3:1 says, "This know also, that in the last days perilous times shall come." The Revelation predicts the same thing. These things are all future. They are yet to come to pass and, when they come, it means the consummation of the age. That is the first reason why I am a Futurist, because these things have not yet happened. They are yet to come to pass.

Now, I have a second reason for believing in the futurist method of interpretation. Look at the text carefully. "Blessed is he that readeth, and they that hear the words of this prophecy." This book that John has written is a "prophecy." It is something that is going to come to pass. We have here delineated the great trends of politics and of government in the future. The Revelation says that the inevitable movement of political power will be toward one great government. Then it points out another thing, that the tremendous movement of religion will be toward one great religion, headed up in one ecclesiastical leader that the Revelator calls the false prophet. All of these words are given here by prophecy; that is, John is foretelling these events that are going to come to pass when the consummation of the age reaches it apex.

The text says that the angel "signified" these things to John. A sign tells you how you are coming along, tells you about the road. As I go down the road, there are signs which say "curve" here, or "railroad crossing" there. So these signs in the Revelation are for the comfort and the encouragement of God's people as we go along the road of history stretching out before us. God has revealed these things to us in order that we might know them, and in the midst of darkness or disaster or wars or tribulations or trials, that we might lift up our faces and rejoice, for our "redemption draweth nigh."

The Meaning of the Prophecy to the Asian Churches and to Us

There are those who say that the words of the Revelation could have been of no help and of no comfort to the people to whom they were addressed (the seven churches of

Asia) unless John meant that the things he wrote were to come to pass immediately. These interpreters deny the Futurist position, on the basis of the preconception that everything written in the book had to be fulfilled in the understanding and in the lifetime of those who read it. "For how else," they say, "could the prophecy have had any meaning to these sorrowing spirits?" Is this true, that John wrote these visions with the thought that the prophecies applied only to the Christian who lived in that trying day? "For the time is at hand." What does that mean?

These above-mentioned critics object to any persuasion except that these words apply just to those people who lived in the days of the seven churches of Asia, and that all of the prophecy was fulfilled in their day. These persons insist that it concerns us not at all. For example, one of the present-day authorities on the Revelation writes in objection to the belief of the Futurists, that "It [the Futurists' belief] is inconsistent with the statement made by John that the events predicted were to come to pass soon." He notices the Greek word "dei" in the belief that, "these things must (dei) come to pass immediately." Then he goes on with the second Greek phrase, "en tachei," to say: "The second Greek term we are interested in is the phrase 'en tachei' which is translated 'quickly or shortly.'" (Remember, now, that the Futurists, those, of which I am one, who believe that the Revelation applies to us and to all the ages, hold that this is a term which means *certainty* rather than *soon* in a temporal sense. But I want you to look at this as I quote from the Professor.) "Paul hardly uses it this way when he says to Timothy in II Timothy 4:9: 'Be diligent to come unto me quickly' (tacheos). We can almost hear him say, according to the Futurists, (the people who believe that the prophecy is yet to come), 'Timothy, I want you to come to me here in Rome. Bring the coat I left with Carpus. I am cold and need it, but there is no hurry — just

On looking further, we see the apostle Paul, in Romans
16:20, encouraging the persecuted church at Rome, saying,
"And . . . God . . . shall bruise Satan under your feet *en
tachei*." That word is translated here exactly as it is in the
Revelation — "shortly." But Satan is not yet bruised under
God's feet, and it was two thousand years ago when Paul
wrote that. Paul is referring to the promise made in Eden,
"God shall bruise Satan under your feet shortly," "en tachei,"
and thus seeks to hearten the saints in the certainty of the
promise of God, although it is long in fulfillment.

Just one other instance is found in the parable of the
unjust judge. Jesus said in Luke 18:7: "And shall not God
avenge his own elect, which cry day and night unto him,
though he bear long with them? I tell you that he will
avenge them *en tachei*," translated here "speedily." "Nevertheless when the Son of man cometh, shall he find faith on
the earth?" Plainly, our Lord indicates here it is going to
be a long delay, so long that the people will begin to believe
He is not going to keep His word.

What has God said in those words written one thousand
eight hundred and some odd years ago, in these great
prophetic revelations which have not yet been fulfilled?
What is the meaning of "en tachei" translated "shortly," and
"eggus," "for the time is *at hand*"? It is very plain what He
means. First, the words contain the element of certainty.
These things must come to pass certainly. Not a syllable
of this prophecy will fall to the ground. It will assuredly
come. It may delay, it may be a long time, but every
prophecy of God will come to pass assuredly and certainly.
That is one meaning.

Second, there is the idea of speed. Some of these things
are already coming to pass. Some of these things, and most
of them, when they begin to come to pass, will come to pass
"en tachei," "speedily." The thing will be done as Babylon
will be destroyed, in an hour. Speedily, these things will

so you get here in the next two or three thou
need those scripture scrolls I left there. Bring
read them. There are some passages I want to
in the next millennium or two. I want to see y
know how long I can hold out, so come in th
thousand years (tacheos). Any time will be all ri
bile dictu! But this is not more absurd than to take
tion that the phrase in Revelation 1:1 means 'cer
fulfillment,' rather than a speedy fulfillment. Here
saying to the suffering, persecuted Christians of Asia
'That's all right. Don't be disturbed. After a few th
years, the nations will gather together for a great ba
the valley of Megiddo and when it is all over, God w
up an earthly kingdom and reign with His saints and a
followers of the antichrist will be destroyed.' Such a
sage would have little meaning and less comfort to t
in need." That is what the professor writes about the me
ing of that word "en tachei" — "shortly" — and "eggus"
"for the time is at hand."

I would like to comment on the professor's opinion. H
says that it would have been no comfort at all to these earl
Christians if these apocalyptic revelations were future, i
they were prophetic; for, he says, in order for them to be of
comfort, they had to come to pass immediately. Let us see
if God says so. In James 5:8, James, in encouraging the
church, says, "Be ye also patient; stablish your hearts: for
the coming of the Lord draweth nigh" — "eggus." Here the
pastor of the church at Jerusalem, James, the Lord's brother,
is encouraging the people of the church by the promised
return of Jesus and uses that same word "eggus" that John
uses in Revelation. Yet it has been two thousand years, and
Christ has not come. What comfort, according to the professor, could that have been to the persecuted church at
Jerusalem, this prophecy of a coming that is thousands of
years distant?

come when they do come. And then, there is no set time
for the consummation in the Revelation. One can study it
and study it, but there is no date in it. God's clock is not
like our clock. God does not compute time as we compute
time. ". . . one day is with the Lord as a thousand years,
and a thousand years as one day" (II Peter 3:8).

Then what does God mean when He says "shortly" and
when He says "at hand"? In the last chapter of the Revelation look at these words: ". . . blessed is he that keepeth
the sayings of the prophecy of this book . . ."; "Behold, I
come quickly . . ."; ". . . Seal not the sayings of the prophecy
of this book: for the time is at hand"; "He which testifieth
these things saith, Surely I come quickly . . ." What does
God mean by that? Why, dear and precious and beloved
fellow Christians, God means by that, this: that the return
of our Lord is always imminent — always. It could be today,
it could be at twilight, it may be at midnight or in the morning. What God wills for His children through all of the
church age is that we be watchful and waiting and prayerful and expectant. It could be today, and it pleases God
for His children to read the words of the prophecy and to
say in their hearts, "It may be today." We are to live our
lives and to minister in the name of our Saviour, expecting
that some day, some hour, soon, we shall see the beloved
and holy face of our Lord in Glory. "Quickly I come," He
says. "Amen, even so come," is our answering prayer.

Sermon 3

THE BLESSEDNESS OF THE VISION

> Blessed is he that readeth, and they that hear the words of this prophecy, and keep those things which are written therein: for the time is at hand. — Revelation 1:3

This message is based upon the whole introduction to Revelation — "The Revelation [the Apocalypse, the Unveiling] of Jesus Christ, which God gave unto him, to shew unto his servants things which must shortly come to pass; and he sent and signified it by his angel unto his servant John: Who bare record of the word of God, and of the testimony of Jesus Christ, and of all things that he saw. Blessed [and this is the first of seven beatitudes in the Book] is he that readeth and they that hear the words of this prophecy, and keep those things which are written therein: for the time is at hand." God says that blessed is the one that reads the book, and blessed are they that hear it, and blessed are they that guard and treasure the words of this prophecy, — "for the time is at hand." These are things which must shortly come to pass.

Two Extreme Attitudes Toward the Revelation

There are two extreme attitudes regarding the study, the reading, the teaching, and the preaching of the book of the Revelation. There are those who say that it ought to be abandoned by all serious students. They look upon the Revelation as a farrago of baseless fantasies. Some of them describe it as a compilation of Jewish apocalyptic fragments that some unknown Christian in the ages past put together and tried to give a Christian turn and a Christian touch. They look upon it as being a parcel of mystery that no man can understand or fathom. For example, even Martin Luther, at one time, refused to include the Apocalypse in his canon of scripture because he said no man could understand it. And following in that vein, those who have that spirit and attitude concerning it have words of sarcasm and belittlement for those who would seriously attempt to study it. They have a deep prejudice against the book and would dissuade all of us from teaching and preaching it. That is one extreme. Now, the other extreme is on the other side. There are those who are persuaded that about the only book in the Bible that is really worth studying is the Apocalypse. They find in the Apocalypse a map, with all details for all of the historical future, and they make chronologies that inevitably include the setting of a date for the time of the end of the age. And when we come to those dates that they have set for the time of the end and their chronological prophecies are not fulfilled, then they make the whole thing look silly and ridiculous.

WHAT GOD HAS DONE IN THE REVELATION

As for us, we are interested in only two things: What has God *done* here and what has God *said* here? So let us take these two fundamental interests and look at the Revelation. Let us see, first, what God has done here. He has done two things. First, He has given to Christ an incomparably, celestially ineffable reward for what He has wrought for us in His redemptive and reconciliatory ministry in this weary, sinful earth. And that great reward that God has bestowed upon Christ for what He has done to save us from our sins, that ineffable honor, is revealed in this Apocalypse, this unveiling, this manifestation, this presentation of Jesus Christ as the Owner and Ruler and King of things in heaven and things in earth. The Lord God raised Jesus from among the dead and received Him up into Glory. But these honors, great as they are, are not the end of what God has given and has yet to bestow upon our exalted Lord. This honor, this reward, this enthronement, this apocalypse, this manifestation, this appearing, as Lord and ruler over all creation and all things therein, God gave to Jesus, in God's judgment a fitting reward for what our Saviour has done. Christ then deemed that honor so great and so worthy that He sent an embassage down to the sons of men to make it known unto us. The holy angels of heaven counted it an honor to signify that unveiling which God has given to our Lord. The apostle John, the disciple of love, conscientiously wrote it down for all of the Lord's children to see and to accept and to believe and to have reason to rejoice.

Consider this: If we gain strength from the mystery of the incarnation and the humbling of our Saviour, from His birth described in the Nativity and the first Christmas, from His life of humility and condescension, from His prayers and temptations, from His sorrows and His griefs; if the veiling of His deity is a strength and an encouragement to us; if we are blessed by the message of His cross, the outpouring of His life and the spilling of His blood; if all of these things are for our salvation and our encouragement and our strength, then with what immeasurably grateful exultation and praise should we look upon the great and ultimate reward that God has bestowed upon Christ for what He has done for us! And the record, the prophecy, the unveiling and the apocalypse of that glorious honor is the book of the Revelation. The bestowal of this celestial reward upon Christ is the first thing that God has done in the Apocalypse.

I have said that God has done two things here. First, He gave this great reward, this Apocalypse to Christ. The second thing God has done here is this: He has given to

us an unsealed Book. John bare record of what God said
and what God did, of the testimony of Jesus Christ and of
all things that he saw. John conscientiously, faithfully and
minutely wrote all these things down that God revealed to
him through His angel. The angel-guide said, "Seal not
the sayings of the prophecy of this Book for the time is at
hand." After God had given this glorious Apocalypse to
Jesus, He did this second thing: He caused the Apostle John
to write it down that all of us might look upon it and might
be encouraged and strengthened by it. "Seal not the sayings
of the prophecy of this Book, for the time is at hand" (Revelation 22:10). "And I John bare record of the word of
God, and of the testimony of Jesus Christ, and of all things
that I saw" (Revelation 1:2).

Some of the great prophetic revelations that were given
to Daniel were closed up. They were sealed. They were
veiled. Daniel 12:4: "But thou, O Daniel, shut up the words,
and seal the book, even to the time of the end." What God
had revealed to Daniel, Daniel was not allowed to write.
The Apocalypse as revealed to John, however, is altogether
different. What was sealed in Daniel is unsealed in the
Apocalypse; what was not made known in Daniel is made
known in the Revelation; what was hidden and covered
away in Daniel is open to view in the Revelation. This
open, unsealed Book of the Apocalypse has been for the eyes
of God's people to look upon from that first day when the
breathless messenger came from Patmos and had in his
hand this glorious manuscript to be delivered first to the
church at Ephesus, then to Smyrna, then to Pergamos, then
to Thyatira, then to Sardis, then to Philadelphia, and finally
to Laodicea. This great apocalyptic vision has been kept
open from that day until this before the churches of the
Lord Jesus Christ. Some of those messages in the Revelation were especially pertinent for those seven churches in
Asia. Some of those messages are especially pertinent for

us in this day and hour. Some of the messages of that Apocalypse are especially pertinent for an accepted and elected time in the future. But all of it, from beginning to end, is pertinent and profitable to all of us in all ages and in all times in the churches of Jesus Christ. God has not given to us a mystery, or an enigma; God has given to us an open, unveiled revelation. "Seal not the things that are written in the book, for the time is at hand."

Did you know that there is a word that sounds like "apocalypse" that you will often find in studying Bible background? There are books that are accepted by the Roman Church which, to us, are just human productions. Sometimes you will find them in a big, family Bible between the Old and the New Testaments, and they bear the name "Apocrypha." "Apocrypha" means "hidden, covered over." It ultimately bears the meaning "not authentic, not true." "Apocalypse" is the Greek word that means exactly the opposite of the Greek work "apocrypha." "Apocrypha" is from the words "apo" and "krupto" meaning "hidden, concealed." But "apocalypse" is from the Greek word for "taking away the covering," "unveiling," "presenting to view." What I have here in the last book of the scriptures is not an apocrypha — "a covering up, a sealing, a hiding away," but, what I have is an "unveiling, an apocalypse, an unsealed revelation" upon which the eyes of the church may always look. There are many people who would seal up what God has unsealed. There are those who would not only take away from the words of the prophecy, but they would take away the prophecy itself. But God has given to us an open Book that we may read it and look upon it and see what He proposes for His Son and for us who trust in Him.

THE BLESSEDNESS OF STUDYING THE PROPHECY

I have now listed the two things God has *done:* He has given to Christ this apocalypse, this unveiling, this manifestation, as King of the Universe, our rightful and only Lord; and He has given to us this unsealed book that our eyes may look full upon it and our hearts may be strengthened and encouraged by it. Now God has also *said* something; not only has He done something but He has said something. What is this which our Lord has said? "Blessed . . . blessed . . . blessed is he that reads. Blessed . . . blessed are they that hear the words of this prophecy, and blessed are they that guard and treasure and keep the words of this prophecy in their hearts, for the time is at hand." God has said a remarkable thing. Why should God have said that the study of, the understanding of, and the meditation upon the words of this prophecy are profitable and blessed? Well, first, because it is the Revelation of Jesus Christ, Himself. The great, all-inclusive hope of the churches of our Lord lies in the coming and reigning of our victorious King. God said that to meditate upon that appearance and to look and watch and wait for that glorious triumph, the second coming of our Lord, is blessed above all things in this earth. "Blessed are they who read and who hear and who treasure the words of this prophecy."

The study of any scripture is profitable. II Timothy 3:16 says: "All scripture is given by inspiration of God and is profitable for doctrine, for reproof, for correction, for instruction in righteousness." All scripture is profitable, but some scriptures are more significantly meaningful than other scriptures, and some scriptures are more preciously dear than others. Thus it is with the Revelation. God says that these words are especially dear and precious and profitable. When we look upon the Revelation in honest perplexity and bewilderment, that is just the more reason why we are carefully to examine it. These words were not written in order that they might mystify the church, but in order that we might be encouraged by them. The author who wrote them down did not do so in order that we might be confused and bewildered, but in order that we might understand. Lest the reader hesitate, God writes at the very door of the book this marvelous beatitude: "Blessed is he that reads and they that hear and treasure the words of this prophecy."

This is the same kind of commitment that confronted Mary, the peasant girl, the maiden-mother of our Lord. She did not understand the things that were spoken by the angel nor the things that were coming to pass, but the scriptures say, "She treasured them, she kept them and pondered them in her heart" (Luke 2:19), and as the days passed the meaning of those words came to full fruition and understanding. When Simeon, in the Temple, said, "And this child shall be a sign that shall be spoken against, yea, and a sword shall pierce through thine own soul also" (Luke 2:34-35), she had no idea what that meant until the day when she stood by the cross and looked upon the Son of God, her child of promise, nailed and lifted up between the earth and the sky. But she, though not understanding the words at the time, treasured them and kept them and pondered them in her heart. With a like humility of faith and of acceptance, we also can listen to the words of the prophecy, and what we cannot understand we can treasure and examine. The darker the mystery, the deeper is the cause for examination and careful study, and, according to the Word of God, the greater the blessing. "Blessed is he that reads and hears and treasures, guards, the words of this prophecy." According to John 16:13, the Holy Spirit stands ready to guide us and to help us. "Howbeit when he, the Spirit of truth, is come, he will guide you into all truth: . . . and he will shew you things to come" (John 16:13).

It is a profitable and precious thing to read the words of this prophecy and to meditate upon them and to treasure them in our hearts, because this is the only prophetic book in all of the New Testament. There are many small apocalypses in the New Testament, like Matthew 24, Mark 13, Luke 17, parts of I and II Thessalonians, the third chapter of II Peter; but there is only one prophetic book and that is the book of the Revelation. This is the last writing of inspiration. This closes the Canon. This is our Lord's last message to His churches after He had ascended into Glory. And what God has done for us is to pull aside the veil and to invite, with uncommon urgency, His people to look through the vistas of the future. There we find recorded and revealed the inexorable apocalyptic judgments that God shall visit upon a denying and unbelieving and blaspheming world. There we also see the frightful and terrible rise and fall of the antichrist. Then we see the unveiling of the Lord in glory and power, the establishment of His Kingdom in the earth, and the ultimate victory of our Christ over sin and death and the grave. There we see God's glorified saints reigning with our Lord forever. This Book is the only book in the New Testament that pulls aside the veil that we might see into the vistas of the future that are yet to come.

There is a third reason why it is blessed to study this prophecy. Christ is not going to be glorified alone. We shall be glorified with Him. This prophecy concerns us. We shall have a glorious, rewarding and triumphant part in these things that are revealed in the Revelation. ". . . Unto him that loved us, and washed us from our sins in his own blood, and hath made us kings and priests unto God and his Father . . ." (Revelation 1:5-6). We shall share in the glory. When we read of the exaltation of our Lord, we are looking upon the exaltation of God's sainted children, those who have trusted in Him. And even the least of those who place their faith in our Saviour shall be remembered and rewarded and glorified and exalted in that incomparably precious and glorious day.

Sermon 4

JOHN — TO THE SEVEN
CHURCHES WHICH ARE IN ASIA

John to the seven churches which are in Asia: Grace be unto
you, and peace, from him which is, and which was, and which
is to come; and from the seven Spirits which are before his
throne. — Revelation 1:4

This is a sermon on the writer and the age and the background of the Apocalypse, of the Revelation. Five times
in the book the writer says that his name is John. In Revelation 1:1: "The Revelation of Jesus Christ, which God gave
unto him, to shew unto his servants things which must
shortly come to pass; and he sent and signified it by his angel
unto his servant John." This is the first time he gives his
name. The second time is in Revelation 1:4: "John to the
seven churches which are in Asia. . ." His name is repeated the third time in the ninth verse of the first chapter:
"I John, who also am your brother, and companion in tribulation, and in the kingdom and patience of Jesus Christ, was
in the isle that is called Patmos, for the word of God, and
for the testimony of Jesus Christ." The fourth time his name
is given is in Revelation 21:2: "And I John saw the holy
city, new Jerusalem, coming down from God out of heaven,
prepared as a bride adorned for her husband." And the
fifth time that he tells his name is in the last chapter — chapter 22, verse 8: "And I John saw these things, and heard
them. . ." The writer says that he is a servant of Jesus
Christ in Revelation 1:1. And in Revelation 1:9 he says

44

that he is a brother to the Christians of the Roman province of Asia and that he is a companion, a fellow-sufferer, with them in their tribulation and in their persecution. Then in the twenty-second chapter of the Revelation the author claims that he has seen and heard the things which are recorded in this Apocalypse.

Who is this John? There were as many Johns in that ancient day as there are Johns today. Even in the New Testament pages there are several Johns. But who is this John who says that he is a servant of Christ, that he is a brother to those Asian Christians, and that he saw and heard and wrote down these things?

About A.D. 250 there lived Dionysius of Alexandria, called Dionysius the Great because he was so famous a pupil of Origen. In the Alexandrian school of theology, Dionysius the Great wrote a famous tract, a famous treatise. In that scholarly work he said that the Apostle John could not have written the Revelation. This Dionysius is the first of a long series of scholars who have been persuaded of such a position ever since his day. He based his persuasion on the difference between the Greek that is used in writing the fourth gospel, the gospel of John, and the Greek that is used in the writing of the Revelation. Dionysius of Alexandria said that the difference between the two is so great that the same man could not have written both of them. He was convinced that John the apostle wrote the fourth gospel, and, therefore, that the same John could not have written the Apocalypse. That is a very common position and one that has been defended up until this present hour. So, who is this John who describes himself five times in the pages of the book? We are going to look inside the book first and find the internal evidence concerning the author.

First, whoever he was, he was a Jewish Christian, not a Greek Christian. He was a Palestinian who thinks in Hebrew but writes in Greek. And almost certainly the author was a Jew who grew up in Galilee. We know that from many things I have not time to discuss. He translates Hebrew idioms into Greek. He does violence to Greek syntax and grammar. He throws the rules of the grammarians to the winds. He is burning in the delivery of a message and if language gets in the way, he disregards the rules of grammar. He has a grammar and a syntax all his own. Whoever this John is, he is a Hebrew, a Jew, who grew up in Palestine, whose soul is saturated with the language and phraseology of an Old Testament that he uses consciously and unconsciously.

A second thing about him, whoever this John is: he is a man of deep spiritual insight. This man looks deeper into the plan of God for the ages to come than any other writer of the New Testament.

A third thing about this John, whoever he is: he is a man of tremendous, positive statements. For example, the hostile Jews of Smyrna and of Philadelphia are called the synagogue of Satan. He calls Rome "Babylon" the mother of harlots and of the abominations of the earth. He refers to the Roman religion as the scarlet whore who commits fornication with the nations of the world. In his depiction of Christ, he exhibits Him as One of unbounded power and authority and One of severe, but just, condemnation and judgment. In the Revelation written by this man John, Christ is a warrior that rules the nations with a rod of iron; Christ is the Lamb of God whose wrath is terrible, ". . . who shall hide us from the face of him that sitteth on the throne, and from the wrath of the Lamb" (Revelation 6:16). John presents Christ as a king who treads the winepress of the fierceness of Almighty God. Whoever this John is, he is a man of uncompromising nature and of tremendous conviction and statement.

A fourth thing about this John: he is a man of unquestioned authority. As he writes to the seven churches of Asia he does so with unquestioned jurisdiction. We shall discuss that word "seven" in the next chapter when we write of the meaning of numbers in the Bible. Seven represents all of them — completion. The seven churches are all of the church, and this man writes to those churches with authority.

THE APOSTLE JOHN, THE AUTHOR OF THE BOOK

Who is this John that could fit a picture like that? There is only one, and there is not any other but that one. This man John is so famous and in a position of such authority that when he writes he needs no other epithet, no other descriptive adjective. When he calls himself "John," that is enough. Immediately all of the churches of Asia knew who he was. There is only one John that answers to the description that we have found of the author in the book itself. That is John, the son of Zebedee, who grew up in Galilee, and who was the beloved disciple of the Lord. In A.D. 69 in the terrible war that destroyed Jerusalem, John came to Asia Minor, and was for over twenty-five years the pastor of the church in Ephesus. He was exiled by the Emperor Domitian on this lonely, rocky Isle of Patmos "for the word of God and for the testimony of Jesus Christ." There is only one John whose name needed no other description as he wrote with authority to the churches of Christ in the Roman province of Asia. That John is the beloved apostle of the Lord.

There are many other things that substantiate that conclusion. For example, John is the only author that uses the word "Logos" — "the Word" — as a personal name for Christ. He personalizes that word "Logos." "In the beginning was the Word [Logos] and the Word [Logos] was with God and the Word [Logos] was God" (John 1:1). The same thing is found in I John 1:1; and again in Revelation 19:11-13: "And I saw heaven opened, and behold a white horse; and he that sat upon him was called Faithful and True. . .

His eyes were as a flame of fire, and on his head were many crowns. . . And he was clothed with a vesture dipped in blood: and his name is called the Word [Logos] of God." John is the only one that uses that word "Logos" to refer to Christ. He does it in all of the Johanine literature, including the Revelation.

Another thing — John is the only one who refers to Christ as "The Lamb of God." "Behold," he says in the first chapter, quoting the great Baptist preacher, "the lamb of God . . ." (John 1:36). And in the Revelation He is referred to as "The Lamb of God" twenty-two different times. John is the only one who calls Jesus that — "The Lamb of God."

Another typical thing — John is the only one that refers to the spear that pierced the side of our Lord. He uses a Greek word that is different from the usual Greek word to refer to that piercing. Zechariah, for example, referred to the piercing of our Lord, and in the Greek Septuagint the usual Greek word is used to translate it. The word used by John, however, is altogether different. That same word by which he describes the piercing of the side of Jesus in the gospel, he uses also here in the Revelation: "Behold, he cometh with clouds; and every eye shall see him and they also which pierced him . . ." (Revelation 1:7). John is the only one who mentions the piercing of Christ in his gospel, and he mentions it again here, using the identical Greek word.

Now, about the difference and the likeness in the grammar and the syntax and the style between the gospel of John and the Revelation. Let us consider the difference first. When John wrote the fourth gospel, he wrote it in a time of quiet meditation when he was surrounded by wonderful Greek friends who loved and honored him. They could help John make his Greek beautiful and correct. But when John wrote the Revelation he was in exile and by himself. There he wrote as he preached — in fervor and in power

and in fury. In the excitement of that hour he wrote this
Revelation just as he saw it and as it burned in his own
soul. This was a man who thought in Hebrew and wrote
in Greek. And when the Revelation was sent to the churches,
they so honored and so revered God's sainted disciple that
no church took upon itself to correct the syntax and the case
sequence, nor to make the relative pronouns correspond.
Rather, they left it just as John wrote it, which is just as
we have it today.

Now, let us see how the gospel of John and the Revelation
are alike. The easiest Greek to read in the Bible, and I suppose in all literature, is contained in the fourth gospel and
the Revelation. If you have a beginner student or you would
like to learn Greek, the way to begin is to read either the
Revelation or the fourth gospel. They are very simple and
very easy to read. The writer of one is the same author of
the other. Both books come from the same pen.

We now turn to the external evidence for the author of the
book. It corroborates the internal evidence. Justin was martyred under Marcus Aurelius in A.D. 166. Justin Martyr lived
and his ministry was in the Roman province of Asia, and he
said John the apostle wrote the Revelation. Irenaeus, who
died in A.D. 190, was the pupil of Polycarp, who was a disciple and convert of John, the beloved disciple of Jesus.
Polycarp was pastor of Smyrna when this Revelation was
written, and Irenaeus says that many times he heard Polycarp talk about John, stating that John wrote the Revelation
in the latter part of the reign of the Emperor Domitian.
This view agrees also with Origen of Alexandria, with Tertullian of Carthage, with Clement of Alexandria, with Hyp-
politus of Rome, and with the Muratorion Canon and so
on and on. I think there is no doubt that this John is the
disciple who leaned upon the breast of our Lord at the Last
Supper and asked, "Lord, which is he that betrayeth thee?"
(John 21:20). That was John, the beloved disciple. "I

John, who also am your brother, and companion in tribulation, and in the kingdom and patience of Jesus Christ. . ."

THE DATE OF THE WRITING OF THE REVELATION

Now a word about the date of the writing of the Revelation. It was written in a time of terrible persecution. In the first Christian century there were only two periods of heavy persecution against the Christians. One was under Nero and the other was under Domitian. Nero died in A.D. 68. Domitian died in A.D. 96. There is practically no reason for any scholar to say that the Revelation was written in the Neronian persecution, but there is every reason for any student or any scholar to say that the Revelation was written in the reign of the Emperor Domitian. It was written in either 95 or 96 A.D.

The reasons for selecting the Domitian date are these: First, there is a great difference in the inner life of the churches in the Revelation from that reflected in the writing of the apostle Paul. Paul was martyred under Nero, and the state of the churches found here in the book of the Revelation is altogether different from the state of the churches when Paul wrote to these same people. For example, in the Revelation, Ephesus has lost its first love, a situation very different from that in the days of Paul. In the Revelation the Nicolaitane Party is widespread and firmly entrenched, but there is no trace of a Nicolaitane Party in the days of the apostle Paul. Sardis is already dead in the Revelation. Laodicea, which was destroyed by an earthquake in the days of Nero, has been rebuilt and boasts of its wealth. In the days of the Revelation the great antagonist of the churches of Christ is the Roman Empire, while in the days of the apostle Paul the opposition of Nero was personal, to avert suspicion from himself concerning the burning of the city of Rome. The time and the day is altogether different in the Revelation from the days of the apostle Paul when he wrote the letter to Ephesus (which I think is a circular letter to all of the churches of Asia just like the Revelation). On the inside heresy has developed, and on the outside there is cruel persecution.

Another thing — the persecution that is reflected in the Revelation is Domitianic. One of the characteristics of the Domitian persecution was the exiling and banishing of the Christians. John was banished to the Isle of Patmos, just as you would expect under Domitian. The persecution of the Christians under Nero was personal. As I have said, he burned down the city of Rome, and the people suspected that he had done it. Nero pointed to this strange sect of Christians and, in order to avert suspicion from himself, accused them of having set fire to the city. It was a personal matter with Nero. On the other hand, when Domitian persecuted the Christians, he did it as a legal policy of the State. He bathed the Empire in Christian blood. He has gone down in history as one of the great persecutors of the churches of Christ. The reason he did it was because he sought to establish himself as the god of all of the Empire and to set images of himself in all of the temples. He demanded, as a loyalty to the State, that the people bow down and worship Domitian in the presence of his image.

One may get a good idea of Domitian in studying some of the Latin historians. For example, Suetonius says that Domitian referred to himself as "Deus et Dominus" — "God and Lord." Suetonius then continues by saying that when Domitian would write a letter or make a command or send out a law, he would always begin it with "Domitian, our God and Lord, commands thus and so." He demanded that everyone who referred to him must do so as "God and Lord," either in writing or in address. It is interesting to read what Pliny says about Domitian. Pliny says that Domitian took any slight to himself as an offense and an impiety against his divinity. Pliny continues by saying that Domitian had statues of himself erected throughout the Empire and that he slaughtered uncounted numbers and myriads of victims because of their refusal to worship his name and to bow down before his image. So you can imagine what a startling conflict immediately arose between emperor worship commanded by Domitian and Christian worship in the churches of Jesus Christ. That conflict came especially in Asia Minor, because, after the destruction of Jerusalem, the stronghold of the Christian faith was in the Roman province of Asia.

Now I want to discuss the Roman Empire at the time of the writing of the Revelation. The Roman Empire toward the end of the first Christian century reached its zenith. It covered the then-known civilized world from the British Isles down to the central part of Africa, from the Atlantic Ocean to the Euphrates River. To the people of that age, Rome was the world. The Roman soldier was looked upon as invincible. Those legionnaires were garrisoned everywhere. Because of the one government and because of the great system of military highways, commerce was expedited. Rome was built upon two things — conquest and commerce. In the eighteenth chapter of the book of the Revelation, a score or more articles are described as a part of the commerce of Rome. They are from India, from China, from central Africa and north Africa, from the Danube, from Gaul, from the British Isles — they are from everywhere. The lavish wealth of the upper ruling classes of Rome was beyond imagination. Look at this: The Roman Emperor Caligula spent over five hundred thousand dollars on one banquet. The wife of Caligula was not to be outdone. She had more than two million dollars worth of emeralds with which she decorated herself. Seneca, the teacher of Nero, one time cynically remarked that the wealthy ladies in Rome had two or three estates suspended from their ears. A patriot gave a dinner in honor of Nero and spent more than one hundred sixty thousand dollars on roses alone. Three out of every five people were slaves. Slaves waited upon the Romans day and night. The poor crowded into Rome to receive doles and to watch the gladiatorial combats. The city decayed in wealth and in luxury.

Why the Roman Empire Persecuted the Christians

Now a word about why the Christians were persecuted. First, Christianity was persecuted by the Roman Empire because its faith was militant, because it was missionary, because it was evangelical and evangelistic, because it sought to win converts. As long as Christianity appeared as just a sect of Judaism, it was unmolested. As a matter of fact, Judaism, the religion of the Jew, was legalized in the Roman Empire. When Rome conquered a province, its religion was automatically recognized by law and was placed in the Pantheon. In Rome today, the most perfectly preserved building of antiquity is the Roman Pantheon, built by the great Agrippa I in the days of Julius Caesar in about 40 or 50 b.c. It is a magnificent building. And whenever Rome conquered a province, its gods and its religion were just added to the Pantheon — "Pan" — "all," "theos" — "God" — "all of God" building. And as long as Christianity appeared to be just a sect of Judaism, it was unmolested, but when Christianity appeared to be not a patch on an old garment but a new faith and a living witness, immediately it ran afoul of Roman order.

The second reason why Christianity was persecuted was because it demanded universal obedience and obeisance to the great king of heaven, Jesus, and not to Caesar. The Roman State looked upon religion as being just an aid to the state and the politicians manipulated it for the state. One of the truest sentences ever written is written by the great historian Gibbon in his famous *Decline and Fall of the Roman Empire.* He said in that history, "To the people all religions were equally true, to the philosopher all religions were equally false, and to the politicians all religions were equally useful." So the politicians used religion as a tool of the state, but when the Christian churches said, "Not so, our allegiance is to Jesus Christ," they ran afoul of the Empire.

The third reason why Christianity was persecuted by the Roman Empire was because Christianity refused to bow down before an idol. Christians refused to have idols in their homes, they refused to tie them on their chariots, and they refused to use them as amulets around their necks. Roman society, like Greek society, was built around guilds and orders, all of which had idols as patron saints. When the Christians refused to belong to the order, refused to bow down before the queen of heaven and refused to enter into an idol temple, immediately they were castigated as atheists and they were hated and persecuted. Every calamity of the Empire was laid at their door. If it was dry and did not rain, those Christians had offended the gods. If the Tiber flooded, those Christians had offended the gods. If there were military reverses, those Christians had offended the gods. Because Christians refused to bow down before idols, they were regarded as enemies of the state.

A fourth reason the Christians were persecuted was because they were looked upon as cannibals. They met secretly at night in subterranean places, in dens and dives and catacombs, and they reportedly ate flesh and drank blood. That is what the Romans said, for they would hear them speak concerning the partaking of the body and blood of Jesus. They were cannibals to the Romans.

There was then a fifth reason for Christian persecution. The Christians offended the passive philosophers of the day because of their enthusiasm. They were evangelistic and fervent.

And then there was a sixth reason why they were persecuted — a commercial reason. They offended those who trafficked in idols. This age-old quarrel of commerce with Christianity continues all over the civilized world today. Christians offended the manufacturers of idols and those who had stock to sell for the sacrifices in the heathen temples.

The Christians were also persecuted for a seventh reason. For the most part, Christians were recruited from among the poor and the slaves, and, as such, were looked down upon by the noble, the rich, and the respectable.

As I have already mentioned, Christianity was persecuted because it refused emperor worship — to bow down before the image and the name of a man. The Christian said, "I will not bow and I will not kneel." The Romans hated Christians and persecuted them and decimated them, and Domitian said, "And I shall annihilate them." And it was in the days of this attempt to annihilate the Christians because they refused to bow down before Domitian, that the Revelation, the Apocalypse, of Jesus Christ was written. It was written to encourage the churches to stand up and to be counted and to be numbered. It was written to comfort them in an hour of their blood and their trial and their death.

When you read the Revelation, you are reading the newspapers of today. When you read of the martyrs of the Revelation, you are reading of the martyrs of today. And when you read of the ultimate victory and triumph of the Revelation, you are reading of the ultimate victory and triumph of the people of Jesus Christ today. "I John . . . your brother and companion in tribulation, and in the kingdom and patience of Jesus Christ." "Grace and peace to you from God the Father, from God the Son and from the seven spirits which are before His throne, from the Holy Spirit of God in the earth." May the Lord bless the word to your hearts.

Sermon 5

THE SYMBOLIC MEANING OF NUMBERS

> John to the seven churches which are in Asia: Grace be unto you, and peace, from him which is, and which was, and which is to come; and from the seven Spirits which are before his throne. — Revelation 1:4

When we read the text, we are immediately confronted with the symbolic meaning of numbers, to be found not only here, but throughout the entire Revelation and throughout the whole Word of God. The text says, "John to the seven churches which are in Asia." Those are not all of the churches that were in Asia, for I read of others in the New Testament. For example, right across the river from Laodicea was the famous Asian church of Hierapolis which Paul mentions in his letter to the Colossians. There is one church that is not even referred to in the Revelation. The famous church of Colosse is another, where Philemon lived and to which church Paul wrote a New Testament epistle. There were also many others. Why, then, does John choose seven? Then, the last part of the text says, ". . . and from the seven Spirits which are before his throne." Did you ever know of seven spirits of God? There is only one Holy Spirit of God, but this verse refers to seven.

You will find such numerals in all of the Revelation. You will find them in the web and warp and the woof of the entire Word of God. For example, the last verse of this first chapter of the Revelation says, "The mystery of the seven stars which thou sawest in my right hand . . . and the seven candlesticks which thou sawest. . ."

56

Let us look at some of these numbers mentioned in the Revelation. Turn to chapter four and verse four: "And round about the throne were four and twenty seats: and upon the seats I saw four and twenty elders sitting, clothed in white raiment. . ." Why were there not four and eighteen seats, or two and twenty seats? Why were there four and twenty? Now look at the sixth verse: "And before the throne there was a sea of glass like unto crystal: and in the midst of the throne, and round about the throne, were four *zoa.*" In Ezekiel they are called "cherubim." Why were there not three, or five? Why were there just four? Now in the next chapter: "And I saw in the right hand of him that sat on the throne a book written within and on the backside, sealed with seven seals" (Revelation 5:1). Why were there not six seals? Could not the book have been sealed just as well with six or eight seals? Why was it sealed with seven seals? Turn to chapter seven and verse four: "And I heard the number of them which were sealed: and there were sealed an hundred and forty and four thousand. . ." Why were there not a hundred forty-three thousand, five hundred sealed or why were there not a hundred fifty thousand sealed? Why is it a hundred forty-four thousand? Then in chapter eight and verse two: "And I saw the seven angels which stood before God; and to them were given seven trumpets." Why could there not have been six angels and six trumpets, or ten angels and ten trumpets? But there are seven angels and seven trumpets. We are just taking a few instances so that you will understand how numerics are woven into all the book. The most famous number in all the Word is found in Revelation 13:18: "Here is wisdom. Let him that hath understanding count the number of the beast: for it is the number of a man; and his number is six hundred three score and six." His number is 666. Let us hastily turn to chapter twenty and verses one and two: "And I saw an angel come down from heaven . . . And he laid hold on the dragon, that old serpent, which is the Devil, and Satan, and bound him a thousand years." Why didn't he bind him eight hundred or eleven hundred years? He bound him a thousand years. Now turn to chapter twenty-one and verses twelve and fourteen: ". . . And this new city of Jerusalem had twelve gates, and at the gates twelve angels . . . And the wall of the city had twelve foundations. . ." Why couldn't it have been eleven foundations or fourteen foundations? Now verse sixteen: "And the city lieth foursquare . . . and he measured the city with a reed, and it was on each side twelve thousand furlongs." Could it not have been eleven thousand furlongs or thirteen thousand furlongs? It is twelve thousand furlongs.

Now, you not only find a significance in the actual stated numbers in the Word — all the way through — but you find it woven into the text itself. Let us look at the three's in the text out of which we are reading, Revelation 1:4-6. I want you to see how the number three is woven into the very text, and into the very words that he uses. "John to the seven churches which are in Asia: Grace be unto you, and peace. . ." Notice first: ". . . from him which is, and which was, and which is to come" — one. "And from the seven Spirits of God which are before his throne" — two. "And from Jesus Christ, who is the faithful witness" — three. One, two, three. Then he will say three things about each one of them and twice three about the third one. Observe the first one: "From him which is [one] and which was [two] and which is to come [three]." Now about the second one. "He is spirit [one], he is seven Spirits [two] and he is before the throne [three]." Now, let us take the third one. "And from Jesus Christ, who is the faithful witness [one], and the first begotten of the dead [two], and the prince of the kings of the earth [three]." You have another three there. "Unto him that loves us [one], and washed us from our sins in his own blood [two], and hath made us kings and priests unto God and his Father [three]." You not only find these numbers said, but you find these numbers woven into the very structure of the book itself. That leads us to a remarkable study, this thing of the symbolism of numbers. And because I could not even begin to encompass this study in one chapter, I have broken it down into two.

NUMBERS IN GOD'S BOOK OF CREATION

In talking about God and numbers, we find that the work of God has a character, a consistency, that is evident wherever His hand has wrought. The workmanship of a particular author will have certain characteristics and idioms and mannerisms and presentations and manifestations that are typical of him. For example, Shakespeare will be somewhat, somehow Shakespeare, in all his authentic writings. Milton will have a certain kind of turn and manner. Milton is Milton, wherever you find him — whether he is writing prose or poetry. Longfellow, likewise, has a certain style and a certain kind of approach. He will use a certain nomenclature and language and style that will be Longfellow's all the way through. And so it is with any author. Unless he is plagiarizing, he will be himself in a way that can identify him.

Just so, the authorship of God is unmistakable. God has two great books. He is the author of the book of creation — the above us, the below us and the around us. His other book is the Bible — the Holy Scriptures that I hold in my hand. Now, I would expect to find the same kind of workmanship and craftsmanship and characteristics in both of them if both of them are by the same author. If I can find the hand of God in creation, I would also expect to find that same hand in the volume of Scriptures. If the works are done by the same Mighty Omnipotence, then I would expect them to be somewhat alike.

One distinctive characteristic of God is this: He works

through laws of numbers and mathematics. He likes them. He invented them and He is true to them in all of the categories of His workmanship, whether up there in the sky, whether down here in the earth or whether in the tiny, infinitesimal molecular universe around us. The hand of God, wherever it is manifested, will be revealed in His great love for proportion and ratio and numbers and mathematical laws. For example, in the world of astronomy, all of it can be reduced to mathematical laws. Astronomers can tell for the centuries past where every one of those heavenly bodies has been, and they can predict for millenniums yet to come where every one of those heavenly bodies will be. The whole universe above us is controlled by numbers that can be reduced into mathematical laws. It is the same way in the world of physics, where everything is governed by mathematical laws of weight and motion and substance. The molecular worlds around us, the atomic world about us, the rocks and the crystals and the gems and the snowflakes, and the things in every landscape and in every cave, speak to us about numbers and mathematical laws. Every time a sound awakens your ear, and every time a ripple of light plays upon your eye, it follows a definite, mathematical law.

It is the same way in God's world of chemistry. All of the elements in their powers to combine with one another are definite in their numerical relationship and in their mathematical laws. They make valence charts for the several elements by which we know the number of atoms and the atomic weight of each one and their abilities to combine. The same order is found in God's great world of biology. In botany, everything that is alive will follow a mathematical law. Every flower will have a certain number of petals in a certain arrangement. Everything that grows will have certain types of leaves that are arranged in definite, mathematical proportion. The same thing is true of zoology. Every living thing has a certain number of chromosomes in the cells, and every cell in that living thing has the same number of chromosomes, as a man has forty-six. In the trillions of cells in your body, every nucleus in every one of those trillions of cells has in it forty-six chromosomes. The little fly, Drosophila, has four chromosomes. All of God's creation is governed by definite, numerical, mathematical laws.

Those mysteries were observed by the ancients. As far back into antiquity as history can go, you will find these philosophers studying the orderliness and the harmony and the numerical proportion of what God has done. For example, the great hero and saint of the entire ancient philosophical world was Pythagoras. He was one of the first and one of the greatest of all philosophers. He was born about B.C. 582 on the Greek isle of Samos across from the Greek Ionian colony in Asia Minor. The central thought of Pythagorean philosophy is this: the idea of numbers and the recognition of numerical and mathematical proportion in all things. Aristotle summed up the doctrine of Pythagoras in these words: "Number is the principle of all things and the organization of the universe is an harmonic system of numerical ratios." The Pythagorean philosopher, Philolaus, summed it up in these words: "Number is great and perfect and omnipotent and the principle and guide of divine and human life." Here is a summary of the entire Pythagorean school of philosophy: It is number and definite mathematical relations that separate one thing from another and so in a sense make them things. Without number and the limitation which number brings, there would be only chaos and the illimitable. Number, then, is the principle of order, the principle by which a cosmos, or ordered world, subsists.

The Pythagoreans, especially, based their principle of philosophy on two observations. One concerned the heavenly bodies, as these philosophers observed how they were kept in order by the mathematical creative workmanship of (and they didn't know His name) the great God. The Pythagoreans made the entire created universe a sphere, and in the center of it they put the sun, and they had the planets revolving around that central fire, that central "hearth," as they called it. When Copernicus discovered the law of astronomy that we accept today (that the sun and not the earth is the center of the universe), an unusual comment that the medieval church used in denouncing it was that it was "heathen and Pythagorean." The other great thing that these Pythagoreans observed, and upon which they first based their philosophy of numbers, was this: They observed that musical tones follow certain definite mathematical proportions, and they linked the musical tones that they discovered — seven of them — with their great seven planets. Their famous theory of the seven planets and the seven golden chords of the heavenly heptachord made the whole heaven and the whole earth in harmony. To the Pythagoreans the whole universe was a harmony of God, a music of the soul. God made it that way, so the Pythagoreans thought.

NUMBERS IN GOD'S BOOK, THE BIBLE

Now, I come to the second Book, the other book of God's handiwork, the Book that I hold in my hand. It would be strange to find the author of the book of creation putting numbers and mathematical meaning into the soul of everything that He made in His great book of creation above and around us and not to find numerical meaning here in this written book of His Word. But I find the same thing in the Book of the Holy Scriptures that I find in the other book of the creative workmanship of God. In these numbers that God uses in the Book that I hold in my hand, there is a central thought. Numbers are used as derived from some natural, inherent significance, from which all other meaning takes its rise. The meaning is never arbitrary, it is never fantastic and it is never disconnected. In each number there is a basic meaning in the mind of God.

Before I start on the one number I have chosen for this chapter (the number seven), I want to show you by illustrations from the Scriptures that these numbers are not fantastic or arbitrary or disconnected, but that they have a central thought arising in the mind of God. It is in the nature of the thing. It is in the essence of the thing. As an illustration, let us take the number *one*. Number one refers to unity and to primacy and to independent existence. One — separate and apart. Deuteronomy 6:4: "Hear, O Israel: the Lord our God is one Lord." My Lord God is one God.

Let us take the number *two*. Two would be addition, an increase. It would be help and confirmation and fellowship. Look at Ecclesiastes 4:9-12: "Two are better than one; because they have a good reward for their labor. For if they fall, the one will lift up his fellow." Is it not logical — how God uses numbers?

Let us take the number *three* as another illustration. Three is the simplest compound unity. It is the first and simplest compound unit of mathematical science. So the manifestation of God. We know Him as a Trinity. We know Him as Father, as Son and as Holy Spirit. Three is the number of God.

Four is the number of the world. This is not fantastic or far-fetched. There are four seasons: winter, spring, summer and fall. There are four points of the compass: north, south, east and west. So in Ezekiel you will find the four living creatures (called by him "the cherubim") having four faces, four wings, four sides and moving on four wheels; that is, they represent the world of God's creation and providence.

Now, one other illustration, the numbers *five* and *ten*. The fingers of the hand are five. Both of the hands have ten. The toes on your foot are five and the toes on both feet are ten. The basis of the decimal system, by which we count our money and run our lives, originated in the practice of counting with the fingers. It is not a far-fetched, fantastic thing, the use of these numbers; rather, it lies in the very character and mind of God.

The Sacred Number, Seven

Now, in this chapter we are going to take up one number, the sacred number *seven*. Look how the number seven was put together, and you can see how it came to symbolize the fulness and perfection of God's Word. The perfect world-number, we said, was four. That represents the world. The perfect, divine number is three. So, they together make the holy and sacred number, seven. Seven is the earth crowned with heaven, the union of earth and heaven. Four and three, the creature manifesting the great Creator. Seven days make up each of the four quarters of the moon. Thus the week originated. One, two, three, four, five, six, seven — then start over again, four times every month. Seven notes make all of our music. God's world, God's universe, God's Book are musical with the numerical imprint. There are seven fundamental notes in music and the eighth is but the beginning of the series again, the beginning of the higher octave. The sacredness of that number, seven, reaches back to the very beginning of all time and creation. The seventh day was hallowed by the Lord after the works of creation, after the creative work of God. The number seven speaks of fulness, of completeness, of accomplishment and of rest.

As far back as is known in antiquity, in secular history, the number seven has been a sacred symbol. In the Chinese Empire, the Chinese emperor divided his empire into seven divisions. The emperor made offerings on seven altars to the seven spirits of God, and he was placed in his coffin on the seventh day and was buried in the seventh month after his death. In Greek and Roman mythology, the number seven occurs time and time again. In the world of the Babylonians, they regarded seven as the number of totality and completeness. The civilization that preceded the Babylonians was the Sumerian (from the country called Sumer). The Babylonians translated the Sumerian word *seven* into the Babylonian word for "completeness" or "all." They equated "seven" and "all." "Seven gods" meant "all the gods." The seven-storied towers of Babylon represented the whole universe. Seven was the expression of the highest power and the highest conceivable force. The number seven is a most distinct thing in the Bible, and it is used at least six hundred times. It means perfection, it means completeness, it means fulness and plenitude.

In Revelation 1:4 ". . . to the seven churches of Asia. . . ." That is, to all of the churches of Asia, and to all of the churches of all time. "To the seven churches in Asia." Now read Revelation 3:1: "And unto the angel of the church in Sardis write; These things saith he that hath the seven spirits of God. . . ." That is, the whole spirit of God. Now read Revelation 5:6: "And I beheld, and, lo, in the midst of the throne and of the four beasts [they represent creation, as we will find later on], and in the midst of the elders [the four and twenty elders representing the saints of the Old and New Testaments], stood a lamb as it had been slain, having seven horns [fulness and plenitude of power] and seven eyes [he is omniscient]." Seven represents fulness, completeness, plenitude, power and perfection. So Jesus Christ is presented here in the Revelation as being all-powerful and all-wise, and the way that the revelator does it is to say it by numbers. God likes numbers.

Now, we are going through the Bible and look at some of these uses of seven. First, the ritual use of seven. In

Genesis 2:1-3, the seventh day of the week is the Sabbath. Exodus 22:30, an animal must be seven days old before it can be offered for sacrifice. Exodus 34:18, the Feast of Unleavened Bread is to last seven days. Leviticus 12:3, the circumcision of a child is to take place after seven days. Leviticus 14:7, 16, 27, 51 — there is a seven-fold sprinkling which is repeatedly mentioned in the rules for the cleansing, the purification of the leper. Leviticus 16:14, 19 — the seven-fold sprinkling of the blood on the day of Atonement. Leviticus 23:18, the seven days of the Feast of the Tabernacles. Numbers 8:2; Zechariah 4:2 — the golden lampstand had seven branches and seven lights. II Kings 5:10, Naaman was to dip himself seven times in the River Jordan. Such is the ritual use of the number *seven*. These are just examples.

Now, the historical use of the number seven. In Genesis 7:4, 10, Noah entered the ark after seven days of grace. In Genesis 8:4, the ark rested on Ararat in the seventh month. In Genesis 29:20, Jacob worked seven years for Rachel. In Genesis 33:3, Jacob bowed seven times before Esau. In Genesis 41:53, following Pharaoh's dream of seven years of plenty were seven years of famine. Joshua 6:8-16, seven priests marched seven days blowing seven trumpets around Jericho, and on the seventh day they marched seven times. Judges 14:12 Samson had seven days of a marriage feast, and he had seven locks in his hair (Judges 16:19). I Samuel 16:10, there were seven sons of Jesse. II Samuel 24:13, David was offered, after his sin, the choice in the awful judgment of God upon him, of seven years of famine or three months of exile and peril or three days of pestilence. In the book of the Kings, Solomon took seven years to build the Temple, and he kept the feast of its dedication seven days. In I Kings 18:43 are the seven prayers of Elijah and the seven times that his servant ascended to the top of Mt. Carmel to look for rain. In Job 1:2, the seven sons of Job;

and his friends sat in silence seven days and seven nights, and they were atoned for at the end of the book by seven bullocks and seven rams for a burnt offering. In Daniel 3:19, we read of the heating of the furnace of Nebuchadnezzar seven times hotter. In Matthew, Luke and John, are the seven words from the cross. Luke 2:36 mentions Anna's seven years of wedded life. Matthew 15:34-37 records the seven loaves of the four thousand, the seven baskets of fragments. Matthew 22:25 tells of the seven brothers of that Sadducean story, each one having the same wife. Mark 10:9 refers to the seven devils cast out of Mary Magdalene. Acts 6:3b describes the ordination of the seven deacons (or ministers) of the Jerusalem church. Acts 19:14 mentions the seven sons of Seva. Such is the historical use.

Now, the didactic, or literary, use of seven. Psalm 12:6, silver purified seven times means completely purified. Matthew 12:45, the seven evil spirits were brought unto the self-reformed man. Luke 17:4 tells of the seven-fold sin and the seven-fold repentance and seven-fold forgiveness. Matthew 6:9-13 gives the seven-fold petition — there are seven petitions in the model prayer. In Matthew 13 are the seven parables of the kingdom; that is, a complete view, a whole view, of the kingdom of heaven. In Matthew 23:13, 15, 16, 23, 25, 27, and 29, there are seven woes pronounced upon the Pharisees. That is, they were wholly condemned. In the apostolic epistles, you will find the following heptads: Romans 8:35, the seven afflictions; Romans 12:6-8, the seven gifts; James 7:17, the seven qualities of heavenly wisdom; and II Peter 1:5-8, the seven virtues proceeding from faith.

Now, in the Apocalypse. The Apocalypse is a book of sevens because it is the Book of consummation, of completion. There is an amazing use of these heptads. There are seven churches represented by seven lampstands; seven stars representing the seven angels of the seven churches; there are seven lamps representing the seven spirits of God;

there is a seven sealed book, sealed securely, completely, that is; there is a lamb with seven eyes and seven horns; there are seven angels blowing seven trumpets; there are seven angels that pour out seven vials (bowls) of wrath in which, as the Book says, "is filled up with the wrath of God," that is all of the wrath of God; there are seven thunders that utter their voices; the beast out of the sea has seven heads (Revelation 13:1); the dragon has seven heads and seven crowns upon his heads (Revelation 12:3); there are seven mountains, seven kings, etc. One could go on and on.

The Multiples and Divisions of Seven

The significance of the number seven extends to its multiples and to its division. Two times seven equals fourteen. Exodus 12:6, 16, the Passover is on the fourteenth of Nisan; Numbers 29:13, 15, there were fourteen lambs offered on each of the seven days of the Feast of Tabernacles; Matthew 1:17, from Abraham to Christ in the genealogy of the first chapter of Matthew, there are three groups of fourteen in each.

Seven times seven is forty-nine. In Leviticus 23:15 following, Pentecost is on the fiftieth day, that is, after forty-nine days from the Passover, seven weeks. Leviticus 25:8 following, Jubilee Year is after seven times seven years, that is, after forty-nine years, the fiftieth year was Jubilee.

Seven times ten is a strong expression of multitude. Seven times ten, seventy, is an intensified seven. In Exodus 1:5, there were seventy members in the household of Jacob who went down into Egypt where they were so fruitful. In Exodus 24:1, 9, there were seventy elders of Israel. In Judges 8:30, there were seventy sons of Gideon. In II Kings 10:1, there were seventy sons of Ahab. In Ezekiel 8:11, he sees seventy idolatrous elders of Israel; that is, the whole country was given to idolatry. There were seventy members of the Sanhedrin, and the Septuagint is the Greek word for seventy, referring to the translated scriptures. The Lord sent out seventy disciples to preach the Gospel of the kingdom (Luke 10:1, 17).

Now, with reference to periods of time: In Genesis 50:3, there were seventy days of mourning for Jacob. In Isaiah 23:15, 17; Jeremiah 25:11b; Daniel 9:2 and Zechariah 1:12; 7:5, we read of seventy years of trial and captivity. In Daniel 9:24, seventy weeks of Daniel; Psalm 90:10, the seventy years in human life span (three score and ten); Matthew 18:22, seventy times seven — unlimited Christian forgiveness.

The significance of the number seven extends to the realm of division. This is important because you are going to meet it time and again in Daniel and in the Revelation. The significance of the number seven extends not only to its multiples, seven times seven equals forty-nine or seven times ten equals seventy, but it extends to the realm of division. The perfect number, seven, cut in half, is three and one-half. That is the incomplete, the imperfect, often the disastrous, the dreadful, and the distressful. It is found in four different terms. Three and one-half years, forty-two months, one thousand two hundred and sixty days, or a time, times and half a time (or a dividing of time). For example, in Luke 4:25: "... in the days of Elijah, when the heaven was shut up three years and six months. ..." James 5:17: "Elijah ... prayed earnestly that it might not rain: and it rained not on the earth by the space of three years and six months." This was a time of great distress. Daniel 7:25: "... and they [the saints] shall be given into his hand until a time and times and the dividing of time [three and one-half]." Daniel 9:27: "And he shall confirm the covenant with many for one week [seven] and in the midst of the week [three and one-half] he shall cause the sacrifice and the oblation to cease. ..." Daniel 12:7: "And I heard the man clothed in linen, which was upon the waters of the river ... when he held up his right hand and his left hand unto heaven, and sware by him that liveth forever that it shall be for a time, times, and a half; and when he shall have accomplished to scatter the power of the holy people, all these things shall be finished." Now, in Revelation 11:3: "And I will give power unto my two witnesses, and they shall prophesy a thousand two hundred and threescore days, clothed in sackcloth [three and one-half years]." Revelation 12:6: "And the woman fled into the wilderness, where she hath a place prepared of God, that they should feed her there a thousand two hundred and threescore days [three and one-half years]." Revelation 12:14: "And to the woman were given two wings of a great eagle, that she might fly into the wilderness, into her place, where she is nourished for a time, and times, and half a time, from the face of the serpent." Revelation 13:5: "And there was given unto him a mouth speaking great things and blasphemies; and power was given unto him to continue forty and two months [three and one-half years]." Revelation 11:9: "And they of the people and kindreds and tongues and nations shall see their dead bodies three days and an half, and shall not suffer their dead bodies to be put in the graves." Revelation 11:11: "And after three days and a half the spirit of life from God entered into them, and they stood upon their feet. . . ."

I just want you to see in this chapter that these things are not fantastic and they are not ridiculous and they are not far-fetched. They are woven into the work of God. When God makes His world on the outside, He does it according to numbers, to mathematical law. When God starts talking to you on the inside of His Book, He will do it in the same way. He will use numbers. He likes them. God likes harmony and music and law and proportion and ratio and numbers, and you will find them in both worlds of His creation.

Sermon 6

THE SYMBOLISM OF NUMBERS

John to the seven churches which are in Asia: Grace be unto you, and peace, from him which is, and which was, and which is to come; and from the seven Spirits which are before his throne. — Revelation 1:4

This chapter concerns the second half of "The Symbolism of Numbers." In the first chapter of the Revelation, the fourth verse, John begins, after his formal introduction, with these words: "John to the seven churches which are in Asia: [and we have said that there are many more churches in Asia than seven, yet he chooses seven]. Grace be unto you, and peace, from him which is, and which was, and which is to come; and from the seven Spirits which are before his throne." In that first introductory salutation twice you find a number. "The seven Spirits of God." There is just one Holy Spirit of God, yet he speaks of "the seven Spirits of God." Then through all of the book these numbers are interwoven into the very context and woof and warp and fabric of the Apocalypse. There are four *zoa* — living creatures — cherubim. There are four and twenty elders. There are one hundred forty-four thousand sealed. There is an army of ten thousand times ten thousand. There are seven spirits before the throne. The Lamb has seven horns and seven eyes. The beast is described in the terms of three sixes raised in their decimal powers. Then you have the holy city of God with twelve gates and twelve foundations and it measured twelve thousand furlongs. The tree of life bears twelve manner of fruits. All through the book are these numbers.

THE NUMBER, ONE

In the last chapter we discussed the number *seven*. In this chapter we are to discuss the rest of the symbolic numbers in the Word of God. First, the number *one*, which is the symbol of unity and independent existence. One — unique, separate, set apart, alone. The unit underlies all continuation and in God all things consist and continue. *One* is for God in the most hidden absoluteness of His being. It speaks of primacy and sufficiency and omnipotence. It speaks of harmony in all parts and attributes. It speaks of individuality and personality. It speaks of headship and sovereignty. In Deuteronomy 6:4: "Hear, O Israel: The Lord our God is one Lord." In Zechariah 14:9: "And the Lord shall be king over all the earth: in that day shall there be one Lord, *and his name one.*" Did you know that the name of God, Jehovah the Lord, is also One? One God and one Lord. In Mark 12:32: ". . . there is one God; and there is none other but he." In Ephesians 4:4-6: "There is one body, and one spirit, even as ye are called in one hope of your calling; One Lord, one faith, one baptism, one God and Father of all, who is above all, and through all, and in you all." One — the personality and sovereignty and uniqueness and separateness and holiness of God.

THE NUMBER, TWO

Now the number *two*. Two means addition, an increase. So it pertains to help, and to confirmation and to fellowship. In the previous chapter I used as an illustration of that in the Bible, Ecclesiastes 4:9-12: "Two are better than one; because they have a good reward for their labor. For if they fall, the one will lift up his fellow: But woe to him that is alone when he falleth; for he hath not another to help him up. Again, if two lie together, then they have heat: but how can one be warm alone? And if one prevail against him, two shall withstand him; and a threefold cord is not quickly broken." Confirmation and help. So in the Bible *two* stands for testimony, for confirmation.

In the last chapter I tried to point out to you that these numbers in their meaning are not arbitrary. They are not far-fetched. They lie in the mind and in the genius of God. God ordained them. God created things that way. God made His universe that way. We find in the normal intercourse of our life the confirmation of these things that God has wrought, using His mathematical laws and His love for numbers and harmony in everything that He does.

As an illustration of the use of *two* for testimony: When at a parliamentary meeting a man stands up and makes a motion and someone else stands up and says, "I second the motion," what is he doing? "I second the motion" — that is, "I am confirming his testimony and what he says — I second the motion." *Two* is for confirmation and witness. There are two testaments, the Old and the New, by which God witnesses to man. The second person of the Trinity, the Lord Jesus Christ, is in Revelation 1:5, "the faithful witness," in Revelation 3:14, "the true witness." Confirmation and testimony. The second man, the second Adam (Jesus Christ) unites the two natures, divine and human, in His own person and He witnesses to us of men and of God. In John 8: 17: "It is also written in your law, that the testimony of two men is true." In Mark 6:7: "And he called unto him the twelve, and began to send them forth by two and two . . .," that is, that they might confirm each other in their witness and testimony to Christ. In Luke 24:4, there are two angels at the tomb to testify that He is raised from the dead. In Acts 1:10, there are two angels on the Mount of Ascension, on Olivet, who encourage in testimony those stricken disciples who are bereft of the Lord, telling them that the Lord will come back again just as they saw Him leave.

In Revelation 11:3: "And I will give power unto my two witnesses [when we reach these numbers they will be increasingly meaningful to us], and they shall prophesy a thousand two hundred and three-score days, clothed in sackcloth." Now, as two confirmed the gospel of righteousness, so evil is confirmed in the same way. There are two beasts, not one beast, as they confirm each other in evil (the secular system and the false prophet, the two beasts). So *two* is for confirmation in witness and in testimony.

THE NUMBER, THREE

Now the number *three*. Three is the number of divinity. Three is the Trinity of God. ". . . baptizing them in the name of the Father, and of the Son, and of the Holy Ghost" (Matthew 28:19). When Patrick was in Ireland, preaching the Gospel, they said, "How can God be three in one?" Patrick stooped down and picked up a shamrock, a three-leafed clover, and holding it up, said, "Behold, three in one." Three is the symbol of the divine, a complete, ordered whole.

God has woven into the heart of His creation — existence, experience and knowledge — a trinity of things. Three in one are these: beginning, middle and end; heaven, earth and sea; father, mother and child; morning, noon and night; right, middle and left; knowledge, action and experience; body, soul and spirit; length, breadth and height.

Many instances of the number three in Scripture could be given. Hebrews 13:8: "Jesus Christ the same yesterday, and today, and forever." Genesis 18:1-2: "And the Lord [singular] appeared unto him [Abraham] in the plains of Mamre: . . . And he lifted up his eyes and looked, and, lo, three men stood by him. . . ." Is not that significant? Three! In Numbers 6:24-26, there is a three-fold benediction from God upon Israel, "The Lord bless thee . . . The Lord make his face shine upon thee . . . The Lord lift up his countenance upon thee. . . ." In Isaiah 6:3 there is a three-fold trisagian sung by the seraphim, "Holy, holy, holy, is the Lord of hosts. . . ." In Psalm 55:17, there is the thrice daily prayer to God, "Evening, and morning, and at noon, will I pray, and cry aloud: and he shall hear my voice." In Daniel 6:10, "Now . . . he [Daniel] kneeled upon his knees three times a day, and prayed, and gave thanks before his God. . . ." In Exodus 29:20 in the consecration of the priest and in Leviticus 14:14 in the cleansing of the leper, the blood is placed (the blood of sacrifice, and consecration and cleansing) upon the tip of his right ear, upon his right thumb and upon the great toe of his right foot. The whole man belongs to God.

In terms of the relationship with deity, in Matthew 4:3, there are three temptations. What were those three temptations? ". . . If thou be the Son of God. . . ." They have to do with the divinity of our Lord. Three times Peter denied the Lord God (Matthew 26:34). There are three prayers in Gethsemane (Matthew 26:44). On the third day Christ was raised from the dead (Matthew 16:21; 28). Thrice did Jesus speak to Simon Peter and thrice did He give him a holy charge (John 21:15-17). In I John 5:8, there are three witnesses: "And there are three that bear witness in the earth, the Spirit, and the water, and the blood: and these three agree in one." So three is the number of divinity, the number of God.

Three is the simplest compound unity. It forms the simplest compound figure in geometry, the equal-sided triangle which is indivisible and unresolvable into anything else. It is the first and fixed compound unit of mathematical science. So the sanctuary, God's dwelling place, is a cube, a perfect cube. In the tabernacle it was ten cubits each way, in the Temple it was twenty cubits each way and in the final city of the Holy Jerusalem, it is twelve thousand furlongs each way (Revelation 21:15-16): "and he that talked with me had a golden reed to measure the city. . . . And the city lieth foursquare [a perfect cube]. . . . The length and the breadth and the height of it are equal." The glory of God lightens it, there the counsels of God realized, and the holiness, fulness and completeness of God is attained. The three, the perfect cube; length, breadth and height, the fulness of God realized.

THE NUMBER, FOUR

Now the number *four*. Four is the number of the world of God's creation. It is the number of earthly completeness and universality. To the oriental philosophers, four was the symbol of the world. There are four seasons — spring, summer, fall and winter. There are four directions of the compass — north, south, east and west (Isaiah 11:12; Ezekiel 7:2; Revelation 20:8). There were four walls to the ancient town. There are four phases of the moon. There are four primeval elements — earth, air, fire and water.

Consequently, in the Bible, in the Scriptures, four refers to God's world, God's creation, God's universe. In the first chapter of Ezekiel, for example, there are four cherubim, with four faces and four wings and four sides and four wheels. Those creatures are a symbol of God's providence and God's creation. They are called cherubim. In Revelation 4:6, 7, there are four *zoa*, translated "beasts," which is the most terrible translation I could imagine. Those are four cherubim. They are the four cherubim of Ezekiel. The Greek word "zoa" means "living ones," "quickening," "alive." They represent the same thing in the Revelation that they represent in the book of Ezekiel. When the four *zoa* bowed down and worshiped the Lord and praised "him that liveth forever and ever," they symbolized all God's creation bowing down and worshiping. The singing of the stars and the glory of God's world, bowing down and worshiping the great Creator.

Four is the number of the world. In Genesis 2:10b, the

river of Eden has four heads and divides into four parts, all of which refers to God's sustaining care for His world. In Matthew 13:19-23, in the parable of the sower, there are four kinds of soil, as there are four kinds of hearers in this earth. In Jeremiah 49:36 and Ezekiel 37:9, there are "the four winds." So in Revelation 7:1, "And after these things I saw four angels standing on the four corners of the earth, holding the four winds of the earth. . . ." In Daniel 2:36-40, there are four kingdoms of Nebuchadnezzar's great dream. In Daniel 7:3b, the four beasts, like the four different parts of Nebuchadnezzar's dream, sum up the Gentile empires with their sovereignty over all the earth. In Revelation 6: 1-8, the four horsemen of the Apocalypse sum up the destructive powers of the world at war. The world in which men live and work and die is symbolized by the number four.

Four is the first number that can be divided by two, a symbol of the weakness of the creature in contrast with the Creator. So it is a symbol of us in this world. It is a symbol of failure and of trial. The book of Numbers is fourth in the Pentateuch, and is a type of our pathway and trial in the wilderness of this world. So the meaning (our weakness and trial) extends to the multiple of four: four times ten equals forty. Forty refers to a time of trial and testing in the earth. In the days of Noah, it rained forty days and forty nights. In the days of Moses, on Sinai, he was there forty days and forty nights while Israel was down in the valley around the golden calf. In the days of Jonah he preached to Nineveh, "yet forty days and Nineveh shall be destroyed." In the days of Jesus, He was driven into the wilderness to be tempted of the devil forty days. Trial and temptation.

THE NUMBERS, FIVE AND TEN

Now we come to the numbers *five* and *ten*. I have put them together because they are of the same thing. Five and ten. So common is that "five and ten" that it refers to a certain type of store, doesn't it?

Ten is integral in the thinking of human life. The tithe is a tenth. That is, all that we have is conceived of as being divided into ten parts, of which one part belongs to God as a token of God's sovereignty. These things are not fantastic, they are not arbitrary; rather, they lie in the very genius of the mind and the creative will of God. Now we mentioned earlier that in the consecration of the priest (Exodus 29:20), and in the cleansing of the leper (Leviticus 14:14), the blood of the atonement and the blood of cleansing was placed on the lobe of the right ear and on the thumb of the right hand and on the great toe of the right foot. Each of those is connected with five. There are five senses by which we are in contact with the world. There are five fingers on the hand by which a man executes his choice. There are five toes on his foot by which he walks in God's blessed ways. The basis of the decimal system, as mentioned a while ago, originated in counting with the fingers. So five, so ten, is the secular digit. It is a significant number in all ages and in all history. In the ancient day, men were often maimed, they were crippled through accident and disease. So, the full rounded man was the man who had all of his fingers and all of his toes. In the law, no man could be consecrated high priest who was maimed. Five doubled to ten came to stand for human completeness. The whole duty of man is summed up in ten commandments. The picture of complete power in human government would be a beast with ten horns, as you find in Revelation 13:1. In Daniel 2:41-42, the great image of world empire stands up and is held in place on ten toes. Ten stands for worldly, human completion.

In Matthew 25:1-13, the ten virgins represent the churches in their entirety, in their mixed and slumbering and earthly condition. The ten virgins — all of the churches — just as you find them: some of them dead and sound asleep; some of them alive and vibrant and quickened. Just as you find them — all the churches. In Luke 19:13, the nobleman calls his ten servants and entrusts to them ten pounds, saying, "Occupy till I come." The whole responsibility and sovereignty of God placed in our hands. In Luke 15:8, the woman in the parable has ten pieces of silver, representing all of the devotion of her life. In Genesis 18:32, ten righteous men would have saved Sodom.

Now, the multiples of ten intensify the meaning of the basic number. Four times ten, that is, four intensified. Seven times ten, that is, seven intensified. One hundred times ten, a thousand, is the number that equals ultimate completeness and completion and is (whatever the number stands for) raised to the nth degree. For example, in Revelation 9:16: ". . . the horsemen were two hundred thousand thousand," that is, the number is twice ten thousand times ten thousand, two hundred million. An immense army. The multiples of ten may be found in Genesis 31:7 where Jacob complains to Laban that he changed his wages "ten times"; in Nehemiah 4:12, the discouraging Jews spoke to Nehemiah "ten times"; in Daniel 1:20, the king found Daniel and his companions "ten times better than the others . . ."; in Revelation 2:10, the church of Smyrna is to have tribulation "ten days." That is, it is to be fierce and intense tribulation. In Exodus 7:12, there were "ten plagues" upon Egypt, terrible in the extreme.

THE NUMBER, EIGHT

Now the number *eight*. Eight is the number of the new order, the number of the new departure. Eight is the number of the new beginning. There are seven notes in the musical scale which are the basis for all our music. God's world, God's universe, God's Book are musical with this numerical impress of seven, which is the sacred and holy number. Now, the eighth note is but the octave, the beginning again of the series in a higher key. It is the beginning again in a series higher.

The eighth day is the first day of the new week. It speaks of the new covenant, a new creation. Genesis 17:2, "And he that is eight days old shall be circumcised among you. . . ." After the seventh day, on the eighth day, circumcision was to be administered to the child. It symbolized a new era, cut off from the old Adamic headship. There is a new relationship with God. So Colossians 2:11: ". . . ye are circumcised with the circumcision made without hands, in putting off the body of the sins of the flesh by the circumcision of Christ." II Corinthians 5:17: "Therefore, if any man be in Christ, he is a new creation." Starting over again — Ephesians 2:10. In II Peter 2:5: ". . . Noah, the eighth person, a preacher of righteousness. . . ." In I Peter 3:20: ". . . his [Noah's] family of eight souls were saved by water." That is, there is to be a new beginning, a new family, a new race and a new population. In Exodus 29:35, there are seven days that are occupied with the consecration of the priesthood and on the eighth day they begin their work. In Leviticus 14:10, 23, the leper is cleansed the eighth day. He is a new man; on the eighth day he is cleansed and free. In Leviticus 23:11, "And he shall wave the sheaf [of the first fruits] before the Lord . . . on the morrow after the Sabbath [on the eighth day, after the seventh] the priest shall wave it." In I Corinthians 15:23, the resurrection of Christ is called "the first fruits." So the sheaf of the first fruits is a type of the resurrection of our Lord. On the eighth day, on the morrow after the Sabbath, on the first day of the new week, our Lord arises. It is a new day, it is a new covenant, it is a new gospel, it is a new creation, it is a new departure. Fifty days later, on the same day of the week, is Pentecost. Pentecost came on Sunday. It is a new dispensation of the Holy Spirit of God. In Luke

9:28, we learn that the transfiguration of our Lord was on the eighth day; that is, it is an adumbration of the new age with the power and coming and glory of our Lord (II Peter 1:16-18). John 20:26: "And after eight days . . . Jesus . . . stood in the midst. . . ." He was raised from the dead on the eighth day of the week, the first day of the new week. He appeared to His disciples on that day and on that same day one week later. It is the Lord's day. It is the new beginning. That is the meaning of eight.

THE NUMBER, TWELVE

Now, the meaning of *twelve*. The elements of the numbers seven and twelve are the same. In one, the elements are added: four plus three equals seven. In the other, they are multiplied: four times three equals twelve. Twelve is the number of the world (four) and the number of the divine manifestation of God (three), multiplied, equaling the manifestation of God in the world of His creation. Twelve represents the elective purpose of God in the story of human life. It is a symbol of religion in the world. God's manifest sovereignty is seen, for example, in the twelve tribes of Israel. Twelve is unity and completeness, sanctioned by divine election and choice.

There are twelve months in the year; there are twelve signs of the zodiac; there are twelve tribes of Israel; there are twelve apostles of the Lamb; there are twelve stars in the crown of the radiant woman (Revelation 12:1); there are twelve gates in the new Jerusalem; there are twelve foundations; and there are twelve fruits from the tree of life. Matthew 14:20, "And they did all eat, and were filled: and they took up of the fragments that remained twelve baskets full." Matthew 19:28: ". . . ye which have followed me . . . shall sit upon twelve thrones, judging the twelve tribes of Israel." And Matthew 26:53, "Thinkest thou that I cannot pray to my Father, and he shall presently give me more than twelve legions of angels?" In Exodus 24:4, there are twelve pillars set up by Moses. In Exodus 28:21, there are twelve jewels on the breastplate of the high priest. In Leviticus 24:21, there are twelve loaves of shewbread. In Numbers 13, there are twelve spies sent into Canaan. In Numbers 17:2, there are twelve rods laid up before the Lord. In Joshua 4:9, there are twelve stones set up in the bed of the Jordan River. In I Kings 18:31, Elijah's altar was erected with twelve stones; that is, it represents God's elective purpose and people in the earth.

In Revelation 4:4, "And round about the throne were four and twenty seats: and upon the seats [thrones] I saw four and twenty elders sitting. . . ." What does that mean? That means the redeemed of the Lord. Four and twenty (twenty-four), twelve patriarchs, twelve tribes representing the Old Testament saints and twelve apostles representing the children of God in the New Testament. So twenty-four, that is, the unity and completeness of the redeemed of God, as God's elective purposes are wrought in the earth. In Revelation 7:4, "And I heard the number of them which were sealed . . . an hundred and forty and four thousand. . . ." That is, twelve times twelve times ten times ten (the intensity) equals one hundred and forty-four thousand. Now by saying these things, I do not mean that there were not twelve patriarchs, and there were not twelve apostles and there were not one hundred forty-four thousand. I am just showing you that the numbers have a symbolic and beautiful meaning which is inwrought by the hand of God in all of God's universe.

So in Revelation 21:12, there are twelve gates. In Revelation 21:14, there are twelve foundations to the city. In Revelation 21:16, there is a cube — twelve thousand furlongs. In Revelation 21:21, there are twelve pearly gates. In Revelation 22:2, there are twelve manner of fruits — God's provision and purpose in electing and caring for His people. So in the new Jerusalem, the number of manifest sovereignty, His elective purpose, is everywhere apparent. Wherever you look at it, there do you find it. This is the blessedness: that God rules entirely. The redeemed belong to Him. This is God's ultimate and final work, His purpose to bring us to the holy city of God. Twelve, twelve, twelve and twelve.

THE NUMBER, SIX

The last number is the number *six*. Seven is the sacred number. Six falls short of it. It represents failure. It is the number of man. He was created on the sixth day. His work-day week, appointed time of labor, is six days. The Hebrew slaves were to serve six years. As the darkest hour immediately precedes the dawn, and as the darkest years are just before the millennial Sabbath, so the number six immediately precedes the perfect, holy number of seven. It is the worst of all: six. The darkness of the cross began at the sixth hour and Jesus was crucified on the sixth day of the week. In I Samuel 17:4, Goliath in his height was six cubits and a span. In I Samuel 17:7, his spear's head weighed six hundred shekels of iron and a giant of his race had six fingers and six toes. In Daniel 3:1, the golden image of Nebuchadnezzar was sixty cubits high and six cubits broad. In Ezekiel 39:1, 2 the host of God was all destroyed except one-sixth, which was spared.

Now we come to the most discussed number used in the Bible. In Revelation 13:18: "Here is wisdom. Let him that hath understanding count the number of the beast: for it is the number of a man; and his number is six hundred three score and six." Six units, six tens, six hundreds. Three sixes, three successively higher powers in the decimal scale. That is evil in its fullest activity: the number of a man vainly and impiously aspiring to be God; the deification of man; the de-throning of the Son of God. He is a leader (this antichrist, whose number is 666) — he is a leader where labor is without prayer, where culture is without scripture, where songs are without Psalms, and where rules are without reverence. His is a world without God.

The sum total of human achievement after six thousand years is still the restlessness of ceaseless activity. Has man reached a Sabbath at last? Has he attained a perfect seven? No! He is as far away as ever. He never gets beyond the number *six*. Failure and shortcoming! As Browning says:

> Oh! The little more, and how much it is,
> And the little less, and what worlds away.

Such is the symbol of the number *six*.

Sermon 7

JOHN'S ASCRIPTION OF PRAISE

John to the seven churches which are in Asia: Grace be unto
you, and peace, from him which is, and which was, and which
is to come; and from the seven Spirits which are before his
throne; and from Jesus Christ, who is the faithful witness, and
the first begotten of the dead, and the prince of the kings of
the earth. Unto him that loved us, and washed us from our
sins in his own blood, and hath made us kings and priests unto
God and his Father; to him be glory and dominion for ever
and ever. Amen. — Revelation 1:4-6

This is John's first ascription of praise, his first doxology.
This is John's dedication of the holy and blessed book. In
all literature, there is no work that opens so sublimely and
with such exaltation as this Apocalypse of Jesus Christ.
There is no other book in Holy Scripture that is marked
with such solemnity and such gracious fulness as is found
in this introduction to the Revelation.

Many salutations are found on the pages of the Bible.
When the Hebrew strangers came into Egypt, Pharaoh's
steward greeted them with these words, "Peace be unto you"
(Genesis 43:23). When David sent word by his servants to
Nabal, he said, "Peace be both to thee, and peace be to thine
house, and peace be unto all that thou hast" (I Samuel 25:
6). When the Assyrian monarch made his great proclamation to the kingdom, he said, "Peace be multiplied unto
thee." In the lands of the Levant, a like address and salutation may be heard to this present day, "Shalom" — "peace
be unto thee." But there never was a salutation or a greeting comparable to this written by John to the seven churches

in Asia. This is a peace that is based upon the grace of
God. "Grace be unto you, and peace." It is a peace founded
upon the forgiveness of our sins and the reconciliation of
our souls unto God.

John extends the salutation in the name of the tri-unity
in the Godhead. "Grace be unto you, and peace, from him
which is, and which was, and which is to come." He writes
a descriptive trinity of the first Person of the Godhead,
"which is and which was and which is to come." He writes
a descriptive trinity of the third person of the Godhead:
"spirit," descriptive one; "seven," descriptive two; "before
the throne," descriptive three. As he had three things to
say about the other two persons of the Godhead, so he says
three things about Jesus our Lord. He is "the faithful witness, the first begotten of the dead, and the prince of the
kings of the earth." His salutation, therefore, in the name of
the triune God, is from the everlasting Father, who is the
same in the absoluteness of His unchanging nature and
eternal existence, "who is and who was and who is to come";
from the Holy Spirit, described as the seven Spirits of God,
in all the plenitude of His fulness and perfection and completeness; from Jesus Christ in the virtue of His blood-
sealed testimony, in the power of His resurrection from the
dead, and in the royal administration of His eternal Kingdom. In this exalted way does the apostle address the seven
churches which are in Asia. No more meaningful greeting
was ever read or heard of in all other literature or in all
the Bible.

John now does something marvelous. Upon the mention
of the name of Christ, he breaks into a glorious ascription
of praise, "Unto him that loved us, and washed us from our
sins in his own blood, and hath made us kings and priests
unto God and his Father; to him be glory and dominion
for ever and ever. Amen." It is as though while John was
dictating the mind of the Holy Spirit, when he came to

mention the name of Jesus, he could be seated no longer, but he arose, and then he knelt in adoration and in glory, in worship and in exaltation at the very name of the Son of God, our Saviour. "Unto him . . . be glory and dominion for ever and ever. Amen." The spontaneity of that paeon of praise is like the bursting forth of a mountain stream in all of its sparkling and songful fulness.

John is not alone in his spontaneous doxology. He is one with the rest of the apostles. For example, in the very midst of the wonderful prayer of the apostle Paul in verses twenty-one and twenty-two of the third chapter of the Ephesian letter, he bursts into a doxolgy: "Now unto him that is able to do exceedingly abundantly above all that we ask or think, according to the power that worketh in us, unto him be glory in the church by Christ Jesus throughout all ages, world without end. Amen." In the first letter to Timothy in the first chapter, verse seventeen, at the mentioning of the name of Jesus, Paul bursts into another doxology: "Now unto the King eternal, immortal, invisible, the only wise God, be honor and glory for ever and ever. Amen." Jude, as he writes his little book, bursts into a doxology: "Now unto him that is able to keep you from falling, and to present you faultless before the presence of his glory with exceeding joy, to the only wise God our Saviour, be glory and majesty, dominion and power, both now and ever. Amen." (Jude 24-25). John is like the rest of the apostles in that adoration. Suddenly, their hearts filled beyond measure in fulness and overflowing, they break forth into glorious ascriptions of praise, as John does here, upon the mentioning of the name of the Lord Jesus. "Unto him that loved us, and washed us from our sins in his own blood. And hath made us kings and priests unto God and his Father; to him be glory and dominion for ever and ever. Amen."

Now, these three things that John ascribes in glory and

exaltation to our Lord are the three great things of our salvation. The first is the motive, "Unto him that loved us." The second is the act itself, "unto him that . . . washed us from our sins in his own blood." The third is the result of that great atonement, "Unto him that . . . hath made us kings and priests unto God and his Father."

The Love of Jesus for Us

"Unto him that loved us." Is not that a marvelous phrase? We can understand how our Saviour could have pitied us, understand easily how He could have had compassion upon us, but what a remarkable thing that He should love us! The love is first, before the washing. "Unto him that loved us and then washed us from our sins in his own blood." That is, He loved us in our unloveliness; He loved us while we were foul and unclean and unwashed. He does not wash us first, sanctify and purify us first, then love us. He loves us in our sins, while we are dead in trespasses. "Unto him that loved us." What a remarkable thing that He loves us as individuals and calls us by our names! What an astonishing thing!

In the days of John, the individual counted for nothing. Kings counted. The state counted. Caesar counted. But the oppressed millions of the Roman Empire were just so many pieces of chattel property, deprived of citizenship and made pawns of government. They counted for nothing. In that regard, John's day is much like our own day. What is a man, what is an individual, what is a soul, in the millions and millions trodden underfoot in Communist China or in Soviet Russia? In our modern day, what is a man, what is one soul, in the multitude of things, things, things? On these vast, modern assembly lines, what is a man who is tightening up a bolt here and screwing the head of a nut there and adding a cog on a piece of machinery as it goes down the line yonder? What is a man in all that? When you think about such things, what is a man in the multitudes of humanity that make up the vast population of this earth to-day? What is he but an autumnal leaf falling to the ground, or an insect that dies in the morning? What is man? Finally, with the Psalmist, you may think about him in terms of the age and the vastness of creation: "When I consider thy heavens, the work of thy fingers, the moon and the stars, which thou hast ordained; What is man, that thou art mindful of him? and the son of man, that thou visitest him?" (Psalm 8:3-4). Yet, He loves us, as individuals, *by name* — ". . . he calleth his own sheep by name . . ." (John 10:3). However many there are in this world, and however vast the creations beyond us, and however complicated all of the ramifications of life, yet He loves us.

"Agaponti" is present linear action, translated here "loved us" in the past tense, but the word that John uses is in the present tense, "he loves us." He uses that word to mean that before the foundation of the world He loved us. In the days of His flesh and in the day of His cross He loved us. Ascended back up to glory, He still loved us. When the sun is gone out and the stars are but cinders like ashes on the hearth, He still loves us. Who can comprehend or enter into the breadth and the length and the height of the love of Christ which passeth all understanding and all knowledge? "For I am persuaded, that neither death, nor life, nor angels, nor principalities, nor powers, nor things present, nor things to come, Nor height, nor depth, nor any other creature, shall be able to separate us from the love of God, which is in Christ Jesus our Lord" (Romans 8:38-39). "Unto him that loved us, and washed us from our sins in his own blood."

WASHED IN THE BLOOD OF THE LAMB

"And washed us from our sins in his own blood." In the English these verbs are here written in the past tense. In the language in which John wrote, differences in tenses made much difference in the text, in what he is saying. The word for "love" is in the present tense, and tense in the Greek language is not the pigeon-hole of time that it is in English. Tense in the Greek language denotes kinds of action. Present tense is linear action, meaning here and now and on and forever. "Who loves us," present linear action, means *loves us all the way through*. Then he uses an aorist verb, the aorist tense, when he uses the word, "Lousanti," "Who washed us" — that is, one great act. "He loves us," continuously, always and forever. But He washed us in one great, mighty, atoning act. "Who washed us." We do not work for cleansing, we are not good for it, we do not reform for it, we do not do penance for it. It is something we receive by faith from the gracious hands of our great God. He washed us in that mighty, atoning act in the day and in the hour of His cross. "Who washed us," and all who receive by faith that atoning grace and favor are cleansed and washed and forgiven and saved.

I have a friend who is a retired Air Force Captain. For twenty-two years he was a chaplain in the Air Force. In this last war he was stationed throughout the conflict in field hospitals at the front lines. He said that the doctors had a little secret sign by which they would tell the chaplains how long a boy would live. Three fingers meant he would live three minutes. Five fingers meant he would live five minutes. Ten fingers meant he had ten minutes to live. If the doctor held up ten fingers twice, the boy would have twenty minutes to live.

The chaplain said that he would kneel by every one of those boys and would ask: "Son, have you been saved? Do you know the Lord? In the forgiveness of your sins, have you trusted Jesus as your Saviour?"

And he said, "I would talk to the boy. 'Son, do you realize you are a sinner?' And the boy would reply, 'Yes, I realize

I'm a sinner.' I would say, 'Then, son, will you trust in Jesus for the forgiveness of your sins?' "

Then the chaplain said, "I would have the boy pray and confess his sins to Jesus and ask Jesus to forgive his sins."

I asked, "What if the boy didn't know how to pray?"

"Then I would have the boy pray after me," he replied, "to follow the words as I said them."

"But what if the boy were a Jewish boy?" I asked.

The chaplain said: "Then I would say, 'Son, will you trust in your great Messiah, the atoning Redeemer, who died for your sins? Will you trust Him?' "

"Chaplain," I asked, "in all of those years of the war did you ever have a boy refuse you?"

"I never did," he said, "I never did. Every boy I talked to about his sins and every boy that I pointed to Jesus in faith, and every boy that I encouraged to pray and to trust his soul to Jesus, every boy I spoke to responded."

He added: "I could not tell you the number of times I have seen the light of the glory of God upon the face of an American boy as he left us to be with the Lord."

The cleansing is an act, one great act of faith. It is the aorist tense, "He washed us." It is not a process. It is not linear, continuous action. It is one great, mighty act of God. "He washed us."

> Have you been to Jesus for the cleansing power?
> Are you washed in the blood of the Lamb?
> Are you fully trusting in His grace this hour?
> Are you washed in the blood of the Lamb?

Many ancient Greek manuscripts have "Lusanti," "*freed us* from our sins in His own blood." The imagery in this word, "freed" is plain. In John Bunyan's *Pilgrim's Progress*, the pilgrim is not only dressed in rags, but he has a burden on his back. As he reads the book, weeping, you remember how Evangelist points him to the hill called "The Hill of a Cross," "The Hill of a Skull," "Calvary," and there his burden rolls away. "Who freed us," who loosed us from our sins. All of us are bowed down by the weight of our iniquities. As one man said, "I am the wretched man of Romans 7, when Paul cries, 'O wretched man that I am! who shall deliver me from the body of this death?'" (Romans 7:24). I, too, am that wretched man. All of the philosophies of the ancients are sterile and barren; all of the ancient religions are powerless and pantheistic; all of the ancient helps and comforts are as dust and ashes until Jesus frees us from our sins in His own blood.

KINGS AND PRIESTS UNTO GOD

Not only does He love us and not only has He washed us and forgiven us, but He has done something glorious with us. He has assigned us places of service and dignity and honor. He has made us kings and priests unto God and His Father. He has conferred upon us a celestial citizenship. John was no citizen. Roman citizenship in his day was for the privileged few. The great throngs and masses of the Roman Empire were slaves and subjects, and John was one of those subjects. He had no citizenship. But in Christ, John was not only a citizen but a king and a priest of the heavenly family itself. By the new birth we, also, belong to the blood-royal. We are made kings and priests. The most astonishing thing that mind can imagine is to see poor fishermen and tax-gatherers, just by listening to Jesus, set upon thrones, judging angels and the twelve tribes of Israel.

It is so with us. The lowliest, humblest man among us, in Christ, is exalted and lifted up, made a king and a priest to God and our Father. From this text one might preach on the universal priesthood of all believers. Every man is a priest when he trusts in Jesus. Every believing Christian is an intercessor for lost men to God and is a channel through whom the blessings and grace of God are poured out upon the human race. We are priests unto God. The priesthood of all believers is a celestial doctrine. For ourselves, we have access to God; for ourselves, we can pray to Him; for ourselves, we can come boldly to the throne of grace and speak to God, and God can speak to us. He can whisper in our ear. God can talk to us. Our common garments are vestments, and our common meals are sacraments. Our homes are temples, and our hearts are altars. Our lives are oblations, and the pots and the pans in our kitchens are bowls before the altar of God. Priests unto God and our Father! What a marvelous thing God has done for us in setting us in places of service and honor in His kingdom.

Then John closes, ". . . to him be glory and dominion for ever and ever. Amen." He began this paeon and outburst of praise and this ascription of adoration and exaltation with reference to Jesus. "Unto him" (unto our Christ). John closes with a like reference to Jesus, ". . . to him be glory and dominion for ever and ever. Amen." To John, the person and the presence of Christ was real, most real. How tragic that He is not this real to all of us! If some of us have any sense of the presence of Christ at all, He is far away. He is gone somewhere, we know not whither. He is to some of us like Julius Caesar or Napoleon Bonaparte. He is a character in history somewhere, or he is like an actor on a stage, fictional and feigned. But not to John. "Unto him that loved us"; "to him be glory and dominion for ever and ever."

Each one of these ascriptions to Jesus, John makes personal. He sees Jesus in every act of which he speaks. Not "unto the love of God" (an attribute or a characteristic or an influence) but "Unto him that loved us," and "Unto him . . . that washed us from our sins in his own blood." Back of the theology of the atonement, he finds the day of the cross. He looks to the wounds from whence the atonement flowed, he gazes on the visage so sadly marred, he even peers into the heart pierced by men. "Unto *him*. . . ." If we have places of service, if we are kings, then it is Christ who made us so. All of his faith was personal to John and it ought to be personal to us. Theology can be cold and removed, and religion can be ritualistic and formal. There is nothing of that in the apostles. To them there is the warm presence of the Son of God. True religion is always personal. It is not an atonement, as such, but Jesus dying for our sins; not the theology of the kingdom of God, but a looking for the "parousia," "the presence," "the manifestation," "the epiphany," "the Apocalypse," "the unveiling" of our glorious Lord. Christianity, to the apostles, was Christ, and theology was Jesus. It is so in this ascription of praise. ". . . to him be glory and dominion for ever and ever. Amen."

In the rest of this chapter I want you to see how these ascriptions and doxologies and exaltations grow. There are many of these doxologies in the Apocalypse. See how they grow. The first one here has two notes of praise in it: ". . . to him be glory and dominion for ever and ever. Amen." When we turn the page to the fourth chapter, verse nine through verse eleven, the doxology has three notes of praise: "And when those beasts (living creatures) give glory and honor and thanks to him that sat on the throne, who liveth for ever and ever, The four and twenty elders fall down . . . and cast their crowns before the throne, saying, Thou art worthy, O Lord, to receive glory and honor and power." See, our doxology has grown from two to three — "to receive glory and honor and power." Now, let us turn over to the next chapter (five), and our doxology has grown from three to four, in verse thirteen: "And every creature which is in heaven, and on the earth, and under the earth, and such as are in the sea, and all that are in them, heard I saying, Blessing, and honor, and glory and power, be unto him that sitteth upon the throne, and unto the Lamb for ever and ever." It has grown to four. Now turn to the seventh chapter of the book of the Revelation, the eleventh and twelfth verses, and the notes finally come to the fulness and the completeness and the perfection of seven: "And all the angels stood round about the throne, and about the elders and the four beasts (cherubim), and fell before the throne on their faces, and worshipped God, Saying, Amen: Blessing, and glory, and wisdom, and thanksgiving, and honor, and power, and might, be unto our God for ever and ever. Amen." From two to three to four, to the fulness of seven. Thus the paeon always grows and grows and grows, as our capacity and our realization and our understanding and our love for Jesus grows and grows and grows. I would suppose that when we are unfettered in the body of this death and are privileged to rise in that immortal and glorified body given us in heaven, our doxologies will grow and our ascriptions of praise and exaltation will grow for ever and ever, as previsioned here in the doxologies of John and in these incomparable ascriptions of praise in the Apocalypse. What a glorious and beautiful thing! Unto Him be power and glory and dominion and blessing, world without end, for ever and ever. Amen.

Sermon 8

THE SUBLIME AND EXALTED ANNOUNCEMENT

> Behold, he cometh with clouds; and every eye shall see him, and they also which pierced him: and all kindreds of the earth shall wail because of him. Even so, Amen. — Revelation 1:7

This is the cry that shall reach to the bottom of every grave. It is the cry that shall sound in the depths of the caverns of all the seas. It is the cry that shall reach to the uttermost part of the world, waking the sleeping millions of our dead, who are buried in the heart of the earth. It is the echoing, trumpet sound of the arch-angel of God. "Behold our Lord cometh."

This is the theme and the text of the book of the Revelation. It is the heart and substance of all of its visions. In the first vision, our Lord's coming is promised to His churches. In the next vision, our Lord's coming is the grand climax of the judgments of heaven upon this earth. In the following vision, the coming of our Lord is the catastrophic climax of the conflict between God and Satan. In the concluding vision, the coming of our Lord is the introduction to the new heaven and the new earth and the new order of God's heavenly things.

THE RECURRING THEME OF THE BIBLE

This grand announcement, "Behold, he cometh with clouds; and every eye shall see him . . .", is the sublime, exalted and constantly recurring theme of the entire Bible. In the garden of Eden, the promise of the Lord that the seed of the woman would bruise the serpent's head (Genesis 3:15) is nothing but this same, glorious proclamation, "Behold, he cometh. . . ." The types of the Old Testament are pre-figurations and adumbrations of the return of our Lord. "But as the days of Noah were . . .; so shall also the coming of the Son of man be" (Matthew 24:37). The trials and sorrows, the psalms and songs of David are prototypes of the return of our Lord, our promised coming and rightful King. The uplifted voices of the prophets spoke of the golden, millennial age, in glorious announcement of the coming of our Lord: ". . . And they shall beat their swords into plowshares, and their spears into pruninghooks; nation shall not lift up sword against nation, neither shall they learn war any more" (Isaiah 2:4). "The wolf also shall dwell with the Lamb, and the leopard shall lie down with the kid . . ." (Isaiah 11:6). ". . . They shall not hurt nor destroy in all my holy mountain . . ." (Isaiah 65:25). "For the earth shall be filled with the knowledge of the glory of the Lord, as the waters cover the sea" (Habakkuk 2:14). "Behold," saith the prophet, "he cometh."

Such is the sublime theme and text of the New Testament. One out of every twenty verses of the New Testament concerns the second advent of our reigning Lord. When our Saviour spoke in His parables, He spoke about His coming again. In the nineteenth chapter of the book of Luke, He spoke of Himself as a nobleman that went into a far country to receive a kingdom for himself. He called his ten servants and gave to them ten pounds and said: "Occupy till I come . . . till I come." When our Lord would comfort His disciples, He does so in words of His coming again: "Let not your heart be troubled . . . if I go . . . I will come again, and receive you unto myself . . ." (John 14:1, 3).

This theme is also the content of the preaching of the apostles. The great preacher, Paul, in I Corinthians 15:50-52 said: "Now this I say, brethren, that flesh and blood cannot inherit the kingdom of God; neither doth corruption inherit incorruption. Behold, I shew you a mystery; We shall not all sleep, but we shall all be changed, In a moment, in the twinkling of an eye, at the last trump: for the trumpet shall sound, and the dead shall be raised incorruptible. . . ." Again, in Philippians 3:20-21: "For our citizenship is in heaven; from whence also we look for the Saviour, the Lord Jesus Christ: Who shall change our vile body, that it may be fashioned like unto his glorious body. . . ." Another example is the entire substance of the letters to Thessalonica, of which every chapter ends with a discussion of the return of our Lord. Or, as Paul writes in Titus 2:13: "Looking for that blessed hope, and the glorious appearing of the great God and our Saviour Jesus Christ." Or, as the author of Hebrews says in Hebrews 9:28: ". . . unto them that look for him shall he appear the second time without sin [apart from sin] unto salvation." Or, as Jude writes in the fourteenth verse of his little epistle: ". . . Behold, the Lord cometh with ten thousands of his saints."

This is the summary and the climactic theme and the glorious text of the whole Bible, "Behold, he cometh with clouds; and every eye shall see him. . . ." This is the immutable truth of God, predicted by the prophets, promised by the Lord Jesus Christ, confirmed by the testimony of the angels, preached by the apostles, believed by the early Christians. It is a part of all of the creeds of the churches, of the prayers and the liturgies of the people, and of the hymn books from which we sing the songs of Zion. Take this promise out of the Christian faith and you have a mutilated fragment and a maimed relic. There is no Christianity of this Book apart from that exalted hope of the return of our living, reigning Lord. As He went away, so shall He come again. Surely His feet shall rest upon the summit of the Mount of Olives. If He went away for our justification, He shall return for our redemption and our ultimate, full salvation.

This book of the Revelation, with its Apocalypse of the
return of our Lord, is the completion of the circle of the
revealed Word of God. What is begun in Genesis finds its
concluding, consummating climax in the Revelation. In
Genesis is the story of the creation of the heavens and the
earth. In Revelation is the story of the creation of the new
heaven and the new earth. In Genesis is the story of how
man lost his first paradise. In Revelation is the story of how
paradise is returned to fallen man. In Genesis is the story
of the tree of life and how man was driven from it. In the
Revelation is the story of the tree of life and how man is invited back to it. In Genesis we are introduced for the first time
to Satan, and in the Revelation he appears for the last time in
his ultimate and certain doom. In the book of Genesis is the
story of the entrance of sin into the world, with the sorrow
and toil and heartache it brings. In the book of the Revelation
is heard the great announcement that ". . . there shall be no
more . . . sorrow, nor crying, neither shall there be any more
pain . . ." (Revelation 21:4). In the book of Genesis is the
story of the first death, the first mound of earth heaped up,
over which our first parents wept and cried. In the book
of the Revelation there is the glorious announcement, ". . .
there shall be no more death . . ." (Revelation 21:4). In
the book of Genesis there is the story of man's vast disobedience and the building of the Tower of Babel, of Babylon.
In the book of the Revelation is the story of the destruction
of Babylon and the world system that it represents. In the
book of Genesis is the story of the creation of the first man,
Adam, and his dominion over all things that God made. In
the book of the Revelation is the story and the revelation of
the second Adam and his dominion over things in heaven
and in earth. In the book of Genesis is the story of the
first woman, the first bride, and how she was made a help-
mate for the man. In the book of the Revelation there is the
story of the Bride, the Church of Christ, and how she shall

share with Him in His great and exalted and eternal glory. Without the book of the Revelation, without this sublime announcement and without the personal coming of our Lord, the Bible is a fragment, a maimed and crippled piece. But in the revelation of the glorious return and coming of our Christ, we have the whole circle of God's elective purpose completed. What is begun in Genesis finds its completion and ultimate consummation in the Revelation.

THE INCOMPARABLE ANNOUNCEMENT

What a startling and amazing announcement! "Behold, he cometh with clouds. . . ." In Greek: "Idou, Erchetai Meta ton Nephelon." In Latin: "Ecce, Venit Cum Nubibus." In German: "Er Kommt Mit Den Wolken." In any language it is a sublime and startling announcement. It is the cry of the Holy Spirit, "Come, come and see." It is the cry of the holy apostle, "Come, come and see." It is the cry of inspiration, "Come, come and see." It is the cry of the enraptured church, "Come, come and see." It is the cry of the exalted armies of heaven, "Come, come and see." Behold, and see if there is any glory like unto this glory. We are called, not to look upon a king in his jubilee, not to share in a nation's sesqui-centennial, but to come and to behold the King of kings in His glory. The fire of the heart of the apostle John flamed and burned as he announced this glorious and final consummation, the grand climacteric of all time: "Come, come, come and see." "Behold, he cometh with clouds."

Of all the glories the world has ever seen, there is no glory comparable to this glory. The children of Israel stood at the foot of Sinai and saw the flaming, burning mount that blazed with the presence of God. It was not comparable to this. When Judah and the ten tribes of Israel gathered for the great dedication of Solomon's temple and the Shekinah glory of God came upon it, it was not comparable to this. When Isaiah saw the Lord high and lifted up, the glorious vision was not comparable to this. When the children of God gathered on Mount Carmel and saw the fire fall from heaven to burn up the altar, and lick up the very water in the trench, it was not comparable to this. When the disciples saw the transfiguration of our Lord on the holy mountain, when His face became radiant like the sun, it was not comparable to this. The glory of the coming of our Lord has no parallel in the history of the human race.

"Behold, he cometh with clouds; and every eye shall see him. . . ." "Behold, he cometh with clouds. . . ." John was present when our Lord went away. He saw the clouds receive Him out of his sight, and he heard also the angel's announcement: ". . . this same Jesus, which is taken up from you into heaven, shall so come in like manner as ye have seen him go into heaven" (Acts 1:11). Our Lord, in His return, shall be attended by a radiant sign. In the days of the wilderness experience of the people of God, they were led by a pillar of fire by night and a cloud by day. It was the Shekinah glory of God, riding in His chariot. When our Lord returns, He shall return with a sign, He shall come with clouds — the Shekinah glory of God. He shall appear with clouds of ten thousand times ten thousand of His angels, the angelic host of heaven. He shall appear with thousands of His saints, in glory, in exaltation, in incomparable beauty, descending. ". . . He cometh with clouds. . . ." The entire pageantry of heaven will arise to greet our Lord at His return.

It is a strange thing in the scriptures, this "coming with clouds." Always, when our Lord is presented as appearing, it is with clouds. In Daniel 7:13ff: "I saw in the night visions, and, behold, one like the Son of man came with the clouds of heaven, and came to the Ancient of days, and they brought him near before him. And there was given unto him dominion, and glory, and a kingdom, that all people, nations, and languages, should serve him: his do-

minion is an everlasting dominion, which shall not pass
away, and his kingdom that which shall not be destroyed."
In chapter twenty-four of the book of Matthew, verses
twenty-nine and thirty: "Immediately after the tribulation
of those days shall the sun be darkened, and the moon shall
not give her light, and the stars shall fall from heaven, and
the powers of the heavens shall be shaken: And then shall
appear the sign of the Son of man in heaven: and then shall
all the tribes of the earth mourn, and they shall see the Son
of man coming in the clouds of heaven with power and
great glory." In the twenty-sixth chapter of the same book
of Matthew, verses sixty-two and sixty-four: "And the high
priest arose, and said unto him [Jesus], Answerest thou
nothing? what is it which these witness against thee? But
Jesus held his peace. And the high priest answered and said
unto him, I adjure thee by the living God, that thou tell us
whether thou be the Christ, the Son of God. Jesus saith unto
him, Thou hast said: [the strongest affirmative in the Greek
language] nevertheless I say unto you, Hereafter shall ye see
the Son of man sitting on the right hand of power, and coming in the clouds of heaven."

"Coming with clouds and great glory." What a contrast
as He bowed under the abuse and the spittle and the buffet-
ing and the stripes of men! What a contrast when He returns with the hosts of glory and the Shekinah of God, with
the clouds of heaven! When He first came, He came in
swaddling bands. When He comes again, He comes with
the royal robes of glory. When He first came, He came to
die. When He returns, He returns with dominion and power.
When He first came, He came to be buffeted and to be
crucified. When He returns to reign, He comes the openly
acknowledged Lord God, King eternal and forever.

The Personal Hope We Have in Jesus

"Behold, he cometh with clouds; and every eye shall see
him. . . ." That is, this coming is to be visibly realized. It is

to be personal. Not, "and every mind shall see him," as though it were a subjective experience, as though it were an apparition, a phantom. ". . . every eye shall see him. . . ." This coming is to be visible, it is to be actual, it is to be real. We shall look upon Him with our eyes. ". . . and every eye shall see him. . . ." As Job said by faith in the nineteenth chapter of his wonderful book, in verses twenty-five through twenty-seven: "For I know that my redeemer liveth, and that he shall stand at the latter day upon the earth: And though after my skin worms destroy this body, yet in my flesh shall I see God: Whom . . . mine eyes shall behold, and not another."

"Behold, he cometh with clouds; and every eye shall see him . . ." The coming of our Lord in the second advent is to be as real and as actual as the coming of our Lord in His promised first advent. He came the first time actually and really. Our hands handled Him, and our eyes looked upon Him. ". . . the Word was made flesh, [God was made a man] and tabernacled among us, and we beheld His glory, the glory as of the only begotten of the Father . . ." (John 1:14). Just as actually and just as really, shall He come back the second time. If He came to Bethlehem, He shall also come to Olivet. If He came to die, He shall also come to reign. If He came to be crucified, He shall also come to be admired in all them that believe and trust in Him. As He went away, so, some day, shall He return. "Behold, he cometh with clouds; and every eye shall see him. . . ."

There is no meaning to the first advent of our Lord if we forget the second. The first is without significance except for glorious consummation in the second. In these holy ordinances that we observe in the church, we look forward to the second coming of our Lord. If we are buried with Him by baptism — what a broken fragment — what a tragic sorrow if we are just buried with our Lord in the likeness of His death! But if we have been buried with Him in the

likeness of His death, we shall also be raised with Him in
the likeness of His resurrection. "Christ, the first fruits of
those that are raised from the dead, and afterwards we that
believe in Christ, at His coming, at His return" (I Corinthians 15:23). Buried with our Lord, as He died; but raised
with our Lord, as He was raised. He, raised on the third day
from the Passover; and we, raised when our Lord shall return again from heaven. "Christ, the first fruits and afterwards we, at His coming."

It is thus with the holy ordinance of the breaking of bread
and of the drinking of the cup. There is no such thing as
discerning the Lord's body unless we discern the return of
our Lord, the second advent as well as the first. There is
no drinking to its fulness the cup of our Lord unless we
also hear Him say, ". . . I will not drink henceforth of this
fruit of the vine, until that day when I drink it new with
you in my Father's kingdom" (Matthew 26:29). The holy
ordinance looks backward to the crucifixion of our Lord, and
it looks forward to the return of our Lord. It sees both of
them, the first advent when He died for our sins, and the
second advent, when He returns for our full and ultimate
redemption. We are to greet one another in that same believing faith as those first disciples greeted one another then
— "Achri Hou Elthe": "till He comes," "till He comes." Eating bread and drinking the cup "Achri Hou Elthe," "till He
comes," "till He comes."

Whether in life or in death, we are to greet one another
with that glorious Aramaic word of encouragement and
faith, "Maranatha," "the Lord cometh." If it be today, if
it be tomorrow, if it be tonight, if it be next week, this
promise is the faith and the hope that binds God's children
together: "Maranatha."

> It may be at morn, when the day is awaking,
> When sunlight through darkness and shadow is breaking,
> That Jesus will come in the fullness of glory,
> To receive from the world "His own."

It may be at mid-day, it may be at twilight,
It may be, perchance, that the blackness of midnight
Will burst into light in the blaze of His glory,
When Jesus receives "His own."

While its hosts cry Hosanna, from heaven descending,
With glorified saints and the angels attending,
With grace on His brow, like a halo of glory,
Will Jesus receive "His own."

Oh, joy! oh, delight! should we go without dying,
No sickness, no sadness, no dread and no crying,
Caught up through the clouds with our Lord into glory,
When Jesus receives "His own."

O Lord Jesus, how long, how long
Ere we shout the glad song,
Christ returneth! Hallelujah!
Hallelujah! Amen.

"Behold, he cometh with clouds; and every eye shall see him . . ." — the exalted and sublime announcement — the glad and incomparably glorious climacteric of all ages and of all time!

Sermon 9

THE COMING OF THE LORD SECRETLY
AND OPENLY

Behold, he cometh with clouds; and every eye shall see him, and they also which pierced him: and all kindreds of the earth shall wail because of him. Even so, Amen. — Revelation 1:7

Behold I come as a thief. Blessed is he that watcheth, and keepeth his garments, lest he walk naked, and they see his shame. — Revelation 16:15

There are passages in the Bible that are all-significant and all-important. This text is one of them. This chapter deals with one of the great fundamental keystones in the understanding of the glorious promises of God about the coming again of our Saviour and Lord. In a previous chapter, we discussed the text which is the theme, the key-text, of the book of the Revelation (Revelation 1:7): "Behold, he cometh with clouds; and every eye shall see him, and they also which pierced him: and all kindreds of the earth shall wail because of him. Even so, Amen." The last chapter was on the first part of that glorious announcement: "Behold, he cometh with clouds. . . ." This chapter concerns the remainder of the text: ". . . and every eye shall see him, and they also which pierced him: and all kindreds of the earth shall wail because of him. . . ."

Now, this glorious proclamation, this marvelous, celestially, incomparably glorious announcement: "Behold he cometh with clouds; and every eye shall see him. . .," is the same thing that you read in the second Thessalonian letter, chapter one, verses seven through ten: ". . . When

106

the Lord Jesus shall be revealed from heaven with his
mighty angels, in flaming fire taking vengeance on them
that know not God, and that obey not the gospel of our
Lord Jesus Christ; Who shall be punished with everlasting
destruction from the presence of the Lord, and from the
glory of his power; When he shall come to be glorified in
his saints, and to be admired in all them that believe. . . ."
That great, public appearing of our Saviour is the same thing
you find in the apocalyptic discourse in Matthew 24:27-30:
"For as the lightning cometh out of the east, and shineth
even unto the west; so shall also the coming of the Son of
man be . . . after the tribulation of those days shall the
sun be darkened, and the moon shall not give her light,
and the stars shall fall from heaven, and the powers of the
heavens shall be shaken: And then shall appear the sign
of the Son of man in heaven: and then shall all the tribes
of the earth mourn, and they shall see the Son of man coming in the clouds of heaven with power and great glory."
In Revelation, in Thessalonians, in Matthew, all of those
passages speak of the same incomparably glorious, dramatic
appearing of our great God and Saviour, Jesus Christ. As
the lightning splits the bosom of the sky, so shall the appearing, the *parousia*, the presence, the coming of the Son
of Man be.

THE COMING OF CHRIST SECRETLY

But, there is also in the Word of God a diametrically
opposite presentation of the coming of our Lord. In Revelation 16:15: "Behold [that same exclamation; here is another
'ecce,' 'behold'] I come as a thief. Blessed is he that watcheth, and keepeth his garments, lest he walk naked, and they
see his shame." So opposite! "Behold, I come as a thief."
Now turn to Revelation 3:3, in the middle of that verse:
". . . I will come on thee as a thief, and thou shalt not know
what hour I will come upon thee." That is the same thing
which you read in Matthew 24:42b: "Watch therefore: for

ye know not what hour your Lord doth come. But know this, that if the goodman of the house had known in what watch the thief would come [there's that same word again] he would have watched, and would not have suffered his house to be broken up. Therefore be ye also ready: for in such an hour as ye think not the Son of man cometh." That is the description that you find in the first Thessalonian letter, chapter five, verses one and two: "But of the times and the seasons, brethren, ye have no need that I write unto you. For yourselves know perfectly that the day of the Lord so cometh as a thief in the night." That is the same figure that you find in II Peter 3:8-9, when he speaks of a thousand years as a day and a day as a thousand years. "The Lord is not slack concerning His promise . . . but is longsuffering to us-ward . . . that all should come to repentance. But the day of the Lord will come as a thief in the night [with sandaled feet; secretly, furtively, softly, clandestinely — a thief]."

Someone may say, "What a violent contradiction!" He is coming as lightning that breaks the livid sky in twain, that floods the earth with the light of its power and its glory. Then, in the next sentence, He is coming as a thief — secretly, furtively, softly — to steal away. Is that a contradiction? No! Oh no! For you see, when we read the text in Revelation 1:7, we must read exactly what the spirit of God has said — not what we think He said, not what we read into the text, but exactly what He said. Revelation 1:7: "Behold, he cometh with clouds; and every eye shall see him. . . ." But it does not say, as so many infer, that all shall see Him at the same time, in the same place, in the same manner, and with the same feeling. There will be some who will see Him when He comes as a thief to steal away His jewels. Then, there are others who will see Him as the terrible lightning breaks the bosom of the sky. There are two acts in this great, final, climactic drama. He is coming as a thief to steal away His people. He is also coming as lightning, brilliant upon the throne of His glory and of His judgment. But all must someday look upon the face of the Lord Jesus. There never has been a human being born, nor will there ever be a human being born, who will not somewhere, sometime, in some place, stand face to face with Jesus Christ. The dead shall hear His voice and live, rising out of their graves, and the living shall be caught up to meet our Lord in the air.

In these comings there is the glad, glorious triumph of the people of God — He cometh, our final vindication and reward. But there is also that terrible, indescribable horror and despair of the impenitent — "and the kindreds of the earth shall wail because of him." Those two acts complete the great drama of the denouement and consummation of our age: coming as a thief, with sandaled soles, with furtive steps, secretly, to take out of the earth His own, coming for His people; then — the other act of the great drama — coming as lightning with His saints, into this earth, visible where every eye of the impenitent and the unbelieving shall see Him, establishing in this weary world a final mandate for peace and for righteousness and for the glory of the establishment of the kingdom of our God. So there are two ways that our Lord is to come. First, secretly, as a thief, unannounced, any moment, any day, any time, any hour, any watch, coming for His people, coming to take out of the world the pearl of price.

The most precious thing God has in this earth or in this universe or in this creation is you, God's people. You cost the most. He made the stars in the universe by fiat, by the speaking of a syllable, "Let them be," and they were. But you, the redeemed of God, cost the tears and the agony and the blood and the suffering and the sorrow and the death of the Son of God. You are the pearl of price for which He laid down His life. The heart of our Saviour is here with His people, and the love and expectation and hope of glory is you.

He is coming for us some day, as a thief, to steal us out of this world (I Thessalonians 4:13-18). For that day and hour, God's children wait and the Saviour waits. The whole creation waits in travail and in agony and in pain until that moment when the Lord shall come (Romans 8:19-25). This is the imminency of the return of our Lord, coming for His people any hour, to take us out of the world. This is called the rapture of the church, meeting our Lord in the air. This is a rendezvous that is secret, that is just for and just includes the children of God; the sainted dead preceding us, and all of us who are alive, transformed, immortalized, transfigured, in a moment, in the twinkling of an eye, when the trumpet of God shall sound and the dead in Christ rise first, when the Christian's ear, attuned to the call of God, hears the great invitation to rise to meet our Lord in the air. He is coming secretly.

This secret call of the Lord is presented in the Bible through type, through promise, through teaching, from beginning to ending. Enoch suddenly was translated with no announcement, no word. The world did not know when. All the world knew was that Enoch was gone. He just was not. The church is an *ecclesia*, a "called out" body. That is the Greek word translated "church." The church is "the called out." The church is "the called away." *Ecclesia*, "called out," "taken away," like Enoch. Matthew 24:40-41 says: "Then shall two be in the field; the one shall be taken, and the other left. Two women shall be grinding at the mill; the one shall be taken, and the other left." Just caught away, just gone, translated, secretly, without announcement.

We find the same kind of a type in the days of Noah. "As it was in the days of Noah, so shall it also be in the days of the coming of the Son of Man" (Luke 17:26). While the impenitent were blaspheming, while they were drinking and carousing, while they were damning and scorning and scoffing, while the world was plunged in its sordid ways, suddenly, without any announcement, God called Noah into the ark, and the Book says, "and God shut the door." God shut the door! Like the story of the five wise virgins who entered in, "God shut the door." There was no announcement; the world did not know; it did not care. For one hundred and twenty years, righteous Noah had been preaching to that sinful and vile and violent race. They scoffed and they scorned. They drank the more and cursed the more and blasphemed the more. Noah entered into the ark and God shut the door. Then the fountains of the deep broke and the sky rained floods. Judgment — but first, God's people safe within.

The same thing happened in the days of Lot: ". . . As it was in the days of Lot . . . so shall it be also in the days of the Son of Man" (Luke 17:26, 28). While the Sodomites fell into their gross, indescribable iniquity; while they revelled in the filth and dirt of their blasphemy; while they drank and caroused and cursed, the angel snatched Lot out of the city. What an unusual thing! For God said, ". . . I cannot do anything till thou be come thither" (Genesis 19:22). Compromising Lot! Lot looked toward Sodom. Lot pitched his tent toward Sodom. Lot moved to Sodom. Lot took office in Sodom. Lot sat in the gate of Sodom. Lot raised his family in Sodom. Lot ceased to be a pilgrim in Sodom. Lot lost his testimony in Sodom. Lot vexed his soul with the filthy, dirty conversation of Sodom (II Peter 2:8). Yet God said, ". . . I cannot do anything till thou be come thither." The Lord snatched him away. ". . . as it was in the days of Lot . . . so shall it be also in the days of the Son of Man" (Luke 17:26, 28).

As compromised and as worldly as God's church is and as God's people are, God cannot rain judgment and the fire of righteous indignation upon this earth until His people

first be taken out. The only thing that stays the heavy hand
of God's righteous wrath upon this sinful earth is the people of God, the church of our Lord, His saints who dwell
here. But secretly, unannouncedly, furtively, upon a time
known only to God, His people shall be taken away, shall
meet the Lord in the air. Then shall take place the second
tremendous act of this final and consummating drama. Then
shall appear the sign of the coming of the Son of Man as
lightning splits the bosom of the sky. ". . . Behold, the Lord
cometh with ten thousands of his saints," says Jude, quoting
Enoch, the seventh from Adam. ". . . Behold, the Lord
cometh with ten thousands of his saints" (Jude 14). First,
He is coming *for* His people, then, after a terrible period of
trial and tribulation in the earth, He is coming back openly,
publicly, announcedly, *with* His people.

THE COMING OF THE LORD OPENLY

God reveals the great publicity of the sublime event. It
is with this public coming that the book of the Revelation
has to do. The book of the Revelation has not to do with
the secret coming of our Lord, the taking out of His people.
The book of the Revelation concerns itself with that great,
final act of the mighty drama when He comes in power and
in glory, including the great judgment and visitations that
precede it. "Behold, he cometh with clouds; and every eye
shall see him. . . ." As the flood of the light of His glory falls
on the mountains and on the hills and through the valleys,
so every eye that is in this earth shall behold Him, the King
in His glory. He shall come in the glory of the Father, God
the Son and the Son of God. He shall come in the glory of
the angels, their Lord and Master, the Captain and the
Prince of the hosts of heaven. He shall come in the glory of
the church, the Bridegroom with the Bride. He shall come
in His own glory as the Son of God, the Son of Abraham,
the Son of David, the Son of Man, the immortal Man, the

infinite Man, the risen Man, our atoning Saviour, born of a woman. Our Lord is coming in the glory of His manhood, God and man, the Man-God, Christ Jesus. He is coming to be king over Israel, He is coming to be king over the nations and He is coming to be the restorer of the earth, its Re-creator, its Prince, its manifest and eternal God — "Behold, he cometh with clouds; and every eye shall see him. . . ."

Then, this inspired apostle John writes of the reception of our Lord in the earth: ". . . they also which pierced him: and all kindreds of the earth shall wail because of him. . . ." That word "wail" is a strong word in our English language but it is not nearly as strong as the word John uses here in his original Greek sentence. "Kopto" is the Greek word for "cut" — as you would cut off a branch, as you would cut down a tree. "Cut" ". . . and every eye shall see him and . . . all kindreds of the earth shall [*kopto* — translated *wail*]." That word is taken out of oriental imagery. When people were in despair and in horror they cut themselves. To paraphrase: *and all kindreds of the earth shall fall into such despair* (it's a picture of the bitterness, of the agony, of the horror of their future) *that they shall "kopto"* (wail) *"cut themselves" because of him.* . . . Such is the scene in the sixth chapter of the book of the Revelation: "And the heaven departed as a scroll . . . and every kindred of the earth hid themselves in the dens and in the rocks of the mountains; and said to the mountains and rocks, Fall on us, and hide us from the face of him that sitteth on the throne, and from the wrath of the Lamb: For the great day of his wrath is come; and who shall be able to stand?" (Revelation 6:14-17) ". . . shall wail because of him. . . ."

In this terrible horror and waiting, John picks out one particular group: ". . . and they also which pierced him. . . ." Those that drove the nails in His hands, those that thrust the spear in His side, those that shared in that shameful murder, some day shall confront the Lord face to face.

I think the reason John wrote it like that was because he was present when Jesus died. He saw their fierce looks, he beheld their hard, impenitent hearts, he saw their cruel hands and he witnessed their blasphemy and their unbelief. John said some day they shall behold the king on the throne of His glory in the day of judgment.

"... and all kindreds shall wail. . . ." Because John, in speaking here of "kindreds," uses the word *phule*, the word for "tribe," some think this refers to Zechariah 12:10, when the house of Israel wailed because of Him, the One they pierced, the One they rejected, their Messiah. Some think this is the fulfillment of the prophecy when a nation is born in a day, when the remnant of Israel is converted. Maybe so. But it also includes all of the families of the earth. These are the impenitent. God's people have been taken away. God's people are with the Lord; they return with Him, the ten thousands and thousands of His saints and of the host of heaven. These who see the Lord coming in judgment, as lightning, are they who blaspheme His name, who curse the thought of Him, who do despite to His spirit of grace, who tread under foot the blood of the covenant. These are the impenitent, and His appearance strikes terror and despair to their hearts. Here is the world, drinking, carousing, living in godlessness, in rejection and in unbelief. Then the great Judge of the world appears and they are lost — lost. In a moment, how the earth changes, from its sinning and its dancing and its carousing and its drinking and its worldliness, into awful despair because of the horror of the judgment of God.

I think of the Titanic. In the nighttime the orchestra was playing for the dancers when occurred that awful tragedy. The orchestra gathered on the bow of the ship as the stern began to sink. They were not playing any "red hot mama." They were playing "Nearer My God to Thee." As the ship sank, the orchestra went down playing that plaintive melody.

As suddenly shall every man stand before God in that awful day, either with Him on the throne of His glory, sharing the beauty of our glorious king, or standing in His presence, impenitent, lost and unsaved, undone and cast out, condemned and destroyed. In that dread hour of judgment, the wicked dead shall be raised and shall stand beside those who are living in unrighteousness and unbelief. O lost sinner, death shall not hide thee, the vault shall not cover thee, corruption shall not deliver thee. Thou shalt be there in that day.

> Oh, what a weeping and wailing,
> When the lost are told of their fate,
> They cry for the rocks and the mountains
> They pray, but their prayer is too late.

If you are going to be saved, you will have to be saved now. God doesn't deceive us with idle dreams of repentance and restoration after that day of judgment arrives and after the hour of our death. If His first coming doesn't save us, His second coming shall certainly condemn us. If we are lost now, we are lost then and are lost forever and forever.

> Oh, then to the Rock let me fly
> To the Rock that is higher than I.

Death is coming. Judgment is coming. Christ is coming, and to those who lift up their hearts in faith and in trust, His return is our redemption, it is our salvation, it is our glory, it is our final and ultimate triumph, it is our heaven forever, world without end. But to those who turn aside from the invitation of mercy and forgiveness, it is the day of horror and of judgment, crying for the rocks and the mountains. Oh! Spirit of God, that we might be delivered in that terrible and climactic hour that shall come upon all of the earth! ". . . every eye shall see him. . . ." God grant that we may look up and say, "Here is our Saviour." God grant none shall look up in terror and say, "Here is the great Judge who stands in rebuke and in condemnation of my rejection and my unbelief." Lord, save our people!

Sermon 10

EVEN SO — AMEN

Behold, he cometh with clouds; and every eye shall see him,
and they also which pierced him: and all kindreds of the earth
shall wail because of him. Even so, Amen. — Revelation 1:7

The text is the answer of the apostle John to the glorious
and incomparable announcement of the coming of our Lord.
In the first chapter of the Revelation, John greeted the
seven churches of Asia in the name of the triune God: the
Father (Him who is and was and is to come); the Holy
Spirit of God (which is before the throne); and Jesus Christ
(who is the faithful witness, the first begotten of the dead,
and the prince of the kings of the earth). Then follows a
glorious ascription of praise to our Lord. When he mentions the name of Jesus, his heart abounds in adoration and
worship. ". . . Unto him that loved us, and washed us from
our sins in his own blood, And hath made us kings and
priests unto God and his Father; to him be glory and dominion for ever and ever. Amen" (Revelation 1:5-6). Then
follows the text, the theme of the Apocalypse, this incomparably glorious announcement: "Behold [ecce], he cometh
with clouds; and every eye shall see him . . ." (Revelation
1:7). Then follows the text of this chapter — the answering
cry of the heart of the sainted apostle: ". . . Even so, Amen."
"Nai, Amen." That same heartfelt expectancy, that same
glorious acquiescence, is found in the concluding chapter
of the Revelation when the apostle said the same two words
again: "He which testifieth these things saith, Surely I come

116

quickly. Amen. Even so, come, Lord Jesus" (Revelation 22:20).

The early apostles and the first primitive Christians lived in the daily expectation and hope of the appearing of our Lord. When they saw one another, when they greeted one another, when they bade farewell to one another, they would use words that expressed the blessedness of the Lord's coming. If they were Aramaic, they used the word "Maranatha," "the Lord cometh." If they were Greek, they would say, "achri hou elthe": "till He come, till He come." "Even so, Amen."

Who Is It That Is Coming?

Who is it that is coming and whom are we to expect? Who is this "him," when in the ascription of praise the apostle John says, "Unto *him* who loved us . . . to *him* be glory and dominion . . ." (Revelation 1:6-7)? Who is this "he" in the great announcement: "Behold, *he* cometh with clouds; and every eye shall see him . . ." (Revelation 1:7)? Whom are we to expect? Who is this "I" in the closing of the Apocalypse: ". . . Surely *I* come quickly. Amen. Even so. . . ." (Revelation 22:20)?

The identification of this One who is coming is sure and certain; in the first chapter John clearly identifies this One who has spoken unto him. Look at Revelation 1:11-13: ". . . I am Alpha and Omega, the first and the last: and, what thou seest, write in a book, and send it unto the seven churches which are in Asia. . . . And I turned to see the voice that spake with me. And being turned, I saw . . . the Son of Man [Jesus Christ]." That Somebody, that Someone, that Some-Person, whom we are looking for, descending in clouds of glory and power, is none other than the Christ-Man, the Lord Jesus. We are looking for *Him*. ". . . this same Jesus, which is taken up from you into heaven, shall so come in like manner as ye have seen him go . . . (Acts 1:11). We are looking for, we are expecting, the Lord Jesus, the one with the stigmata, the nail prints in His hands and His feet and the scar of the spear thrust in His side. We are looking for the man, Christ Jesus. We are looking for our Saviour, whom death could not kill, whom the grave could not hold and the sepulchre could not keep. We are looking for the same Lord Jesus who sat wearied on the well in Sychar of Samaria. We are looking for the same Lord Jesus who taught by the blue waters of Galilee, who climbed the steep hills of Judea. We are looking for the same Lord Jesus who took into His arms little children and blessed them, who spoke words of comfort to His disciples, who bare our sicknesses and carried our infirmities. We are looking for the man, Christ Jesus, the same Lord and the same Saviour, that same blessed face, that same holy voice, that same heavenly emissary, that Saviour who opened for us the gates of glory. We are looking for Him, the man, Christ Jesus.

We are looking for Him in the flesh, our living Lord. God, the Father, has no body; He has no bones and no flesh; God is spirit. The Holy Spirit has no body. He is spirit. But Jesus is not a spirit. Jesus has flesh and bones such as we have. Look at Luke 24:38-43: "And when they saw Him they were terrified and affrighted and supposed they had seen a spirit. Jesus said, Why are ye troubled? and why do thoughts arise in your hearts? Behold my hands and my feet, that it is I myself: handle me, and see; for a spirit hath not flesh and bones, as ye see me have. And when he had thus spoken, he shewed them his hands and his feet. And while they yet believed not for joy, and wondered, he said unto them, Have ye here any meat? And they gave him a piece of a broiled fish, and of an honeycomb. And he took it, and did eat before them." Flesh and bones — immortalized, glorified, resurrected! Compare the marvelous, inexplicable miracle that happens when we eat and by the mysterious process of God, the alchemy of heaven, things on the table are translated, transmuted, sublimated, quickened, into lives, into *you*. Only there is one other and higher step: the corrupting body is immortalized, quickened, glorified, transfigured into the heavenly, spiritual body of Christ. One miracle is just as inexplicable as the other. You can as well explain one of them as you can the other: the miracle of assimilation (common, everyday eating) and the miracle of glorification (the resurrection of the body). It is the same Lord Jesus, raised from the dead. We are looking for and expecting that same Christ-man in the flesh, descending on clouds of glory from heaven.

Jesus is in heaven. His spirit is in our hearts; but our Lord Himself is in heaven and He looks down upon His children. He bows His ear low to hear us when we pray. He encourages us by making the way before us. He sends the power and presence of His Holy Spirit into our hearts and into our services. But we are looking for the man, Christ Jesus from heaven. Stephen saw Him in heaven when they stoned him to death. Before the first Christian martyr was crushed into the dust of the earth, he lifted up his eyes and saw the Lord Jesus. Paul met Him on the road to Damascus, the man, Christ Jesus. ". . . Who art thou, Lord? And the Lord said, I am Jesus whom thou persecutest" (Acts 9:5). "Jesus of Nazareth," the same Lord Jesus. John saw Him on the Isle of Patmos; "And I turned to see the voice that spake with me. And being turned, I saw . . . the Son of man. . . ." (Revelation 1:12-13). "The Son of Man" — the same Christ Jesus. And I have talked to Christians who have seen Him since. Sometimes as our aged saints near the great divide, they speak of the green pastures and the still waters and they speak of the angelic music and heavenly choirs and sometimes they will say, "And I behold His glorious face; I see the Lord."

Isn't it Jesus we want to see? It is not enough to have a

letter from Him. It is not enough to have the third person of the Trinity in our hearts and in our services. "We would see Jesus," cried the Greeks at the great feast, and the cry of the Greeks is the cry of God's people today. "Sirs, we would see Jesus." It is Jesus some day that we shall see. "Even so, Amen."

There was once a man, an immigrant, unlettered and unlearned, who was converted. He was gloriously happy in his conversion. His heart so welled with joy and gladness that he said as he stood to testify for his Saviour: "Some day, when I go to heaven, I want to see Jesus first of all. I want to see Him first of all." When his father and his mother died, they asked him, "Is it still Jesus first?" The immigrant replied, "When I get to heaven, I still would see Jesus, first of all." Then other members of his family died. A child died, and a son died, and his wife died and finally the immigrant, in his old age, was left alone, and they asked him then, in the twilight and sunset of life, if it was Jesus still first of all. At the end of the way, after all of his friends and all of his family had gone on before, the convert still replied, "I want to see Jesus first of all." Maybe this story is the basis of the beautiful hymn by blind Fanny Crosby. It is in our hymn book and it is entitled, "My Saviour First of All."

> When my life-work is ended, and I cross the swelling tide,
> When the bright and glorious morning I shall see;
> I shall know my Redeemer when I reach the other side,
> And his smile will be the first to welcome me.

> Oh, the dear ones in glory, how they beckon me to come,
> And our parting at the river I recall;
> To the sweet vales of Eden they will sing my welcome home;
> But I long to meet my Saviour first of all.

> Thro' the gates to the city in a robe of spotless white,
> He will lead me where no tears will ever fall;
> In the glad song of ages I shall mingle with delight;
> But I long to meet my Saviour first of all.

Is It True, That We Shall See Jesus?

Shall we see Him? Can it be really true? The same Lord
Jesus? To avow the reality and visibility and the personality
of Christ Jesus in His return, Scripture again and again
emphasizes promise by reiteration and re-enforces reiteration by repeated assertion. ". . . this same Jesus . . . shall so
come . . . in like manner." "The Lord *Himself* shall descend
from heaven . . ."; "every eye shall see Him . . ."; our Lord
in the flesh. It is Jesus we are going to see. "Behold — behold, he cometh with clouds; and every eye shall see him.
Nai, Amen. Even so. Amen."

In our modern world and in our modern theology and in
our new day, what strange identifications are made with
respect to the coming of our Lord. Who is coming? What
is the coming of the Lord and what are we to expect? Ah!
Such strange things as are said by the theologians. In my
reading as I look at the writings of some of our most famous
preachers, I can hardly believe my eyes. I quote from one:
"What then is the coming? It is the divine unexpectedness
of our experience — temptation, sorrow, opportunity, gladness, grief — watch, therefore." May I choose one other?
From another book I have copied this little excerpt. "I believe Jesus came in 70 A.D. in the destruction of Jerusalem.
I believe Jesus came in the fall of the Roman Empire. I
believe He came in the Mayflower which brought the little
company from Holland. I believe He came when the Consti-
tution of the United States was dedicated. In July, 1914,
when the Serbians shot the Arch-Duke of Austria, I have
the feeling that Jesus came when the nations of Europe
plunged the earth into a bloody holocaust." On and on it
goes. They say Jesus came at Pentecost. They say Jesus
came in the philosophical truths of modern metaphysics.
Some of them say Jesus came in the enlightenment and in
the technical advances of the nineteenth century. Some say
that Jesus comes in death. Others say that Jesus comes in

the diffusion of the Christian message over the world. Still others say that Jesus comes in the civilization that has up-lifted the standards of mankind. In every way you can imagine, as you read, they identify the coming of our Lord.

As I read these books and sometimes as I listen to these men, I pick up THE Book and I say again, who is this "He" who is coming in Revelation 1:7? Who is this "I" in "Surely I come quickly" in Revelation 22:20? Who is this precious, comforting Saviour, who says in the fourteenth chapter of John: "I go to prepare a place for you. And if I go to prepare a place for you, I will come again . . ." (John 14:2-3)? Who is this "I"? Whom are we to expect? Is this what He meant? "Let not your heart be troubled, I will come in the destruction of Jerusalem in 70 A.D.?" "Let not your heart be troubled, I will come again in the downfall of the Roman Empire?" "Let not your heart be troubled, I will come again in the diffusion of the Christian message over the world?" "Let not your heart be troubled, I will come again in the technological and scientific advancements of the nine-teenth and twentieth centuries?" "Let not your heart be troubled, I will come again." Whom are we to expect? Who is this "I"? My dear people, they have so diffused Him in history, they have so confounded Him with death, they have so spiritualized Him into a shadowy, vague phantom, they have so allegorized Him into myth and fairy-tale and fiction that I can almost hear our Lord saying to us as He said to His disciples: ". . . handle me, and see . . . that it is I my-self . . . for a spirit hath not flesh and bones, as ye see me have" (Luke 24:39). Whom are we to expect? Who is this "I" who will come again? Of whom is this great announce-ment made in Revelation 1:7: "Behold, He cometh with clouds and every eye shall see him"? If I can believe the Book, and if I can accept in faith the promises of our Lord, I am to look for Him, the same blessed Lord Jesus.

It is our Saviour who is coming. That same blessed face,

those same gracious hands. Our living, loving, worshipful Lord. Mary knew Him by the sound of His voice when He pronounced her name. He had a way of calling her, unlike anyone in the earth, and when He said just, "Mary," she turned and, falling at His feet, cried, "Rabboni, my Master." He was known in the way He pronounced her name. John recognized Him in the way that He folded up a napkin. Our Lord had an idiosyncrasy, a turn, a way of folding up a napkin, and when John followed Simon Peter into the sepulchre and saw the napkin folded up in a place by itself, he said, "This is my Lord." He believed. Cleopas and the other un-named disciple knew Him in Emmaus by the way He said grace at the table. At an eventide, as they sat down for the breaking of bread, He prayed and they recognized Him in the kind of a prayer that He said. In the gray mist of the early morning, a dimly outlined figure stood by the side of the sea of Galilee saying, "Put the net on the right side and thou shalt catch." When they caught, the disciple Jesus loved said to Simon, "Simon, that's the Lord, that's the Lord." He still has the personality, the traits, the idiosyncrasies that make us *us*, that make you *you* and that make Jesus *Jesus*. When He comes, it will be the same, blessed Lord Jesus. "For I know," said Job, "that my redeemer liveth, and that he shall stand at the latter day upon the earth: And though after my skin worms destroy this body, yet in my flesh shall I see God: Whom I shall see for myself, and mine eyes shall behold, and not another . . ." (Job 19:25-27). "Behold, he cometh with clouds; and every eye shall see him." "*Nai*, Amen." "Even so, Amen" (Revelation 1:7). We are looking for the Christ-man, the same Lord Jesus.

THE MARK OF THE TRUE DISCIPLE

May I make one other observation? The mark of the true disciple and the true believer in Christ is this, that he is

looking for our Lord in the flesh. Turn in your Bible to II
John. The same apostle John who wrote the Revelation,
who wrote the Apocalypse, the same apostle John is writing a letter to an Elect Lady and her chilidren. In verse
seven, he says: "For many deceivers are entered into the
world, who confess not that Jesus Christ is come [the Greek
word here is *erchomenos*] in the flesh." Now, in the Revelation I want to show you how that word "erchomenos" is
translated. In the first chapter of the Revelation and in the
next verse from my text, verse eight, we read: "I am Alpha
and Omega, the beginning and the ending, saith the Lord,
which is, and which was and which is to come [*erchomenos*]." You cannot translate the passage any other way.
"I am Alpha and Omega, the beginning and the ending,
saith the Lord, which is, and which was, and [*erchomenos*]
is to come." Many deceivers are in the pulpits, in the
theological chairs, in the world of philosophy and metaphysics, in the secular and materialstic world, many deceivers who say, "You'll never see His face; there is no
Lord who is actually coming." ". . . who confess not that
Jesus Christ [*erchomenos*] is coming in the flesh. But we
who believe and who bow in His presence, we who lovingly
read and are persuaded of this blessed Book, *we* are looking
for the same Lord Jesus in the flesh, with body and bones
as we have — our risen and glorified Christ Jesus. "*Nai*,
Amen." "Even so, Amen."

In the last World War when the Japanese military took
over Korea from the civil administration of Japan, we had
in that country forty churches, forty little Baptist churches,
with five thousand members. Because they were so faithful in meeting together, the Japanese military called the
President of the Convention and with endless questions that
continued hour after hour, demanded what these Korean
Baptists believed. After hours of exhausting interrogation,
they finally got down to the second coming of Christ and

the interrogators of the Japanese military authority said, "And what do you believe about the second coming of the Lord?" The pastor and the president of our Convention said, "We believe that this same Jesus shall so return as He went away." The Japanese military said, "And then what?" The pastor said, "And then shall every knee bow and every tongue confess that He is Lord to the glory of God the Father." The Japanese military said, "Does that include our great, divine Emperor?" The pastor replied, "Sir, it includes your Emperor, for our Saviour is the King of Kings and the Lord of Lords." The Japanese military said, "Do you believe this for yourself alone, or do all of you believe it?" The pastor replied, "Sir, we all believe it."

They gathered up all forty of our pastors and put them in prison. After three or four years of trial and persecution beyond description, the pastor, who was the Convention President and who was answering the questions, died of the terrible exposure and privation. One by one, most of the other pastors died. When finally the few that remained were liberated, two of them died upon their liberation. That is the fabric of God's believing disciples. "Do you believe this for yourself or do all of you believe it?" Our pastor and president replied, "Sir, we all believe it." "Behold, he cometh," and we all answer with the apostle John, "Nai, Amen." "Even so, Amen, Lord Jesus." "He which testifieth these things saith, Surely, I come quickly" (Revelation 22:20). "I" come. Our Lord cometh. Amen. Even so, Lord Jesus. That is our faith, that is our hope, that is our comfort, and that is the consummation of this age for God's children. Some day, to look upon His blessed, blessed face! We ourselves immortalized, a body like His, glorified, a new creation, in a new city, in a new home, in a new fellowship. Amen. Even so, Lord Jesus.

Sermon 11

IN THE ISLE THAT IS CALLED PATMOS

> I John, who also am your brother, and companion in tribulation, and in the kingdom and patience of Jesus Christ, was in the isle that is called Patmos, for the word of God, and for the testimony of Jesus Christ. — Revelation 1:9

The brother of Titus, the Roman Caesar, was named Domitian. Titus was a gifted general, a mighty man of war, and the man who led in the destruction of Jerusalem when his father, Vespasian, was called to be the Roman Caesar. Titus was an able and wise ruler, but before his reign was extended he died and his brother, Domitian, ascended to the throne. Domitian was altogether unlike his father, Vespasian, and his brother, Titus. Domitian was bloodthirsty and cruel. He was the first of the Roman Caesars who demanded that all of his subjects address him as "our Lord and god." He was the first of the Roman Caesars to make images of himself, place them in all of the places of worship in the empire and demand that the people worship him. In these circumstances the lot of the Christians was extremely cruel, for to them, as to us, there was no God but God, and to bow down to a graven image of any kind was idolatry. Especially was the lot and the life of the Christians difficult in Asia Minor because they were so numerous in that part of the Empire. Their very numbers demanded that the mandate that they bow and worship the image of Domitian as God be carried out with extreme cruelty.

The pastor of the church in the capital city of the Roman province of Asia was named John, the sainted disciple of the Lord, now in the old age of his life. In that Domitianic persecution, John was exiled to the island of Patmos. Patmos was just one of the many places to which Domitian sentenced those who had incurred his wrath. Patmos is a little rocky island about twenty-four miles west into the sea off the Asia Minor coast, directly opposite the ancient town of Miletus. It is about twenty-five miles in diameter, rugged and mountainous. Apparently John was not chained or guarded nor was he cast into a dungeon. He had free access to all of the confines of the little island. In that rugged place he saw the sublime revelation called the Apocalypse of Jesus Christ.

The Sufferings of the People of God

John speaks of himself in this first chapter in the words of our text: "I John, who also am your brother, and companion in trial and in suffering and in persecution and in tribulation. I was in the isle that is called Patmos, because of the preaching of the word of God, and because of the testimony of Jesus Christ." It is not strange or new or unusual that John is in trial, in exile and in suffering. Jesus had said that the mark of His disciples was their persecution and their suffering. In the Sermon on the Mount, our Master said: "Blessed are they which are persecuted for righteousness' sake. . . . Blessed are ye, when men shall revile you, and persecute you, and shall say all manner of evil against you. . . . Rejoice and be exceeding glad . . . for so persecuted they the prophets which were before you" (Matthew 5:10-13). In the Apocalyptic discourse of our Lord in Matthew 24:9, our Saviour said: "Then shall they deliver you up to be afflicted, and shall kill you: and ye shall be hated of all nations for my name's sake." In the sixteenth chapter of the gospel of John, verse thirty-three, in the comforting discourse spoken in the upper room, our Lord said: ". . . In the world ye shall have tribulation. . . ." The apostle Paul, in the last letter that he wrote, addressed to Timothy, his young son in the ministry, said: "Yea, and all that will live godly in Christ Jesus shall suffer persecution" (II Timothy 3:12). The endurance of suffering and trial is a mark of the favor of heaven and the blessing of God.

The whole New Testament is a record of the sufferings of the people of our Lord. John the Baptist died in his own blood. Our Saviour was crucified beneath the open skies, raised from the earth on the tree. The story of the church from the beginning is written in blood and in tears. In the eighth chapter of the Book of Acts and verse one: ". . . at that time there was a great persecution against the church which was at Jerusalem. . . ." Then begins that long list of illustrious martyrs that continues to this present hour. Stephen is stoned outside the city of Jerusalem. The head of James, the brother of John who wrote the Revelation, is severed from his body by the cruel sword of Herod Agrippa I. In the Revelation, chapter two and verse thirteen, our Lord speaks of His faithful martyr, Antipas, who was put to death for the Word of God in the city of Pergamos. The book of the Hebrews was written in a time of great trial and trouble. The author made appeal to the little Hebrew church that they be willing to go outside the gate, without the camp, bearing the reproach of the Lord (Hebrews 13:13). When the book of the Revelation was written, Polycarp was pastor at Symrna and Polycarp was burned at the stake. When the book of the Hebrews was written, Ignatius was pastor of the church at Antioch. He was condemned to die. He was taken to Rome and there torn by wild beasts, the first Christian to die in the Roman Colosseum which had just been completed. This is the story of the people of our

Lord through all of the generations and through all of the centuries.

Why, in the elective purpose of God, does the Lord permit His people to be persecuted? The first reason is this: out of the trial, the martyrdom, the imprisonment, the sorrows and tribulations of God's people, God speaks His truth to our souls. This is seen plainly in the epistles of Paul. Most of Paul's ministry was spent in prison. Does not that seem a vast waste of life when he could have been preaching to the Dalmatians, to the Spaniards, to the Gauls, or to the Ionians? But most of his life as a Christian was spent in the confines of a dungeon. Why did God allow that? Because from the chains of those prisons Paul sent the letters that comprise so large a part of our New Testament. Out of the sufferings of the life of Paul, we have revealed the great truths of God that are the very foundation of the life of the churches of Jesus Christ. Out of a life that was bruised and hurt and buffeted and beaten, these great revelations were made known. Had it not been for the sufferings and the tears and the incarcerations, there would never have been made known to us these mighty truths of the living God.

We find an illustration of this truth in the Apocalypse itself. There would never have been the writing down of the Revelation had John remained in place as the pastor of the church at Ephesus. It was the hour of heavy trial that called for an unusual word of comfort to God's people. In the solitary, lonely exile on the mountainous, rocky Isle of Patmos, John saw these great Apocalyptic revelations that are given for our comfort and encouragement in the final book of the Word of God.

We also find an illustration in the life of our great Baptist preacher, John Bunyan. Because he refused to turn aside from preaching the Gospel of the Son of God, he was placed in Bedford jail for twelve years. One of the most

pathetic passages in all English literature was written by
John Bunyan as he described the hurt in his heart, as he
looked out of the jail window upon the face of his poor,
little, blind girl, Mary — selling laces (that Bunyan had
made in jail) in order that the family might have food to
eat. It brings tears to our eyes as John Bunyan describes the
hurt in his soul as he watches his blind, little girl in hunger
and in rags. Yet, out of that incarceration and out of that
tragic imprisonment, in those twelve years of lonely con-
finement, we have the holy allegory of *Pilgrim's Progress*.
Next to the Bible itself, the most loved, the most read and
the most famous of all of the literary productions in human
life is *Pilgrim's Progress* — the vision of the triumph of the
Christian Pilgrim in the weary journey from this world to
the world that is to come. Had it not been for the trial and
tribulation through which John Bunyan passed, he had not
seen those visions nor written that allegory.

TRUTH BROUGHT TO LIGHT IN THE FIRES OF MARTYRDOM

A second reason why God allows the suffering, the martyrdom, the imprisonment and the trial of His people is found
in the discovery, the rediscovery of the truth of God that
has been darkened by the devices of men. It is brought to
light in the fires of the martyrdom of God's people. Truth
that is buried by the devices of men, truth that is hidden
away, even by these who propose to be the priests of the
most high God — that truth would die, it would perish from
the earth, had it not been resurrected by the martyrdom of
God's people. In the early fourteenth and fifteenth centuries,
our forefathers recovered for the world the faith of the living God. They did so by the martyrdom of their lives. We
are familiar with the famous couplet,

> In Flander's fields the poppies blow,
> Between the crosses, row on row.

But before there was any battle fought in Flander's fields, our forefathers died for the truth of God. One family which so suffered was that of John Deswarte, his wife and six sons. The inquisitors came and arrested John Deswarte and his wife and four of his sons, the two younger being away from home. The neighbors told the two younger boys of the tragic plight that had overwhelmed their father and mother and brothers. They told the two younger sons to escape for their lives. Those boys said to one another, "Let us not save ourselves but let us die with our father and with our mother." When the father saw the two younger boys coming to him, he asked, "Sons, are you ready to go with us to the New Jerusalem?" Those two boys replied, "We are." In the city of the Lisle the father and mother and six sons were burned at the stake. Out of the martyrdom of God's children was born again the knowledge of the Word of God.

When they burned Master Ridley and Bishop Latimer in Oxford, Master Ridley began to cringe before the mounting flames. Bishop Latimer said, "Master Ridley, be of good cheer. We shall this day light a fire in England that, please God, shall never go out."

One of the famous sonnets in all literature was written by John Milton who, when he wrote it, was secretary to the great commoner, Oliver Cromwell. How he came to write it was this. Without warning, the Romanists descended upon the Waldensian Christians, faithful believers who lived in the Piedmont Valley in northern Italy. The attack came, unannounced, the latter part of December in the year 1400. Having no opportunity to defend themselves, the Waldensians fled in the dead of winter to find refuge in the snow-covered heights of the towering Alps. Many of them were slaughtered in the valley before they could escape to the heights of the mountains. The flight was tragic beyond description — mothers, carrying in one hand a cradle with a baby and leading with the other hand such children as could walk. After the first night, the next morning more than four-score little babies were found dead, frozen in their cradles or lying in the snow by the side of their dead mothers. When the furious attack was launched, the Romanists took one mother holding an infant in her arms and hurled her down to death. Three days later the mother was found dead, but the baby was still alive in her arms. With great difficulty rescuers were able to free the stiff, cold arms of the mother from the living child. I tell you these things so that you can understand this famous sonnet, one of the greatest in all literature, written by John Milton. Listen to the words of the sonnet as he writes:

> Avenge, O Lord, thy slaughtered saints, whose bones
> Lie scattered on the Alpine mountains cold;
> E'en them who kept thy truth so pure of old.
> When all our fathers worshiped stocks and stones,
> Forget not: In thy book record their groans,
> Who were thy sheep, and in their ancient fold
> Slain by the bloody Piedmontese that rolled
> Mother and infant down the rocks. Their moans
> The vales redoubled to the hills, and they
> To heaven. Their martyred blood and ashes sow
> O'er all the Italian fields, where still doth sway
> The tripled tyrant; that from these may grow
> A hundred fold, who, having learned thy way,
> Early may fly the Babylonian woe.

(Later in the Revelation we shall understand what John Milton referred to when he said, "may fly the Babylonian woe.")

Out of that martyrdom of our forefathers and out of the sufferings and tribulations of those Christians, arose the dawning of the great Reformation and the preaching of the Gospel of the Son of God and the far-flung missionary endeavor that has blessed the continents of the world. That is God's way of bringing to light His glorious truth that is hidden underneath the strange and peculiar devices of men.

The Recovery of the Word of God

There is a third reason why God, in His elective purpose, allows the persecution of His people. It is found in the bringing to light and to life and the scattering abroad of the holy Scriptures themselves. It was the avowed purpose of those who claimed to be the followers of Christ that the Bible should be an unknown book, buried out of sight, never read, never translated, never known, never preached. The light of the Gospel of the Son of God destroys error and is mighty for the pulling down of the households of those who bow before graven images and who worship idols. This accounts for the Romanist fear of the Bible.

In those dark days of Romanist hegemony, there arose a man by the name of John Wycliffe. He did for the English language what modern Martin Luther did for the German language. Martin Luther practically created the modern German language. John Wycliffe practically created the modern English language, the language you and I speak today. He was the first man to translate the entire Bible into English. Out of that format, out of that Word of God, there was solidified that spoken word that is your mother-tongue and mine. But the Romanists, in hatred, sought the life of John Wycliffe. By a kind Providence, he died before they could lay hands on him, but their cruel hatred was not to be robbed of its intended victim. His dead body was disinterred from the ground. John Wycliffe's body was dug up out of the earth in which it had been laid. John Wycliffe's exhumed body was burned and his ashes scattered on the bosom of the river Swift. But the river Swift pours into the Avon, and the river Avon runs into the river Severn, and the river Severn pours into the sea, and the sea laves the shores of the continents of the world. The book that John Wycliffe translated into English became the Bible that I hold in my hand and was preached wherever the civilization of the English nation did proceed. Out of

that glorious testimony of John Wycliffe, Martin Luther
wrote this famous hymn:

> Flung to the heedless winds,
> On the water cast,
> Their ashes shall be watched
> And gathered at the last.
>
> And from the scattered dust
> Around us and abroad,
> Shall spring a plenteous seed,
> Of witnesses for God.
>
> Jesus hath now received
> Their latest, dying breath.
> Yet vain is Satan's boast
> Of victory in their death.
>
> Still, still, though dead, they speak,
> And triumph-tongued proclaim,
> To many a waking land
> The one availing name.

When the converts of Wycliffe were burned at the stake,
the Bible of Wycliffe was hung around their necks, that
the Scriptures might burn with the martyred bodies of the
preachers of the Gospel of the Son of God. But the fires
lighted the world and the fires gave to the nations of the
earth a knowledge of the name of the Son of God. Out of
its light and out of its burning, God's Word was given to
the world.

THE BIRTH OF RELIGIOUS FREEDOM

Why does God allow His people to be persecuted? Out
of the travail of their sorrows and out of the tears of their
troubles and sufferings, out of it liberty and freedom are
born. It is hard for us to realize that in the United States
of America, on the shores of this American continent, the
preaching of the Son of God was interdicted. The fourth
day of June in 1768 there were three Baptist preachers ar-
raigned in the courthouse in Spotsylvania County, Virginia,

in the town named Fredericksburg. On this fourth day of
June, those three Baptist preachers were brought before
the King's Court. In great decorum the King's judges took
their places behind the bar, and the King's attorney stood
ready to prosecute the three Baptist preachers. The offense
was slowly, formally, read by the Clerk of the Court, "for
preaching the Gospel of the Son of God contrary to the
statute in that case provided and consequently disturbers
of the peace." But while those pompous preparations and
formalities of the Court were proceeding and while the
Clerk was getting ready to read the indictment, there
dismounted from his horse in front of the Courthouse a
plain man, a young fellow who was becoming known as a
brilliant patriot. His name was Patrick Henry. He had heard
of the arraignment of those three Baptist preachers, and
he had ridden sixty miles from his home in Hanover County
in order, unsolicited, to defend those three men before the
King's Court. As he entered the house unnoticed, the Clerk,
in that slow, formal manner, was reading the indictment
— "for preaching the Gospel of the Son of God." When
he had finished, the King's attorney arose and said what
few words he thought were necessary to condemn the men.
The judges seated in the Court were preparing to pronounce
sentence against those three Baptist preachers.

At that moment, Patrick Henry, who, unnoticed, had gone
into the bar to sit with the lawyers, reached out his hand
and took from the Clerk the indictment and, holding it in
his hand, he said (and I quote from one of the most eloquent pleas in recorded history): "May it please your worships, I think I heard read, as I entered this house, the
paper I now hold in my hand. If I have rightly understood,
the King's attorney of this county has framed an indictment
for the purpose of arraigning and punishing by imprisonment three inoffensive persons before the bar of this court.
. . . May it please the court, what did I hear read? Did I

hear it distinctly, or was it a mistake of my own? Did I hear
an expression, as if a crime, that these men, whom your
worships are about to try are charged with — What? 'for
preaching the Gospel of the Son of God!'" Patrick Henry
paused and three times waved that indictment around his
head, then lifting his eyes up to heaven, exclaimed, "Great
God!" Then he continued: "May it please your worships: In
a day like this, when truth is about to burst her fetters,
when mankind is about to be raised to claim his natural
and inalienable rights — when the yoke of oppression which
has reached the wilderness of America, and the unnatural
alliance of ecclesiastical and civil power is about to be dis-
severed — at such a period when liberty — liberty of conscience — is about to awake from her slumberings, and I inquire into the reason of such charges. If I am not deceived,
according to the contents of the paper I hold in my hand,
these men are accused of preaching the Gospel of the Son
of God. Great God!"

There was another long pause, in which Patrick Henry
held up the indictment in his hand. Then the brilliant young
lawyer proceeded: "May it please your worships: There
are periods in the history of man when corruption and depravity have so long debased the human character, that
man sinks under the weight of the oppressor's hand, and
becomes his servile, his abject slave; he licks the hand that
smites him; he bows in passive obedience to the mandates
of the despot and in this state of servility he receives his
fetters of perpetual bondage. But, may it please your worships, such a day has passed away. From the period when
our fathers left the land of their nativity for settlement in
these American wilds, for liberty — for civil and religious
liberty — for liberty of conscience, to worship their Creator
according to their conceptions of Heaven's revealed will;
from the moment they placed their feet on the American
continent and in the deeply imbedded forests, sought an

asylum from persecution and tyranny — from that moment despotism was crushed; her fetters of darkness were broken, and Heaven decreed that man should be free — free to worship God according to the Bible. Were it not for this, in vain have been the efforts and sacrifices of the colonists; in vain were all their sufferings and bloodshed to subjugate this new world if we, their offspring, must still be oppressed and persecuted. But, may it please your worships, let me inquire once more, for what are these men about to be tried? This paper says, 'for preaching the Gospel of the Son of God.' Great God! For preaching the Saviour to Adam's fallen race!" When Patrick Henry reached that culmination, the Court, the audience, the spectators were amazed and the face of the prosecuting attorney was pale and ghastly and he was unconscious that his whole frame shook as in a quake. The judge, in a tremulous voice, speaking for the Court, said, "Sheriff, discharge those men!"

Out of the sufferings of those Baptist preachers observed by Jefferson and Madison and Monroe, came religious liberty for all America. Those statesmen, moved by the example of those faithful Baptists, wrote into the basic document that governs the United States of America our amendment on freedom of religion and liberty of conscience. Where did it come from? Out of the sufferings and the imprisonment and the tribulation and the tears and the heartache of our brethren. "I John, who also am your brother, and companion in tribulation . . . was in the isle that is called Patmos, because of the word of God, and for the testimony of Jesus Christ." God has an elective purpose in these sorrows and in these trials. Out of them His truth is made known to the world and in its travail these great gifts that bless our lives forever are born. In this day and in this hour I hear the call of the author of the book of the Hebrews, "Let us go forth therefore unto him without the camp, bearing his reproach" (Hebrews 13:13).

I have not time to speak of the refugees from Red Communist China with whom I spoke when I was in Hong Kong. One pastor's wife, her mind deranged, demented, insane, because of the awful horrors of the persecution; and her husband, our Baptist pastor of a little church in interior China, crippled and maimed and waiting for the summons of God that he die — both destroyed by the awful trial and persecution. We have had men in our pulpit who have later been assassinated in China. Others who have been guests of our people are now in prison, in vile and filthy dungeons in China. Throughout the world such persecutions have spread. "Our brethren and companions in tribulation . . . in the isle of Patmos, for the word of God, and for the testimony of Jesus Christ."

Just a few days ago, I read this from the pen of one of our professors in the Seminary at Southwestern: "It was a beautiful Sabbath day and the Christians sang worshipfully as they prepared for the preaching service in the home of a friend. But the solitude was only temporary. The first inkling the evangelical Christians got of their attackers was when armed men burst into the room and began beating men and women alike. Lined up like cattle, they were marched into the main part of the city, mocked on public display and thrown into jail. Sounds like a description of the persecutions of the early Christians, doesn't it? But it isn't. It occurred only a few months ago in Colombia, South America."

All over this world, Christians are in prison, Christians are beaten and hurt, their homes burned, their houses of worship destroyed, the preachers slain. All over this world, clouds of darkness loom as those in power would destroy the testimony of God and the Word of our Lord Jesus Christ. Why does not the Gospel die? Why is it not killed? Because "the blood of the martyrs is the seed of the church." The more men die for the faith, the more men turn to it.

The more the churches of Christ suffer, the more brilliant and able and mighty for the tearing down of empires is the testimony of the Word of God. Such is our call and our place. This is God's will for us — a great commitment — a lifelong and everlasting devotion, at any cost and at any price. We are the servants of God. We are to be ready to lay down our lives for the preaching of the Word of Jesus Christ. ". . . in the isle of Patmos, for the word of God, and for the testimony of Jesus Christ."

> Am I a soldier of the cross,
> A follower of the Lamb?
> And shall I fear to own His cause
> Or blush to speak His name?
>
> Must I be carried to the skies,
> On flow'ry beds of ease,
> While others fought to win the prize,
> And sailed through bloody seas?
>
> Are there no foes for me to face?
> Must I not stem the flood?
> Is this vile world a friend to grace,
> To help me on to God?
>
> Sure I must fight, if I would reign;
> Increase my courage, Lord;
> I'll bear the toil, endure the pain,
> Supported by Thy word.

"I John . . . your brother, and companion in suffering and tribulation . . . was in the isle of Patmos, for the word of God, and for the testimony of Jesus Christ." This is our witness, sealed with our lives and our blood unto death.

Sermon 12

THE GLORIFIED VISION OF THE LORD JESUS

> I was in the Spirit on the Lord's day, and heard behind me a great voice, as of a trumpet, Saying, I am Alpha and Omega, the first and the last; and, What thou seest, write in a book, and send it unto the seven churches which are in Asia; unto Ephesus, and unto Smyrna, and unto Pergamos, and unto Thyatira, and unto Sardis, and unto Philadelphia, and unto Laodicea. And I turned to see the voice that spake with me. And being turned, I saw seven golden candlesticks; and in the midst of the seven candlesticks one like unto the Son of man, clothed with a garment down to the foot, and girt about the paps with a golden girdle. His head and his hairs were white like wool, as white as snow; and his eyes were as a flame of fire; and his feet like unto fine brass, as if they burned in a furnace; and his voice, as the sound of many waters. And he had in his right hand seven stars: and out of his mouth went a sharp two-edged sword: and his countenance was as the sun shineth in his strength.—Revelation 1:10-16

This is the first vision of the Apocalypse and, significantly and appropriately, it is a vision of our reigning Lord Christ. On the Isle of Patmos, an exile for preaching the Word of God, somewhere on that rocky mount rising out of the Aegean Sea, on the Lord's day, John is in the spirit of worship and praise and adoration. While he is worshiping God, he hears behind him a great voice as of a trumpet. The One who speaks, first identifies Himself. This is all-important because of the amazing, incredible chronicle of events that is to follow. These apocalyptic revelations of the consummation of the age are beyond what mind could imagine or heart could conceive. It was vitally important

140

that the Author of these apocalyptic revelations first be identified. Who is the authority for this unusual open door that
gives to us in these words the vistas of all the future ages?
Who is this Speaker who says that He executes this divine
plan that in time will faithfully come to pass? The signature,
the author, the authority, the great voice that speaks as a
trumpet is the voice of the Lord God, the eternal Christ,
Himself. Twice in these few verses does He identify Himself. Here in verse eleven, and again in verse eight: ". . . I
am Alpha and Omega, the beginning and the ending, saith
the Lord, which is, and which was, and which is to come,
the Almighty." So the author of this great Apocalypse is the
Eternal God, the Christ, Himself. "I am Alpha and Omega,
the beginning and the ending." All of the words of wisdom
from heaven and all of the revelations from God are in
Him. The only communication between the absolute and
the creation is in the self-disclosure of God in Christ. He
is the sum and embodiment of the words and wisdom and
utterance of the invisible God-head. He is the Alpha, the
first of the alphabet, and the Omega, the last of the alphabet, and all of the words in between.

Then He describes Himself — "which is, and which was,
and which is to come." In the first chapter and the fourth
verse is the greeting: "John to the seven churches which are
in Asia: Grace be unto you, and peace, from him which is,
and which was, and which is to come [the Father]; and
from the seven Spirits [the Holy Spirit]. . . . And from
Jesus Christ." In that great trumpet voice, this Christ identifies Himself as that holy God, which is, which was, and
which is to come. He is the great "I Am," the same yesterday, today and forever. The complete, unqualified, unchangeable God, the Almighty. That is the final and con-
clusive name, the Almighty, the *Pantokrator,* beyond which
there is no other one. This is the author of the Book and
this is the voice that speaks like a trumpet.

THE COMMAND TO WRITE TO THE CHURCHES

Then He also says: "What thou seest, write in a book."
In the nineteenth verse, He repeats the same mandate:
"Write the things which thou hast seen, and the things
which are, and the things which shall be — [*meta tauta* —
after these things] hereafter." Daniel was commanded not to
write: ". . . seal the book, even to the time of the end. . . ."
(Daniel 12:4). John is commanded to write. It is now, in
Christ, an open vision. Write so that every man can look
upon its page and see.

The commandment came with the voice of a trumpet.
That harbingers an all-important message, an all-important
revelation. When God spoke to the people from Mount
Sinai, from the mountain that burned with the presence
of God, He spoke to them in the voice of a trumpet. When
the door was opened in the Temple and the people were
called to worship each morning, the call was made with
the sound of a trumpet. When the great and final resurrection day of the Lord shall come, it shall be with the voice
of the trumpet of God. The great year of Jubilee was announced by a trumpet. When that final silence of the dead,
of the grave, of the tomb, of the sepulchre, is broken, it
will be with the voice of a trumpet, calling God's people to
their great, final and eternal Jubilee. With the voice of a
trumpet, John is commanded to write these things for the
people of God.

Then He said, "Send it unto the seven churches which
are in Asia." The seven churches were located in a rough
geographical circle in the ancient Roman province of Asia.
Beginning with the first church, Ephesus, the leading city
of the province, all of them were connected by ancient
Roman roads. The messenger who carried the document
from one church to another could easily make the journey,
going from one church to the other over the highways, from
Ephesus to Smyrna, to Pergamos, to Thyatira, to Sardis, to

Philadelphia, to Laodicea and back to Ephesus. In this Revelation is found the apocalyptic vision of what God's intention is for His churches in this church age, in this present age, until He shall come again. There are seven churches. There were many more churches in the Province of Asia than seven. The number seven (according to its symbolic meaning in the Scriptures) represents the whole, the complete. It represents all of them, the divine, full and completed number. When Christ addresses the message to the seven churches of Asia, He addresses the churches of all ages and of all time.

One can speak of "the government" of the Roman province of Asia, but there is no such thing as "the church" of Asia. There are "churches of Asia" just as there are "churches of Judea," just as there are "churches of Macedonia," and just as there are "churches of Galatia." So there are "churches of Asia." But there is no "church" of Judea; there is no "church" of Macedonia, and there is no "church" of Galatia. There is no such thing in the Word of God. The only time the Word of God will use the word "church" in its all-inclusive sense is as we use a word to symbolize the abstract idea of an institution. As a great orator in his speech will refer to "the family" or to "the home" or to "the state" or to "the school," he may also refer to "the church," that is, the idea of the institution of the church. It is thus used in Matthew 16:18: ". . . upon this rock I will build my church. . . ." But when the church is actually materialized, when the idea comes out of the abstract into an organized form, it is always a local, independent congregation. The "churches of Asia" would include the "church" at Ephesus, the "church" at Philadelphia, the "church" at Thyatira, or at Laodicea. In these churches there is individual responsibility with pastor, with deacons, with people. Any time churches cooperate, it must be voluntary.

There is no such thing as a hierarchy in the New Testament. There is no such thing as a modern "bishop" in the New Testament (the word translated "bishop" refers to the local pastor). There is no such thing as an over-organization in the New Testament. These churches are all free, independent, local congregations. The Word of God presents no other organization. "Send the message," He says, "to the churches of the Roman province of Asia." Our First Baptist Church in Dallas is one of God's independent congregations. In its pastor, in its deacons, in its organization, it is responsible to God alone. We are chargeable to no man that lives, whether he is high in government or high in princely, self-arrogated, ecclesiastical authority. The church is free, is independent and is responsible to God alone, just like the church in Ephesus, like the church in Smyrna, like the church in Pergamos. "To the churches [plural] of the Roman province of Asia." That is God's conception of a church for all of this age.

"And I turned to see the voice that spake with me." "And I turned to see the voice." Here is a sermon in itself. Our eyes are on the wrong thing most of the time and especially now. How easy it is to fall into despair and into discouragement! Especially is it true for people like us, who believe as we do, who have committed themselves to great principles such as we have found in the Word of God, and who stand defending them in this modern world. We are not to set our eyes upon some crack-pot Napoleon or upon some petty dictator or upon some self-styled prince who allocates to himself the authority to lord it over the people of God. Turn your eyes upon Jesus. Turn and look unto Him.

THE VISION OF THE RESURRECTED CHRIST

"And being turned I saw . . . in the midst of the seven candlesticks [in the midst of the churches — the lampstands are the churches] one like unto the Son of man." That is to say, "I saw in the midst of the seven lampstands — the churches — [and this is the apocalyptic vision of the Son of God, of the Lord in glory] one like unto the Son of man." Every syllable of that passage is meaningful. John had not seen the Lord for over sixty years. The last time he saw Him, He was ascending up into heaven. He sees in the midst of the churches (the lampstands) one like unto the Son of Man.

There are two things most emphasized in that little passage. "One like unto the Son of Man" — first, he saw the humanity, the human form of God, the Son of Man. Eighty-five times that phrase is used in the gospels, and eighty-three of those eighty-five times Jesus uses it Himself, referring to Himself. The Son of Man — God in His humanity — in His human form. Yet, he says, "one *like* unto the Son of man." This is highly mystical and highly symbolical, deeply so. The description which follows (which is the only description that you will find of the Lord in the New Testament) no man could put on canvas. No man can translate it into line and into delineation and into color. For God is unrealizable by a finite mind, inconceivable by a finite soul and undelineable by the genius of a painter's brush. Is it not strange that there is no description of the Lord in the Bible? None! None! In the days of His flesh, there is no word as to how He looked. In this description we have "one like unto the Son of Man," a semblance, a mystery, a symbol — but also glorious beyond compare. This is the way that He will look when we gaze upon Him. It is beyond what a man could describe or what he could put down on canvas. That figure that he saw in glory is the Alpha and the Omega, the beginning and the ending, which was, which is, which is to come, the Almighty, the Lord God *Pantokrator* — God Himself.

I often wonder at people who think that in heaven they are going to see three Gods. If you ever see three Gods, then what the Mohammedan says about you is true and

what the Jewish neighbor says about you is true. You are
not a monotheist, you are a polytheist. You believe in a
multiplication of Gods, plural. "Hear, O Israel, the Lord thy
God is one God." We know God as our Father, we know
God as our Saviour and we know God by His Spirit in our
hearts. But there are not three Gods. The true Christian
is a monotheist. There is one God. "I and my Father are
one." "He that hath seen me hath seen the Father." The
Lord God is He that speaks. It is He that John saw when
he turned around. The only God you will ever see is the
Lord God whom John saw in the vision of the lampstands.
The only God you will ever feel is the Lord God's Spirit in
your heart. The only God there is, is the great Father of us
all. The one Lord God, Christ. In the Old Testament we
call Him Jehovah. In the New Testament, the New Covenant, we call Him Jesus. The one great God, standing in
authority and in judgment and in judicial dignity among
His churches, here today, watching over us. "I saw one like
[a great mystical symbol] unto the Son of man."

In the following description, John presents Him with the
symbols of function and with the symbols of character. The
symbols of function: ". . . clothed with a garment down to
the foot, and girt about the breast with a golden girdle. . . ."
Clothed with a long, flowing garment that refers to His
dignity, that refers to His judicial authority, that refers to
His kingly presence. "In the year that King Uzziah died,"
said Isaiah, "I saw the Lord sitting upon a throne, high
and lifted up, and his train [His robes, His dress, His skirts]
filled the temple" (Isaiah 6:1). Such is the dignity of the
presence of God. He was clothed with a garment, a flowing garment, down to the foot, the priestly dress of a priest,
the regal robes of a king, the judicial attire of a judge. This
represents His celestial majesty and His judicial authority
and His kingly, priestly presence. "Girt about the breast
with a golden girdle." In that ancient time, when a man was

to serve, when he was to run, when he was to work, he girded up his loins. He gathered up the skirts of his flowing garment underneath the girdle in order that he might move without hindrance. But this girdle is about His breast. He is in repose, the kingly repose of the Son of God who sits down upon the throne of the Almighty. The symbol also refers to His affection, His understanding, His sympathy and His love for His people. Though exalted, glorified and immortalized, His heart is still the same. He is the same Lord who took babes in His arms and blessed them, who put His hands upon the blind and they could see, who had compassion upon the people. "Girt about the breast [the heart] with a golden girdle."

A Seven-fold Description of Our Living Lord

Then follow seven descriptions of our Lord's character: First, His head, His hair, was white like wool, white as snow. That refers to the purity and the elevation and nobility of His thoughts. It refers to the eternity of His character, "the Ancient of Days." Here is patriarchal honor. Here is eternal dignity. Second, His eyes were as a flame of fire, picturing the omniscience of the Almighty God. As the author of Hebrews says in chapter four, verse thirteen: ". . . but all things are naked and open unto the eyes of him with whom we have to do." The knowledge, the omniscience of God whose eyes are like a burning flame. Third, "And his feet like unto fine brass, as if they burned in a furnace." All of the instruments in the outer court of the Tabernacle were made out of brass because they had to do with the judgment of God upon sin. The altar (where the fire burned), brass; the laver (where they washed), brass; the tongs and all the instruments, brass. This represents the judgment of God upon human iniquity: "and his feet like unto fine brass, as if they burned in a furnace." No man can look upon the holy righteousness of the presence of God. He treads upon His enemies. He walks upon sin. He condemns iniquity. "His feet like unto brass, as if they burned in a furnace." Our Lord is later pictured as treading the winepress of the wrath of Almighty God. It is the judgment of Christ upon human sin. Fourth, "And his voice as the sound of many waters." "Many waters" refers to many messages, many messengers, many prophets, although there is but one great, eternal word, one great voice. As a mighty river pouring over the falls is gathered from many streams and many sources, so His voice is as a sound of many, many waters, the great eternal Word of God. "God, who at sundry times and in divers manners spake in time past unto the fathers by the prophets, hath in these last days spoken unto us by His Son, whom he hath appointed heir of all things, by whom also he made the worlds . . . the express image of the invisible God" (Hebrews 1:1-2). Many others. Many waters, but one great voice.

Fifth, "And he had in his right hand seven stars." (The seven stars are the "*aggeloi*," translated "angels," "messengers," "pastors," of the seven churches.) In the hand of authority, in the hand of command, in the hand of might and skill and strength and power, God holds up, God holds out, God holds fast His servants. Possibly far away, twinkling somewhere, is God's humble servant that no one has observed, ministering in obscurity; no matter, he is held up by the right hand of God and is dear to the heart of the Almighty. Here is a vision of the ministry of the servant of Christ in all of this church age. There he stands as a star, upheld by the hand of Christ. The star to guide through the trackless way, the star to herald the morning sun — that is the great commission of a true preacher of Christ, to herald the coming of Christ, who came the first time to die for our sins, who is coming the second time in victorious splendor to rule over this creation and to take God's people home to Himself. The preacher is a star, reflecting the light of the glory of God. The minister does not create the light. The lampstand is a place to hold it up. The star reflects the glory of the light of the Son of God, preaching Christ, preaching the Lord, preaching Jesus as the Saviour and the hope of the world and held in the right hand of the Son of God. One of the most effective pieces of statuary I have ever looked upon is that of Phillips Brooks placed by the side of Trinity Church in Boston. There is a pulpit, there is an open Bible and there stands Phillips Brooks with his hands outstretched, preaching the Gospel of the Son of God. Back of the preacher, the sculptor created a likeness of Jesus, standing with His right hand on the shoulder of His faithful servant. "And he had in his right hand seven stars," upholding the preachers, the pastors of the churches.

"And out of his mouth went a sharp two-edged sword." That is the power of the delivered message of Christ. Did you ever think of this? Bring any actor in radio or in television, any lecturer in politics and economics, bring anybody you could name and place him in an auditorium. Then invite the public to come and to hear. There would be someone to hear him one time and a few might come back another time. Some would came back a third time and maybe a fourth. But after a few appearances, the people would get so tired of his jokes, they would get so weary of his lectures that they would feel as Jesus said of Laodicea, "I will spue thee out of my mouth." We are that way about anything. Listen to a comedian and listen to an economist or a politician until you are sick of him. But the most astonishing, the most amazing thing in this world is this: Let any faithful preacher, *any* faithful preacher, stand up anywhere — in a theater, in an empty store building, on a vacant lot, under a tabernacle with sawdust on the floor — and let him preach the Gospel of the Son of God. Let him do it faithfully. People will be there to hear; they will come again and they will be back the next Sunday morning and night. Like my own congregation in the eighteen years of my ministry, the congregation grows and grows and grows. Oh, the power of the preached Word of Christ!

> How to reach the masses,
> Men of every birth,
> For an answer Jesus gave the key,
> And I, if I be lifted up from the earth,
> Will draw all men unto me.

". . . and out of his mouth went a sharp two-edged sword," the Word of God. "For the word of God is quick [living] and powerful, and sharper than any two-edged sword, piercing even to the dividing asunder of soul and spirit, and of the joints and marrow, and is a discerner of the thoughts and intents of the heart" (Hebrews 4:12). The Word of God is a sharp, two-edged sword. There is a judicial process in the preaching of the Son of God that is inevitable. It is the word of life unto life to them that believe. It is also the word of death unto death to them that refuse. It is a sharp sword that cuts both ways. In the sixth chapter of Ephesians, verse seventeen, it is written: ". . . the sword of the Spirit . . . is the word of God." In the second Thessalonian letter, chapter two, verse eight: "And then shall that Wicked be revealed, whom the Lord shall consume with the spirit of his mouth . . ." In Revelation 2:16: "Repent; or else I will come into thee quickly, and will fight against thee with the sword of my mouth," ". . . and out of his mouth went a sharp two-edged sword. . . ." The Word of God is the living, burning judgment of the Almighty upon the world.

"And his countenance was as the sun shineth in his strength." The stars are the preachers of the Word, but Christ is the power, the glory, the triumph, the victory, the life and the light of it all. ". . . and his countenance was as the sun shineth in his strength. . . ." On the mount of transfiguration, His face was as bright as the sun: ". . . his face did shine as the sun . . ." (Matthew 17:2). On the road to

Damascus when Saul of Tarsus met Him, he appeared above the brightness of the noonday sun. In the new Jerusalem there are not any stars that shine; there is not any moon that shines; and there is not any other light, for the light of the city is the glory of the Son of God. We shall walk in the glory of His presence, world without end. "For God, who commanded the light to shine out of darkness, hath shined in our hearts, to give the light of the knowledge of the glory of God in the face of Jesus Christ" (II Corinthians 4:6). ". . . and his countenance was as the sun shineth in his strength."

Sermon 13

OUR LIVING LORD

And when I saw him, I fell at his feet as dead. And he laid his right hand upon me, saying unto me, Fear not; I am the first and the last: I am he that liveth, and was dead; and, behold, I am alive for evermore, Amen; and have the keys of hell and of death.—Revelation 1:17, 18

"And when I saw him, I fell at his feet as dead." One could not write a stronger expression than John writes here as he describes his response when he looked upon our glorified, resurrected, reigning and living Lord. ". . . I fell at his feet [Hos Nekros] as dead. . . ." He could not see, his eyes were blinded by the glory of that light, the face of Jesus shining as the sun in his strength. He could not hear; he was stunned by that voice of many waters. His soul was overpowered and overwhelmed. His consciousness, his very life, seemed to ebb away. ". . . I fell at his feet as dead. . . ." That response is most strange. It would seem that he would have looked upon the face of his Master with ecstatic bliss and joy beyond words to describe. I would suppose that John, this beloved disciple, knew the Lord all of his life. Their mothers were sisters, which would mean, according to the flesh, that John and Jesus were first cousins. He was a beloved disciple in that inner circle who lived next to the very heart and ministry of our Saviour. He laid his head on Jesus' bosom at the Last Supper. He stood at the cross. He saw the blood and the water flow out like a fountain from His heart. It was this beloved disciple John who, in obedience to the loving, tender, shepherdly word of the Saviour, took Mary, the Lord's mother, to his home and cared for her. Yet, when he sees the Master on this Isle of Patmos he falls at His feet as dead. I repeat, it would seem that he would have looked upon the Lord with joy unspeakable, with a bliss and a gladness that would be indescribable. Instead, great fear fell upon him, so much so that it caused the first word of the Lord spoken to him to be one of comfort and encouragement, "Fear not."

THE REVERENTIAL AWE OF JOHN BEFORE CHRIST

Why this great fear that prostrated the beloved disciple when he looked upon the face of his Lord? There are two reasons for it. The first is this: The beloved disciple is looking upon unveiled deity. In the days of His flesh, in the days of the Lord's ministry in the earth, His Godhead was covered over, it was shrouded, it was curtained in the flesh. His flesh, His body was a veil that covered the glory of His Godhead. Just once in a while did the glory of the deity of Jesus shine through, such as on the mount of transfiguration, when His face shone like the sun and His garments were white as no fuller could make them. But for the most part, the Godhead of our Lord shined through the veil of His face with only an occasional and softened light. But here, John is looking upon the unveiled glory and deity of our Lord Christ. He is looking upon the Ancient of Days, whose countenance shone like the sun. He is looking into the eyes of the Judge of all the earth, eyes that burn and flame like fire. He is beholding the presence, the face of the great living God Himself. As such, he falls down before our Lord as one dead. John could look with undimmed and undaunted eye upon the throne made of jasper and upon the emerald rainbow. He could look, unabashed, upon the seven lamps that burned before the throne of God. He could gaze in glory and wonder upon the crystal sea like unto beautiful, burning glass. In fact, when the Lord opened to him the doors into heaven and into hell, his soul did not tremble nor did his spirit quail.

But when he looked upon Jesus, God in the flesh, deity resurrected, incarnate, glorified, immortalized, he fell at His feet as dead.

A second reason why John trembled when he stood in the presence of the great God and Saviour, Jesus Christ, was this: He became conscious of the burden of his own nothingness, his own folly, his own insignificance, his own shortcoming, his own humanity, his own sin and iniquity. How can an insect live in the furnace of the sun? How can a sinful mortal look upon God? How can a man's ear hear the voice of the Almighty? How can folly and insignificance and shortcoming look upon Omnipotence and Omniscience? In awe and in reverence, in godly fear, John fell down as dead at the feet of our Lord Christ.

A similar emotion overtook Daniel at the river Hiddekel when he saw the vision of that glorious one, the Son of God. He says that his strength went out of him and his comeliness turned into corruption (Daniel 10:8). A like feeling overwhelmed Isaiah when he saw the Lord, high and lifted up. The prophet cried, ". . . Woe is me! . . . for mine eyes have seen the King, the Lord of hosts." An identical sense of awe swept over the children of Israel when they stood in the presence of Jehovah God who, on the top of Mount Sinai, came in lightning and thunder and burning fire. The people in fear, in dread and in awe, drew back to the other side of the valley, as far from the burning mountain as they could and said unto Moses, ". . . let not God speak with us, lest we die" (Exodus 20:19). In the presence of deity, all human flesh is as grass. A reverential awe comes upon the true follower of Christ as is exemplified here in the prostration of this beloved disciple, John, who fell at Jesus' feet as though dead. For this reason I have never been able to understand the familiarity that some of our people assume in the presence of God. That is the reason my soul abhors some of these songs I have asked the choir not to sing in my church. Any time

a man assumes a familiarity with the living God, he is just
that much beyond and beside and away from these great
apostles and prophets who have seen the vision of the Lord
God Himself. The place of a sinful, mortal man is in deepest
humility and contrition and confession at the feet of the
Lord God, "as dead." As Abraham cried, "Who am I that
I should speak unto the Lord, which am but dust and ashes?"
(Genesis 18:27). Our attitude and our spirit in the presence
of the living Christ ought always to be one of deepest,
profoundest reverence and humility. ". . . I fell at his feet
as dead."

THE SAME BLESSED LORD JESUS

John lay at Jesus' feet, lifeless, blinded, stunned, overwhelmed, overpowered by the vision of the glorious Lord;
then "He laid his right hand upon me, saying unto me,
Fear not." The contrast is an astonishing thing. In awe, in
reverence, in wonder, John heard the voice of the Son of
God and looked upon His face. He seemed greatly different
from the Christ of the hills of Galilee. He seemed utterly
different even from the Christ of the Emmaus Road, of the
resurrection forty days. He seemed very different from the
Christ John knew as a boy, whom he followed as a disciple,
whom he saw on the cross, whom he looked upon raised
from the dead. This exalted Lord in glory seemed entirely
different. In wonder, in awe, in trembling fear John fell
at His feet. Then this amazing contrast: ". . . And he laid
his right hand upon me, saying unto me, Fear not." That
is one of the tenderest passages in all of the Word of God.
Deity, Godhead, before whom John fell as one dead; then,
this: ". . . And he laid his right hand upon me." It is the
right hand, the hand of favor and of power, supporting
the weak, lifting up the fallen, giving strength to those
who have no strength. ". . . he laid his right hand upon me."
He needed not have made that gesture. Our Lord could
have spoken to John. He need not have put His hand upon

the fallen and prostrate disciple. He could have spoken a word and John would have been resurrected. But how like the Lord, as the Lord always was and always did!

When our Lord ministered to the needy, did you ever notice that He put His hands upon them? If it was a blind man, He would put His hands upon the eyes of the blind. If it was a deaf man, He would put His hands on the ears of the deaf. If it was someone sick, He would put His hands upon the sick. If it were little babies to be blessed, He would put His hands upon them and bless them. And even if it was a leper to be cleansed, He would put His hands upon the foul and unclean leper.

One of the most dramatic stories in the life of our Lord is in the eighth chapter of the book of Matthew. Great multitudes thronged our Lord on every side. "And, behold . . . a leper." How could a leper, crying with his hands over his mouth, "Unclean, unclean," always in the tombs or outside of the city — how could a leper in a great throng come and speak to the Lord Jesus? Because wherever he went there was an opening circle around him. Always he stood by himself. When he walked toward the crowd, the throng began to fall back and away from him. "A leper! a leper! a leper!" Everyone moved except the Saviour. He just stood in the midst. The leper walked straight up to Him and when the Lord touched him, the crowd gasped. The Book says, "And Jesus put forth his hand and touched him." That gesture was half the cure. That leper had forgotten what the warm pressure of a human hand felt like. "And Jesus put forth his hand . . . saying . . . be thou clean."

The hand of our Lord rests upon John. It is the same Lord, ". . . And he laid his right hand upon me." He is still the same. He has not changed. The outward glory has changed, but His nature, His identity, His heart, is still the same. The Jesus of Galilee and of Judea, the Jesus of our healing and our seeing and our hearing and of our

resurrection from the dead — He is still the same. He has
not changed. The heart beneath that golden girdle is the
same heart that was moved with compassion when He saw
the multitudes. The hand that holds the seven stars is the
same nail-pierced hand that was extended in love and
invitation to doubting Thomas. The eyes that flame with
fire are the same eyes that wept over Jerusalem and at the
tomb of Lazarus. The feet that burn like molten brass in
a furnace are the feet that walked the weary ways of this
world, when He sat down wearied by the well. He has
not changed. He is still the same. That is why the beautiful
type of the life of Joseph is so precious. On the throne, a
very Pharaoh himself, with the whole nation and empire
in his hands, and life and death in his authority, exalted,
raised up, reigning, Joseph looked upon the need of his
brethren and he wept. He had not changed. Joseph was
still the son of Israel and a companion in love and sympathy and understanding with the sons of Jacob. It is thus
with our Lord in glory. With all authority and all power,
deity Himself, He is yet the same. He is still our loving,
tender, compassionate, sympathetic, understanding Lord.

Christ said unto him, "Fear not — fear not." It does not
matter what ails us, just so long as we lie at the feet of
Jesus. Better to be dead there than alive anywhere else.
". . . fell at his feet as dead." The Lord put His hand upon
John at His feet and said, "Fear not." "Fear not." That
tender, gracious voice is described in the book of Matthew
in the twelfth chapter, verses nineteen and twenty: "He
shall not strive, nor cry; neither shall any man hear his
voice in the streets. A bruised reed shall he not break, and
smoking flax shall he not quench." "Fear not." It is the
voice that Isaiah described in chapter forty, verse eleven:
". . . he shall gather the lambs with his arm, and carry them
in his bosom, and gently lead those that are with young."
It is the same God who in Psalm 103 said: ". . . he knoweth

our frame; he remembereth that we are dust." It is the God of the shepherd's Psalm when the Psalmist says: ". . . He restoreth my soul." ". . . he laid his right hand upon me, saying . . . Fear not." "Fear not." Oh, how can tongue describe this or word find syllables to say it? Bowing in the presence of the great God and our Saviour, John is lifted up in compassionate love.

CHRIST'S SELF-DESCRIPTION

We turn now to Christ's self-description; how He speaks of Himself; how He describes Himself. ". . . And he laid his right hand upon me, saying unto me, Fear not." Then He describes Himself. What does the Lord say of Himself? "I am the first and the last: I am he that liveth, and was dead; and, behold, I am alive forevermore, Amen; and have the keys of hell and of death."

First, He says: "I am the first and the last." Those are words that belong unto deity, unto God alone. They are the same words that He said in the eleventh verse: "I am Alpha and Omega, the first and the last." It is the same description that we find Him giving in the eighth verse of the first chapter: "I am Alpha and Omega, the beginning and the ending, saith the Lord, which is, and which was, and which is to come, the Almighty [the Pantokrator] the Almighty." "I am the first and the last." "I am the first"; here is His eternal pre-existence. Only God can be first, as only God can be last.

If we had time in this chapter, we would follow through the New Testament to show how the apostles thrust back and back and back the life of our Lord into pre-existent days and ages and eons. ". . . Lo, I come (in the volume of the book it is written of me) to do thy will, O God . . . a body hast thou prepared for me." This is the pre-existent Christ. John the Baptist said: ". . . This was he of whom I spake, He that cometh after me is preferred before me: for he was before me" (John 1:15). This is the pre-existent Lord Christ. Similarly we find in the twelfth chapter of John when, in describing Isaiah's vision in the sixth chapter of Isaiah, he ". . . saw the Lord . . . high and lifted up, and his train filled the temple." John says Isaiah saw Christ and His glory when he saw Jehovah high and lifted up. Again observe in the first Corinthian letter in the tenth chapter, where Paul speaks of the Rock that followed Israel in the wilderness, "and that Rock was Christ." Paul further said, "Let us tremble, let us fear, lest any one of us should tempt Christ as they tempted Christ and were bitten of serpents." The repudiation of God in the wilderness on the part of the children of Israel was the repudiation of Christ. Another such reference is found in the third chapter of I Peter in verse nineteen, where the apostle says the Spirit of Christ in Noah preached unto the antediluvians. Also in the first chapter and the first verse of the gospel of John: "In the beginning was the Word, and the Word was with God, and the Word was God." This is the pre-existent Christ. ". . . I am the first. . . ." "All things were made by him; and without him was not any thing made that was made." He is our great Lord God, this pre-existent Christ. ". . . I am the first and the last." He is the great King and High Priest after the order of Melchizedek, who, in the book of Hebrews in chapter seven, verse three, is presented as being without beginning of days nor end of life, but whose ministry is forever and forever, after the power of an endless life.

The Master says further, ". . . I am . . . the last." When all the kings of earth sleep in the dust of the ground and their power has passed away, when all of the enduring monuments of the earth have turned into the mists that the morning sun drives away, when all of the great of the earth sleep in the grave, He shall live and abide and reign forever and forever. ". . . I am the first and the last."

"I am he that liveth." "I am the living one." All other life is derived. All other life borrows its breath. It lives according to the brittle thread held in the hands of God. There is only one whose life is self-existent and that is God. "I am the living one and I am the one that was dead." "*Egenomen,*" "I became dead." It is the same verb used in John 1:14: "And the Word was made [became] flesh." The life "became" dead. It is a voluntary laying down of His life for the atonement of our sins. There are two natures in Christ, though one personality, one person. One of those natures is His human body. In His human flesh He died. He bowed His head and gave up the ghost. He was dead. Be careful to notice here that John writes in the past tense. No crucifix. No dead Christ. No bowing down before a Jesus still on the cross or still in a tomb. That would be the travesty of all sorrows, were God to do that to us. But our Lord "was" dead, past tense. It was an atonement that we are to remember. But, our Lord Christ now is alive, raised from the dead. We serve a risen Saviour. ". . . was dead; and, behold, I am alive for evermore." That is one of the strongest characterizations you will find in this Greek text. "*Idou,*" — "behold," "look," — "*zon,*" "living," — "*eis*" "into," — "*tous ainoas,*" "the always," — "*ton aionon,*" "of the always." "Living — behold — living — I am living into the forever of the forevers, into the ages of the ages." What a remarkable sentence!

Listen! Listen with all of your heart's ability to hear. If that is true, then He is somewhere now. If that is true ("I am alive forever more"), then He is alive this minute. If He is alive this minute, and He is somewhere, we ought to be able to know it. Listen with all of your heart! Testimony two thousand years ago, no matter from whom it came, is not comparable to a testimony offered this moment. Though every human soul who lived in the days of Jesus Christ in the Roman Empire, though the Roman Caesar himself, and though his officers in their historical records, said that He is alive, yet the testimony of people two thousand years in the grave would not be anything comparable to testimony right now. Right now! It is as if in a trial a man were accused of murder. Then during the trial, the supposed corpse (the supposed murdered man), walked into the court! Could you imagine testimony more dynamic and virile than that? While one man was being accused of murdering another one, the man who was supposed to have been murdered walked into the court! There he was alive. This is what I am describing concerning the testimony about the Lord Jesus Christ. If He is alive, where is the testimony *now?* Not two thousand years ago. Where is it *now?*

Here is a summary of a long sermon, I would like to preach some day. Our Lord is alive. He is here. This is the testimony: listen to it. First, the testimony of healing. Our Lord was dead, was resurrected, and ascended back into glory. Yet, afterward, John and Simon Peter at the beautiful gate of the Temple said to an impotent man, "In the name of Jesus Christ of Nazareth, rise up and walk" (Acts 3:6). He that was impotent rose and walked. Years still later Paul, the apostle of Christ, at Lystra, looked upon a man that was impotent from his mother's womb and in the same name of the living Lord said, "Stand upright on thy feet. And he leaped and walked" (Acts 14:10). Through these ages since, and today, there is power in the name of Christ to heal. "In the name of Jesus Christ rise and walk." I may not believe in paid divine healers, but I believe in divine healing. He heals today.

A second testimony is found in answered prayer. Did you ever try to pray to Lincoln? Did you ever try to pray to Napoleon? Why not? Get down on your knees and try praying to some great character who is dead. Then get on your knees and pray to Jesus. There will be an ear that will bend low to hear. There will be a voice that will speak to your heart. There will be an answer from heaven.

A third testimony is in the salvation of souls. The Lord

saved Matthew: He saved Simon Peter; He saved the apostle Paul; but He also saved Polycarp, and Chrysostom, and Savonarola, and John Wesley, and Charles Haddon Spurgeon, and B. H. Carroll. Everyone ought to read B. H. Carroll's *My Infidelity and What Became of It.* The Lord saved George Truett. He saved me. He saved you. He is saving today.

A fourth testimony is found in our Lord's present kingdom. He has a kingdom. When Alexander the Great died, his kingdom ended. He no longer had any subjects. But our Lord reigns in heaven and He reigns on earth in the hearts of His disciples. Even in this earth every Christian is a witness to the reigning Lord Christ.

A fifth testimony is found in His coming again. "Behold, he cometh with clouds." If He is alive, then He is coming again. Do you look for Apollos to come back to this earth? Do you look for Jupiter or Juno or Jove or Neptune to come back to their ancient temples? But millions of us lift up our hearts and our faces, looking, expecting, when that day shall come and our Lord shall return to this earth.

A sixth testimony is to be found in the presence of Christ among His churches. Walking, walking, walking in the midst of His churches. Walking in the midst of the seven lampstands that represent our churches. Walking in the midst of His people. Walking in the congregation. His presence felt in His churches. Convicting, wooing, inviting, saving, directing, blessing. Oh! Our Living Lord! Our living Christ! Oh, the depths of the unsearchable riches of God in Christ Jesus! They are past finding out. They are unfathomable, unspeakable and inexpressible. I never felt so much in my life like bowing down in reverential worship before our great God and Saviour as I do this very moment. "How dreadful," said Jacob, "is this place! this is none other but the house of God, and this is the gate of heaven" (Genesis 28:17). How dreadful, how awesome is this place. Christ standing in the midst of His people!

Sermon 14

THE KEYS OF HELL AND OF DEATH

> I am he that liveth, and was dead; and, behold, I am alive
> for evermore, Amen; and have the keys of hell and of death.
> —Revelation 1:18

"I have the keys of hell and of death." This is a symbolic word that testifies to and presents the universal Lordship of our great Christ. His sovereignty is presented likewise in Philippians 2:9-11: "Wherefore God also hath highly exalted him, and given him a name which is above every name: That at the name of Jesus every knee should bow, of things in heaven, and things in earth, and things under the earth; And that every tongue should confess that Jesus Christ is Lord, to the glory of God the Father." Whether it is in heaven, on earth, or in hell, our Lord reigns.

Julian (called the Apostate) a nephew of the Roman Caesar Constantine, was reared in a Christian family. But in his youth he renounced his Christian faith and embraced paganism. When he became emperor in A.D. 361, he sought to blot out Christianity. In the days of his Caesarship one of his admirers and subjects said to a humble, quiet Christian, "And your Jesus — what is your Carpenter of Nazareth doing now?" The humble Christian simply replied, "He is building a coffin for your Emperor." In 363, after he had reigned two years, Julian died on the battlefield, facing a Persian army. One of the most famous incidents of history is this: As they carried the emperor off the field and as he lay dying, he lifted up his eyes to heaven and cried, "Oh, Galilean, Thou hast conquered."

163

Our Christ is Lord; He is king over all. It is said here in these words: "I have the keys of hell and of death." "I have the keys of hades and of the grave." The imagery is this, that He is king over men in the unseen world in the vast beyond, king over men's souls; and He is king over death, over the grave, that is, over men's bodies. Now and in this world, tomorrow and in the world that is to come, in the terrestrial, mundane, physical world around us and in the unseen, spiritual world beyond us, whether it is now, whether it is then, whether it is here, whether it is there, Christ is king forever. Whether in heaven, whether in hell, whether in earth, whether in life, whether in death, "I have the keys of hades [men's souls] and I have the keys of death [men's bodies]."

The Authority of Christ Over the Unseen World

The keys are a symbol of authority, of control, of possession and of government. As Isaiah prophesied in Isaiah 9:6: ". . . and the government shall be upon his shoulder. . . ." As terrible as they are, the powers of hell and of death are not allowed to run riot without authority and control. Hell is a horrible region. There evil and profanity and blasphemy hold high court and dread assembly. But even hell trembles at the presence of Christ. The throne of the Lord God is higher and mightier than the throne of evil and iniquity. Death is darkness itself, and it wastes in riotous plunder. But even death is surveyed by a sovereign eye and a master hand holds the key. There is nothing in heaven or under heaven, there is nothing in earth or under earth, there is nothing in life or in death, there is nothing in this time or in the time that is yet to come, that is not under the surveillance of the great God and our Saviour, Christ Jesus. Eternally, above the flood, He reigns serene forever. Nothing happens by chance. All history lies in the elective purpose of God and under the review of heaven.

"I hold in my hand the keys of hell and of death." He reigns by right and by fact. He reigns by right. He is Lord and King. This truth can be illustrated by what happens when a king comes to one of his royal cities, and the mayor, representing the people, presents to his majesty a key to the town. The mayor and the people are in the presence of this rightful and reigning lord, and the sign thereof is the key presented to the king. Christ also reigns by actuality, by reality, by possession, in fact. It is as though a tenant were surrendering the key to the landlord. The landlord then takes possession in actuality, in reality. So Christ rules in heaven, in hell, in earth, and under the earth. Christ rules by right, "de jure," and He rules by fact, "de facto." He is king over all and the things that happen, happen in His permissive will.

Now, let us speak of the keys of hades. "I hold in my hand the keys of hades." That is, Christ is the ruler of the unseen world, the world of men's souls and the world of the heavenly spirits. Whether souls are damned and in torment or are glorified and in paradise, He is king over all. He is adored in heaven and feared in hell. (May I turn aside for a moment to clarify the difference between "soul" and "spirit"? The difference between spirit and soul is this: Spirit is always un-incarnate, if I may manufacture a word. Spirit is always spirit. "Soul" always carries with it the idea of body. There is never any exception to that. Spirit can be pure spirit, un-incarnate, un-associated with body. But soul must always have a body.) Our Lord God is Christ and King over the souls of men; that is, men who are disembodied. Their bodies lie in the heart of the earth, but their souls are either in damnation and perdition or in paradise and glory. Our Lord is King over glory. He is King over heaven. He is King over those who have died and are in the presence of the Son of God. He is King over all the spirit-world of glory. The angels are His ministering servants. Our Lord has the key that keeps stedfast and forever the souls of men who have trusted in Him. We need never fear of falling from our high estate or of ultimately perishing. He has the key of the unseen spirit-world to which we go after we lay down this mortal flesh. He shuts out of that world all that would harm or destroy. He shuts in all that belong to Him. The door is faithfully kept by the hand and authority and control of God. You have a picture, a symbol, of this great truth in the story of the ark. When the great judgment day fell and the floods rose, when the winds tore and beat, God took Noah into the ark and the Bible says, "And God shut the door." God shut that door. God locked that door and Noah was kept by the hand of Almighty God. That is exactly the same picture given to us when we shall go over the river Jordan into that other more glorious world. We are kept by the hand of God. "I have the keys of heaven. I have the keys of glory. I have the keys of paradise and no one is able to pluck my own out of my hand." We are safe forever and eternally.

THE KEYS OF HELL

He also has the key of torment, of Gehenna. In that world beyond, unseen by us, in the spirit-world, in the world of the soul, there is a place called Gehenna. It is also called torment. It is also called damnation and perdition. When we die, we are with our Lord in paradise, in glory. But when the damned die, when the lost die, when the unbelieving die, they fall into torment. They fall into damnation. They fall into perdition. Our Lord is King over hell. He is King over the damned. They would not recognize Him in this life. They would not touch the silver scepter extended to them in this life. They would not turn and believe in Him in this life. Now, in the life to come, they bow and they confess in horror and in torment and in agony. There will never be an infidel in hell. They all believe there. As the unbeliever falls into the flame of torment and damnation, he confesses then the Lord God *Pantokrator*.

"He has the keys of hell." When a soul goes beyond the day of mercy and grace, and that key is turned, it is turned forever and forever. In the third chapter of the book of the Revelation, verse seven, our Lord introduces Himself as "he that hath a key in his hand and he openeth, and no man shutteth; and shutteth, and no man openeth." In the twenty-fifth chapter of the book of Matthew is told the story of the five foolish virgins, who were not prepared when the Lord came. They knocked at the door after it was shut and said, "Lord, Lord, open to us." But the Lord said, "I know you not." In the sixteenth chapter of the book of Luke, you have the story of Dives and Lazarus between whom there is a great gulf fixed. No man crosses over to this side nor does any man cross over to the other side. These things are in the hands of God, and when that key is turned, it is turned forever.

I see that terrible fact in this life. I see it all the time. I am thinking now of a man who believed in selling liquor. He had a drugstore in which he sold it. He stood one day over the silent, still form of his dead son who had come to be an alcoholic and who had died, drunk, in an automobile accident. To this day I can see that man stand and wring his hands and weep and cry. But that key was turned, and turned forever — the key of damnation and of misery and of perdition.

That key some day will be turned on Satan. In the ninth chapter of the book of the Revelation, there is a picture of an angel who has a key to the bottomless pit. In the twentieth chapter of the book of the Revelation, the mighty angel comes down from heaven and that angel has in his hand a key and a chain. Satan is chained for a thousand years. After he is liberated for a space, he is finally cast into a damnation and torment that lasts forever and ever. The

key is turned forever and forever. Christ has the key in his
hand. What Satan does, he does in the permissive will of
the Lord Christ. "Thus far, and no further," God says as He
did to Satan concerning Job. "Thou shalt have permission
thus to do but beyond that thou shalt not do." Things that
happen in this world happen according to the elective purpose and the permissive will of God. He holds the key in
His hand. "I have the keys of hell (of hades, of heaven and
of torment) and I have the keys of death."

The Keys of Death

In the remainder of this chapter we shall discuss men's
bodies fallen into the grave. Death is a horrible spectacle.
All the poetry of the world and all the songs of the saints
and all the flowers of the earth cannot cover the horrible,
decaying, decadent visage of death. God calls death an
enemy. It is an intruder. It was not planned. Death is the
exact opposite of the spirit and the will and purpose of God.
Death is an implacable enemy. The footprints of death, the
sepulchre and the tomb and the grave, seem inscrutable,
unfathomable, black and horrible. Death is a horrible fortress, a castle of despair, a bourne from which no traveler
ever returns. Death is a black camel that kneels at every
gate. With impartial fate, with certain pace, death knocks
at every palace and every cottage gate. If he has not visited
your house, look down the road. If he has not broken up the
circle of your family, wait awhile. We shall not escape.

But does death reign forever? Is there never to be any
triumph over the tomb and the sepulchre and the grave?
Is death, and not God, king of the universe? Do we all
finally fall into his offensive arms and does he hold us forever? No, for our Lord-Christ says, "I have the keys of hades
and of death." Death is in the hands of God, in the hand
of our Christ.

Death moves only in the permissive will of heaven. The

issues of death lie in the hands of the Almighty. There is
no such thing as death's running riot, without the surveillance and the sovereign eye of God. Our Lord holds the
key to that mystic door of death. No man enters it unless
our Christ shall open it. Even the ungodly and the unsaved
owe their spared lives to Christ Himself. No man ever dies
except by the permissive will of our Lord. He has the key
to death, and no man enters that dark and forbidding land
unless Christ wills it. The key is in His hand. *When* you die
is known to Him. *How* you die is known to Him. The circumstances under which you die are known to Him. He
controls them all.

If it is not His will that a man die, neither fever, nor pestilence, nor earthquake, nor bomb, nor war, nor circumstance,
nor providence, nor a thousand angels could drag that man
down to the grave or hurl his soul into the world that is yet
to come. Our lives are in the hands of Almighty God and He
holds the key of death. Not till He opens that mystic door,
does anyone enter into the grave. Listen again to the words
of Psalm 91: "Thou shalt not be afraid for the terror by
night; nor for the arrow that flieth by day; nor for the pestilence that walketh in darkness; nor for the destruction that
wasteth at noonday. A thousand shall fall at thy side, and
ten thousand at thy right hand: but it shall not come nigh
thee" (Psalm 91:5-7). Our lives are immortal until the Lord
God says, as in the ninetieth Psalm, "Return." I shall not die
until Christ opens the door, the door of death. When that time
shall come, I shall die, even though I am sleeping safely
and calmly and quietly in my bed. But I shall not die if it
is not His will, though I be in the furor and in the cauldron
and in the maelstrom of a livid war. Death is in the hands
of Christ and He holds the key.

Death, to the Christian, is not death. We fall asleep in
Jesus. Those pierced hands when they were nailed to the
tree, and those pierced feet when they were fastened to the

cross, began to trample and to destroy the dominions of death. When our Lord entered the tomb, He grappled with that last great enemy face to face and hand to hand, and He destroyed forever death's sovereignty.

Death to the Christian is just a falling asleep, a laying aside of this house of clay for a little while, while we wait with the Lord. "Today thou shalt be with me in paradise." In death we wait with the Lord for that great and final consummation, the full redemption of the purchased possession, soul *and* body. For when Christ died for us, He not only bought our souls, but He also bought our bodies. We are not wholly redeemed until we are redeemed in soul *and* in body. There shall not a bone be left behind, not a relic for the devil to gloat over. We shall all be raised and live in eternity.

Death to the Christian is a going to be with Jesus — "absent from the body, present with the Lord," awaiting the adoption, namely the resurrection of our body. Therefore, a Christian is never to tremble in the presence of death. "For me to live is Christ and to die is gain." We are to be unafraid. I am not saying that if the visage of death were to knock at your house, that *now* you would not tremble. I think God gives us grace for this hour and grace for that hour, grace for this day and grace for that day. We do not need dying grace now — not until the time comes. But when the hour comes and Christ opens for us that door of death, He will give us dying grace. We are not to be afraid, for, to us, death is being with our Lord.

I do not know what sermon it was, but I read a sermon delivered by Dr. Truett. In that message he described a little Sunday school girl who died in our congregation. She belonged to our Sunday school. The little girl, as she lay dying, said to her mother, "O Mother, O Mother, it is growing dark and I am afraid. I am afraid, O Mother, come closer, come closer. It is growing dark and I am afraid." Dr. Truett said the mother took the little girl into her arms and said, "My child, Christ is in the dark just as He is in the light, and you need not be afraid for He keeps all who place their trust in Him." I don't know who that little girl was, now with Jesus. But what that mother said is true. Our Saviour is Lord of the night as He is Lord of the day. He is Lord of death as He is the Lord of life. He is the King of the soul as He is King of the body. He keeps in His hands those who place their trust in Him.

Where are our fathers and our mothers and our loved ones who have gone on before? Where are they? They live in paradise. They live in another world, unseen by us. Their life is expressed in this beautiful poem. No one knows who wrote it, but listen to its sweet, precious assurance. It is called "The Rose Beyond the Wall."

> Near a shady wall a rose once grew,
> Budded and blossomed in God's free light,
> Watered and fed by morning dew,
> Shedding it sweetness day and night.
>
> As it grew and blossomed, fair and tall,
> Slowly rising to loftier height,
> It came to a crevice in the wall,
> Through which there shone a beam of light.
>
> Onward it crept, with added strength,
> With never a thought of fear or pride,
> And it followed the light through the crevice length,
> And unfolded itself on the other side.
>
> The light, the dew, the broadening view,
> Were found the same as they were before,
> It lost itself in beauties new,
> Bathing its fragrance more and more.

Then the author applies the sweet lesson to our sorrowing hearts:

> Shall claim of death cause us to grieve,
> And make our courage faint or fall?
> Nay, let us faith and hope receive.
> The rose still grows beyond the wall.

Scattering fragrance far and wide,
Just as it did in days of yore,
Just as it did on the other side,
Just as it will forever more.

Growing, blooming, blossoming, on the other side of the wall, for He is king over there as He is king down here. "I hold in my hand the key . . ."

Then what? When we go to be with the Lord Jesus and our souls are in His presence, but our bodies are buried here in the depths of the sea or in the dust of the ground — then what? Oh! What a Gospel and what a message! Some day, some great and final and glorious day, some triumphant and consummating day, Christ shall use the keys of death and say to these that sleep in the heart of the earth and in the dust of the ground, "Arise, Arise." Death shall not hold our bodies forever. Death shall be forced to give up his treasure some day at the voice and at the call of Almighty God, when the trumpet shall sound and the dead shall be raised incorruptible. "For He must reign until He hath put all enemies under His feet and the last enemy that shall be destroyed is death." This body, sown in corruption, shall be raised in incorruption; sown in dishonor, raised in glory; sown in weakness, raised in power; sown a natural body, raised a spiritual body. "Now this I say, brethren, that flesh and blood cannot inherit the kingdom of God; neither doth corruption inherit incorruption. Behold, I shew you a mystery . . . In a moment, in the twinkling of an eye, at the last trump . . . the dead shall be raised incorruptible . . . when this corruptible shall have put on incorruption, and this mortal shall have put on immortality, then shall be brought to pass the saying that is written, Death is swallowed up in victory. O death, where is thy sting? O grave, where is thy victory? . . . But thanks be to God, which giveth us the victory through our Lord Jesus Christ" (I Corinthians 15:50-57). "I hold in my hand the keys of hell and of death."

Sermon 15

GOD'S OUTLINE OF THE APOCALYPSE

Write the things which thou hast seen, and the things which
are, and the things which shall be hereafter.—Revelation 1:19

This chapter is the key to the interpretation of the Revelation. The text is God's outline and foundational meaning
concerning the unfolding of this Apocalyptic vision.

On the Isle of Patmos, John, the Seer, hears a great voice
behind him and turning, he sees the Son of God in the midst
of seven golden lampstands. Then follows the description
of this glorious Lord of heaven. After the description of the
Lord, the narration reads: "And he had in his right hand
seven stars: and out of his mouth went a sharp two-edged
sword: and his countenance was as the sun shineth in his
strength. And when I saw him, I fell at his feet as dead.
And he laid his right hand upon me, saying unto me, Fear
not; I am the first and the last; I am he that liveth, and was
dead; and, behold I am alive for evermore, Amen; and have
the keys of hell and of death. Write the things which thou
hast seen, and the things which are, and the things which
shall be hereafter; The mystery of the seven stars which
thou sawest in my right hand, and the seven golden candlesticks. The seven stars are the angels of the seven churchs:
and the seven candlesticks which thou sawest are the seven
churches." Our text is verse nineteen: "Write the things
which thou hast seen, and the things which are, and the
things which shall be hereafter."

In the Textus Receptus, the Greek manuscripts from

which the King James Version was translated, there was left out an illative particle that is all-important. What John wrote in that original manuscript was this: "Write *therefore* [Gr. *oun*] the things which thou hast seen, and . . . which are, and . . . shall be hereafter." That little particle "oun" looks very small, but it is very significant. To illustrate: In Matthem 28:19 are written these words: "Go ye, therefore, and make disciples of all nations, baptizing them in the name of the Father, and of the Son, and of the Holy Ghost: Teaching them to observe all things whatsoever I have commanded you. . . ." That "therefore" — that little Greek illative particle *oun* — refers to some great previous statement of the Lord. What was it? In Matthew it was this (Matthew 28:18): "And Jesus came and spake unto them, saying, All authority — all authority — all power is given unto me in heaven and in earth." Then follows Matthew 28:19: "Go ye *therefore* [on the basis of all authority and all power given unto me] go ye therefore." This is the commandment of Him who reigns supreme and forever. On the basis of His might and His power and His authority, we are commissioned to preach and to evangelize. The identical emphasis is here. "Write — *therefore*." The *therefore* refers to the incomparable vision of the Son of God, who identifies Himself and authenticates Himself, saying, "I am the first and the last — the Almighty — the Alpha and the Omega, who was dead and is alive for evermore and who has the keys of all destiny and of all creation and of all the future." "Write therefore"; that is, "On the basis of the Lordship and the kingship and the sovereignty of the Son of God, write, for these things are sure and stedfast and will certainly come to pass." The great Executor of this divine plan is none other than Deity Himself. Christ is not one thing in one age for one time and one country and one people and then another thing for another age and another time and another country and another people. Christ is the Lord God, "the same yesterday and today and forever" (Hebrews 13:8). On the basis of His deity and insuperable authority, He commanded John to write this great outline of the plan of the ages. That little particle has a tremendous, significant meaning. It means that the Lord God Himself, the *Pantokrator*, the first and the last, the Almighty, the Alpha and the Omega, He who has the keys of hell and of death, has commissioned John, on the basis of His authority and His ableness to execute this divine plan, to write it out that His people may see it and know it. Then follows that divine plan. That is why this chapter is the most significant in our discussion, for it is the basis of the interpretation of this Book, the Bible. This is the grand foundation; this is the great starting point. After Christ has identified Himself and authenticated His signature, He presents the vast unfolding of the ages yet to come. "Write — therefore."

Three Outlines of the Revelation

There are many wonderful man-made divisions and outlines of the Apocalypse. Every commentator upon it will present one. They are all interesting, every one of them. I have chosen three here in order that you may get a good idea of how men divide this book. Then we are going to see how God divides the book. Here are three illustrations that I have chosen to show you how well scholars, students and commentaries divide up the Revelation — how they analyze it, how they outline it.

The first is a division into just two parts. This author says the goal of the establishment of the kingdom of heaven is reached twice in the book. He is correct in that. One time the goal is reached in Revelation 11:15-17 and again it is reached in Revelation 19:6 and 7. So he says the book falls, naturally, into two complete and distinct sections. He divides the book exactly in the middle: the first eleven chapters when the kingdoms of this world become the kingdoms of our Lord and of His Christ, and the last eleven chapters when it reaches that glorious climax again. That is simple, fine, true. That is one outline.

Here is another. One of the authors has divided the Revelation into four distinct sections, according to the visions. They are there, just as he has described them, just as I now present them to you from him. There are four visions of unequal length and of differing content, introduced in the same manner with almost identical phraseology. Each one of these four divisions is introduced like this: Each mentions the Seer personally, mentions John personally. Each begins with the phrase, "I was in the spirit," and each takes the Seer to a different place where he sees things not ordinarily seen by mortal eye. Those four visions, each introduced in the same way, are these: In Revelation 1:9-10, the Seer is in Patmos and he sees the vision of the Lord Christ, walking in the midst of the lampstands. Then, Revelation 4:1 and 2, locates the Seer in heaven. Then, Revelation 17:3 locates the Seer in the wilderness. Revelation 21:10 locates the Seer in a great and high mountain. Therefore, these four visions follow respectively the four different locations of the Seer. So if you divide the Revelation according to these four visions, it would be divided like this: I. Chapters one through three. II. Chapters four through sixteen. III. Chapters seventeen through twenty. IV. Chapters twenty-one and twenty-two.

Then I copied one other very fine and somewhat typical division that you will find men making of the Apocalypse. This one has seven parts, with a prologue and an epilogue. The first division — the seven churches, roughly chapters one through three. Second — the seven seals, chapters four through seven. Third — the seven trumpets, chapters eight through eleven. The fourth — the seven personages, chapters twelve through fourteen. The fifth — the seven vials or the seven bowls, chapters fifteen and sixteen. The sixth — the seven dooms (the seven great judgments), chapters seventeen through twenty. The seventh — the seven new things, chapters twenty-one and twenty-two. This is a beautiful outline and a magnificent one. It divides the Apocalypse into seven divisions; namely, the seven churches, the seven seals, the seven trumpets, the seven personages, the seven vials, the seven dooms and the seven new things.

Now, all of these outlines are fine, but they are also manmade. The genius and the scholarship and the studious ferreting out on the part of scholars arranged these outlines. They are all commendable and they are all good. Most any study of the Apocalypse by a devout student is a profitable study to read and to follow. But we are not interested much in what men would do in outlining it and in presenting its analysis and its great truth. What we would like to know is this: Is there a key to this book from God? Does God have an analysis of it? Does God have an interpretation? Is there something from heaven by which we can study the meaning of these visions? Yes, there is. When I was a student in school, I remember some lecturers saying that there was a key to the interpretation and the meaning of the Revelation, possessed in ancient times, but that key has been lost and we do not possess it today. Therefore, those lecturers concluded, the book is an enigma to us. I have learned just the opposite of that as I have studied the book. The same key that those first and primitive Christians had in the Roman province of Asia to whom the letters were addressed, we have today; because the key is written here in the first chapter of the book itself. This is the grand foundation. This is the great starting point. This is the key to the meaning of this vast outline of God's future. The outline is simple. God outlines according to a good homiletician. Every fine sermon, they say, should have three points. God has written His Revelation in three divisions — in three parts. He tells you what those three parts mean and what they signify.

GOD'S SIMPLE OUTLINE OF THE APOCALYPSE

Look at it, in its simplicity. "Write, therefore, first, the things which thou hast seen." That is part one. That is the first division. Second, "and the things which are." That is part two. Third, "and the things which shall be [*meta tauta*] after these." That is part three. So we have this three-fold division of the Apocalypse, its meaning and its analysis, according to the Revelation of God. First, John is going to write the things which he has seen. Second, he is going to write the things which now are. Third, he is going to write the things that are after these things that now are. When we look in the book we can see exactly what God has done and what God means, for He follows that outline to the letter, to the exact syllable and the exact word. So let us take God's outline and look at the Revelation in view of what God has said.

First, "write the things which thou hast seen." In obedience to that command, John sat down and wrote the things that he had seen. He had seen the seven golden lampstands, and in the midst of the seven lampstands he had seen One like unto the Son of God. John wrote all this down. John described the vision of the Living Lord, what His eyes looked like, His head and His hair, what His clothing looked like and His feet, what He had in His hand, and what His face looked like above the shining of the sun. Then he wrote down what Christ said. That is the first vision. "Write the things which thou hast seen." That is chapter one. John wrote down these things which he had seen.

Now, the second great division of the Revelation is: "Write the things . . . which are." He is talking about the churches, the things which now are. Revelation 1:20 ". . . the seven lampstands *are* the seven churches." "The mystery of the seven lampstands." He doesn't refer to a riddle or an enigma. That is the reason for reading the third chapter of the Book of Ephesians. A "mystery" — Greek, "*musterion*" —

is something that God has in His heart that man could not ferret out until God discloses it. What is the mystery of the seven lampstands? The mystery of the seven lampstands is this: they represent all God's churches. There is a divine arithmetic. Just as there are divine personages and divine places, there is a holy and sacred arithmetic. A number in the Apocalypse is just as significant as a word of a syllable. That "seven" represents all of the churches, the complete household of God. "The *mystery* of the seven lampstands"; that is, God's churches through all of the ages. The *seven* represents all of the churches, the whole age. They represent our church age, our church dispensation, our age of grace, this hour in which we now *are*. The reason John uses that word "are," ("write the things which *are*"), the reason Christ told him to write about the things that "are," was because John lived in the same age, in the same dispensation, under the same government that you and I live in today. John lived in this age, in this day of the church, in this day of grace, in this hour of the goodness and the mercy of God. He lived in the time of the preaching of the Gospel of the Son of God. John puts himself in the same age in which we are, the age of the churches. So the second great division of the Revelation concerns the things of the churches. That you will find in Revelation two and three. In these two chapters we have a remarkable prophetic preview of the history of the churches, through all of the years that they are to exist in the earth. We have this preview of the spiritual progress of the kingdom of God in the hearts of men in this sinful world. It is a remarkable condensation of the story and condition of the churches as long as churches last. That is the great message of Christ as He speaks to His churches through all ages and in all times.

Every once in a while I come across a man who thinks that these letters to the seven churches of Asia have no longer any significance for us, but that their messages concerned only the local congregations in Asia to whom they were addressed. Why, such a thing is the most impossible conception that mind could dream of. What our Lord says here in these letters to the seven churches of Asia, he is saying to His churches through all the ages and through all time as long as churches last in the earth. The message is for us today. Read it and hear what Christ says to us about our past, about our present and about our future development. He speaks of things of which we ought to be aware. He has written them beforehand for the admonition, edification and encouragement of the saints.

We have here, then, the second section that God has written in His Book. It is a very complete division. It is not fragmentary, it is not partial, it is not sectional; rather, it is a complete unit in itself. The seer is in the same place, the Speaker is the same, and the manner of communication is the same. All the way through this second section there is an identical position on the part of the Speaker and on the part of the Seer, concerning what God is doing and what Christ is saying. It is a complete unit in itself. It is an age. It is the age of the churches of Jesus Christ. This is the second division, chapter two and chapter three.

Then the third part, the great, amazing Revelation of things beyond the church age. First, "write the things which thou hast seen," and John wrote them down, what he had seen. Second, "And the things which are," and John wrote about the churches, all of the story of the churches until Jesus comes again. Then, the third section, "write . . . the things which shall be [*meta tauta*] after these churches." When I turn, then, to the fourth chapter of the book of Revelation, I see there the identical words, "*meta tauta.*" The Lord God is picking up here the third part of His great outline. Listen to it. "After this I looked, and, behold, a door was opened in heaven: and the first voice which I heard was as it were of a trumpet talking with me; which said,

Come up hither, and I will shew thee things which must be [*meta tauta*] after these." After the church, after the day of grace, after the day of the mercy of the preaching of God through His ambassadors in His churches. "Come up here, and I will show you this great period of time after the calling away of the churches," after the day of the preaching of the Gospel of the Son of God in the churches, after that is passed, — *meta tauta.* After these things of the churches, the third great division of the Apocalypse opens to view.

THE MEANING OF "META TAUTA"

May the Holy Spirit help us to get a clear picture of what those two words, "*meta tauta,*" mean. That is all-important. First, "Write the things which thou hast seen," the vision of Christ. Second, "Write the things . . . which are," these churches and this church age and its story to the end. Third, "Write the things . . . which shall be [*meta tauta*] after these things." Now, let us get in our minds a clear idea of the meaning of those two words, "*meta tauta.*"

The greatest intellectual philosopher the world ever produced was named Aristotle. He was the pupil of Plato. He was the teacher of Alexander the Great. Natural science began with Aristotle. He looked at practically everything in God's world, and he wrote down observations concerning what he saw. He wrote down things about astronomy as he observed the sky and the stars. He followed the course of the weather, and he wrote many observations about it. We call that science meteorology. He looked at the whole world of botany, the world of plant life, and he wrote down volumes about plants. Then he observed the world of zoology, animal life, and he wrote down his observations about animal life. He was a tremendous observer. He followed the armies of Alexander the Great, looking and writing down everything he could see and find.

Following the incomparable Aristotle by a few hundred

years, in the first century A.D., there was a Greek scholar by
the name of Andronicus, who lived in the cultured Greek
city of Rhodes. Andronicus edited all of these many works of
Aristotle. He put them together and called them *Ta Phusika,*
"the things of physics"; that is, things concerning the physical world. The Greek word for nature is *"phusis."* *"Phusika"*
refers to the things of nature. *"Ta Phusika"* means natural
things, physical things. So, Andronicus put together all of
Aristotle's observations on things physical, such as astronomy
and meteorology and botany and zoology, and labeled them
"Ta Phusika." But Andronicus had left over many, many
things that Aristotle had written concerning things that were
not physical; for example, the science of knowledge and
logic and the nature of existence and being, the cause of
things and the existence of God — discussions that had not
anything to do with physical things like stars or plants or
animals. So this is what Andronicus, the editor of Aristotle's
works, did. He placed first all of those studies that were
physical, such as astronomy, botany, zoology, collected all
of them together and called it *"Ta Phusika,"* the physical.
Then he took all of these other things that were left and put
them together and called them *"Meta Phusika"* — Meta-
Physical. That is, things beyond the physical, things after
the physical. This is the derivation of the word, metaphysi-
cal," "things beyond the physical," things beyond what Aristotle had written on nature. Now, that is the identical thing
that you find here in the Revelation. "Write the things
which are," the revelation of the course of the churches until
the churches are taken away. "Write the things — meta tauta
— beyond these things." When the church is taken out of the
world and when God's people are caught up to be with
Jesus in the air, then write the things, *"meta tauta,"* beyond
these things of the churches.

Beginning at the fourth chapter of the book of the Revelation, John discloses what God is going to do in His judg-

ment upon Jew and Gentile after the church has completed its history, after Christ comes for His sainted people, after the church has been taken away. When I turn to the fourth chapter of the book of the Revelation, I do not see the church in the earth any more. It is gone. The Revelation follows this identical outline that God has given and when the course of the church is finished, and when the story of the church is complete, and when its history is entirely written and we come to the end of it in chapter three, we never return to it again until the end of the age. There is no mention of the church thereafter. The next time we meet the church is in the nineteenth chapter of the book of the Revelation at the Marriage Supper of the Lamb. After chapter three, it has absolutely disappeared and that is exactly what God said in His outline: *"Meta tauta,"* "after these things," after these churches, beyond these churches, *meta phusika,* metaphysics, beyond the physical. After the churches, God reveals the things that are going to happen in His great, final visitation upon the earth.

This outline is in keeping with the whole book of God. For example, in I Peter 4:17, the apostle says: ". . . judgment must begin at the house of God." If judgment begins at the house of God, then, the judgment upon the nations and upon the Gentiles and upon the heathen, upon the unbelievers, begins subsequently, after the judgment upon the house of God. That is exactly what you find in the Apocalypse. First, God deals with His churches; the judgment of God is first upon His people. God completes what He is going to do with His churches and then after, *"meta,"* beyond that, we have the story of what God is going to do with a gainsaying and blaspheming and unbelieving world. This is the section beginning at chapter four in the Book of the Revelation, the things beyond the things of the churches. Revelation 7:14 calls it "the great tribulation" with emphasis upon "the." These are the things that are yet to come, written so dramatically and so vividly in chapters four through nineteen, preparing for the final consummation described in chapters twenty through twenty-two. May the Lord give to us an understanding spirit as we study the book together in the succeeding volumes of this series.

Expository Sermons on Revelation

Volume 2—Revelation 2 and 3

Expository Sermons on Revelation

VOLUME 2—REVELATION 2 AND 3

by
W. A. CRISWELL, PH.D.

To
CLARE ZACHRY
God's True Business Man
The Church's Faithful Deacon

FOREWORD

In the foreword to the first volume of *Expository Sermons on Revelation* I wrote that it was my hope to follow the initial book with a second and thus to continue until all of the sermons I have preached on the Apocalypse have been printed. The time has come when this second volume is ready for publication and it is my humble prayer that God will bless this one as fully and as richly as He has blessed the previous one.

The first volume contained the sermons preached on the first chapter of the Revelation. This volume contains the sermons delivered on the seven churches of Asia, which comprise, along with a few texts in the first chapter, the second and third chapters of the Apocalypse. Having published these two books, it is my prayerful hope that each year we shall be able to place in book form a portion of the remainder of the sermons delivered on the Revelation until the entire series has been published. This will mean possibly three more volumes beyond the present two.

It was my intention to leave out some of the sermons that I have delivered on chapters four through twenty-two in order to encompass them in fewer volumes and in smaller books. However, some of my preacher brethren have said to me that it is these middle chapters of the Revelation that are rarely mentioned. They have expressed the earnest wish that any sermons I have prepared on these middle chapters will be printed. God willing, we shall do just that. Next year we shall seek to present the sermons prepared and delivered through the first part of the great central section of the Apocalypse.

Once again let me express my profound and everlasting appreciation for Mrs. B. B. Binford, who has so kindly gone through the messages with an eye sensitive to every grammatical construction. Her help in this regard is invaluable. In the fire and fury of a pulpit delivery, this preacher sometimes does not keep his subjects and his predicates even in the same tense, much less in the same mood, case, number, antecedent or reference. Mrs. Binford sees to it with her red pencil that all these parts appear correctly. And again let me express my deepest gratitude to Mrs. Bailey Forester for the hours and hours she has spent in typing and retyping the manuscript. The Lord's richest blessings be upon them both in their vital contribution to this work.

And now may the Lord reward the mind that follows the meaning of these sermons, and may God bless the heart that opens itself to the spiritual connotation of the message itself. I could pray that these sermons will be preached and repreached and kept alive in a thousand pulpits unknown to me.

"Till He come," God keep us in His shepherdly care.

— W. A. CRISWELL

Pastor's Study
First Baptist Church
Dallas, Texas

TABLE OF CONTENTS

Expository Sermons on Revelation

Volume 2—Revelation 2 and 3

Chapter 1

The Seven Churches of Asia

... What thou seest, write in a book, and send it unto the seven churches which are in Asia. — Revelation 1:11

The first chapter of the Revelation closes with these words: "Write the things which thou hast seen, and the things which are and the things which shall be after these; The mystery of the seven stars which thou sawest in my right hand, and the seven golden lampstands. The seven stars are the angels of the seven churches: and the seven lampstands which thou sawest are the seven churches." These words also close the first of the three divisions with which God divides the Book: "Write the things which thou hast seen." So John wrote down the things that he had seen, the vision of Christ as He walked in the midst of the lampstands. Then, "write the things which are," and the Book describes the things which are ("the seven lampstands which thou sawest *are* the seven churches"); so "the things which are" are the things that belonged to the same era and age and dispensation to which we belong. "The things which are" — the churches. John lived in the day of grace and the preaching of the Gospel. He lived in the day of the churches, just as we do. John belonged to a church, just as we belong to a church. We are all fellow-citizens of the household of faith, brought together in the love and mercy and forgiveness of Jesus Christ. So, the second great division — "write the things which are" — refers to the things of the churches. This is the day in which we live. This is our administration and dispensation.

Then the third division is beyond — *meta* — after these things: "and write the things which shall be [*meta tauta*] after these things." That is to say after the churches are

13

taken away, after there is not another church in the earth, after God's people have all been taken out of the world, "write the judgments that are to fall after the history of the churches." The fourth chapter of the book of the Revelation is introduced with these words: "... come up hither, and I will shew thee things which must be [*meta tauta;* i.e., after these things concerning the churches]." Then the church is never mentioned again. It is not in the earth. The next time the church is seen is at the end of the book, at the Marriage Supper of the Lamb in glory. "After these things," after the age of the church, when Christ has stolen away, like a thief in the night, His jewels and His gems and His pearl of price in the earth, after He has taken these away, then comes those awful judgments upon unbelieving and blaspheming mankind that are called the Tribulation, the Great Tribulation. Thus God divides the Apocalypse into these three tremendous divisions.

We begin now at the second division. We have written of the first one, the vision of Christ that John saw and which he wrote down. That is the first chapter of the Apocalypse. Now we begin the second division: "The mystery of the seven stars which thou sawest in my right hand and the mystery of the seven golden lampstands. The seven stars are the angels of the seven churches and the seven lamp-stands which thou sawest are the seven churches." "Unto the angel in the church at Ephesus write"; "unto the angel in the church in Smyrna write"; "unto the angel in the church at Pergamos write"; "unto the angel in the church at Thyatira write"; "Unto the angel in the church in Sardis write"; "unto the angel in the church in Philadelphia write"; "unto the angel in the church of Laodicea write." These seven churches are a "mystery" and the angels of the seven churches are a "mystery." They have a profound and signifi-cant meaning, far more meaningful than appears on the surface.

Seven is a number which is sacred and symbolic. There is a sacred arithmetic as there are a sacred place and sacred persons. There is a holy arithmetic. These numbers have in themselves a profound significance. The number *seven* represents completeness, fulness — like the seven spirits which are before the throne of God. There is only one Holy Spirit of God, but the number *seven* represents the fulness and the plenitude of God's spirit. All of Him. So these seven churches represent all the churches through all the ages and through all times. When Christ speaks to the seven, He speaks to all of the churches of all time, including us today. Now, these churches are actual, local congregations, just like this church. Here in the Revelation we are not on cloud nine or in some ethereal, intangible, mythical fantasy that has nothing to do with actuality and reality. These things that Christ is saying are things that pertain to us. If we would know the course of God's work in the world — its destiny and consummation — we have it written here, by Him who can see the end from the beginning. These things that Christ is saying are things that pertain to us. These churches are actual congregations. "The lampstands which thou sawest *are* the seven churches."

THE GREEK WORD TRANSLATED "CHURCH"

The word translated "church" is a compound Greek word made out of two parts. The first part is *ek,* which means "out of," "from among." The other part is *kaleo,* which means "to call." So, *ek kaleo* is "to call out from" — "to call out from among." An *ek kaleo, ecclesia* translated "church" is a group of people who have been "called out from among." That word *ecclesia* was as common in the Greek language as the word "assembly" is in our language. The basic meaning of the Greek word has never been changed. Whether it is used in the New Testament or in the Septuagint (the Greek translation of the Old Testament), or whether it is used in profane, secular Greek literature, always it is the same. It refers to an assembly that is called out.

Three times in the New Testament the word *ecclesia* is translated "assembly." Acts 19:32,40,41: "Some therefore cried one thing, and some another: for the assembly [the *ecclesia*] was confused... But if ye enquire any thing concerning other matters, it shall be determined in a lawful assembly [ecclesia]... And when he had thus spoken he dismissed [the ecclesia] the assembly." The assembly was the "called out citizens" who gathered in convocation for purposes of transacting business of state. In the democracy of those first Greek settlements and organized political units, no slave could belong nor any stranger. It was a called out-assembly of citizens. The same use of the word is made by Stephen in Acts 7:37-38: "This is that Moses, which said unto the children of Israel, A prophet shall the Lord your God raise up... This is he, that was in the church [assembly, ecclesia] in the wilderness... " Stephen looked upon that group coming out of Egypt and on the way to the promised land as an ecclesia — "a called out assembly" — a "church" — called out of Egypt on the way to the promised land.

Again, you find the eloquent author of the book of Hebrews using the word to refer to all of God's called out people who are in glory: "For ye are not come unto the mount that might be touched... But ye are come unto Mount Sion, and unto the city of the living God, the heavenly Jerusalem, and to an innumerable company of angels, To the general assembly and church [ecclesia] of the firstborn . . ." (Hebrews 12:18,23) — "To the general assembly and church of the firstborn." The word refers to all of God's people who are called out of this gainsaying and unbelieving world. There they are in heaven — every one of them — without loss of a one. There is a calling and there is an election in the Bible that is woven into the very warp and woof of the whole fabric of the Word of God. A calling and an election. The word ecclesia is about as meaningful a portrayal of that fact as anything you could find in the Scriptures. The word ecclesia is an exact and true delineation of the "church." The church is a called out group. It is an election. It is a demonstration of the grace of God that reached down for you and that included us. So these congregations all over God's earth are called-out assemblies, saved by the grace of God, separated from the world, on the pilgrim road to the great glory that is yet to come, an *ecclesia,* a church, a called out body of believers saved by the loving grace of God.

Almost always that word *ecclesia* is used to refer to a local congregation, such as the *ecclesia* in Corinth, the *ecclesia* in Jerusalem, or in Antioch, or in Caesarea. The scriptures say, "the church*es* [plural] of Judea"; "the church*es* [plural] of Galatia"; "the church*es* [plural] of Macedonia." These called out assemblies that love God and believe in Christ, separated from the world, elect by the grace and loving mercy of Jesus, are His churches in the earth.

In the book of the Revelation are seven of these representative congregations. They are historical; they are actual; just as this church is historical, having a history; just as it is actual. Look at it: here we are a people who have been saved from our sins by the grace and forgiveness of Jesus, called of God and set apart unto these ministries in which we share in the life of our church. With its pastor, with its deacons, with its teachers and leaders and fellow-helpers, we are one of God's churches. Our Lord addresses these letters to seven such churches — actual, historical congregations. As an introduction, just to feel at home, just to get acquainted, we are going to visit these seven different cities in which God's seven elected congregations are gathered together.

THE CITY OF EPHESUS

First, we visit the church at Ephesus. Ephesus was the flourishing, commercial city on the western side of Asia Minor, three miles up on the Cayster River opposite the Greek island of Samos. It had a large artificial harbor that could accomodate the biggest ships in the world. The great trade routes from the East poured into Ephesus. It was the most accessible city in the Levant. Trade between East and West passed through the city of Ephesus. As such, it enlarged mightily and grew to be one of the richest cities of the Roman Empire. It had a history that ran back into dim antiquity. The Amazons, a tribe of people who were ruled by vigorous and capable women, believed that the mother-goddess of the world was born in Ephesus, and they built there a city and a temple in which to worship that mother-goddess. The city flourished until the days of the Greeks, who conquered it. They dedicated the city to the Greek goddess, Artemis (in Latin called *Diana*). There they built for her the greatest Greek temple in the world. It was looked upon as one of the seven wonders of the world. When the time comes, we shall describe that temple in detail. The temple was a center of interest and adoration and worship not only for the province of Asia but for the entire world. People poured into Ephesus from the ends of the Roman Empire to share in a worship full of pageantry and cere-mony, bowing down before the Ephesian Diana.

The city also had a marvelous Christian history. Paul, in his ministry, spent two full years in Ephesus and there wrought wonderful miracles. Even handkerchiefs that Paul would touch would be taken to the sick, and the sick would be healed. There Paul wrote the first letter to the Corin-thians. Paul wrote to the church itself a marvelous letter that is called the letter to the Ephesians. It was in Ephesus that the most brilliant pulpiteer who ever preached the Gospel of the Son of God was converted. In Ephesus, Apollos was converted to the Christian faith. I think Apollos wrote the letter to the Hebrews. He was the most polished of all the orators and expounders of the faith who have ever lived in Christian history. There, also, Timothy was pastor. The first epistle to Timothy was written to him when he was pastor of the church in Ephesus. There John, the author of the Apocalypse, and of the fourth Gospel, and of the three epis-tles that bear his name, was pastor. John came to live in Ephesus about 69 A.D., fleeing the terrible war in Judea that ended in the destruction of Jerusalem. For about thirty or forty years the sainted John was pastor of the church in Ephesus. It was there, under the reign of Domitian, that he was exiled to the Isle of Patmos, which is located about twenty-five miles from Ephesus itself.

As the years passed, Ephesus declined, and today it is nothing but a scene of endless desolation. The great harbor has filled with silt. The site of the city is now located several miles from the sea. When it is visited by archeologists, startled giant lizards, amazed at the presence of a man, dart over great stones of porphyry and marble and hide in and out of great cornices and capitols and columns that at one time were the amazement and wonder of the world. You can still see the outline of the great theater that held its vast crowds shouting, "Great is Diana of the Ephesians." It was in apostolic times the biggest theater on earth. You can still see the outline of the great temple of Diana, one of the seven wonders of the world. Its beautiful stones are broken and scattered over a vast area, and the exact location of the temple is sunken into the ground and covered over with a miasmic pond that breeds malaria-bearing mosquitoes. For miles and miles over the hills and through the valleys, you can see the ruins of this once great and wonderful city that belonged to the Ephesians. It is now brooded over by disease and silence and death. "Repent therefore and do the first works or else I will come unto thee quickly and remove thy lampstand out of its place except thou repent." Such is Ephesus.

THE CITY OF SMYRNA

Thirty miles to the north, magnificently situated, is the city of Smyrna. It is located at the end of a beautiful bay of the Aegean Sea. The bay comes inward for thirty miles, and where the bay reaches the mountains and the hills, there the glorious, mercantile city of Smyrna was built. It was founded by the Aeolian Greeks after the destruction of the city of Troy. It has always been and still is one of the most magnificent cities in the Levant. Smyrna, at this time, had been laid out according to the finest tastes of Greek architectural perception.

The streets were wide and straight and spacious. The most famous of the streets was called the Golden Street. It ran from the sea, where the great temple of Cybele (the goddess of Nature) was built, straight through the entire length of the city to Mount Pagos, on the summit of which was built the great temple to Zeus. As one walked on the Golden Street from the sea up to Mount Pagos, to the right and to the left were the glorious temples of Apollo and Aphrodite and Aesculapius. On that street one of the famous monuments was dedicated to Homer, who was supposed to have been born in the city of Smyrna.

In that ancient day the Romans looked upon Smyrna as being the queen and the glory of all Asia. It must have been an unusually impressive city. Today it is still the largest city in the Levant; it is the largest city in Asian Turkey, in Anatolia. It has a population today of about two hundred and fifty thousand. It was burned down by the Turks after World War I when an Allied treaty gave it to the Greeks. But even though it was rebuilt squalidly and meanly, yet it is the center of the mercantile trading for all that part of the eastern Mediterranean. It is the headquarters of the great complex of railroads that fan out to all of present-day Turkey. It is called today *Izmir* and the bay is called the bay of Izmir. *Izmir* is a Turkish corruption of the ancient word *Smyrna*. This is the second of those great cities of the Apocalypse.

THE CITY OF PERGAMOS

About fifty miles north and fifteen miles inland from the sea was located Pergamos. Pergamos from the beginning was a capital city. For three hundred years Pergamos was the capital of all that part of the world. A capital city has an air about it that is unlike any other metropolis. Pergamos was not a mercantile city. It was not a city of flourishing trade routes. It was a pagan, cathedral city, a university city, a city on which the chiefs and kings of succeeding kingdoms lavished untold wealth and in which they built beautiful temples and colonnaded arcades and streets and monuments. It was built on an acropolis at the point of two rivers, built where it could be easily defended. It was the capital of ancient Mysia. It was the capital of the Kingdom of the Attalids (one of the portions into which the Empire of Alexander the Great broke up). When the Romans took it over it was made the capital of the newly created province of Asia.

Pergamos was famous for two wonderful things. First, it

was noted for its library. Pergamos had a library of more than two hundred thousand volumes, which was an immense number of books in those days. The word *parchment* comes from the word *Pergamos*. The first time writing was ever done on skins — called parchments — was in Pergamos. You see, papyri was a government monopoly of the Ptolemies down in Egypt. The word *paper* comes from *papyri*. It was made from a plant that grew on the Nile. The fiber of the reed-like plant, when flattened out and criss-crossed, was substantial enough to write on. The government of Egypt, under the Ptolemies, had a monopoly on the manufacture of papyri. Ptolemy, in Egypt, became angry with Eumenes, king in Pergamos, and refused to sell him any more papyri on which to write his books. So, having nothing to write on, the King of Pergamos and his librarian invented writing on skins. Hence, the word *parchment* from *Pergamos*. The library of parchment in the city was one of the wonders of the world.

The other thing for which Pergamos was famous was its temple to Aesculapius. He was the god of healing. In Pergamos was the greatest medical school in the world. There students came from all over the Mediterranean world to study the science of healing. You notice Revelation 2:13 says, "in Pergamos where the throne of Satan is." It was pre-eminently a city of pagan worship. It was the city of heathenism and paganism and the adoration of many, many gods.

As the years passed, Pergamos also fell into ruin and is now just a vast scene of desolation and destruction. It has a small Turkish village nearby, called *Bergama*, a town of about ten thousand people. *Bergama* is a corruption of the ancient word *Pergamos*.

THE CITY OF THYATIRA

About thirty miles to the south (we have been going north, from Ephesus, to Smyrna, to Pergamos; now the circle is coming back again) from Pergamos was the ancient city of Thyatira. Nothing is known of its history. It was a flourishing mercantile community situated at the confluence of two valleys, where the ancient roads came together. It was noted for its manufacture of purple and of copper and of silver. The entire city was organized into trade guilds: a trade guild for the coppersmiths, a trade guild for the silversmiths, a trade guild for the dyers and the weavers. Lydia was from Thyatira, selling her goods, selling her purple cloth in Philippi, a Roman colony in Macedonia. Thyatira has also fallen into ruin and decay and is hardly recognizable today.

The City of Sardis

Thirty miles south from Thyatira was the ancient and glorious capital of the Lydian kings, Sardis. The history of Sardis goes back into dim antiquity, but we know it mostly as the capital of the Lydian king whose name was Croesus. Sardis had an impregnable, unassailable position. It was located on the north wing of Mount Tmolus, and at its base ran the Pactolus River, which acted as a moat around the mountain. The city was built upon an acropolis, where no storm troopers could get to it and no army could conquer it. There the Lydians built their beautiful capital city named Sardis. The wealth of Croesus was partly due to the gold in the sands of the Pactolus River that ran at the base of his beautiful capital. There money was invented. The first gold and silver coins ever minted were the work of Croesus in the capital city of Sardis in the kingdom of Lydia. Solon, the great Greek legislator, visited Croesus in Sardis. When Cyrus conquered it and took the kingdom of Lydia, it was at that time one of the most impressive cities in the world. Sardis also has fallen into decay and into ruins.

The City of Philadelphia

About thirty miles south of Sardis is the city of Philadelphia. Philadelphia was built by Attalus II — Attalus Philadelphus — who was the king of Pergamos. He built the city of Philadelphia on the edge of the vast, interior province of Phrygia in order to try to teach Greek culture and Greek life to the wild tribes of Phrygia. It was the market place for the Phrygians. It was a town which never grew to great proportions because of the frequent earthquakes. It had no

Roman law courts; these were located in Sardis. It also has fallen into ruin and decay.

THE CITY OF LAODICEA

About forty-three miles to the southeast was the ancient city of Laodicea. There were three famous cities in the Lycus Valley. To the Asia Minor seacoast, below Ephesus, flowed the Maeander River. Inland about a hundred miles from Ephesus, it is joined by the Lycus River. The Lycus River pours into the Maeander River. We know of three famous churches among others in the Lycus Valley. All three of them are mentioned in the New Testament. On the north side of the Lycus was the city of Hierapolis, where Papias was pastor. On the south side of the Lycus was the city of Laodicea. About eleven or twelve miles up the Lycus to the east was located the city of Colosse, where Philemon lived, and to which church Paul wrote the letter to the Colossians. So the last of these seven Asian cities is Laodicea, in the Lycus Valley. Laodicea was a mercantile town, on the great trade route from east to west. It was a flourishing city. The people were so wealthy and the inhabitants so affluent that when it was destroyed by an earthquake in 60 A.D., the citizens refused the financial aid of the Roman Empire in order to do the work themselves. Laodicea also has fallen into ruin. There is nothing there except desolation. It sits in an abandoned widowhood beyond that of Ephesus, for at Ephesus you can see the rolling Aegean Sea, where once in a while the white sail of a fishing boat goes by, but Laodicea sits in loneliness and desolation.

These are the seven churches of Asia. This is just an introduction, as we shall go into those cities later to look at the churches in them and to see what Christ has to say to the individual congregations. The purpose of this sermon is to show us that these things which He said touch reality. Christ is talking about actual people. He is speaking to actual churches.

I make just one further brief observation. Out of all of the churches that were in Asia, just like the churches that were

in the Lycus Valley, why choose Laodicea? Why not Hierapolis? Why not Colosse? Out of all of the churches of
Christ — great ones — such as at Rome, Corinth, Antioch,
Alexandria, Caesarea, Jerusalem — why these seven? They
were chosen because of "the mystery of the seven stars
which thou sawest in my right hand" and "the mystery of
the seven golden lampstands." There is a significance, there
is a profound spiritual meaning, beyond the reference to the
local congregations themselves. There is a message for us
today in these seven lampstands, in these seven historical
churches. As we enter into this meaningful and significant
section, it will be astonishing (that is, it was to me) how
much there is to learn and to know, as we bow in the
presence, as John did, of our exalted Lord, who sees the
end from the beginning and who pleads, "he that hath an
ear let him hear what the spirit saith to the churches."

Chapter 2

The Angels of the Seven Churches

And he had in his right hand seven stars . . . — Revelation 1:16

Our text is Revelation 1:16: "And he had in his right hand seven stars . . ." and Revelation 1:20: "The mystery of the seven stars which thou sawest in my right hand, and the seven golden lampstands."

(By the way, several children have asked: "Why do you read that 'lampstands'? In the King James version it is 'candlesticks.'" The reason is this: When Shakespeare put a clock in the play "Julius Caesar," he created an anachronism. There were no clocks in the days of Julius Caesar. Clocks were invented hundreds and hundreds of years after Caesar lived. The same thing is true here in this translation. There were no candlesticks when John wrote. Candles were an invention many hundreds of years later than this. What the people had were lampstands; so "the seven golden lampstands." A lamp is a far more beautiful and effective representation and symbol of what the Spirit of God is saying to His churches than a candlestick.)

"The mystery of the seven stars which thou sawest in my right hand, and the seven golden lampstands. The seven stars are the angels of the seven churches . . ." Then begins the second chapter of the book of the Revelation. Each time the address to a church is made in the same language: "Unto the angel of the church of Ephesus"; "unto the angel of the church in Smyrna"; "unto the angel of the church in Pergamos"; and so with Thyatira and Sardis and Philadelphia and Laodicea. All the way through, the address is "to the angel of the church."

In this message we are to discuss the angel of the church.

25

"And he had in his right hand seven stars . . . The mystery of the seven stars which thou sawest in my right hand." The seven stars are the angels of the seven churches. The *aster* (the Greek word for "star") is the *angelos* (actually in Greek spelling *aggelos*), the Greek word translated here "angel." Then "angel" cannot be a symbol, for, if that is true, the *aster*, the "star," is a symbol of a symbol, which reduces the Apocalypse to foolishness and would make it so enigmatic that there would be no possibility of understanding it at all. If symbols are symbols of symbols, we would find ourselves lost in a maze of inexplicables. This *aster*—"star" — is not a symbol of a symbol. An *angelos* (the *aster* — "star") refers to a definitely responsible person who is in charge of a church.

THE MEANING OF THE GREEK WORD TRANSLATED "ANGEL"

The word *angelos* in the Greek language, and *malaka* in the Hebrew language, immediately open up in their meaning what it is for which the star stood. The Greek word *angelos* refers to a "messenger," one entrusted with a communication. Because so many times those *angeloi*, those messengers, were heavenly, in time men began to think of them as having wings (which is altogether alien to the Scriptures; there are no wings on angels in the Scriptures), and they came to be looked upon as the holy, heavenly hosts, the messengers of God who wait upon Him before His throne of grace. But that is medieval imagery and poetic fancy. The messenger of God, the *angelos*, the *malaka*, was a servant of God who was entrusted with a communication from heaven. It could be a heavenly person and once in a while it was. An angel appeared unto Manoah announcing the birth of Samson, and an angel stood by the side of the altar and spake unto Zacharias. But, most of the times the *angelos* is a man. He is a prophet, an apostle, a preacher, an evangelist, a missionary. He is a man of God entrusted with a communication from the courts of heaven. The word *angelos* refers to that messenger.

Turn in your Bible, for example, to Haggai, chapter one

and verse thirteen: "Then spake Haggai the Lord's messenger [malaka] in the Lord's message unto the people,
saying, I am with you, saith the Lord." The Septuagint
translates malaka as angelos. "Then spake Haggai the Lord's
angel [angelos in Greek — malaka in Hebrew]." The Lord
spake His message to Haggai, the Lord's messenger, the
Lord's angel. He is God's anointed servant for the delivery
of the Word of the Lord. Now, turn to the last book of the
Old Testament, Malachi. The first thing I see here in Malachi is his name. The word for messenger in Hebrew is
malaka, and Malachi is described as "my messenger" — "my
angelos" — "my angel." Now, turn to Malachi 2:7: "For the
priest's lips should keep knowledge, and they should seek
the law at his mouth: for he is [the angelos — the malaka]
the messenger of the Lord of hosts." The priest in the Old
Testament economy and administration and dispensation
is called the Lord's messenger, the Lord's spokesman, the
Lord's prophet, the Lord's priest, the Lord's star, the Lord's
angel, the Lord's malaka, translated "messenger." Now turn
the page in Malachi to chapter three, verse one: "Behold, I
will send my messenger [my angelos, my angel, my malaka],
and he shall prepare the way before me: and the Lord,
whom ye seek, shall suddenly come to his temple, even the
messenger of the covenant . . . ." Now, the word, "messenger
of the covenant," I think, should have been translated the
"angel of the covenant." The "angel of the covenant" refers
to the Son of God, to Jesus when He was incarnate. But the
first reference should be translated as it is, "Behold, I will
send my messenger [my angelos]." That refers to John the
Baptist — "my messenger," "my preacher," who will stand
up saying, "Prepare ye the way of the Lord."

Let us notice two other instances of the use of these
words. In Luke 7:24: "And when the messengers [the
angels] of John were departed, he began to speak unto
the people . . . ." In verse twenty-seven: "This is he, of whom
it is written, Behold, I send my messenger [quoting Malachi:
'Behold, I send my angel'] before thy face, which shall
prepare thy way before thee." Again, in James 2:25: "Like-

wise also was not Rahab the harlot justified by works, when she had received the messengers [angels], and had sent them out another way?" Therefore, when I come to the reading of this passage in the book of the Revelation, I know exactly what God means when He says the *aster*, the "star," is the *angelos* — the messenger of the church which is at Ephesus, or Smyrna, or Pergamos, or Laodicea. By "the star," by "the *angelos*," He means God's appointed servant, sent of the Holy Spirit and called of heaven to be God's spokesman to His people. He is talking about God's preacher, God's man.

THE MESSENGER A STAR

The messenger is called a star because he is an illuminator. A true servant of Jesus is a star. He takes the Word and the message of God and he makes it shine before the people. He is not talking about passing fancies, momentarily significant for the dying hour. He is standing in God's sacred place, telling the people what God has to say, how we can be saved from our sins, how our souls can be delivered from judgment, how some day we must stand before God and give an account for the things we have done in the flesh. He is to deliver God's message. He is a star. He is called an *angelos* — a *malaka* — a "messenger," because he does not invent his words. He does not ingeniously contrive, with palatable remarks, to say soft things that please itching ears. Rather, he is standing as a messenger of God, delivering God's Word to the people. So, he is called an *angelos*, or as Paul says, an ambassador for Christ, a steward of the mysteries of God. "The mystery of the seven stars [*the angeloi*], the messengers of God to His churches . . ."

I think one reason why such an enigma has been made of these stars, these angels, is that when we begin to read the Revelation, we assume that now we are going into things constructed of myth and fancy and we are preparing to think about the ethereal and the intangible. On the contrary, the Revelation is what God has to say to His churches, and it is couched in this beautiful, symbolic language that it might be the more impressive for God's people through the years, as truly it is. But that does not mean that these truths are hidden and enigmatic and mysterious. They are down to earth. They talk about us in our daily lives and our daily walk. They are what God has to say to His people. They are God's message to us.

Let us look now at the passages of Scripture in which these angels, these messengers, are addressed. First, when He spoke to the angel, He spoke to the churches. "He that hath an ear, let him hear what the Spirit saith unto the churches" (Revelation 2:7). Yet, the address, in each instance, is to the angel of the church. What that angel is to say is what God wants His people to hear. The message he is to deliver is what God wants preached to His people. So, what the angel delivers is as from the mouth and lips and heart and mind of the Lord God, Himself.

And yet, though entrusted with so heavenly a message, the messengers are fallible men. How do I know they are fallible men? For one reason, because there is no intimation in scripture that churches are under the tutelage and instruction of heavenly beings. In the book of Daniel there is a guardian angel over a nation; but there is no intimation anywhere in scripture other than that our churches are under the direction and sponsorship of God's appointed servants, the pastors and the preachers whom the Holy Spirit sets over His congregations. Then, another reason I know these angels are fallible men — just listen to what God has to say here to those angels! It makes your ears burn. Their derelictions, their shortcomings, their failures, their faults, and their downright sins are fearlessly delineated. I could not conceive of heavenly angels, pure and holy, ministers of light in the very presence of God — I could not imagine those angels in glory, those messengers of God in heaven, being castigated as Jesus castigates some of these angels over His churches. For example, turn to what He says to the angel of the church of Laodicea. It is a scorching word our Lord has to say. The Lord is about ready to cast him on the ash-heap. If that angel has wings he is surely going to get them clipped. No! It is a man He is talking about. He is addressing that servant of God who presides over the church at Laodicea.

Notice that there is an ordained, ecclesiastical, ministerial office which the Lord God Himself created for His churches. It is in the sacred, divine economy of the Lord God, Himself, that His people should have an ecclesiastical churchly ministry. I attended one time (because I had never gone to one of a like denomination before) a church in Pennsylvania, a very famous one. The church does not believe in a ministry. We went to the service and sat down and just sat. That is all we did. After we had sat there an hour, one of the men in the church turned to his wife and shook her hand, and someone else shook someone else's hand, and that was the signal that it was over. Members of that church do not believe in ordinances nor in a ministry. As I sat there in attendance upon the service, I felt that here was a vast departure from the ordained economy and wisdom of God as He established His churches in the earth. I do not mean that in the Book we have bishops like modern bishops, for the words "bishop" and "elder" and "pastor" all refer in the Bible to the same office. But there is in God's economy and in God's wisdom a ministry for each one of God's churches. Such is the wisdom of the Almighty. We have a God-appointed man to preside over and to deliver God's Word to God's church. That is the way the Lord has organized it.

GOD'S MESSENGER TO THE PEOPLE

Now, let me say another thing. What kind of a ministry is included in the work of the angel, the messenger, the pastor? There is no intimation that this servant, this *angelos*, this "messenger" of God, is to lord it over God's heritage as though he were a dictator or a tyrant, or that he be above being reprimanded and rebuked. What kind of a messenger is he? What kind of an *angelos* is he? This is the kind that he is. He is a servant of God, to hear the word that God speaks, to hear from God. He is an *angelos* to receive the word from God, to take it from God's hand, and to deliver it to God's people. The very thought of this sacred assignment bows the pastor in prayer. It humbles a true pastor beyond any way to think of it — that God should have chosen a mere man to do His work on the earth. The Lord appointed men to hear God's Word, to receive God's Word and to speak God's message to His people. This *angelos*, this "messenger," is an under-shepherd. He is a guardian, he is a keeper, he is a watchman. "And thou, O son of man, I have appointed thee a watchman for my people Israel; thou shalt hear the word of my mouth and warn them from me." If a man will hear, he will be saved; if he will not hear, his blood is then upon his own head. But the watchman has delivered his soul when he delivers God's message. He that hears the messenger hears God. He that obeys the messenger, obeys God. He that despises the messenger, despises God. In the economy and the wisdom of heaven, the Lord has chosen this way to guide and to build up His churches in the earth.

Look at this in the Book. Turn to Matthew 16:19. This is what the Lord says about His messenger, His *angelos*, His *presbuteros* (elder), His *episcopos* (overseer), His *poimen* (pastor): "And I will give unto thee the keys of the kingdom of heaven: and whatsoever thou shalt bind on earth shall be bound in heaven: and whatsoever thou shalt loose on earth shall be loosed in heaven." Lest someone say, as certain people do, "That means Simon Peter has the keys," just turn the page to chapter eighteen, verse eighteen, where He says the same thing to all of the disciples: "Verily I say unto you, whatsoever ye shall bind on earth shall be bound in heaven: and whatsoever ye shall loose on earth shall be loosed in heaven." He is talking about these *angeloi*, these "messengers," these "angels" of the churches.

Now, when you look at that passage in the Greek, it looks different from what it does in English. This is the exact Greek translation: "Whatsoever thou shalt bind on earth *shall have been* bound in heaven." The verbal form is paraphrastic, future perfect. "Whatsoever thou shalt loose on earth *shall have been* loosed in heaven," a paraphrastic future perfect. That is, Christ is saying to His disciples: "When you are in the Spirit of God, true to the commandment of

God, obeying the great commission and ordinance of heaven, the thing that you do on earth is the thing that shall have been ordained of God in heaven. Whatsoever you do not do, when you act under the aegis and direction and inspiration and power of the Holy Spirit of God, is the thing that God would not have done in heaven."

You find that same, identical thing in John 20:22-23: "And when he had said this, he breathed on them and saith unto them, Receive ye the Holy Ghost [the Holy Breath, the Holy Spirit, the Holy *Ruach*, the Holy *Pneuma*, the Holy Spirit of God, the divine in-breathing]. Whose soever sins ye remit, they are remitted unto them; and whose soever sins ye retain, they are retained."

These passages mean this: that God entrusted to His *angeloi*, to His "messengers," the keys of the kingdom of heaven. No man is ever saved apart from the preaching of the Son of God. Are the heathen lost? If we do not preach to them the Gospel of the Son of God they are, and their blood is on our hands, for no man is ever saved apart from the preaching, the delivery, the knowledge of the Gospel of the Son of God. "For whosoever shall call upon the name of the Lord shall be saved. How then shall they call on him in whom they have not believed? and how shall they believe in him of whom they have not heard? and how shall they hear without a preacher? And how shall they preach, except they be sent?" (Romans 10:13-15a). There is a holy office, and there is a separate, a unique, a sacred calling. We may be called to be Christian teachers, and I believe that. We may be called to be Christian physicians, and I believe that. We may be called to be Christian civil servants, and I believe that. But there is also over and aside and beyond, a sacred and heavenly calling whereby God sets aside a man for this special high and holy office, to be an *angelos*, to be a "messenger" for His people.

SHINING IN A DARK WORLD

Let us look at the background of that *angelos* (pastor) and that *ecclesia* (church). Wherever there are stars and there are lampstands, the background is darkness. The church shines, the *angelos* shines in a dark, dark world. This world is filled with beauty and glory and power. But underneath, it is brutal and savage. Once in a while this depravity bursts open like an eruption, and the world is staggered at the inhumanity and ruthlessness of the human heart. But in the midst of violent evil, the star shines and the lampstand holds up the light. Always there will be some who are drawn to the burning, some who open their hearts to the transforming power and message of God. Always! In Asia, He has His own. In Africa, He has His own. In every city, He has His own. There will always be some who will come to the light and be saved.

There they are, the two together, the light and the darkness, the wheat and the tares, the good and the evil, the Christ and the anti-Christ, warring in ever increasing intensity until the great Harvester shall send forth His reapers to separate the one from the other. We stand, as the apostle said, in the midst of a dark world; we stand as lights, shining in the brightness of God. This is a poem dedicated to the angels, the "messengers" of the churches:

> Draw near, O Son of God, draw near,
> Us with thy flaming eye behold,
> Still in thy church vouchsafe to appear,
> And let our lampstand be of gold.
>
> Still hold the stars in thy right hand,
> And let them in thy luster glow,
> The lights of a benighted land,
> The angels of thy churches below.
>
> Give them an ear to hear thy Word,
> Thou speakest to the churches now,
> Let all tongues confess their Lord,
> Let every knee to Jesus bow.

This is the mystery of the seven stars: The seven stars are the *angeloi* of the seven churches. "Unto the angel of the church at Ephesus, write" and "unto the angel of the church at Smyrna, write." What is said is God's message today to His people.

Chapter 3

The Symbolic Meaning of the Seven
Churches of Asia

> The mystery of the seven stars which thou sawest in my right hand, and the seven golden candlesticks. The seven stars are the angels of the seven churches; and the seven candlesticks which thou sawest are the seven churches. — Revelation 1:20

This message is a delineation of the spiritual significance of the seven churches of Asia. These seven churches represent and are symbols of all of the churches of Jesus Christ through all the centuries. If we would know what the church was, what its history has been, and what the churches will be, we shall find it here in the seven churches of Asia. They represent all of the churches and are symbols of all of them. The spiritual significance and message of the seven churches pertain to all of them, even to us today and to this church here. There is a message from God to us as the Lord addresses these seven churches of Asia. The word is as pertinent, as up-to-date, as significant, and it is as certainly and really applicable to us today, as it was to these seven historical, local congregations. The seven churches represent all of the churches of Christ throughout their past and present and future history. We know that assumption is true for five reasons:

THE CHOSEN NUMBER "SEVEN"

First, because of the number "seven." As there is a sacred place or a sacred scripture or a sacred book or a sacred person, so there is a divine arithmetic. The number seven refers to plenitude and to fulness and to completeness. The Revelation speaks of the seven Spirits of God; but there is only one Holy Spirit of God. Then why the reference to the *seven* Spirits of God? Because the Lord, in His arithmetic, in the use of the number seven, refers to the plenitude and the fulness of the ever-present, living, quickening Spirit of God. Now, when the word "seven" is used of these churches, it refers to the fulness of the message of Christ to His people, the completeness of all His congregations. They all are included in that number seven.

But were there not other churches in Asia beside these seven? Yes! Many, many others. Were there not other great churches far more famous than these to whom Christ addressed this message? Yes! Far more famous. In fact, some of these seven churches are located in cities that are hardly known and would have long been forgotten had it not been for the Book of the Revelation. Thyatira was a most insignificant city, comparatively. So was Philadelphia. Laodicea would never have been heard of had it not been for the Revelation.

Why did not Christ address some of His messages to the church in Antioch, or to the church at Rome, or to the church at Jerusalem, or to the church at Corinth, or to the church in Alexandria, or to any one of the others of the great, famous churches of the world? Simply because these chosen seven have in them those spiritual characteristics that Christ finds in His churches throughout the centuries. These seven are chosen out of a multitude of others even in Asia. In the Roman Province of Asia was Hierapolis. There was Colosse, to whom Paul addressed a letter. Along with these in the Lycus Valley, there was Apamea. All of these were famous churches in that day. Yet, Christ chose just Laodicea out of all the churches of the Lycus Valley. Now, these things are in the elective purpose of God, and those seven were chosen because they have characteristics that will be significant in the development of the churches of our Lord in the earth. These seven represent all of them. Did not other churches need reprimanding and rebuke and encouragement and warning? Yes, they did. But in speaking to these, Christ was speaking to them all, and in encouraging these He encouraged them all. In warning these, He warned them all. In the messages He addressed to these, He delivered messages to them all.

The *second* reason why we know that these seven churches represent all of the churches of Christ is because of the solemnity, the sobriety, the urgency, the immediacy with which these letters are composed and addressed. Look at the introduction. Each time that the letter is addressed to a church, it is based upon the authentication of the Lord God Christ Himself in one of His attributes. For example, to the church at Ephesus: "These things saith he that" (and always there follows an attribute of the great Lord God who reigns over us, our Jesus the Christ); "These things saith he that holdeth the seven stars in his right hand, who walketh in the midst of the seven golden lampstands." Look at the next one: "And unto the angel of the church in Smyrna write: These things saith [then another attribute] the first and the last, which was dead, and is alive." Then the next one: "And to the angel of the church in Pergamos write: These things saith [then another attribute] he which hath the sharp sword with two edges." Thus all the way through with the seven. So it is the living Lord who is authenticating Himself, who is addressing these churches. These letters are just like the parables. Every syllable of them is a spoken word by our Lord Christ, addressed for all time to all of His people.

A *third* reason: Because of their conclusion, the ending of the letters. They are ended with the most impressive sentence that mind could imagine: "He that hath an ear, let him hear what the Spirit saith unto the churches" — plural. The letter is written to the angel of the church at Ephesus, to the pastor of the church at Smyrna, to the spiritual leader of the church at Pergamos. Yet each time, as though there is an immediacy and an urgency in the message for all of Christ's people, it stops, it ends, it concludes in the same way: "He that hath an ear, let him hear what the Spirit saith unto the churches." What He says to Ephesus, He says to us; what He says to Sardis He says to us; what

He says to Philadelphia He says to us: "He that hath an ear let him hear what the Spirit saith unto the churches."

A *fourth* reason: I would suppose that there is something significant, over and beyond what I see on the written page, that there are deep meanings in these messages, because they are referred to as "mysteries" (Greek *musterion*), a secret meaning that a man could not know. It has to be revealed of God. "The *musterion* of the seven stars which thou sawest in my right hand and the *musterion* of the seven golden lampstands. . . . ." The stars are pastors, the ministers of the seven churches. "The seven lampstands which thou sawest are the seven churches." So it is a mystery — a *musterion* — that Christ is going to reveal to us. Therefore, I am to look beneath the syllable and the sentence. I am to look for a deep, significant, pertinent, spiritual, and universal meaning in what Christ has to say to each one of the seven churches.

Then, the *fifth* reason: I would know that there is significance in these addresses to those seven churches beyond those local historical congregations because the messages are found in a book of prophecy. Twice in the book of the Revelation there is reference to "this prophecy." In Revelation 1:3: "Blessed is he that readeth, and they that hear the words of this prophecy." Then the book concludes in the same spirit, "For I testify unto every man that heareth the words of the prophecy of this book . . ." (Revelation 22: 18). I find, therefore, right in the heart of "this prophecy," and in a deeply significant part of this book, these chapters dedicated to the seven churches of Asia. They are a vital and significant part of a book that refers to itself as a book of prophecy. Therefore, I would expect to find in these addresses of our Lord to the seven churches a great, prophetic outlook and foreview of the churches of our Lord through the centuries.

THE ENCOURAGEMENT OF THE SEVEN PROMISES

When we look at the letters we see in them many, many things that are marvelously enlightening and encouraging.

Let us notice, to begin with, one beautiful thing in the epistles. These seven letters contain a promise, a presentation of the giving back to us all that we lost in the sin of our first parents, as the Lord has worked out His plan in ages past and will continue to work it out in the ages that are yet to come. Look at the letters for just this moment, by way of introduction, to see the richness and depth of meaning of these seven significant addresses of our Lord to His people, to His churches.

In the first letter: In the Garden of Eden we lost our access to the Tree of Life and we were driven out of the Paradise of God. Now, in the first letter to Ephesus, the Lord says that He will give to us the right to eat of the Tree of Life which is in the midst of the Paradise of God. In the beginning we lost it. Now, in the first letter, Christ says He will give it back to us again, the paradise of glory and the Tree of Life.

In the second letter: In the beginning and through these ages since, God has afflicted us with the curse of our sin, which is death, not only to die in our bodies but to die in our souls, which is the second death. In the second letter, Christ says that all of us who overcome in Him shall have no fear and shall not be hurt by the second death.

In the third letter: When the pilgrims from Egypt were on their way to the promised land they were fed in the wilderness with manna from heaven. The High Priest bore the names of the people of God over his heart, on the breastplate. In the third letter it says that Christ will give to us, His people, to eat of the hidden manna and that we shall have our names inscribed upon the whitestone, the Urim and the Thummim of the breastplate of the High Priest. In the pilgrimage of God's people through the wilderness, He cared for His own and fed them with manna and bore their names upon the heart of the great High Priest. So God will care for us and keep us forever.

In the fourth letter: In the story of the Scriptures is recorded the triumph of God's people under Joshua, under David, under Solomon, over the heathen, over the nations of the earth, over their enemies. In the fourth letter: "I will give unto my people power over the nations: And they shall rule with a rod of iron." Our promised victory in Joshua and in David and in Solomon is ours as the morning star is the harbinger of the glorious sunrise soon to come. The victory symbolized in that ancient story is actually ours in Christ.

The other three promises pertain to the future that is yet to be experienced by God's children.

In the fifth letter: To the church at Sardis, Christ speaks of those who believe in Him as being raised from the dead. The book of life is opened and our names are found written therein. God's people are pictured as walking in pure white, a symbol of righteousness of the saints, the "yet-to-come" victory of the church.

In the sixth letter: To the church at Philadelphia, Christ says to His people in this promise that we shall be citizens of the new Jerusalem which cometh down from God out of heaven. He speaks of the temple, the house not made with hands, eternal in the heavens. This is ours, for us who are the people of God.

In the seventh letter: To the church at Laodicea is written the climactic consummation of all God's promises to His people. To them who trust and overcome in Christ it is granted to sit down with our Lord on the throne of glory and to rule with Him forever and forever. In session with Jesus at the right hand of God, beyond which there is no other thing that could excel or glorify or make glad! What a wonderful thing!

THE SEVEN PERIODS IN THE HISTORY OF THE CHURCH

These seven churches are parodigmatic of the whole story of the churches through all of the centuries. They are panoramic views of the history of the churches, the whole story written out before us. The seven churches represent historical periods in the history of the people of Christ.

There is an Ephesian period, a period that witnessed the cooling of love and devotion. Such is the church at the conclusion of the apostolic days. There is a waning, a lessening, an ebbing and a cooling of first love and zealous consecration.

There is a Smyrnian period in the history of the church. To the church at Smyrna, Christ had no word of condemnation. It is the only one of the seven letters that is all praise and encouragement. The Smyrnian church is the church of martyrdom. This is the story of the churches of Christ from the latter days of the apostles until the days of Constantine. This is the church of the catacombs. This is the church of terrible suffering.

Fox's Book of Martyrs (a book like *Pilgrim's Progress* that changed the course of this world) begins with the ten great Roman persecutions, which occurred in the days of pagan Rome. The Smyrnian church is the church of the days of the martyrs under the terrible oppression of the Roman Empire. Jesus says to the church at Smyrna, "Ye shall have trial and martyrdom and tribulation, blood and suffering, *ten days*." In that *Book of Martyrs* there are ten great persecutions of the people of God. To the church at Smyrna, "Ye shall have trial and martyrdom and tribulation *ten days*." What an unusual coincidence! This is the church of blood, the church of the baptism of fire, the church of the terrible persecution, the church of Smyrna. There is a Smyrnian period in the history of the church.

There is a Pergamian period in the church. Christ says, "You are now seated where Satan's throne is." The church is married to the world. Constantine performed the ceremony. The church now is seated on the throne where Satan is, and it is decimated by the doctrine of Balaam. The church at Pergamos is introduced to the doctrine of the Nicolaitanes which is the exaltation of the clergy, dressed in gold and in purple. There is a Pergamian period in the life of the church.

There is a Thyatirian period in the development of Christianity when Jezebel ruled the church, as described in the seventeenth chapter of the book of the Revelation. The church becomes like a whore, a harlot, a scarlet woman. The

Book says she commits adultery with the nations of the earth, that she gaudily costumes herself in chains of gold and colors of red, and that she lives like a queen. Have you not seen this development in history, and do you not look at it now with your eyes? God says that there is a Thyatirian period in the history of the church, but God also says that there is a faithful remnant. In the twenty-fourth verse of the second chapter, He speaks of God's faithful servants who are put to death; history records fifty million of them, slain by that blood-thirsty, murderous, false system. Jesus saw it all from the beginning.

There is a Sardian church, the church of the Reformation. There are "some names in Sardis who have not defiled their garments." Great names — Balthazer and Hubmaier and Felix Mantz, our Baptist preachers, besides Wesley, Calvin, Luther, Zwingli, Knox, Whitfield, Edwards. There is a Sardian period in the church. Great names of men who stand up and preach the Gospel of the Son of God!

There is a Philadelphia period in the church, the era of the open door, the saga of the far-flung missionary endeavor, the story of William Carey, Adoniram Judson, Luther Rice, preaching the Gospel of the Son of God. There is a Philadelphian period in the church. "I have set before thee an open door."

And last, seventh, there is a Laodicean period in the history of the church, when the church says, "I am rich, and increased with goods, and have need of nothing"; but the Lord says to it, "You don't know you are wretched and miserable and poor and blind and naked." I remember when a traveler from afar stood in the Vatican and the prelate said: "Look look! The riches, the gold, the silver, the accumulated wealth of the world; no longer does the church need to say, 'Silver and gold have I none.'" The visitor from afar answered, "And no longer can the church say, 'In the name of Jesus Christ of Nazareth, Rise up and walk.'" "I am rich and increased with goods." But Christ is on the outside knocking at the door. The Laodicean period is one of ease in the history of the church.

So we learn from Christ and read in history concerning the growth of Christendom that there is an Ephesian period of waning love, there is a Smyrnian period of martyrdom, there is a Pergamian period of identity with the world, there is a Thyatirian period when the church is dressed in purple, there is a Sardian period when men stand up and preach the Gospel of the Son of God, there is a Philadelphian period of an open door, and there is a Laodicean period of wealth and affluence and apostasy.

THE SEVEN CHURCHES IN EVERY AGE

But those periods also co-exist through all the ages. In every year, in every age, in every country, and in every denomination there are Ephesian churches who cool off, who once had a fire and a flame and an evangelistic zeal and who now are cooling in their drive for the souls of men. In every age there are these seven churches. There are Ephesian churches in this age. There are Smyrnian churches in this age, churches of the martyrs.

Could I ever forget in the days that I preached in Hong Kong soon after the cruel, crushing tyrant of Red China swept away the government of liberty and freedom and the churches of the Lord, the stories of Christian suffering told by the refugees from that cruel state? I listened to a man from the interior of China as he described the martyrdom of every member of one of God's little churches in the interior of China. We have the Smyrnian church today. So all the seven churches are represented today.

There is a Laodicean church today. In another city I went to see a Laodicean church. In that great magnificent pile, a monument to wealth and affluence, there is a dance hall on every floor. As I went from floor to floor and looked at the card tables and the polished floors, I thought of this passage in Revelation 3:17, 18. As I left the church and looked back upon it, I shall never forget this scene. Framed in the doorway of that magnificent cathedral-like pile was, half-leaning against a great stone arch in the main entrance, a woman dressed in mink, leisurely smoking a cigarette, waiting for her liveried chauffeur to bring the limousine close enough for her dainty steps to make it from the gorgeous cathedral to the beautiful automobile. I never heard of a prayer meeting in that church, I never heard of a revival meeting in that church, I never heard of the preaching of the Gospel of the Son of God in that church. There is a Laodicean church today.

All seven co-exist together: some that are aflame with missions (Philadelphian churches), some that are paying the price with their lives (Smyrnian churches), some that are cooling off in their devotion and dedication, (Ephesian churches) and some that are Laodiceans, taking it easy in Zion.

All seven co-exist in almost every church. There are Ephesian members in our church. Their love is cooling off. They used to be afire, aflame, burning for God. Now, they are not nearly so enthusiastic about Jesus. There are Ephesian members in our church. There are Smyrnian members in our church that pay for their devotion with their very lives. I can walk down some of these aisles and put my hands on some of those people right here who are Christians at a great cost and a great sacrifice. There are Smyrnian members in this church. There are Laodicean members of this church. They love social life more than they love God. They love to be accepted in a certain circle more than they love to be praised of God. If you were to ask them to take a place of responsibility, to help us with our children, they haven't time. "Pastor, I'm busy." But you'll see them at the Country Club day after day, wasting their lives on trivialities and insignificancies when we need them to help us with the children in the church, visiting the lost, winning people to Christ. There are Laodicean members in this church.

I am trying to get you to realize that the message of the Revelation is not some mysterious enigma, wrapped up in a riddle. This is a burning, flaming message that Jesus has for His people today. "He that hath an ear, let him hear what the Spirit saith unto the churches." These are not messages from an absent Lord. They are sentences from a present and living Judge. Our Lord walks among His lampstands, among His churches today, and the appeal today is as it was then, "Remember from whence thou art fallen, and repent, and do the first works; or else I will come unto thee quickly, and will remove thy candlestick out of his place . . . as many as I love, I rebuke and chasten: be zealous therefore, and repent" (Revelation 2:5; 3:19). The Lord with flaming eyes, walks among His churches, even up and down the aisles of this church, saying to us as He said to the Laodiceans, "Behold, I stand at the door, and knock: if any man hear my voice, and open the door, I will come in to him and sup with him, and he with me."

Chapter 4

Good and Evil in the Churches

Nevertheless I have somewhat against thee . . . — Revelation 2:4

Not in any sense as a text, but as representative of the messages to all the seven churches, we read the letter to the first church:

> Unto the angel of the church of Ephesus write: These things saith he that holdeth the seven stars in his right hand, who walketh in the midst of the seven golden lampstands; I know thy works, and thy labour, and thy patience, and how thou canst not bear them which are evil: and thou hast tried them which say they are apostles, and are not, and hast found them liars:
> And hast borne, and hast patience, and for my name's sake hast laboured, and hast not fainted. *Nevertheless I have somewhat against thee,* because thou hast left thy first love. Remember therefore from whence thou art fallen, and turn, and do the first works; or else I will come unto thee quickly, and will remove thy candlestick out of his place, except thou turn — except thou repent. But this thou hast, that thou hatest the deeds of the Nicolaitanes, which I also hate. He that hath an ear, let him hear what the Spirit saith unto the churches; To him that overcometh will I give to eat of the tree of life, which is in the midst of the paradise of God.

"He that hath an ear, let him hear what the Spirit saith unto the churches." With a listening ear, we shall open our hearts to a truth of God that the Lord's people ought always to remember. As Christ Himself judges these congregations, they are all a mixed society of good and evil. Six out of the seven He severely condemns. With one out of the seven, He finds nothing right at all. In only one (Smyrna) out of the seven, He finds nothing to condemn. But even the background of that Smyrnian church is one of darkness and contact with iniquity, which He does condemn. Some of these churches are filled with people who have lost their first love. They have cooled in their ardor. Some of them are downright false in their professions, workers of iniquity. Among the churches there is true faith, there is false faith, and there is no faith at all. Even among the devout and the most worshipful and the most dedicated there are those whose hearts are in the world. There are tares among the wheat. Among the children of light there are children of darkness. There is an admixture, an intermingling of good and evil, through all the ages, through all the centuries and through all of these churches. Good and evil exist together in all of them.

THE PRIMITIVE CHURCHES A MIXED SOCIETY

In these seven churches we have a delineation of the primitive churches as they were in the days of the apostles. Would you not have thought that the first churches, founded and shepherded by the apostles, would be paragons of purity, that they would be models of the faith, exemplary in doctrine and in life and in deportment? But the very opposite is true. Even the churches under the shepherdly care and guidance and teaching ministry of the apostles were filled with heresy and schism and false doctrine and corruption. Even in that first church, the members were always having trouble. They were constantly disagreeing and quarreling. Such has been the story of the church ever since. Just as you find discord in the beginning in those first apostolic congregations, so you find it in the history of the church through all of the centuries since. There are interminglings and admixtures and composites of good and evil; children of the kingdom and children of the evil one; wheat and tares. The story repeats itself. In fact, ecclesiastical history is largely a recounting and chronicling of corruption and defection and a falling away from the faith. Every one of the great creeds of the church was promulgated because of heresies that had entered into the congregations. These creeds were protestations against those false doctrines that crept into and preyed upon the true churches of Christ.

Once a false doctrine is introduced it is never completely eradicated. Someone has said, "Happy is the nation whose history is brief." It is wars that make the story of a nation long and arduous. That same thing is true of the history of the church. The history of the church is long and extremely ramified because it is a recounting of the terrific conflict of good and evil, of false doctrine and true doctrine of tares and wheat, of the kingdom of light and the kingdom of darkness, enmeshed in the same group and the same congregations.

Is not that a remarkable development? Yet, it is the same history our Lord describes in His parables. In the parable of the tares He says: "The kingdom of heaven is likened unto a man which sowed good seed in his field: But while men slept, his enemy came and sowed tares among the wheat, and went his way. But when the blade was sprung up, and brought forth fruit, then appeared the tares also. So the servants of the householder came and said unto him, Sir, didst not thou sow good seed in thy field? from whence then hath it tares? He said unto them, An enemy hath done this. The servants said unto him, Wilt thou then that we go and gather them up? But he said, Nay; lest while ye gather up the tares, ye root up also the wheat with them. Let both grow together until the harvest: and in the time of harvest [which He said is the end of the world] I will say to the reapers [and they are the angels], Gather ye together first the tares, and bind them in bundles to burn them: but gather the wheat into my barn" (Matthew 13:24-30). Both are growing together through all of the dispensations and through all of the ages and through all of the story of God — good and evil together. It was so in the sowing of the Lord in the beginning. There has never been a sowing of God that was not over-sown by Satan. There have never been the plantings of grace where also the plantings of the world did not hinder.

So it has been through all the ages. The Lord sowed good seed in heaven, and when the harvest came, one-third of the angels left their first estate and forsook their thrones of adoration and glory. God sowed good seed in the paradise of Eden, and when the harvest came, it contained tares and thistles and death. At the world's first altar there appeared by the side of the saint, the first murderer. Cain was there beside his brother Abel. Before the flood, God had His sons, but the sons of the wicked one were far more numerous. In the days that followed the deluge, there were children of the Lord, children of righteousness, but they were a minority who were hounded and persecuted throughout the earth.

So it has been in the Christian dispensation and in the story of the churches, this mingling of good and evil all the way through. In the little band chosen by our Lord, one of them was a devil. When Christ was raised from the dead and appeared on an appointed mountain in Galilee to about five hundred (Paul says) at one time, Matthew writes that as they looked upon the Lord God Himself raised from the dead, heard Him speak, listened to His commission, "some of them doubted." There was a lack of faith even among that little band of the faithful five hundred who were looking upon the figure and the face of the risen Lord Himself. In the first church at Jerusalem there appeared Ananias and Sapphira. In the great revival in Samaria under Philip the evangelist, there came down the aisle Simon Magus the Sorcerer. He said he was converted when he was not converted at all, and later history records that he led the people into great heresy. In the first churches the public servants sometimes were like Demas and Diotrephes who renounced the faith of God and were the enemies of Christ.

Christ always has His anti-Christ. Wherever the temple of God is, there is the Man of Sin. This truth is revealed by the apostle Paul in the letters to Thessalonica. This is what Jesus was saying in the parable of the tares. Both good and evil are together. They are in every age, they are in every dispensation. It was that way in heaven; it is that way down here in the earth. It is so here and in every church in the earth.

THE MYSTERY OF EVIL

Now one could ask, "Why?" Why does the permissive will of God allow the intrusion of evil into His most sacred institutions? Why is it that the Lord Christ, Himself, either is not able or does not choose to keep evil and grievous pain and folly and false doctrine out of His church? That is an unanswerable question. Paul, in II Thessalonians 2:7, refers to "the *mystery* of evil." There is an elective choice and permissive will of God concerning iniquity in the earth and in heaven — a mystery into which a man's mind cannot enter. God's thoughts are not our thoughts, and God's ways are not our ways. This world is an altogether different kind of a world from what a man's wisdom would have chosen for it. In the elective purpose of God, evil is present. In the assembly celestial, there was rebellion in heaven and God Himself was blasphemed. The leader of that rebellious blasphemy was the archangel, the cherub who walked in the fires of burning and the gems of beauty, the one to whom even Michael dared not say other than, "The Lord rebuke thee." Apparently, the highest created being God ever set forth in glory, whom He made crown-prince of all of the hosts of heaven, rebelled. Sin was found in him; pride and iniquity became a part of the church celestial. When Lucifer was cast out, behold, one-third of the angels of God chose to fall with Satan rather than serve God in heaven (Revelation 12:4, 9). No man's mind can enter into that mystery of evil.

The same thing true of the church in heaven is true of the churches here in this earth. Evil is allowed to admix among all of the church's parts and people and institutions. Wherever you go, there I will show you tares among the wheat. Among our finest harvests on our mission fields, anywhere that God sows the seed of His children, there you will find Satan sowing the seed of the evil one. The church is nothing other than a circle within the great circle of creation. From the time of the beginning until the time of the final consummating end, there is to be that admixture of

good and evil together. I cannot understand it. No man's
mind can enter into it.

In passing, I have this observation to make: This strange
fact is certainly one proof of the inspiration of the Word of
God. For, had a man been saying it, he would have spoke
of the golden ages that we were going to achieve in the
preaching of the Gospel of the Son of God. In fact, in my
youth-time I used to hear eloquent preachers speak so.
They do not talk like that any more. That is one thing that
Stalin and Lenin and Tojo and Hitler and Khrushchev and
their like have done for theology. There is not a pulpiteer
living today who lifts up his voice and speaks as our preachers did when I was a young man. Those preachers spoke
contrary to the Word and revelation of God. God said from
the beginning, as He saw the end, that there would be tares
among the wheat, that there would be bad among the good,
that as long as this world lasted, there would be a mixed
society in the churches, in government, in all of the multiplied, multifarious ramifications of life. Good and evil exist
together. That is exactly what God said. But a man would
not have said that. He would have spoken in great perorations, in eloquent tones and stentorian voices, of the glorious
achievements and the golden age that was coming through
the preaching of the Gospel of Christ and through the work
of the churches. God did not say that. God's prophecies are
all alike. In the bad times and in the evil times, we have the
last times; "perilous times," God says, until the end of the
world.

The Struggle of the Christian Faith with Evil

This inevitably raises one other question. If we are helpless before the presence of evil in God's universe — evil in
heaven, evil in earth, evil in the churches, evil on the mission
fields, evil in the over-sowing of Satan, then has not Christianity failed? Have not the purposes of Christ failed? The
church has never been able to bring to fruition a golden age
and to empty this world of iniquity. It has not been able
to preach out or to educate out of mankind the claw and

the tooth and the tiger and the ape. We stand today in dread
of the most terrible, ominous future that the earth ever
looked upon, after two thousand years of Christian history.
Then, has it not failed? No. If God had said that the Gospel message would never be diluted and mixed with false
doctrine and the leaven of evil, if God had said that the
purity of heaven would never be soiled by the touch of
earth, if God had said that in the circle of the church there
would never come false professions and false teaching and
false doctrine, if God had said that the life of the church
would be like a pure and a peaceful river flowing unob-
structed, with unpolluted waters, gathering force and size
and expanse through the centuries until finally the churches
with outpoured blessings would cover the earth as the waters cover the sea, if God had said that, then I would be
forced to admit that the verdict of history necessitates the
judgment that the sunny picture and the felicitous pattern
has grossly failed and turned to despair and to dust and to
ashes.

But did God ever say such things? He said exactly the
reverse, the very opposite. Every reference to the estate of
the world is the opposite of that sunny dream. For example,
what did the ministry of Christ Himself issue in? When the
Lord had done His task and had finished His work and
had gone back to heaven, what was the result of His ministry? It was a little, believing flock — a little flock, a small
flock. The great mass of the nation and of the people rejected Him. When the abundant labors of the apostle Paul
were described by the apostle himself, what did he say? He
said, ". . . that I might . . . save some" (I Corinthians 9:22).
The great mass of the Roman Empire never listened to the
preaching of the Gospel, even when preached by Paul himself. But he labored prodigiously in order that, and I quote
him, ". . . that I might . . . save some."

James was the pastor of the church at Jerusalem. In the
fifteenth chapter of the book of Acts is found the pronounce-
ment of James regarding the great religious controversy
that brought to Jerusalem representative converts from the

heathen world, converts who came directly into the Christian churches without becoming Jews. Now, in that address, James said that the elective purpose of God was to take out of the Gentiles a people for His name and then he added, "And to this agree the words of the prophets" (Acts 15:15). All the prophets and all apostles speak of this minority. There is no exception to it. No exception. The very word "ecclesia" translated "church" means a "called out group." That is, the great majority will not listen. They will not turn. They will not heed. They will not be saved. But the church is an election, an "ecclesia," a group called out of the great mass.

The people who are presented as God's people in the Bible are always an election, a remnant, a small minority. "Fear not, *little flock;* for it is your Father's good pleasure to give you the kingdom." It is always a *"little flock."* We are taught that we are ambassadors from God in a foreign court. We are taught in the Book that we are strangers and pilgrims in the earth, that here we have no abiding home. We are taught that we are to *bear witness to* the nations of the world. We are taught that in the end, at the consummation of the age, "as it was in the days of Noah, so shall it be in the days of the coming [the *parousia,* the presence, the appearing] of the Son of Man . . . Likewise also it was in the days of Lot . . . even thus shall it be in the day when the Son of man is revealed" (Luke 17:26, 28, 30). When the fire fell on unbelieving Sodom and Gomorrah, only Lot, his wife and his two daughters were saved. That is the Bible. That is the revelation of God. That is what the Lord says, who sees the end from the beginning.

We repeat the question. Has not the Christian dispensation failed then? Have not the churches failed? Has not the Gospel of Christ failed? No more so than the first dispensation failed. For what the Mosaic dispensation was to the Old Covenant, to the Old Testament, the preaching of the Gospel is to this dispensation and to this government and to this administration. Back there the Jews subverted the Mosaic revelation by their traditions; they even crucified

Him for whom the dispensation was a preparation. But the crucifixion did not nullify the promises. To the Jew they were everlastingly yea and amen if they had qualified and if they had obeyed. But the Jew rejected and disobeyed. The promises were taken away and the dispensation came to a conclusion. But did it fail? No! For the Mosaic dispensation in the elective purpose of God prepared a people for His name and presented the Lord Messiah to the earth. In His crucifixion He overruled the wrath of men, and Christ became an atoning Saviour for our souls. Out of the apparent failure of the Mosaic law and legislation as it was lived and preached by the Jew, there came the birth of the Son of God and the churches of Jesus Christ.

So with the congregations of our Lord. This dispensation is nothing other, Paul says, than the grafting into the original stem of new branches instead of the branches which were torn off in the Mosaic dispensation and the Jewish nation. God has ingrafted now the churches of the Gentiles in this age and in this dispensation. If the first branches were torn out and torn off because they rejected God and were disobedient to God, it will be no more fatal to the economy of heaven if the ingrafted branches go Laodicean (are "spewed out of God's mouth") and are torn off. The kingdom of God will not fail. In the economy of grace, the elective purposes of God shall continue. Remember, God has promised only this: that in every age and in every generation there shall be a true witness to the saving grace of the Son of God. Remember this, that His promise is that the effect of the preaching of the Gospel will be to take out of the nations, out of the masses, out of the multitudes, an election for His name's sake.

THE FAITHFUL REMNANT

I cannot tell you the comfort that truth is to my heart. No matter where a man may preach, there will be many, many people who will turn him down. No matter how high a man may raise the cross, and with what fervent, earnest voice he may offer the saving grace of God in Christ, there will always be those who will reject the message. They will turn it down, they will refuse it. But there will always also be those (even as Paul found in Athens) who will turn and repent and open their hearts to the truth of God and who will be saved. There will always be an election. There will be a response. When I preach the Gospel of the Son of God in the center of Dallas, there will be thousands who will pass it by. But there will also be great numbers who will turn and believe and be saved. In every age and in every generation, God has promised that He will have His preacher and His witness and He will have His election and His people. The darker the hour, and the more blasphemous the generation, sometimes the greater shine the names of those who have uplifted the marvelous Gospel of the grace of the Son of God. So it has been throughout all the history of the churches through the ages and the centuries.

Sometimes there is darkness; sometimes there is blackness; sometimes there is defection; sometimes there is repudiation; and sometimes there is false doctrine that threatens to sweep the churches away. But simultaneously, in every instance, there continues in other places the vigorous preaching of the Gospel of life and light and regeneration and conversion. So it has been through all of the centuries.

When piety was waning in the church at Antioch, great revival and spiritual surging was characterizing the church in Milan. When the churches of Alexandria and of Carthage were falling into empty formalism, the churches of Gaul were battling the vices of imperialism and were winning converts among the rude barbarians. When the church at Rome was falling into vain ceremonialism and pretense, the whole country of Ireland was turning to the beauty and holiness of the Lord Jesus, our Saviour. When Mohammed, whose sword was as the avenging hand of God against the idolatry of the churches (and whenever you pass by a church and see an idol in it, remember the sword of Mohammed), when Mohammed was destroying the churches of Egypt and of Syria and of Asia Minor, at that same time the scholars of Iona (the little island off of the coast of Scotland) were

studying the Word of God, and their preachers were convert-
ing the Anglo-Saxons (your forefathers and mine). When
the papal, pontifical court at Avignon in France was being
sold to vice and debauchery, and religion was made a disgrace and an infamy, at that same time, in the Teutonic
cities of Germany, godly, pious men were preaching sermons, were practicing the virtues of the Christian faith and
were winning converts to the Gospel of the Son of God.

When the harvest was rotten and the stubble was withered in Italy, the fields were whitening unto the harvest
in Bohemia. When France fell into the darkness and blackness of superstition and despotism, the morning star of the
Reformation was rising in England. When the Unitarian
defection destroyed and emptied the churches of New
England, the pioneer preacher was crossing the Alleghenies
into the wilderness of Kentucky and Tennessee and pressing
westward across the prairies. He came even to the far western town where I grew up as a boy and preached the Gospel
of the Son of God. That flaming pioneer preacher founded
our churches and our institutions and won men to Christ
all over the heartland of America.

Today, there may be drought and there may be empty
ritual and ceremonialism and there may be downright paganism and repudiation and blasphemy and rejection in
some places. But there is revival in other churches. Young
people are turning to the Lord. Children are being saved.
Families are being put together in the love and in the
patience and in the name and in the Spirit of Jesus. That is
the way it is to be to the end, according to the Book of God.
Good and evil, pure faith and false faith, wheat and tares,
children of light and children of darkness, citizens of the
kingdom and citizens of the world are to be here, side by
side, living in the same town, listening to the same gospel
message, some of them coming in repentance and faith to
the Lord, and some of them saying, "No," hardening their
hearts against the spirit of appeal and conviction and grace
of the Son of God.

The thing for us to do is not to try to improve upon the

Word and revelation of God. This is the way the Lord says it is. So, when I preach, I am not to be discouraged if not everyone is saved. When I try to win people to Christ, I am not to be crestfallen if some of them reject my message. There will be others, the called out, the elect of the Lord, who will say, "Yes." Beside the great host that say, "No," there will be some who will say, "Yes." In that election, in that "ecclesia," in that calling out, we have our joy and our gladness, our stipend and our ultimate and final reward. Look around you. There are thousands who will not get up. They will not rise out of their beds to go to church on Sunday morning. There will be uncounted numbers of children playing in the streets or children whose families are taking them out in boats or on fishing trips or on outings or on picnics, people whose hearts are hardened against the appeal of the Gospel of Christ. I know.

But look around you. There are thousands of others who call this a holy day, who say "this is the day the Lord hath made," and who rejoice and are glad in it. They rise to say: "This is the Lord's day and we were glad when our fellow-Christians said, 'Let us go up to the house of the Lord.' Let us pray together, let us sing together, let us open the Book together and let us listen to a man preach the everlasting Gospel of the Son of God." We are here, the elect, the called out, the "ecclesia" of heaven. God has done it that way from the beginning. God says it will be that way to the end. So we are not to be discouraged. We stand as witnesses to the peoples and nations of the world, crying, "Turn ye, turn ye, turn ye, for why will ye die?" Some will reject, but some will always turn and be saved.

Chapter 5

The Reward of the Faithful

To him that overcometh will I give . . . — Revelation 2:7

All the seven letters of our Lord to the seven churches of Asia are designed exactly alike. They all follow a distinct and unusual pattern. There are seven parts to each one of the letters.

The first part contains the address, the salutation, the one to whom the letter is sent. "Unto the angel of the church at Ephesus," or "at Smyrna" or "at Pergamos" and so through the seven. All seven of the letters begin with those identical words.

The second part of all seven of the letters contains the citation of one or more of the wonderful, marvelous, celestial attributes of the glorified speaker. All of these attributes are found in the first chapter of the Revelation in John's incomparable vision of the Lord Jesus on the Isle of Patmos. "These things saith he that holdeth the seven stars in his right hand, who walketh in the midst of the seven golden lampstands." ". . . These things saith he which hath the sharp sword with two edges." So all seven of these letters follow that pattern.

Now the third part. In all seven of the letters the Lord states that He knows all about the works of the ones to whom the letter is addressed. He makes an avowal of His omniscience, knowing all that is being done by the churches. All seven letters have that same avowal. "I know thy works," writing to the church of Ephesus, writing to the church in Smyrna, writing to the church in Pergamos. "I know thy works." All seven of these letters contain those words.

This third part is followed by a fourth, a characterization of the works of the churches. He describes what they are

57

and what they are doing. He praises them in some instances. He condemns them in some instances. He warns them and He pleads with them and He admonishes them. In all seven of the letters this part is always present. After He speaks of His omniscience, there often follow words of praise or condemnation or admonition or warning.

Then follows the fifth part. He always makes a reference to His second coming, showing, in the case of each church addressed, how His coming will appear to that church and how it will be received. To some of them the second coming of the Lord will be a great judgment. To some of them the coming of the Lord will be a great triumph and relief. In every instance, the coming of the Lord to different churches and to different people has different aspects, different receptions and different characterizations.

The sixth part of each one of the letters is a universal admonition to hear. "He that hath an ear, let him hear what the Spirit saith unto the churches ..."

The seventh part of each one of the letters is a final promise to the one that overcomes. For example, the promise to Ephesus reads: "To him that overcometh will I give to eat of the tree of life, which is in the midst of the paradise of God." In the last four letters the seventh part (the promise to the overcomers) is placed where the sixth part (the admonition to hear) is, and the sixth part is placed where the seventh was heretofore. John just turned the parts around in the last four letters. Thus all of these seven letters have these seven distinct divisions and they all follow that same pattern.

We are going to discuss one of those parts, the seventh part, the last part, the reward that is promised to the faithful. It is highly instructive and wonderfully inspiring to look upon the reward that Christ promises to His people, to His faithful churches.

REWARD IS BESTOWED AT CHRIST'S COMING

The first thing I notice about the reward that is promised is this: It is last. The reward is not first, it is not middle, it is not almost to the end, but the reward is always last. The reward is bestowed as the last thing in the age. It is not given until the end. It is not given until the consummation of all time and all history. As it is written in Revelation 22:12: "Behold, I come quickly; and my reward is with me, to give every man according as his work shall be." So the reward of the Christian is given at the end, at the time of the consummation, at the time of the ending of the age. Why is the reward not given in this earth? Why is it not given in this life? Or, at least, why is the reward of the Christian not bestowed upon him at death? Why does he not receive it, at least, when he dies? Why is the reward of the Christian withheld until the time of the end, at the consummation of the age, at the end of the world? The reason is obvious. A man's life and work and influence keep on beyond this day and this life. A man's influence does not die when he dies. The work that he has done keeps on and on and on, like the reverberation of a sound wave or the going out of a light wave or the rippling of the water on the sea. It goes on and on and on until it reaches the farthest shore. So God unravels, in the skein of life, the thread of every man's work and every man's influence through all of the years. The reward of the man is given to him at the end of the age. The reward cannot be given to us now and cannot be given to us when we die, because what we have done keeps on bearing fruit, whether good or evil. No man in the world could trace out the influence of a man's life through all of the ramifications of story and of history. But God can do it and God does do it and will do it. At the end-time all of the influences of a man will be gathered together to determine his reward.

A man's influence does not die when he dies. I went to high school with a young friend. We were graduated together. He and I were in the same university together. To the amazement of all of us, he turned out to be an infidel, an atheist. It was an astonishing development. So, upon a night, some of us who loved him and had known him all those years went up to his room to talk to him. When we walked into his room, he was seated at his desk reading infidel Tom Paine's *The Age of Reason.* Tom Paine died in 1809. He has been dead more than one hundred and fifty years. But the influence of the man lives on. It lives on today. It has been but a few days ago that a beloved member of this church, after looking through the attic, found and gave me a copy of Tom Paine's *The Age of Reason.* It is there on my desk right now. I am reading it to see what the infidel has to say. You do not die when you die. Your influence goes on for good or for evil.

Now, let me turn the matter around. I know a young preacher whom God has honored. He said to me the other day, "I have never been so blessed in my life as I have been by reading Matthew Henry's *Commentary on the Bible.*" He said, "As I prepare my sermons I read Matthew Henry and he blesses my heart and he enriches my messages." George Whitfield read that commentary (and it is long) through four times, the last time on his knees. Do you know when Matthew Henry died? In 1714. That man has been dead all of these two hundred and fifty years. Yet, to this day the blessed influence of his life goes on and on and on. It is because of the abiding nature of influence that we do not receive our reward when we die. That is why it is not given to us in this life or upon our entrance into heaven. Our rewards are given to us last — when Jesus comes and when all time in history for us is ended. Then Christ gives to us the reward of our life, whether it is good or evil.

SEVEN FACETS OF FUTURE REWARDS

In these letters we have seven facets of the reward that God has in store for His faithful people. Like a beautiful gem that shines through seven beautiful faces, so in these seven letters we have seven sparkling presentations of the reward God has in store for His children. Those seven facets gather up the light of all the ages. Whatever God has proposed, has promised, has offered to His children in any age past, God gathers it up and gives it to us in the age that is yet to come. However in days past, in any age, we have lost what God had prepared for us, some day all of it is to be given back to us. We have this promise here set forth in these seven rewards as they are described in reference to the seven churches.

For example, in the first church, to the church at Ephesus, He says: "To him that overcometh will I give to eat of the tree of life, which is in the midst of the paradise of God." The Lord never intended for the tree of life to be taken away from us. We lost it in our first sin. We were shut out from it when God took the tree of life and transplanted it in the paradise of heaven. But there God is keeping it for us, that we may eat thereof and be young and vigorous and active and gloriously alive forever and forever. This is the first facet of the reward of the faithful.

Now look at the second one. To the church at Smyrna, He says: "He that overcometh shall not be hurt of the second death . . . I will give thee a crown of life." Death was never intended. Death is an enemy. Death is an intruder. Death was not in the scheme and plan and promise of God for us. Death is a fruit of the seed of unbelief and rejection and sin and transgression on the part of our first parents. But God has said that those who trust in Him and commit their lives to Him shall not be hurt by that second death, the death of judgment and perdition. ". . . in the day that thou eatest thereof thou shalt surely die" (Genesis 2:17). Ultimately, Adam and Eve died physically. But the death by which they died the day they ate was that spiritual and second death. God delivers us from it. That is one of the rewards of the faithful.

Look at the reward He promises to the angel of the church of Pergamos: "To him . . . will I give to eat of the hidden manna, and write his name upon the white stone." This is our new name which is given us of God. Upon the breast-plate of the high priest were written the names of the children of Israel, the children of God. He fed them with manna from heaven. What did the curse say? "In the sweat of thy face shalt thou eat bread, all the days of thy life. The soil shall bring to thee thorns and thistles and the very ground is cursed because of thy sin" (Genesis 3:19). But in glory there is no more curse. The harvest is never thorns and thistles and briars and brambles and weeds. God feeds us with manna, the heavenly angel's food. Our names are written on the Lamb's heart, on his breast. There are we cared for, not as in a wilderness and a desert, in a cursed earth, but in a world that is new and beautiful and abundant. There does God love us and keep us.

The promise to Thyatira is: "I give you power over the nations: And ye shall rule them with a rod of iron." God's people for just a little while, under David and Solomon, conquered their foes and ruled over their enemies, but in glory we shall rule forever and be triumphant forever.

The promise to Sardis: "He that overcometh, the same shall be clothed in white raiment." The reference is to the resurrection of the dead and our gift of a pure, white and sinless character in the glory that is yet to come. In this life we are stained. No man can walk through a coal mine and not get dirty. No man can walk through this life and not be hurt by its sin and its perils. If there is any man reading these words who can walk through the pilgrimage of these years and can stand up and say, "I have never been touched by the sin of the world in which I live," I would like to see him. There is not a man living that could stand up and say that. Thus it is in this life. But in the life that is yet to come, God will give us white raiment, a pure, spotless and stainless character. God will make us anew. The blind will be able to see again. The crippled will be able to walk again. The hobbling and maimed and lame will be strong again. The weak will be made whole. The sick will be made well. The dying will be given life, and all of us shall be perfect in His sight. What we have lost here, God has in store for us there in heaven.

To the church at Philadelphia the promise is: "You are to be pillars in the temple of God ... in the city of the new Jerusalem, which cometh down out of heaven from God." We are going to have a place and an assignment in the holy and beautiful new Jerusalem. It will be blessed. Maybe those who love to sing will be given places in the choir. Maybe those who love to preach, God will give a planet somewhere to praise His name world without end. We are going to have assignments in the kingdom of God. As Jesus said in the parable, some of His servants are going to rule over ten cities, some are going to rule over five cities. All of us are going to be busy in God's house, serving the Lord in this new and beautiful Jerusalem.

Then the last facet. To Laodicea, He said: "To him that overcometh will I grant to sit with me in my throne, even as I also overcame, and am set down with my Father in his throne." We are going to be fellow-rulers with the Lord Jesus Himself. That is the highest reward that mind could think of. Beyond that, there is nothing. To be in session with Christ! Did you ever visit the Supreme Court of the United States? Imagine being one of those justices, one of the high, chosen judges of the nation. Or, fancy sitting on the throne of the British Empire. Think of being the Prime Minister who lives at 10 Downing Street. Or consider what it would be like, as President of the United States, to live in the White House. So, on and on all over the world, go in imagination into the places of honor. But these worldly honors are small as compared to those of God's people, who are to sit on the thrones of glory, judging angels and men, and ruling over all the peoples and nations of God's whole creation. Our finite minds cannot grasp such a thought. What an amazing thing, that clay and dust and ashes, such as we are, could be thus exalted, to be fellow-heirs with Christ in His kingdom and to sit with Him on His throne!

THE CERTAINTY OF CHRIST'S REWARDS

That leads me to the next point, the certainty of these rewards. The profound respect that the hearers of these letters had for those promises of Christ moves one's soul. There was a paradise of God upon which their hopes and visions were cast. There was a crown of life for which their hearts longed and their hands reached out to receive. To them the promise was true. There is a city of God that exists and there are promises of God that never fail. To these people who heard them, the promises were meant for them. God had the promise in store for them. That faith is characteristic of God's saints through all of the ages. These promises are, they exist, and God has them in store for us. For example, in the eleventh chapter of the book of Hebrews, we are told that Moses renounced the throne of Egypt, refusing to be called the son of Pharaoh's daughter, choosing rather to suffer affliction with the people of God, because he had respect unto the recompense of the reward (Hebrews 11:24-26). He believed there was some greater, finer and better thing for him than to be ruler over the greatest civilized empire in that day. To Moses the vision was real.

Similarly, in the eleventh chapter of the book of Hebrews about Abraham, and Isaac, and Jacob, we read that they "looked for a city which hath foundations, whose builder and maker is God." It says that they confessed that they were strangers and pilgrims in the earth. It says for them, because they looked for that city and lifted up their eyes to behold it, for them God is not ashamed to be called their God and He has prepared for them that city. We find the same persuasion when Paul says: "I press toward the mark for the prize of the high calling of God in Christ Jesus" (Philippians 3:14). He believed that it was there. Just as the racer, the runner, the athlete, reaches out with all his strength toward the prize held in store for those who win the race, so we, as Christians, ought to be busy, like runners, like athletes, reaching out to our utmost for those rewards that God has prepared for us.

I read recently that General Sherman said that as long as he was on the front lines, in the firing line, directing and leading his troops, he was filled with hope and the assurance of certain victory. But he said that when he was in the rear with the stragglers and the deserters, he felt despondent and depressed and full of doubts and fears. So it is with the Christian. If we are on the front line with God, pressing toward the mark, we are filled with joy and victory and hope and assurance. But when we are sitting back, afar off,

with the stragglers and deserters, we are filled with doubts
and fears and despondency and failure.

These churches had a profound assurance that these
rewards of God were for them. But what about those promises? And what about the people themselves? They have
been dead these centuries and now for two millennia. What
about them and these promises? What about them and
their profound persuasion that these things God had promised should be certainly theirs? They have all been consigned to the tombs, and the wasting ashes of God's sainted
children have been mingled with the dust of this planet
ever since. What about these promises? What about these
people who believed them? May I point out to you one
thing? Have you observed as you have read these letters
and as you have followed through these words of the Revelation, that death is hardly taken into account? It is hardly
considered. It is hardly worth mentioning. Christ has passed
through it and Christ has the keys to it. Death is so small
and trivial, so brief a hiatus in the life of the saints, that they
do not even bother particularly to mention it. Death is as
nothing. According to the revelation given to the apostles,
this thing of death is so small in consequence that it is not
even to be considered. Paul says, whether we die and the
Lord comes, or whether we remain until that hour, makes
no difference at all. One does not have any advantage above
the other, either way. For, he says, those who sleep in Jesus
will rise first. They will see Him first. Then we who are
alive and remain until the coming of the Lord shall be
caught up with them to meet the Lord in the air. There is
no advantage of one above the other. So whether we fall
asleep in Jesus or whether we are alive until the time of
His coming, it is all the same. There is no advantage either
way.

As some of you know, I read Spurgeon a great deal. He
is my ideal of the greatest pulpiteer who ever preached
the Gospel of the Son of God, after the apostle Paul. The
great preacher in London said that he wanted to have the
experience of death such as the Lord Jesus had. He said,

"If I had my choice of being here when the Lord comes or of going through the deep waters of the Jordan River, I would choose for myself to go through the experience of death in order that on the other side I might know what it meant when it says, 'And my Lord tasted death for every man.'" I use this as an illustration for us, that death is nothing at all. It is a hiatus of a moment, of a second, of the twinkling of an eye. There are even some among us, like the great Spurgeon, who avowed, "I would rather go through the deep waters and experience the resurrection rather than be alive and remain when He comes."

There are many, of course, and most of us possibly, who pray to see the coming of the Lord while still in this body of flesh.

> Oh, joy! oh, delight! should we go without dying,
> No sickness, no sadness, no dread and no crying,
> Caught up thro' the clouds with our Lord into glory,
> When Jesus receives "His own."

But it is immaterial, either way. Whether we die and He comes, whether we fall asleep in the Lord until He comes, or whether we are translated, in a moment, in the twinkling of an eye, at the sound of the trumpet, at the shout of the arch-angel. It does not make any difference. So, when we look upon these Christians of the seven churches and the promises made to them, death is not to be considered. The promise of God is theirs as it is ours now and forever.

I close with a word regarding the reward promised to Philadelphia (Revelation 3:10): "I will keep you from the hour of trial which shall come upon the whole world." What is this marvelous thing and how is it going to come to pass? How will the Lord translate His people out of the trial coming upon this vast world? The answer is found in a mystery revealed to the apostle Paul. Paul said, "Now this I say, brethren, that flesh and blood cannot inherit the kingdom of God; neither doth corruption inherit incorruption. Behold, I shew you a mystery . . . ." What is the great mystery? "Behold, I shew you a mystery; we shall not all sleep, but we shall all be changed, In a moment, in the twinkling of an eye, at the last trump; for the trumpet shall sound, and the dead shall be raised incorruptible, and we shall be changed" (I Corinthians 15:50-52). That is what is meant when our Lord refers to this reward. It is one of the mysteries of the kingdom of God revealed to Paul, the mystery of how God will keep His people from that hour of trial. He is going to take us up. Those that sleep in Jesus shall be caught up and be with the Lord when these great judgments of God fall upon the earth; and we who remain on earth to the coming of the Lord shall be, with them, gathered together to our blessed Saviour, delivered from the terrible judgments that are to be visited upon the unbelieving world.

Chapter 6

The Artemesian City of Ephesus

Unto the angel of the church of Ephesus write . . . — Revelation 2:1

The second chapter of the Revelation records the first letter of our Lord. Thus he speaks: "Unto the angel of the church of Ephesus write ..."

There were seven wonders — famous, beautiful, glorious, incomparable — in the ancient world: the Pharos lighthouse at Alexandria, Egypt; the pyramids near Cairo, Egypt; the wall and the hanging gardens of Babylon; the tomb of King Mausolus at Halacarnasis; the Colossus at Rhodes; the statue of Zeus on Mount Olympus by the incomparable Greek sculptor, Phidis; and seventh, the temple of Artemis, the temple of Diana, in Ephesus. Of those seven great wonders of the ancient world, the most impressive and the most beautiful was the temple of Artemis at Ephesus. There has never been a structure raised in the story of mankind as impressively beautiful as this incomparably glorious temple to the Greek goddess Diana. Her name in Latin is *Diana*. In Greek it is *Artemis*. The temple was larger, far larger, and far more famous than the Parthenon on the Acropolis in Athens. Pausanius said of the temple in Ephesus, "It surpasses every structure raised by human hands." Another ancient Greek writer said: "I have seen the walls and hanging gardens of old Babylon, the statue of Olympian Jove, the Colossus at Rhodes, the great labor of the lofty pyramids and the ancient tomb of Mausolus. But when I beheld the temple at Ephesus, towering to the clouds, all these other marvels were eclipsed." You notice that ancient writer names six of those seven wonders. The only one he had not seen, apparently, was the Pharos lighthouse at Alexandria.

THE LOST TEMPLE AT EPHESUS

For many, many centuries the temple at Ephesus was lost. In its destruction and in the annihilation of the city, it disappeared not only from view but also from history. No one knew where it had been built, neither its site nor its place. It had positively vanished. There was a book written by a man named Edward Falkener entitled, *The Lost Temple*. In that book he attempted to reconstruct what the temple must have looked like. The book was read by an Englishman named J. T. Wood. He resolved to find that lost temple. Financed by the British Museum, he made his way to the ancient site at Ephesus and began, with his archeological background and training, to seek for the lost temple in the ruins of that vast city. For six, solid, seemingly interminable years, J. T. Wood sank pits all over the extensive site of Ephesus, with no hint of success whatsoever.

Any other man would have given up years before, but not this man. Upon a day (and here follows one of the most romantic stories in all archeological history), this Victorian, wearing his formal top hat and frock coat even in the hot summer time, working down in the bottom of a pit in the theater (the theater of which you read in the nineteenth chapter of the book of Acts where the riot was staged against Paul), came upon a marvelous discovery. While he was digging in the spacious area (it was the largest theater in the world; it would seat twenty-four thousand people) he found an inscription. It was to a Roman named Caius Vibius Salutarius. The inscription was to the effect that this Roman had given to the Temple of Diana several gods (images) of gold and silver, each weighing about six or seven pounds. The inscription said he also had left to the Temple an estate, a trust for the cleansing and repairing and keeping of the images. Then, the inscription said one other thing. This man, Caius Vibius Salutarius, decreed that when the images were displayed on the birthday of the festival of Artemis, the goddess in the temple, the images were to be taken to the theater through the Magnesian

Gate; and on the return journey they were to be taken out through the Coressian Gate.

Immediately this man, Wood, saw the importance and the significance of the inscription. If he could find the Magnesian Gate and the Coressian Gate and follow the roads, they would come to the exact site of the temple. With renewed energy Mr. Wood began to dig. First he found the Magnesian Gate. Then he found the Coressian Gate. He followed the roads and where they met he found the lost Temple of Diana. You see, this man, Caius Vibius Salutarius, was a man of great pomp and pride and vanity. He wanted the largest possible multitude of viewers to see his magnificent gifts to the temple. He directed that they would be taken in on one side of the city, marched through the entire length of the metropolis and out on the other side. Because of the vanity of that man, dead eighteen hundred years, searchers found the site of the temple the last day of the year 1869. There, buried twenty feet beneath the alluvial silt and mud of the Cayster River, on the plain below the hills on which Ephesus was built, they found the pavement and the broken columns of the once proud edifice. The pillars were easily identified by a distinguishing architectural feature. The only temple in the world where the columns were sculptured in heavy relief up to the height of a man's head was the Temple of Diana. The workmen dug them up. They carried them to the British museum, and you may go there today and look upon them. We are now going to visit that temple and the city of Ephesus when Paul was there in 54, 55, 56 and 57 A.D. and when John was there in 69 to 100 A.D.

THE PRE-EMINENCE OF THE CITY OF EPHESUS

Ephesus was one of the truly great cities of the ancient world. It was important commercially. In the three great river basins that pour into the Aegean Sea in Western Asia Minor, the Hermus, the Cayster and the Maeander, the central river basin is the Cayster. At the mouth of Cayster River, inland about three miles from the Aegean Sea, on the slopes of the hill rising out of the valley of the river, was built the great commercial city of Ephesus. The ships came up the river and then, through a man-made canal, to the turning basin and to the docks within the city. There were four great roads that led into Ephesus. One came from the north, from Pergamos and Smyrna down to Ephesus. One came from the northeast, from Sardis and Galatia and Phyrgia and so into Ephesus. One came from the southeast, the great trade route from the Euphrates that went by Colosse and Laodicea and so into Ephesus. The fourth road came from the south, from the great Maeander Valley and Miletus and so into Ephesus. In the eighteenth chapter of the book of the Revelation is enumerated a long list of articles that were traded and sold in the marketplace of that ancient world. Had you gone through the shops at Ephesus, you would have seen all of those variegated wares brought from the ends of the earth and the continents of the world. The commercial city of Ephesus was most impressive.

Ephesus was a tremendously important political center. It was a free city; that is, the Romans had given it the right of self-government, and it never suffered the indignity of having compulsorily quartered upon it Roman troops (such as in Jerusalem). It was what the Romans called an "assize city"; that is, the district courts were there. The governor sat there and tried the cases that were brought from all over the province of Asia.

Once a year the great Artemesian games were held in Ephesus. They rivaled the Olympic games in Hellas in their glory, in their grandeur and in their worldwide interest. In the Greek language the month of May was named for their world-famous Greek goddess. The Greek name for May is *Artemesion* and it was dedicated to Artemis. Throughout the month of May, these Artemesian games were held. They were spectacular beyond description. One could see in Ephesus the pageantry and the brilliance and the glory of the entire Graeco-Roman world. There were athletic contests. There was glorious drama in the theater where the great Greek plays, tragedies and comedies, were presented. There were solemn sacrifices; there were great parades; there was everything that human mind and genius could present in colorful pageantry. When Paul said, in the sixteenth chapter of the first Corinthian letter, the eighth verse: "But I will tarry at Ephesus until Pentecost," that is, until after the month of May, the reason for his choice was obvious. There poured into Ephesus for the Artemesian games the pilgrims of the entire ancient Mediterranean world. It afforded an excellent opportunity for missionary work. One is reminded that when the great World's Fair was held in Chicago, Dwight L. Moody conducted revival meetings in every part of the city, and many people went to Chicago to the World's Fair just to attend the revivals of Dwight L. Moody. Thus it was with the apostle Paul. The entire month of May was given to the world-famous Artemesian games in Ephesus, and it was a fine opportunity for Paul to preach the Gospel to the whole civilized world. As you know, he was not able to remain because of the riot, but his purpose was obvious and good.

The Splendor of the Temple of Diana

Above all, though, Ephesus was a religious city. It was the center of the worship of the most sacred goddess in the civilized, ancient, Graeco-Roman world. The incomparably beautiful temple would have made it so were there no other valid reason. Let us take the trip to the city.

Had we been going to the Artemesian games and had we come by ship, we would have sailed in from the Mediterranean Sea into the Cayster River, through the canal and up to the turning-basin and the docks at the edge of the city. As we came up, we would have seen the city of Ephesus on the hills rising to the right. Then to the left, about a mile from the edge of the city, on the plain of the Cayster, we would have looked upon the most breath-taking architectural spectacle the world has ever seen. Rising out of the plain, in brilliant colors and hues of gold and red and scarlet and blue, before our very eyes, would be the pile of glittering Parian marble, the seventh wonder of the world, the ancient Temple of Diana. It was four hundred and twenty-five feet long. (An average city block is three hundred feet.) It was two hundred and twenty-five feet wide. The columns stood sixty feet in height. There were one hundred thirty of those columns, in rows of twos, all the way around the magnificent edifice. Each one of the columns was the gift of a king, and thirty-seven were embellished with gold and jewels and intricate carving. No house of worship in the world possessed such ornate columns as this Temple of Diana in Ephesus. As we entered the temple, so impressive, so glorious, so glittering white, so embellished with colors of red and gold and scarlet and blue, before us in the center we would have seen one of the most beautiful and impressive altars in the earth. It was carved by the great Greek sculptor, Praxitiles. Beyond that beautiful altar hung a rich and gorgeous drapery-veil made of velvet. Beyond that was the shrine of the goddess herself. Beyond that was an inner shrine where all of the sacred and valuable things of the nation were kept.

The temple was first a museum. Through the passing of the centuries, the rich and great of the world bestowed gifts upon the goddess. Many treasures of art from throughout the Graeco-Roman world were brought and displayed in that glorious temple. For example, the famous picture by Apelles of Alexander the Great holding a thunderbolt in his hand belonged to the temple at Ephesus.

It was also an asylum. If any man committed a crime, anywhere, if he could reach the sanctuary of the Temple of Diana, he was free from arrest and prosecution and prison. When he reached the precincts of the temple, he was beyond the law. The boundaries of the temple were changed and enlarged through the years to take care of this increasing population. Mithradates set them at a bow-shot. That was two hundred yards all the way around. Mark Anthony extended them to include a part of the city. Augustus Caesar made the boundary one-quarter of a mile and built a wall all the way around the temple. Incidentally, the most notorious collection of criminals in the ancient world could be found in the Temple of Diana. Naturally, it drew to itself murderers and thieves and villains from all over the world. If they could get to the temple, they were free and unmolested.

It was also the greatest bank in the world. Is it not unusual that in the same place where the biggest criminals were harbored, the greatest and safest bank in the world was built? It was true of Ephesus. Beyond the inner shrine of the goddess there was another shrine, and in that sacred and holy place kings and merchants made their deposits of valuables and precious stones and money and gold and silver. A temple was rarely violated and this temple was the safest in the world. It became the bank of all the eastern Mediterranean.

The temple was also a great business. Pilgrims poured into Ephesus and into the Temple of Diana by the uncounted thousands. There the temple-keepers sold little gods. The buyers took the little gods, fastened them on their chariots, placed them in their houses, hung them up on the walls and carried them around their necks and on their arms and their ankles. There was nothing in the world to protect one from the perils of a journey like a little shrine from Ephesus. There was nothing in the world to keep one healthy and well like hanging a little shrine around one's neck. There was nothing like going to Ephesus itself and letting the priests bless the idol in order that it might be a wonder-working charm. For example, in the Olympian games, there was a wrestler who was invincible. No one could throw him. The people discovered that he was wearing around his ankle a little Ephesian charm he got from the temple at Ephesus, blessed by the priest there. When they made him take it off, he was weak, they said, just like any other man.

It is evident that when the Roman Church took over the idolatrous worship of the Roman Empire, it took over the whole practice. Instead of an idol being an Ephesian goddess, it was named Saint So-and-So. Instead of its being blessed by the priest of a pagan god or goddess, it was blessed by a priest of the most high Jesus. Instead of being a little picture of a pagan goddess, or a little shrine image of pagan deity, the church said it was a little shrine and a little image of Saint So-and-So or of a Virgin So-and-So. The whole idolatrous arrangement — holy days, pilgrimages, temples, with the craftsmen selling images and people wearing medallions around their necks, hanging them on the walls, putting them in their vehicles — was taken over from the pagan Roman world by the Roman Church.

The practice is sheer, unadulterated superstition. That is what it was then. That is what it is now. It is no different in any century. Just because one calls a little goddess not Diana or Artemis, but Saint So-and-So, does not make any difference. Such idol-worship came out of the darkness of the superstition of man. God said, in His second commandment written by His own finger on tables of stone, "Thou shalt not make unto thee any graven image." One will never find images in true Judaism. Never! One will never find them in the great monotheism of the Moslem, Islamic, Mohammed religion. The only place where idolatry can be found outside of heathenism is in the Catholic church. But it is grossly pagan. The Roman Emperor married together the Christian church and the pagan, idolatrous religion practiced in the temples in Olympus, on the Acropolis in Athens, in the Ephesian temple of Diana and around the Mediterranean world.

There had always been a temple at Ephesus. In the dim antiquities the half-mythological Amazons believed that the mother-goddess of the world was born there and that they were her high priestesses. There in Ephesus they built a temple to their goddess. On the inside of that temple was an image that they said had fallen down from heaven. No one knew from where it came. That was the world-famous temple image of the goddess Diana. In the eleventh century B.C., Androclus came down (he was the son of an Athenian king) with his Ionian Greeks and conquered the city. Thereafter, the story of Ephesus is mostly a conflict between Graeco-Hellenistic customs and ancient Asiatic customs. In

356 B.C., the night that Alexander the Great was born, a man named Herostratus sought to make a name for himself, if only by a monstrous crime, by setting fire to the temple and burning it to the ground. It was then that the cities of Asia and the kings of the world rebuilt it into the temple that Paul saw, which was one of the seven wonders of the world.

The image inside the temple was an altogether different thing from the Greek Artemis, the swift, beautiful and graceful virgin sister of Apollo. The image was a gruesome thing, a far cry from the graceful Diana. Yet the Greeks named it Artemis. The reason it was called Artemis is this: When the Ionian Greeks came, they found the people devoted to that image. Because the Amazons, the war-like Amazons, loved the hunter's chase, they gave to that image the Greek name of Artemis. But that is the only thing the two goddesses had in common, namely, love of hunting. The goddess in Ephesus was actually the goddess of fecundity, of fertility, of life, of sex, of reproduction. She was a gruesome, dark thing, like some ogre out of the past of man. From her waist up she was covered with rows of breasts. From her waist down she looked like a mummy with all kinds of strange symbols that had been lost in meaning to the memory of man.

The worship of the Ephesian Diana was beyond anything that can be translated or described. She had scores of eunuchs, thousands of priestesses and temple prostitutes along with unnumbered heralds and singers and dancers and flute players and singers to lead in her homage. The worship was a kind of hysteria when the people, with shouts and music, worked themselves up into frenzies of shameless sexual mutilation. One of the most famous citizens of Ephesus was the gifted Greek philosopher, Heraclitus. He was known as the weeping philosopher who never smiled. That philosopher wrote a letter. This is the summary of it. He said that the darkness of the approach to the altar of the temple was the darkness of vileness. He said that the morals of the temple were worse than the morals of animals, for even the promiscuous dogs do not mutilate each other. He said that the inhabitants of Ephesus were fit only to be drowned, and that the reason why he could never laugh or smile was because he lived amid such terrible uncleanness. When we become discouraged and think it is difficult to live in this modern world and be a Christian, remember that some of the greatest victories of grace that were ever won were won in the city of Ephesus. There were Christians there also.

THE DECAY OF EPHESUS

Our Lord said to Ephesus, "Except thou repent, I will remove thy lampstand." In 252 A.D., the Goths destroyed the temple along with the entire city. It never recovered its glory. The great ruins of the temple were used as a quarry for the beautification of Constantinople, used by the Turkish conquerors for all of their palaces and used by the medieval Italians as a source of beautiful Parian marble. The Cayster River had an estuary, beautiful and fair, and a lagoon, blue and impressive. Centuries of floods have silted it up, and it is now filled with wiry grass and reeds, and the malarial mosquitoes it breeds have driven man out from the face of the earth around Ephesus.

The great stadium, the huge amphitheater carved in that oval of rock, is but ruins. Remember the reference Paul makes to it in I Corinthians 4:9? He says: "For I think that God hath set forth us the apostles last, as it were appointed to death: for we are made a spectacle unto the world, and to angels, and to men." Paul had seen in that very amphitheater, that very stadium, the spectacle of men fighting with beasts, for he said, "If after the manner of men I have fought with beasts at Ephesus." The spectacle he saw was this: after the day's pageantry and drama and racing and athletic contests were over, the last thing on every day's program was the marching into the amphitheater, into the great stadium, of the prisoners who were going to be consigned to death by the fangs of the wild, starved beasts. These prisoners were marched into the arena, the iron gates were opened, and the hungry, starved lions, wolves, dogs, tigers and other wild beasts were turned loose upon them. This bloody spectacle was always last. It was the diabolical kill that ended the day. The people wildly cheered as the fangs and claws of the beasts tore apart those helpless men and women down there on the sands of the stadium. That is what Paul means when he says, "God hath set forth us the apostles last, as it were appointed to death: for we are made a spectacle unto the world, and to angels, and to men." The stadium where these terrible atrocities were held was cursed of God and is now in ruins.

The great temple is now a stagnant pond. After the workmen excavated the place, it filled up with water. It is covered over with a green scum, breeding malarial-bearing mosquitoes. If a passerby comes, the frogs raise a din of croaking. In their croaking one can hear the refrain, "Great is Diana! Great is Diana! Great is Diana of the Ephesians!" Two thousand years from now do you suppose that some archeologist, interested in English history, will be searching among the marshes around Ludgate Hill on the banks of the Thames, trying to find a relic from Saint Paul's cathedral? Or do you think some student of American history, having heard of Texas, and having read somewhere about the city of Dallas, will probe among the mounds, two thousand years from now, to see if he can find something that depicted the size and the glory of the great city of Dallas? For remember, when Paul looked upon that temple and when John wrote this letter to Ephesus, it seemed to them that that glorious temple was invincible and permanent and impregnable. No man who lived at that time ever dreamed the day would come that the temple would be a stagnant, scum-covered, frog-croaking, malarial-mosquito-producing pond.

The glory passeth by. "Turn, repent, or else I will come unto thee quickly and remove thy lampstand from its place." Remember this, in the day and the hour in which we live, the imponderables of life and death, whether our nation exists or not, do not lie in how many atomic bombs we have or how many Polaris submarines we have launched, but they lie in the elective purposes of God. "Turn, turn, lest I come unto thee quickly and remove thy lampstand out of its place." Our destiny lies in the hand of God.

Chapter 7

The Message to Ephesus

Unto the angel of the church of Ephesus write; These things saith he that holdeth the seven stars in his right hand, who walketh in the midst of the seven golden candlesticks; I know thy works, and thy labor, and thy patience, and how thou canst not bear them which are evil: and thou hast tried them which say they are apostles, and are not, and hast found them liars: And hast borne, and hast patience, and for my name's sake hast labored, and hast not fainted. Nevertheless I have somewhat against thee, because thou hast left thy first love. Remember therefore from whence thou art fallen, and repent, and do the first works; or else I will come unto thee quickly, and will remove thy candlestick out of his place, except thou repent. But this thou hast, that thou hatest the deeds of the Nicolaitans, which I also hate. He that hath an ear, let him hear what the Spirit saith unto the churches; To him that overcometh will I give to eat of the tree of life, which is in the midst of the paradise of God. — Revelation 2:1-7

This sermon is an exposition of the letter that the Lord writes to the church at Ephesus. The content of that letter may be easily divided into three main and separate parts.

First, there is a word of congratulation, of commendation. Second, there is a word of complaint, of condemnation. Third, there is a word of counsel, of warning. This is the reading of the letter in Revelation 2, the first seven verses: "Unto the angel of the church of Ephesus write; These things saith he that holdeth the seven stars in his right hand, who walketh in the midst of the seven golden lampstands; [now the word of commendation] I know thy works, and thy labour, and thy patience, and how thou canst not bear them which are evil: and thou hast tried them which say they are apostles, and are not, and has found them liars: And hast borne, and hast patience, for my name's sake hast laboured, and hast not fainted. [Then, His word of complaint] Nevertheless I have somewhat against thee, because thou hast left thy first love. [Then, His word of warning] Remember therefore from whence thou art fallen, and repent, and do the first works; or else I will come unto thee quickly, and will remove thy candlestick out of his place, except thou repent. But this thou hast, that thou hatest the deeds of the Nicolaitanes, which I also hate. He that hath an ear, let him hear what the Spirit saith unto the churches; To him that overcometh will I give to eat of the tree of life, which is in the midst of the paradise of God." We shall follow those three main sections of this letter of our Lord to the church at Ephesus.

CHRIST'S WORDS OF COMMENDATION

His word of commendation comprises seven things. First, "I know thy works." It was, therefore, an active and energetic church. They were in business for the Lord. They were working at it. I do not suppose in that day they had district associations to which, as we do, annually the churches sent letters, summations of the work for the year. But if they did have any such thing as that, the letter from the church at Ephesus would have been encouraging and inspiring, indeed. They would have listed their attendance in all organizations. They would have summed up the number of baptisms and new members. They would have summed up their gifts to missions, to the cooperative program and to the local church budget. After they had added these all up, the whole would have summed up a magnificent letter that Ephesus would have mailed or sent by messenger to the annual district association. They had, indeed, a fine work going in the church at Ephesus.

Often a church letter will read just the opposite. I heard of a church that sent in their annual letter, filling in the blanks like this: new members — none; baptisms — none; gifts to missions — none. Then the clerk wrote at the bottom: "Brethren, pray for us that we may be faithful unto the end." Every once in a while I come across a minister or a Christian leader who says that he does not believe in statistics, he does not believe in reports, he does not believe in summations and he does not believe in figures and in numbers. "For," he says, "these do not reflect the true work of the Holy Spirit." Whenever I hear a man talk like that, I think of what Spurgeon said: "Brethren who say those things are brethren whose report humiliates them." They don't have anything to report. They have not baptized anyone, they have received few, if any, new members. They have not given anything to the Lord and they do a poor work. Therefore, they say, "We believe in culture and in the development of our own. We believe in taking care of these we already have instead of going out and winning others to the Lord." But, did you know the mightiest oaks grow in the greatest forests, and the tallest trees are to be found thick together in a vast panorama of foliated green? I stood one time and looked at the tallest tree in the world. It was surrounded by trees that seemed to me just about as tall, crowded together in a vast redwood forest in northern California. It is thus in a church. Good works beget more good works. Soul winning begets more soul winners. "I know thy works." Ephesus was an energetic church.

A second thing. The Lord commends them for ". . . thy labour. . . ." Now the difference between *ergon*, translated "work," and *kopos*, translated "labour," is this: *Kopos* (labour) has in it the ideal of toil, of working at a cost. The task was not something incidental to them. As David said: "Neither will I offer burnt offerings unto the Lord my God of that which doth cost me nothing" (II Samuel 24:24). They not only worked for God, but they worked for God at a price, at a cost. They toiled at it. They labored at it. It took something out of them.

A lifetime of the labor of some of us would not exhaust a butterfly. Today some church members are very happy to ride on the gospel wagon and take the chief seats, the box seats up high. But they do not get out and push. They do not get down and pull. Many love to eat of the clusters of the vineyard, but how few of us love to toil in its cultivation. Once in a while I hear someone in our church say to me: "Do you know, the activities in this church are too many. You have too much going on. It takes too much of our time." The conclusion is that we should limit our activities in order that our people may be more holy and pious and may be more given to God; that we should cut the choir program in two, cut our educational program in two, cut our recreational program in two, cut our ministry in two, in order that our people may be more pious and given to God. O yes? I know exactly what would happen. Our members would look at the TV programs twice as much. They would be parked out on the roadside twice as much. They would be everywhere else twice as much.

Do not ever get the idea that when we cease going to church we are going to do more for God in the world. Just the opposite is true. The only way to get people out of the world is to get them into a vigorous program in the church. If we do not do so, they will be in the world altogether. Some of our churches on Sunday nights are closing down, locking the doors and turning out the lights in order for the family to be home worshiping God. I know where they are likely to be: looking at television or going to the theater or to the picture show or picnicking or otherwise entertaining one another. There is no such thing as bringing people closer to God by closing down churches. But the people in Ephesus were staying with the faith. "Thy toil and thy labour." They were pouring their lives and their souls and their hearts into it. They meant business for God.

A Splendid Example for Us

The third thing our Lord commends them for is *hupomone* (thy patience). That does not mean passively bearing anything. It means triumphant fortitude. No matter how the Ephesian Christians were beaten down, discouraged or persecuted, they did not quit. They stayed with the work.

In preparing this message I read of an evangelist who told a most interesting story. He loved to hunt. He bought two new bird dogs, setters. He put them in his backyard.

One morning there came down the alley a mean, vicious-looking bulldog. He meant business. The evangelist said his first impulse was to take his setters and put them in the basement so that they might not tear up that bulldog. But, he said, he had a second thought. He would just let that bulldog learn a lesson he would never forget. The bulldog jumped over the fence into the backyard, and those two bird dogs and that bulldog went around and around and around. When the bulldog had enough, he ran away. All the rest of that day he spent licking his sores. The evangelist said he thought that was the end of it. There would be no more bulldog around the yard. But, he said, the next day at the same hour and at the same time, over the fence jumped that bulldog and the fight started again. Those two bird dogs beat the stuffing out of him and chewed him up and after a while, when the bulldog had enough, he went back home with more sores and more scars and he spent that day licking his wounds. The evangelist said, "I thought that would be a sure lesson to that bulldog." But on the third morning, at the same time, down the alley came that bulldog. He jumped over the fence and they had it again. The same thing happened. Those two bird dogs chewed him up. After the bulldog had all he could take, he jumped back over the fence and went back home to lick his wounds. Then the evangelist said, "I had to leave for a revival meeting. I was gone several weeks. When I came back, I asked my wife about that bulldog." She said, "Husband, I don't know what in the world. I want you to know that at the same time every morning that bulldog came back and he had it out with those two setters; and I want you to know that the time has come when those two setters, just looking at that bulldog, start whining and running into the basement. The bulldog jumps over the fence and just walks around, the master of every place he puts his foot on." That reminds me of a poem:

> No one is beaten 'til he quits,
> No one is through 'til he stops,
> No matter how hard failure hits,

No matter how often he drops,
A fellow is not down 'til he lies
In the dust and refuses to rise.

Fate may bang him around
And batter him 'til he is sore,
But it is never said that he's down
While he bobs up serenely for more,
A fellow is not dead 'til he dies,
Nor done 'til he no longer tries.

You cannot beat someone who just persists. That is what
Jesus said He liked about this church at Ephesus: *hupomone*
— staying with it despite persecution and discouragement.
Chewed up, beaten down, cast out, they endured everything. But they remained steadfast, serving God.

Now look at this fourth thing our Lord says: "And how
thou canst not bear them which are evil." They noticed,
they were cognizant of, they were sensitive to, the presence
of evil. Did you know it is possible to get so accustomed
to evil that you hardly notice it? When I was in Oklahoma
the state was "dry." One of the great and blessed things
about prohibition is this: the advertising of liquor is taken
away. You do not see it in neon signs and on billboards. It
is not advertised. When you buy it, you have to buy it from
underneath a counter and in the back alley and from a bootlegger. You cannot do it openly and respectably and legally.
When I came to Dallas, the thing I noticed about Dallas
was the liquor stores. On every prominent corner, there
were neon signs and the lights blinking and all kinds of
that poisonous stuff being sold to the people. When I came
to the First Baptist Church in Dallas, the thing I especially
noticed about the church was the liquor store within thirty
feet of the St. Paul entrance where all of our children come
in. I was very sensitive to that years ago. To my amazement,
I have almost become so accustomed to that store with
that sign that I do not notice it any more. All evil is like
that, even as Alexander Pope said,

Vice is a monster of such frightful mien,
As to be hated needs but to be seen.
But seen too often, familiar with her face,
We first endure, then pity, then embrace.

The fifth thing for which He commends them refers to the fact that Ephesus was an orthodox church. They had a holy decision about them. They tried the big ones as well as the little ones. There were those that came by and said, "We are apostles of Jesus Christ," and they tried them and found them liars and could not bear them. Did you know that just about the contrary is true in our modern theological world? The more rank a heretic you are and the more you challenge every doctrine of the faith, the more you will be received as a great liberal, as a man of scholarship and advanced thought. That is as true of my own denomination as it is of any other. Let someone deny every doctrine of the Bible and be a heretic of the reddest hue, and the so-called scholars will love him, follow after him, sit at his feet and listen to him. That is not what the church at Ephesus did. When a man showed that he was a doubter and a heretic who denied the faith, they could not stand him. They called him a liar. They never had him appear before the church or the congregation or any of their schools. They tried them which said they were apostles and emissaries of God and found them to be liars.

Then the sixth thing He commends them for: "and hast borne." You notice the things that they cannot bear? They cannot bear evil men and they cannot bear false doctrine and doubts. But they can bear toil and sacrifice and persecution and self-negation.

Then the seventh: "and hast patience, and for my name's sake hast laboured, and hast not fainted." There they are, staying with it, at a cost, and not fainting. Many people say: "I'm going to quit; they don't appreciate me. I'm tired; I've been doing this all the years of my life and I've done my part." They quit running the heavenly race and start walking. Then, soon, they stop altogether. Diligence is turned to indolence and they faint. All of us ought to be like a piece of iron on the gospel anvil. If the Lord wants to beat us into a plowshare, and plunge us into the earth to break fallow ground, that is fine. Or, if the Lord wants to beat us into a spear-point, that we might challenge the enemies

of God, that is fine. The heart of a real Christian is just this,
that he is willing in God's hands to be God's servant as God
shall choose. And he does not faint.

THE COMPLAINT OF OUR LORD

Those are the seven things for which our Lord commends
the church. What a wonderful church! But He has a complaint. What an astonishing thing, that He would find
anything wrong with that church. It was the assignment
of the High Priest to go into the Holy Place and there to
trim and light and care for the seven golden lampstands. In
the glorious picture of our Lord here in the Revelation, He
is dressed in His regal and priestly robes, and He is walking
in the midst of these seven golden lampstands. As He walks
among His lampstands, He pours in sacred oil, He takes out
impurities, He trims the wick and He makes the light to
shine. He walks among His churches with eyes as a flame
of fire, with penetration and with accuracy. He sees everything among His people. Our eyes are covered with the
smoke of the world and we cannot see very well. But our
Lord sees perfectly and penetratingly. But how could the
Lord find anything the matter with a church like this apparently faultless church at Ephesus? Its order and its decorum
and its work are matchless. Every fine thing the Lord could
say about that church He did say. Surely, surely there is not
anything that God could say about this church that would
be condemnatory.

This is one of the best churches in all the world. Yet, the
keen, clear, penetrating eye of our Lord in looking at the
church at Ephesus found the fatal fault. "Nevertheless I have
[that word *somewhat* in the King James Version is in italics,
meaning that it is not in the Greek] . . . Nevertheless I have
against thee, namely this, thou hast left thy first love."
The old, abounding joy and the overflowing gladness and
the old enthusiasm is altered. It is beginning to wane. Their
service is becoming mechanical. Their devotion is becoming
routine. They do not have that old flame and the old fire
and the unction from above. They are getting faultily fault-

less, icily regular, and splendidly null. They do not like enthusiam, they have no place for emotion and they have become cold and regular, without moving devotion and spirit and love. To my amazement, I find that practically all churches like it that way. Emotion is discounted, and enthusiasm represents intellectual weakness. They like it icy and dead and dull and routine, with no great enthusiasm, no great, abounding, overflowing gladness. They are pleased with the mechanical, the routine, the ritualistic and the cold in all of church life. "We like it that way."

I was preaching in an evangelistic conference in a great state on the eastern seaboard. There was a doctor in a certain denomination other than ours who happened to attend. He went to his denomination and said, "I want you to get that preacher from Dallas, Texas, and I want you to call a convocation of our churches and let us have an evangelistic conference and let him preach to us." Because he was a man of great influence and wealth and fame, the dignitaries of his denomination felt that they had to do as he asked. So they called a convocation of all of their pastors and people and sent for me to preach to them. They were very careful to see that I was followed by a man who stood up and negated everything that I had said. It came out just as I thought it would. They did not like anything I had to say, and least of all did they like the way I said it. They like their religion cold. They like it without enthusiasm. They like it icy. They like it faultlessly faultless.

I copied this from A. J. Gordon. Discussing the spiritually destitute of the churches in Boston, Dr. Gordon said: "Ecclesiastical corpses lie all about us. The caskets in which they repose are lined with satin and are decorated with solid silver handles and abundant flowers. Like the other caskets, they are just large enough for their occupants with no room for converts. These churches have died of respectability and have been embalmed in self-complacency. If, by the grace of God, this church is alive [referring to his Clarendon Street Baptist Church], be warned to our opportunity or the feet of them that buried thy sisters will be at the door to carry thee out."

The enemy of a church is formalism. We do it "just so." The Holy Spirit of God has no opportunity to say anything, no opportunity to do anything, no opportunity to work. If a man really expressed his love for God and were enthusiastic about it, he would be told: "Now listen, you get out; you do not belong here with us." Devotion, enthusiasm, all-out-for-God-at-any-cost-and-at-any-price were gone from Ephesus. "I have this against thee, that thou hast left thy first love."

OUR LORD'S WORDS OF COUNSEL

Then the Lord speaks words of counsel: "Remember, therefore, from whence thou art fallen, and repent, and do the first works." Look at that. "Remember . . . and repent, and do . . ." He says they are fallen, because they do not have a deep devotion and love and commitment in their hearts to Him any longer. O God, come, come, and trim our lamps! Come, Lord, among our people and with eyes of fire probe us and look at us. So much of our labor is mechanical. We have lost the joy and the drive and the enthusiasm and the gladness of it. We do our service because the time has come to do it, because we feel it a matter of duty. O God, give us an abounding soul and an overflowing love. Often our heart is in the world. We used to love sermons, prayer meetings, the reading of the Word of God, the services of the Lord. But now our interest is some other place, and we seek to build up a jaded appetite by strange novelties out there in the world. We are not content with just the things of God. O Lord, come and probe our hearts.

Lord, could it be, could it be that we have ceased loving Thee? "Nevertheless I" — more precious to the Lord Jesus than the constellations in the heavens are the churches He bought with His own blood. Christ loved the church and gave Himself for it. He died for His people. The church was born in like manner as Eve was taken out of the side of Adam. The church was born out of the side, in the blood and tears and sacrifice of Jesus. He loves His church. "I have this against thee, you do not love Me any more, you have left your first love. Remember therefore from whence thou art fallen." The lamp does not burn apart from personal love to Jesus; and when love dies, the light goes out.

Uselessness invites disaster. If one of the church light bulbs ceases to shine, the custodian has it thrown away. "I will remove thy lampstand . . . except thou repent . . . for you do not love the Lord any more." Remember the words of Paul, "Though I speak with the tongues of men and of angels, and have not love, I am becoming as sounding brass, or a clanging cymbal. And though I have the gift of prophecy, and understand all mysteries, and all knowledge; and though I have all faith, so that I could remove mountains, and have not love, I am nothing. And though I bestow all my goods [and put it in the collection plate], and though I give my body to be burned, and have not love, it profiteth me nothing . . . And now abideth faith, hope, love, these three; but the greatest of these is love." "Thou hast left thy first love." The foundation for all of our singing and teaching and preaching; for all of our laboring and ministry ought to be a great, deep-seated love for Jesus. "I love the Lord," ought to be the refrain and the reverberation and echo of every one of God's true children. When we love Him, we have no cause to worry about all the rest. It will fall into place. But when we do not love the Lord, and have ceased to adore Him in our hearts, then everything else will finally come to dust and to ashes. "From whence thou are fallen . . . thou hast left thy first love — remember, and turn and come back." Lord, we are on the way, coming back to Thee.

Chapter 8

The Martyr City of Smyrna

And unto the angel of the church in Smyrna write; These things saith the first and the last, which was dead, and is alive; I know thy works, and tribulation and poverty, (but thou art rich) and I know the blasphemy of them which say they are Jews, and are not, but are the synagogue of Satan. Fear none of those things which thou shalt suffer: behold, the devil shall cast some of you into prison, that ye may be tried; and ye shall have tribulation ten days: be thou faithful unto death, and I will give thee a crown of life. He that hath an ear, let him hear what the Spirit saith unto the churches; He that overcometh shall not be hurt of the second death. — Revelation 2:8-11

Coming to this second letter and to this second church, we are introduced to one of the most significantly meaningful messages in all of the Word of God. "And unto the angel of the church in Smyrna write . . . ." Three times that word "smyrna" is used heretofore in the New Testament. In the second chapter of the Gospel of Matthew the evangelist tells us that the Wise Men coming from the east opened their treasures and presented before the young king gold and frankincense and *smyrna*. In the fifteenth chapter of the book of Mark, when the evangelist describes the crucifixion of our Lord, he says that some of them who stood by offered to the suffering Lord wine mixed with *smyrna* in order to help alleviate, in the anesthetic, the sufferings Jesus was bearing. The third place it is used in the New Testament is in the nineteenth chapter of the book of John. There the evangelist says that when Jesus died, Nicodemus came with Joseph of Arimathaea, and the two men, after carefully taking down the body of our Lord from the cross, wrapped it in a long, linen cloth in the folds of which they placed an hundred pound weight of aloes and *smyrna*. In each of these instances, the word is translated in the King James Version of the Bible, "myrrh."

It is said that the great port city of Smyrna received its name from the traffic in that balsam herb for which it was world-famous. It was the port of the fragrance and perfume of Myrrh. In the providence of God, the name came to symbolize that era in the story of the Christian church when it entered severe and terrible persecution. Myrrh, *smyrna*, is a type of suffering. It was used in the embalming of the dead. "And they brought unto Him gifts, gold and frankincense and *smyrna*." The gold is a picture of the deity of our Lord. The frankincense is a picture of His great mediatorial office, interceding for us in heaven. Myrrh, *smyrna*, typifies the suffering of our Lord for our sins. Thus the very name of this city and the church in it brings to our minds the figure and the type of tribulation and persecution. This is the church, therefore, of great trial and tribulation. It is the only church to which the Lord has none other word but commendation and encouragement. He finds no complaint. He voices no criticism. Every sentence that He speaks of Smyrna is one of appreciation and encouragement. "... be thou faithful unto death [for you will be cast into prison and you will have hard trial ten fierce days, the number of days in itself a figure of the fierceness and intensity of the persecution] be thou faithful unto death, and I will give thee a crown [the reward] of life."

THE BEAUTIFUL CITY OF SMYRNA

This city of Smyrna is one of the truly great ancient cities of the world. As far back as history goes there was a city located at Smyrna. Today it is by far the largest metropolis in Asia Minor. It has at present a population of about two hundred and seventy or seventy-five thousand people. The name of it is *Izmir*, the Turkish corruption for Smyrna. It has had a continuous history from the earliest dawn of human story, and its name has been the same through all of the centuries and through all of the milleniums. The harbor at Miletus has silted up and disappeared. The harbor at Ephesus has silted up and disappeared. The great, maritime cities that were contemporary with Smyrna — Miletus and Ephesus — have ceased to exist, but Smyrna has lived through the centuries and is one of the teeming cities of the world today. It was in Roman times a great city. The harbor is one of the finest in all of the world. The gulf of Smyrna reaches back into the inland of Asia Minor for about thirty-five miles. It is beautiful and spacious. It had an added attraction in that the inner harbor could be entirely closed off in times of war. The fleets of the world could enter the gulf of Smyrna and find space to dock and discharge passengers and exchange cargo. The city stood at the end of the great road that poured down from the interior, through the Hermus Valley. Consequently, the market wares, the market-place and the traffic at Smyrna, between the sea and the interior, made for the building of a flourishing metropolis.

Smyrna was a great political center. It had the unusual fortune, in the civil wars of the Roman Empire, of always being on the side of the winner. The city never lost a cause; it was always right. Whether the war was between Brutus and Cassius on one side and Anthony and Octavius on the other side, or between Octavius (Augustus) Caesar and Mark Anthony, Smyrna was always on the right side. The triumphant, conquering Romans were not forgetful. They made Smyrna a free city. That is, it had its own government and was not under tribute and tax to the Roman Empire. They made it an assize town; that is, a town where the Roman courts were built and where the Roman judges sat in justice.

It was the proudest of all of the cities of Asia. It vaunted itself as being the first city of Asia, as being the glory of Asia, as being the most beautiful city of Asia, as being the center of Caesar-worship in the eastern part of the Roman Empire, and as being the birthplace of the great incomparable Greek poet, Homer. Mommsen, the famous historian, says that Smyrna was a municipality of pride and vanity. To Smyrna, worldly things were "the first and the last"; God was not supreme. When the Lord Jesus introduced Himself

here as being the first and the last, to Smyrna the first and
the last were the glories of Greek culture and the magnificence of their incomparably beautiful city.

Not only was Smyrna a great trade town and a great
political center, but it was also one of the most beautiful
cities in the ancient world and one of the most beautiful
Greek cities ever erected. It was built at the head of the
gulf of Smyrna, where the hills of Asia Minor run down to
the blue waters of the Aegean Sea. The city was built from
the low lands of the dock area up the rising slopes of the
hillsides. When one came in from the sea, he saw that glis-
tening and beautiful city, tier upon tier upon tier, one of the
most magnificent sights in all of the world. At the dawn of
history there was a city of Smyrna. About 1000 B.C., the Ionian
Greeks conquered it, and for the centuries thereafter it was
a member of the Green Ionian league. About 650 B.C., it was
reconquered by what the Greeks call "the barbarians." For
over 300 years it lost its place in the list of the Greek cities
of Ionia. But when Alexander the Great conquered the
world, he conceived the idea of rebuilding Smyrna and of
making it a model Greek city in beauty and in layout. The
idea of Alexander the Great was continued and furthered
by Antigonus and by Lysimachus, generals of Alexander
who followed him in military authority. They made Smyrna
the model Greek city of all time. They did the same thing
at Smyrna that the Mormons have done in building Salt
Lake City. They made it a model town.

The streets of Smyrna were wide and spacious and well-
paved and ran at right angles to each other from one end
of the city to the other. The most famous of all of its beautiful streets was called the Golden Street. It began at the
seaside, at the harbor, and ran the entire length of the city
up to the Acropolis on Mount Pagos. That street was one of
the most impressive of all of the streets that have ever been
built in human history. At the beginning of it, on the sea
side, was the beautiful Greek temple to the goddess Cybele.
Then, farther up, there was the gorgeous temple to Apollo.
Still farther, there was the incomparable temple to Aescu-

lapius, the god of healing, beyond which stood the beautiful
temple to the goddess, Aphrodite. Following that street,
one would pass by the glorious monument to Homer, whose
birthplace Smyrna claimed to be. The Golden Street led to
the Acropolis on Mount Pagos, where stood the imposing
temple to Zeus (Latin, *Jupiter*).

No city in the east had the impression, the glory, the
magnificence of the city of Smyrna. It claimed to be, and
rightfully so, the most beautiful Greek city in the world.
One entering the city could not but be impressed by the
intensity of Greek culture and life teeming everywhere.
Between a hill on the northeast side of the city and Mount
Pagos on the southeast side of the city, ran the road from
Ephesus, through the Ephesian Gate. Close by the Ephesian
Gate was the gymnasium. Then southward, toward Mount
Pagos, was located the great stadium. On the slopes of
Mount Pagos, on the northern side, was the theater, seating
more than twenty thousand spectators, and said to be the
largest Greek theater in the world. The life of the people
was centered around cultural theater-programs and athletic
contests and festival days and worship in the beautiful
temples.

THE SUFFERING CHURCH IN SMYRNA

This church in Smyrna, in its suffering and tribulation,
came to be used of the Lord as the story and prophecy of
that era of the church when it would enter the fiery furnace
and would know the heavy hand of persecution. There are
reasons why this bitter persecution was the daily lot and
life of the poor and humble church in Smyrna. There are
three reasons why in that city the Christians were especially
persecuted and why they lived in continual jeopardy of life.

The first reason was this: the Christian church there
stood in the sight of a continuous and spectacular display
of paganism. How poor and insignificant did that little
church appear as it lived in the midst of those marvelous
Greek temples and those pagan festivals and the colorful
Greek worship honoring the gods and goddesses! The humble places where the Christian church met would not begin

to compare with the glories of those magnificent temples. Now, had those Christian people taken their new cult and their new God, Jesus, and put Him in a Pantheon, the citizens of Smyrna would have been most happy to receive Him. After all, they had gods all up and down this street and that, and gods and their temples on all the hills and on all of the Acropolises. It would have been as nothing to receive just one more god to worship. Had the Christians been willing to take their Saviour and put Him alongside Aesculapius, Apollo, Aphrodite, Jove, Poseidon, Hermes, Mercury, Dionysius, or any other of a thousand pagan deities, He would have been received with all gladness. But that was the one thing the Christian would not do. He would not put Jesus in any Pantheon, nor would he worship the Lord Jesus by the side of any other god or goddess.

Remember, the economic and mercantile and social life of those Greek cities was organized around the cults. Every man that worked belonged to a guild, and every guild had a certain patron god or goddess. The life of the guild and of the merchant-man and of the workman and of the people was organized around goddesses and gods. Days of festivity and of worship were set aside as sacred to the deity. When the Christian stood aloof and refused to share in such things, he was immediately marked off. He stood practically alone. His faith cut him off from the job that he would hold, from the work that he would do and from social life, without which a man can hardly exist. His religion set him apart as being strange, peculiar, queer. It was terribly different to be a Christian.

The second thing that contributed to the terrible trial and persecution of the church at Smyrna was this: Smyrna was the great center of Caesar-worship in all of the eastern part of the Roman Empire. As early as 196 B.C., Smyrna was the first city in all of the Empire to erect a temple to *Dea Roma*, the goddess Rome. In 26 A.D., there were six great cities in Asia Minor that were striving for the honor of building a temple to the reigning emperor, Tiberius. Of those six cities, Smyrna won the privilege. The citizens were

proud of their Caesar-worship, and they made it one of the
distinctive glorifications of their city.

But what was there in Caesar-worship that was so tragic
and that brought such suffering to those early Christians?
The answer is plain when you probe into how the cult of
Emperor-worship arose and how the worship functioned.
Now listen to this, for this is one of the keys to the understanding of the book of the Revelation. The background of
all of the Revelation is against this cult of Emperor-worship.
This is the way it arose. The Roman Empire covered the
then-known civilized world. Inside that Roman Empire was
every kind of a city and language and race and nationality.
It was a veritable polyglot. There had to be some way by
which the Roman government could unify such diverse
elements and fragments. What could be done? There was
no extant religion that could be universalized. But there was
one thing about Rome that could be universalized and that
was the Roman spirit, the thing that made Rome Rome.

THE PROVINCES AND THE ROMAN EMPIRE

We have a wrong impression about the attitude of the
provincials of the conquered nations that made up the
Roman Empire. The reason we have that attitude is because
in our study of the Roman Empire practically all of it
centers around Judea. (Were it not for Christ, were it not
for the apostles, we would have no particular interest in
the Roman Empire any more than in the Assyrian empire
or in the ancient Egyptian dynasties.) From the bitterness
of Judea about the Roman yoke, we get the idea that the
Roman Empire was filled with the spirit of insurrection
and hatred. Nothing could be further from the truth. More
than one king willed his dominion to the Roman government and the possession of the Roman people. For example,
the king of Pergamos willed his empire and his kingdom to
Rome. For, you see, the Roman government was an untold
blessing to the multitudes of the population of the Roman
Empire, to these provinces around the Mediterranean Sea.
For one thing, the Empire enforced the *Pax Romana,* the

Roman peace. Instead of letting their subjects live in jeopardy of life and of incessant wars, Rome did away with war. By their iron hand the Romans made it impossible for tyrants and despots to rise to battle one another. There was a world of peace in the Roman Empire. That made it possible for a man to live and provide for his family and do business all over the civilized world. The Romans, for example, built great roads and they made them free from brigands and thieves and robbers. The Romans cleared the high seas of pirates. A man could do business anywhere in the Empire. He could travel where he pleased, he could go where he wished, and he could make his journey without fear of molestation and robbery and assault and death. The government brought to the provinces marvelous blessings.

Again, the Mediterranean world was made up of many differing nations. Each had its own despot and its own tyrant. The man who lived under that petty government lived under the caprice of whoever happened to be a ruler, a ruler who was accountable to no one. The Roman government brought to the Roman Empire, the civilized world, Roman law. A man no longer lived under the caprice of a tyrant or a local despot. He lived under the impartial justice of the application and rule of the Roman law. In this and in many other ways, the Roman Empire was a blessing to the civilized world. The provincials, for this fact, were not ungrateful and they were not forgetful. The citizens of the Empire were everywhere ready and willing to do worship to the *Dea Roma*, the goddess, the spirit of Rome.

But, as time went on, it was discovered that "the spirit of Rome" was rather vague. It was an intangible thing. So gradually, it was natural that the peoples of the Empire began to concentrate in the person of the Emperor "the spirit of Rome." He became the personalization of what Rome was and what Rome stood for, of the might and strength and power of the Empire. Thus the cult of Emperor-worship, the cult of Caesar-worship, began to grow. The first emperors looked upon it with stark amazement. They deprecated it. The first emperors shrank from it. It was not a thing chosen by the Roman emperors themselves. In the passing of the years, however, it became increasingly acceptable and popular. Finally, the Emperor of the Empire was officially created a god. Then, eventually, the final step was taken. Heretofore, the worship of the Roman Emperor had been voluntary. If any man worshiped the Emperor as a god or called upon him as a deity, he did it of his own free will and choice. But as the centuries passed, in the days of Domitian, in the latter days of the first Christian century, in the days when the Revelation was written, the last step was taken and Emperor-worship, Caesar-worship, became compulsory. A man had to do it in order to show himself a loyal citizen of the Empire. It was demanded by law.

I have in my possession a request on the part of a Roman subject for a certificate to show that he has worshiped at the shrine of the Emperor. I also have a certification that this family received when they worshiped at the shrine of the Emperor. It was by law that every subject of the Empire was forced to take a pinch of incense and burn it in the temple dedicated to the Emperor. He had to confess, in the burning of that little pinch of incense, that Caesar was lord. The worship was in no wise a test of his orthodoxy; it was a test of his political loyalty. For, after he burned that pinch of incense and said that Caesar is lord (*Kaisar kurios*) he could go his way and worship any god and goddess that he pleased. But all this was precisely the one thing that the Christian would not do. He would not take that little pinch of incense and burn it at the shrine of the Emperor. He would not say that Caesar is lord. Because the Christian refused to burn that little pinch of incense and to bow down and acknowledge the lordship of Caesar, the Christian was marked out. He was looked upon as being a traitor to the state; he was looked upon as being disloyal to the government.

In a vast empire like Rome, rulers could not tolerate traitors and they could not have disaffected citizens, who might grow to be storm centers of insurrection and rebellion.

Thus the heavy hand of the state was on the Christian wherever he lived in the Roman Empire. To be a Christian anywhere in the Empire was to take one's life in his own hands. This was especially so in the city of Smyrna, a place that prided itself upon being the center of Caesar-worship in all of Asia and of the east. Rather than bow down and burn a little pinch of incense and rather than say that Caesar is lord, the Christians in Smyrna laid down their lives. "Fear none of those things which thou shalt suffer," said the Lord. "Satan shall cast you into prison, ye shall be tried; and ye shall have tribulation ten days." *Fox's Book of Martyrs* describes ten persecutions of the Roman Empire. "Be thou faithful unto death, and I will give thee a crown of life." Martyrstuff — that is where we came from. These are our Christian forefathers, our Christian forebears, our Christian ancestors. The Lord says to us today the same words of encouragement. Stand up. "Be thou faithful unto death." Be counted. "And I will give thee a crown of life."

Chapter 9

The Martyred Christians of Smyrna

And unto the angel of the church in Smyrna write; These things saith the first and the last, which was dead, and is alive; I know thy works, and tribulation, and poverty, (but thou art rich) and I know the blasphemy of them which say they are Jews, and are not, but are the synagogue of Satan. Fear none of those things which thou shalt suffer: behold, the devil shall cast some of you into prison, that ye may be tried; and ye shall have tribulation ten days: be thou faithful unto death, and I will give thee a crown of life. He that hath an ear, let him hear what the Spirit saith unto the churches: He that overcometh shall not be hurt of the second death. — Revelation 2:8-11

The word *Smyrna* or "myrrh" has to do with embalming, with suffering, with death. So the church in Smyrna is the church of myrrh, the church of tribulation, the church of suffering and martyrdom. This is the only church to which our Lord has no other word but one of commendation. To the other churches of Asia He has a pointed sentence or paragraph of criticism; but not against Smyrna. Every word that He says to this congregation is one of commendation, of encouragement, of approbation.

There are three things, our Lord says, that the Christians in Smyrna faced. First, "I know thy . . . tribulation . . ." The word translated "tribulation" is seldom used. It is the strong word, *"thlipsis."* The actual and literal meaning of the Greek word *"thlipsis"* is "pressure." Our English word "tribulation" has in it the background and the idea of a Roman whip, which, of course, is fearful enough. But it carries nothing of the connotation of this word *"thlipsis,"* for *"thlipsis"* is "pressure," like the execution of a man by placing a heavy boulder upon him. The weight of the great rock gradually crushes him to death. The word *"thlipsis"* has the picture of

101

grinding millstones, the pressure of which, in heavy weight, grinds the wheat into flour. The word contains the idea of the pressure that forces the blood out of the grapes. "I know thy *thlipsis* — the pressure of persecution and sorrow and death."

The second thing our Lord says these Christians of Smyrna faced is this: "I know thy tribulation and thy poverty." There are two Greek words for poverty. One is *ptocheia* and the other is *penia*. Our English word "penury" comes from the Greek word *penia*. *Penia* is the Greek word for a man who has to work for a living, the man who just barely makes a living. He has nothing superfluous. He just gets by. He is a poor man and he is forced to work for a living. That is *penia*. But that is not the word used here. The word used here is *"ptocheia."* That word actually means "beggary." It means absolute and utter destitution. "I know your poverty; I know your absolute and utter destitution." Why were these Christians at Smyrna so destitute? Smyrna was one of the richest cities in all the ancient Roman Empire. Yet, these people lived in absolute beggary and destitution. The reasons are not hard to find.

THE POVERTY OF THE CHRISTIANS IN SMYRNA

The first reason is this: the Christians in that ancient day were, almost without exception, poor anyway. Most of us account greatness and success in terms of riches, acceptability, fame and fortune. Yet, these Christians — the followers of the Lord who remade this world — were almost without exception the poorest of the poor. When the scribes and Pharisees and learned doctors of the law looked upon and listened to the apostles of Christ in Jerusalem, they called them *"agrammatoi kai idioti"*: that is, plain, unlearned, untaught, unschooled men of the poor and deprived. There was nothing professional, nothing learned about them. They were the poorest of the poor. Is not that a remarkable thing? One would think that for His work, God would need extraordinary personalities and people. Not at all. He needs just plain, ordinary people whom He can fill with His power to do extraordinary things. Those Christians in that New Testament day, outside of a few exceptions, were all plain, common, ordinary people. So, to begin with, if the Christians in Smyrna were like the Christians everywhere else, they were very poor.

There was another reason why they were unusually poor in Smyrna. They were severely persecuted. They were plundered and deprived of the right to work and make a living. No trade union would have them, and no business would hire them. They were boycotted on every hand. In their loss of home and work and possessions, they lived in beggary, "*ptocheia.*" They lived in destitution and in utter want. You might remember their plight if you have a job, if you own a house, or if you have a few possessions, something that you own. In gratitude to God, you might express thanks to Him for the bread you have to eat, for the house built as a shelter over your head, for the things that you have to wear, besides, maybe, a car to drive and other extras that God has given you. The Christians in Smyrna had none of these things. They possessed nothing. They were in utter want and destitution. So the Lord says, "I know thy *thlipsis* — the pressure unto death and the agony under which you live — and I know thy *ptocheia* — thy destitution and thy absolute want and need."

Then our Lord says, "I know another thing; I know the *blasphemia* of them which say they are Jews and are not but are the synagogue of Satan." "*Blasphemia.*" Blasphemy usually refers to words against God. It can have that meaning, but here it means "slander." The word refers to the things that were said about them by false Jews who were "of the synagogue of Satan."

It is a tragic thing, and one of the darkest in human history, the way religious people persecute each other. Give them an opportunity and practically every major religion that has ever lived has used an iron fist to grind dissenting minorities into the dust of the ground. The Christians have persecuted the Jews for centuries and centuries. That is why, for one thing, it is difficult to reach a Jew for Christ. The

Christian people have so bemeaned him and so reviled him and have so persecuted him that the name *Christian* is synonymous to the Jew with an enemy, with a persecutor, with an instrument of death and spoilation.

But, back there in the beginning of the Christian era, it was just the other way around. In the Roman Empire, where so many of the wealthy Jews had the ear of the Roman authorities, they sought to blot out the infant Christian church. The first Roman Emperor who ever persecuted the Christians was Nero. He had an actor, Aliturus, whom he admired very much. He also had a paramour named Poppaea. They were both Jewish proselytes. They took advantage of their intimate positions to feed ill will and slander into the ear of Nero. The result was that first terrible Christian persecution. It was so here in the city of Smyrna. There was a large Jewish population in that wealthy, flourishing mercantile city. They poisoned the minds of the populace against the Christians.

Brought about by the Jewish people, one of the most famous martyrdoms in all the world happened in this city of Smyrna. The pastor there at the time (who doubtless is the angel to whom this letter is addressed) was named Polycarp. He was the leader of the Christians in the city. Upon a festival day, when the crowds were inflammable and excitable, the cry went out from the mob about Polycarp and they brought him before the Roman governor. He was given the choice of saying, "Caesar is Lord" or "Jesus is Lord." He refused to say that Caesar was Lord. The governor urged him, saying: "Swear! I will set thee at liberty. Reproach Christ." Polycarp answered with one of the famous avowals in all history: "Eighty and six years have I served Him and He never did me harm. How, then, can I blaspheme my King and my Saviour?" When the proconsul again pressed him, the aged pastor answered: "Since thou art vainly urging that I should swear by the fortune of Caesar and pretendest not to know who and what I am, hear me. I am a Christian." A little later the governor threatened: "I have wild beasts at hand. To these will I cast thee except thou change." Later the proconsul said, "I will cause thee to be consumed by fire, seeing thou despisest the wild beasts, if thou wilt not change." Polycarp said: "Thou threatenest me with fire which burneth for an hour, and after a little, is extinguished. But thou art ignorant of the fire of the coming judgment and of eternal punishment reserved for the ungodly. But, why tarriest thou? bring forth what thou wilt." Soon after, the people, led by the Jews (it was on their Sabbath day and in contradiction to their law) gathered the wood and the faggots and burned the faithful pastor. In the flames, Polycarp prayed this moving prayer: "I thank Thee that Thou hast graciously thought me worthy of this day and of this hour, that I may receive a portion in the number of Thy martyrs in the cup of Thy Christ." So died the pastor, the angel messenger of the church of Smyrna. "I know thy *thlipsis* — the pressure and agony unto death — and I know thy *ptocheia* — thy utter destitution and want — and I know the *blasphemia* of them which say they are Jews and are not but are the synagogue of Satan. I know. I understand."

OUR LORD'S WORDS OF ENCOURAGEMENT

We have come, now, to our Lord's words of encouragement and praise and commendation. Encouragement is found even in the way that He introduces Himself. "To the angel of the church in Smyrna write: These things saith the first and the last. Through all of the trial you have or shall ever have, I am at the beginning of it; and I shall be at the end of it and I shall be all the way through. I am the first and the last." When the world was largely unexplored and the lands beyond were mysteries, in that ancient day when a man made a map, he would write over an unknown country, "Here be dragons." Over another unknown place he would write, "Here be burning and fiery sands." Over another unknown place on the map he would write: "Here be the abyss." Just so the Christian can take the map of life, the map of the world and the map of all the eternity that is yet to come, and in every unknown place he can write: "Here is Christ. Here is my Lord. Here is my Saviour. Here is my Advocate and my Mediator and my Redeemer." "I am the first and the last." The words were designed to lift up the hearts of those suffering Smyrnian Christians.

Our Lord continues His introduction of hope and encouragement when He adds, "I am he which was dead, and is alive." In the authorized King James Version, the Greek word for "is alive" is translated in the present tense. But the Greek *ezesen* is an aorist, a tense that describes a definite, complete act in past time. He refers to His resurrection, that great event in the past. "Who was dead, who became dead (*egeneto nekros*) and am now alive (*ezesen*)." He is referring to the great enemy that He conquered when He died and was buried and was raised from the tomb. There is nothing in death or in persecution or in destitution to fear.

For, our Lord said, "I know thy works, tribulation, poverty, *blasphemia* — I know." The word "I know" is not the "I know" of observation, as if He had said: "I observe, I see, I know, having seen it in you; I know thy works, tribulation, and poverty." This "I know" (*oida*) comes from His own experience. "I know thy tribulation." Think of His tribulation. "I know thy poverty." Think of His poverty. "I know the slander against thee." Think of the reviling against Him. "I know." This suffering, and this persecution and this death — He had experienced it all. He knew all about it. "I know. I know."

Our Lord's encouragement is further found in the words by which He addressed them. "Fear none of those things which thou shalt suffer . . . Satan shall cast you into prison, that you may be tried; and ye shall have tribulation (*thlipsis*) — pressure unto death — ten days." The number "ten" is an intensive number. Forty is four intensified. Seventy is seven intensified. The word *ten* refers to a fierce and intense persecution, like the ten plagues in the land of Egypt. But the Lord said, "Fear none of these things." One might have expected the Lord to say: "Fear not for I will mitigate and alleviate and palliate the suffering. Fear not, the days will soon be past. Do not be afraid for I will destroy those who

persecute you and I will cut them short." But the Lord said
the contrary: "You're to have more of the same." To which
the Christian may have cried: "O Lord, we have so much
now, we cannot bear it. Our property is despoiled, our homes
are taken away from us. We live in rags, in misery, in
agony, in beggary, in hunger, and in want. We are outcast
and despised." Yet the Lord said: "Fear not. There will just
be more of hardship and persecution. There will just be
more. Is not anything promised to the Christian besides
suffering, want, tribulation, poverty, misery, agony and
death? Is not there something else? The Lord never promised us freedom from tribulation in this world."

When James and John, the sons of Zebedee, came to Him
and said, "Lord, Lord, that we might be on thy right hand
and on thy left hand," the Lord said, "Can you be baptized
with the baptism I am going to be baptized with and can
you drink the cup that I am going to drink?" They said,
"We can." How little they understood! James was beheaded
by the sword of Herod Agrippa, and John, as you know,
was left on the Isle of Patmos to die of exposure and privation. When the Lord called Simon Peter, in the last chapter
of the Gospel of John, he called him unto crucifixion and
unto death. When the Lord called Paul, He said, "I'll show
him how great things he must suffer for my name's sake."
What an amazing thing! The Lord says here: "You are
going to have more trouble. You are going to have more
suffering. You are going to have more trials."

FAITHFUL UNTO DEATH

But our Lord also said something else. When you see the
wicked prosper and God's people having a hard time: when
you see these of the world apparently with everything that
life could want, and you are having a difficult, difficult time,
remember this: the Lord never said anything to us in this
life about having the abundance of all the things that this
life has to offer, about being rich, or about having health,
or about having all the amassed things that the people of
the world think are necessary to the joys of living. What the

Lord said is this: "Although as a Christian you may suffer and be deprived and many times be persecuted and cast out; although as a Christian, you may not be free from agony and disease and death, yet do not be afraid, for I know all about these things, and in them there is nothing to fear."

I may say to the little child, "Fear not, do not be afraid." I do that same thing with my parishioners. Many times I will say to one of my church members, "Do not be afraid," when at the same time there lurks in my heart the shadow of fears that I am afraid to speak of and to discuss. But our Lord gives complete assurance. "I know," He says. "I know." Because He knows, He says to the suffering Smyrnian Christians: "Fear not. Fear not. I am the first and the last. I'll be there all the way through. I see the end from the beginning. I know all about it." There is nothing to fear for a Christian. Do not be afraid. Do not tremble. Do not hesitate. Do not despair. Fear none of those things. None of them. "Yea, though I walk through the valley of the shadow of death, I will fear no evil: for thou art with me; thy rod and thy staff and thy strong arm support me" (Psalm 23:4). When Rupert Brooke went to the World War, he wrote a poem called "Safety":

> Safe shall be my going,
> Secretly armed against all death's endeavor,
> Safe tho' all safety is lost,
> Safe where men fall,
> And if these poor limbs die,
> Safest of all.

John Greenleaf Whittier wrote with the same confidence:

> I know not where His islands lift
> Their fronded palms in air;
> I only know I cannot drift
> Beyond His love and care.

Or, as Paul wrote: "For I am persuaded, that neither death, nor life, nor angels, nor principalities, nor powers, nor things present, nor things to come, nor height, nor depth, nor any other creature, shall be able to separate us from the love of God, which is in Christ Jesus our Lord" (Romans 8:38-39). "Fear not — fear not." There are some of you who are going

through trials and God knows. There are some of you who
are fighting desperately for life and health and the Lord
knows. There are some of you who labor in persecution and
God knows. There are some of you who are depressed in
spirit and in heart and God knows. "Fear not, fear not,
fear not."

Then our Lord speaks this marvelous promise: "Be thou
faithful unto death, and I will give thee a crown of life . . .
He that overcometh shall not be hurt of the second death."
The man of the world lives to die, but the Christian dies
to live. Beyond death for the lost lies death. But the Christian
is encouraged by the Lord, "Do not be afraid." He has
been through it all. There on the other side He waits with
the wreath and the laurel-crown for the Christian victors,
for the martyrs of Smyrna, for His children, for you who
live in this weary world today. Oh, what a blessing and what
a comfort! God is with His children.

Chapter 10

The Church in Pergamos

And to the angel of the church in Pergamos write; These things saith he which hath the sharp sword with two edges; I know thy works, and where thou dwellest, even where Satan's seat is; and thou holdest fast my name, and hast not denied my faith, even in those days wherein Antipas was my faithful martyr, who was slain among you, where Satan dwelleth. But I have a few things against thee, because thou hast there them that hold the doctrine of Balaam, who taught Balak to cast a stumblingblock before the children of Israel, to eat things sacrificed unto idols, and to commit fornication. So hast thou also them that hold the doctrine of the Nicolaitans, which thing I hate. Repent; or else I will come unto thee quickly, and will fight against them with the sword of my mouth. He that hath an ear, let him hear what the Spirit saith unto the churches; To him that overcometh will I give to eat of the hidden manna, and will give him a white stone, and in the stone a new name written, which no man knoweth saving he that receiveth it. — Revelation 2:12-17

On the ancient site of Pergamos there is today a village called Bergama which is a Turkish corruption of this Greek name, *Pergamos*. In that far-away day the original Pergamos was a most beautiful and illustrious city. In legend it was supposed to have been founded and built by a son of Hercules on a lofty hill in the broad and fertile plain of the Caicus Valley fifteen miles inland from the Aegean Sea. In the time of Xenophon it was a small, fortified town on the top of that Acropolis. It came to fame and to great fortune in the days of Lysimachus, who was one of the mighty generals of Alexander the Great. It became the capital city of an increasingly enlarged territory under the Attalid kings, a kingdom that finally came to cover most of what we now call Asia Minor. In 133 B.C., Attalis III bequeathed the kingdom to the Roman Empire. The Romans took the great area and, making it into the province of Asia, kept the capital city at Pergamos. When John wrote this letter to the church at Pergamos, Pergamos had been a capital city for more than three hundred years.

The Attalid kings, along with merchants and princes, increasingly beautified the metropolis through the centuries. It became one of the most imposing of all the Greek cities of the ancient world. The Attalids loved art and wisdom and all things pertaining to sculpture and painting and architecture. For example, they built in Pergamos one of the most famous libraries of antiquity. It had on its shelves more than two hundred thousand volumes, which is an immense number for that ancient day when every volume had to be copied by hand. The use of parchment, of skins of animals, as writing material was invented in Pergamos. The name "parchment" comes from this town of Pergamos. The story goes that Eumenes, the Greek king of Pergamos, cast longing eyes upon Aristophenes, the great librarian at Alexandria. He tried to entice the librarian at Alexandria to come to Pergamos to head his library, which thing infuriated Ptolemy, the Greek king of Egypt. Ptolemy promptly placed Aristophenes behind bars so that Eumenes could not get him. Then he did a second thing against the king of Pergamos. He interdicted the export of papyri to Asia Minor. Papyrus was the ancient material used in the making of books. Our word "paper" comes from the Greek word *papyrus*. It is a bullrush that grows along the banks of the Nile River. The pulp of it can be pounded down, cross-woven and made into a paper able to sustain a writing pen. It was a nationalized industry in Egypt, and Ptolemy had complete control over it. When the king, therefore, prohibited the export of papyri to Pergamos, the authors and librarians there had no material upon which to write. That forced them into the discovery and the perfection of writing material made out of skins of animals. Even today, for instance, if you are graduated from college they call your diploma a "sheep-skin." That refers to the material on which the diploma is written. The use of skin, called *parchment* or *vellum*, was invented here by those illustrious librarians and authors in Pergamos.

THE GRIM SITUATION OF THE CHURCH AT PERGAMOS

The letter of our Lord to this church begins with a grim tone: "I know thy works, and where thou dwellest, even where Satan's seat is: and thou holdest fast my name, and hast not denied my faith, even in those days wherein Antipas was my faithful martyr, who was slain among you, where Satan dwelleth." That word translated "seat" ("where Satan's seat is") is in Greek, *thronos.* In the nineteenth chapter of Matthew the word *thronos* refers to the seat of the judge. In the first chapter of the book of Luke, it refers to the throne of a king. So, when the Lord says, "I know where you dwell, where Satan's throne is," He is referring not only to the fact that these Christians live where Satan exists but also that these Christians are dwelling where Satan has great authority and great power.

What was "Satan's throne," "Satan's seat," there in this beautiful capital Greek city of Pergamos? The reference could have been to those gorgeous, impressive, idolatrous temples that the Greeks built everywhere. As one would expect, in this capital city there was a temple to the four greatest Greek gods: to Zeus (the Latin name for him is *Jupiter*), to Dionysius (the Latin name for him is *Bacchus*), to Athena (the Latin name for her is *Minerva*), and to Aesculapius. Zeus was the head of all of the gods. Dionysius was the god of wine and of drama. Athena was the god of wisdom in art and in war (planned war, astute war). Aesculapius was the god of healing. This latter god was known all over the ancient world as the Pergamene god. His impressive temple had also with it medical wards and the most famous medical school in the world. His emblem was a serpent. In the courts of the temple, harmless snakes slithered on the ground and sufferers came from the ends of the earth to sleep in the sanctuary. If a sufferer happened to be touched by one of those sliding, slithering snakes in the night, he was touched by the healing presence of the god Aesculapius. Much of what they called medicine we would call sheer, unadulterated superstition. But it was a famous shrine and effectively drew the sick from the ends of the Empire to be healed by the god. It may be, therefore, that the Lord called the idolatry of the city "Satan's seat." Certainly pagan worship was an institution opposed only at the peril of death.

The reference to Satan's *"thronos"* could have focused attention on another thing that was world-famous in Pergamos. One of the ancient wonders of the world was the magnificent altar to Zeus. On a jutting ledge out from the Acropolis, was built the most ornate, the largest and the most famous altar in the world. It was ninety feet square and forty feet high (according to one authority), and around the frieze at the base of it was one of the most impressive pieces of sculpture created by ancient art. The German government in the last century sent an expedition to excavate Pergamos and they found a large part of that frieze. It is in the museum at Berlin to this day. The great altar of sacrifice to Zeus, high on the side of that Acropolis and jutting out from it, was the most impressive thing in the city. It looked somewhat like a throne, and maybe that is the reference of our Lord when He says, "You dwell where Satan's seat is."

Or, "Satan's seat" could have been a third thing. It could have referred to emperor-worship, the worship of the Roman Caesars. Much of the Roman Empire was put together by conquest and by war, but the Attalid kingdom which was made into the Roman province of Asia came by will, by choice. Attalis III bequeathed his kingdom to the Romans. The citizens followed their king in his devotion to the Roman Empire. An illustration of that devotion can be seen in the fact that there were three different temples in Pergamos dedicated to Roman emperors. Like Smyrna, Pergamos was the head of a district that enforced Caesar-worship. It may have been to that coercive idolatry the Lord had reference when He said, "Satan's *thronos*."

Notice especially in this letter that our Lord says, "And thou hast not denied my faith, even in those days wherein Antipas was my faithful martyr." That word "denied" (*erneso*) is in the aorist tense; that is, it refers to a thing in the past, a thing completed and done. Evidently, sometime there had been a great persecution that suddenly burst out against the Christians in Pergamos. In that angry day, Antipas was martyred. It has been said that the first martyr put to death by the Roman Empire was this Christian, Antipas, of Pergamos. In His faithfulness to Christ and in protest against Caesar worship, Antipas laid down his life. Let me point out one of the great tributes of Jesus to this martyr Antipas: He calls this faithful martyr in His own name. In Revelation 1:5 we read, "And from Jesus Christ, *ho martus — ho pistos.*" Those are the exact words by which the Lord refers to Antipas. "Antipas — *ho martus — ho pistos.*" In Revelation 1:5 the word *martus* is translated "martyr." It became the same thing. *Ho martus* in the days of the New Testament was a man who witnessed for Christ. In many instances he sealed his testimony with his blood. Thus the word *martus* — "witness" became our English word "martyr." Antipas was that faithful leader in the church at Pergamos who, in a violent outburst against the Christians, laid down his life for Christ.

Observe one other thing here in the Greek of this text: "I know thy works, and where thou dwellest, even where Satan's seat is." There are two different Greek words for "dwell." One of them, which is almost always used, is *paroikeo.* That means to dwell as a foreigner, as a sojourner, as a stranger. The Greek word for stranger, sojourner, is *paroikos.* So, the word for dwell almost always used in the New Testament is *paroikeo.* That is, we are dwelling here in this earth as strangers, as pilgrims, as sojourners. Our home, the New Testament says, is in heaven. But in this text the other Greek word is used for dwell, namely, *katoikeo,* which is the Greek word for a permanent resident. "I know where thou dwellest [*katoikeo*] where Satan's seat is." When you think about that just a moment, you will understand why the Lord used that particular Greek word. "I know where you are staying; I know where your house is; I know where your home is; I know where you dwell and you have to stay there; you cannot escape; you cannot run away; you cannot flee the dangerous situation, even there where Satan's seat is." What a description of our lives in this sin-cursed world! We cannot run away. There are many fine Christian men and a multitude of dedicated Christian women who work under situations that are trying. But they cannot run away. They have to dwell there. So, with most of God's true people in this dreary earth. They live in a world that is difficult and hard and they cannot escape. They have to stay even as Antipas stayed, "my faithful *martus*."

THE DOCTRINE OF BALAAM

With verse fourteen the tone of our Lord changes. "But I have a few things against thee, because thou hast there them that hold the doctrine of Balaam." The doctrine of Balaam is the teaching and counsel of a shrewd sage. He was hired by Balak to curse Israel. He could not curse Israel. God would not let him. But he did something worse to corrupt God's people. He introduced them to strange Moabite women. Those strange Moabite women did the work. They corrupted Israel, a thing that Balaam, himself, could not do. But they did it. That is the method of Balaam. So the Lord says to those Christians in Pergamos, "I have this against thee, that there are those in your midst that hold the doctrine of Balaam and they encourage you to eat things sacrificed to idols and to commit fornication."

One of the most astonishing things in the Graeco-Roman world is this: with all of their magnificent philosophy and ethics and their achievements in every realm of art and science and literature, they looked upon prostitution as a needful and acceptable way of life. For example, I read from Demosthenes. "We have prostitutes for the sake of pleasure. We have concubines for the sake of daily cohabitation. We have wives for the purpose of having children legitimately and of having a faithful guardian of our household affairs." That was the accepted pattern of ancient Greek life as illustrated by this greatest of all orators, Demosthenes.

I have copied this from Cicero, which is a description of the accepted pattern of life among the Romans. "If there is anyone [says Cicero] who thinks that young men should be absolutely forbidden to love a prostitute, he is extremely severe. He is at variance, not only with the license of what our age allows, but also with the customs and concessions of our ancestors. When, indeed, was this not done? When did anyone ever find fault with it? When was such promiscuousness ever denied? When was it that this which is now lawful was not lawful?" The passage truly sounds like the great Roman Cicero in his oratorical manner of speech, interspersed with rhetorical questions. But what a debased moral code he was defending! However, Cicero was but echoing the accepted life of the ancient citizen of the ancient Roman world. There were those in the church who stood up and said: "That is the way to live, as everyone else lives around you. What do you want to do — be cut off from society? What do you want to do — alienate all your friends? What do you want to do — stick out like a sore thumb? What do you want to do — be a wallflower? What do you want to do — be peculiar?" So they said that the accepted standards of the world are to be the accepted patterns of life for every Christian. He is to have his prostitutes and his concubines and just as many of them as his affluence would allow. Such practices were taught in the church!

It would surprise you to know the number of people today in our church, in every church, who have the persuasion that we ought to go along with the crowd. Why certainly! Do you think we would want to cut ourselves off from the social intercourse of people? The pattern of life calls for certain things. Therefore, if we conform, we do not look peculiar. The doctrine of Balaam is the same thing today as it was then.

Our Lord refers to "things sacrificed unto idols." To us that reference is remote. Yet, in the days when the Lord wrote, and when this New Testament was written, the most agonizing, personal problem that Christians faced was this, "concerning things sacrificed to idols." Let me explain. When the ancient worshiper made a sacrifice to an idol, as on that great altar to Zeus, the animal was not burned. Many times no part of it was burned except a little piece of the forelock. The priest would cut off a few hairs and burn them. The animal, however, when it was sacrificed, and offered unto the god on the altar, was always divided, with a small portion given to the priest, but most of it was returned to the worshiper to eat. The sacrifice was a communal meal. (Could I pause to say, as I often say when I come to an exegesis of a passage like this, that I am amazed at people who do not believe in eating at the church. Those are the most peculiar, theological exegetes that I have heard of. For, practically all of worship from the beginning was some kind of a communal meal. Even when the Christians met together they always ate. Every day they were eating together. Every day! I am in favor of it. God invented eating, and I would think He likes it.) Anyway, when the heathen worshiper made his sacrifice, a little part of the animal was burned, a part was given to the priest and the rest was given to the votary. What he did with it was this: he called his family, his friends, and they ate the animal sacrificed to the gods. What was the matter with that? Would there be anyone who would be so narrow-minded, could there be anyone who was so straight-laced as to refuse an invitation to the feast, to the party given by the best of friends? Everyone did it — ate the meat sacrificed unto idols. I have one comment to make. Had these false teachers succeeded in saying that it was all right for the Christian to eat the holy bread of the Lord's Supper and to drink the holy cup of the Lord's Supper and then the next hour or the next day drink and eat at these feasts dedicated unto idols, Christianity would have been swamped and would have died in the surrounding seas of paganism. The social customs of idolatry were a threat to the Christian faith on every side. But the true Christian said, "I will not drink and I will not eat." So he was cut off from the social intercourse of the world and the pattern of life in which he lived. He was separate, he was distinct, he was apart, he did not share. But those first Christians had a thrust in them, a drive in them, a march in them and a dedication in them that astonished the world. Satan's seat and Antipas. "*Ho martus,*" "*ho pistos.*" The Christian's devotion cost him his life.

THE HIDDEN MANNA AND THE WHITE STONE

The Lord says, "He that hath an ear, let him hear what the Spirit saith unto the churches; To him that overcometh will I give to eat of the hidden manna." They were not to eat and to drink according to the customs surrounding Satan's throne. Especially notice here the reference to "hidden manna." Manna is called in the seventy-eighth Psalm, "Angel's food, corn of heaven." In Exodus 16:4, it is called "bread of heaven." When it came down from heaven, they gathered an omer of it and after placing it in a golden bowl, laid it up in the Ark of the Covenant before the Lord, hidden behind the veil. Thus the Saviour says, "You may not share in the social life, eating and drinking things sacrificed to idols, but I will give you to eat of the hidden manna, bread of heaven." God will do that for us if we are willing to cut ourselves off from the compromise of the world. He will give us a better thing. "I will give to him hidden manna to eat, if he will turn aside from eating and drinking things sacrificed unto idols."

Then our Lord says He will give to the overcomer "a white stone." Many are the strange interpretations as to the meaning of that "white stone." Some say it refers to an acquittal from God concerning our sins. When a man was tried, if the jurors voted to acquit him, they dropped in an urn a white stone; if they voted to condemn him, they dropped in a black stone. So the white stone, some say, refers to the acquittal on the part of God of our sins. There are others who say the stone was used in calculation and that we are numbered among the children of God. There are those who say it refers to victory and to happiness. As we say a "red-letter day," Pliny one time refers to a "white stone day." There are those who think it refers to the circuses and the games that were provided free to the people to which the admission was a white stone. If we are faithful, God will give us a white stone, an admission to all the wonderful things from Heaven. Then, there are those who think the white stone refers to an amulet, and they make the suggestion very plausible. An amulet often had a mystic name on it that maybe no one knew but the man who possessed it. "To him that overcometh will I give . . . him a white stone, and in the stone a new name written, which no man knoweth saving he that receiveth it." These amulets, little charms, little superstitious gadgets, little fetishes, were worn in order to keep people safe and to keep them away from disease and death. I see certain people wear them around their necks today. The Lord would say: "You do not need that; you have me, the true stone."

But I do not think the true interpretation is to be found in any of these suggestions. This is what I think the meaning is: "a white stone" does not mean a little white rock; rather, it means a beautiful, crystal-clear gem, a diamond. I think the Urim on the breastplate of the priest was a diamond. Those who sought to know God's will could look into that crystal-clear diamond, which had on it the mystic name of God, and they could learn Jehovah's answer to their questions. Many, many times the people of Israel would inquire of the ephod, of the Urim and Thummim to find God's will. The priest wore it upon his breast along with the other gems in which were written the names of the people of God. I think the reference is to that. I think "a white stone" refers to a diamond, that beautiful Urim, that brilliant gem on the breastplate of the high priest. On it was written the mystic name of God and the Lord gives it to us. To us who love Him there is wisdom to know the way, and there is direction for all of the things we must face, and there is

the love and presence and comfort of God. The Lord gives
it to us. He gives us His own self, His own spirit, His own
precious presence. "I will go before you and I will help you
and I will see you through." This is the faithful promise of
God to us who possess the mystic stone.

Chapter 11

Living Where Satan's Seat Is

And to the angel of the church in Pergamos write; These
things saith he which hath the sharp sword with two edges;
I know thy works, and where thou dwellest, even where
Satan's seat is . . . — Revelation 2:12, 13a

In this letter of our Lord to the church at Pergamos, note
especially the words of the text: "I know where thou dwellest, even where Satan's seat is." The Authorized Version
has toned down the text. When John wrote it, he wrote it
like this: ". . . dwelling where Satan's *thronos* is." The Greek
word is *thronos*, Satan's throne. The Authorized Version
softened it to Satan's "seat." But John wrote, "Satan's throne."
So let it stand. Satan has a throne. It is in this earth. It is
in the city. When Lucifer fell from heaven, he dragged
down with him one-third of all of the angelic hosts. He built
his kingdom in this planet, and with him are those multitudes of fallen angelic beings. They are evil spirits. No man
could ever convince me that I have not seen an evil spirit
enter into a home, a heart, a life. Sometimes it is the spirit
of rejection, of unbelief, of blasphemy; sometimes it is the
evil spirit of covetousness, of hatred, of lust, or murder; but
always it is an evil that hurts and destroys and wastes.
That is the part of the over-sowing of Satan in God's earth.

When Lucifer fell he kept his brilliance. He is as shrewd
and astute and ingenious this hour as he was when, as the
covering, sheltering, reigning cherub, he presided over God's
heavenly hosts in glory. Fallen, ruined, an enemy of God
when he came down to this earth, he set up his throne on
this planet. From the beginning, from the time of the multiplication of people in this earth, his throne has been in the
city. In the previous letter, the Lord addressed Smyrna.

There the opposition to the church was in the synagogue. In the period of ecclesiastical history represented by Smyrna, the opposition to the church was veiled under the cloak of religion. But in Pergamos the opposition to the church takes an altogether different turn. Satan invites the church and the people of God to share with him the glamor and the glitter of all things that mammon has to offer of worldly greatness and glory. "Yea," said Satan to our Lord Himself, "if thou wilt fall down and worship me the riches of the kingdoms of the earth will I give unto thee." "Share it," says the devil. This is "dwelling where Satan's throne is."

THE CITY THE SEAT OF SATAN

When I live in the city, I live where Satan's seat is. There is evil in the country. There is evil in rural areas. I grew up in a small village, and for the first ten years of my ministry I was a country preacher. I know the evil that is in the country, and I know the evil that is in rural areas. But there is no evil and no vice like the iniquity that one finds in a city. There are sins, gross sins, that I never heard of until I came to live in the city. Somehow in a great, pressing, metropolitan area, vice, iniquity, lewdness and wickedness are much implemented and activated. Sin becomes a thousand times more villainous in the city than it is in any other part of the earth. The waste and sacrifice of young lives on the altar of Satan in the city must make God weep. Clear-brained, strong-bodied young men and women come out of rural areas and out of small villages. Their faces are set toward the city and here they are debauched and sold for a price. They are sacrificed on the altar of white slavery and liquor and narcotics and every vile and vicious and empty pleasure that Satan himself could devise. I see this evil before my very eyes every day of my life.

I do not mean to minimize the sin that exists in the open country. There is liquor in the country. Where once I preached in Kentucky, on most any clear day, I could stand in the little village and see in the distance the soft curl of smoke from a moonshine still. In the little town in which

I grew up, there was the bootlegger. Everyone knew him. Those who so desired, in the darkness of the night, could do business with him. But one never sees liquor organized and become corporate and powerful except in the city. Most of the country area is dry. If an election is held in a county that is sparsely populated, most of the time the vote will be dry. But it matters not to the liquor industry if the whole countryside is dry, just so that the cities are wet. In the city are found those incorporated, vested interests of evil which are represented not only by a man who sells the poison, but also by the virulent power of Satan himself. How do you think those great evil empires are built and those vile corporations exist except as they teach every rising generation to use their wares? Thus these entrenched monopolies of wickedness destroy the lives of our youth. To the organization, the liquor traffic is money. To the city, it is revenue. The young people come and are sacrificed on the altar, "where Satan's throne is."

In my reading I copied from a court this record:

"What is your name, my woman, and where were you born?"

She answered, "My name is Aileen Burn, your honor, and I were born in Aberdeen, off the Scotland coastland."

"And you are charged with striking a man?"

"I am, your honor."

"McGinnis, here, testifies that he never laid a hand on you," returned the Judge.

"He stabbed me to the heart, your honor."

"Stabbed you? Suppose you explain."

"I will, You might not know what was, your honor, to have one bonnie laddie and none else. I left the good father o' my lad asleeping in the kirkyard, when I brought my wee bairnie to this land. For many a year I toiled in sun and shade for my winsome Robbie. He growed so fine and tall that he was taken to a gentleman's store to work. Then this man, McGinnis, set his evil eye on the lad. I was forced to pass his den on my way to and from a breadstore he minded and I hated to look on his place. One morn' as I passed by he said I needn't be so grand about my boy, he were no above taking a drink o' liquor with the rest. I begged my child fro' the love of God to let the stuff alone. Me Robbie promised to bide my wishes, but this man McGinnis, watched for the night when it was cold and storming and gave the lad a drink to warm him, he would say. I got on my knees to my bairn and pled him pass the place no more, but to gang to home by some other road. Then I went myself to the man and perhaps, your honor, you can understand, how a mither would beg and pray for the bone of her bone and the flesh of her flesh. But he laughed in me face. Last night, your honor, the noise at me door frightened me. I run with all me might to see what were the trouble. Me Robbie swayed into the room and fell at me feet. He were drunk, your honor. When McGinnis poked his face in at the door and said, 'What think ye now, Mrs. Burn?' did I mean to strike the man, your honor? If I could, I'd have struck the breath out of his body. You had better keep me with lock and key til me gloom dies out. But, O Judge, Judge, I wish me bairn and me lad were in the kirkyard aside the good father. They tell me if I could prove the mon sold liquor to the bairn under age, the law could stop him. I tell you, Judge, there is naught but God's vengeance can stop his ilk. It were enough to arrest the mither that strikes the mon as ruins her bairn, but wait til the Lord God Almighty strikes. Aye! Wait for that!"

If the liquor interests did not teach our youth to drink, they would soon run out of business. So through every ingenious way they can contrive, they teach them. If they failed, there would be no one to whom to sell their evil wares. So the young people come, they pour into the city where Satan presides, and there they are debauched. One young man I am thinking of, destroyed and ruined, said, "I went to hear the minister and the minister said there was no harm in a man's drinking, provided he didn't drink too much." So the boy followed the advice of the minister. He happened to be the one out of every nine that drinks who becomes an alcoholic. One out of every nine cannot leave it alone. Five hundred thousand every year turn in destruction and in hopelessness into that downward road where Satan's seat is, and many of the ministers encourage them in it. Any man, I do not care what his ordination, who says to a boy, "It's all right to drink," has on his hands the blood of one young man out of nine. The right to destroy these lives cannot be legalized before God. Young man, do not drink. As this dear, blessed, Scotch woman fell down before her bairn and plead and begged and prayed, so you pass it by, pass it by. You may be one of the eight that can learn to

carry your liquor. You may be; I do not deny it. But I say
to you, for the sake of the ninth one, it is not worth it. The
destruction of his life is not worth it. Give it up! Give it up!
Pass it by!

Satan's throne is in the city where mammon dwells. Satan
likes to have his throne in the glitter and the greatness of
worldly power and influence. The Lord Jesus said, "You cannot serve God and mammon." Look at that sentence out of
the Sermon on the Mount. He did not say that you cannot
serve God and the devil. He said, "You cannot serve God
and mammon." God controls the spiritual life of a man
through his heart, through the great commitment of his soul
to Jesus. But mammon controls the life of a man through his
affinity and love for the world and the things of the world.
There are men who sell their souls, there are women who
trade their lives, for the tinsel and tin foil and the cheap
reward of this present, weary world. Satan has his seat in the
city where mammon reigns.

False doctrine is found in the city, far more than in rural
areas. Heresy is in the city. It is in city institutions and in
city pulpits. There was placed in my hands recently a book
by one of our supposedly great and intellectual theological
professors. It is an affront to God. Another man brought me
two or three days ago an article in a current magazine he
had obtained from a news rack. It proposes to be the attitude of the present modern-day Protestant minister regarding some of the sacred relationships of human life. Had
Freud written it, had an outright infidel written it, it would
have been no more offensive and repulsive to God.

The Witness of the Church in the City

It is a strange thing that the Lord says here: "To the
angel, to the pastor of the church in Pergamos write . . . I
know . . . where thou dwellest . . . where Satan has his
throne." Well, of all the places, where is God's church, but
there, *there*? Located where Satan has his throne. There
where Aesculapius, the god of healing, whose symbol was
a serpent, presided over the orgies and incantations that

went along with that heathen worship; located there where further up the hill, Zeus (Jupiter), and where a little below the hill, Athena (Minerva), and where toward the heart of the city, Apollo, bestowed their blessings upon indescribably licentious rites. Surely you would not find a church in a place like that! What a trying, perilous, difficult place to locate God's house! But there where it is most difficult and trying, there where it is most needed, even there did Jesus build His house, did God establish His church, "where Satan's throne is." But that is where it needs to be. In the midst of these towering monuments to wealth and industry and commerce, right down in the district where the night-clubs are and the hotels and all of the passing throngs of humanity are, there, where Satan has his throne, there is the church of Jesus Christ. There it ought to be. "I know thy works, where you dwell, where Satan's throne is and thou hast not denied my faith, but you have been true like a bridge of stars, like a lighthouse set on a hill; thou hast not denied my faith."

How do we deny the faith in the city where Satan's throne is? We deny the faith by refusing to confess it. "Hush. Hush. I am a Christian. Hush. Hush. I am a member of that dear and precious church, but hush, hush. It is not to be said. It is not to be confessed. It is to be hid. It is to be taken out of sight. It is to be made a deep, inward, clandestine secret. It is not to be said or confessed." But Christ said, "I know where you dwell, where Satan has his throne, and *thou hast not denied my faith,* even in those days when Antipas, my faithful martyr was slain among you." When the Lord says here, "You have not denied my faith," and He mentions His faithful martyr, Antipas, I would suppose that He refers to a martyrdom on the part of Antipas like that of Polycarp. The world says: "Just deny you are a Christian and we will receive you. You will be one of us. Do violence to the great commitment in your soul and we will take you in. You can join our club. You can walk by our side. You can sell our merchandise and we will buy from you." The Christian pilgrim ought to answer, "If I

starve to death, I will not compromise." That is Christ's
faithful witness, His faithful martyr. "Whosoever will confess me before men, him will I confess before my father
which is in heaven. But whosoever will deny me before men,
him shall I deny before my father which is in heaven."
Openly, publicly, let us come down that aisle and here to
the front, saying: "I am a Christian, baptized in obedience
to the command of the Lord Jesus Christ, I am a Christian,
working in the world. I do not deny the faith."

How, sometimes, do we deny the faith? We deny it by
exchanging it for another gospel and another saviour. Some
seek to persuade us that in the ancient New Testament days
the saints were saved by the sacrifice of the Son of God, but
that today they are saved by a new theology. Would not that
be a strange thing? After God has gathered His saved into
glory, we would discover that these first century Christians,
saved in the days of the apostles, were saved by one kind
of a gospel; that the third century Christians were saved by
another kind of a gospel; that sixteenth century Christians
were saved by yet another kind of a gospel; then that the
twentieth century Christians were saved by still another
kind of a gospel. When all of these different clients of these
separate ways ascribe praise and glory to the One who
saved them, what a motley conglomeration it would be!
There would be discord from one end of the quarters of
heaven to the other. That is not the way God has worked.
Back there in the first century, the saints were saved by the
blood of the crucified One; in the third century, in the fifteenth, in the nineteenth and today, we all are saved by the
same atoning grace. All glory unto Him who washed us in
His blood, to Him who reigneth forever and ever, to the
Lamb of God, the same through all the centuries, to whom
we offer the same ascription of praise through the unending
millenniums! No new gospel, no other saviour, just Jesus
and His love! "Thou hast not denied my faith."

How do we deny the faith? By forsaking it, by quitting it.
We can do it individually. Many a fine Christian family
comes to the city and is lost to God. Many a man who once

served Jesus has forsaken the faith. Many a youth who loved God as a child, or as a teenager, now is sold unto sin with a load on his back and misery and blackness for his lot every day, who weeps at night, whose heart hungers, who is wandering out in the world.

JESUS WEEPING OVER THE CITY

Our Saviour weeps over the great cities of the world. The population of humanity every day presses more and more inwardly toward the city. Do not ever persuade yourself that these great cities are emptying themselves of their populations. Every day that passes, the population of the heart of the great city increases and shall increase. Every day that I drive home and back to the church, where there used to be a single dwelling, now, stacked on top of each other, are those multiplied units that constantly increase, up and up and up. They will continue to increase. Diagonally across from our church in Dallas is going up this minute a great towering apartment building. Directly across from our church is going up another one. These great cities tower and tower and tower, and the populations of the earth flood into them. But the churches of Jesus Christ go farther out and out and out and away. I copied from a Boston pastor: "Only two churches remain on the ground first occupied by the gospel in Boston. The sepulchres of Increase and Cotton Mather are with us to this day. They sleep hard by the scenes of their useful labor but the churches to which they ministered have moved out." Those vast, teeming thousands and thousands are left, forsaken, "where Satan's seat is," where Satan has his throne.

The Lord said, "I understand the trial of the church in the heart of the city. I know her peril and the difficulty. I understand. I understand." And He does. Sometimes when the clusters from the vineyard are few, He sees that the ground is barren. Sometimes when the yield is small, He sees the plowshares that break against the rock in the soil. He understands. That is why there is no reason to quit, why there is no reason to cease to pray, why there is no reason to stop our thrust for God in the heart of this city where Satan has his throne. We challenge every inch of ground that Satan battles for, every vile and vicious thing that he offers. We challenge him to his face. These young men belong to God, not to the world. These beautiful girls, we dedicate to Christ, not to Satan. The power and the glory and the influence that God has placed in this world and in the hands of men rightfully belong to heaven and not to hell. God has set His church, even us, where Satan's seat is, where Satan has his *thronos*, that we might build up the household of faith in the name and in the spirit of our all-conquering Lord Jesus. God help us, thus to do!

Chapter 12

The Doctrine of the Nicolaitanes

> But I have a few things against thee, because thou hast there
> them that hold the doctrine of Balaam, who taught Balak to
> cast a stumblingblock before the children of Israel, to eat
> things sacrificed unto idols, and to commit fornication. So
> hast thou also them that hold the doctrine of the Nicolaitanes,
> which thing I hate. — Revelation 2:14, 15

In the message of our Lord to the third Asian church,
Pergamos, He says in Revelation 2:15 and 16: "So hast thou
also them that hold the doctrine of the Nicolaitanes, which
thing I hate. Repent, or else I will come unto thee quickly,
and will fight against them with the sword of my mouth."
In His letter to Ephesus, the first Asian church, our Lord
said: "But this thou hast, that thou hatest the deeds of the
Nicolaitanes, which I also hate" (Revelation 2:6).

Seven churches are here addressed in a book that calls
itself "a book of prophecy." So I am thereby instructed that
these seven churches represent seven successive prophetic
portrayals of the history of the Gospel and the story of the
churches of Christ in the earth. They depict Christian history from the beginning to the end. In the chronicles of the
church there is to be an Ephesian period, a Smyrnian period,
a Pergamean period, a Thyatiran period, a Sardian period,
a Philadelphian period, a Laodicean period. They are prophetic presentations, delineations, descriptions of the course
of Christ's church in the earth. The Ephesian period, the
first one, represents the church in the days of the apostles.
It is the apostolic church. The Smyrnian church is the
church of martyrdom and persecution, the church under
the heavy hand of imperial Rome. The Pergamean church
is the church of the establishment. It is the church after

300 A.D. when it became a part of the state religion of the Roman government.

Notice how Christ changes the description of Himself from His address to Smyrna, the church of martyrdom and persecution, to the description of Himself when He addresses Pergamos, the church of the establishment. Look at Revelation 2:8: "Unto the angel of the church in Smyrna write; These things saith the first and the last, which was dead, and is alive." That is the description of a Saviour who presents Himself as comfort and strength and assurance to a church that is undergoing the fiery trials and the blood-bath of heavy and terrible persecution. "I am the first and the last. Do not be afraid. I also was slain, but in the power of the spirit of God, raised to live forever more." Now observe the difference when He addresses Himself to the Pergamean church: "And to the angel of the church in Pergamos write; These things saith he which hath the sharp sword with two edges." He is a God of love and of mercy, but He is also a God of justice and righteousness and judgment. The winnowing fan is in His hand and the axe is laid at the root of the tree. "These things saith he which hath the sharp sword with two edges." How greatly our Master changes from the church of martyrdom to this church of the establishment!

WHO ARE THE NICOLAITANES?

It is in this church at Pergamos that He says: "So hast thou also them that hold the doctrine of the Nicolaitanes, which thing I hate." What is the doctrine, the system, the teaching of the Nicolaitanes? Some of the most fantastic suppositions imaginable are written by some expositors in explaining this passage. For example, one of them says that the Nicolaitanes were the apostatizing followers of Nicolas of Antioch, who was one of the seven ordained deacons in the church at Jerusalem. There is no basis, no substantiation for such a theory either in profane or in sacred history. Now, there are many, many expositors (and it seems to me the majority) who follow the line of the great expositor, G. Campbell Morgan, who identifies the Nicolaitanes with the

Balaamites. In the verse above, the Lord said to the church at Pergamos: "I have a few things against thee, because thou hast there them that hold the doctrine of Balaam, who taught Israel to eat things sacrificed to idols and to commit fornication." Now Balaam was hired by Balak to curse Israel, but God would not let him. However, in order to receive his hire from the King of Moab, Balaam had to do something. Being unable to curse Israel because of the interdiction of God, Balaam told Balak to bring in all of his strange Moabitish women and those strange Moabitish women would seduce Israel (which they did).

Now the doctrine of Balaam is the doctrine of sensuality, of carnality, of lust. G. Campbell Morgan and most of these expositors say that the doctrine of the Nicolaitanes is that same antinomian doctrine, the doctrine of carnality and lust and fornication, the doctrine of sensuality. But if the doctrine of the Nicolaitanes is the same as the doctrine of the Balaamites, why mention it? If they are the same, then when Christ described the doctrine of Balaam, He also described both of them. Why mention the Nicolaitanes if they are the same as the Balaamites? Notice also the wording of the text: "I have these things [plural] against thee, because thou hast there them that hold the doctrine of the Nicolaitanes." I would suppose, just from looking at the text, that the doctrine of the Balaamites and the doctrine of the Nicolaitanes were two different things. One was one thing and one was another thing. I am much persuaded that this is true. The doctrine of the Nicolaitanes is not the doctrine of the Balaamites. It is something else.

What then is this doctrine of the Nicolaitanes? It is important that we know because of this: twice in this one chapter the Lord says concerning this doctrine, "This thing I hate." Our Lord's emphasis upon His hatred of the doctrine demands our earnest, prayerful, unwearying search as to its meaning. This message is the answer to that question: "What is the doctrine of the Nicolaitanes?" We find the answer in two areas. The first area is in the name itself. Names have great significance in the Word of God. The second area is in the Pergamean church itself — the Pergamean period of church history.

First, consider the name itself. The word *Nicolaitane* is composed of two simple Greek words. The first is *Nike*. We have a *Nike* missile. One can also go to any trophy shop and buy a *Nike* (a winged victory) and give it to a contestant who is victorious, who has conquered and excelled in a game. The Greek word *Nike* is the word for "victory." The other simple word that makes up the word *Nicolaitane* is the word *laos*. *Laos* is the simple word of the Greeks for "people." The word "laity" is derived from the Greek word *laos*. When these words are put together, *Nike* and *laos*, we have in English "Nicolaos," "Nicolaitane." The word refers to a group, to a class, who exalt themselves above the people. They subjugate the people. They are oppressors of and conquerors of the people — Nicolaitanes.

The other area in which we can learn the meaning of the doctrine of the Nicolaitanes is to be found in the Pergamean period of the church. This is the church of the establishment. This is the day when the church is married to the world. Look at the name *Pergamos*. Learned linguists say that that little prefix *per* refers to something that is objectionable. The Greek word for marriage is *gamos*. You will find that word *gamos* appearing in "polygamy" or "bigamy." The Pergamean period of the church is the period of the marriage of the church to the world. This is the day when the church has become wealthy and popular and exalted and lifted up. This is the day when the church enters the great field of power and political aggrandizement and when men seek through it personal advancement and preferment. This is the day when the church is married to the Roman government.

Let us now put all these meanings together and we shall have a good idea of what the doctrine of the Nicolaitanes is: *Nico-laos*, the conquerors, the victors, the subjugators of the people; *Pergamos*, the Pergamean period of the church when it is exalted and lifted up and married into the very household of the Roman Empire. The doctrine of the Nicolaitanes, then, is this: the rising up of a class separate, apart and exalted over the great mass of God's people. This class arrogated to themselves, above the people, the powers of life and of death. They had the power to forgive sins, to excommunicate, the power to damn in hell; they alone had the power to interpret and to mediate the Word and will of God. The doctrine of the Nicolaitanes is the subjugation of the people. The Nicolaitanes entered the political, imperial and governmental arena of the world. Both government and church became pawns in a game of political power, and the two are married together. In James 4:4 the pastor in Jerusalem said: ". . . the friendship of the world is enmity with God." "Which thing I hate," says God.

THE EARLY GROWTH OF THE EVIL DOCTRINE

This doctrine of the Nicolaitanes began early. In the Ephesian church the Lord said, "But this thou hast, thou hatest the deeds of the Nicolaitanes, which I also hate." By the time of the Pergamean period of the church, however, those "deeds" of some had become a system and a theology. "So hast thou also them that hold the doctrine of the Nicolaitanes, which thing I hate." What was just sporadic doctrine then has become a great system now.

The law of degeneration works in all the areas of life apart from the presence and power of God. Corruption, corrosion, rust, disintegration are the common lot of all created things. The sun, the rain and even the air itself are arms of destruction and disintegration. Even the stars grow old and worn out. So it is with spiritual life. Spiritual life has a tendency to degenerate, to go down, to lose its fresh thrust and spiritual power. It was so in the case of the churches of our Lord. They began in miraculous, heavenly unction, only to fall into the hands of that priestly class which lifts itself above the people and arrogates to itself the whole prerogatives of God to save and to forgive. For example, in III John the apostle says: "Diotrophes lifts himself above his brethren and will not receive our messengers." He uses the church and the people for his personal preferment, and he arrogates to himself authorities that are never deposited by God in the hand of a man. Such even in apostolic days were the deeds of the Nicolaitanes. In the Pergamean period of the church, those deeds had become a great system, a great teaching, held by the churches themselves. Priest-craft was supplanting the preacher of the Word of God; ceremony was taking the place of the regenerating power of the Holy Spirit; and the church had opened its heart to the love and the power and the emolument of the world. This was the doctrine of the Nicolaitanes.

All of these things came to pass in the days of the Pergamean church, after 300 A.D. The class distinction between clergy and laity grew ever wider. The church was no longer a company of believers, of saved, regenerated souls; but the church became a channel through which a sacramental and a hypothetical salvation was offered.

In the Old Testament, in Exodus 19:5 and 6, the Lord said to all Israel: ". . . if ye will obey me and keep my words . . . ye shall be unto me a kingdom of priests." What was conditionally offered to Israel was actually realized in the Christian church. Everyone became a priest of God, mediating the truth of the Lord. Peter said two things that undermined forever priestcraft, sacerdotalism and salvation by ritual and ceremonialism. The first, in I Peter 1:23-25, was this: "Being born again [saved, regenerated] . . . by the word of God." Not by baptism, not by ritual, not by sacramentalism, but "born again . . . by the word of God." "And this is the word that by the gospel is is preached unto you." The second thing that Peter said is in I Peter 2:5: "Ye . . . are . . . a spiritual house, an holy priesthood, a chosen generation, a holy nation, a peculiar people." The old day of the priest is gone. The veil is rent from the top to the bottom, and any man can go to God for himself anywhere. "Come boldly," the invitation says, "to the throne of grace and find help in the hour and the time of need." That is the true Christian faith. But in a relatively short time, in less than three hundred years, the shadow had become the substance. Gone were all of the spiritual liberties and endowments of the Christian household. The whole church was led back into the sacerdotalism, the priest-craft, the ceremonialism, the salvation by ritual, that had developed in the Judaistic system of the Old Testament dispensation.

THE STATE ESTABLISHED CHURCH

The establishment of the church, not upon the Rock of Christ, but upon governmental power and worldly favor under the oppressive hand of a ruling hierarchy was an amazing thing. It came to pass suddenly, quickly, in one great event. That one great event that married the church to the world and established it in the favor and popularity of the Empire under the iron heel of a privileged, sacerdotal class was the so-called conversion of Constantine, who became an unconverted and unbaptized Christian. In the early part of the fourth century A.D., the Roman Caesar died and left in question his successor. One of the contenders for the great place of imperial master of the civilized world was an able Roman general by the name of Constantine. In October of 312 A.D., at the Milvian Bridge near Rome, the armies were bivouacked on either side. The destiny of the Empire was to be decided the next day. That night Constantine, this Roman general who had been introduced somewhat to Christianity, made a vow saying that if he should be victorious on the morrow he would become a Christian. The next day, when the battle was joined, the traditionalists say that Constantine saw at noonday a flaming cross in the sky, and in that cross were written these Greek words: "En tauto niko." As someone else writes it, the words were Latin, "In hoc signo vinces." I cannot find what was written up there in the sky. Some say God wrote in Greek, "En tauto niko"; others say the Deity wrote in Latin, "In hoc signo vinces." In any event, the vision was supposed to have said, "In this sign conquer." Well, as you know, Constantine won the war, and Constantine became the sole Caesar of the Roman Empire. He embraced, nominally, the Christian faith, and immediately, like a clap of thunder, like the explosion of a meteor, like the snap of your finger, like the twinkling of an eye, the Christians were no longer persecuted. They were popular. Like boys in the presence of heavy drinkers, their heads were turned with the wine of the world.

The priests of Jupiter, of Juno, of Dionysius, of Bacchus, of Venus, and of Adonis, all had been paid out of the purse of Caesar. But now that Caesar was a Christian, the priests of the temples hastened to their baptism to remain on the imperial payrolls. They turned their idol-temples into churches, and they said, "These are no longer images of Jupiter or Juno or Venus; these are images of the saints." The same rituals by which they had worshiped Astarte, Aphrodite or Venus they now employed to worship the true Queen of Heaven. They bowed down in the same way, in the same ceremony, in the same temples, before the same idols, only now the idols were named after so-called Christian saints. Even the days by which the priests honored their gods were made days on the calendar to honor these saints. The astonishing thing took place overnight. Heretofore, humble homes and catacombs and dungeons had echoed with the hymns of God's children, whose singing was sometimes changed into shouts of the martyrs as they were dragged forth into the arena. All of that now was past. The rags of persecution were changed for the plush silk of the imperial palace. The Pergamean period of the church had begun.

What of the conversion of Constantine and what of that miraculous sign in the sky? That was the shrewdest political move that a man ever made in the history of power politics. The early church historian Eusebius said that the miracle actually happened; Constantine told him so. But Eusebius was about as gullible as any man who ever lived. Edward Gibbon, who wrote the great volume, *The Decline and Fall of the Roman Empire*, ridicules the story as a fable. It was Edward Gibbon who said, "To the people all religions were equally true; to the philosophers all religions were equally false, and to the politicians all religions were equally useful." Constantine was a shrewd politician. He saw an opportunity to gain his objective to be Caesar of the Roman Empire by employing the great might of those who were Christians, who by that time had pervaded the whole civilized world. Was he really saved, born again? Consider these things: First, he kept all of his heathen and pagan superstitions — all of them. Second, he planned to combine the worship of Christ with the worship of Apollo. For example, on his coins he would put the picture of Apollo and then the name of Christ. In the celebrated decree of March 321 A.D., when he ordained the observance of Sunday, he did it as "*Dies Solis,* the Day of the Sun." In 325 A.D., when he presided over the Council of Nicea, he was unbaptized. He came into the assembly of God's preachers as a pagan would, dressed in gold, studded with glittering gems. As he made his way to the golden throne, all of the people stood up in reverential awe and were seated only when first he was seated. He went to the assembly having murdered, brutally, his eldest son, one of the finest, ablest generals the Roman Empire ever produced. Such was Constantine. With him, with his glittering robes and jewels and infinite power as Caesar, Nicolaitanism triumphed. Thus arose "the princes" of the church.

The Monstrous System Today

This is not an ancient story but a monstrous system of error that girdles this globe to this day and to this present hour. Those princes arrogate to themselves the power to cast into hell, to forgive sin, to offer sacramental salvation; and their word "ex-communication" is to their people the word and sentence of death. That awful power they hold over their people strikes terror to their hearts when they even think of deviating from it. This is the doctrine of the Nicolaitanes, "Which thing," God says, "I hate." The doctrine of the Nicolaitanes is a doctrine of sacramental salvation. According to that doctrine, one is converted not by the power of the regenerating spirit of God through the acceptance of the saving message of Christ, but by an act of parliament. As you are born a citizen of the state, you are christened a member of the church. The world and the church become one and the same.

There is no fictional theology that mind could imagine that could be further from the great revelation of the truth of the New Testament than that system, "the doctrine of the Nicolaitanes, which thing I hate." It turned the church into the pawn of a political prize. Men courted it; men made concordats with it; men sought its favor and men, world without end, used it for personal preferment and for great unspiritual power. Just read the story of Cardinal Richileu; just read the story of a Cesare Borgia and his sister, Lucretia Borgia; just read the story of a Metropolitan of the church in Russia.

The day came in Russia when the people rose up and crushed the state church with a mailed fist. We face that horrible antipathy to the power of the church today in a supplanting system that parades its antagonism and its atheism across the horizon of our present world. All of this revolt had roots in the history of the church which formerly was used to suppress and subjugate the people. Do not forget that Stalin was trained as a priest in the Greek Orthodox Church. In this day and hour and age, there is a need, as high as heaven itself and as deep as the earth itself, to call our people back to a personal religion. We are saved not through some intermediator but through the great intercessor, Christ Jesus. Religion of the soul, religion of the heart, religion of the homes, religion of the people, the religion that saves, that calls to repentance and to faith is a great personal commitment to God. O Lord! if we are saved, if God shall spare us, our hope lies in those areas where men stand up and proclaim the simple truth of the redemption offered for our poor souls in the sacrifice and atonement of Jesus, a salvation that a man can receive for the taking and have for the asking.

Chapter 13

The Thyatiran Jezebel

And unto the angel of the church in Thyatira write; These things saith the Son of God, who hath his eyes like unto a flame of fire, and his feet are like fine brass; I know thy works, and charity, and service, and faith, and thy patience, and thy works; and the last to be more than the first. Notwithstanding I have a few things against thee, because thou sufferest that woman Jezebel, which calleth herself a prophetess, to teach and to seduce my servants to commit fornication, and to eat things sacrificed unto idols. And I gave her space to repent of her fornication; and she repented not. Behold, I will cast her into a bed, and them that commit adultery with her into great tribulation, except they repent of their deeds. And I will kill her children with death; and all the churches shall know that I am he which searcheth the reins and hearts: and I will give unto every one of you according to your works. But unto you I say, and unto the rest in Thyatira, as many as have not this doctrine, and which have not known the depths of Satan, as they speak; I will put upon you none other burden. But that which ye have already, hold fast till I come. And he that overcometh, and keepeth my works unto the end, to him will I give power over the nations; And he shall rule them with a rod of iron; as the vessels of a potter shall they be broken to shivers; even as I received of my Father. And I will give him the morning star. He that hath an ear, let him hear what the Spirit saith unto the churches. — Revelation 2:18-29

Heretofore, in the circle of the seven churches, we have been going north, from Ephesus to Smyrna to Pergamos. Now we are turning south and east in the great circle. The distance from Pergamos, the capital of the Attalid Kingdom and the capital of the Roman province of Asia, to Sardis, the capital of the ancient kingdom of Lydis, is about sixty miles. Halfway between them, thirty miles from Pergamos, thirty miles to Sardis, is this town of Thyatira. It is one of the oddest facts that the longest letter of the seven was written to the church in the least important of the cities. Pliny dismisses Thyatira with these contemptuous words: "Thyatira and other unimportant communities." Thyatira emerged into history in about 290 B.C. It was a military town. It was built as a sentinel block to guard the capital city of Pergamos. It was one of those outposts fated to fight a delaying action while the capital city was preparing for the attack — a town destined to be destroyed, to be rebuilt, to be destroyed again. In the days of the Roman Empire it came to some eminence as a commercial city. It was on a great trade route followed by the railroad that runs through it today. In ancient days it was the center of a wool and dyeing industry. Lydia was from this city of Thyatira. She was, as you know, a merchant princess dealing in purple. The ancients obtained that costly, precious dye of purple from two sources: one, from the madder root which grew around Thyatira; second, from a little seashell fish called the murex. From the throat of that tiny sea animal could be extracted one tiny drop of that precious dye. Pliny, the elder, says that one pound of it could not be bought for a thousand denarii. One denarius was an ordinary working man's one-day's pay. Lydia must have been a wealthy merchant princess, indeed, dealing in one of the most costly substances in the Roman Empire. Today, Thyatira is a little city of about twenty-five thousand people, their means of subsistence found in the weaving of Oriental rugs.

THE LORD INTRODUCES HIMSELF

As the Lord introduces Himself to these churches, the description of Himself is always pertinent. He introduces Himself to the church at Ephesus as the one who is walking among the seven lampstands. Then He says to Ephesus: "Except thou repent I will remove thy lampstand." He introduces Himself to Smyrna as the One who is the first and the last, who was dead and is alive again. He speaks thus to comfort those Smyrnian Christians in their great trial and agony of persecution. He had been through it Himself. He had been slain. He had been raised victorious. Then, in

His address to the church at Pergamos, He introduces Himself as the one who has a sharp two-edged sword. He then speaks of His warring with that sword against the doctrine and the deeds of the Nicolaitanes. So, to this church of Thyatira He introduces Himself: "These things saith the Son of God." The Lord uses this description because of a Jezebel who refers to herself as an oracle of God, an infallible authority, denying the Word of the Lord. Because of her claim to infallibility as an oracular prophetess, the Lord introduces Himself as the Son of God. Then He adds: ". . . who hath eyes like unto a flame of fire," penetrating into the deepest recesses of the heart. "His feet are like unto burning, burnished, flaming, molten brass." This letter, then, is going to be a letter of wrath because brass is a symbol of the wrath of the judgment of God. So the Son of God, whose eyes penetrate to the hidden secrets of the soul, is going to tread the winepress of the fierceness and wrath of the Almighty. The central theme of this letter is God's judgment upon this prophetess. She calls her works, "the deep things of God," but God calls them "the deep things of Satan."

It is an unusual situation: "Thou sufferest that woman Jezebel, which calleth herself a prophetess, to teach and to seduce my servants." Who is that Jezebel? Her name immediately takes us back to Israel. Ahab, the king, married a daughter of the King of Sidon whose name was Jezebel. When she came to live in the capital city of Samaria she brought her heathen gods with her, and she introduced into Israel its worst days of apostasy. She was a brilliant woman, an able woman, a zealous woman. She so slew the prophets of Jehovah, and she so swept Israel off its religious feet and she so subverted the doctrine of God that she brought the mighty prophet Elijah himself down to his knees as he fled before her face for his life and prayed that he might die. But who is this Jezebel of Thyatira who claims to be an oracle of God, a prophetess, and to deliver the infallible words of heaven, and who teaches and seduces God's servants? Who is she?

THE IDENTIFICATION OF JEZEBEL

Various commentaries and discussions offer some of the most fantastic identifications that mind could imagine. Here is one identification. In some ancient Greek manuscripts, by the side of that word translated "woman" there is a *sou* ("thy"). Now the Greek word for woman is *gune* which is also the Greek word for "wife." So some of those ancient Greek manuscripts read: "To the angel [to the pastor] of the church in Thyatira, I have this against thee, because thou sufferest thy wife, Jezebel [who claims she is a better preacher than you are and certainly more able] to seduce my servants." There are expositors who say that Jezebel was the wife of a pastor who subverted the good work of the man of God. However, the word *sou* ("thy") rests upon small textual evidence.

There is a second guess as to who this Jezebel was. In Thyatira was a famous oracle called the Sambathe. In it was a pythoness, a priestess, who was most famous, exerting a tremendous influence over the people. There are those who think she sought to bring her influence against the Christian faith and thus to destroy it. So they say that Jezebel was that pythoness. That supposition is not pertinent, however, because this Thyatiran Jezebel was on the inside of the church, not on the outside.

There are those who say that since this commercial city of Thyatira was organized into guilds, and since all of the commercial people belonged to guilds, and since every guild was dedicated to a patron god or goddess, there was opportunity for an influential woman, an able woman in the church, to teach the people that for them to belong to the guilds and to enter into the sacrifices and orgies that went along with oriental pagan, idolatrous worship, was altogether acceptable. A Christian could compromise and do both. This suggestion has some merit.

There are some expositors who identify Jezebel with Lydia. They say that Lydia could have come back to her home town of Thyatira and found that her business interests conflicted with her religious devotion; therefore she proposed a compromise. "Let us," she is supposed to have said, "serve God and also worship idols." So they say this Jezebel was Lydia. To me, such a conjecture is puerile and certainly religiously fantastic.

THE PROPHETIC MEANING OF JEZEBEL

But who was this Jezebel who called herself an oracle of God, a prophetess who spoke infallibly and who taught God's servants to turn aside from the revealed word of the Lord? Her identification is plain. This book is a book of prophecy, and these letters to the seven churches of Asia are imbedded in the heart of a book that refers to itself as "this book of prophecy." God is speaking here of a development in the church, in the age of the Thyatiran history of His people. The Ephesian period was the day of the apostles, the apostolic church. The Smyrnian period represented the church of persecution and tribulation, the church of the catacombs, when the heavy iron hand of the Roman Empire was upon it. The Pergamean church was the church of the establishment, when the church was married to the Roman government, no longer persecuted and no longer hated and despised, but now exalted and lifted up; the days when the pagan priests rushed to their baptisms as ministers now of the religion of the Caesar of the Roman Empire. Then follows the age of the church of Thyatira. She is dressed in purple and in silk, with golden chains around her neck, and she speaks as the infallible prophetess of God, subverting the word of the Lord Himself. Thyatira is the apostate church, who looks upon herself as the infallible oracle of the Almighty.

There are many reasons for this identification. The church is always represented by a woman. The church is always referred to as a "she" or as a "her," never as a "he" or a "him." The "Him" in our religion is the Great God and our Saviour, Jesus Christ. The church is always described as the Bride of Christ, espoused to Christ, subject to Christ. Paul said, "I suffer not a woman to teach or to usurp authority over the man": that is, the church is to be subject to Christ, the Word of God. So in this passage, when we see a woman, we see a figure of the church; and when that woman is called Jezebel, we immediately know that the Lord is speaking of an apostate church. When she claims for herself to be an oracle of God, a prophetess, who speaks the Word of God to replace the words of the Lord God Himself, then I know exactly what period of history He refers to. The church now is rich, dressed in purple and silk and gold, and she speaks as an oracle of God Himself, an infallible authority. What she teaches is a seduction of God's people from the plain, simple revelation of the words of the Lord in the Holy Scriptures.

Let us see how all of this interpretation fits together. Whenever the Bible is interpreted just as the Bible is, every piece of it will enmesh into a divine pattern. When all the pieces are placed together correctly, everything will fit perfectly. But if that is not done, we fall into expositional impossibilities. Let me explain how this pattern fits. When I turn to the parables of our Lord in the thirteenth chapter of the Gospel of Matthew, I find that the fourth parable is identical in meaning to Christ's letter to this fourth church. They are one and the same. This is the fourth parable: "The kingdom of heaven is like unto leaven, which a woman took, and hid in three measures of meal, till the whole was leavened." The letter to the fourth church: ". . . thou sufferest that woman Jezebel, which calleth herself a prophetess, [an oracle, an infallible authority] to teach and to seduce my servants [my own people]." The meaning is plain. The meal offering represents our Lord. He is the Bread of Life, he is the food from heaven, He is our staff and stay. The meal offering, the fine flour, represents the Word of God, the Bread of Life, the true manna from heaven. The woman took leaven, which is a symbol of corruption and evil, and placed it in the Word of God. That leaven corrupted the great truths of the doctrine of the Son of God. The leaven represents evil doctrine and teaching. This prophetess, this woman, this infallible oracle, delivers not the true message of God, but her own evil, corrupt doctrine. However the Bible may teach, *she* teaches thus and so; although the revelation of God may be very clear and very plain, *she* says this and that. The woman took that corruption, that false doctrine and teaching, and she seduced God's servants until the whole was leavened. All Christendom became corrupt, outside of the few who remained true to the faith. This is the parable of the loaves, and this is the Thyatiran Jezebel.

THE CORRUPTION OF THE WOMAN

The dream that the Gospel of the Son of God will ever convert the world is a fantastic thing out of man's imagination. It is not revealed in the Bible. In the thirteenth chapter of the Gospel of Matthew, there were four kinds of soil, and it was only one of them that produced for God. In the thirteenth chapter of the Gospel of Matthew, the tares grow with the wheat, and the leaven grows in the lump until the time of the end. There is never a time without tares. It is only in the days of the end, when God's judgment comes, that God separates the tares from the wheat and burns up the tares with unquenchable fire. They are both together until the end. There is never a time when the Gospel converts the world. This, the parable of the leaven teaches. Corruption and men's false doctrine enter into the truth of God and pervade it. The kingdom of heaven in the thirteenth chapter of the Gospel of Matthew refers to the kingdom here in this world as it is administered by men. It is what we call "Christendom," the great nations of the world who are called "Christian nations." This corruption works and it is furthered by this woman, Jezebel. God refers to what she teaches as "the depths of Satan." She, of course, would call what she teaches "the depths of God." "You cannot learn this Book for yourself," she says; "you must come to me and let me teach you the deep things of God." Man cannot read the simple Gospel for himself. He cannot listen to the Word of God and repent of his sins and trust Jesus and be saved. He must come and be instructed by lectures, classes, in the deep things of God. The Lord says, "I call their instruction the deep things of the devil, the deep things of Satan."

One stands in awe before the unfolding of prophecy as it has been written by the finger of God in this amazing Book. He says a thing will come to pass, and it comes to pass just as He has written it in the Book. This woman, Jezebel, subverts almost all Christendom — almost all of it. But there are a few, there is a minority, there are some who are faithful to the Lord and He says: "Unto you who have not this doctrine, who do not follow this teaching, unto you I have two words of reward. To you who overcome, you shall rule with a rod of iron and break as a potter the vessel into pieces." This passage in Revelation 2:27 is a quotation from the second Psalm.

There is a limit beyond which false doctrine and false teaching cannot go. Some day God Himself shall destroy that system. It is referred to thus: "I will cast her into a bed, and them that commit adultery with her into great tribulation . . . and I will kill her children with death." This judgment is described at length in the seventeenth chapter of the book of the Revelation when the scarlet whore who sets on the seven hills of Rome is destroyed. God will not put up forever with Jezebel and the seduction of His people. God will judge this woman who claims to be an infallible oracle, thereby perverting God's Word. God will give His people a great victory, a victory that is minutely delineated in the book of the Revelation.

But God has a second reward to the faithful: "And I will give him the morning star." In the twenty-second chapter of the book of the Revelation, the sixteenth verse, the Lord describes Himself: "I am the . . . bright and morning star." When Christ gives us the morning star, we have *Him*. The morning star is also the announcement of the dawn. If we have Christ and are with Him, then we have been caught away unto Him and shall appear when He appears in glory. Caught away with our Lord, the morning star! There, when the day dawns, with our Saviour, announcing the glorious consummation of the age! "He that hath an ear, let him hear what the Spirit saith unto the churches."

Chapter 14

Immortal Names in Sardis

And unto the angel of the church in Sardis write; These things saith he that hath the seven Spirits of God, and the seven stars; I know thy works, and thou hast a name that thou livest, and art dead. Be watchful, and strengthen the things which remain, that are ready to die; for I have not found thy works perfect before God. Remember therefore how thou hast received and heard, and hold fast, and repent. If therefore thou shalt not watch, I will come on thee as a thief, and thou shalt not know what hour I will come upon thee. Thou hast a few names even in Sardis which have not defiled their garments; and they shall walk with me in white: for they are worthy. He that overcometh, the same shall be clothed in white raiment; and I will not blot out his name out of the book of life, but I will confess his name before my Father, and before his angels. He that hath an ear, let him hear what the Spirit saith unto the churches. — Revelation 3:1-6

Sardis is the fifth church of the seven. In the great circle of the seven churches in Asia, the messenger carried the letter to Ephesus, then north to Smyrna, then further north to Pergamos; there he turned south and somewhat east to Thyatira and so down to Sardis. Sardis is about thirty miles from Thyatira, about sixty miles from Pergamos and east of Smyrna about fifty miles. Sardis is the name of one of the noblest and greatest and most storied of all of the cities of the East. For more than two thousand years, it was a famous city under successive empires. It first is introduced to us in glory and splendor as the capital of the ancient kingdom of Lydia, whose king was Croesus, whose name is a synonym for riches. But Sardis was not only famous for its rich men, it was also famous for its wise men. Thales, the first great Greek philosopher, was a citizen of Sardis. Solon, whose name is another name for a wise legislator, was for a while a resident of Sardis. When Xerxes prepared his mammoth conflict with the kingdom of Hellas, he massed his vast forces before Sardis.

One of the most brilliant and interesting of all the stories of ancient history is told by Herodotus, the first Greek historian, regarding the topography of Sardis. It concerns an incident which happened when Cyrus, king of the Medo-Persians, was besieging Croesus, shut up in the citadel of this capital city. Sardis was considered an impregnable fortress. It was built on the slope of Mount Tmolus, at the base of which ran the gold-bearing Pactolus River. Like a pier jutting out from Mount Tmolus was a ridge of rock with great cliffs on either side. On that pier of solid rock, precipitous and high, Sardis had built its impregnable citadel. When Cyrus besieged the city, he could not advance farther until first that fortress was taken. So the Persian general said that if any man would find a way to storm the fortress and overwhelm it, he would give large rewards. He had in his army a Mardian soldier by the name of Hyeroeades. This soldier was standing one day watching the cliff and the battlement on top and a Lydian soldier on top of the battlement. As he watched, the Lydian soldier accidentally dropped his helmet over the battlement and it fell down to the base of the cliff. The Lydian soldier climbed over the battlement and picked his way slowly to the base of the cliff to recover his helmet, and so climbed back to his place of sentinel duty. The Mardian soldier in his memory carefully watched as the Lydian came down and back up, and that night with a picked band of Persian soldiers, he made his way up to the height. It was absolutely unguarded, and Sardis fell into the hands of the Persians. Back of that story and that topography can be seen the emphasis of our Lord when He says, "Be watchful . . . if thou wilt not watch, I will come on thee as a thief."

THE SARDIAN CHURCH

The church in the city of Sardis is a church that "has a name to live and is dead." What an unusual thing! "I know thy works, that thou hast a name that thou livest, and art dead." The church was contaminated with the world, inward decay, spiritual disintegration and dry rot. In museums of natural history are the animals of America, lifelike in their natural habitat, mounted exactly as they lived; but they are dead. Almost every school child brought up in our modern grades is compelled to read somewhere in his English literature, *The Rhyme of the Ancient Mariner*. That poem reflects the strong imagination of Coleridge, its author. In the story, corpses of dead men rise to man the ship; dead men pull the oars, dead men hoist the sails, dead men steer the vessel. Preposterous though it seems, such a condition may obtain in Christ's churches: dead men in the pulpit, dead men filling the pew, dead men running the machinery, spiritually dead. "I know thy works, that thou hast a name that thou livest, and art dead."

But even when the drift of things is into decadence and disintegration, yet there is always a possibility of individual devotion and individual spiritual commitment. So it is that the Lord says here, "Thou hast a few names even in Sardis . . . who are worthy." These seven churches in this book of prophetic history are a foreview of seven great developing periods in the church: the Ephesian period in the days of the apostles, the apostolic church; the Smyrnian period, the church of martyrdom under the heavy hand of the Roman Empire; the Pergamean church, the church of the establishment; the Thyatiran church, the church when Jezebel leads God's people into illimitable apostasy, the church that clothes herself with scarlet and purple, with chains of gold, and looks upon herself as the prophetess, the infallible oracle of God; and now this, the fifth period, the church of the dark ages, with a name to live, yet dead. And yet, even in that dark time there were stars that shone in the hand of God. There were immortal names in Sardis of those who walked before God, worthy to overcome in the name of the living Christ.

There is never a time so dark but that the Lord has His stars, His men. In the dark days of the Antedeluvian period, there were righteous Enoch and God-fearing Noah. In the

days of the Imirs of Arabia, there was Job, God's best man
in all the East. In the tragic days of universal idolatry,
there was Abraham, called out of Ur of Chaldea. There was
a Lot even in Sodom. The Lord says, "In the midst of the
earth and the drought and the darkness of the dead church,
even in Sardis there are a few immortal names." The Lord
says, as He introduces us to them, "I am he that hath the
seven Spirits of God and the seven stars in my hand." The
Holy Spirit of God in any hour of darkness is able to illumi-
nate, to guide, and to comfort. "I am he that hath the seven
Spirits of God, the plenitude, the overflowing abundance of
the ableness of Almighty God. I am he that hath the seven
stars in my hand." Even in the dark age in the dead church
of Sardis, there were bright and brilliant stars shining in the
chalice of God's firmament. We are never to think that the
sky is so overcast that these stars never shine. Even in the
snow fields and in the ice rivers of the Alps and the Hima-
layas, one may find a solitary flower that blooms. There is
no wilderness in this earth so sterile and so barren that it
is without oases and springs and vegetation. I flew once
over the entire breadth of the Sahara Desert; and to my
surprise, as I watched, enraptured, hour after hour over
those burning sands, I saw great cloud formations and on
my left a vernal shower. So in the midst of the darkness
and the deadness of the church of God, there are His stars
that shine like luminaries in the sky.

SEVEN STARS THAT SHINE IN THE NIGHT

"Immortal names even in Sardis." I have picked out seven
of God's stars from the dark days of the Sardian church.
First, there was Peter Waldo. In 1170, on a street he heard
a Christian hymn. It interested him in the gospel message.
Being a wealthy merchant of Lyons, France, he was able
to hire two eminent scholars to translate for him the Word
of God. As he read the gospels, he was converted. Immediately, he began to preach the good news of Jesus Christ in
the city. He also had the Gospel translated into the vernacu-
lar of the people and had his followers, the Waldenses, to

give out copies. The Waldensian church began to sow the seed of the Word among the darkened, illiterate and superstitious people of central and southern Europe. God blessed them in their fervor and evangelism. Then in 1208, a horrible Papal "holy crusade" was inaugurated; and soon more than one million of the Waldensians and the Albigenses were wiped from off the face of the earth, cruelly persecuted, decimated, destroyed. One of God's seven stars was Peter Waldo.

In 1320, John Wycliffe, reading the Holy Book, translated it into the language of our English forefathers. John Wycliffe, with the Bible in his hand, taught his Lollard brethren to memorize the scriptures. They went up and down the highways of the English countryside preaching the unsearchable riches of the grace of God in Christ Jesus. Before the Church could seize him, John Wycliffe died. After he died and was buried, men dug up his body. They burned it publicly and scattered his ashes over the bosom of the River Swift. But the River Swift pours into the Severn, and the Severn pours into the Avon, and the Avon pours into the sea, and the sea laves the shores of the continents of the world. Thus John Wycliffe's Bible, his preaching and his writings were scattered abroad by the harsh hand of cruel oppression, for one does not destroy an idea or a gospel by blood and fire.

The teachings of Wycliffe spilled over into Bohemia; and there, in 1367, a man, a star, John Huss, read the scripture translation of John Wycliffe, read the writings of the English preacher, and having the fire and the furor of God's evangelist in his soul, began to preach the Gospel of the Son of God in Bohemia. Thousands turned and listened. Other thousands were converted. He was called before the church council of Constance. He was given a pledge and a signed covenant by the king for safe conduct as he left his city of Prague. But the Church said that no promise should be kept to a heretic. They sentenced him to be burned at the stake. They put a crown, a mitre, on his head and on it they wrote the words, "The Great Heretic." John Huss, as he made his way to the martyr's stake, said, "With joy I wear this crown of shame for the love of Him who wore the crown of thorns." As the flames began to roar, he sang a hymn and prayed a prayer. Though his lips continued to move, others could not hear what he said as the fierce fires began to flame upward to take the soul of the great preacher to the throne of grace in the heavens. One of God's stars was John Huss.

In 1452, was born Savonarola of Florence, one of the most flaming preachers who ever lived, one of the most eloquent, one of the mightiest of all the expositors of the Word of God who ever opened the sacred Book and expounded to the people, "Thus saith the Lord." The Papal legate came and denounced him before the council. Savonarola was condemned to be hanged and burned. In the city square of beautiful Florence, he was first hanged from the gallows and then burned with fire. One of God's stars was Savonarola.

The tenth day of March, 1928, a little band of Baptist people gathered in the square of Vienna. They held a service there in memory of the great preacher, Balthazar Hubmeir, who four hundred years before was burned at the stake by the Church in Vienna. After the memorial service in the square, the little band went to the blue waters of the Danube River and there laid a wreath on the bosom of the waters in memory of his faithful wife who had been drowned for her love and devotion to Jesus. Balthazar Hubmeir was a man who preached the Gospel out of the original Hebrew and Greek languages. God blessed him. In Moravia, year after year, he would baptize six thousand, eight thousand, ten thousand, twelve thousand — this great Baptist preacher of the unsearchable riches of the grace of the Son of God. Because of his preaching, men burned him at the stake and drowned his wife in the river. One of God's stars was Balthazar Hubmeir.

A contemporary of Balthazar Hubmeir was Felix Mantz, who lived in the city of Zurich. He was brought up under a learned father who, himself, was the minister of the great Cathedral in Zurich. The son, Felix, began to read the scriptures in the original languages and thus became a Baptist. In the fields, on the streets, in the home of his mother, he lifted his voice proclaiming and expounding the Word of God. People by the thousands began to listen and to turn. He was brought before the Council, and the church condemned him to death. As they marched him through the streets of Zurich, his faithful mother, walking by his side, exhorted her son to be faithful even unto death. Where the Lammont River in the city of Zurich pours out of the Zurich Lake, there they said to Felix Mantz: "So he likes water. Let's give him lots of water." They drowned him where the beautiful Lammont River pours out of the Zurich Lake. One of God's stars was Felix Mantz.

In 1628, was born John Bunyan. One of the most pathetic passages in all English literature is the famous writing of John Bunyan as he described his looking through the bars of his prison at this little blind girl, Mary, as she sold the laces that he had made to help support the preacher's family while for twelve years he languished in jail for preaching the Gospel of the Son of God. One of God's stars was John Bunyan.

Even in Sardis, in the days when the church was dead, "Thou hast a few immortal names." The Lord who said, "He that hath the seven spirits of God, [the plenitude of the grace and ableness of heaven]" also said, "And I hold my seven stars in my hand."

THE REWARD OF THE FAITHFUL

Observe the reward: "And they shall walk with me in white: for they are worthy . . . I will not blot out their name out of the book of life, but I will confess them before my Father, and before the holy angels." Three things are in the reward: First, ". . . I will not blot their names out of the book of life." The church, in terrible anathemas of excommunication, separated these saints from the family of God and consigned their souls to hell. When the Papal legate stood in the presence of the great Florentine, Savonarola, he lifted his hand and said, "And I separate thee from the church militant and from the church triumphant." Savonarola, before his martyrdom, replied, "From the church militant, yes; but from the church triumphant, never, for it is not in thy power so to do." From the church-roll in this life, yes; but from the church of the first-born whose names are written in glory, never. "For it is not in thy power so to do." "And I will not blot out his name out of the book which I have written." On the 21st day of October, 1617, Martin Luther was excommunicated from the church, and his soul consigned to everlasting hell and damnation. But God says, "I will not blot his name out of the book of life which I have written." Stars shine even in Sardis.

". . . and they shall walk with me in white." The ministry is referred to as "men of the cloth," of the vestment, men who have dressed like the minister. So, when the minister is excommunicated, he is defrocked. For example, the first thing they did to John Huss when they brought him to the stake and the flames began to rise, was to tear off his ministerial garb, the sign of his being a preacher of Christ. They tore off his ministerial clothing and threw it on the fire and burned it first. They may burn his raiment, but the Lord says: "I shall clothe them in white raiment and they shall walk with me." To the Jew white raiment was a sign of purity and holiness and devotion to God. To the Romans the white robe was no less meaningful. There were three classes of Romans: the Patrician, the Knight and the Plebe. The Patrician, the senator, wore a long garment of pure white, expressive of the dignity, the sublimity, of his calling and his office. God says, "I will clothe them in white. Defrock them, burn up their garments of ministerial attire, I shall clothe them in the purity and sublimity and dignity of the raiment of Almighty God." ". . . for they are worthy . . . I will confess their names before my Father, and his angels in heaven." These stars of God shine even in Sardis.

The Covenanters in Scotland were hunted and shot down like animals. Poor, humble people gathered together in their cottages to pore over the Scriptures, to pray to God, and to exhort one another in the faith. They were called Covenanters because they covenanted together to read the Book, to pray and to exhort one another in the faith. Isabel Weir was married to John Brown, the Covenanter. When he performed the ceremony, the minister said to Isabel: "Hold him close to your heart. But also keep close by a winding-sheet; you will need it." John Brown had twenty sheep. That was his living. But he loved God and into the humble homes of the people he went to read the Word, kneel in prayer and teach them the riches of our Lord. Men hunted and tracked him down. An emissary of the church by the name of Claverhouse took six soldiers to shoot him before his own humble cottage. They brought out his wife with a baby in her arms that she could witness the execution of her husband. John Brown asked if he might pray. He knelt down and prayed and then stood up fearlessly, courageously, as a man of God ought to stand. The soldiers lined up before him to execute him. They looked at the man of God, they looked at his noble, courageous wife and the little baby in her arms. All six of the men put down their muskets. "We cannot do it," they said. Claverhouse cursed them in the name of the Church, took his pistol, walked up to John Brown and blew out his brains. When the martyr fell in his own blood, the murderer turned to Isabel Brown and said, "And what do you think of your fine husband now?" Isabel Brown replied, "Sir, I thought much good of him in life and now much more in death." "For they are worthy . . . and I will confess their names before my Father, and before his angels."

Even in Sardis, in the dark ages, in the days of a dead and decadent church, God's stars announce the coming of a reformation, the infusion of new life and the glorious day of the Philadelphia church to whom Christ sends His next mesage, the church of missions and evangelization and brotherly love. So the message of hope and of salvation lives in fire and in blood. It lives today. O bless His name, we also are a part of and belong to that blessed company of God's immortal saints!

Chapter 15

The Open Door of Philadelphia

And to the angel of the church in Philadelphia write; These things saith he that is holy, he that is true, he that hath the key of David, he that openeth, and no man shutteth; and shutteth, and no man openeth; I know thy works: behold, I have set before thee an open door, and no man can shut it: for thou hast a little strength, and hast kept my word, and hast not denied my name. Behold I will make them of the synagogue of Satan, which say they are Jews, and are not, but do lie; behold, I will make them to come and worship before thy feet, and to know that I have loved thee. Because thou hast kept the word of my patience, I also will keep thee from the hour of temptation, which shall come upon all the world, to try them that dwell upon the earth. Behold I come quickly: hold that fast which thou hast, that no man take thy crown. Him that overcometh will I make a pillar in the temple of my God, and he shall go no more out; and I will write upon him the name of my God, and the name of the city of my God, which is new Jerusalem, which cometh down out of heaven from my God: and I will write upon him my new name. He that hath an ear, let him hear what the Spirit saith unto the churches. — Revelation 3:7-13

About 28 miles southeast of Sardis was the city of Philadelphia. As cities go, it was relatively new. It was founded in 140 B.C. by the king of Pergamos, Attalus II, whose other name was Philadelphus. The city was named Philadelphia after him. It is interesting how much the letter of our Lord to this sixth Asian church reflects the topography, the history and the situation of the city. Let us recount some of these references.

For one thing, the Lord says to the church, "Behold, I have set before thee an open door." Philadelphia was located where three great countries joined together. The ancient lands of Mysia and Lydia and Phrygia all bordered at Philadelphia. It was for that purpose that Attalus founded the city, that it might be a missionary city, Hellenizing (spreading Greek language and culture and literature and manners and way of life) the wild tribes of interior Phrygia.

Another thing is here reflected in the letter from the life of the city: "Him that overcometh will I make a pillar in the temple of my God." It was a magnificent custom in Philadelphia that if a magistrate, a civic servant, a benefactor or a philanthropist had done some unusual thing, some noble thing, the citizens would honor him by placing a great pillar in one of their temples with his name inscribed upon it. Such a commemoration thus became a perpetual memorial for the great man whom the city delighted to honor.

Then our Lord says again: "And he shall go no more out." Philadelphia was located before a vast, volcanic field, and was itself subject constantly to severe earthquakes. Many times the whole city would be destroyed by the tremors. When those quakes came the people fled for fear. But here Christ speaks of the perpetual, everlasting, eternal security that we have in Him. Again our Lord says: "And I will write upon him the name of . . . the new city . . . new Jerusalem." In 17 A.D., one of those earthquakes destroyed the city completely, the same earthquake that destroyed Sardis. Tiberius at that time was the Caesar of the Roman Empire. What Tiberius did for Sardis in rebuilding it, he also did for Philadelphia. In gratitude for this kindness, Philadelphia renamed their city Neo-Caesarea, "the new city of Caesar." It reverted to its old name in later years, but the incident in history corresponds with the words of Christ to this city: "And I will write upon him the name of . . . the new Jerusalem."

Philadelphia was the last bastion of Christianity when Asia Minor was overrun by the Islamic Turks. One of the most interesting commentaries upon prophecy and the Word of God is to be found in the works of the famous historian, Edward Gibbon. This is a quotation from him as he speaks of the seven churches of Asia:

> In the loss of Ephesus, the Christians deplored the fall of the first angel and the extinction of the first candlestick of the Reve-

lation. The desolation is complete and the temple of Diana, or the church of Mary, will equally elude the search of the curious traveler. The circus and the three stately theaters of Laodicea are now peopled with wolves and foxes. Sardis is reduced to a miserable village. The God of Mohammed without a rival or a son, is invoked in the mosques of Thyatira and Pergamos. The populousness of Smyrna is supported by the foreign trade of the Franks and Armenians. Philadelphia alone has been saved by prophecy or courage. Among the Greek colonies and churches of Asia, Philadelphia is still erect, a column in the scene of ruins.

It is to this day largely a Christian town. Our Lord had nothing but words of commendation for Smyrna, the martyr church. He had almost nothing but words of commendation for this missionary church of Philadelphia.

Each one of these churches represents great periods and eras in the history and development of Christendom. The Ephesian church is the church of the apostles, the apostolic church of Peter, Paul, James and John. The Smyrnian church is the church of martyrdom and trial and persecution, oppressed under the heavy hand of the Roman Empire. It is the church of the catacombs. The Pergamean church is the church of the establishment, when it was married to the authority and power of the Roman Empire. The Thyatiran church is the church of so-called oracular infallibility, wrapped in gorgeous robes of purple and scarlet and gold, speaking forth as the prophetess of God. The Sardian church is the church of the dark ages in whom are found the burning, shining stars of the Reformation, immortal names that Christ has lighted to shine forever in the galaxies and the glories of His people. The Philadelphian church is the church of our closing era. The Philadelphian church is the church of the missionaries; it is the church of the evangelists; it is the church of the Bible societies; it is the church of the soul winners; it is the church of the world-wide preaching of the Gospel of the Son of God. "And unto the angel of the church in Philadelphia write: These things saith he that is holy, he that is true, he that hath the key of David, he that openeth, and no man shutteth; and shutteth, and no man openeth . . . behold, I have set before thee an open door."

This text describes great opportunities of the age in which our fathers have lived, and to some extent, the age in which we now live.

THE CHURCH OF THE OPEN DOOR

"I have set before thee an open door." That door is Christ, personally. In the tenth chapter of John, our Lord says: "I am the door: by me if any man enter in, he shall be saved, and shall go in and out, and find pasture." Like a cared-for-sheep, finding pasture and grass and life and water for thirst and guidance and security in the love of the shepherd, we are within our Lord's remembrance. "I am the door."

The beautiful passage here in Revelation 3:7, "I have the key of David; [I am] he that openeth and no man shutteth; and shutteth, and no man openeth," is a quotation from Isaiah 22:22, which itself is a characterization of Eliakim, the steward of King Hezekiah. The noble, trusted man was given the key to the palace. No one came to approach the king except through Eliakim. So it is with us in Christ. There is an open door to God in our Saviour and no man can shut it. No man! Were we in prison, we would still have access to God. In illness, in death, in life, in youth, in age, in trouble, in sorrow, or on the highest pinnacle of gladness and achievement, always in Christ there is an open door to God, and no man can shut it. The door of prayer and intercession, of asking, is always open. "Come boldly," said the author of Hebrews, "come boldly and find grace to help in time of need." There is an open door.

This Philadelphia church is the open door of testimony and witness and soul-winning. Any man, anywhere, is endowed with the God-given privilege to invite to faith and salvation in the redemptive mercy of Christ. This is an open door God has set before us. A man, moved by the Spirit, went to the great London preacher, Charles Haddon Spurgeon, and said: "Mr. Spurgeon, I have it in my soul to win people to Christ. What shall I do?" Mr. Spurgeon asked: "What is your job? What do you work at?" The man replied: "I drive an engine. I'm an engineer on the railroad." Spurgeon said, "Is your fireman a Christian?" The man replied,

"I don't know." Mr. Spurgeon said, "Go back and find out and start with him." This is the kind of open door all around us. This is the Philadelphian church. Is your friend a Christian? Invite him, ask him, after calling him by name in private prayer. In how many ministries has God given to us illimitable opportunities! There is an opportunity with children. There is an opportunity with young people. There is an opportunity with adults. Oh, how many facets and in how many areas are there opportunities to serve God! "Behold, I set before thee an open door."

The Philadelphian church describes the illimitable opportunities that God gave to His people in the Philadelphian age, the great missionary age of His church. I know we are getting close to the end of this Philadelphian era because the doors are beginning to close. We can no longer go to Russia and preach the Gospel openly there. We can no longer go to China and preach the Gospel openly there. The doors are beginning to close in India and Africa and in other sections of this earth. I was in India some years ago. My companion and I had been asked to seek visas for our missionaries to enter India. The request was denied. We have no Southern Baptist missionary in India. The doors are beginning to close. But in the Philadelphian era of the Christian church every nation and the hearts of all the people of the earth were open to the gospel message. Oh, the illimitable opportunity that the people of Christ had in this great missionary story of His churches!

In 1792, William Carey went before his brethren and pleaded for the world-wide cause of missions. The moderator of the Baptist association said: "Sit down, young man. Sit down. When God wants to convert the heathen, He will do it without your help or mine." But the Lord said, "Behold, I will make them to come and worship before thy feet and to know that I have loved thee." Our people today look back in amazement that the moderator and learned pastors in our communion in England should look askance and in disdain upon a young minister of the Gospel whose heart burned for the salvation of the lost of the world.

When Carey went to India, the East India Company interdicted his presence in the part of India governed by England. He was forced to leave. Eighteen miles up the Ganges River, in the Danish colony of Serampore, there he built his schools and his college and sent out his preachers with the Gospel of the everlasting Son of God. "I will make them to come and worship before thy feet and to know that I have loved thee. . . ." The great commerce of the English-speaking world has followed in the steps of the missionary. Today there would not be a Christian businessman of acumen and understanding in the earth who would not know that the best thing that could happen for a nation and its commercial life is the evangelization of the tribes and races within its borders. This is the Philadelphian church of the open door.

A like thing happened with our great American missionary, Adoniram Judson. In 1813 he was interdicted in India because of the East India Company. He then went down to Rangoon in Burma, where for six years he labored without a convert. But God was in him and with him. In that terrible war of 1824-1826 between England and the Burmese, Adoniram Judson was placed in prison, filthy and vile, and was fettered down with five pairs of chains, sick with fever, suffering from the excruciating heat of the jungles. He was almost destroyed by the terrible treatment of his keepers. He was fed, nurtured and kept alive by his faithful wife, Ann Hasseltine. But he lived to see the day when the Lord turned thousands of natives to the saving faith in Christ Jesus. We have not time to recount the stories of these incomparable heroes of the cross whose illustrious exploits glow on the pages of human time and history. It is the great open door of the Philadelphian church.

THE LORD'S PROMISES TO OVERCOMERS

Look briefly now at the reward God has promised: "Because thou hast kept the word of my patience, I also will keep thee from the hour of trial [*peirasmos*, translated here "temptation," but a better translation is "trial"] that is com-

ing upon all of the world, and on them that dwell upon it."
In Luke 21 the Lord admonishes us to pray that we might
be delivered from that great hour of trial that is coming
upon the earth. Through the sweep of all time, there are
three great ages: the present one, the one that is to come,
and in-between the day of the Lord, the day of trial and
tribulation. This is the day that is described in the book
of the Revelation. As we come to the end of chapter three
and begin chapter four, we come to that great hour of the
judgment and fury and wrath of Almighty God. "Because
thou has kept my word, I also will keep thee from the hour
of trial and tribulation." God will take His people out and
away. "Behold I come quickly," the Lord says of the approaching time of the denouement and the consummation of
all history. But not one of God's little ones will perish or
will have to go through the flame and the fire of those days
of judgment. "Because thou hast kept my word, I also will
keep thee from [take thee out of] the great hour of trial."

"I will make him a pillar in the temple of my God." What
magnificent imagery! It is beyond anything into which
we can enter. John says that in the new Jerusalem, in the
heavens above us, he saw no temple, for the Lord God and
the Lamb are the temple therein. How can you enter into
such imagery? In heaven, in the new Jerusalem, there is no
movable temple like that erected by Moses, nor is there a
fixed, perishable temple like that built by Solomon. But the
Lord God and the Lamb are the temple. When He says
we are to be a pillar in the temple of God, He is saying that
in heaven God's people have an eternity with God Himself.
What is a pillar? It is for strength, it is for adornment, it is
for beauty, it is for commemoration. For example, the church
is called "the pillar and ground of the truth." The church
is for conspicuousness, for perspicuity, that Christ might be
seen always in the view of men. Peter and John and James
(the Lord's brother, the pastor of the church at Jerusalem)
in Galatians 2 were called "pillars" of the church. So God
has chosen us in the eternities of the eternities to be the
witness of, to be an adornment to, to be the commemora-

tion of His grace and His love and His mercy. Never forget that man was created in the first instance to be the image and the likeness and the expression and the glory of God. In that new Jerusalem, we are the adornment and the embellishment and the expression of all that God is, love and mercy and grace and beauty and holiness, world forever and without end.

We are to be "pillars" and "we shall go no more out." In the courses of the priests, death took them out of their ministries. Even our first parents were driven out, there beyond Eden to water the ground with their tears and their sweat and to be buried beneath its sod. But in the new Jerusalem we shall "go no more out."

"And I will write upon him the name of my God, and the name of the city of my God, which is new Jerusalem." In the Revelation, as he looked on the saints in glory, John said, "And his name was written in their foreheads." Like the high priest of old, we also shall have the dignity of his high office, carrying with it the right of access to God forever. We shall see His face and live. And we shall be citizens of the new Jerusalem. In the eleventh chapter of the book of Hebrews, Abraham saw the city which hath foundations, whose builder and maker is God, and in the same chapter we are told: "Wherefore God is not ashamed to be called their God for He hath prepared for them that city," the new Jerusalem. We shall be citizens of the new and heavenly kingdom.

"And I will write upon him my new name." I know some of our Lord's old names: "And his name shall be called Wonderful, Counselor, The Mighty God, The Everlasting Father, The Prince of Peace" (Isaiah 9:6). I know some of His old names: "Thou shalt call His name Jesus for He shall save His people from their sins." And in the glory that is to come he does not lay these names aside. He will continue to be known by His old names. In the second chapter of Philippians: "Wherefore God hath also highly exalted him, and given him a name which is above every name: That at the name of *Jesus* every knee should bow, of things in heaven, and things in earth, and things under the earth." He never lays aside His old names. But there are also achievements, victories and triumphs of which man has never heard or dreamed, to be accorded to our Lord Jesus. Oh, the fulness of the riches of His grace! For example, in the nineteenth chapter of the book of the Revelation, John sees Christ the Conqueror, and calls Him "the True" and "the Faithful" and "the Word of God" and "the King of Kings and the Lord of Lords." In that one little passage are all those marvelous names. Then John adds: "And he had a name . . . that no man knew, but he himself." There are worlds and universes and infinite areas in which our Lord Christ shall live and reign triumphantly beyond anything that a man can imagine. These conquests also are ours. We are hid with Christ in God, from grace to grace and from glory to glory, until the fulness of our Lord is the fulness of His people and we and He are one, world without end. Oh, the blessedness of it all! Amen.

Chapter 16

The Laodicean Church

And unto the angel of the church of the Laodiceans write;
These things saith the Amen, the faithful and true witness,
the beginning of the creation of God; I know thy works, that
thou art neither cold nor hot; I would thou wert cold or hot.
So then because thou art lukewarm and neither cold nor hot,
I will spue thee out of my mouth. Because thou sayest, I am
rich and increased with goods, and have need of nothing; and
knowest not that thou art wretched, and miserable, and poor,
and blind, and naked; I counsel thee to buy of me gold tried
in the fire, that thou mayest be rich; and white raiment, that
thou mayest be clothed, and that the shame of thy nakedness
do not appear; and anoint thine eyes with eyesalve, that thou
mayest see. As many as I love, I rebuke and chasten: be
zealous therefore, and repent. Behold, I stand at the door and
knock: if any man hear my voice, and open the door, I will
come in to him, and will sup with him, and he with me. To
him that overcometh will I grant to sit with me in my throne,
even as I also overcame and am set down with my Father in
his throne. He that hath an ear, let him hear what the Spirit
saith unto the churches. — Revelation 3:14-22

In the great circle by which the messenger carried these
seven letters from our Lord to each one of the separate
congregations, we have come to the last, the most south-
easterly. The background, the topography and the history
of the city are most evident in this letter. The very name,
"Laodicea," is rich in meaning. It was founded by Antiochus
II who named it after his wife, Laodicea. It was located at
the narrow glen of the Lycus Valley where it pours into the
Maeander river, which river runs through Ephesus. It was
founded because it controlled the entrance into the interior
province of Phrygia.

The churches of the Lycus Valley were among the most
famous of all the ancient Christian world. There were four

of them: Hierapolis on the north side of the Lycus; Laodicea on the south side of the Lycus; then about fifteen miles further east up the river, there was Colossae; and a little further up was Apamea. There is a most interesting reference to the churches in these cities at the close of the letter of Paul to Colossae. For example, in speaking of Epaphras, who had evangelized them, Paul says: "I bear him record, that he hath a great zeal for you at Colossae and for them at Laodicea . . . And when this epistle [the one that he is writing to the church at Colossae] is read among you, cause that it be read also in the church of the Laodiceans; and that ye likewise read the epistle from Laodicea." So this church and the valley in which it was located belong to a famous group of ancient Christian churches. Papias was doubtless the pastor at Hierapolis when this Revelation was written. Both Papias and Polycarp, who was pastor at Smyrna, were disciples of John, the aged pastor at Ephesus, who wrote the Revelation. Archippus was pastor at Colossae, in whose congregation was Philemon, the wealthy slave-owner, and Onesimus, his runaway slave whom Paul won to Christ and sent back to Colossae no longer a slave but a brother beloved.

THE CITY REFLECTED IN THE CHURCH

Our Lord draws from the topography of the country when He says: "Thou art neither cold nor hot . . . because thou are tepid [lukewarm] . . . I will spue thee out of my mouth." In the district around Laodicea and Hierapolis were hot mineral springs. As long as the water is boiling hot, one is somewhat able to get it down. But if you have ever tried to drink tepid, lukewarm mineral water, it is of all things most nauseating and ill-tasting. So our Lord uses the background of those hot mineral springs, cooled off and making the drinker sick.

Then He says: "Thou sayest, I am rich." From the beginning Laodicea was a success story. It was not ancient, as oriental cities go. It was founded by Antiochus in 250 B.C. But every one of those Selucid kings (and you remember when Alexander's empire was divided by his generals into four parts, the Selucids took Syria and Palestine), in building a city (and they built many), offered free citizenship to the Jews to entice them to come and to live in the new area. The reason was that the Jews brought trade with them. Trade meant wealth, commerce, banking and manufacturing. That was especially true of Laodicea. We know, for example, when this letter was written how many Jews lived in the country.

It is a strange thing how we can find out. In 62 A.D., in the same generation in which this Revelation was written, Flaccus, who was the Roman governor of the province of Asia, made an interdiction. It sounds modern. Flaccus interdicted the export of any more gold out of the province. They were running out of gold, and they needed to keep it in order to bolster their currency. Does not that sound like modern United States, trying to keep its gold supply in order to keep our money sound? Well, Flaccus did that in 62 A.D. As you know, all over the civilized world, once a year every male Jew above twenty-one years of age sent one-half shekel to the temple in Jerusalem to support the worship of Jehovah there. In order not to have too heavy a package, the money was sent across the sea in gold. However, the Jews in the district around Laodicea proposed to disregard the ban of the governor against the export of gold and to send their contributions in gold, anyway. The governor promptly seized it and confiscated it. It weighed twenty pounds. Twenty pounds of gold is fifteen thousand drachmas. Each adult male Jew had to send one-half shekel. One-half shekel would be two drachmas. So each male Jew had to send, in Roman currency, two drachmas to the temple. If there were fifteen thousand drachmas represented in that twenty pounds of gold, divide fifteen thousand by two to arrive at the number of adult male Jews in Laodicea. Fifteen thousand divided by two is seven thousand five hundred. There were seven thousand five hundred adult Jewish men above twenty-one years of age who lived in and around Laodicea at the time this Revelation was written. That is a great population of Jewish familes. Wherever so many Jews work and build and trade, there is always an accumulation of riches.

Another instance of the wealth of Laodicea can be seen in the story of the life of Cicero. When Cicero made his extensive trip through the East in 61 A.D., he cashed his letters of credit in the great banking center of Laodicea. Another instance of the wealth of the city can be seen in the description of Tacitus as he speaks of Laodicea when it was destroyed by earthquake in 60 A.D. The citizens refused the help of the Emperor, the reigning Caesar, and rebuilt their city themselves.

Another background of the city reflected in the letter can be seen when the Lord admonishes them to buy white raiment "that thou mayest be clothed, and the shame of thy nakedness do not appear." Laodicean wealth came in no small part from the garment industry in the city. They had a breed of sheep raised in that district that was different from any other in the world. The wool of the sheep was black and its glossy, raven-colored beauty was superior to any other to be found in the world. Laodicea manufactured four different kinds of garments, one being an outer garment, which they called a "trimata," similar to a toga. Sometimes Laodicea is referred to as Trimataria, so famous was it for this manufactured cloth.

One other thing our Lord refers to in the background of the city: ". . . and anoint thine eyes with eyesalve, that thou mayest see." There was a medical center in Laodicea, and one of the things manufactured and exported, among other medicinal products, was a "Tephra Phrygia" which was a tablet bought all over the Roman Empire. The users crushed it and put it on their eyes in order to heal any eye ailment.

This is an interesting city and an interesting church, but most of all, it is meaningful for us because it represents the last of the churches. What will the churches be like when our Lord comes again? The church at Laodicea represents the last period in church history. The Laodicean church is the church of the end. That fact makes every syllable of

what God says to this church very important and pertinent
to us. What is it like, this church of the end-time, when the
Lord shall come and knock at the door; what is it like? It
is like everything bad. This is the only church of which God
has nothing good to say. To all of the others, there is something that greatly appeals to the Lord. To one of the
churches, the Smyrnian church, He had nothing but good
to say. Of the great Philadelphia outreach, the church of
missions and evangelism, He had almost everything good to
say. There is only one of these churches for which He has
nothing to say in the way of commendation and encouragement, and that is the church of the Laodiceans. Of the last
age of the church, He finds nothing good at all. Let us look
at it more closely.

Not Cold, Not Hot, But Lukewarm

First of all, the Laodicean church is a lukewarm church
— not cold, not hot. It is vastly indifferent. It is indifferent
to doctrine and to truth and to the teaching of God. To
the Laodiceans, one church was about as good as another.
Why find yourself exercised over any difference between
religions? Is not one just about as good as another? Passing
for Christianity, there is a "goodishness" that is insipid and
that makes our Lord sick. The "goodishness" that poses as
Christianity is a sort of civic betterment program; a sort of
"pay your debts and don't kill anyone" teaching; a sort of
"love your mother" attitude. It is a maudlin sentimentality
that is supposed to be the Christian faith. It makes God sick.
Such religionists are lukewarm, indifferent to the great
fundamental truths that God reveals in His Book.

This Laodicean church was not only lukewarm and indifferent about the great truth and doctrine of God, but its
members did not even know the truth and the doctrine of
God. So today one may accost almost any Christian and ask
him any simple question about God, about the Bible and
about the revelation of Christ, and he has no idea what to
answer. The Laodiceans were untaught and mostly did not
care. What does the church believe? What does it stand for?

What is its teaching? What is its goal? It does not matter particularly, just so there is a "goodishness" identified with the name — such was the Laodicean church.

Indifferent to commitment, the Laodicean church was that queer kind of a hybrid that worshiped Baal and Jehovah at the same time. It worshiped God and mammon at the same time. So today, men try to worship Christ and the world at the same time. I am simply overwhelmed by the identity of God's people with the world. I cannot, for the most part, see any difference in them. Recently I heard a distinguished lecturer tell of a student over here from a Communist land who had said that the most overwhelming thing to him was that he could not tell a Christian from one who is not a Christian. "They both look alike to me," he said. Such was the lukewarmness of the church of Laodicea. The lukewarm church lives in the world, is a part of the world, worships and loves the same things that the world does. One cannot tell the difference between such a church and the world.

The Laodicean church was indifferent in devotion, in zeal, in energy, in whole-souled earnestness. To the Laodiceans, in their tepid, in-betweenness and their spiritual lukewarmness, to be enthusiastic about God and Christ and His work would seem to be offensive to cultivated tastes. We are enthusiastic about everything else. At the Cotton Bowl the whole thing rocks from side to side as one of the teams makes a touchdown. We are enthusiastic about entertainment or emoluments or advancements or art or literature or a thousand things. But when it comes to Christ and religion and the church, there is no enthusiasm, no zeal, nothing but deadness of soul and heart. How earnest this world is! Military armies are in earnest, business is in earnest, the whole world is busy in hand and heart and mind. But God's people are apathetic and lethargic, lukewarm. Such was the Laodicean church. But there is no religion without enthusiasm. Religion is a fire in the bones. It is a moving in the soul. It is a stirring of the heart. It is a vast, illimitable commitment of life. If it is not that, we do not have it.

Another characteristic of the Laodicean church is that it

was self-deceived. I cannot imagine how people could be persuaded of such good things about themselves as was the Laodicean church. Self-deceived! They said, "We are rich"; Christ said, "You are poor." They said, "We have increase in goods to make us happy"; Christ said, "You are wretched and miserable." They said, "We have need of nothing"; Christ said, "You are blind and naked." Strangely enough, in proportion to their lukewarmness, they were filled with self-content and self-satisfaction, as much as to say: "We do not need God; we do not need man; we do not need anything; we are complete and self-sufficient in ourselves." I do not know a more common attitude in this world today than that of humanism: "We can do it without God. We do not need to pray; we do not need to cry to God; we do not need to repent; we do not need to turn; we do not need to ask. All we need to do is just get our scientists at work, get the human energies of our great people hitched up to these great programs, and we will work out all these things ourselves. We do not need anything. We are self-sufficient and self-content." Such was the spirit of the Laodicean church.

CHRIST ON THE OUTSIDE

Observe another thing, a last characteristic, an astonishing thing: Christ is on the outside, knocking. He is on the outside of the Laodicean church. He has been gone a long time. The ages and the centuries have witnessed the development, the progress and the regress of His church. During all of that vast story, the Lord has been gone. Now He comes back. Is the door open to receive Him? Is He there with His people? No. He is on the outside. This is the end of the age. The words Christ speaks are, "I will come in to him, and will sup with him." The last meal of the day before the dawn was *deipnon. Deipneo* would be to eat that last supper and that is the word used here: "I will come in and eat supper [*deipnew*] with him." The next thing is the dawn. This is the coming of our Lord, and the next thing is the dawn of the new creation of God. But when He comes, He is on the outside. He is not on the inside of the church. He is "out

there." What a tragedy and what a sadness! When the Lord
came the first time (John 1:11), He was refused by His
people: "He came unto his own, and his own received him
not." But how infinitely more sad when the Lord shall come
back to the earth and, according to Luke 18:8: ". . . when
the Son of man cometh, shall he find faith on the earth?"
Will there be anyone watching, will there be anyone believing, will there be anyone waiting, in true devotion, the
appearing of Christ Jesus? He is on the outside; He is not
inside.

Let us sum up the blessedness of this hope we have in
our Lord. One of the most striking of all of the things said
by our Lord to His churches is this: "If any *man* hear my
voice . . . I will come in to *him* . . . To *him* that overcometh
will I grant to sit with me in my throne . . . *He* that hath
an ear, let *him* hear what the Spirit saith unto the churches."
The letters, like this to Laodicea, are addressed to congregations, to ministers and to churches; but always the appeal
is to the individual heart, to the individual soul. The Lord,
as He speaks to His congregations, to His people, to His
churches and to His ministers, rebukes, counsels, exhorts,
threatens. But when He makes appeal, it is always addressed
in the singular, to the individual. "*He* that hath an ear, let
him hear what the Spirit saith unto the churches." The appeal is always in the singular. "If any *man* hear my voice . . .
To *him* that overcometh . . . be *thou* faithful unto death
[*thou, singular*] be *thou* faithful unto death and I will give
thee [singular] the crown of life." What an impressive thing!

It is the duty of the individual Christian to hear. We
cannot cover ourselves or hide ourselves under the great
blanket of the vast congregations of Christendom. The faith
is individual. That fact is the very genius of the Christian
religion. What is said to the churches and what is addressed
to the congregations must be individually heard by the
people, each one. Like the great wall of the temple, the
church of God is built one stone at a time. So the burden
of the prophet to the nation: "Yet if one will repent, he
shall be saved." Hearing is always individual. The word,

the sermon, the message of God may be addressed to the congregation; but the only way that the congregation hears is through the individual soul, each one. As each man must eat for himself, sleep for himself, so each soul must repent for himself. He must trust God for himself. Each man shall some day die for himself and be judged for himself. Although the address may be to the congregation, always it is the individual who is to hear, who is to repent, who is to turn, who is to be zealous, who is to overcome, who is to be judged, who is to be saved. "*He* that hath an ear, let *him* hear what the Spirit saith unto the churches." "To *him* that overcometh."

The promise of our Lord to the believing soul is this: "To him that overcometh will I grant to sit with me in my throne, even as I also overcame, and am set down with my Father in his throne." There are two thrones. One is God's throne, the Father's throne, the throne of the essential, absolute, invisible, Deity, the throne of the Omnipotence of God. High above the highest heavens does God sit upon His throne. Invisible, unapproachable, omnipotent, eternal. Christ as God and co-regent with the Father is set down in the Father's throne, unapproachable, awesome, removed. But there is another throne. There is Christ's throne, the throne of our Lord, the throne of Him who was the Son of Mary, who was the son of David, who was the son of Abraham, who was the son of Adam, our brother, made in the likeness of men, with flesh and bone, such as we are. He shall have a throne some day. He shall be our visible king, our reigning Lord, and all of the power of kingdom and empire will be in His hands. And in that day we shall reign with Him, according to the Word of God. Remember the words of our Lord to a faithful servant: "Thou hast been faithful, be thou ruler over ten cities; thou hast been faithful, be thou ruler over five cities."

I do not know where the idea came from that in glory we are going to rest in eternal idleness, to luxuriate in nothingness and emptiness. It would bore me to death to contemplate such a prospect. There is no such idea as that in the Word of God. We are going to have an intense life and share with Christ in the rulership of the whole universe. We shall judge angels, the Bible says. We shall sit with our Lord upon His throne and judge the saints, He says. We shall have great cities to govern, planets to visit and congregations to preach to, and all of us shall be worshiping God and serving the Saviour. We do not know what is included and what is entailed in what God hath in store for His people. But it will be wonderful beyond compare. "He that hath an ear, let him hear what the Spirit saith unto the churches."

Chapter 17

Christ Knocking at the Door

Behold, I stand at the door, and knock: if any man hear my voice, and open the door, I will come in to him, and will sup with him, and he with me. — Revelation 3:20

Our text is the third chapter of the book of the Revelation, the tenderly beautiful and precious passage in Revelation 3:20: "Behold I stand at the door, and knock: if any man hear my voice, and open the door, I will come in to him, and will sup with him, and he with me."

That is an unusual text because of the place in which it is found. Of the seven churches in Asia, our Lord had words of commendation for everyone of them except this one, Laodicea. For the last and the seventh church He had no other words but severity and rebuke and condemnation. No word of approval is to be found in His letter to the Laodiceans. Yet, in the midst, in the very heart, of this severe rebuke is this compassionate text. It is as though one found a lovely flower in a vast, burning, searing desert. It is as though one heard a mockingbird sing on a bleak, cold wintry morning. This text, loving, gentle, tender, is strangely in the midst of a severe condemnation and rebuke.

It is an amazing text because of its presentation of our Lord as being very near. It is Jesus, the Christ, who has come our way, who is at the door. What a wondrous Visitor! What an astounding reality that it should be our Lord Christ who has come, who is near, who is even knocking at our door! Consider His kingly presence. The first chapter of the Revelation describes Him: "I turned to see the voice that spake with me. And being turned, I saw . . . in the midst of the seven lampstands one like unto the Son of man [then this description], clothed with a garment down to the foot, girt about the breast with a golden girdle [the King of

177

Glory]. His head and his hairs were white . . . white as
snow: and his eyes were as a flame of fire; And his feet . . .
as though they burned in a furnace; and his voice as the
sound of many waters. And he had in his right hand seven
stars: and out of his mouth went a sharp two-edged sword:
and his countenance was as the sun shineth in his strength."
That is the One who is standing at the door. To have a visitor from heaven, like the angel who came to see Abraham,
or the angel who visited Manoah, or the angel who stood
before Zacharias on the right side of the altar, would be
an overwhelming thing. Were the visitor a great emperor
or king or prime minister, that would be marvelous indeed.
But this One who knocks at the door is the King of Glory,
vested with all of the power of heaven and of earth, whom
the heaven of heavens cannot contain. It is an amazing text:
"Behold, I stand at the door" — this Lord Christ who is thus
near.

LEARNING ABOUT OUR SEEKING LORD

We can learn from this passage a great many things about
our risen Saviour. First, He is on the same quest in His
exalted and glorified life as He was in the days of His flesh.
The same yearning that brought Him from heaven to this
world when He became incarnate, is the same love that
engrosses His life and His entreaty now. When He came into
this world the first time, He came to seek and to save those
who were lost. Now that He is in glory, He is upon the same
identical mission: "Behold, I stand at the door and knock."
He is our seeking Saviour. Notice that He seeks aggressively
like the shepherd finding the sheep that was lost; like the
woman with a lighted candle, searching through the house
and sweeping with a broom, seeking the coin that was lost.
So our Lord seeks aggressively today. It is not that we seek
Him, but that He seeks us. It is not that we love God, but
that God loves us. Many times we are persuaded that it is
the other way around, that it is our seeking and our searching. Sometimes people have the impression that the Lord
holds us at arm's length and will not let us into His presence
and will not allow us to come before His glory, when exactly

the opposite is true. The aggressor is our Saviour. He is seeking us: "Behold, I stand at the door and knock."

In this passage we learn that there is a limit to His aggression. He stops in reverence before our personality. He does not violate our moral freedom nor does He crush our volitional choice. He stops at the door. He will do all in His power to gain our attention, to attract our love, to woo our hearts, but He never forces an entrance. In the parable of the lost sheep, I suppose when the shepherd found the sheep, by force he picked him up, put him on his shoulder and carried him home. But in the third part of that parable, the story of the prodigal son, the father waits and prays and hopes and yearns; but he does not force the boy. If the boy chooses to live in a far country, he has the right of the choice; and the Father waits and prays and hopes. When the elder brother was angry and would not go in, the parable says the Father went out and entreated the older boy and spoke to him and pleaded with him.

So it is with us. The King of Glory never breaches a man's will nor violates a man's freedom. When the Lord comes in, it is because we open the door. Unless that door is opened, He never forces an entrance into a man's life, never. Even so it is with sunshine and the mystery and the glory of God's light. We have to open the shutters and raise the blinds or the sunshine will never come in. If we open wide the window, the mystery of God's creative glory will flood the whole room; but we have to let it in. It never forces entrance itself. In the eighteenth chapter of Matthew, the rich young ruler turned away and Jesus let him go. Why did not the Lord seize him with both hands, compel him? God has a reverence for personality and the Lord will never violate our choice and our will. The decision is ours to make. He never comes where He is not invited; He never enters the heart that is not open; He never saves a man who does not ask Him. Ask, open the door, let Jesus come into your heart!

How Christ Knocks at the Door of the Heart

Some say, "I can see that He knocks at the door of that man's heart and He knocks at the door of yonder heart, and

He speaks to those, I'm sure; but He doesn't knock at my door, and He doesn't stand before my soul, and He never seeks entrance into my heart." No! Our Saviour stands before every heart. Even if you say, "I'm a bad man," the text replies, "Behold, I stand at the door and knock." Even if you say, "I'm not interested and I don't want religion," yet He answers, "Behold, I stand at the door and knock." If you say, "But I wouldn't have Him if I could," yet He replies, "Behold, I stand at the door and knock." If you say, "But I'm lost and undone and have drifted too far, and my heart is too calloused to listen to Him," yet He pleads, "Behold, I stand at the door and knock." Wherever there is a beating heart in this world, there is a yearning Saviour knocking at the door.

How does He knock? There is no soul anywhere, any time, in all of life before whom Christ does not come, knocking at the door. But how does He knock? In a multitude of ways. Our Lord knocks at the door of a man's heart through the Word, through the Book, through the Bible, through the revealed message of truth. Our Lord knocks at the door of a man's heart through every service of the church. The very spire of the church pointing to God is an invitation to a man to reverence his great Maker. Every song that is sung, every word that is spoken, every knee that is bowed, every public offering of prayer, every assembly of God's people, everything that a man hears on the radio that might point to God, all are a knocking at the door of a man's heart. The Lord Jesus knocks at the door of a man's heart in his own sense of unworthiness, sin, shortcoming and neglect, and there is no soul without its consciousness of wrong and of sin. That is a knocking at the door. The Lord knocks at the door of a man's heart through the disappointments, the sufferings and the bitter trials of life. Every tear that falls, every heartache that comes, every disappointment we know, all are knockings at the door of our heart by the Lord. Every tender memory of childhood or of the love of a mother or of the prayers of a father, every memory of yesterday

is a knocking at the door of our heart. "Behold, I stand . . .
and knock."

When I was a youth, I held a revival meeting in the great,
broad ranchland of New Mexico. In that country was a big
rancher who was an unbeliever. They said he was an infidel,
hard and rough. They said there was no need to go to that
rancher's house. One would be met by insults and refusals.
I went anyway. At the house, I was told he was out on a
certain part of the ranch, taking care of a windmill and the
water for his cattle. So I went out to the windmill, found
him there and introduced myself. He was amazed to see
me. He put down his tools, put one foot on the corral-fence,
looked at me and we began to talk. The folks were correct:
he was rough and an unbeliever. But as I began to talk to
him, I asked him if he had a Christian mother. I suppose
he had not thought about her in years, and certainly not at
the invitation of a young preacher who represented God.
"Yes," he said, "I had a wonderful Christian mother." I said:
"Tell me about her. Did she ever pray for you? Did she
ever cry over you? Did she ever ask you to be a Christian?
Tell me about your mother." He went back into the years
and the years, and, as though he were sweeping cobwebs
out of a window of glory, he began to tell me about his
mother and her godly Christian life and her prayers and her
tears. I tell you truly, it was no time at all before the tears
of that rough cattleman were falling on the ground by the
side of the corral-fence as he began describing to me the
godliness of his mother. When I shook hands with him, he
said, "Young fellow, I'll be there tonight." Christ was knocking at the door.

He knocks at the door when two are joined together, asking that their home be Christian. He knocks at the door
when a little one is born into the home. He knocks at the
door when the two are parted, and the heart is empty and
the casket is full. He knocks at the door in every gracious
providence of life. "It is the goodness of God," said the
apostle Paul, "that leadeth to repentance." Whenever a man
feels in his soul that he would like to thank God for health

and strength or gladness and happiness, all these are invitations of our Lord to reverence the great God and our Saviour. "Behold I stand at the door and knock." There is no soul without the experience of God seeking entrance into his life. A man has to wrench his life, choke his soul and do violence to his spirit to turn away from God; for, you see, God made us with a capacity to love, to honor, to adore and to reverence Him.

It is as natural for a little child to pray as for the little one to breathe. Try it, try it on any child. Teach the little fellow to kneel down, and before he can even understand language, he will say his prayers. When he is able to say any word, he will say "Jesus" and he will love the Lord — any child. God made the soul for Himself. It is the image and the expression of the great Creator, Himself. You have to teach a man to be an infidel; for by the love of our souls and the way God made us, we reflect the loving personality and the yearning, shepherdly care of our Saviour. It is sin that blights us and destroys us, and it is unbelief that shuts Him out. A man has to do violence to himself to say, "No," to the Lord. "Behold, I stand at the door and knock."

THE EAGERNESS OF OUR LORD'S ENTRANCE

With what eagerness He enters in when the door is opened! One cannot buy salvation. "Ho," said Isaiah, "come, buy without money and without price. Wherefore spend for that which does not feed? Come, let your soul delight itself in affluence and prosperity and fatness. Seek ye the Lord while He may be found. Call upon Him while He is near." Salvation is at the door. You do not have to buy it. You do not have to entreat. You do not have to work. You do not have to follow an outlined program. Jesus is at the door. Open it, and the Lord Himself will come in. "Lift up your heads, O ye gates, and be ye lifted up ye everlasting doors and the king of glory shall come in. Who is this king of glory? The Lord, great and mighty. The Lord, mighty in battle. The Lord of hosts. He is the king of glory." That such an One should stand at the door of my soul! And that, when

I open the door, He, God our Saviour, should come in and sup with me! Marvelous text!

When I was in London the first thing I wanted to do was to go to St. Paul's Cathedral. The first thing I wanted to see there was the picture by Holman Hunt, "The Light of the World." The title illustrates the spiritual genius of the artist. I would have called the painting, "Christ Knocking at the Door"; but it was the spiritual insight of the artist that gave it the title, "Jesus, the Light of the World." It is a picture of a cottage, run down and neglected. Thistles have grown up to the height of the window. Grass has grown in the pathway. The trailing years of vines and weeds are everywhere. The hinges are rusty. Yet, in the midst of that dishevelment and neglect, there stands the kingliest form that mind could imagine, the Lord in His regal robes. He has in one hand a lantern from which the light falls upon every crevice, and with the other hand He is knocking at the door. The sense of the artist and the wonder that overwhelmed his soul seems to have been that the light of blessedness and of glory is very close to the soul of any man. There Jesus stands, knocking at the door, and the glory of that light falls upon the neglected cottage. One of the most familiar stories I have read is of a discerning man who looked at the picture, went to see Mr. Hunt, the artist, and said: "You have made a mistake. You did not put any handle on the door. It is just a plain door." The artist replied: "No, not a mistake. You misunderstand. The handle is on the inside. We must open the door." When we do, the glory of that light falls upon the soul. And what a difference! The Lord says, "I will come in to him, and will sup with him, and he with me."

Martin Luther said: "Before my conversion, had you knocked at the door of my heart and asked who lives there, I would have said, 'Martin Luther lives here.' Had you come in to see me, you would have found a monk with his head shaved, sleeping in a hair shirt, under his head two tables of stone, a scourge hanging down by the side of the bed. But now if you knock at the door of my heart and ask who lives there, I will reply: 'Martin Luther no longer lives here; Jesus the Lord lives here now.' "

There is light for darkness. There is gladness for mourning. There is joy for sorrow. There is hope for despair. There is cleansing for sin. There is forgiveness for transgression. Instead of the dark and the hopelessness and the despair of life, there is glory.

> If you are tired of the load of your sin,
> Let Jesus come into your heart.
> If you would like a new life to begin,
> Let Jesus come into your heart.
>
> Just now your doubting give o'er,
> Just now reject Him no more,
> Just now throw open the door,
> Let Jesus come into your heart.

Would you? Would you? It is as simple as that. Just open the door and say, "Lord Jesus, come in," and give to Him the destiny of every future moment. He will come in to abide forever.

Expository Sermons on Revelation

Volume 3—Revelation 4 through 10

Expository Sermons
on Revelation

VOLUME 3—REVELATION 4 THROUGH 10

by
W. A. CRISWELL, Ph.D.

EXPOSITORY SERMONS ON REVELATION — *Volume Three*
Copyright © 1964 by Zondervan Publishing House
Grand Rapids, Michigan

DEDICATION

To my father and mother, who believed the
Word of God and who instilled that belief in
my soul as deep and as enduring as life itself.

FOREWORD

It has been my thought to condense the expositions on these middle chapters of the Revelation and to present them in one volume, not two. But many people have said to me, "Every one preaches on the first and the last chapters of the Apocalypse and no one preaches on the middle chapters; please include those middle chapter sermons." The observation seemed all too pertinent and the appeal too urgent to deny. Very few congregations ever hear a sermon from the visions John beheld on Patmos concerning the consummation of this age. Maybe, therefore, God will so bless these volumes that the blessed hope we have in the ultimate victory of Christ will ring forth more vibrantly than ever.

These messages have been most difficult to prepare. There is so much I do not understand, so much that God has not revealed. In the exposition on "The Seven Thunders" I have particularly spoken of that knowledge denied to us by the counsels of God. But what the Lord has revealed He caused John to write for our encouragement and we should take it to heart as the very breath of life. It is a privilege, therefore, to walk down Scriptural paths I have never walked before, and to look upon scenes that I never knew God had revealed. I can truly say that in the eighteen years of my preaching through the Bible, the studies in the Apocalypse most blessed my soul. Everything of God and of man seems to find summation in the Revelation.

Once again I express deepest gratitude to Mrs. B. B. Binford for her invaluable help in correcting the sermons transcribed from tape recordings and to Mrs. Bailey Forester for typing them so accurately. Their contribution is almost the publication of the book itself.

God bless the eyes that look upon these pages and God bless the truth so triumphantly revealed in these Apocalyptic chapters. Truly, the battle is the Lord's and we shall yet see the full salvation of our great God and Saviour, Jesus Christ. Maranatha.

— W. A. CRISWELL

Pastor's Study
First Baptist Church
Dallas, Texas

TABLE OF CONTENTS

Foreword

Expository Sermons on Revelation

Volume 3—Revelation 4 through 10

Chapter 1

A Door Opened in Heaven

After this I looked, and, behold, a door was opened in heaven: and the first voice which I heard was as it were of a trumpet talking with me; which said, Come up hither, and I will shew thee things which must be hereafter. — Revelation 4:1

In chapter four of the Revelation, we come to the third and final great section of the Book as it is outlined by the Spirit of God. Every word of this verse is meaningful — Revelation 4:1: "After this I looked, and, behold, a door was opened in heaven: and the first voice which I heard was as it were a trumpet talking with me; which said, Come up hither, and I will shew thee things which must be here-after [meta tauta]." I recognize that meta tauta is the key word in God's great outline of the Book. When I turn the page back to Revelation 1:19, I find that meta tauta. "Write the things which thou hast seen, [that is section one] and the things which are [section two], and the things which shall be [meta tauta, section three]."

Thus God divided the Revelation into three great parts, and He commanded John to write down those three great parts. First, "the things which thou hast seen." What he had seen was the vision of the exalted and glorified Lord. So John faithfully wrote that down, as one may read in chapter one of the Revelation. Then the second part, "Write the things which are." The "things which are" are the churches. Look around you. Here is a church, there is a church, yonder is a church. So it was in John's day. There was a church at Ephesus, there was one at Smyrna, another at Pergamos, one at Thyatira and again at Sardis, yonder

13

at Philadelphia and at Laodicea. "Write the things which are." So John faithfully wrote down "the things which are." In chapters two and three of the Apocalypse, we have read an epitome of the story of the churches from the days they were founded by Christ and the apostles until the day of the end of the churches. Seven great periods of the church are revealed to us in chapters two and three.

Then the third part, "Write the things which shall be [meta tauta]." Meta tauta, translated literally, means "after these things." We have it translated in the King James Version "hereafter." The meaning is: "Write the things which shall be after the churches, when the churches are no more; write the things which shall be after the things of the churches." When we come to chapter four we are told by the Spirit of God through the revelation made to John, that now we are to see what God is to do after the things of the churches, after the churches are no more, after the churches are gone, after the churches are taken out of the world — meta tauta, "after the things of the churches." When we come, therefore, to Revelation four, we are entering the final consummation of the age. All church history now is past. The thousands of years that God has been preaching the Gospel through His ministers and the thousands of years that God has upheld the light of Christ in His churches — all are no more. They are taken away. Beginning with chapter four we enter the great period of the judgment of God upon this earth after God's people are taken away.

The Churches Disappear

It is an astonishing program, these things we read in the Book of God. For example, the churches disappear in chapter four. That is an amazing thing. Heretofore, the churches have occupied the central place as God views history. But at the end of chapter three and beginning with chapter four, the churches disappear. There are no more churches. They are never mentioned. If anyone thinks they are referred to under the name of Israel, do the churches have twelve tribes and are we divided according to the tribe of Judah, the tribe of Simeon, the tribe of Reuben and the tribes of all the rest of the twelve? When we read about the twelve tribes of Israel and what God is doing with those Jewish people, the reference is to Israel and to the twelve tribes. When we come to chapter four, the churches disappear. They are no more and they are never referred to and they are never seen again on this earth. Up until chapter four, the whole revelation has had to do with the churches. Beginning with chapter four, they disappear and the next time we see the church is in chapter nineteen at the end of the age. She is there, the bride of Christ, coming with her Lord in glory, marching in the armies of heaven to the last great victory in the denouement of the age.

How did the church get up there? She disappears at the first verse in chapter four, and the next time we see the church is in chapter nineteen at the end of the age, at the end of the revelation, coming with the Lord in glory. How did she get up there with the Lord? That is a *musterion*, Paul calls it, which is revealed to the apostles. Now, if you want to follow the message, turn to I Corinthians 15:51: "Behold, I shew you a *musterion* [translated a 'mystery']." To us a mystery is an enigma, a riddle, something devious and hard to find out. But in the Bible a *musterion*, a "mystery," is a secret in the heart of God that a man could never learn by himself, but God has to reveal it. So a *musterion*, a "mystery," is a great purpose and plan in the heart of God that no man would ever know, that no man could ever find out, until God chose to reveal it. Now Paul says, "Behold, I shew you a *musterion* [a 'mystery,' a thing that we could never know except as God revealed it]. We shall not all sleep, but we shall all be changed." That is the *musterion*. We are not all going to die, but there is coming a time when all of us shall be translated like Enoch, we shall be lifted up to glory and immortalized like Elijah. We shall not all sleep, but we shall be immortalized, we shall all be glorified, we shall all be changed, "in a moment, in the twinkling of an eye, at the last trump; for the trumpet shall sound, and the dead shall be raised incorruptible, and we shall be changed." Paul says that is going to happen instantaneously, in a moment, in the twinkling of an eye. Now do not translate that "in the blinking of an eye." It takes a little piece of a moment to blink an eye. It does not say "blinking of an eye," which is a long time compared to this. The twinkling of an eye is that little sudden something that happens when you recognize somebody. I look at you and I recognize you. The recognition happens instantaneously, before you could describe it, before you could hardly delineate it, that light of recognition that comes into the eye. That is how quickly, that is how suddenly, that is how immediately, that is how miraculously God will change these lives at the secret, clandestine, furtive, thief-like coming of the Lord. "Behold, I shew you a *musterion;* we are not all going to die." There will be a generation of God's people who are alive at the coming of the Lord. Paul prayed that he would be in that generation. Every true Christian has prayed that same prayer. Even as John closed the Book, he prayed, "Even so, come, Lord Jesus, in my day, in my time."

> O Joy, O Delight, should we go without dying,
> No sickness, no sadness, no dread and no crying,
> Caught up with our Lord through the clouds into glory,
> When Jesus receives His own.

Notice that same *musterion* in I Thessalonians 4:16, 17. "For the Lord himself shall descend from heaven with a shout, with the voice of the archangel, and with the trump of God: and the dead in Christ shall rise first; Then we which are alive and remain shall be caught up together with them in the clouds, to meet the Lord in the air: and so shall we ever be with the Lord." That is the *musterion*. Not that the dead are going to be raised. The *musterion* is that we who are alive and remain until the coming of the Lord shall be caught up with our Saviour in the air and shall be immortalized, shall be glorified, shall be translated, instantaneously, in the twinkling of an eye. This is the great mystery which God has kept in His heart from the foundation of the world and revealed through His apostles to His churches.

THE OLD ENGLISH WORD "RAPTURE"

That is why we used the word "rapture." The word "rapture" is an old English word built upon the Latin word *rapere, raptum.* It means "to transport," "to take away," "to snatch away." "Rapture" has come to mean "ecstasy" to us in the English language because, in our modern language, when a man is transported out of his senses and is in ecstasy, he is just beyond himself. We say he is "enraptured." He has been swept off his feet. We have come to apply the word to our senses, to the way we feel. That is a good use of the word, remembering that the great basic meaning of the word "rapture" is *rapere*, "to snatch away." So when we speak of the rapture of the church, we are speaking of the taking away of the people of God, the transporting upward to glory of the great household of faith. That, Paul says, is a *musterion*, something that God has revealed to His churches.

Let us turn back to Revelation 4:1 and see that marvelous thing happen in type and in symbol before our eyes: "After this I looked, and, behold, a door was opened in heaven." That is a type and a picture of the door of the ascension of God's sainted people, the door opened wide to receive God's children from the earth. "And I heard a trumpet voice . . ." That trumpet voice is the type and symbol of the voice of the archangel of God, sounding like a trumpet, that raises the dead from their graves and that, according to the word of our Saviour, gathers His elect from the four winds of the earth. That is the great trumpet voice that summons to heaven God's sainted children in the earth. "Then I heard that voice saying, 'Come up hither.'" That is the type and the picture of God's children rising to be with their Lord in glory. When John was transported to heaven he was a type and a picture of the transporting, the rapture, the snatching away, the taking up of God's people into glory. Then, after the door is opened in heaven, after the great call of God to His sainted dead and His sainted living, after the rapture and the transporting of the church, the Holy Spirit writes, "I will shew thee things which must be [*meta tauta*, the things after the things of the church, the things after the churches are taken away, the things after the people of God are in heaven]." The rest of the Revelation is a description of that awful and terrible period when God has taken His people out of the earth and when He pours upon this world the judgments of the wrath of the Almighty. Beginning at chapter four to the consummation, we have the delineation, the revelation, the unveiling of the end time of the world, the great and terrible days of the tribulation. Matthew 24:21 calls it "the great tribulation." Revelation 7:14 calls it *he thlipsis he megale*, literally meaning "*the* tribulation *the* great."

THE DELIVERANCE OF GOD'S PEOPLE

In the thirteenth chapter of the Book of Isaiah, in the first chapter of Joel, in the second chapter of Joel, in II Thessalonians 2:2, that time is called "the day of the Lord." In the thirtieth chapter of the Book of Jeremiah, that time is called "the day of Jacob's trouble." In the twelfth chapter of the Book of Daniel, in the first verse, that time is described as being a time of trouble such as the world has never seen nor shall ever see again. It is a day of awesome horror and terror. "*The* tribulation *the* great." The world has known terrible times. It was a time of tribulation in the days of the Spanish Inquisition when God's children were tortured and uncounted thousands were put to death. It was a day of great tribulation in the days of the French Revolution when, as it was in the days of Titus in A.D. 70 when Jerusalem was destroyed, the streets ran red with blood. Those were terrible days. It was a terrible time when Hitler, taking advantage of the defenseless Jews of

Germany, exterminated thousands and millions of those help-less people. But those tribulations and sorrows in days past are not to be compared with the indescribable out-break of judgments of God upon mankind which are yet to come. Heretofore we have seen the outbreaking of the wickedness of man, but this day that is coming is the out-breaking and the outpouring of the judgments of Almighty God upon human iniquity, upon human sin, upon those who reject the overtures of grace, when God shall say, "It is enough, it is enough, thus far and no longer." It will be the days of the Great Tribulation.

Will our people, God's people, will the church, God's churches, will the saints, God's redeemed believers, will they go through that terrible tribulation? No! No! No! Every answer of Scripture is an emphatic "No!" When that day of awful judgment comes and God shall rain down hailstone and fire and brimstone, the great day of the Lord, when God shall deal with this world in its iniquity, in its blas-phemy and in its unbelief, when that day comes, God's people will be in glory with their Saviour. We shall be taken away. As long as we are here in this earth, those judgments cannot fall. As long as God's people are present in this earth, those horrible and terrible things cannot come to pass. They will come to pass only after God's people are taken away.

These things are written plainly on the page of God's Book. In reading them, in understanding them and in see-ing them, we discover untold encouragement for our souls and at the same time become aware of a vast, marvelous flood of knowledge that God gives us about the end time. "For," says Paul, "we are not of those without knowledge as though that thing should overtake us unawares, but we are those who live in the daytime, in the full splendor of the glory of the light of the knowledge of God in the Reve-lation and in the faith of our Lord Jesus Christ." God's people are to be a knowing people, a knowledgeable people, a spiritually-intelligent people. They are to be a people aware. They are to be a people who live in triumph when the clouds of this world are dark and lowering. The darker the times, the more glorious does the Christian, in triumph and in faith, lift up his face, for he knows that His redemption draws nigh. This is an admonition of our Lord. Look up, look up. For when these things begin to come to pass, know that your redemption, the final work of God for His people, is nigh, even at the door. Watch! Look! Be aware! For God has revealed to us these things that are yet to come, even the blessing and the glory and the triumph of His people.

Chapter 2

God's Churches and the Great Tribulation

> After this I looked, and behold, a door was opened in heaven:
> and the first voice which I heard was as it were of a trumpet
> talking with me; which said, Come up hither, and I will shew
> thee things which must be hereafter. — Revelation 4:1

This sermon concerns the church and the awesome, un-
paralleled Tribulation, described in the Revelation. This
is one of the most awesome subjects which mind could
consider or imagination could dread. It concerns the inevitable judgment toward which all history is moving. It is called
in Matthew 24:21 and in Revelation 7:14 *he thlipsis he
megale, "the* tribulation *the* great." This message discusses
why the churches of Christ will not go through this terrible
period of trial and judgment. I have four reasons why it
seems to me, as I study these Scriptures, that God's people,
Christ's churches, will not go through that terrible time of
trial and trouble.

The first reason lies in the structural outline of the Book
of the Revelation itself. The outline is given to us by the
Lord:

    I. "Write the things which thou hast seen."
    John wrote in Chapter 1 of the vision on Patmos
    which he had seen.
   II. "Write the things which are." (The things of the
    churches)
    John wrote in Chapters 2 and 3 concerning the
    churches.

*III.   "And the things that shall be hereafter [meta tauta]"
        John wrote in Chapters 4 to 19 of the things that
        were to come to pass after there would be no more
        churches upon the earth.

But how had the church come to be in heaven? She was
taken up, snatched away, raptured (an old English word),
which was the *musterion* revealed by the Apostle Paul. The
church will be taken up to God in glory, in a moment, in the
twinkling of an eye, at the last trump, when the dead in
Christ rise first and all of us who are remaining shall be
changed, caught up to be with them and with the Lord in
the air. In the Revelation, in symbol, a door was opened in
heaven and a voice as of a trumpet was heard saying,
"Come up hither," vividly portraying the calling away of the
people of Christ, of whom John is a representative.

The delineation of judgment in the Revelation follows the
same pattern found in the whole Word of God. The Tribulation at the end-time is the visitation of God upon sin and
upon Satan and upon the lawless system of Satan in this
world, both upon Israel and upon the Gentiles. All of the
blaspheming unbelievers who reject Christ are to be judged
by the Lord God. It is to be a time of unprecedented outpouring of the wrath of the Almighty. The judgment falls
upon a godless world. God's people, God's churches are
not thus to be judged. The only judgment that God's people
shall ever face is that described in II Corinthians 5:10,
when we shall all stand at the judgment seat of Christ,
each one to receive according to what he has done in the
body. That is a judgment of rewards. Some of us shall be
rulers over ten cities, some over five, some of us shall be

---

*Note that in the part of the Revelation before Chapter 4, the whole heart
and circumference of that message of Jesus is to His churches. But with
the beginning of Chapter 4, there is no more reference to the churches.
All through this great period of trial and tribulation, Chapters 4 to 19, the
church is never mentioned. Not until the nineteenth chapter does the
church appear, when in the great, concluding, climactic, consummating
end of the age, she is represented as the Bride of Christ in heaven and
comes with Him in glory.

saved as if by fire, just by the skin of our teeth. But God's
people are not going into that great final trial and wrath
of Almighty God inflicted upon the ungodly. Romans 8:1
says: "There is therefore now no condemnation to them
which are in Christ Jesus." John 5:24 says: "Verily, verily,
I say unto you, He that heareth my word, and believeth on
him that sent me, hath everlasting life, and shall not come
into judgment, shall not come into condemnation; but is
passed out of death into life." In II Thessalonians 5:9, Paul,
talking about the day of the Lord, the day of the wrath and
the judgment of God, says that God hath not appointed us
unto that wrath and that judgment and that terrible day,
but to obtain salvation by our Lord Jesus Christ. In Revelation 3:10, the Lord says to His people: "Because thou hast
kept my word, I also will keep thee from the great trial that
shall come upon all the world." So the structural outline in
the Book of Revelation is the same pattern that I find in
all the rest of the Book. God's people are judged already.
We have passed through the great judgment upon our sins
in Christ's death on the cross. Christ has assumed for us
the penalty of our sins and died in our stead. Before that
awesome day of the final judgment of God upon this world,
God's people are to be taken away.

Paul and "The Mystery of Iniquity"

The second great reason why it seems to me God's people
will not pass through those days of terrible Tribulation is
found in the exposition of Paul in II Thessalonians 2. The
Christians in Thessalonica were in great trial. They thought
that they were in the days of the Tribulation. The authorized version in II Thessalonians 2:2 uses the term, "the day
of Christ." The best manuscripts and the true text is "the
day of the Lord," which is the day of the end-time. These
Thessalonians, because of their trials, thought that they
had come to the end-time, the terrible Tribulation. Paul
had told them before that they were not going through
that awful day of the Lord. So they asked Paul, "What is

this that has overwhelmed us?" They thought the day of trial and the Great Tribulation were here and they were in it and suffering it now. Paul explains to them in chapter two of II Thessalonians: "Let no man deceive you as that the day of the Lord is at hand [*enesteken,* is here, that you are now in it] for that day is not coming, until first there be the calamitous falling away, [or, as some texts have it, 'the rapturous taking away'] of God's people first."

Then Paul continues with the explanation that the first thing that shall happen in that awful day of the Lord in the trial and judgment of God upon this earth is to be the revelation of a man of sin. "That day shall not come except first that man of sin be revealed, the son of damnation and perdition; who opposeth and exalteth himself above all that is called God, or that is worshipped; so that he is as God sitteth in the temple of God, shewing himself that he is God . . . And now ye know what withholdeth, what restraineth, what keeps this back, that he might be revealed in his time. For the mystery of iniquity doth already work: only he that restrains, restrains until he be taken out of the way. And then shall that Wicked one be revealed, whom the Lord shall consume with the spirit of his mouth, and shall destroy with the brightness of his *perousia,* [his presence, his coming]; Even him, whose coming is after the working of Satan with all power and signs and lying wonders, and with all deceivableness of unrighteousness in them that perish . . . for this cause God shall send them strong delusion, that they should believe a lie: That they all might be damned." That is the final judgment of God upon this unbelieving world, "who believed not the truth, but had pleasure in unrighteousness."

Paul says here that the mystery of iniquity has been working for centuries, moving toward the revelation of Satan's masterpiece. In some places in the Bible that Satanic leader is called the ultimate and the final Antichrist. Here He is called "the Man of Sin," the son of damnation. Paul says that the only thing that keeps the ultimate and final day of trial and judgment of God from coming on this world and the revelation of that Ultimate Man of Sin is the presence of a "Restrainer." I think Satan always has his "man of sin" prepared and ready. In every generation I think there is a candidate for that world dictator. In one generation it will be one, in another generation it will be another. After Hitler comes Stalin; after Stalin, Khrushchev; after Khrushchev, another will arise. Satan always has his man.

But there is a Restrainer in this earth. To me that Restrainer, the only one who could stand in the way of Satan (not even an archangel could do that, for Michael dare not speak to Satan and rebuke him to his face, but says, "The Lord rebuke thee")— the only Restrainer on this earth is the Holy Spirit of God. The Holy Spirit of God is in His people. Some day the Holy Spirit of God in His churches, in His people, is going to be taken away. When that is done, when the Holy Spirit of God in Christ's people is taken away, then, unrestricted, the Man of Sin will be revealed. He is the ultimate world dictator, the ultimate and final Antichrist.

From my study of the Scripture passages referring to the Antichrist, I have come to certain conclusions about him, as follows: I think he is coming on the world scene as the champion of peace and unity and will be received as such. He is to reign seven years. In the midst of that seven years he will prove to be an impostor and a deceiver. The last half of the seven years is called *he thlipsis he megale*, "*the* tribulation *the* great." (We shall come across that time period again and again, sometimes referred to as three and one half years, sometimes as time and time and dividing of time, sometimes as time, time, and half a time, sometimes as forty-two months, sometimes as one thousand two hundred and sixty days.) He is going to organize this world into its last disastrous war that ends with the Battle of Armageddon. One-third of all the earth will be destroyed and the whole earth would perish were it not that in that final battle of that final war the Lord appears in glory (in the nineteenth chapter) with His people.

But we are not going to be in that terrible trial in those awful and awesome days. For, as long as the churches are here and the Spirit of God is in these churches, there is a restraining of this ultimate, energized Satan-incarnated spirit of defilement and blasphemy and wickedness, the dark kingdom of Satan. The only thing that keeps governments together is the children of God. The only thing that sustains the pillars of this world is the presence of the children of God. As long as God's people are here, that ultimate wrath will not come. Only when God's people are taken away, then will those monstrous, horrible, awesome things in the hands of Satan be permitted. Then unrestrained shall he, as a roaring lion, devour this earth.

THE TYPES OF THE OLD TESTAMENT

The third reason why I do not believe that God's people, His churches, will go through that Great Tribulation is because of the types, the illustrations, that are used in the Bible to describe those awful and awesome times. For example (and this is just one) in Luke 17 our Lord says: "And as it was in the days of Noah, so shall it be also in the days of the coming, the appearing, of the Son of Man; likewise also as it was in the days of Lot, even thus shall it be in the day when the Son of Man is revealed." Now, to take just this one instance of how the Scriptures follow a certain type and use certain illustrations: "As it was in the days of Noah." In the days of the judgment of God upon the earth, in the days of the flood, Enoch was taken out before the flood, Noah passed through the flood, and the vile, wicked, blaspheming, unbelieving world perished in the flood. Enoch is a type and a picture of God's people who are taken to Himself before this Tribulation. Noah is a type of that remnant that is saved through it, even in those terrible days of the Tribulation. Of course the unbelieving are those who perish in it. Now that same kind of an illustration, that same kind of a type, is used by our Lord with reference to Lot. Lot was a carnal, compromising Christian (II Peter 2:8). But the angel said to Lot, "I can do nothing until thou be come thither." As long as Lot was in Sodom, the fire could not fall and the brimstone could not burn and the judgment could not come. The angel said, "I can do nothing until thou be come thither." But the moment that Lot came out, that moment, the Book says, the judgment of God fell upon Sodom and Gomorrah. Thus it is, says our Saviour, in the time of the coming of the Son of Man. Before that judgment falls and before these awesome days of the Tribulation, God's people must be taken away, for God will not let that judgment fall until first the restraining spirit of God in His people, with His people, is taken away.

Enoch was taken out, taken away, in glory. Lot, compromising as he was, was also taken away. Both of them. Godly Enoch and compromising Lot, who vexed his soul with the filthy living of Sodom, both of them alike, were taken away. Read the passage in the third chapter of I Corinthians. When we are taken away, some of us, spiritual Christians, having built for Christ, gold, silver and precious stones, will receive a glorious reward. But some of us taken away who are compromising and worldly Christians, having built with wood, hay and stubble, at the great judgment of Christ will be saved as if by fire, just like Lot, by the skin of our teeth. Some of us will be saved like glorious Enoch, who entered into the fulness of an inheritance that is indescribable and unimaginably precious and dear. They both, alike, are taken out, even the carnal, compromising Lot, as was the glorious and devoted Enoch. In the Scriptures, in the types, in the illustrations used, God's people first are taken out, then the terrible judgment of the Lord falls.

The Promises to God's People

My fourth reason why it seems to me that we shall not go through that awesome judgment and trial and the pouring out of the wrath of God upon an unbelieving world, lies in

the scriptural presentation of the comfort and hope of the
Christian. What are we looking for? There are some who
are looking for the Man of Sin and the Son of Damnation.
There are others who are looking for the Beast and the
False Prophet. There are some who are looking for Armageddon and the last great battle of this earth. There are
others who are looking for the Tribulation and the trials and
the judgments of God. But what are God's people told to
look for? Read the Book. God bids His people to look only
for the blessed, holy Saviour. We are to look for *Him*. Even
as Paul wrote in Titus 2:13: "Looking for, waiting for, praying for that blessed hope, and the glorious appearing of the
great God and our Saviour Jesus Christ." God's people are
not told to look for the Battle of Armageddon. God's people
are not told to look for the Great Tribulation. God's people
are not told to look for the Beast and the Antichrist and
the Son of Damnation and Perdition. But the hope and the
comfort of the church is Christ. We are told to look for
and to pray for and to love the appearing of our "great
God and Saviour." Paul calls Him God. We are to look for
and to be comforted by the "glorious appearing of our great
God and Saviour, Jesus Christ."

I think it is false, always, to put anything between the
promise of the imminent, immediate return of Christ and its
actual fulfillment. I do not think it is right to put any program, to put any years, to put any days, to put any development, to put anything in the world between us and the
coming of the Lord. I think the coming of the Lord is always
imminent, any moment, any second, at the twinkling of an
eye, this hour, this day, this evening, in the twilight, at midnight, in the morning, the next day, any time He might come
for us, for His own. Whenever anyone inserts a program
that delays the coming of the Lord, I think he does violence
to the Word of God. For the coming of Christ is always at
hand. The disciples believed it in their day. Their greeting
was "Maranatha" (the Lord is at hand) and they were
comforted by it. We are to live in that imminency that the

Lord will come, that He is at the door, with nothing to separate between us and the appearing of our Saviour. When
He comes, it will be without announcement; there will be
no signs. The signs are for other things but not for that.
He will come silently, quietly, furtively, clandestinely, coming for the pearl of price that He purchased with His own
blood, coming for His jewels in the world. And like Enoch,
who was miraculously, gloriously, but silently and secretly
transfigured, immortalized, translated, taken away, so will it
be when the Lord comes for His people. That is what we
are to look for. Not for those terrible days of the judgment
and wrath of Almighty God, but we are to look for the
"glorious appearing of the great God and our Saviour, Jesus
Christ."

At the end of the Philadelphian age, the door is beginning
to close. All over the world the doors are beginning to close.
In the Laodicean age, the door is closed and Christ is on
the outside knocking, individually gleaning. But when the
door begins to close at the end of the Philadelphian age, and
when the door is closed in the last Laodicean age, that is
the signal for the door to open in heaven. When it is thus,
then God takes to Himself in symbol this Apostle John who
represents us all. The door, the voice as of a trumpet, the
"Come up hither," are symbols of the rapture of the church.
We are ambassadors for Christ in this world and when a
country declares war, first it calls home its ambassadors. So
it is in the Lord's plans for His own. Before those judgments
come and before the awful hour of the visitation of God
upon the earth, first God must take out His Enochs and provide for His Noahs and even snatch out His Lots, for the
fire cannot fall and the judgment cannot come until we be
come hither. May the Lord encourage us and bless us in
the faith. To all those who love His appearing shall He
come the second time, apart from sin, unto salvation. This
is the hope and the deliverance of the children of God.

Chapter 3

The Four and Twenty Elders

And round about the throne were four and twenty seats: and upon the seats I saw four and twenty elders sitting, clothed in white raiment; and they had on their heads crowns of gold. The four and twenty elders fall down before him that sat on the throne, and worship him that liveth for ever and ever, and cast their crowns before the throne, saying, Thou art worthy, O Lord, to receive glory and honour, and power; for thou hast created all things, and for thy pleasure they are, and were created. — Revelation 4:4, 10, 11

The vision opens with a throne set in heaven, the exalted throne of the Lord God Almighty (Revelation 4:2). Around that central throne John saw twenty-four *thronoi*, thrones, translated in the King James version, "seats." On these twenty-four lesser thrones, around the great central Deity, were seated twenty-four elders.

Who are these twenty-four elders? They are not spirits. It is incongruous to our thinking and it is certainly foreign to the revelation of God that spirits should be clothed, should be crowned and should be seated. There is no such conception as that either in the mind of a rational man or in the Word of God. They are not spirits. These twenty-four elders are not angels. In the description of these who give praise to God, they are always separated and separately delineated from angels. For example, in chapter five, verse eleven, "And I beheld, and I heard the voice of many angels round about the throne and the cherubim and the elders." They are not angels. Angels are never numbered. Sometimes they were referred to as myriads by myriads by ten thousands of thousands of thousands. Hebrews twelve refers

30

to an innumerable company of angels. But, angels are never numbered. These elders are numbered. They are definitely four and twenty. Angels are never crowned. These elders are crowned. The Greek word for "crown" here is *stephanos* (of Stephen). There are two Greek words for crown: *diadema*, which is a crown of a potentate, a king; then there is the word *stephanos* which is the crown of a victor. It is the garland of success. These elders are crowned as those who came out of great trial. Then if we accept the Textus Receptus, the Greek text used in the translation of the King James Version, in the fifth chapter, these elders sing to the Lamb of God: "Thou wast slain, and hast redeemed us to God by thy blood out of every kindred, and tongue, and people, and nation. And hast made us kings and priests: and we shall reign on the earth." Whoever these twenty-four elders are, they were once sinful people, redeemed unto God by the blood of the Lamb. Such a thing could never be said of angels.

Who, then, are these four and twenty elders? They are God's saints. They are the redeemed of mankind. They are His blood-bought people. They are in heaven enthroned around the great central throne of God. They are seated, they are not standing and waiting on the Lord, but they are seated as God's royal counselors and co-laborers. They have won the victory over this life, and they are crowned with the garland of attainment. They are redeemed out of all of the languages and tongues and families and tribes and people in the earth. These twenty-four elders are the redeemed saints of God. They number twenty-four, twice twelve, representing the twelve patriarchs of Israel and the twelve apostles of the Lamb. Together, they make up God's redeemed society. This is the same system of numbers you will find in John's description of the beautiful city, the new Jerusalem. There are twelve gates, and on those gates are the names of the twelve tribes of Israel. On the twelve foundations are written the names of the twelve apostles of the Lamb. The twelve of Israel and the twelve of the church make up the twenty-four elders, seated on the thrones before the throne of God. Some of these Old Testament saints have already been raised from the dead. After the Resurrection of our Lord, they appeared unto many in the holy city of Jerusalem. Some of these Old Testament saints, such as Enoch and Elijah, are already raptured, are already translated. Both Old Testament saints and New Testament saints are presented together in the Bible in passages such as Hebrews 12:22-23: "But ye are come unto mount Sion, and unto the city of the living God, the heavenly Jerusalem, and to an innumerable company of angels. To the general assembly and church of the firstborn, which are written in heaven, and to God the Judge of all, and to the spirits of just men made perfect." All twenty-four of them are before the throne of God.

THE NUMBER TWENTY-FOUR

That number *twenty-four* is a descriptive symbol of the all-inclusiveness (without loss of one) of all of God's people. In I Chronicles 24 and 25 the priesthood of the Levites was divided into twenty-four courses and that included all of them. Every Levitical priest was included in those twenty-four courses. In I Peter 2:5 and in I Peter 2:9 we are told that God's people are a royal priesthood. The twenty-four courses of the priests represent all of God's people. There is a definite number of God's people. Their names are written in the Lamb's Book of Life. When the last one comes in, when that last soul is saved, that will be the end, that will be the consummation of history. God's people are definitely numbered. They have a certain arithmetical delineation and denomination. It is not a matter of guess; it is known to God. It is not that it might be this or it might be the other; there is a definite number of God's people who are registered in God's Book and that number is represented by the inclusive twenty-four, the definite number that included all of the priests of the Lord.

These twenty-four elders represent, therefore, the redeemed of humanity. And where are they? They are in heaven. At the beginning of chapter four in the Revelation, we come to an altogether different kind of a scene. A great event has transpired. A great thing has come to pass. Heretofore, in the previous chapters in the Revelation, the Lord is seen walking among the lampstands of His churches in the earth. But here He is seen as the Lamb on the throne with His Father in heaven. Heretofore we have had the description of God's churches on earth. But now we have God's redeemed in heaven, and from here on the church is always in heaven looking down upon the things on earth. The church never again appears on earth until the people of God come with Christ, as recorded in the nineteenth chapter of the Book of Revelation, at the end of the consummation of the age. Beginning at chapter four, these sainted people of God are always with the Lord in heaven. So something marvelous has transpired. What is it? It is the rapture; it is the translation; it is the resurrection of those who sleep in Jesus. It is the great assembly of the Lord's people as they have been taken up into glory. Thereafter the church, the people of God, the redeemed of the Lamb, look down upon the events that are transpiring in that awesome and indescribably terrible tribulation, which begins with chapter six, in the Book of the Revelation. These four and twenty elders, the people of God, look and observe in heaven these things that transpire on the earth. They are there in heaven first, and then these things follow.

They are in heaven as they watch the Lamb take the sealed Book in chapter five. They worship God and fall down and praise Him forever as He receives the Book to open the seals thereof. Those twenty-four elders, mentioned twelve different times in the Revelation, are in their places as they watch the mighty accession of those who are coming out of the Great Tribulation, their robes washed in the blood of the Lamb, entering through the gates of glory, tribulation saints, the martyred of the Son of God. Those elders are in their places, in the eleventh chapter of the Book of the Revelation, when the seventh angel sounds and the kingdoms of this world become the kingdoms of our Lord and of His Christ, and they glorify Him who is to reign forever and forever. They are in their places and in their positions when, in the fourteenth chapter of the Revelation, the one hundred and forty-four thousand are gathered unto the Lord upon Mount Sion. They are in the nineteenth chapter, verse four, where they are last mentioned, where they last appear. They are there rejoicing over the conquest of Babylon and the fall of that awful system that blasphemes the name of God. They rejoice in singing Alleluia's to the Lord God, world without end. They are first in heaven; then all of these things transpire in the days of the Great Tribulation upon the earth.

THE JUDGMENT OF THE CHRISTIAN

The remainder of this sermon is a description of what happens to us when we are taken up into glory. There are two great events that transpire when we are resurrected, or (if we are alive when the Lord comes) when we are changed, in a moment, in the twinkling of an eye, to meet our Lord and to be taken up into the Father's house in glory.

The first is this. We shall stand at the *Bema*, the judgment seat of Christ. The Greek word *Bema* is the word for "a step," and it came to refer to the raised step upon which the judge would sit when he crowned a victor in a race or when he gave the rewards of state. Finally, of course, the word came to refer to a tribunal, a judge's seat. Now, the Scriptures are very plain in teaching that all of us some day shall stand at the *Bema* of Christ. For example, in II Corinthians 5:10: "For we must all appear before the *Bema* of Christ; that every one may receive the reward of the deeds done in the flesh, whether they be good, whether they be bad." We shall all stand at the judgment seat of Christ, all of us. In I Corinthians 3, there is delineated in detail what shall happen when God's children are standing before the *Bema*, the judgment seat of Christ. Our works shall be

tried. ". . . for the day shall declare it, because it shall be
revealed by fire; and the fire shall try every man's work of
what sort it is . . ." If any man's work be made out of gold,
silver, precious stones, his work shall abide and he shall
receive a reward. But if his work be made out of wood,
hay and stubble, his work shall be burned, but he himself
shall be saved, as though by fire [as though a naked man
ran out of a house and everything he possessed burned
down, but he himself escaped with his life]." These last
words refer to those whose works perish at the *Bema* of
Christ.

Now the *Bema* of Christ is not the judgment as to whether
we are saved or damned. That judgment is here. That
judgment is in this earth and life. That judgment is in your
heart and in your soul. You are judged now according to
the damnation or salvation of your soul. For those who will
accept Jesus, the judgment and the wrath of God against
our iniquities fell upon Him. His sufferings, His agony, His
tears and His blood made atonement for our sins. But to
those who refuse the overtures of mercy and say "No" to
God and "No" to Jesus, that judgment is now. They are not
going to be lost; they are lost now. They are not going to
be damned; they are damned now. They are not some day
going to perdition; they are on the way to perdition now.
The road of rejection leads to no other thing. There is death
and the burning judgment of God upon those who refuse
the mercies of grace. There is an awesome judgment going
on now in the hearts of all mankind.

But this judgment at the *Bema* of Christ is an altogether
different kind of a judgment. When we are taken up into
glory, this judgment has to do with our rewards. We receive
the fruit of our hands and of the labor of our lives at the
judgment seat of Christ. That judgment is always at the
end of the age. That judgment is always connected with
resurrection and with the return of our Lord. A typical passage is in the fourteenth verse of the fourteenth chapter of
the Book of Luke, where the Lord says to us that when we

make a dinner, we are not to invite those who can call us back again and so recompense and repay us. But when we prepare a dinner, we are to call in the poor, the blind, the maimed and the halt, for they cannot recompense us, but we shall be recompensed at the resurrection of the just. The reward for a man's life, for the good that he does, is always at the time of the end, at the resurrection. That, of course, is connected with the return of our Saviour. Paul, in the last chapter of the last letter that he wrote, said: "I have fought a good fight, I have finished my course, I have kept the faith: Henceforth there is laid up for me a crown of righteousness, which the Lord, the righteous judge, shall give me at that day: and not to me only, but unto all them also that love his appearing" (II Timothy 4:7-8). The great reward is not when the man dies, not when he is deceased, but when Jesus comes again, at the resurrection. In Revelation 22:12: ". . . behold, I come quickly; and my reward is with me, to give every man according as his work shall be." Our reward is at the resurrection day, it is at the return of our Saviour.

It is very, very plain why this should be. No man could be given the reward of his life when he dies, because when he dies, he does not die. The influence of his life goes on. It lives on and on and on, and it continues until Jesus comes again. Only God, at the *Bema* of Christ, is able to unravel the skein of the influence of a man's life and make it all one, that the man may receive the reward he deserves. A man that does good — think of the illimitable reward that will come to a man like the Apostle Paul, a man like the sainted disciple John; or the great reward that will come to some of those mighty preachers of other days and the sainted of God through the years. Their lives live on and on and on in others. But, also think of the tragic reward that will come to those who have sown seeds of death and destruction. Think of those who have precipitated these horrible wars. If a man died when he died, the greatness of his reward or the terribleness of his reward might not be so much. But it goes on and on and on and on until the end of time, and at the end of time we appear before God. The Lord's people will appear at the *Bema* of Christ where we shall receive all of God's goodnesses to us. The wicked and the unbelieving will appear at the Great White Throne Judgment of God where they will receive the bitter rewards from what they have sown by their Christless lives and godless influence. The shadow of our lives extends beyond the grave. When we are resurrected, when all of us are changed, we shall appear immediately before the *Bema* of Christ, there to receive the rewards of our lives. In a thousand ways is it possible for a Christian to reap and to sow and to work for God now and until Jesus comes again.

THE MARRIAGE OF THE LAMB

Now the second great event in heaven is the marriage of the Lamb and the marriage supper of the great King. It is described in the nineteenth chapter of the Revelation: "Let us be glad and rejoice . . . for the marriage of the Lamb is come, and his wife hath made herself ready. And to her was granted that she should be arrayed in fine linen, clean and white: for the fine linen is the *Dikaiomata*, the righteousnesses [plural, the good deeds, the rewards at the *Bema;* that fine linen, clean and white, is the righteousnesses] of the saints. And he saith unto me, Write, Blessed are they which are called unto the marriage supper of the Lamb. And he saith unto me, These are the true sayings of God." The second great event is the marriage of the Lamb. "For his wife hath made herself ready. And to her was granted that she should be arrayed in fine linen, clean and white: for the fine linen is the righteousnesses of saints." That is, the *Bema* of Christ is over. The Judgment Day for God's people is over and the Lord hath given to us our rewards. That is what is referred to when it is said that His wife has made herself ready and is arrayed in white robes, the righteousnesses of the saints. At the wedding God has already given us our rewards. At the *Bema* of Christ, God's people are prepared to be married to the Lamb of God. All of our filthinesses are taken away.

The Bride of Christ is the church. It is not Israel nor is it a remnant of Israel. There is a special blessedness to us who have been saved and who love Jesus in this day of grace. All of the saints, from the beginning of the church in the days of our Lord and His Pentecost until the resurrection and translation when God takes us to heaven, all of the saints of God in this era, in this dispensation, are the Bride of Christ and there is a special blessing for us. Everywhere in the Scriptures the church is presented as the Bride of our Lord — just the church. Read Ephesians 5. Christ loved the church and gave Himself for it that He might present it to Himself without spot, without wrinkle, without any such thing, a chaste and beautiful maiden. The Bride of our Lord is the church.

But there is also a great marriage supper prepared to which there are guests invited. The Bride is married to the Lamb: the church is married to Christ. Beautiful, holy, spotless, perfect, are all of God's sainted people in the church. Then there is a marriage supper to which guests are invited. Who are they? This is what I think. These four and twenty elders are referred to the last time in this chapter nineteen of the Book of the Revelation. After that the term is never used again. I think those four and twenty elders divide. I think the twelve representing the church of Christ are married to the Lamb. That is His church, the Bride of Christ. I think the other twelve represent the saints of the old dispensation. I think they are the guests at the marriage supper of the Lamb. Why do I think that? Because the idea is presented in the Word of God consistently. For example, our Lord will say of John the Baptist, "of those born of woman there has never been a greater than John the Baptist, yet the least in the kingdom of heaven is greater than he." Then this great Baptist preacher will say in the third chapter of the gospel of John: "He that hath the bride is the bridegroom: but the friend of the bridegroom which standeth and heareth him, rejoiceth greatly because of the bridegroom's voice; this my joy therefore is fulfilled." The mighty Baptist preacher was martyred before the church was formed, and it is the church that is the Bride of Christ. That is why Jesus said, "Of those born of woman there has never been a greater than John the Baptist, but the least child in the church, the least child in this age of grace, is greater than John." As the concluding verse of the eleventh chapter of Hebrews says, "these all died in the faith in the Old Testament, but they did not receive the promise, that they without us should not be made perfect." The blessing of the Bride is that she is married to the Lamb.

But what of these Old Testament saints? Is there a blessing for them? Did God forget them, and are they not also honored and remembered? Look at Revelation 19:9: "And he saith unto me, Write [that means a specialty in the commandment] Blessed are they which are called unto the marriage supper of the Lamb." Without doubt there is a special and particular blessing for us who belong to the church. We shall be the Bride of Christ, married to Him. But there is also a blessing for those who are called to the marriage supper of our Christ, such as John the Baptist, who died, was martyred before the church was built, but who, standing, rejoiced in the bridegroom's voice. At that glorious banquet, which I think will last for a thousand years, when God's people sit down with Him to rejoice in the kingdom forever, there shall come in God's guests. I would think maybe that the greatest of them all will be that Baptist preacher. "Of those born of woman none is greater than John the Baptist." When John comes, he will be the most honored of all of the guests. Then will come in Abraham, who rejoiced to see His day and he saw it and was glad — Abraham rejoicing in the voice of the bridegroom. And so, God's saints are to come in and be seated around our glorious Lord, rejoicing in Him and in one another, world without end!

To think of these things staggers the imagination. Oh,

the glory, the wonder, the incomparable goodness, the great-ness, the sweetness, the celestial favor and shepherdly care of the Lord for those who love Him! Do you belong to the household of faith? If Jesus were to call us today, is it with gladness and rejoicing that we would behold His face? Is it right with you and God? Is your name written in the Lamb's Book of Life? Have you given your heart to Jesus? When you listen to a preacher preach about these glorious days that we some day shall see, does your heart lift up in gladness? Do you raise up your face with anticipation? Or is it a foreboding and a dread and a darkness to you? Which is it? Oh, that it might be the light and the glory of heaven! Make it that today by giving your heart in trust and in saving faith to the Lord Jesus.

Chapter 4

The Four Living Cherubim

And out of the throne proceeded lightnings and thunderings and voices: and there were seven lamps of fire burning before the throne, which are the seven Spirits of God. And before the throne there was a sea of glass like unto crystal: and in the midst of the throne, and round about the throne, were four beasts full of eyes before and behind. And the first beast was like a lion, and the second beast like a calf, and the third beast had a face as a man, and the fourth beast was like a flying eagle. And the four beasts had each of them six wings about him; and they were full of eyes within: and they rest not day and night, saying, Holy, holy, holy, Lord God Almighty, which was, and is, and is to come. And when those beasts give glory and honour and thanks to him that sat on the throne, who liveth for ever and ever, The four and twenty elders fall down before him that sat on the throne, and worship him that liveth for ever and ever, and cast their crowns before the throne, saying, Thou art worthy, O Lord, to receive glory and honour, and power: for thou hast created all things, and for thy pleasure they are and were created. — Revelation 4: 5-11

The King James version of the text reads: "And before the throne there was a sea of glass like unto crystal: and in the midst of the throne, and round about the throne, were four beasts . . ." There is a separate, different Greek word for "beasts" — *theria*. It is used in the thirteenth chapter of the Revelation. *Theria* refers to wild animals. But the word here is *zoa*, an altogether different kind of nomenclature. *Zoa* refers to living ones. The word "zoo" comes from it, as does the word "zoology." So the version usually reads: "Round about the throne, were four *zoa* [four living ones]

41

full of eyes before and behind. And the first *zo-on* [the first living one, singular] was like a lion, and the second *zo-on* like a calf [like an ox], and the third *zo-on* had a face as a man, and the fourth *zo-on* was like a flying eagle. And the four *zoa* had each of them six wings about him; and they were full of eyes within: and they rest not day and night, saying, Holy, holy, holy, Lord God Almighty, which was, and is, and is to come. And when those *zoa* [when those living ones] give glory and honour and thanks to him that sat on the throne, who liveth for ever and ever, the four and twenty elders fall down before him that sat on the throne, and worship him that liveth for ever and ever, and cast their crowns before the throne, saying, Thou art worthy, O Lord, to receive glory and honour, and power: for thou hast created all things, and for thy pleasure they are and were created."

We are to discuss the four *zoa*, the four living creatures. In the Old Testament we have been introduced to them in years past. In the first chapter of the Book of Ezekiel the prophet saw a whirlwind, and before the whirlwind a great black cloud and in the black cloud a fire enfolding itself; and out of the enfolding fire, he beheld the likeness of four living ones, four living creatures, four *zoa*. In the tenth chapter of the Book of Ezekiel, verse twenty, he gives them a familiar name: "This is the living creature that I saw under the God of Israel by the river of Chebar [the vision that he saw in the first chapter]; and I knew that they were the cherubim." The four *zoa*, the four living creatures, that Ezekiel saw, he names the four cherubim of God. They represent the animated life of all of the hosts of God in heaven and all of the manifold, maniform forms of life in this world, the four cherubim. Many times have we seen them in the Old Testament Scriptures.

In the third chapter of the Book of Genesis, when the man and the woman were cast out of the Garden of Eden, it was the cherubim who were placed on the east side of the Garden to guard and to keep the Tree of Life. In the

building of the Tabernacle, the pattern of which God gave
to Moses from heaven, there were cherubim interwoven in
the sacred veil before the holy of holies. There were cherubim interwoven in the ten curtains that covered the tabernacle. Above the ark of the covenant that contained the
ten commandments, which if a man kept he should live,
which if a man broke he should die, was the mercy seat,
the propitiatory, the lid made out of solid gold. Out of the
one piece of solid gold there were beaten the two forms of
cherubim, whose wings arching over formed the throne of
God, and whose eyes looked down upon the blood of expiation. Throughout the Old Testament, Jehovah God is called
"the One who dwells between the cherubim." In the construction of the temple of Solomon there were cherubim
interwoven in the veil between the holy place and the holy of
holies. Beyond the veil, King Solomon made two gigantic emblems, the cherubim of olive wood who were ten cubits high,
who were covered with pure gold, under whose overarching
wings the ark of the covenant was placed, and whose faces
looked forward toward the veil. Solomon also carved the
likenesses of cherubim around the lower part of the lavers,
he placed the likeness of the cherubim on the olive doors,
and he carved the likeness of the cherubim on the cedar
plans, covered with gold, that formed the inside of the
beautiful temple.

In the days of our Lord, in Herod's temple, pictures of
supposed likenesses of cherubim were painted on the walls.
But Josephus says that by that time and in his day, they had
forgotten what the scriptural form of a cherub looked like.
We have no idea what cherubim were like in shape and
figure except that they had wings. It is strange that in the
scriptural pattern of the Tabernacle we have God's delineation of every little hook and curtain and rod, but no description of the cherubim. What they looked like is known but
to God. In the Bible, however, in Ezekiel and here in the
Revelation, we are given symbolic forms of those glorious
creations. In Ezekiel and in the Book of the Revelation they

have wings, they are filled with eyes, penetrating into the inmost purposes and decrees of Almighty God; and they have four faces, the face of a man, the face of a lion, the face of an ox, and the face of a flying eagle. In Ezekiel each cherub has four faces; in the Revelation each cherub has one representative face.

THE MEANING OF THE CHERUBIM

As we read the Book and follow the course of the Apocalypse, we can easily see the part that the cherubim play in the administrative decrees of Almighty God. There are three things to be said about them in the Revelation. First, they have to do with this world. They have to do with God's purposes in this created life. They are four in number, and four is the scriptural numeric for the world. As seven is the number of the fulness of God, as three is the number of the diety of God, so the number *four* refers to the world that God made. There are four seasons, four points to the compass, four elements, four winds; four, the number that refers to this earth. These cherubim, four in number, represent and are emblems of God's great, animate creation. The Jew of old time in the Talmud said that there were four who were primary among the forms of life that God made: first, among all created life, man; second, among all domestic life, the ox; third, among all wild, untamed life, the lion; fourth, among the birds of the heavens, the flying eagle. These are the four faces of the cherubim: the face of a man, the face of an ox, the face of a lion and the face of a flying eagle. They have to do with God's created life in this world.

The second thing about the cherubim is that they have to do with the implementation and the execution of God's purposes and decrees for this world and for the life that He has created. They stand on the steps leading up to the throne of God, one on each side, ready and equipped to execute God's decrees anywhere in His world. Their assignment is the execution of the decrees and purposes of God in human history and in the destiny of this created universe.

In this chapter four we read, "out of the throne proceeded lightnings and thunderings and voices." We know, therefore, that the throne set in the Book of the Apocalypse is a throne of judgment. It is by the decrees and judgments of God that the Lord will redeem this lost and fallen creation. This truth is plainly delineated in the assignment given the cherubim in the Revelation.

In chapter six there is recorded the opening of the seven seals: "And I saw when the Lamb opened one of the seals, and I heard, as it were the noise of thunder [it is to be a day of judgment and visitation of the wrath of God] I heard and I saw one of the four *zoa* [one of the four cherubim] saying, Come, and when that cherub said Come, there came a white horse [the Antichrist, a false prophet of peace, conquering and to conquer] . . . And when he had opened the second seal, I heard the second of the cherubim say, Come, and there came in response to his command a red horse of war and of blood and of pillage . . . And when he had opened the third seal, I heard the voice of the third of the cherubim say, Come . . . And there came a black horse of famine and awful agony . . . And when he had opened the fourth seal, I heard the voice of the fourth of the cherubim say, Come, and there came a pale horse and the rider was named Death." In the providence of God and in the decrees of God, the nations of the world that oppose Him and the men who blaspheme His name shall be destroyed in a day of dark and terrible judgment. It has pleased God that in blood and agony this world is to be redeemed, and the instruments of that judgment and the implementation of those decrees are committed to the four cherubim.

Once again, in the fifteenth chapter of the Revelation, observe verse seven: "And one of the four cherubim gave unto the seven angels seven golden bowls full of the wrath of God, who liveth for ever and ever," and in those seven bowls is filled up and poured out the sum of the final wrath of God against the iniquity of this world. Not forever, God says, shall iniquity abound and the nations be cursed and mankind and all of animate life be in corruption and in bondage, but in the decree and elective purpose of the sovereign Lord Almighty there is a day coming when this world shall be judged in its sin, when it shall be redeemed from its corruption, when the Lord shall make a new creation. The instruments of the execution of those decrees of God lie in the hands of the four cherubim.

The third thing about the *zoa*, the living creatures, the cherubim: They are not only representative of the life that God has made, all animate life; they are not only the instruments of God in executing His decrees, sovereign and elective in this earth and in this world; but they are also the emblems and instruments and insignia of the love and purposes of grace for us and for God's creation. In the Garden of Eden, when the man and the woman were driven out, cherubim were placed at the gate on the east side, to guard and to keep the Tree of Life, lest the man, in his sin and in his mortality, eat thereof and live forever. That was a part of the provision of God for our blessing, in His mercy and grace and goodness toward us. For, had the man eaten of the Tree of Life after he had fallen into sin, he would have been confirmed forever in this body of death.

The Book says that flesh and blood cannot inherit the kingdom of God. In the Revelation there is a picture of men who seek death and cannot die. For a man to be confirmed forever in this body of death would be a horrible sentence beyond any imaginable word to describe it, for in this body, in this house, we are crippled, we are hurt, we are blinded, we are diseased, we are senile. Forced to live forever and forever in this house of clay, blinded, destroyed, senile, mind gone, man would be condemned to die a thousand deaths. Lest the man, in his sin, in his depravity, in his corruption, put forth his hand and eat of the Tree of Life and live forever, bound down in this body of death, the Lord took the Tree and placed before it the cherubim that it might be guarded for that holy and redemptive day when the man, resurrected, blessed, glorified, could partake of the Tree of Life in the Garden of Paradise which is in heaven. This body is to be planted in the earth that it may be resurrected to the glory of God. In body we must die that we may live unto the Lord. This body must be taken away in order that we may be given a house made without hands, eternal in the heavens. In this body we groan, earnestly desiring to be clothed upon, to be given our glorious house, our new body, which God is fashioning for us in heaven. The guarding, keeping, protecting care of the cherubim is that we may some day inherit that final glory that God has prepared for those who trust in Him.

Another function of the cherubim is to signify blessing in our earthly life. The old Rabbis in the Talmud, in commenting on the second chapter of the Book of Numbers, said that the twelve tribes of the children of Israel, in marching three tribes on each side of the encampment, marched under four banners, four standards, four ensigns of the administrative and judicial purposes of God. The standard of Judah was the lion, and on that side three tribes gathered. The standard of Reuben was a man, and on that side three tribes gathered. The standard of Dan was a flying eagle, and on that side three tribes gathered. The standard of Ephraim was an ox, and on that side three tribes gathered. So the twelve tribes gathered round the central glory of God, marched through the wilderness under the banner of a lion and an ox and a man and a flying eagle, the four *zoa*. In the purposes of God, He took His children out of the bondage of Egypt, He preserved them through the wilderness, He settled them in the Promised Land of Canaan under the symbols of the cherubim. Such is God's care for His elect in this weary world. He guides us and directs us through the wilderness of this life until finally He gives to us our ultimate, promised inheritance in heaven. The four *zoa*, the four living ones, the four cherubim, are emblems of God's protecting care.

THE SONG OF REDEMPTION

Now, we come to the last and most glorious of all of the emblems of blessing which God has purposed toward His people in these four cherubim: in the fifth chapter of the Revelation is a song of redemption. There is a great deal of textual difference in this song. Some of the ancient Greek manuscripts refer the song of redemption to just the four and twenty elders, to the church and the redeemed of the Lord. But most of the ancient Greek manuscripts include in that song not only the four and twenty elders, but also the four *zoa:* "And when the Lamb had taken the book, the four *zoa* [the four cherubim] and the four and twenty elders fell down before the Lamb . . . and they sung a new song, saying, Thou are worthy to take the book, and to open the seals thereof: for thou wast slain, and hast redeemed us to God by thy blood out of every kindred, and tongue, and people, and nation . . . and we shall reign on the earth."

It is very plain why a scribe would choose a text that kept the song to the four and twenty elders and excluded from it the four *zoa.* But as I read the scriptures and pore over these pages, I can see why those four cherubim can also join in that ultimate, glorious paean of praise and glory to the redemptive work of the Son of God. Read the eighth chapter of the Book of Romans. Paul says in that passage that not only shall fallen humanity be redeemed, not only shall we be delivered from the bondage of corruption, but that the entire creation of God and every one of God's living creatures shall be delivered from the bondage of corruption into the glorious liberty of the children of God. "For," he says, "the earnest expectation of the creature [God's animal life, all of God's life] waiteth for the manifestation of the sons of God. For the creature was made subject to death and carnivorous viciousness and to the wildness of life, not willingly, but by reason [by the permissive will of the sovereign Lord God] of him who hath subjected the same in hope, Because the creature itself [animate life itself] shall be delivered from the bondage of corruption into the glorious liberty of the children of God. For we know that the whole creation [all of animal life, whether it be domestic like an ox or whether it be wild like the lion or whether it be fowl like the flying eagle] groaneth and travaileth in pain together until now." The agony of the animal world in their vicious carnivorousness was not a thing intended of God. It was a judgment. It was an execution of the wrath of God upon sin.

Where did that sin come from? Who initiated it? Who destroyed God's perfect creation? It was one out of the number of the heavenly cherubim. In the twenty-eighth chapter of the Book of Ezekiel he is described. In Ezekiel 28:12 ff., his name is given: "Thou sealest up the sum, full of wisdom, and perfect in beauty. Thou hast been in Eden the garden of God; every precious stone was thy covering . . . Thou wast perfect in thy ways from the day that thou wast created, till iniquity was found in thee . . . Thine heart was lifted up because of thy beauty, thou hast corrupted thy wisdom by reason of thy brightness."

Who is that Lucifer whose pride, whose beauty, whose wisdom lifted him up against God Almighty? The Book says: "Thou art the anointed cherub that covereth," the one whose wings outstretched over God's creation and in whose beauty and wisdom and care, God gave the keeping of all of His vast universe. In his pride and his beauty, he lifted up himself against God and brought sin into heaven, brought sin into this world and destroyed God's beautiful creation. It was one of their number, it was one of the celestial cherubim, whose heart was lifted up against God and in whose soul sin was born. He destroyed God's creation, and he was the instrument of destroying the man and the woman God made. In that iniquity the earth was cursed. The wild beasts grew claw and fang and carnivorously destroyed each other. Was that the purpose of God? Was that the initial creation of the Lord God, that the earth should be stained with blood and that life should destroy life and that God's creatures should devour each other and that the whole world should face animosity and horror? The attack upon one another of the untamed animals, and the war by which the man destroys and slaughters his friends and his neighbors — was that the purpose of God in the creation? No! No! The throne of God is a throne of judgment.

Those four cherubim represent God's great work of animate life. When one of their number fell, in the wisdom and choice of God, He gave to that group, He gave to the cherubim the execution of the decrees of the Almighty whereby this whole creation shall be delivered from the bondage of corruption until it be again as God made it in the beginning, full and sweet and beautiful, living to the glory and the worshipful, reverential awe and love of the Lord God our Creator.

So this fourth chapter ends, in the paean of praise of the four cherubim in the redeemed creation, as it worships and serves the just and only God. When those four cherubim give glory and honor and thanks to Him who sat on the throne, the four and twenty elders fall down to worship and they say, "Thou art worthy, O Lord, to receive glory and honour and power; for thou hast created all of these things, and for thee they were and are created." When the four *zoa* bow before God, singing that song of creative redemption, they represent all of God's creation bowing before God, serving the Lord in the purposes for which God created them. That is the holy and incomparably beautiful picture of that millennial age when the earth shall be filled with the knowledge of the Lord as the waters cover the sea; for, says the prophet, in that day and time, when God has executed these purposes, and when He has delivered the creation from its bondage, "the wolf shall dwell with the lamb and the leopard shall lie down with the kid, the lion shall eat straw like the ox, the sucking child shall play on the hole of the asp and the weaned child shall put his hand on the cockatrice's den, and none shall make them afraid."

All of animal life that is now vicious and carnivorous, God will remake into that beautiful Edenic peace by which He decreed their life in the beginning. The lion and the leopard and the wolf shall lose their claw and their fang and their vicious, carnivorous spirit. The wolf, the lamb, the leopard and the kid shall live in peace and beauty and glory to the great Lord God who created them and placed them in the Edenic garden of this world.

All of creation shall be redeemed — not just the man. All of God's creation shall be redeemed. Animal life, bird life, human life, domestic life, the stars, this earth burned and seared with drought and desert and burning sand: all shall be redeemed unto God. It is the purpose of the Lord for us that we shall live in a beautiful, holy and godly world. The instruments of the decrees by which He shall bring it to pass are the cherubim, who stand in the midst of the throne day and night, ready to carry out the final, ultimate, elective purpose of God for us in this world.

What ultimate blessedness and glory the Lord has purposed for His people! Until then, precious beyond compare it is to call on His name now, to love Him now, to trust in Jesus now. That is our appeal and invitation to your heart.

Chapter 5

The Seven-Sealed Book

And I saw in the right hand of him that sat on the throne a book written within and on the backside, sealed with seven seals. And I saw a strong angel proclaiming with a loud voice, Who is worthy to open the book, and to loose the seals thereof? And no man in heaven, nor in earth, neither under the earth, was able to open the book, neither to look thereon. And I wept much, because no man was found worthy to open and to read the book, neither to look thereon. And one of the elders saith unto me, Weep not: behold, the Lion of the tribe of Juda, the Root of David, hath prevailed to open the book, and to loose the seven seals thereof. And I beheld, and, lo, in the midst of the throne and of the four beasts, and in the midst of the elders, stood a Lamb as it had been slain, having seven horns and seven eyes, which are the seven Spirits of God sent forth into all the earth. And he came and took the book out of the right hand of him that sat upon the throne. And when he had taken the book, the four beasts and four and twenty elders fell down before the Lamb, having every one of them harps and golden vials full of odours, which are the prayers of saints. And they sung a new song, saying, Thou art worthy to take the book, and to open the seals thereof; for thou wast slain, and hast redeemed us to God by thy blood out of every kindred, and tongue, and people, and nation; And hast made us unto our God kings and priests: and we shall reign on the earth. — Revelation 5:1-10

Chapters four and five in the Revelation go together. There is a chapter division in between them, but this device must not be allowed to destroy their continuity. The two chapters belong together. Chapters four and five record the scenes that the incredulous eyes of John looked upon in glory. He saw the throne of God, he saw the cherubim of the Lord, he saw the four and twenty elders (the redeemed of the Lord), and as he looked in wonder and in amazement, all heaven was astir with a coming scene, a development of vast significance and of celestial, eternal importance. As that scene unfolds, it is unlike anything we might have thought for. The scene, as it develops, brings into focus an all-important scroll that is laid upon the hand of God. "And I saw in the right hand [*epi* — 'upon' the right hand of God] a scroll, a book, written within and on the backside, sealed with seven seals." On God's extended right hand lies a scroll, a book, as if for one who could take it, open it, read it and execute its mandates and its elective purposes.

There are several books mentioned in the Revelation. There is the Book of Life, a register of the names of all those who have been redeemed by the blood of the Lamb. There is another book, the Book of Works, wherein God writes down all the deeds that are done in this human life. Again, in the tenth chapter of the Revelation, there is a book of the testimony that is given to John by which he speaks in prophecy to the peoples and the nations. This book described in Revelation five is most unusual. It is unique. It is sealed with seven seals.

Remember, when we use here the term, "book," we refer to the book as it was in an ancient day, a scroll. The Christian people took the long roll and cut it up into leaves and tied the back part together, like this book you are reading. The book we use in modern times was invented by the first Christian preachers, martyrs, missionaries and evangelists as they took the scrolls of the Scriptures and preached to the people, showing out of the Holy Scriptures that Jesus is the Christ, the Son of God. It takes time to unroll a scroll; so the Christian people cut it up and bound the back side of the leaves together into what was called a "codex." That was done so the Christian could testify and the preacher could easily turn to a place in the Bible when he could show God's Word presenting the Son and our Saviour. But the scroll was the only kind of a book known when the Bible was written.

This scroll that lay in the hand of God was sealed with seven seals. It was *really* sealed. The Greek text reads, *katesphragismenon sphragisin kepta*. You couldn't write it more strongly than that. Literally, it was "sealed down with seals seven." Now the vision that John saw was this: There was a scroll rolled up, then that part sealed, then rolled again and sealed, and rolled again and sealed; so through all six seals, and the seventh seal sealed the entire scroll. When it was unsealed, the process was reversed. When the first seal was broken, a portion of the scroll could be unrolled and could be read. When the second seal was broken, another portion of the scroll was unbound and could be read; and so on down until, when all seven of the seals were broken, the entire scroll was opened and could be read. There is immeasurable significance in that book. In fact, as we shall see in proceeding with these messages, this is the most important, the most vital, the most significant of all of the scenes that we are looking upon as they are depicted in the Apocalypse.

THE SYMBOLIC MEANING OF THE BOOK

What does this book mean? There are excellent suggestions concerning the meaning of the scroll that lay on the extended hand of God. For example, there are those who suggest that the scroll represents the investiture of the Lord Christ with the reins of sovereignty and government in the earth. That is a fine suggestion. Our Lord said in Matthew 28:18: "All authority is given unto me in heaven and in earth." Here is another suggestion. It is said that the Book represents the eternal counsels and decrees of the Lord God Almighty, His elective purposes in the earth. The reason it is written on the backside and on the inside is because those great decrees of God so crowded the pages of the scroll, being so many. In that event, the sealed scroll, the unbroken book, would represent the unrealized purposes of God, the unknown and the unexecuted decrees of heaven. Then the open book, the unsealed book, would represent the decrees and the purposes of God made known and executed and realized in the earth. That is a fine suggestion. Then, there is another suggestion as to what that Book might mean, which comprises a splendid suggestion. The last chapter and among the last words of the prophecy of Daniel in chapter twelve, verse eight reads: "And I heard, but I understood not: then said I, O my Lord, what shall be the end of these things? And he said, Go thy way, Daniel: for the words are closed up and sealed till the time of the end." (Here is that same *sprageso,* the word used to translate the Hebrew word in the Septuagint, the Greek Bible, which is the Bible the Christians employed in their preaching; here is the same word which is found in the fifth chapter of the Revelation, that "sealed" book.) According to this interpretation, the Book means, in the Revelation, that the time of the end has come, as the book is to be unsealed, as the purposes of God are made known and executed in the earth. That is a fine suggestion, also.

Now, this is what that book means to me. I shall first point out four significant things about it. First, it is *that* book which brings into the heavenly scene the Son of God, the Prince of Glory, the Redeemer of creation and the great architect of the events that follow, events that finally ensue in the creation of the new heaven and the new earth. It is a very significant thing that *that* book brings into the scene of heaven the Prince of Glory and the great Author of the new creation. Second, that book, when the great Redeemer comes to receive it and John turns to look upon Him, introduces us to the Lamb of God. The Prince of Glory who takes it does so in the character of a lamb slain on the sacrificial altar, a lamb with its blood poured out upon the earth. The character of the One who comes, the great, matchless Son of God, is the character of a sacrificial lamb. Third, when that One comes to take the book, He comes in a character and in a work from which all creation has shrunk away in unworthiness and in ability. Fourth, when the Book is taken by the hand of Him who is the great Redeemer of the world, then all creation bursts into song. When that book is taken and when the Christ holds it in His hand, all the hosts above and in the earth beneath and all creation, animate and inanimate, sing to the glory of the Lamb. What are their praises and their doxologies and their words of wonder and worship and reverence? They are all words of redemption. "Worthy art thou to take the book and to open the seals thereof, for thou wast slain and hath redeemed us unto God by thy blood."

Therefore, it is my understanding that the primary, fundamental, chief reference and significance of this book has to do with the redemption of God's created universe and everything in it. That book is a book of redemption. It is a book of the final acts of God, concerning the liberation of this destroyed and cursed and ruined universe. That book is a book of the judgment of God upon the alien and the usurper who has cursed this earth and destroyed it and now occupies it. That book is the book of the casting out of the usurper and the destroyer. That book is the book of the casting into hell of Satan, of the dragon, of the grave, of death, of sin. That book is the book of the redemption of the whole purchased possession of God.

The Meaning of Redemption

When we refer to this book that lies in the hand of God as "a book of redemption," we must understand the larger meaning of that word "redemption." Usually, when we think of the word "redemption," our minds go back to one act, the act of Christ when He redeemed us to God by His own blood. That truth is the great root and fundamental basis upon which all salvation reposes — the sacrificial act, the atonement of Christ. But the word "redemption" encompasses far more than that. The word "redemption" goes back in its meaning through thousands of years of history. It includes all of the story of God of the ages past, all the dispensations of the past, all of the marvelous theophanies of God in the past, the advent of our Lord into the world, this present age, the age of grace, and of the church; all of those things are included in that word "redemption." But it also includes that vast consummation that is yet to come. The word "redemption" also includes the dispensations that are yet to be; it includes the glorious, incomparable, celestial theophanies of the Lord that are yet to be given to man, and it includes the more glorious advent of Christ and the far more significant things that are yet to be wrought through the wondrous hands, the redeeming hands of the Lord Messiah, the God Christ. The blessings of redemption have hallowed and sanctified this earth through the generations. It was the redemptive purpose of God in Christ that made Adam not ultimately die, that delivered the race from extinction and upholds this world from destruction. The redemptive love and mercy of Christ girdles this globe like a golden chain binding it to the heart of God. But, however great the seas and the oceans and the mercies of God in days past and now, they are not worthy to be compared with the glorious things that God has in store for this creation and for us in a future day.

There is a future in that word "redemption" that encompasses the entire consummation of the purposes and elective decrees of God. Read the twenty-first chapter of the Book of Luke. In the Apocalyptic discourse of our Lord, He said, "When these things begin to come to pass, then look up, and lift up your heads; for your redemption draweth nigh." There is a future in that word "redemption." It rests upon the great basis of the sacrifice of Christ. It is founded upon the atonement of our Lord. But it reaches out to the great ultimate purpose of God for all creation. When this end time comes of which we are speaking in the Revelation, and when these things begin to come to pass, "then look up, lift up your heads, for your redemption draweth nigh." There is a future to our salvation, more and more excellently glorious than any we have ever known in the past or that we could experience now. As much as he gloried in the cross of Christ, Paul will say in I Corinthians 15:19: "If in this life only we have hope in Christ, we are of all men most miserable." There is a future to redemption beyond what we have known now or what we have ever known in the past. In the first chapter of the Book of Ephesians, Paul will say, "God hath sealed us with the Holy Spirit." But he says, "That is but an earnest [it is a token, it is a small part] of the inheritance that will be ours when God redeems the whole purchased possession." However much we may have now or know now or experience now, it is but an earnest, it is but a pledge of the great, glorious, entire redemption of all God has purchased that lies in the future. That word "redemption" includes the entire purpose, the elective choice and decree of God for His entire creation.

The inheritance belongs to someone else now. There is a usurper who possesses it. There is an interloper, there is an intruder, there is an alien, there is a stranger, who has cursed God's world. The world does not rightfully belong to him; it rightly belongs to us. It was created for Adam and it belongs to Adam's seed. It is rightfully Adam's race and some day God will redeem, will take back, the entire purchased possession and He will cast out that interloper and intruder. The story of how that is to be done is revealed in the seven-sealed book, as the seals are broken one after another.

THE FORFEITED INHERITANCE

From the Word of God let us consider why that Book is seven-sealed and how it reflects perfectly the manners and customs of the ancient Jews as we know them here in the Bible. "And I saw upon the right hand of him that sat on the throne a scroll written within and on the backside, sealed with seven seals." That seven-sealed book represents a forfeited inheritance. That is what it means in the Word of God. According to the custom of the ancient Jew, and according to Mosaic Law, the estate, the land and possessions of a Jew, a Hebrew, in God's land, Palestine, could never be sold or given away. Forever it belonged in that family and in that household.

In the Word of the Lord, one reads that at the Year of Jubilee (after seven times seven, forty-nine years, the fiftieth year was a Jubilee), the trumpet was to sound and every man was to return unto his possession. "In the year of Jubilee ye shall return every man unto his possessions" (Leviticus 25:8-13, 23-25). So at the fiftieth year every man was given back the inheritance of his father. Now, if between those two Jubilees, ". . . if thy brother be waxen poor and hath sold away some of his possessions, if any of his kin come to redeem it then shall he redeem that which his brother sold, either his uncle or his uncle's son may redeem it or any that is nigh of kin unto him of his family may redeem it." We have an instance of such redemption in the fourth chapter of the Book of Ruth. Boaz, a kinsman, a goel, a kinsman-redeemer, redeemed the lost inheritance of Naomi and of Mahlon, the dead husband of Ruth. How they did it is beautifully told in the story of Ruth. The story of Ruth is a story of redemption. The thirty-second chapter of Jeremiah records how Jeremiah brought back the inheritance of his uncle: "So I took the evidence of the purchase, both that which was sealed according to the law and custom, and that which was open: And I give the evidence of the purchase . . . then said the Lord . . . take these evidences, this evidence of the purchase, [of the redemption], both which is sealed, and this evidence which is open; and put them in an earthen vessel . . ."

Let these passages explain this sealed book in the Revelation. According to the manner and the custom of the ancient Hebrew, when an inheritance was forfeited because of distress or anguish or poverty, and the family had to give up the inheritance of their fathers, two scrolls were written. One was a scroll that recounted the reason for the forfeiture of the inheritance, and that scroll was sealed. I have thought (and this is just my guess) that the reason the scroll was

sealed was because the family would not want the curious
to read of the distress and agony and travail that forced
them to give up the inheritance of their fathers. So it was
written on a scroll, in a book, and it was sealed. That
sealed book was a sign of the forfeiture, of the giving up of
the inheritance. Then, according to custom, another scroll
was written, which was open, which anyone could see, and
in that scroll were written the terms of its redemption if a
legally qualified goel appeared. As time went on, the family
did not take two scrolls. They just used one. On the inside
of the scroll was written the reason, the secret reason, historical reason, for the forfeiture, and that was rolled up and
sealed. Then on the outside were written the terms of the
redemption and the names of the witnesses.

Such is the book which we see here in the hand of God.
That sealed book is a sign of the forfeiture of Adam's inheritance. The world now belongs to someone else. An
intruder, an interloper, an alien, an enemy took it and cursed
it and damned it. The Lord never created Adam to die.
Death is an enemy, God says, an interloper. God never
made the earth to groan and to travail in agony and in pain,
a place where the animals eat one another, where the earth
is blasted with desert and with the burning of the sun and
the cold of the winds. God never intended this earth to be
bathed in tears and in blood. "An enemy hath done this,"
saith the Lord, "an interloper." The sign of that forfeiture
lies in the hand of God. The Book represents the instruments, the mortgages, the bonds, of our lost inheritance.
The completeness of that forfeiture and the terrible encumbrance upon it is signified by seven seals — seven of them.
Adam's race has forfeited the inheritance altogether.

The breaking of those seven seals represents the restitution of the creation to God and to Adam's fallen race. If
the breaking of those seven seals is the restitution of the
inheritance to the seed of Adam, then the sealing of those
seven seals represents the vast encumbrance that lies upon
Adam's inheritance. It is lost; it is completely lost. That

sealed book represents the forfeiture of our lost inheritance. It lies on the hand of God. Who in heaven above, in earth beneath, who is worthy to take that book and to buy back the lost inheritance? Who is worthy?

THE WHOLE CREATION TO BE REDEEMED

I conclude this sermon with just a word concerning that lost inheritance which that book represents. The record of our lost inheritance is written within and on the backside. Inside is the story of how we lost it, the distress and the agony and the tears and the sorrow by which we lost our father's inheritance. Written on the outside are the terms of its redemption, waiting for a kinsman-redeemer to buy us back to God. That book represents the entire creation of God. Everything you have ever seen, everything you have ever read about, everything that your eye could behold at night, everything that your heart has ever experienced, the whole earth around us, the whole creation of God, all of it, all of it is lost to us.

Adam was cursed in death. "In the day that thou eatest thereof thou shalt surely die," and being the federal head of the race, in him death passed upon us all and we all die. We inherit that backdrop. The curse that fell upon Adam falls upon us, and the death that fell upon him falls upon us. Adam was cursed. He lost the glory and the beauty of his soul. He lost the perfection of his mind and character. He lost the wonder of the glorious, celestial mechanism of his body; and he became a prey to every evil thing, every wind of violence, every disease in death and age and senility, all of which fell upon Adam and upon us. The house in which we live is cursed, the mind with which we think, cursed, the heart with which we feel, destroyed. The curse fell upon Adam. The ground was cursed, "Cursed is the ground for thy sake," said God. Great desert wastes, all things that are sterile and barren on this earth — the ground was cursed for Adam's sake. The vegetable kingdom was cursed. "Thorns also and thistles shall it bring forth to thee," said God, and the vegetable kingdom lost its glory and its beauty. The animal kingdom was cursed. "And the Lord God said unto the serpent . . . thou art cursed above all cattle, and above every beast of the field; upon thy belly shalt thou go, and dust shalt thou eat all the days of thy life." Adam cursed — death, death — the ground cursed, the whole vegetable world cursed and the whole world of animal life cursed — all are cursed! Our lost inheritance! The stars cursed, the planets cursed; the whole creation of God lost to an interloper, lost to an intruder, lost to a Satan, lost to a devil, lost to a dragon, lost to a serpent, lost to an enemy! That evil messenger reigns. Death seems to be supreme, and the grave seems never to be satiated. The whole earth seems forever to burn in its blistering heat in the summertime, and to die in its frigid cold in the winter.

But there is a decree of God and there is a purpose of God to redeem the whole purchased possession. Is not that what we read? "Ye were sealed with that holy Spirit . . . Which is the earnest of our inheritance until the redemption of the purchased possession" (Ephesians 1:13-14). Just for a while we wait, just for a while in agony and tears now, just for a while in death, just for a while in this veil of tears; but there is coming a time, there is coming a day when God in Christ shall redeem this whole purchased possession. That is the story of this little book: how God shall redeem the world and cast out the interloper and bring back to Adam the lost inheritance; how God shall bring it back to us. That is the story of the opening of those seals. When that last seal is opened, the last enemy is cast out. The grave and death, the false prophet, the false beast and the devil are cast into hell. God has redeemed to Himself and given back to Adam's lost race the inheritance that He purchased for them when the Lamb died on the tree.

When God restores to us our inheritance, He is going to redeem our bodies: "For we know that if our earthly house of this tabernacle were dissolved, we have a building of God, an house not made with hands, eternal in the heavens"

(II Corinthians 5:1). Our bodies, planted in the dust of the ground, are to be raised in the likeness of His own glory. We shall have a new house, a new body. The blind will see and the crippled walk and the broken-hearted will be made well again and the diseased will be strong.

Second, there will be a redemption of this earth. Oh, the promises in the Book! "And the desert shall blossom like the rose and the waste places shall be gardens of paradise." This whole earth shall be redeemed. The curse shall be taken from the soil of the ground. The vegetation of the earth shall be redeemed. When God shall take away the curse from the fields and the grass and the flowers, then all the vegetable creation shall be redeemed. The animal creation shall be redeemed. All animate life shall be redeemed unto God. Then the wolf shall dwell with the lamb and the leopard shall lie down with the kid and the lion shall eat straw like an ox, no longer carnivorous and vicious, wild, with that curse that the interloper put into animal hearts. "The sucking child shall play on the hole of the asp, and the weaned child shall put his hand on the cockatrice's den, when they shall not hurt nor destroy in all God's holy mountain."

Finally, there will be the redemption of the whole creation. As Paul writes, incomparably, in the eighth chapter of Romans, verses 21 and 22: ". . . the creation itself also shall be delivered from the bondage of corruption into the glorious liberty of the children of God. For we know that the whole creation groaneth and travaileth in pain together until now." The creation is waiting for the redemption of God's children. But when it comes, the whole creation shall be redeemed unto the Lord. How that is to be is in the book that lies in the hand of God.

But who can redeem us, who can buy us back, who can remake us, and who can create the new heaven and the new earth? Therein is the worthiness of the Lamb. May God sanctify the next message as we speak of the Lion of the Tribe of Judah who casts out the interloper. When John

turns to look, behold, it is the Lamb that taketh away the
sin of this world. Oh, whoever thought such things? I
never saw them before. But there they are, written large
upon the open page as God shall give us spiritual eyes to see
and spiritual ears to hear and a spiritual heart to praise
and to love and to respond. God sanctify these words to
our souls.

Chapter 6

The Worthiness of the Lamb

And I saw in the right hand of him that sat on the throne a book written within and on the backside, sealed with seven seals. And I saw a strong angel proclaiming with a loud voice, Who is worthy to open the book, and to loose the seals thereof? And no man in heaven, nor in earth, neither under the earth, was able to open the book, neither to look thereon. And I wept much, because no man was found worthy to open and to read the book, neither to look thereon. And one of the elders saith unto me, Weep not: behold, the Lion of the tribe of Juda, the Root of David, hath prevailed to open the book, and to loose the seven seals thereof. And I beheld, and, lo, in the midst of the throne and of the four beasts, and in the midst of the elders, stood a Lamb as it had been slain, having seven horns and seven eyes, which are the seven Spirits of God sent forth into all the earth. And he came and took the book out of the right hand of him that sat upon the throne. And when he had taken the book, the four beasts and four and twenty elders fell down before the Lamb, having every one of them harps, and golden vials full of odours, which are the prayers of saints. And they sung a new song, saying, Thou art worthy to take the book, and to open the seals thereof: for thou wast slain, and hast redeemed us to God by thy blood out of every kindred, and tongue, and people, and nation; And hast made us unto our God kings and priests: and we shall reign on the earth. — Revelation 5:1-10

These messages concern one great, sublime, celestial theme, the redemption of the creation of God. It is the substance of the seven-sealed book. It is the content of the songs of the saints and of the antiphonal responses of the *muriades, muriadon* angels, the uncounted millions of millions and multiplied millions of the innumerable of God's hosts in heaven. Men are numbered, the cherubim are numbered, the elders are numbered, the elect are numbered. But there is never a number to God's heavenly host, the angels in glory. Redemption's song and what the angels say will be the message.

The last message discussed the seven-sealed book. "And I saw [*epi*, 'upon'] upon the palm of the hand of God a scroll written within and on the backside, sealed with seven seals." The scroll was rolled and sealed, rolled and sealed, rolled and sealed, rolled and sealed, until finally the seventh seal sealed the entire scroll. Then, when it was opened, one seal was broken, and that much of the scroll unrolled to view; then the next seal was broken, and that much unrolled; until finally, when all seven seals were broken, the entire scroll was opened to view. That book represents a forfeited inheritance. The inheritance is what God created for us, for Adam's seed. We lost it in sin and transgression. A usurper took it; sin, death, hell, Satan, iniquity, judgment, wrath and the curse took away our inheritance as it is unto this day. According to the law and customs of the ancient Jewish people, the sign of a forfeited inheritance was a sealed book. The fact that it is seven-sealed emphasizes the encumbrances that are upon this inheritance. An interloper, an intruder, an alien, an enemy, has taken it, and that book of redemption awaits a goel, a kinsman-redeemer, a worthy, qualified and legal kinsman to buy it back and to restore it to its rightful owners. When that book of redemption is taken by one who is worthy, and those seals are opened, then that interloper, that intruder, that alien, that enemy is to be cast out; and finally the whole purchased possession is to be redeemed, and sin, hell, death, and Satan are to be cast into the lake of fire, forever destroyed. The judgment of God creates for us a new heaven and a new earth, and gives us back the inheritance that we lost in Adam. Such is the meaning of the seven-sealed book that lies upon the hand of God. It is the symbol of a forfeited and lost inheritance. It represents the encumbrances laid upon the property awaiting one to redeem it, to buy it back, to retrieve it, to lift those deeds of mortgage and restore the possession to the rightful owners.

The vision begins with these words: "And I saw a strong angel proclaiming with a loud voice, Who is worthy to open the book, and to loose the seals thereof?" All the moral and intelligent universe is focused upon that sealed book. The voice of the strong angel calls, saying that the time has come, if there is a legal representative, if there is a qualified goel, if there is a kinsman-redeemer who is worthy and able to buy back this inheritance, for him to step forward to redeem the purchased possession. The voice of that strong angel penetrates to the farthest corners of glory; it searches the entire earth, and it reaches down into the realm of the departed dead. Where is one thus worthy? The search is made in heaven. Where is one thus able? The search is made in earth. Where is one thus qualified? The search is made in the nether-world. Where is one who is able to come and lift these title deeds, to retrieve this mortgaged inheritance and to buy it back from the interloper, the intruder, the alien, the enemy who now possesses it? Who, says the strong and mighty angel, who is worthy to open the book and to loose these seven seals and to rid the inheritance of these heavy and weighty encumbrances?

Observe the Greek word for "no one" in the next verse: "*oudeis* in heaven," and "*oudeis* in earth," and "*oudeis* under the earth," was able to open the book or to look thereon. The Greeks built up words as the Germans build them up today. Such words are most expressive. The translation here is: "And no man in heaven, nor in earth, neither under the earth, was able to open the book." Look at the emphatic Greek word for "No one." The Greek word for "no," "not," is *ou; de* is a little participle meaning "even"; and the Greek word for "one'" (the cardinal number *one*) is *heis*. Placed together, the three little words make *oudeis*, meaning "not even one." Search was made in heaven, and not even one in all heaven was able or worthy. When the angels and the principalities and the powers and the archangels and all of the order and ranks of heaven looked at that sealed book and read on the backside the qualifications of those who were worthy and able to break those seals, they shrank back in unworthiness and inability. They were mute. All heaven turned silent. *Oudeis,* "not even one" could be found in the whole realm of the spirit world, not one could be found who was worthy. "And *oudeis,*" "nor was there even one" who could be found in the earth, not one, not one.

THE LAMENTATION OF JOHN

From the way that sentence is framed, "Who is worthy to open the book, and to loose the seals thereof?", it would seem that there were those who had attempted to do so, who had sought to achieve it. If that sentence is so framed and the question so asked that it could thus refer to other attempts to open the seals, it is certainly historically true. For during the ages and ages since Adam lost his inheritance, there has been the constant attempt on the part of men to buy it back, to win it back, to find that ultimate good, to give to us our lost inheritance, the Utopia for which our souls long. The arts of civilizations have sought to do it. All of the political science of the centuries has sought to do it. These revolutions, these different forms of government, are trying to find some way to bring back to humanity that lost inheritance. Philosophy, men's finest thinking, has sought to think it through. Man-made religions have sought to buy it back. Through the centuries, through all the story of mankind, that attempt has been made. Who is worthy, who is able, to buy back, to give us back, this lost inheritance? Who? Not even one in heaven above, in the earth beneath, or on the earth where now we live, not one was found able to open the book or to look thereon.

Then is written this expressive clause in the Greek language as John describes his agony of soul: "And I wept much." The emphasis is upon the distress and the agony of heart and the grief of the Seer as he breathlessly waited for someone out of heaven, or out of the nether-world, or out of the earth, to come forward to redeem this lost inheritance, God's destroyed creation. As he waited, there was no one found, not in the earth, not in heaven, nor under the earth; there was no one found. The Seer writes in such a way that you can see the deep agony of his soul. *Kai ego*, "And I," then the personal pronoun is also in the verb, "And I *eklaion*," "And I burst into open lamentation and audible sobs." We find that same verb in its imperfect tense, just as it is here in the Revelation, in Luke 19:41: "And when the Lord was come near, he beheld the city, and [*eklausen*, the same imperfect verb] he audibly lamented over it." He burst into tears looking upon it. That is John's description of the agony of his soul as he breathlessly waited for some qualified redeemer to come forward and take that possession and give it back to a lost and destroyed humanity. As he waited and waited, and as all heaven was breathless and silent, there was no one, no one who came forward, who was able and worthy to take the book of the mortgage deeds of God's creation and to redeem it to those to whom it rightfully belongs. John, as he waited and as no one came forward, burst into audible lamentation and tears.

These represent the tears of all God's people through all the centuries. Those tears of the Apostle John are the tears of Adam and Eve, driven out of the Garden of Eden, as they bowed over the first grave, as they watered the dust of the ground with their tears over the silent, still form of their son, Abel. Those are the tears of the children of Israel in bondage as they cried unto God in their affliction and slavery. They are the tears of God's elect through the centuries as they cried unto heaven. They are the sobs and tears that have been wrung from the heart and soul of God's people as they looked on their silent dead, as they stand beside their open graves, as they experience, in the trials and sufferings of life, heartaches and disappointments indescribable. Such is the curse that sin has laid upon God's beautiful creation; and this is the damnation of the hand of him who holds it, that usurper, that interloper, that intruder, that alien, that stranger, that dragon, that serpent, that Satan-devil. "And I wept audibly," for the failure to find a Redeemer meant that this earth in its curse is consigned forever to death. It meant that death, sin, damnation and hell should reign forever and ever and the sovereignty of God's earth should remain forever in the hands of Satan. "I wept much because *oudeis*" — i.e., "not even one" — in heaven, in earth, under the earth, was found worthy to open the book and to loose those seven seals and to cast out these who curse and damn our earth. "I wept much."

"And one of the elders saith unto me, Weep not: behold . . ." Notice it is not a strong angel proclaiming with a loud voice, but it is one of the elders. "Blessed are they that mourn for they shall be comforted." One of the elders, one who, himself, had known what it was to be regenerated in his heart, one who, himself, had known what it was to be redeemed, his body raised out of the dust of the ground and out of the heart of the earth, — one of the elders, one of the redeemed, one of the blood-bought, "one of the elders saith unto me, Weep not: behold . . ." That has been the cry of the church through all of the centuries. "Weep not. Weep not. Lift up your eyes. Lift up your hearts. Raise up your soul. Look! Behold! Behold! Behold the Lamb of God, the hope of Israel, the Saviour of the world!" That is what the prophets saw, and they saw it and were glad. That is what the first Christian herald announced to the world. That is what they said, that is what they preached. This is the Gospel of the Son of God: "Weep not, weep not, behold, behold." "And one of the elders saith unto me, Weep not: behold, the Lion of the tribe of Juda, the Root of David, hath prevailed to open the book, and to break the seven seals of encumbrances and to lift the mortgage and to buy it back and to redeem it to Adam's fallen race. Weep not: behold, the Lion of the tribe of Juda, the Root of David . . ."

THE LION IS THE LAMB

Every syllable of this book, every word and sentence, is fraught with unfathomable meaning. "Behold the Lion of the tribe of Juda." We know who that refers to. In the forty-ninth chapter of the book of Genesis, when Israel was prophesying of his twelve sons, he turned to the fourth boy, Judah, and said: "Judah, thou art he whom thy brethren shall praise [his name means 'praise']: thy hand shall be in the neck of thine enemies; thy father's children shall bow down before thee. Judah is a lion's whelp: from the prey, my son, thou art gone up: he stooped down, he crouched as a lion, and as an old lion; who shall rouse him up? [Who would dare?] The sceptre shall not depart from Judah, nor a lawgiver from between his feet, until Shiloh come; and unto him shall the gathering of the people be" (Genesis 49:8-10). The Lion of the tribe of Judah! In the last chapter of the Revelation (Revelation 22:16), our Lord says: "I, Jesus, have sent mine angel to testify unto you these things in the churches. I am the root and the offspring of David . . ." The root of David! Before David was, our Lord and Saviour was. John the Baptist said in the first chapter of John, the fifteenth verse: "He that followeth after me is preferred before me because he was before me. Here I am, the messenger, proclaiming the way of the Lord and announcing to the world that there follows after me the Lord Christ Messiah, but he was before me." The Root of David!

That same subject is discussed by our Lord in the twenty-second chapter, verses forty-two and forty-three, of the book of Matthew, as He said to those who sought to destroy Him: ". . . What think ye of Christ? whose son is he? They say unto him, The Son of David. He saith unto them, How then doth David in spirit call him Lord, saying, [then He quotes Psalm 110] The Lord [God] said unto my Lord [Christ the Son], Sit thou at my right hand, until I make thine enemies thy footstool. If David then called him Lord, how is he his son?" They could not answer him a word. How is it that David the great king bowed down before his son and called his own son, "Lord"? That is the same name used for God — "Lord." "How is that?" asked the Lord Jesus. The answer is in the words of John, "for he was before me," the Root out of which David sprang.

Why the Root of David? Why not the root of Abraham? It could have been. Why not the root of Moses? It could as well have been said. Why not the root of Elijah? It was also true. But David is chosen because David was preeminently the King and that kingship represents God's purposes for His Son in the earth. He shall reign over the whole creation. The sovereignty of the earth and the authority of all creation is in His hands, David's son, the root and offspring of David. Abraham is of promise, Moses of the law, Elijah of the prophets, but David of the kings. The kingdom is the Lord's. It belongs to the Lion of the tribe of Judah, the root and the offspring of David.

"And I beheld, and, lo, in the midst of the throne and of the four cherubim, and in the midst of the four and twenty elders, stood . . ." the Lion of the tribe of Judah? Does it read thus? *Stood* the root and the offspring of David? Does it read thus? *Stood* our reigning Lord and monarch? Does it read thus? What an amazing thing! "In the midst of the four and twenty elders and of the throne and of the cherubim, stood a Lamb as it had been slain."

A lamb, I repeat, every little syllable of this revelation, every word of this chapter, is fraught with eternal and unfathomable meaning. He saw a lamb. Now the Greek word for lamb is *amnos*. The Greek word for a little pet lamb, a baby lamb, is *arnios*. It is used only twice in the New Testament. The first time is in John 21:15: "Simon . . . lovest thou me . . . Yea, Lord; thou knowest that I love thee . . . Then take care of my *arnios* [my little pet lambs]." The other time, it is used is here. In the midst of the throne, in the midst of the cherubim, in the midst of all God's creation, in the midst of the four and twenty elders, in the midst of all God's redeemed saints, John saw an *arnios*, a little pet lamb. Remember, in the directions for the Passover, the people were not to go out and slay just *any* lamb. The lamb was to be carefully chosen from the firstlings of the flock, for its beauty and perfection, and it was to be placed in the bosom of the family for four days; that is, until the children loved it and it was looked upon as a member of the family, a pet lamb, held next to the hearts of those who lived in that household. That little *arnios* was identified with the family, loved, cuddled, petted, caressed. John saw it *sphazo*, "slain"; the word means violently slain. It is the word used for the blood and sacrifice and suffering of the victim on the altar. The little pet lamb was violently slain. The signs of its suffering are in its body. In His body were the marks of His passion; in His hands, the print of the nails; in His side, the scar of the terrible spear-thrust; in His body, the signs of His suffering. "A lamb as it had been slain."

THE REDEMPTION BY THE LAMB

The Lamb that John saw is standing. Standing, slain, destroyed, with blood poured out onto the earth. He saw Him *estekos*. The translation given here is "there stood a lamb." Oh, no! *Estekos*, "standing." The lamb slain *standing*. There Christ, the Lamb of God, *stands*, in the midst of the throne, preparing to receive the sovereignty of God's universe; *standing*, on the basis of His sacrifice, having identified Himself with us as our kinsman-redeemer; *standing*, to take the purchased possession and to cast out the interloper, the dragon. "I saw the Lamb, slain, *standing*."

Standing in the majesty of the lion, yet in the meekness, the yieldedness, of the lamb. The picture of the Lamb is the picture of our Lord Christ in His first coming as He stood and they spit upon Him. Ah! The filth of that insult. His face and His beard were covered with vile spittle. And they plucked out His beard and they smote Him in the face and they said, "Who smote thee? What is my name?" They thrust on His brow the crown of thorns and they mocked Him with a reed for a sceptre and a filthy, cast-off, dirty robe in the palace for His raiment as a king. They nailed Him like a common malefactor to a cross, raised Him up for the whole world to see, an exhibition of ignominy and shame, the curse of the earth. A crown of thorns pressed upon His brow, He stood as a lamb slain, with its throat cut, with blood pouring out unto death. That is the basis of redemption, the blood that washes sin away, the sacrifice that paid the price and the penalty of our iniquity. The basis of redemption is a lamb slain. But now the time has come when God's suffering servant who paid the price of our sin, who redeemed us and bought us back to God, the time has come for that Lamb of God to take us out of the hand of the interloper, out of the hand of death, out of the hand of that grief, out of the curse and the damnation of sin; the time has come when, in the majesty of the Lion and as the King of Glory, He will receive us back and bestow upon us our lost and defiled inheritance. He stands, He stands, He stands, the Lion of the tribe of Judah, the root of David, that all-conquering, all-prevailing Lord.

The text says in chapter five, verse five, "He hath prevailed." *Nikao, Nike.* We are familiar with that Greek word. We have a Nike missile. That is the Greek word for "victory," a *nike*, a victory. A winged victory is called a *nike* if you buy it in the likeness of a little statue. That is the word in its verbal form here. *Nikao,* "he hath prevailed," "he is victorious," "he is the conqueror." The Lion of the tribe of Judah, the Root of David, he hath prevailed, he is victorious. He prevailed in the day of temptation in the wilderness. He prevailed in the day of the cross, when He was delivered into the bonds of death. He prevailed when He broke those bonds asunder and was raised from the dead. He prevailed when He entered back into heaven, carrying captivity captive and giving gifts unto men. He prevails now when He opens the seals and takes from the hands of the intruder our purchased possession to bestow it back and to give it to us, Adam's fallen race and Adam's seed.

"And I beheld, and, lo, the lamb slain as he stands, having seven horns and seven eyes." The seven horns are representative of the fulness of power that has been placed in His hands; and the seven eyes of the vigilance, the intelligence by which Christ takes care of His people, watching, directing, counseling, marshalling, against the final day of which the Revelation here speaks, when He shall take unto Himself His great power and shall reign in the earth. He is a lamb, redemption by blood, by suffering, by atonement; and He is the lion, redemption by power and by conquest. We see both of these symbols in the Bible, and we have both of them here in the Revelation: a lamb slain, offering His life for our sins, and the Lion, taking in His great, mighty and powerful hands the sovereignty of the universe.

"And he came and took the book out of the right hand of him that sat upon the throne." That is the greatest act in all the story of God's creation. That is the greatest act in the Apocalypse. That is the greatest act in the history of mankind. "He came and took the book," He lifted the title deeds of forfeiture to give back to us our lost inheritance. In that act is the answer to the prayer of all of the saints through all ages. In that act is the judgment of God upon sin and upon Satan and upon death and upon the grave and upon hell. In that act is cast out all those enemies who would deny to us what God purposed for us when He saw us in the beginning and before the foundation of the earth. Weep not. Weep not. Behold, behold. He saw our Saviour who is also our Lord and our coming King. Behold! Lift up your hearts, lift up your face, lift up your eyes, lift up your souls, behold! Beyond the grave there is Jesus, the Lord of life. Beyond our tears there is Jesus, the God of all comfort. Beyond the heartbreaks and heartaches and the despairs of this life there is the King of Glory with gifts in His hands. Behold! Behold!

Chapter 7

The Songs of Heaven

And they sung a new song, saying, Thou art worthy to take the book, and to open the seals thereof: for thou wast slain, and hast redeemed us to God by thy blood out of every kindred, and tongue, and people, and nation; And hast made us unto our God kings and priests: and we shall reign on the earth. And I beheld, and I heard the voice of many angels round about the throne and the beasts and the elders: and the number of them was ten thousand times ten thousand, and thousands of thousands; Saying with a loud voice, Worthy is the Lamb that was slain to receive power, and riches, and wisdom, and strength, and honour, and glory, and blessing. And every creature which is in heaven, and on the earth, and under the earth, and such as are in the sea, and all that are in them, heard I saying, Blessing, and honour, and glory, and power, be unto him that sitteth upon the throne, and unto the Lamb for ever and ever. And the four beasts said, Amen. And the four and twenty elders fell down and worshipped him that liveth for ever and ever. — Revelation 5:9-14

This describes the worship of God in heaven, and these are the doxologies of the redeemed creation and of the hosts of angels.

The fifth chapter of the Revelation opens with God upon the throne. Around the throne of God are the enthroned redeemed, the four and twenty elders. In the midst of the throne, on the steps upward on each side, are the four cherubim. In the right hand of God, on the palm of the hand of the Almighty, lies a seven-sealed book. That book is a sign of a forfeited inheritance. It is sealed with seven seals, significant of the heavy encumbrances upon that inheritance. Then there is heard the voice of a strong angel, whose trumpet-heralding question penetrates to the farthest corners of God's universe, in heaven, in earth, in the unseen world: "Where is there one," says the angel, "who is able to come and to take that book of the forfeited inheritance that lies on the hand of God and open the seals thereof?" Search was made in heaven, in earth, under the earth, in the unseen world, and no one was able — *ou de heis* — "not even one" — no one in heaven, in earth, in the unseen world, was able to open the book or to loose the seals thereof. When that tragedy faced the holy seer, the sainted Apostle John, he burst into lamentations and open cries. The unbroken seals meant that the inheritance God made for Adam's seed was forever forfeited, forever lost. No redeemer could be found to buy it back. Sin, death, hell, Satan are to reign forever. But in the midst of the weeping and the audible lamentation of the apostle seer, there came one of the elders, one of the redeemed, who said, "Weep not, behold the Lion of the tribe of Judah, the Root of David, the Lamb of God, has prevailed to take the book, to break the seven seals, to cast out the usurper, sin and death and hell and Satan, and to give to Adam's race the lost inheritance, our redeemed creation, the new heaven and the new earth."

When the Lamb of God comes, He who alone is worthy and able, our kinsman-redeemer, when He comes to take the book, then all creation bursts into exuberance and triumphant joy. John describes the worship in glory, the songs of heaven. In chapter five he records three of these incomparable doxologies. First, the cherubim and the four and twenty elders lead off. Then they are joined by the hosts of heaven, the angels. One of the most expressive Greek phrases we find in the book concerns the number of these angels. The number of them was *chiliades chiliadon, muriades muriadon*, the innumerable thousands upon ten thousands, multiplied by tens of thousands and thousands of thousands. Then the paean of praise rolls on and gathers force and momentum, and wider and wider it extends until everything that God has created joins in the song of adoration. Every created thing in heaven and every created thing on earth and every created thing in the sea and every created thing that God made began to extol the Lord Almighty, saying, "Blessing and honour and glory and power be unto him that sitteth upon the throne and to the Lamb forever and ever unto the always of the always." And the four cherubim said "Amen," and the redeemed of God, the four and twenty elders, fell down and worshiped Him that liveth, world without end. What a wonderful scene!

Now we are going to speak of it in three ways: first, the worship of the redeemed; then the worship of the angels; and third, the songs, the doxologies, which they sing.

THE WORSHIP OF THE REDEEMED

First, the worship of the redeemed: "And the four and twenty elders fell down before the Lamb, having every one of them harps, and golden bowls full of incense, which are the prayers of the saints." That is, at this climactic, all-meaningful and all-significant moment in human story, when the Lamb of God is invested with the kingship of the universe, and when the inheritance is to be bought back for Adam's fallen race and the usurper cast out, when the Lamb, who alone is worthy, takes the book to break the seven seals and to cast out Satan and sin and death, then these four and twenty elders, God's redeemed, bring to remembrance before the Almighty all that the prophets have spoken and all that God's saints have prayed. The burden of their intercession through the years is represented in the golden bowl of incense. All that the prophets have said in promise and in comforting assurance is represented by the harp. The high priest has his bowl of incense, the prophet, his harp.

The harp is a sign of the prophet. For example, in I Samuel 10:5, the prophet Samuel says to Saul: ". . . and it shall come to pass, when thou art come thither to the city, that thou shalt meet a company of prophets coming down from the high places with a psaltery . . . and a harp, before them; and they shall prophesy: And the Spirit of the Lord will come upon thee, and thou shalt prophesy with them, and shalt be turned into another man." The prophets are coming with harps. Again, in II Kings 3, the spirit of prophecy was not upon Elisha. As he stood before the two kings, Elisha said (in verse 15): "But now bring me a minstrel. And it came to pass, when the minstrel played upon his harp, that the hand of the Lord came upon him. And he said, Thus saith the Lord . . ." There is a ministry in the prophetic deliverance of God's message. There is also a ministry in the singing that is ordained of God. Elisha said, "The spirit of prophecy is not upon me; bring a minstrel. And it came to pass as the minstrel played that the Spirit of the Lord came upon the prophet." God ordained that in the sounding of those notes, in the plucking of those chords and in the making of that melody, His spirit would move. Compare I Chronicles 25:1: "Moreover David separated to the service . . . Asaph and Heman and of Jeduthun, who should prophesy with harps." In that glorious service that David prescribed for the worship of God in the temple, these courses, Asaph, Heman, Jeduthun, would prophesy with harps. The third verse reads: "Jeduthun, who prophesied with a harp, to give thanks and to praise the Lord." I quote again from the forty-ninth Psalm, verse four: "I will incline mine ear to a parable: I will open my dark saying [I will open these things God hath given me to say] upon the harp." God's spirit moved in the songs of the minstrel. A man would have to be a dead man, a man would have to be made out of brass, a man would have to be composed of solid iron, not to be moved in his spirit when God's unction falls upon the choir and they sing the praises and the glory of God. "And unto him be power, and honour, and blessing and glory, even unto him that sitteth upon the throne and unto the Lamb for ever and ever." These things are marks of the spirit of prophecy. That is why in the hands of each of the elders was a harp. The scene calls to mind all that God has spoken as He prophesied through His prophets, as He gave visions to His seers, and as He delivered His Word and His message through His God-filled, God-anointed servants. The elders have in their hands, each one, an harp, bringing before the remembrance of God all that the Lord God has said through His holy prophets.

Then each elder has also a golden bowl full of incense. The text says this represents the prayers of the saints. I do not need to expatiate upon that. As the high priest went into the holy sanctuary and the people remained outside praying, the high priest carried within a bowl of incense; and as the smoke of it and the perfume of it ascended up to heaven, so the prayers of God's people were thus poured out before the great throne of the Almighty. In that golden bowl are the intercessions, the pleadings, the burdens, the agonies of all God's children through all of the centuries. For, did not He teach us to pray, "Thy kingdom come"? These prayers are not lost. Apparently, they fall to the ground. "Thy kingdom come" and the kingdom does not come. We pray, "Thy will be done," and everyone's will in the earth is done except the will of God. Violence is rampant and darkness and error fill the land. Nevertheless, God's children are commanded to pray, "Thy kingdom come, Thy will be done."

It is part of the elective purpose of God that His children pray; and it is a part of the effectiveness of prayer that at this great, final, consummating moment, every prayer of every faithful intercessor is brought anew and afresh before the Lord God, as the four and twenty elders pour out before the throne of the Almighty these bowls of the incense of the burden and the agony of God's sainted children through the centuries and through the ages. So it is that in heaven, as they worship, they pour out their bowls of remembered prayer, and as they worship they bring to God's mind the promises that He made to the prophets. I often marvel at these modern spiritualizers who stand up in their pulpits and say the things spoken by the prophets are not to be fulfilled, that those things the men of God said back there in the Old Testament under the unction and power of the Holy Ghost are not to be fulfilled. How different is our covenant-keeping God, who remembers every promise that He made and who, in this great, final, climactic hour, will bring to pass every word that He said! A part of the adoration and the worship in glory is the bringing to the remembrance of the Almighty, through the harp that prophesied and through the golden bowl full of prayer, all that God has promised to His sainted children.

THE WORSHIP OF ANGELS

Then, the worship of the angels: "And I beheld, and I heard the voice of many angels round about the throne . . . and the number of them was ten thousand times ten thousand, and thousands of thousands." Everywhere in the Word of God angels are unnumbered. They are innumerable. In the center on the throne is the Lamb of God; and around the throne are the four cherubim and the four and twenty elders; and then beyond, beyond, beyond, as far as eye can see are the innumerable, celestial hosts of glory. It is significant that they are introduced here. This is the first time the heavenly hosts, the angels, are mentioned. It is unusual how it is done. For, observe that when the elders sing, they sing directly to the Lamb: "Thou art worthy . . . for thou hast redeemed us . . . and hast made us . . . kings." They sing directly to the Lamb. The angels, in keeping with their inferior (and is it not an astonishing thing that God's redeemed are greater than the angels?) stations of service, do not address the Lamb directly when they speak of Him. They speak *about* Him, not *to* Him. They say: "Worthy is the Lamb that was slain to receive power, and riches, and wisdom, and strength, and honour, and glory, and blessing."

Another thing which is astonishing to me is that angels never sing. Never! When I stumbled into that fact, it was an amazing discovery. But I have already made up my

mind, before I say these things, that I am going to keep on
referring to angels singing, even though it is not true. To do
so is traditional. So, from now on as in the past, I am going
to speak of angels singing — the celestial choir, the angelic
hosts. But, actually angels never sing. Surely they sang
when Jesus was born, did they not? Always people have
spoken about the angels singing when Jesus was born.
"Glory to God in the highest and on earth . . ." — you know
— "the angel's song." So I turned to Luke 2:13 and read,
"And suddenly there was with the angel a multitude of the
heavenly host *saying* Glory to God in the highest and on
earth peace." It is thus here in the Book of the Revelation:
"And there was a great host of angels *saying* with a loud
voice." Never in the Bible do the angels sing. Never! They
always *say*. They are in a doxology, in a chorus, they are
in a recitative, they are all together, *saying*, but never in
the Bible do the angels sing.

That was an astonishing discovery to me. So I began
reading, studying, probing and trying to find out why
angels do not sing, and this is the best reason that I can
find. Always the redeemed sing. God's blood-washed sing.
God's children sing. But angels do not sing. Here is my
conclusion: Music is made up of major chords and minor
chords. The minor chords speak of the wretchedness, death
and sorrow of this fallen creation. Most of nature moans
and groans in a plaintive and minor key. The sound of the
wind through the forest, the sound of the storm, the sound
of the wind around the house, is always in a minor key.
It wails. The sound of the ocean moans in its restlessness,
in its speechless trouble. Even the nightingale's song, the
sweetest song of the birds, is the saddest. Most of the
sounds of nature are in a minor key. It reflects the wretchedness, the despair, the hurt, the agony, the travail of this
fallen creation. But an angel knows nothing of it. An angel
knows nothing of the wretchedness, nothing of the despair,
nothing of the fall of our lost race.

The major key and the major chords are chords of tri-

umph and victory. Surely God has taken us out of the
miry clay, He has taken us out of the horrible pit, He has
set our feet upon the rock and He has put a new song in
our souls and new praises on our lips. But an angel knows
nothing of this. An angel has never been redeemed. An
angel has never been saved. An angel has never fallen and
been brought back to God. That is the only reason that I
find as to why angels never sing. It is God's people who
sing. Shelley one time wrote:

> We look before and after
> And pine for what is not;
> Our sincerest laughter
> With some pain is fraught;
> Our sweetest songs are those
> That tell of saddest thought.

Our sweetest songs with deepest sorrows are fraught. Somehow it is the sorrow of life, the disappointment of life and
the despair of life that makes people sing, either in the
blackness of its hour or in the glory of its deliverance. That
is why the redeemed *sing* and the angels just *speak* of it.
They see it, they watch it, but they know nothing about it.
For it takes a lost and fallen man who has been brought
back to God, who has been forgiven of his sin, who has
been redeemed, it takes a saved soul to sing!

The Heavenly Doxologies

I speak lastly of the songs that they sing, the three doxologies here in this chapter. I want to show you something
in the Book. Leaving out the doxology of the angels who
do not sing, and following just the songs of the redeemed,
I want to show you how the doxologies grow and grow and
grow. The first doxology is in the first chapter of Revelation,
verse six. It is a twofold doxology: ". . . Unto him that
loved us, and washed us from our sins in his own blood,
And hath made us kings and priests unto God and his
father; to him be glory and dominion for ever and ever." A
twofold doxology: "To Him be glory and dominion for ever

and ever." Now, the next doxology will be threefold. Turn to Revelation 4 and the last verse: "Thou art worthy, O Lord, to receive glory and honour and power." This doxology that the redeemed sing is threefold: "Glory and honour and power." Now, the next doxology that the redeemed sing is fourfold, in Revelation 5:13: "All did I hear saying, Blessing, and honour, and glory, and power." Here is a fourfold doxology. Now, in chapter seven, verse twelve, is a sevenfold and final doxology: "Saying, Amen: Blessing, and glory, and wisdom, and thanksgiving, and honour, and power and might, be unto our God for ever and ever." As the Revelation progresses and as the redeemed are made more aware of what God has done for them, the doxologies grow and grow and grow in glory, in majesty, in adoration, in wonder, in reverential awe and worship. Now let us look at these three doxologies in Revelation, chapter five, for a moment.

The King James Version translates Revelation 5:9, *adousin* as "and they sung." But the verb is present tense, emphasizing the intensity of that singing, "and they *sing* a new song." There are two Greek words for "new." *Neos* is new in type and *kine* is new in character, in kind. This word is *kine*. They sing a new kind of a song. They sing a song the world has never heard before. There are three Greek words for "song." The Greek word *psalmos* is a psalm. The Greek word *hymnos* (is not it interesting how these Greek words are in our own language?) is a sacred song. The Greek word *ode* is a song in general. The latter word is used here. "And they sing a new *ode*, they sing a new song, saying: . . .", and there are four things in their song. First they speak of our redemption for the glory of God, "redeemed us to God." That is the thought in the first chapter of Ephesians. Second, they speak of our redemption by the blood of the cross. "Thou wast slain and hast redeemed us by thy blood." Third, they speak of our redemption as illimitable. "Out of every kindred and tongue and people and nation." And fourth, they speak of our redemption as resulting in our actual reign in an actual kingdom in this actual earth. ". . . and thou hast made us unto our God kings and priests and we shall reign on the earth." Notice the last one, the fourth one. So many say, "How crass, how crude, how carnal, how sensual and how unspiritual, that we should look for a kingdom and that we should be real people in it and that we should be kings and priests unto our God and that we should reign upon this earth!" They say, "How absurd to think of a real resurrection and a real body, a real redemption, a real earth, a real Christ, a real kingdom and God's people living in His presence a real life!" "How crass!" they say and "How carnal and how crude and how unspiritual!" Yet, as I study the Book, these things are the avowed disclosure and revelations of the Lord God Almighty. We are going to be real people. You are going to be you, and all of us will be ourselves. We shall live in a redeemed body like the body of our Lord and we shall be real people. We shall reign upon the earth.

I close with the ascription of praise recorded in Revelation 5:13. Look at it. The number four is the number of the world. These four ascriptions here are very significantly and signally set apart. Each one has an article in front of it. "And I heard everything in heaven and earth and in the sea and under the earth, I heard all creation saying, Blessing [ha eulogia], honour [he time], and glory [he doxa], and power, [he kratos]." Each one is set apart. All creation is praising God. "And every creature which is in heaven, and on earth, under the earth and under the sea, heard I them saying, Blessing, and honour, and glory, and power, be unto him that sitteth upon the throne, and unto the Lamb for ever and ever."

Hereafter in the Book, the Lamb and the Lord God Almighty will be together. In the next chapter they are together in wrath; in the next chapter, chapter seven, together in consolation; in chapter nineteen, together in triumph; and in chapters twenty-one and in twenty-two, the Lamb and the Lord God are together the light of the new Jerusalem; they are the temple of it, they are the refreshment of it and the sovereignty of it. The only God we shall ever see is the Lord Jesus; the only God we shall ever feel is the Holy Ghost; and the only God there is the one Great Lord God Almighty. Do not think that in heaven you are going to see three Gods. You will not see three. There is one God. When you get to heaven you will see the Lord God Almighty, Jesus Christ. We are going to worship Him and adore Him. We are going to look into His face, and He is going to be our Lord and our King; and we shall love Him and worship Him and sing to Him and serve Him, world without end.

'Tis the church triumphant singing,
Worthy is the Lamb.
Heaven throughout with praises ringing,
Worthy the Lamb.
Thrones and powers before Him bending,
Incense sweet and voice ascending,
Swell the chorus never ending,
Worthy the Lamb.

Every kindred, tongue and nation,
Worthy the Lamb.
Join to sing the great salvation,
Worthy the Lamb.
Loud as mighty thunder roaring,
Floods of mighty waters pouring,
Prostrate at His feet adoring,
Worthy the Lamb.

Harps and songs forever sounding,
Worthy the Lamb.
Mighty grace o'er sin abounding,
Worthy the Lamb.
By His blood He dearly bought us,
Wandering from the fold He sought us,
And to glory faithful brought us,
Worthy the Lamb.

Sing with blest anticipation,
Worthy the Lamb.
Through the veil and tribulation,
Worthy the Lamb.

Sweetest note, all notes excelling,
On the theme forever dwelling,
Still untold, though ever telling,
Worthy the Lamb.

— Author unknown

"And they sung a new song, saying, Thou art worthy to take the book, and to open the seals thereof: for thou wast slain, and hast redeemed us to God by thy blood out of every kindred, and tongue, and people, and nation; And hast made us unto our God kings and priests: and we shall reign on the earth." That is what they sing in glory. God sanctify unto us that love, that adoration, that worship, even now. Amen.

Chapter 8

The Four Horsemen of the Apocalypse

And I saw when the Lamb opened one of the seals, and I heard, as it were the noise of thunder, one of the four beasts saying, Come and see. And I saw, and behold a white horse: and he that sat on him had a bow; and a crown was given unto him: and he went forth conquering, and to conquer. And when he had opened the second seal, I heard the second beast say, Come and see. And there went out another horse that was red; and power was given to him that sat thereon to take peace from the earth, and that they should kill one another: and there was given unto him a great sword. And when he had opened the third seal, I heard the third beast say, Come and see. And I beheld, and lo a black horse; and he that sat on him had a pair of balances in his hand. And I heard a voice in the midst of the four beasts say, A measure of wheat for a penny, and three measures of barley for a penny; and see thou hurt not the oil and the wine. And when he had opened the fourth seal, I heard the voice of the fourth beast say, Come and see. And I looked, and behold a pale horse: and his name that sat upon him was Death, and Hell [the grave] followed with him. And power was given unto them over the fourth part of the earth, to kill with the sword, and with hunger, and with death, and with the beasts of the earth. — Revelation 6:1-8

This is not a pretty picture. But God is the Lord of truth, and He writes here things as they are, as they will be. It is for the cheap and worldly optimists to speak words of peace, peace when there is no peace, to paint rosy pictures of human nature and of the destiny of nations, when God says it will end in a flood. "War and desolations are determined to the end," so God says. Whatever man may say, however false leaders may deceive, God says, "This is the future," and He unveils it to us that we might prepare ourselves and save our souls and deliver our people.

The action of the Book of the Revelation begins here in chapter six. Here begins the word of our goal, our kinsman-redeemer, in whose hands God Almighty has placed the authority of this universe. This is the act of that great, sovereign Lord who takes our forfeited inheritance out of the hands of the usurper, the interloper, the intruder, the stranger and the alien. This is the act by which, in the judicial proceedings of God, our Lord and Saviour takes back out of the hands of Satan our rightful inheritance. This is the casting out of the dynasties of evil. This is the destruction of the powers of darkness and the bringing in of light, life, liberty and everlasting righteousness. These seven seals encompass all of the story of God from the rapture until the return. These seven seals include the whole proceedings of the Almighty after God's people are taken out of the earth until they come back with their reigning Lord, given the possession of God's inheritance. The seventh seal is the seven trumpets, and the seventh trumpet is the seven bowls of the seven vials of the wrath and plagues of Almighty God. When they are finished, the seventh seal and the seventh trumpet and the seventh bowl, then is finished the judgment of God upon iniquity, then is the cleansing of this earth, then is the binding of Satan, then is the establishment of the millennium kingdom in which God's children shall reign with Him in the earth.

THE FIRST SEAL IS OPENED

"And I saw when the Lamb opened one of the seals, and I heard, as it were, the noise of thunder, one of the four cherubim saying, 'Come' [or 'Go', or 'Proceed']." In the King James Version the translation is "Come and see" as though addressed to the Apostle John. No. For John is already there looking, and if he needed to be told to come nearer, then there would be no need for the words to be repeated four times. If the comment were addressed to John, there would be no need that the cherubim cry in a voice of thunder. The cherubim are the administrative agents of God toward this earth. Here the Lord God Almighty is casting out the powers and principalities of darkness. When the cherubim say "Come," it is addressed to one of the agencies by which the denouement of history comes to its final consummation. The best way to see what it is that the word refers to is to see what happens when one of the cherubim cries "Come." This happens: in each instance, when one of the cherubim cry "*Erkou*," "Go," "Proceed" or "Come," there comes across the stage of human history a horse and a rider.

It would be almost impossible for us today to realize the awe and reverence with which an Oriental looked upon the strength and power of a horse. In Job 39, verses nineteen through twenty-five, is a magnificent tribute to the strength and power of a horse. We find a similar reference in Zechariah 1, and especially in Zechariah 6:1-7. These tremendous beasts, these great animals, represented to an Oriental mind conquest, march, attack, battle. We see this representation in the four horses which proceed across the stage and history of the world at the command of the cherubim: "And I heard one of the cherubim, with a noise of thunder, [a commandment] say, '*Erkou*' and behold a white horse [a charger, a sign of conquest and of victory]. And he that sat on him had a bow; and a crown [*a stephanos*] was given unto him: and he went forth conquering, and in order that he might conquer."

The first horse is a charger of victory, a white horse. He that sat upon him is a conqueror, a victor. He has a crown and a bow. Now, because in ancient processions of triumph, the victor, the conqueror, rode on a white horse; and because, in the nineteenth chapter of the Book of the Revelation, when our Lord comes again out of heaven, He comes riding a white horse; and they who follow Him, God's people, blood-bought, blood-washed, victorious, follow Him on white horses: therefore, practically all commentators and scholars and students will identify this rider as Christ. There are several things to be said about that before such an identification is made.

The first objection is this: the scene creates an obvious incongruity. I do not know whether there are any rules in dramatics concerning such a procedure, but this would be an unusual thing to do. Here the Lord Jesus Christ, the Lion of the Tribe of Judah, pulls aside the curtain in order that you may see the impending Judgment. When He does so, instantly He changes into the garb of a soldier and comes riding out on a white horse. The idea is somewhat confusing.

There is another thing about this interpretation that is somewhat incongruous. Evidently these four horsemen have a common denominator. There is something common to all of them. They all four ride in some particular meaning together — the white, the red, the black and the greenish pale. Now, if the first one is Christ, then He is associated with the bloodiest, the most pestilential, and the most horrible of all of the associates that mind could imagine. Now, I can imagine the Lord with Shadrach, Meshach and Abednego in the fiery furnace. The Lord walked with His three children. I can imagine the Lord Christ with His disciples, with Peter, James and John. But somehow I do not associate the Lord with Ahab and Jezebel or with Baal and Aphrodite. Somehow I do not associate the Lord with Herod the Great, who killed the babies of Bethlehem; and with Herod Antipas, who slew John the Baptist; or with Herod Agrippa I, who slew James, the brother of John. Likewise, I cannot connect the Lord Christ with the blood of war and carnage and murder following the red horse; and with the awful raging famine following the black horse; and with the pestilential death following that pale, ghastly, green horse. The Lord Christ and they just do not belong together.

Another thing is to be considered. When the Lord Christ comes, He comes in the nineteenth chapter and the eleventh verse of the Apocalypse, in its consummation and in its great, final, crowning, victorious day. We look for the Lord from heaven, we look for Him to come with His people, we look for Him to come in triumph and in glory. He does so come. His coming is described in the nineteenth chapter of the Book of the Revelation. His coming does not occur here in this sixth chapter. It does not fit.

There is yet another discrepancy. Compare the two riders in the two chapters that mention a white horse. In chapter nineteen of the Book of the Revelation, the man who rides on the white horse, the Lord God our Christ, has on His head a *diadema*, a Greek word referring to a diadem. Never in the language is that word used for any other except the crown of a reigning, a sovereign monarch. That is the kind of a crown that one would expect to grace the brow of the Son of God, our Saviour. He comes with a diadem, a *diadema*, and His weapon is the sword of the Word. But the white horseman in Revelation six is not so described. His crown is a *stephanos*, something a man could win down here on earth as in a race. He has in his hand, not a sword of the Word of God, but a bow, and that with no shaft and no arrow. Who is this white horseman who precedes the red of carnage and blood, who precedes the black of famine and dearth and want, and who precedes the ghastly green of hades and of death?

THE TEMPORARY TRIUMPH OF THE ANTICHRIST

Our Lord has given us, in the twenty-fourth chapter of the Book of Matthew, in the Apocalyptic address recorded there, the outline of this time of the end. If the Revelation is a picture of the time of the end, then it ought to fit exactly with the outline that our Lord gave in Matthew twenty-four. Surely what our Lord said in Matthew twenty-four will fit what our Lord revealed to John here in the Apocalypse.

The outline that our Lord Christ gives in His great Apocalyptic discourse in Matthew twenty-four corresponds to what occurs in the visions given to John in the Revelation.

Observe the outline in Matthew twenty-four, starting at verse four. First, Jesus says in answer to the question of the disciples as to what shall be the sign of His coming and of the end of the world: "Take heed that no man deceive you. For many shall come in my name, saying, I am Christ, and shall deceive many." Many will come saying, "I am Der Fuehrer; I am the great Il Duce; I am the great saviour; I am the deliverer of the people; I am the leader of the world; I am the great Stalin; I am the great Tojo to bring my nation to victory." There will be many deceivers, there will be many deliverers, there will be many self-styled saviours. That is the first thing the Lord says about this outline of history. There will be false Christs. The next thing He says is this: "And ye shall hear of wars and rumours of wars . . . nation shall rise against nation and kingdom against kingdom." That is the red horse of carnage and blood. Then He says: "And there shall be famines." That is the black horse. "Our faces," says Jeremiah, "were black like an oven because of the terrible famine." Then He says: "And there shall be pestilences." That is the fourth horse of pestilential death, following bloodshed and war and carnage and famine.

If I can trust the Lord in what He says in Matthew twenty-four, then I have the identification of these four horsemen. The first one represents the great deceiver, the great and final Antichrist, the great and final false deliverer, of whom all of these others are but adumbrations, portents, prefigurations. They are just sketches, they are just shadows of that final world dictator who is yet to come. (I am just following the outline of our Lord.) Our Lord describes a deceiver, a false Christ. He comes in peace, promising victory and making treaties. The eyes of all the nations of the earth are upon him. But following him there are these indescribable wars of the red horseman. Then, following him, come the awful want and famine that inevitably goes with war. Following that comes the terrible pestilential presence of death and the grave unsatiated, swallowing up of its illimitable victims.

If I can follow the outline of our Lord in Matthew twenty-four, I can comprehend what is revealed to the Apostle John in the Apocalypse. First, the Lord says there will come on the scene the great deceiver, the great world deliverer, the great world saviour. He is Satan's masterpiece. Satan always is an imitator. In the court of Pharaoh when Moses and Aaron showed their signs before the king, Satan had his sorcerers and his witch doctors and his necromancers, able to do those same marvelous signs. He is an imitator. There is nothing original about Satan. He has never whispered a single new reason why man should reject God since the days of the Garden of Eden. The things he whispers in your heart today about rejecting God are the same things he has been whispering ever since the beginning of the creation. There is nothing original in Satan. Nothing! There is no new work, there is no new device, there is no new appeal. Satan is a great imitator. So he imitates the Lord Christ here. As Christ is God's man, so Satan has his man. His ultimate Antichrist finally will appear when God's people are taken away and the days of that terrible tribulation begin. In the restlessness of nations and in the revolution of the masses and in the prospect of catastrophic war, the first thing that will happen is to be the appearance of this great, final dictator, this great, final world-tyrant. He will promise peace and he will bring with him every token of affluence and prosperity; and the nations of the world and the peoples of the earth will flock after him. "This is our Fuehrer, this is our Il Duce, this is our great leader, this is our saviour and the hope of the world." He comes riding on a white horse, conquering and to conquer. The entire military and economic and political resources of the world are at his disposal and in his hands.

When we make this identification, we find that it will fit every prophecy in the Bible precisely. For example, in the second Thessalonian letter, the second chapter, God says that after the falling away, after the apostasy, and after God's people are taken away, the man of sin will be revealed. That is the first thing that happens — the coming across the horizon of history, this white horseman. The first development is the appearance of this man of sin, the son of damnation, who opposes and exalts himself above all that is called God. "For the mystery of iniquity doth already work: only he who now preventeth will prevent, until he be taken out of the way." God's Holy Spirit and God's people are here in this earth, and as long as we are here that great denouement will not come to pass. Satan's masterpiece cannot be revealed, the tribulation cannot come. The fire and the flame and the fury cannot fall upon Sodom until Lot be taken hence. So said the angel. "I can do nothing until thou be come thence."

First, God's people have to be taken out. Even though Lot was a compromising Christian, vexing his soul with the filthy conversation of Sodom, even though he was a compromising Christian, yet he was God's man. He was a saved man. The angel said, "I can do nothing until thou be come thence," and after Lot was taken away, the fire and the flames fell, the brimstone and the judgment of God. So it is here. There is in this world that which prevents the final judgment. It is God's people. But, there is coming a day when the Holy Spirit, housed and templed in the hearts of God's people, will be taken out of the way. It is then that this first thing shall come to pass, this wicked one shall be revealed. This is Satan's masterpiece, whom the Lord shall consume with the spirit of His mouth and shall destroy with the brightness of His *parousia,* His appearing, His coming, as it is recorded in the nineteenth chapter of the Book of the Revelation. The identification of the white horseman as the final Antichrist fits the prophecy all the way through.

THE SEVENTY WEEKS OF DANIEL

Let us take one other prophecy, out of many that we could discuss. In the ninth chapter of the Book of Daniel is one of the most significant of all the prophecies in the Word of God. It is the prophecy of the seventy weeks. It says that this prince, this Antichrist, this masterpiece of Satan, this great false deceiver, will come in peace and will make his covenant with the people. He is going to have the great systems of religion in this world back of him and for him. The Roman Church is going to acclaim him just as it did Il Duce, just as it does any other Fuehrer or dictator by which they think they can strangle the life of a nation and of a people. The Roman Church is going to hail this dictator, this coming world-tyrant. And the Jewish people will find in him a marvelous refuge from the terrible afflictions that beset them on every hand. He is going to enter into a treaty with the Jewish nation, according to the ninth chapter of the Book of Daniel. He is going to write a treaty with the Jewish people by which they will have their homeland, and according to which they will be enabled to rebuild their temple and reinstitute the Mosaic rituals and the sacrifices. For a while he is truly the saviour of the world. The whole unbelieving world acclaims him, this masterpiece of Satan.

Then, according to Daniel 9:27 and according to the thirteenth chapter of the Book of the Revelation, in the midst of his rise to power and to conquest, this deceiver reveals himself for what he really is. He is the fiend of hell, he is the masterpiece of the devil, he is the great Antichrist, the opposer and blasphemer of God. In the midst of his career he turns and becomes the enemy of the Jewish nation, following which there is a wave of anti-Semitism such as the earth has never known before. Then he turns on the Roman Church and, according to the seventeenth chapter of the Book of the Revelation, he destroys her. That leader, that beast, that ruler, shall take the whore and he shall make

her desolate and naked and shall eat of her flesh and burn
her with fire. Oh, what this world dictator does as he goes
across the stage of human history!

Bear in mind that what we are reading here is not a
peculiar thing, separate and apart from anything else that
we have ever heard. This is the pattern of all history. This
is the story of all such Fuehrers. I have followed the career
of four of them in my brief lifetime. All four of them
appear in this same way. First he is the liberator of his
people. He is the conqueror in the name of the great nation
he represents. He leads his people to conquest and to victory. Then, the fiendish spirit of hell appears in him and
the world is plunged in blood. Whether Der Fuehrer, Il
Duce, Napoleon Bonaparte, Frederick the Great, the Kaiser,
Hitler, Tojo, Mussolini or Stalin — whatever his name —
Caesar, Alexander the Great, name him any time in history
— he follows the same pattern. These principles that God
exhibits here in the Bible are eternal principles, and these
things that happened before and these things that have
happened in this generation are but adumbrations, they are
but sketches, they are but outlines of that great, final denouement that shall come across the history of the world
in that ultimate tribulation. So he comes, first as the friend
of humanity. He is the patron of the Roman Church. He
is the friend of the Jewish nation and people. He gives
each one what each one wants. He leads this world out
of debt, out of war and out of all of the restless, convulsive,
revolutions by which it ferments. He leads them into great
heights, on a white horse, with a bow (that is, a bloodless
conquest, no arrow, no shaft) and a *stephanos,* (a crown of
victory) conquering and to conquer. He is the world's great
dictator, earth's sovereign leader.

The Tragedies That Follow the World Deceiver

But such a world tyrant never rides alone. What inevitably follows him is depicted here in the Revelation. The
second of the cherubim said *"Erkou,"* "Come," "Go," "Pro-

ceed." Then "there came a red horse: and power was given
to him to take peace from the earth, and that they should
kill one another: and there was given unto him a great
sword." There is a Greek word for the sword of a soldier
when he goes marching to war. It is *romphaia*, the sword
of a soldier as he marches into battle. But there is another
Greek word for a sword. We call it a "dirk," or a "knife."
It is a *machaira*. The word that is used here is *machaira*.
That is the kind of a weapon that could be hidden, concealed beneath a coat. A *machaira* was the kind of a knife
with which to cut the throat of an animal or of a man. The
red horseman represents not only nation rising against nation and kingdom against kingdom, but, more nearly, the
terrible slaughter of class fighting class and party fighting
party, as in civil war. The fighters ambush in the night;
they assassinate in the day; they murder at twilight and at
noontime, and everyone lives in the fear of his life. There
is murder and bloodshed everywhere. The red horseman
bathes the earth in blood. "That they should kill one another." Americans are killing Americans, Britishers killing
Britishers, Frenchmen killing Frenchmen, Germans killing
Germans, Russians killing Russians, the whole world in a
ferment of blood and revolution.

Then comes that black horse with the voice crying, "A
choinix of wheat for a denarius." The Greek word *choinix*
refers to just a little bit of wheat. A *choinix* of wheat sells
for a denarius and a denarius is the wage of a working man
for one day. A man works hard for a whole day, and he is
able to win just enough for one meal for himself, beside the
need of all the rest of his household. It is a picture of
famine, a black horse of want.

Finally comes that *chloros* horse, pale, ghastly green. In
Leviticus that is the color of leprosy. "And I saw the pale,
ghastly horse: and his rider was Death, and by his side the
grave swallowing up his victims. And power was given
unto them . . . to kill with the sword, and with hunger,

and with death, and with pestilence and with the beasts, the vermin, of the earth." What a picture! This is evil running rampant, when God's spirit and God's people who now prevent this are taken out of the way. This is the ultimate issue of unbelief and rejection and blasphemy and refusal. This is the world plunged into death under the leadership of the powers of sin and darkness. This is the lot of any man who turns aside from the true God and follows after the will 'o the wisp promises, the deceiving promises, of these who entice into the life of this earth.

O Lord, may it be that we shall bow only before the one, true God, that we may give our lives to the one true Prince, that we shall be numbered among those who call upon His name, that His spirit may live in our souls and that the praise and honor and adoration and love of lives may flow unto Him. It is always dark for the wicked. It is always dark for Satan. It is always dark for his dupes and his followers. It is always dark when sin reigns in the earth. But it is always light for the people of God. In the days of the flood there was an ark for the family of the people of God. In the days of the Israelites there were cities of refuge for the one who had inadvertently shed innocent blood, who fell into sin, who asked God's forgiveness. In the days of the destruction of Jerusalem in A.D. 70 there was a *Pella*, the refuge for the saints, for those who loved Jesus. There is a refuge today for God's people. Though I face death tomorrow, yet, if I face Him today, my home, my refuge is not in the grave. The glory of God is not under the ground. The glory of God is in the pavilions of the heavens. God's people have their house and their home and their destiny beyond the skies. For God's people there is glory and light and victory and heaven. That is the call the Lord extends in this day of grace to your heart. Come. Come. Come with us. In our march to glory, march with us. In a prayer of adoration, pray with us. In a hymn of love, sing with us. As we avow publicly our faith in Jesus, come with us. Do it, and God speed you and bless you as you come.

Chapter 9

The Martyr Seal

And when he had opened the fifth seal, I saw under the altar the souls of them that were slain for the word of God, and for the testimony which they held: And they cried with a loud voice, saying, How long, O Lord, holy and true, dost thou not judge and avenge our blood on them that dwell on the earth? And white robes were given unto every one of them; and it was said unto them, that they should rest yet for a little season, until their fellowservants also and their brethren, that should be killed as they were, should be fulfilled. — Revelation 6:9-11

The Revelation is a book of judgment. The Old Testament describes the days of the law. The New Testament describes the days in which we now live, the days of grace. But the Apocalypse is a revelation of the days of the visitation of the wrath of God. It is described as such in Revelation 4:5: "And out of the throne proceeded lightnings and thunderings and voices." The four cherubim, who stand before God to administer His decrees, are instruments of the wrath of God upon this earth. As they speak, there appears on the horizon of history the four horsemen of the Apocalypse. The four horsemen are, themselves, the instruments of judgment upon this earth. The first seal brings on the state of human history the ultimate Antichrist, which the world receives with open arms. The opening of the second, the third and the fourth seals are the judgments of God that follow the acceptance of that tyrannical world dictator. The sixth seal is a seal of the judgment day of God when the heavens are rolled back like a scroll, when the great men of the earth cry for the rocks and the mountains to fall upon them, when the great day of God's wrath is come. The seventh seal, of course, is the seven trumpets of the judgment of God, and the seventh trumpet is the seven bowls of the final wrath, the last plagues of the Almighty. The Book is a book of judgment from the beginning to the end. The fifth seal is also a seal of judgment. These who are martyred have born witness to the visitation of the wrath of God, and in their disembodied state in heaven, as souls, they cry for that day of vengeance. All of this Book, all of these seals, all of these trumpets, all of these bowls of wrath, the whole Book is a book of the final judgment of God upon this earth.

This fifth seal is different from the rest of the seven in that we see not the action itself, but the result of action, the result of what has happened. Heretofore and hereafter, as a seal is broken or a trumpet is blown or a vial is poured out, across the stage of human history we shall see the judgment develop; we shall see what happens. But not here. This is a picture of the result of what has happened. John sees under the altar the souls of those who have already been slain. Back of those souls that are slain, we must imagine, though it is undepicted and undescribed, the blood and fury and fire of awful persecution, the blood bath in which they lost their lives.

Who are these martyrs whose souls John sees under the altar of heaven? As they cry to God they say, "O Lord, how long dost thou not judge and avenge our blood on them that dwell on the earth?" So, these martyrs are a special group and their murderers still live in the earth. Therefore, these are not the martyrs of all time, the saints of God of all ages, who have lost their lives in days past. Also, we know they are not the souls of those who have been martyred through all the ages because in the fourth chapter of the Book of the Revelation, John sees the four and twenty elders around the throne of God, and these four and twenty elders represent God's saints of the days past who are raptured, who are resurrected, who are clothed, who are crowned, who are in the presence of the Almighty. Then who are these who have lost their lives and who cry unto God for vengeance? These are the martyrs who have lost their lives under those first four seals, in the first half of the Tribulation. The other martyrs of the Tribulation, in the last half, are referred to when God says to these, "You rest for a while until these other martyrs that are to be slain are slain," that is, those who are to be slain in the last half of the Tribulation. At the end of the Tribulation and at the beginning of the millennium, in Revelation 20:4, we shall find all of the martyrs standing in the presence of God and preparing to enter that millennium kingdom where they reign with the Lord for a thousand years. So, these are they who have lost their lives under those terrible blood baths of the opening of the first four seals.

THE ALTAR OF SACRIFICE

John says, "I saw them under the altar." That is unusual. But the whole book is unusual. The Book of Hebrews describes the heavenly tabernacle, the heavenly temple. The Book of Hebrews says what Exodus says, that Moses saw the pattern of the tabernacle, the temple, the form of it in heaven, and he made a material copy of it down here on earth. So, the heaven of God's throne, where the Lord now dwells, has a temple. In the eleventh chapter of the Revelation, John sees the temple of God in heaven, the pattern of which was given to Moses, who made a material copy on earth. Therefore, like the earthly tabernacle, the heavenly one has two altars, both of which are described in the Book of the Revelation. There is the altar of brass which is the altar of sacrifice, mentioned several times in the Revelation. There is the altar of gold, which is the altar of burnt incense and prayer, which is mentioned several times in the Revelation. This altar in our text is the altar of sacrifice, the brazen altar that stood in the courtyard of the tabernacle and of the temple.

The Word of God always presents the devotion of the

lives of His children as being sacrificed upon the altar unto God. We find that idea all through the Scripture. For example, in Romans 12:1, Paul exhorts us to offer our lives a living sacrifice on the altar of God. In the passage of II Timothy 4:6 Paul says, "For I am now ready to be offered," the word "offered" being a technical word for sacrifice. As he anticipated his approaching martyrdom, he looked upon it as a sacrifice unto God on the altar of heaven. That is the way God beholds all of His children who pour out their lives unto Him. It is in that degree of devotion that we are to live and to work and to serve our Lord. If it is pleasing to Him that the sacrifice be a living sacrifice, wonderful and well. But, if it is pleasing to God that the sacrifice be one in death, then whether in death or whether in life, we are to offer our lives unto God.

I read of a young fellow in England who offered his life to go as a missionary to the jungles of Africa. But the doctors said to him: "You cannot go. You are sickly and anemic. You are not physically able to go." But the student replied: "In every bridge, underneath in the foundations unseen, there are stones imbedded in the earth without which the bridge could not stand. So," said the youth, "there are lives that are unknown, that are sacrificed unto God, upon which God's kingdom is built. If I am one of those stones buried in the earth and unknown and unseen, that is in the elective purpose of God. I am called. I go." He went and in keeping with the judgment of the physician, he soon died in that hot, equatorial jungle. In doing God's will, whether we live or die is in God's elective purpose. Our part is to offer our lives on the sacrificial altar of God and if it is here to live, if it is here to die, if it is here to stay, if it is yonder to go, the choice lies in the elective purpose of God. Our part is to offer our lives unto Him. It is a tremendous conception, "I saw under the altar." There is an altar of God in heaven, and all through the Scripture the idea is presented that on that altar God's people are sacrificed unto Him.

Now John says, "I saw these souls under the altar." Had the text said they were on the altar, the picture would be of the holocaust itself, of the action itself, of the burning itself. But when he says, "I saw these souls *underneath* the altar," the sacrifice has already been made, the action has already passed, the life has already been poured out. "Under the altar," as in Leviticus, the blood is poured out at the base of the altar. "Under the altar." And in keeping with another glorious symbolism of the Word of God, they are at rest, they are at peace, under the protecting, sheltering care of Christ, for the altar is always our Lord Christ. Under His wings and in His shepherdly care, protected from evil and judgment and wrath, they rest.

THE CAUSE OF MARTYRDOM

Why were these martyrs slain? The Greek text says that they were sacrificially slain. There is a Greek word for the slaying, the cutting, the terrible slaughter of a sacrifice. It is *sphazo*. That is the word used here describing the death of these martyrs. To the world they were destroyed, but to God they were offered as a sacrifice unto Him. They gave their lives for the Lord and the Lord looked upon them as His. They are *His* martyrs. And why were they slain? They were slain "for the Word of God and for the testimony which they held." The truth of God always brings opposition and turbulence and many times the destruction of those who deliver it. They were slain for the Word of God. They were also slain "for the testimony which they held." There is an added difference in the clause. In Revelation 1:9 it is said of John that he was exiled to Patmos "because of the Word of God and because of the testimony of Jesus Christ." But these are slain "because of the Word of God and because of the testimony which they held." It is a little different here. John was exiled "for the Word of God and for *the testimony of Jesus.*" But these were slain "because of the Word of God and *the testimony which they held.*"

As we think upon their situation, it becomes very apparent what they did which caused their martyrdom. They were living in the days of the visitation of the judgment and the wrath of Almighty God, and they were saying that these things that were happening were happening because they were the judgments of God. Of course, to the world, these things "just happen." Just as today, these things "just happen." But a prophet of God who lived in America today would see in our national calamities an altogether different story. To a prophet of God, the great troubles that face America are due to the sins of America. Our country is more debauched every day. The fear and anxiety in which we live is a part of that judgment. Nations do not build bombs and not use them. They do not invent jet-propelled planes and not use them. The prophecy was made that if atomic fission was ever discovered it would first be used in a bomb. That prophecy came to pass precisely. These things, to the world, are just happen-sos. But to the prophet of God they are the visitations of the judgment of the Almighty. If the day comes when bombs rain down upon the cities of America, the worldly man will say this is just a happen-so. But the prophet of God will say that this is the visitation of the judgment and the wrath of the Almighty.

Now, that is what happened here. The people are in great tribulation. They are in the horrible holocaust of final wrath. The prophets of that day are saying what is happening. The blood and the slaughter, they say, is the judgment of God upon drunkenness, debauchery, iniquity, worldliness and upon crass, cheap materialism. But the people do not like to hear it. The restraining power of God which we feel today has been taken out of the earth in that day and these prophets are mercilessly slaughtered and massacred. These are the martyrs who cry unto God.

Now I would make this observation: wherever there is a true prophet of God, he will preach judgment. These modern so-called ministers of God speak all things nice. Modern pedagogical methods admonish never to mention things

negative. Ignore them and they will not exist. There is not
any hell and there is not any devil and there is not any
judgment of God. All of that now is intellectually passé.
We have evolved beyond that. Centuries ago they may
have had a hell, and years ago they may have spoken of
a devil, and way back yonder they may have spoken of the
wrath and the judgment of God, but in our enlightened
and sophisticated day we do not do things like that. So we
stand up and we speak of the love of Jesus, and we speak
of peace, and we speak of all things pretty and beautiful.
But remember, these other things are as real. The same
Book that tells us about the good, tells us about the bad.
The same Revelation that speaks about heaven, speaks about
hell. The Bible that presents us the Lord Jesus as the Saviour, is the same Bible that presents to us the devil as our
enemy and adversary of damnation and destruction. The
two go together. If there is not anything to be saved from,
we do not need a Saviour, and if we can evolve into angels,
just give us time and maybe we shall be archangels by
and by.

The observation I started to make was this: Wherever in
this Bible we find a true prophet of God standing up, this
will be his message: that unless we repent and get right
with God, and unless we turn, there is coming down upon
us a judgment and a visitation from the Almighty. There
is no exception to that. For example, when Samuel as a
little boy delivered his first message from God, it was a
message of judgment upon the house of Eli because of the
sins of his sons, Hophni and Phinehas, whom Eli did not
rebuke. That was the first message of Samuel. When Isaiah
came and delivered his message, it was that because of the
sins of Judah the people should be carried away into Babylon, the temple should be destroyed, Jerusalem should be
destroyed, the nation should be destroyed. When Jeremiah
came to preach, they put him in stocks and in chains, and
finally they cast him into a miry pit because he predicted
the destruction of the armies of Israel and the destruction

of the temple and of the nation. But people do not like to hear those things. We love to hear things beautiful and things encouraging and things fine. Let us be positive. Let us not speak of these other things. But they are things that God speaks of. God says them. Did you ever notice what these modern pedagogues say? "Let us teach our children always the positive side and never the negative." Look at that. All ten commandments are thou shalt what? Thou shalt *n o t, not.* When we get smarter than God, we are going to raise up a generation of children that are on the road to the damnation of judgment. We cannot escape it. It is God who put this world together, and the Lord did it with a whole lot of "Thou shalt not's." Yet we are not to teach our children, "Thou shalt not!" These modern pedagogues say that such negative approaches give the little divinities inferiority complexes. It mixes up their personalities. It does all kinds of things to them. But God says "Thou shalt not," and when we rear our children according to the Book, and not according to pedagogical pseudo-science that sends our children to destruction, we shall have a new generation and a new family. Why, this thing of the recalcitrance and rebellion of juveniles is beyond anything the world ever saw and it comes from this modern approach.

I was saying that these true prophets of God were all alike in that they spoke of judgment. When Jonah entered Nineveh, he lifted up his voice and said, "Yet forty days and Nineveh will be destroyed." It was a prophecy of the judgment of Almighty God. When Jesus gave His great Apocalyptic discourses, He spoke of judgment. He said days are coming that if it were not for God's graciousness, even the elect would be deceived and would be lost. He spoke of wars and rumors of wars, floods and earthquakes and stars falling out of their places in the day. When Paul wrote II Timothy, his last letter, he said, "Perilous times are coming"; and when he spoke to the Ephesian elders in Acts 20, he said, "After I am gone, grievous wolves shall enter in, not sparing the flock, destroying God's people." Always, when a true man of God stands up to preach, he will warn and he will threaten and he will speak of the Judgment Day of the Almighty. Some day we shall all stand before Him. Some day.

THE CRY TO GOD

The text continues, "And they cry unto the Lord." This is the only place in the Revelation where this word, translated here "Lord," is used. In the Greek it is *ho Despotes.* Our English word "despot" is the exact Greek word. I presume the best way to translate it is "O Sovereign Ruler." You see, it is a scene of judgment. "O Sovereign Ruler, how long, holy and true [these promises God has made are true], how long dost thou not judge and avenge our blood on them that dwell on the earth?" That is the same thing that John the Baptist asked in the eleventh chapter of the first gospel when he said to Jesus: "I can see, Lord, thy ministry of good and healing and helpfulness, but where is that Messiah who lays the axe at the root of the tree, where is that Messiah who brings fire and judgment upon the earth, where is he? Are we to look for another one? Is there still another Messiah?" He did not understand that the first time the Messiah comes, He comes as a sacrifice for our sins on the cross. The next time He comes, it will be in judgment against those who refuse His mercy, who blaspheme His name and who turn aside from His gracious appeal. We ourselves ask the same question: "Lord, when is that day of visitation and judgment and consummation going to be? Lord, when? How long? How long?" Now, observe the answer of the Lord. He deigns to listen to His children. He listens to us in this life. He listens to us in the life to come. First, God presents to each one a beautiful gift. "Each one." Is not that a magnificent thing? To "each one" there was given a white robe. Now, I do not think a spirit can wear a white robe. I think the gift is an earnest, a pledge of the resurrection which is soon coming. There was given to them the promise that they should have this beautiful garment of the Lord, manifest righteousness, the glory of what God can do with a life that is devoted unto Him. Then, God said to them, "Rest yet for a little while, a little season, until thy fellow-servants and thy brethren that are to be killed are killed." Many times we are of the persuasion that when we are gone, that is to be the end of the witness to Christ. No, He always has other testifiers, witnesses, prophets, preachers. Always. There is never a time when God does not have His true servants in the earth. They will be speaking and preaching and declaring the Word of the Lord and when these who are martyred are in heaven, God says to his martyrs in heaven: "Down there in that bloody earth there are other of thy fellow-servants and of thy brethren who are speaking the Gospel of Christ and bearing witness to the truth of the Almighty. They are also to be killed, martyrs to the faith."

All of this tragedy happens in the elective purpose of God. God has His book and in His book are the names of these who are going to be martyred. The list reads down to this point in Revelation 6:9, but it does not stop there. From there God's list continues and does not cease until that last martyr has been slain. What a mysterious thing! That God holds all of this in His hands — the blood, fury, furor, holocaust, and the suffering and the offering of the lives of God's people — all of it is in His plan. I do not understand why. Why does not God do all this without the suffering of His people? Why martyrs? Why martyrs? Why their blood? Why this suffering? I do not know. There is a mystery of evil that is known but to God. We can trace evil back, back, back. It is in the father and the mother; they received it from their grandparents, and thus we trace it back until finally we come to Adam. Where does it come from in Adam? It came from Lucifer, who fell out of heaven because he rebelled against God. "Well, then, Lord, why did you make Lucifer, and why did you create a being capable of evil and why did you create Adam and Eve capable of listening and falling?" There is a mystery of evil that we cannot understand. Our minds, finite, circumscribed, limited, cannot enter into that question. There is no solution for it ever in this time or in this life. We just read it. We just see it. We just know it. In the providence of God and in the life and choice of the Almighty, it is decreed that we shall suffer because of evil. That is a part of the fabric of this life. When you find that judgment in your own life, and you go through the deep valley, and you weep by the side of those who weep, and you stand by the side of open graves, and the sentence finally comes in your own heart and you agonize in pain and in the sleepless night — that is a part of the inexplicable of how God is purging this earth. That is why we have the Revelation. He is bringing in His righteous kingdom, and He is bringing in the great and final consummation of a new earth and a new heaven and a new people. How does God do it? He does it in blood and in suffering and in fire and in smoke. That is the way it is described here in the Book. These martyrs are listed up to here, but God says that there are others listed who are yet to be slain! When that last one has laid down his life, the great consummation shall come.

Is it not a startling thing that whether our souls are disembodied and in heaven, or whether we are here in the flesh in this weary world; that whether it is they in glory, or whether it is we in this earth, we are taught to pray: "Lord, O God in heaven, thy kingdom come, thy will be done." Lord, when will You cast out evil? When will death be no more? When will the usurper, Satan, be destroyed? When will the righteous be vindicated? Lord, when will our new kingdom be given to thy saints? Lord, when? How long? How long?" And the Lord replies, "In a little while, *eti chronon nikron,* yet a little time, just a little while." While we are waiting, of course, time seems long. But it is not. Just a little while and He who comes will come and will not tarry. In just a little while, God will vindicate His people. In just a little while sin and death will be cast out. In just a little while even Hades, the intermediate state, will be destroyed. In just a little while, we shall see our Saviour. We shall be resurrected and glorified. We shall find our place in His presence. We shall live with God's people in glory. In just a little while. That is their prayer in heaven as it is our prayer in the earth: "Oh, Lord, that thy kingdom might come, that God's will might be done, in this sin-cursed earth as it is done in God's beautiful heaven."

Chapter 10

The Soul After Death

And when he had opened the fifth seal, I saw under the altar the souls of them that were slain for the word of God, and for the testimony which they held: And they cried with a loud voice, saying, How long, O Lord, holy and true, dost thou not judge and avenge our blood on them that dwell on the earth? And white robes were given unto every one of them; and it was said unto them, that they should rest yet for a little season, until their fellowservants also and their brethren, that should be killed as they were, should be fulfilled. — Revelation 6:9-11

This is a sermon on the intermediate state. The sermon concerns the fact of living, the existence, the conscious life, of those souls that John saw in heaven.

The difference between soul and spirit is this: Pure spirit has no relationship to a body. God is a Spirit. He has no body. Angels are spirits and they have no bodies. Satan is a spirit and he has no body. But a soul must have a body. If a soul is separated from the body, if the soul is disembodied, it may be referred to as a spirit. But that word "soul" always implies a body. There is no such thing as a soul that does not have somewhere a body.

John says though these martyrs were slain, though they were dead, their souls still live. John says, "I saw their souls in heaven and I heard their cry." One might say that this is an unreal situation, that it is merely a vision. But it is a vision of reality. It is a supernatural vision of facts before the time, but it is a vision of the facts themselves. It is a reality that John sees before the time. If these martyrs still live, then death is not the end of them. Their bodies lie

moldering in the ground, corrupting in the grave. Their
blood has been spilled out on the earth. But their souls
are still alive, in conscious existence in heaven. They speak
and they know what is happening here on earth. Human
eyes, eyes of the flesh, cannot see them. But they are known
to the eyes of God. In the supernatural, prophetic state in
which God elevated John and brought him up into heaven
to see things that were to come, John says, "I saw them
and I heard them."

It is a common relevation throughout all Scripture that
death is not the end of life but rather that there is a conscious existence beyond the grave. Whether one be saved
or unsaved, righteous or unrighteous, good or bad, wicked
or holy, the soul lives beyond death. There was a certain
rich man and a certain beggar. It came to pass that the
beggar died and was carried by the angels into Abraham's
bosom. It also came to pass that the rich man died and
was honored with a funeral. The poor man did not have
a funeral. They just dumped him out in some potter's field.
But the rich man died and was buried sumptuously. But
there is more to the story. In Hades the rich man lifted up
his eyes, being in torment, crying for Abraham to send
Lazarus, the poor man, to minister unto him. He had been
in the habit of ordering people around all his life. Why not
continue to do so beyond the grave? "Send Lazarus," he
cried, "that he may dip the tip of his finger in water and
cool my tongue for I am tormented in this flame." These
men are what you call "dead." But they are in a conscious
existence in another world. We take these two as typical
of all.

THE STATE OF THE UNRIGHTEOUS

We discuss first the unrighteous, the unbelieving, the
blaspheming, the repudiating, the scorning, the scoffing.
They also live beyond death. This rich man in the story
told by Jesus spurned the Word of God. He would not
listen to the prophets or to Moses. In his affluence he lived

in big houses, north in the summer and south in the winter. He had servants to be commanded. He lived and fared sumptuously. But he was like the Book says: He did not repent, he did not turn, he did not look to God. Then he died, as all inevitably die. But he is like all others who die like that. Whether they are poor or whether they are rich, when they die in unbelief and in unrepentance and in unforgiven sin, they go into a netherworld that is filled with agony and pain and torment. When this rich man died, when he shut his eyes between sheets of silk, on eiderdown pillows in that palatial home, he opened them in torment. What an indescribably horrible and tragic thing! So the soul of any unbeliever who dies without the atoning sacrifice of Christ, falls into torment. He is in misery, he is in pain, he is in agony. There is also another thing about these who die unrepentant. They are imprisoned somewhere in God's netherworld. They are imprisoned, awaiting the great White Throne Judgment Day of the Lord. I Peter 3:19 describes lost souls as imprisoned. These referred to in this passage are those who laughed at Noah when Noah for one hundred and twenty years preached righteousness and called a vile and blaspheming world to repentance. Those blasphemers are imprisoned, awaiting the great judgment day of the Lord. Such imprisonment is referred to again in II Peter chapter two, verse four and verse nine: "God spared not the angels that sinned, but cast them down to hell, [it is not hades here, but hell] and delivered them into chains of darkness, to be reserved unto judgment." The ninth verse thus depicts all who are lost: "The Lord knoweth how to deliver the godly out of temptations, and to reserve the unjust unto the day of judgment to be punished." There is, then, a fire, a flame, a burning, a torment, a misery, an agony, a gnashing of teeth, a madness for the soul that dies without Christ. Oh, the weight of these things! They bow us down. We ought to give ourselves to soul winning, to evangelism, to praying, to appealing to the soul lest it die without Christ.

But there is, also, that sinful life, that lost soul, that turns in faith to Christ. Are you one of them? Have you done that? Have you? Have you asked Jesus to forgive your sins? Have you? If you were to die today (and you could) is it right between you and God? There are souls that turn, that repent, that confess, that ask the mercy of God. What of them? What of them? Three things about them:

THE STATE OF THE RIGHTEOUS

First, they enter immediately into paradise. Luke 23:29: "And one of the malefactors turned to Jesus and said, Lord, we die justly for our sins, but Lord, in that day, when thou comest into thy kingdom, Lord, remember me, have mercy upon me." Jesus answered and said, "Verily, truly, I say unto thee, today shalt thou be with me in paradise." Today, today. As with the poor man who died and the angels carried him into Abraham's bosom. "Today shalt thou be with me in paradise." "Paradise" is a Persian word meaning "park," that beautiful, beautiful park of God. But where is that? In II Corinthians 12:2, Paul says that he was carried out of the body or in the body, he did not know, but he was carried up into the third heaven. The first heaven is the heaven where the birds fly and the clouds overspread. The second heaven is the heaven of the great sidereal universe, the milky-way, the heaven of the stars. The third heaven is the heaven of God where God's throne is, where the saints of the Lord are, where Jesus is. In the fourth verse of chapter twelve of the second Corinthian letter, Paul says he was carried up into paradise. So Paul said that when he was carried up into the third heaven (in verse two), he was carried up to paradise (in verse four, the twelfth chapter of II Corinthians). That same identification is made again in Revelation 2:7, where the Lord says to the people of Ephesus, "You be overcomers and I will give you to eat of the tree of life which is in the paradise of God." When I turn the page in the Revelation to chapter 22 and verse two, there John says: "And I saw the river of life proceeding out of the throne of God and of the Lamb . . . and on either side of the river, was the tree of life . . . and the leaves . . . were for the healing of the nations." The tree of life, which Jesus said was in the paradise of God, is in heaven. That is where our sainted loved ones have gone. We close our eyes to the weary things of this world, and we open our eyes to the glory of God's great heavenly home.

The second thing about the saved soul, we now discuss. What is it for the Christian to die? For the believer to die? It is to be with our Lord. In our church paper we list our beloved dead under this passage of Scripture, ". . . absent from the body, present with the Lord . . ." (II Corinthians 5:8). When one who believes in Jesus dies, immediately he is with the Lord. That is the meaning of the passage in the twenty-third chapter of the Book of Luke: "Today shalt thou be with me [with *me*] in paradise." That statement is the great foundation that lies back of what Paul writes in the precious book of Philippians: "For me to live is Christ, and to die is gain. But if I live in the flesh, this is the fruit of my labour; yet what I shall choose I wot not. For I am in a strait between two, having a desire to depart, and to be with Christ, which is far better: Nevertheless to abide in the flesh is more needful for you."

I was asked recently to see one of our members who is dying. He is at the door of death. It is just a matter of whether it is five minutes from now or this evening. As I stood with the family around that hospital bed, what assurance could I give to the bereaved group? God says it is better over there with Him. Here is languishing and lingering and suffering in the dissolution of this house of clay. What is it for a Christian to die? To depart and to be with Christ, which is far better. A real Christian ought to come to the edge of that great eternity with triumph and assurance, with a song in his heart and a smile on his face. "For me to live is Christ, and to die is gain." The Christian soul is a soul that is with Jesus in death, God having prepared a better thing for us. Nothing ever shall come between the

Christian believer and his Lord. Remember how the eighth chapter of Romans ends: "For I am persuaded, that neither death, nor life, nor angels, nor principalities, nor powers, nor things present, nor things to come, nor height, nor depth, nor any other creature, shall be able to separate us from the love of God which is in Christ Jesus our Lord." To die is the gain of being with Jesus. Nothing shall ever separate God's child from his blessed Lord.

A third thing about saved souls: they rest in blessedness. "The Lord said unto them that they should rest yet for a little season." That is, they have been resting and will continue to rest. They are not wandering, melancholy ghosts. Rather, they are blessedly at home with our Lord. Remember the verse in Revelation 14:13, "And I heard a voice from heaven saying unto me, Write, Blessed are the dead which die in the Lord . . . Yea, saith the Spirit, that they may rest from their labours." For the soul that has trusted in Jesus, to die is to go to heaven, into paradise. It is to be with our Lord. It is to rest in the blessedness and in the holiness and in the glory of God.

SCRIPTURAL OBSERVATIONS CONCERNING THE DEAD

Some deductions from these passages of Scripture are: (1) There is no such thing in the Word of God as soul-sleeping. Even those passages in the Old Testament that appear to indicate it, are describing the rot and the ruin of death. They are speaking of the appearance, the corruption of the body. There is nothing in the Word of God about the sleeping of the soul. When we die we go to be with our Lord in heaven. (2) There is no such thing in the Word of God as a purgatory. For one thing, such a supposition is inconsistent with the all-sufficient satisfaction, the all-sufficient adequacy, of the atonement of Christ. The triumphant author of the Book of Hebrews closes his ninth chapter with these words: "And as it is appointed unto men once to die, but after this the judgment: So Christ was once offered to bear the sins of many; and unto them that

look for him shall he appear the second time without sin
unto salvation." All of our salvation is in Christ. We do
not enter any purgatorial fires. We are saved by the grace
of God, not by any suffering on our part. We are saved by
His suffering. When we close our eyes to this world, we
open our eyes in heaven to see His blessed face. (3) At
the end of this life, after death, there is no second chance.
Death fixes our estate for eternity. As the eleventh chapter of the Book of Ecclesiastes says: "As a tree falls so shall
it lie." As the twenty-fifth chapter of the Book of Matthew
says, those five foolish virgins knocked and knocked, but the
door was closed. As the Book of Revelation says in its last
chapter, verse 11: "He that is unjust, let him be unjust still;
and he which is filthy, let him be filthy still." The matter
is settled forever. As Luke 16 describes it, there is a great
gulf fixed between the lost and the saved, a gulf so deep
and so wide that it prohibits the possibility of any crossing
over from one side to the other. It is an eternal fixedness.

The last avowal concerns the resurrection of the body.
This, I think, is the very heart of the Christian faith. Many
pagan philosophies taught immortality or a shadowy existence of some kind beyond the river Styx. But the immortality of the soul is not the Christian hope. The intermediate
state of disembodied souls is not the hope of the Christian.
The hope of the Christian is that we shall be raised from the
dead, that we shall experience a resurrection by the same
power of God that raised the Lord Jesus from the dead, and
that we shall be His people, God's redeemed creation, in a
new world and in a new heaven. Remember the passage in
II Corinthians 5:1-4: "For we know that if the earthly house
of this tabernacle be dissolved we have a building of God,
an house not made with hands, eternal in the heavens. For
in this do we groan, earnestly desiring to be clothed upon
with our house which is from God; not that we would be
unclothed [that is, not disembodied spirits, for heaven abhors disembodiment as nature abhors a vacuum] but clothed
upon, that God might give us the resurrected body, that

mortality might be swallowed up of life." In the great, triumphant chapter of I Corinthians, chapter fifteen, verses 53-57 read: ". . . For this corruption must put on incorruption, and this mortal must put on immortality. So when this corruptible shall have put on incorruption, and this mortal shall have put on immortality, then shall be brought to pass the saying that is written, Death is swallowed up in victory. O death, where is thy sting? O grave, where is thy victory? . . . But thanks be to God, which giveth us the victory through our Lord Jesus Christ." When the early first century Christians found that it was against Roman law to bury their dead (the Romans cremated the body), they carefully took the bodies of their sainted dead and in deep, hidden caverns, beneath the city, they reverently laid them away. They believed, as Christians, that God one day would speak life to these who had fallen asleep in Jesus. Do not let any man rob you of your hope. That is what it is to be a Christian. These crippled limbs will be strong and straight and these blind eyes will see and these dumb ears will hear and this weak body will be remade into the strength of God and we shall be like unto our living Lord. O the blessedness and the preciousness of the hope God hath given to us who in faith look up to Him!

Chapter 11

In the Great Day of His Wrath

And I beheld when he had opened the sixth seal, and, lo, there was a great earthquake; and the sun became black as sackcloth of hair, and the moon became as blood; and the stars of heaven fell unto the earth, even as a fig tree casteth her untimely figs, when she is shaken of a mighty wind. And the heaven departed as a scroll when it is rolled together; and every mountain and island were moved out of their places. And the kings of the earth, and the great men, and the rich men, and the chief captains, and the mighty men, and every bondman, and every free man, hid themselves in the dens and in the rocks of the mountains. And said to the mountains and rocks, Fall on us, and hide us from the face of him that sitteth on the throne, and from the wrath of the Lamb: For the great day of his wrath is come; and who shall be able to stand? — Revelation 6:12-17

This, the sixth seal, and the passage we have just read describing its opening, is not the end of history, but it is the beginning of the end. Those who live in the earth in that awful, terrifying hour think it is the great Judgment Day of God, that it is the end. But it is not. It is just the beginning of the end; it is an adumbration, a harbinger of that final and consummating denouement. The Book of the Revelation follows in broad outline the twenty-fourth chapter of Matthew which presents the apocalyptic discourse of our Lord. Our Lord in turn follows the pattern in the Book of Daniel. In the ninth chapter of the Book of Daniel, the prophet divides the end time into two equal parts. He calls it a seventieth week, and he divides that week that brings the end of the world into two halves. If the week

121

represents a week of years, then it is three and one-half years to the first half and three and one-half years for the second half. Our Lord suggests that division of time in His apocalyptic discourse in Matthew twenty-four. The first part of it He calls "the beginning of sorrows," and the last part of it He calls "the great tribulation." The Apocalypse will refer to this time period in the same terms in which it is described in the prophetic discourses of the Old Testament. Sometimes it is called "three and one-half years," the second half of Daniel's seventieth week. Sometimes it is called "a time, times and half a times." Sometimes it is called "forty-two months." Sometimes it is called "one thousand, two hundred and sixty days." But all those designations refer to the same period of time, whether it is in days or weeks or months or years or times. They all refer to this final day of judgment, the judicial administration of God in the earth. So we come in seal number six to the beginning of the end. This is the end of the first three and one-half years. This is the end of the beginning of sorrows. After the great parenthetical chapter, chapter seven, we enter into the final consummation of the age. These first six seals, then, cover that period of time of the first half of that final week.

The first seal, as you remember, is the seal that brings across the horizon of history the final dictator, the world tyrant, the man of sin. He comes in with the applause and with the admiration of the nations of the world. He comes in by a bloodless coup, a bloodless revolution, without war, without destruction, without the shedding of human blood. He comes in as the promised saviour of the world. The cry is made: "This is the man who delivers us from war." "This is the man who has the answers." "This is the leader who can deliver us from all of the economic ills and disturbances of mankind."

All dictators come in like that. They are the saviours of the world. Whether they are in ancient history, medieval history, or today, they all come in alike. "This is Demetrius

Soter," "this is Ptolemy *Soter,*" "this is Philadelphius *Soter,*" "this is Antiochus *Soter,*" "this is Seleucus *Soter.*" That word *soter* is the Greek word for "saviour." The same pattern obtains in modern history. "This is Napoleon Bonaparte who delivers France"; or "this is Frederick the Great; or a Bismarck, who delivers Germany"; or this is the Iron Duke of Wellington who saves the British Empire." In our generation, the pattern goes: "This is Der Feuhrer who delivers the homeland"; or "this is Il Duce who delivers our native Italy"; or "this is Stalin who delivers mother Russia"; or "this is Tojo, who finds a place for Nippon in the Sun." They are all alike, as described here in the Word of God.

The concomitant, the corollary, the accompaniment is likewise always the same. The history of these so-called "saviours," without exception, is written in blood, in tears, war, death, just as it is in the Revelation. After the world emancipator, the self-styled saviour, the dictator who liberates and emancipates mankind — after him comes war. The second horseman of the Apocalypse is red. He has in his hand a great sword and the world is bathed in blood. The third horseman of the third seal inevitably follows after. The horse is black, and there is famine and dearth and want in the earth. Then the fourth horseman of the fourth seal always follows after. There is pestilence and the black plague. There is death, with the grave opening its mouth to swallow up the vast multitudes of humanity who fall in the wake of the leadership of these so-called saviours of the world. All of them in the past are but types and figures of that ultimate dictator who will seize the reins of the governmental and military powers of the earth.

Then is opened seal number five. In this fifth seal the action is not seen; just the results of it are seen. In heaven John beholds the souls of those who have been martyred for the testimony of God and for the faith of Jesus in the earth. They cry unto God in heaven for vengeance that they might be avenged for their blood shed on the earth.

They cry unto God: "How long, O Lord, holy and true, dost thou not judge and avenge our blood?" That cry certainly does not fit modern-day, soft, saccharin Christianity. The modern pulpit of modern faith and new theology presents a God who is soft and easy. He would not think of hell, nor the flame of vengeance, nor the judgment of a righteous indignation. Their God is easy and soft. Anyone can push Him around. He is malleable. He is like putty. He is like clay. That is the modern God in the modern pulpit. But how different is the God of vengeance and wrath found in this Book. Read the first chapter of the second Thessalonian letter: "And to you who are in trouble and trial rest . . . for it is a righteous thing with God to recompense trouble to them that persecute . . . And to you who are troubled . . . the Lord Jesus shall be revealed from heaven . . . In flaming fire taking vengeance on them that know not God, and that obey not the gospel of our Lord Jesus Christ: Who shall be punished with everlasting destruction from the presence of the Lord . . . When he shall come in glory." What a different kind of a God is this God in the Bible! He is a God of holiness and of righteousness and at the same time a God of judgment and of indignation. Men who do wickedly in the earth, who destroy and waste and murder and make war and shed blood, are held accountable before God in that final day. The fifth seal is the cry of God's righteous who have been bathed in their own blood.

TERRIFYING PHENOMENA IN CREATION

The sixth seal is the beginning of that final judgment of heaven. The rest of the Book of the Revelation describes the judicial administration of God when He deals with sin, when unrighteousness and villainy and wickedness, when violence and wrong are cast out forever. These are the proceedings of an indignant, wrathful and righteous Lord. In the sixth seal there are these startling and paralyzing and terrifying physical phenomena: "And I beheld when he had

opened the sixth seal, and, lo, there was a great earthquake."
There was a great *seismos*. That word *seismos* is a Greek
word meaning "quaking," "shaking," "agitating." It is usually
translated in the Bible as "earthquake." In the English language a *seismograph* would be a graph that recorded the
quaking in the crust of the earth. The underlying meaning
of the word has reference to a "shaking." For example, in
the next verse here in the Revelation, when the author likens
the entire universe of God's creation to a great fig tree, he
says that the tree will be shaken by a mighty wind. The
word "shaken" is the same word previously translated
"earthquake." In the eighth chapter of the Book of Matthew,
the word is translated "tempest," when the fury of the
wind and the waves poured across the sea of Galilee. In
the second chapter of Joel, verse ten, the prophet refers to
the heavens (in the Greek Septuagint) "trembling." It is
the same word. In that same Greek Septuagint, in Haggai,
the second chapter and sixth verse, it is translated "shaking," ". . . when God shall shake the heavens, and the earth,
and the sea, and the dry land . . ." So what this seal reveals
to us is that there is to be a universal shaking of all God's
creation. That is a part of the judicial administration of
God. Throughout the Bible is seen that same thing, the
shaking of this earth in His awesome presence. When the
Lord came down on top of Mount Sinai and there gave to
the people the law of the Lord, the Book says: "And that
mountain trembled and the earth shook and the rocks were
rent." It is the presence of the righteous, holy, Almighty
God. We find that same accompaniment when Elijah com-
plained to God that the prophets of the Lord were destroyed
and the altars of the Lord were cast down. As Elijah described the tragic situation, the Lord passed by and when
He did great winds hit the rocks and great earthquakes
tore the mountain apart. The same thing occurred when
Jesus was murdered. When He died, the whole earth quaked
and the rocks were rent. We find that same thing when

Silas and Paul prayed at midnight in the Philippian jail. The Lord came down and shook that jail to its foundations and the whole earth quivered and shook. That is a part of the judicial coming of God. "There was a great earthquake."

John continues the description, Revelation 6:12: ". . . and the sun became black as sackcloth of hair," black like a Bedouin's tent. That also is an accompaniment of the presence of God in His judicial proceedings. When the Saviour died, God's judgment fell upon our human sin. The whole sun was blotted out. There was a darkness over the face of the earth from high noon until three in the afternoon. In the day of the judgment of God upon Egypt, there was a blackness of night that could be felt. It was dark, terrible, terrifying. When the Lord came down on Mt. Sinai, the mountain was shrouded in blackness of smoke, a part of the sign of the judicial presence of God. John continues the description: ". . . and the moon became as blood." The ensanguined appearance of the moon looked like blood. The same description is found in Matthew 24:29 and in Joel 2:51. John continues, "And the stars of heaven fell unto the earth." He conceived, I have just said, the earth and the whole creation as a fig tree that is shaken by a mighty wind. So God will shake this creation. "And the heavens recoiled as a scroll that is rolled up together"; and the configuration and the topography of this earth are changed when every mountain and every island are moved out of their places. What a day! What a day!

THE MEANING OF THE SIGNS

What do those signs mean? We find them described exactly like that in the apocalyptic discourse of our Lord in Matthew twenty-four. These things He described as the beginning of sorrows, are depicted here in the first six seals of the Revelation. He speaks of famines and pestilences and of wars and of earthquakes. That is the way our Lord spoke of it — just as it is written here in the Revelation.

Our Lord refers to the time when the sun shall be darkened and the moon shall not give her light and the stars shall fall from heaven and the powers of the heavens shall be shaken. "Then shall appear the sign of the Son of Man," the second half of this Great Tribulation. That same description we find in the prophets. They were enabled to see these visitations from afar. Read Isaiah 13:10-13; 34:4, 8; Ezekiel 32:7, 8; Joel 2:10, 11; 3:15; Haggai 2:6 (quoted in Hebrews 12:26-29). We find those same things in the configurations, in the contortions, written in the very stone and rock and strata of this earth. All of us have seen mountains that are on end, great, vast fundamental rock structures that are turned upside down. These gigantic geological upheavals are written in the Palisades, in the Grand Canyon, written over the face of this earth, the contortions and the agonies of nature under the hand of an Almighty God. We do not find anything here in this Book that we do not find in God's other Book, the Book of Nature. The things that God is doing, the things that God has done, the things that God will yet do, are all part of a pattern. They are alike because the same great God does them and is doing them and shall do them.

What is the meaning? I do not know of a more interesting assignment than to read what men of God think as they pore through these pages. I came across one interpreter who had a vivid imagination. I wish you could read his eloquent description of what he thought these descriptions referred to. He thinks that when the moon turns to blood, that is a figure referring to the fires of destruction that burn in this earth and the redness of the flame is reflected in the blood-redness of the moon. He says that the sun blotted out in blackness like a Bedouin's tent is a picture of the smoke that rises from the furnace of this burning world and for those ninety-three million miles it blots out the face of the sun. Those theories are interesting.

Then there are others (and most of the interpreters are

of this group) who say that these physical phenomena are pictures of the break-up of civil, social and ecclesiastical authority. They are pictures of the breaking up of civilized government and the breaking-down of human institutions. These expositors point out that, following war and bloodshed and destruction, there is always an orgy of violence and sin indescribable upon the earth. They say that the sun blotted out refers to the fall of a sovereign, central authority, and the blood-red moon pictures the fall of a lesser governmental authority. The stars represent the fall of still lesser governmental authorities. They say the mountains represent kingdoms, and the islands represent lesser kingdoms, and when they are moved out of their places, it is a picture of a breaking up and the dissolution of governmental and civil authority in the earth, a revolution and a catastrophe the like of which has never been found in the pages of history. That is possibly true.

Certainly the Book says those are terrible and tragic days, and they bring out the bestial and the vile and the wicked in mankind. When the Bible uses these terms of the sun in blackness and the moon in blood and the stars falling like a fig tree shaken and the mountains and the islands moved out of their places, certainly it is no exaggeration of the awful passions of men that lie smouldering underneath. Beneath the crust of this earth upon which we walk, down underneath, there are great, volcanic possibilities, molten rock, fire and fury, and many a Tromboli and many a volcano elsewhere proclaims the fury of the burning of this earth. So it is with the passions of men. Underneath the quiet and the civil order of the human heart, there is an indescribable villainy. All we have to do to realize this is to read of the rape of Nanking or the violence of the Russians in Warsaw or Berlin, atrocities that happened in our lifetime. Even here in America, whenever there is a destructive tidal wave or a violent hurricane or a sweeping flood, there we find the Ranger and the soldier and the police set with orders to shoot on sight those who would ravage and steal the property and the possessions of those who have lost what they have in their homes. Can you imagine that? Can you conceive of that? Families driven out because of a great tidal wave or a great hurricane and before the family can come back to retrieve what little they might have left in what once was a home, there is the thief and there is the scoundrel searching to steal whatever he might be able to find! No wonder the government says to shoot him on sight, like a dog. This evil in humanity comes to the surface in that final day of anarchy and riot and chaos and the breakdown of civil government.

The Response of Men

Then we come to the most astonishing revelation of all. What do those who live on earth do in that great Judgment Day of the Lord? First the Book says they are terrified. The kings, the great men, the rich men, the chief captains, the mighty men, the bondmen, the free men, all are terrified. They hide themselves in the dens and in the rocks of the mountains. They are frightened, they are terror-stricken at these disasters coming from God. They are correct in their interpretation. They say God is on His throne and that these things come from His righteous and indignant hand. They say sin is a reality, and God has come down to judge our naked and depraved souls. As they interpret what is happening, they use a phrase that is fraught with eternal, profound meaning, "For the great day of *the wrath of the Lamb* is come." What a phrase! What a phrase! For a lamb is gentle, a humble creature that one might carry in the arms. "The great day of *the wrath of the Lamb* is come." The Lord is good and gracious to those who love Him. He is merciful and patient and long-suffering to those who lift up their faces toward Him. But God, the Lamb, the Saviour who died for our sins, is also the Lord who is full of wrath and judgment and indignation toward those who spurn His

overtures of grace and forgiveness. That great English poet,
William Cowper, wrote of that awful and tragic truth like
this:

> Hear the just law, the judgment of the skies,
> He that hates the truth must be a dupe of lies.
> And he who *will* be cheated to the last,
> Delusion strong as hell must bind him fast.

When a man turns from God and from truth and from the
appeal of Christ, then he turns to damnation and to perdition, and to hell. That judgment is inevitable. It comes.
It always comes. "For if we sin willfully after that we have
received the knowledge of the truth, there remaineth no
more sacrifice for sins, but a certain fearful looking for of
judgment and fiery indignation, which shall devour the adversaries. He that despised Moses' law died without mercy
under two or three witnesses: Of how much sorer punishment, suppose ye, shall he be thought worthy, who hath
trodden under foot the Son of God, and hath counted the
blood of the covenant, wherewith he was sanctified, an unholy thing, and hath done despite unto the Spirit of grace?
For we know him that hath said, Vengeance is mine, I will
repay, saith the Lord. And again, the Lord shall judge his
people. It is a fearful thing to fall into the hands of the
living God" (Hebrews 10:26-31). Our God is a consuming
fire. That is the judgment of the Lamb.

Another strange thing happens. One would think that
when they call that mammoth prayer meeting, the greatest
prayer meeting this earth has ever seen or will ever see, with
every big man there and every small man, every famous
and every infamous man, every wise man and every foolish
man, every leader and every captain, every bondman and
every free man, the whole earth in the prayer meeting, that
in repentance they would call upon the name of the Lord.
But are they turning from sin, are they trusting in Christ,
are they looking up to God? No! Rather, they are praying
to the dumb rocks, they are beseeching the deaf and inert

stones. It is an astonishing, an amazing performance. As the wrath of heaven grows more intense through the remainder of the judgments of God depicted in the Revelation, these evil men grow more obdurate. Here their consciences are stricken and their hearts are somewhat soft, but when the end does not come at once, they grow harder and harder and harder, with each separate and coming judgment. They are more confirmed in their obstreperous, incorrigible rebellion and negation of God, until finally when Christ comes as we see in the nineteenth chapter of the Book of the Revelation, these are found boldly, flagrantly opposing and fighting against the Lord. How amazing! Even John, himself, is astounded at their lack of repentance. In the ninth chapter of the Book, when John describes the indescribable horrors that come upon the men of the earth, he says, "and yet they did not repent." He closes the chapter saying: "Neither repented they of their murders, nor of their sorceries, nor of their fornication, nor of their thefts." John records his amazement again in the sixteenth chapter as he looks upon these men who are judged of God and who are scorched with heat. He says that they blasphemed the name of God and they repented not. In the eleventh verse: ". . . they blasphemed the God of heaven because of their pains and their sores, and repented not of their deeds." One would think that men ground under the judgment of God would be the first to cry out to God, "Lord, Lord." But they do just the opposite.

The most notorious criminal of my generation was named John Dillinger. The FBI hunted him down like a rat. Placarded over the face of America as a public enemy number one, he was the most sought-after man in the nation. How that man suffered in his evil and in his violence! He cut off the ends of his fingers to destroy any finger prints. He went through terrible surgery to change the configuration of his face. Every footfall, every noise, was an announcement of the terror he fought, secreted behind every door and walking down every dark street. Why did not he turn to God? Because judgment does not save men. The penitentiary would be an effective instrument of salvation if incarceration and pain and deprivation turned men to God. It never does. Only the grace of God can change a human heart and save a human soul. When you say "No" to God, something happens to your soul. When you say "No" to the invitation of the spirit of Jesus, something happens to your heart. When you continue in that negation, the day comes when your heart is as insensible to God as a rock. These condemned men under the sixth seal prayed, not to God who could save, but to the rocks to fall on them and to hide them from the face of Him who sits on the throne and from the wrath of the Lamb, "For the great day of his wrath is come; and who shall be able to stand?"

But thank God, there is a Rock to which we can fly; there is a great, eternal, immovable Rock of Ages to whom we can flee.

> Rock of Ages, cleft for me,
> [open for me, torn asunder for me,
> crucified for me, rent for me,]
> Rock of Ages, cleft for me,
> Let me hide myself in thee.
>
> O my loving brother, when the world's on fire,
> Don't you want God's bosom to be
>   your pillow.
> Oh, hide me ever, in the Rock of Ages,
> Rock of Ages, cleft for me.

There is refuge, there is peace, there is salvation, there is victory, there is deliverance, there is keeping, in "the Rock of Ages cleft for me." There was an artist who drew a picture. It was a painting of a great cliff of solid rock facing the sea. As the storm rent and the waves rolled, beating against that great rock, high in a cleft was a little bird, sound asleep with its head under its wing. The artist captioned the picture "Peace." Peace, peace, rest, security in the cleft of the rock.

Jesus, Lover of my soul,
Let me to Thy bosom fly,
While the nearer waters roll,
While the tempest still is high!
Hide me, O my Saviour, hide,
Till the storm of life is past.

Rock of Ages, cleft for me,
Let me hide myself in Thee.

There is a rock in a weary land, there is a foundation un-
shakable, there is a refuge in the hand of God. Yea, Lord,
I believe, I trust, I come.

Chapter 12

The One Hundred Forty-Four Thousand

And after these things I saw four angels standing on the four
corners of the earth, holding the four winds of the earth, that
the wind should not blow on the earth, nor on the sea, nor
on any tree. And I saw another angel ascending from the east,
having the seal of the living God: and he cried with a loud
voice to the four angels, to whom it was given to hurt the earth
and the sea, Saying, Hurt not the earth, neither the sea, nor
the trees, till we have sealed the servants of our God in their
foreheads. And I heard the number of them which were
sealed: and there were sealed an hundred and forty and four
thousand of all the tribes of the children of Israel. Of the
tribe of Judah were sealed twelve thousand. Of the tribe of
Reuben were sealed twelve thousand. Of the tribe of Gad
were sealed twelve thousand. Of the tribe of Aser were sealed
twelve thousand. Of the tribe of Nepthalim were sealed twelve
thousand. Of the tribe of Manasses were sealed twelve thousand. Of the tribe of Simeon were sealed twelve thousand. Of
the tribe of Levi were sealed twelve thousand. Of the tribe of
Issachar were sealed twelve thousand. Of the tribe of Zabulon
were sealed twelve thousand. Of the tribe of Joseph were sealed
twelve thousand. Of the tribe of Benjamin were sealed twelve
thousand. — Revelation 7:1-8

Chapter seven is divided into two parts. The first words
of verse one are translated into English, "and after these
things I saw": then verse nine is translated, "after this I
beheld." But the Greek is identical. *Meta tauta eidon, meta
tauta eidon,* are the exact words in both verses, "after these
things I saw." There are two visions in chapter seven. The
first vision is of the children of Israel. The second vision —
"After this I beheld . . . a great multitude . . . of all kindreds, and people, and tongues . . ." — is of the Gentiles.

This sermon concerns the first vision, the vision of the one hundred forty-four thousand of all the tribes of the children of Israel. "After these things I saw four angels standing on the four corners of the earth, holding the four winds of the earth . . . And an angel arose from the east, having the seal of . . . God: and he cried with a loud voice to the four angels." "Four" is the number of this world, and there is a four-fold repetition of the numeral in these verses. These four angels standing on the four corners of the earth, at the four quarters of the earth, represent the universality of God's administration. In the seventh chapter of the Book of Daniel, the prophet saw four winds striving over the mighty sea, and out of the turbulence arose the four beasts that represent the four great empires of the world. So the vision has to do with this world, this created world. The vision here says: "I saw four angels standing at the four quarters of the earth, holding the four winds." *Krateo* is translated "holding." The word *kratos* means "power," "might," "dominion." In Revelation 1:8 and in Revelation 4:8, with the Greek word *pan*, it is translated "Almighty," referring to God. *Panto-Krator* — *panto* referring to everything, and *kratos*, "power"; so *panto-krator* is the name of an All-powerful, Almighty God. We have the word translated here "holding." In Revelation 2:25 it is translated "holding fast."

The picture is vivid. These winds are striving to be turned loose, but they are held in abeyance by the omnipotence of Almighty God. They are not to blow on the earth, the scene of settled government (Revelation 10:2; Psalm 46:2). They are not to blow on the sea, which represents the restlessness and confusion of mankind (Daniel 7:23; Isaiah 57:20). They are not to blow on any tree — the trees represent the majesty, the dignity, the culture, the civilization, the glory and the beauty of man (Daniel 4:10, 22; Ezekiel 31:3-9, 14-18). The winds are held in abeyance by the Lord God Almighty. There is a judgment that is ready and restless to fall upon this vile and evil world, but it is held in abeyance by the omnipotence of God.

This passage, this whole chapter seven, is plainly an interlude, a parenthesis. It is placed here between the opening of the sixth seal and the opening of the final seventh seal. The first six seals were opened in chapter six. The seventh and final seal is opened in chapter eight. Between the two, between "the beginning of sorrows" and the beginning of "the great and final tribulation," there is this parenthesis, this interlude. These four angels who have in their hands the storms of Almighty God, to wither and to blast and to destroy, but who in this chapter seven are held back, are in chapter eight turned loose. As they sound the first four trumpets, there is vast waste and destruction and judgment in the earth. But before that judgment falls and before this visitation comes from an Almighty God, the Lord says, "Wait, wait, stay thy hand; for first, before that judgment falls, we must seal the servants of God." Care must be taken to protect those who belong to God before that terrible judgment falls. It is thus in all the story of human history. God's elect are precious in His sight, and for their sakes judgment is stayed. The reason this world stands, the reason governments exist, the reason civilization endures, is because of the elect of God. Were it not for them, the world would be destroyed like a withering branch. Had there been ten righteous men found in Sodom, Sodom would not have been destroyed. For the lack of ten, it was wasted and judged. So it is on this earth. The reason judgment does not fall and the reason condemnation does not come is because of God's elect in the earth. For their sakes the storm is stayed and the destruction waits. In between these awful visitations from heaven recorded in the sixth and eighth chapters of the Revelation, the veil is pulled aside in this seventh chapter and the mercy and grace and love of God are revealed to His elect.

THE NUMBER ONE HUNDRED FORTY-FOUR THOUSAND

"I saw an angel ascending from the east, having the seal of the living God: and he cried . . . to those four angels, to stay . . . until we have sealed the servants of our God in their foreheads. And I heard the number of them which were sealed: and there were sealed an hundred and forty and four thousand." That is one of the symbolic numbers in the Bible, a numerical group about whose identification there has been considerable argument. There are many theologians who say it is impossible to know who those thousands are; so they do not try to identify them. They just dismiss the subject. Then those who do try to explain it offer every conceivable kind of explanation.

The Seventh-day Adventists say that these one hundred forty-four thousand pertain to their communion, who are found observing the Jewish Sabbath when the Lord comes again, and they are raptured up to glory. The Jehovah's Witnesses say that these one hundred forty-four thousand belong to them. They are to be the saved at the end time. They are the great "Over-comers," and each one of these Jehovah's Witnesses is trying to be one of that select number. That is why we see them on the street corner, that is why we see them knocking at the door from house to house. Each one of these Jehovah's Witnesses is striving to be one of that elect group in order that he might be caught up to heaven and might be saved. There is a strange esoteric sect called the sect of "The Flying Roll." They believe the vision pertains to them and that they are going to be the one hundred forty-four thousand when their blood is cleansed and they are given immortal life upon this earth.

And finally, there are those theologians without number who identify the group as the true church. These children of Israel represent the church, the redeemed by the grace of God of all ages and of all time. To them, "Israel" equals "the church," Israel represents the church. There are many things to be said against that belief. For one thing, we have just seen the church, under the name of the redeemed Elders, raptured up to heaven, where they are crowned and robed and enthroned. Another objection to that identification of Israel as the church is that in the fourteenth chapter of the Book of the Revelation, John sees that one hundred forty-four thousand in the presence of those Elders who represent Christ's church. Each group is there, the Elders and the one hundred forty-four thousand, in his own character, with his own blessing, in his own place. The two groups are not the same. John sees them together, one in the presence of the other, the one hundred forty-four thousand in the presence of the Elders, who are the redeemed church of Christ.

What is wrong with taking the text as it is? What is wrong with understanding it as it is worded? "I heard the number of them which were sealed: and there were sealed an hundred and forty and four thousand of all the tribes of the children of Israel." That is what God said. Let us accept the text as meaning just what He said. The one hundred forty-four thousand were of all of the tribes of the children of Israel. Now, where are those tribes of the children of Israel? The Israelite is here. He is everywhere. We see him in every nation, in every city. But where are these tribes? If you were to ask an Israelite what tribe he belongs to, he would have great trouble answering. He does not know. But God knows. All through those genealogical tables, following the male of the family, those tribes were kept distinct as long as their records were kept. When the records were destroyed and the nation was dispersed, the people became known as "lost tribes." But they are not lost to God. In their genealogies every Israelite belongs to a certain family, to a certain group, to a certain tribe. In the Book of Matthew, in the thirteenth chapter, is told the parable of the treasure hid in a field. In the one hundred and thirty-fifth Psalm, Israel is called God's "peculiar treasure." Though that treasure of God, His people, His chosen family, the descendants of Abraham, are buried and hid by their families in the grave of the nations of the world, yet they are known to God.

Twelve thousand from each one of the tribes of the children of Israel are to be sealed. That word "twelve" in the Bible with reference to the people of the Lord always refers to Israel. Twelve is their number. There were twelve tribes. In the nineteenth chapter of Matthew, the twenty-eighth verse, our Lord says that the twelve apostles will sit on twelve thrones judging the twelve tribes of Israel. The High Priest had a breastplate on which were twelve precious stones representing the twelve tribes. On the table of shewbread were twelve holy, consecrated loaves, representing the twelve tribes of Israel. In the great city, the new Jerusalem, there are twelve gates. On each one of those gates is written the name of one of the tribes of Israel. There are twelve gates in the city of God, representing the twelve tribes. All through the Bible, from its inception until its ending, that number *twelve* refers to the children of Israel. So, finding it here, I conclude that its reference is the same as that in the rest of the Scriptures. Here are twelve thousand sealed, elect, called, from the twelve different tribes of the children of Israel.

GOD'S ELECTIVE PURPOSE FOR THE JEW

We have a confirmation here again of a revelation we have met time after time in preaching through the Word of God: The Lord is not done with the Jew. The Lord is not through with Israel. The visible pledge of this fact can be found on every page of history and in every newspaper that we read each day. God's promise to Israel is that same *genus*, that "kind," that "race," "generation" will be here until the Lord comes again (Matthew 24:34). Inside of the Jewish universal heart is that presentiment that God has some greater and better thing for the Jews. All the ravages of the centuries, and all the adversaries of the generations, and all the waste and persecution of time, have never yet been able to destroy that hope of the Jewish heart, nor to destroy the Jewish race, itself.

The only reason I know to deny to a literal Israel the blessings, and to arrogate to a literal Israel the curses, while we appropriate to a so-called "spiritual Israel," the church, the promises of the prophets and the apostles, is Jewish prejudice on the part of the interpreters of the Bible and on the part of the people of Christ. That position I do not understand. A woman came to me in the church a few weeks ago. Wanting to insult me, she called me, half a dozen times, "Rabbi Criswell." I do not object to that title, though she thought it was a great insult to me. "Rabbi" is God's word for "Teacher," as the Latin word for teacher is *Doctor*. The Hebrew would say *Rabbi*, meaning "Teacher." We would use the word "Professor." I was not offended, though the woman thought she was insulting me.

We must never forget, though many people do, that the prophets were all Jews, our Lord was a Jew, the apostles, all of them, were Jews. It was the Apostle Paul who said in the ninth chapter of the Book of Romans: "For I could wish that myself were accursed from Christ [damned from Christ] for my brethren, my kinsmen according to the flesh." He began the tenth chapter of the Book of Romans with this word: "Brethren, my heart's desire and prayer to God for Israel is, that they might be saved." He concluded the eleventh chapter with the discussion: ". . . Hath God cast away his people? God forbid . . . but blindness in part is happened to Israel, until the fulness of the Gentiles be come in." The Jews are blinded in part, and that only until the fulness of the Gentiles be come in. Then shall the scales drop from Israel's eyes, and then shall God send them the Redeemer who shall turn sin and unbelief and blasphemy away from Jacob, and God shall keep His covenant that He made with the patriarchs. All of that prophecy is in the New Testament and is an integral part of the revelation and ministry of Jesus Christ. It is inexplicable to me why people spurn things Jewish even to the denying of their place in the providence and elective purpose of God.

In the time of the most vicious of all the Jewish persecutions on earth, Adolf Hitler wrote out a mandate to be read in all of the state churches of Germany. The tragic procedure went like this: "Will all of the men in this church who are Jewish stand up? Those standing will now turn and leave the church. Now, will all of the women in this church who are Jewish stand up?" Here and there and there they stood up. "Those standing, now leave the church. Will all of those in this congregation who had a Jewish grandparent on the maternal side stand up?" Some stood up. "You will now leave. Now, will all of those who have a Jewish grandparent on the paternal side stand up?" Here and there and there they stood up. "You will now leave. Now will all of those who have any Jewish blood anywhere in the family line on the maternal side stand up?" Here and there they stood up. "Now, you are ordered to leave." When they were ordered to leave, we can imagine the Lord God Christ coming out of the stained glass window high over the altar, down from the cross, and walking the length of the aisle and leaving.

We cannot dissociate, we cannot take out of the Holy Scriptures of God, His elective purpose in His people and have anything left. The more I study the Book, the more I read of its sacred page, the more I observe human history, the more I read the daily newspaper, the more I am confirmed in the persuasion that God lives, and that the great prophecies of the Lord regarding His people shall be fulfilled. To this very day, their land in Palestine has never been a refuge, a security, a peace, for any Gentile who has overrun it. It will never be, according to the Word of God, until it is given back to those to whom God sware it in Abraham and Isaac and Jacob. So, when I read here in the Book: ". . . there were sealed an hundred and forty and four thousand of all of the tribes of the children of Israel

. . .," I read a plain, simple sentence from the Word of God. There is a program, there is a destiny, there is a choice, there is an elective purpose, there is a will of heaven that shall be wrought for those people, and in God's time it will come to pass.

Now, we have the revelation here of what it is that shall come to pass for Israel. Let us look at it. Revelation 7:2 reads, "I saw from the *anatole heliou*, from the dawning of the sun, from the sunrising . . ." I think that is far more beautiful than to say I saw it "from the east." This Greek language is beautiful. "I saw from the dawning of the sun" or "I saw from the sunrising an angel descend having the seal of the living God: and he sealed these who are out of the elect of Israel." That sealing is not a unique or peculiar thing. All through the book, all through the Word of God, we find the Lord placing a mark, sealing those that belong to Him. In the days of Abraham the mark was in the flesh. He set the rite of circumcision. These so marked belonged in an especial way to God. In the days of the judgment of Egypt, the mark was in the form of a cross, on the lintel above the door and on the door posts on either side, and the destroying angel of death looked for the mark, the seal, and passed over those who possessed it. In the days of Rahab, it was a scarlet line hanging in the window. She was to be preserved from the wanton destruction that wasted the city. In the ninth chapter of the Book of Ezekiel, the prophet saw a man clothed in linen with an inkhorn at his side, and the man was commanded to go through Jerusalem and mark on the forehead those who sighed and cried because of the abominations and the wickednesses of the people. In the thirteenth chapter of the Book of the Revelation, Antichrist, who mimicked Christ, has a mark that he puts on the right hand and in the forehead of men, without which mark one cannot buy or trade or sell. This arrangement of marking of God is a custom found often in the Book.

The Sealing of the Servants of God

Why were these one hundred forty-four thousand marked? Why were they sealed? Because they were Jews? No, not at all. This is an election, morally conditioned. God never does anything adventitiously, summarily, arbitrarily. There are great spiritual reasons why God does as He does, and there are great spiritual reasons why God sealed these twelve thousand out of each of the tribes of Israel. Why were these particular men chosen? Because of deep moral, spiritual characteristics. In the fourteenth chapter of the Book of the Revelation they are called "virgins." They have no predecessors and no successors. No virgin ever has a child. So they were not born of virgins nor, being virgins, would they have any progeny, any succession. These are men who are chosen for a separate and elect purpose. They have no predecessors and they have no successors. That is, they do not multiply themselves. They are chosen for a very definite reason, an elective purpose of God. Again, they are called "the servants of our God," in contra-distinction to those who were not servants of the most high God. These are they who have given themselves to the ministry of Christ when the whole world around them is blaspheming and cursing and wallowing in the seas of mire and filth and dirt and sin and unbelief. These are men of unusual spiritual stature. Read their description in the fourteenth chapter of the Book of Revelation. They are described as being undefiled in the midst of a defiled world. They live in purity in the midst of an impure world. They are fearless and brave in their testimony to God in the midst of a world that blasphemes Christ and damns the name of heaven. These are men of great spiritual stature.

Observe, too, that these one hundred forty-four thousand are called "the first-fruits unto God and to the Lamb," and while He is calling them that, there stand the Elders representing the church. They could not be first-fruits in time or the first-fruits of all God hath done, because the Elders

are the raptured, enthroned church, the first-fruits of Christ
in the earth. In I Corinthians 15:23, Christ Himself is
called the first-fruits, followed by those who are raised from
the dead at His coming. Yet, these also are called "the
first-fruits unto God and to the Lamb." What could the
name mean? It means very simply this (and here is that
Jewish matter again which we find in the Word of God):
they are the first-fruits unto God in another order and in
another calling. In the eleventh chapter of the Book of
Romans, Paul disclosed unto us this great mystery: that
there is a time coming when the blindness, when the scales,
when the veil over the heart, shall be taken away from Israel
and God shall reveal unto them their great Messiah; when
a nation shall be born in a day; when Israel shall turn to
God and accept their Messiah in atoning grace, in the
forgiveness of sin; when Israel shall accept in love their
elder Brother. Now, the first-fruits of that promise are the
one hundred and forty-four thousand; and the ultimate of
it, in the day of the harvest of God, is when Jesus comes
again and appears to His own. These are the first-fruits of
that order, such as Paul referred to in the fifteenth chapter
of I Corinthians, verse eight, when he said: "And the Lord
appeared unto me as unto one born out of due time," — an
abortion, before the time. Paul says that before the Lord
appears to His people, He appeared unto me, "before that
time." So it is here. These are the first-fruits unto God,
but the great harvest will come when the whole nation shall
either be saved in turning faith to Jesus or be judged and
cast out forever. The great harvest is to come when the
Lord appears. That prophecy is in the nineteenth chapter
of the Revelation.

What is meant by the "sealing" of these one hundred
forty-four thousand? This is one of the mighty revelations
in the Book. What is meant by being sealed? What is the
seal of God? In the fourteenth chapter, the first verse says
it is their Father's name written in their forehead. What is

the seal of God? We have much mention of that seal in the Bible. In the first chapter of the Book of Ephesians, the thirteenth verse reads: "Ye were sealed after that ye trusted in Christ, ye were sealed with that Holy Spirit of promise"; and in Ephesians 4:30: ". . . grieve not the Holy Spirit of God, whereby ye are sealed unto the day of redemption." The same reference occurs in II Corinthians 1:22. Again in the sixth chapter of John, verse forty-seven, Jesus says that He was sealed by the Holy Father in heaven. The Holy Spirit is the seal of God. If a man has the seal of God upon him, he has the power and unction and presence of the Holy Spirit in his heart and life. When Jesus speaks of being sealed by the Father, He indicates the gift of the Holy Spirit descending upon Him and enabling Him mightily to do the work that God had sent Him in the world to do. So it is here. In the sealing of the one hundred forty-four thousand, they were endued with Pentecostal power; and the Holy Spirit of God, in unction and in glory, came upon them. Fearlessly and in bravery, they gave witness to the Word and to the salvation in Christ in that dark and evil day.

How would that kind of a seal appear? If you were to meet one of those men who had been sealed of God, how would he appear? I think he would be much like Moses, when the Israelites saw him coming down from the mount after he had communed with God for forty days and forty nights. There was a glory about him, there was an unction about him, and his face shone like the sun. The Holy Spirit lived and moved in his heart in unction and in power, and it shone in his face. I would say he would be like Stephen when he stood in the Sanhedrin amidst his murderers. They were not able to withstand the power and wisdom by which he spoke. That same glory is upon these one hundred forty-four thousand. They are endued, endowed and glorified of God, and their eloquence, their witness and their testimony to the truth of Christ are beyond compare. Just to see them and to hear them is to be moved by the presence and the glory of God in their lives. Such is the seal of the Holy Spirit of God. ". . . and there were sealed an hundred and forty-four thousand . . ." Twelve thousand from each of the tribes of Israel. Think what a day that is going to be!

I have never seen one genuinely devout, converted Jew who did not put many Gentile Christians to shame. The Jews are an amazing people. When they turn, they turn completely. We have a marvelous Christian in this church by the name of Lilli Wolff. I want you to get the pamphlet that tells the story of her conversion. It reads like another chapter in the Acts of the Apostles. A Jewish preacher, wherever he is, has a certain power with him beyond anything that a Gentile could ever possess. Those twelve apostles, the eleven along with Matthias, were visited with the Holy Ghost of God at Pentecost, and the whole world shook under the impact of their testimony to Christ. We are to see the same thing again. We are to have the Pentecostal baptism of unction and power upon these twelve thousand from each of the elect tribes of Israel, and they are going to witness to the grace of God in such power as the world has never known.

These judgments that are described in the following chapters of the Revelation will be interpreted by these Jewish evangelists as being interpositions of God and the heralding of the great day of the Lord. And how marvelously effective they are! In the ninth verse one reads: "After this I beheld, and lo, a great multitude, which no man could number . . ." These Jewish elect, these Jewish evangelists and preachers, upon whom the presence of the Holy Ghost has fallen, are a definite number. But these converts no man could number. They are a multitude of all nations, and kindreds, and people, and tongues. There is going to be a revival such as this earth never saw, even in those dark and tragic days of the visitation of God. The Lord never withdraws His hand. Sometimes it falls in judgment and a nation is destroyed. Sometimes it falls in terrible visitation and the whole world is convulsed. But look up through the fire and the blood and the furor and the flame and the smoke, and there will you see God watching over His own, saving the lost, writing names in the Book of Life, electing these and these and these to do His will in the earth. Oh, bless His name forever! Our *panto-krator,* our Almighty God!

Chapter 13

The Blood-Washed Multitude

After this I beheld, and, lo, a great multitude, which no man could number, of all nations, and kindreds, and people, and tongues, stood before the throne, and before the Lamb, clothed with white robes, and palms in their hands; And cried with a loud voice, saying, Salvation to our God which sitteth upon the throne, and unto the Lamb. And all the angels stood round about the throne, and about the elders and the four beasts, and fell before the throne on their faces, and worshipped God. Saying, Amen: Blessing and glory, and wisdom, and thanksgiving, and honour, and power, and might, be unto our God for ever and ever. Amen. And one of the elders answered, saying unto me, What are these which are arrayed in white robes? and whence came they? And I said unto him, Sir, thou knowest. And he said to me, These are they which came out of great tribulation, and have washed their robes, and made them white in the blood of the Lamb. Therefore are they before the throne of God, and serve him day and night in his temple: and he that sitteth on the throne shall dwell among them. They shall hunger no more, neither thirst any more; neither shall the sun light on them, nor any heat. For the Lamb which is in the midst of the throne shall feed them, and shall lead them unto living fountains of waters: and God shall wipe away all tears from their eyes. — Revelation 7:9-17

This is truly one of the most meaningful, comforting and precious of all the passages in the Word of God. But, at the same time, it is one of the most unusually difficult. There are about as many different opinions and explanations concerning this great multitude as there are concerning the identification of the one hundred forty-four thousand sealed out of all the tribes of the children of Israel. Who is this great multitude out of all of the nations and kindreds and peoples and tongues and tribes who stand before the throne of God?

There are some expositors who say these are people who live in the flesh on the earth; that it is a scene of the different nationalities down here in the world who have been saved by trusting in Christ. There are those who say that the great multitude is a vast host of disembodied spirits, souls of dead people, whom Jesus saw in heaven. As he saw the souls of those who were martyred under the fifth seal, so these are the souls, the disembodied spirits, of those who have died for the Lord in the earth. John sees them before the final resurrection. Then there are those who say this great multitude is the redeemed of the Lord who are resurrected and glorified and now immortalized in glory. Then there are some who say this great multitude represents the early primitive Christians as, in persecution and trial, they came out of those sorrows of the first Christian century. There are still others who say this great multitude represents the triumph of the Christian faith under the conversion of Constantine, when the Christians were given liberty and victory at the conversion of that Roman Emperor. Others say this great multitude represents those who were added to the church, in the great accession to the church in the centuries following the conversion of Roman Caesar. Still others say this great multitude is the one hundred forty-four thousand who were sealed in the first vision. Then there are those who say this great multitude represents the church in its millennial glory. Then, finally there are those, especially those who spiritualize the Scriptures, who say the multitude does not represent anything except the triumph of the gospel message on the earth; that it has no particular significance in itself, no particular pertinency. These are just a few of the many identifications of this great multitude that John sees standing before the throne of God and of the Lamb.

THE PERPLEXITY OF JOHN

Who are the uncounted numbers of this multitude and where did they come from? I think that you have a most pertinent key, a suggestion as to who they are, in the fact of the perplexity of John himself. "One of the Elders answered saying unto John . . ." John had not said anything. There is no recorded conversation before, yet "one of the Elders answered saying unto John." That is, he recognized John's perplexity and astonishment and ignorance as to who that great multitude was. The Elder places in language John's questioning spirit, ". . . Who are these arrayed in white robes? and whence came they?" And John said: "Sir, I do not know. I never saw them before. There is not a face in that vast throng I recognize. I do not know who they are." Is not that astonishing? For, if this multitude represents the church, the saved, the redeemed of Christ in this age, there would have been no perplexity on the part of John. That is what he would have expected, to see the redeemed of Christ in heaven. And he would have recognized some of them, just as you would today if you were to see the redeemed of Christ's church in heaven. There are many, many of those faces that you would recognize: your family, your people, your friends. There are many of them you would know. But John recognizes none of them. "I never saw them before. I have no idea who they are."

There is another thing that enters into the astonishment of the Seer. At the end of chapter three, the church age runs it course and the church disappears from the Revelation and is never mentioned, never referred to, until finally the church is seen coming with Christ in glory at the end of the age in the nineteenth chapter. At the end of chapter three, the Book says that John was raptured up into glory, and when he was caught up into heaven, he saw there the church of Jesus Christ, the Bride of our Lord. He saw that church enthroned, crowned and glorified, resurrected, immortalized, raptured. He saw that redeemed throng under the form of the four and twenty elders. Those elders represent the church of the Living God. At the end of the church age, when John is caught up into heaven, he sees the church enthroned before God. Now, he sees both of them here, both the elders (the glorified church) and this vast, blood-washed multitude. In the seventh chapter of this Revelation there is again pictured the throne of God, the four and twenty elders and the four cherubim. Around them, glory upon glory, are the serried ranks of the angels. Then, beside and over and beyond the elders, the glorified church, he sees in amazement this great multitude of Gentiles out of every tongue and kindred and language and people, clothed in white robes, with palm branches in their hands, worshiping and serving God day and night. No wonder John is perplexed! So are we. Who are these aftercomers, this congregation of the after-born, who are they and whence came they?

Notice the great distinction between this group and the church, the enthroned elders. This great multitude has no thrones. They stand in the presence of the thrones. They have no crowns; they have palm branches. They have come after the resurrection and after the rapture and after the church has been taken up into glory. "Who are these that are arrayed in white robes and whence came they?" And John said: "Sir, I do not know. I do not understand. I am surprised. I am amazed. I am astonished." Then we have the answer of the elder. "These are they who [*erchomenoi*, present linear action. We would say in English present tense. There are no tenses in Greek. There are just kinds of action.] . . ." "These are they," explains the elder, "who are coming out of the Great Tribulation." John, from his vantage point in heaven, sees them as they are coming out of the Great Tribulation [*He thilipsis — he megale — "the* tribulation — *the* great" — "the Great Tribulation"]. They have washed their robes and made them white in the blood of the Lamb. These, then, are tribulation saints. These are they whom God has saved in His mercy during those dark, dark days. These are they whom God has saved and is saving in that great and final trial that shall come upon the earth. Is not that astonishing? No wonder John did not know who they were. No man would ever have known or guessed such a thing had it not been by the grace of the revelation of God Himself.

For this time of terrible trial is not only a time of universal damnation and perdition; it is also a time of God's grace and salvation and forgiveness. Most unbelievers, after the church is taken away, become more confirmed in their defiance of God, until finally the waves of hell roll over them forever, and the smoke of their torment ascends up throughout the endless ages. But even in those dark and tragic days, in wrath God remembers mercy. He elects those one hundred forty-four thousand. He seals them. He empowers them with the unction of Pentecost; and in that awful, final day, there are those who, listening to these preachers of Christ, turn in faith to Christ, and wash their robes and make them white in the blood of the Lamb. Daniel the prophet foresaw those tribulation saints, and Simon Peter writes of them in the spirit and language of the prophet Daniel, as he speaks of those who will be saved in that last season. So this great multitude is a saved throng from among those who were left in the earth at the coming of our Lord when He takes His church to glory. These are from among those who were left behind. For, when the Lord comes for His own and His church is taken out of the earth, most of this earth will be full of gainsayers and blasphemers and rejectors and unbelievers. Most of the professing church will be apostate and will be left behind. When the Lord comes, so bad will be the evil and the blackness on the face of this earth that Christ Himself asks, "When the Son of Man cometh, will He find faith in the earth?" Two shall be in a field, one taken and the other left; two sleeping in a bed, one taken and the other left;

two grinding at a mill, one taken and the other left. These are they who were left behind in this earth. They were among those who blasphemed God. They were among those who said "No" to Christ. They were among those who were not born again. They were left behind in their unbelief. But, oh, what a change, what a change! As they listen to the incomparable preaching of the Gospel of the Son of God by these one hundred forty-four thousand sealed evangelists and missionaries (who sow the world down with the seed of the Word of the blessed Jesus), these are they who turn in repentance and in faith to God. Their stained garments, they wash in the blood of the Lamb. Their empty philosophizing, they exchange for the simplicities of the Gospel of faith. Their rejection of Christ, they change into an affirmation of the Sonship and the Deity and the Saviourhood of our Lord. They were sinners, and now they are saints. They were lost, and now they are found. They were rejectors, and now they are acceptors. They were repudiators and blasphemers, and now they are the servants of the most high God. This is the great multitude that no man could number, of every nation and tribe and tongue, standing before the Lord with robes washed white and with palm branches in their hands.

THE SAINTS COMFORTED IN HEAVEN

There is another thing to note about them: they are in heaven. Many of the interpreters who read this passage think of this group as being still on earth. I cannot understand such an identification; for, to me, plainly, the group is in heaven. I think that because, for one thing, when John was taken up into heaven at the beginning of the fourth chapter, the first thing he saw was the throne of God. Then he saw the four and twenty elders who sat around the throne of God. Then he saw the four cherubim. Then he saw the unnumbered angels in serried ranks, beyond and beyond and beyond the innumerable hosts of the heavenly worshipers of our Lord. Now, in the seventh chapter in this vision, John sees the same thing. There is the throne of God, and there is the throne of the Lamb, and there are the elders, and there are the cherubim and there are the angels. Then he sees this great multitude coming out of the Great Tribulation. To me the scene is in heaven. The language is heavenly. The very nomenclature of the passage is like that in the twenty-first chapter of the Book, wherein is described the glories of our Lord in heaven. In the fifteenth chapter of the Book, this group is described as standing on the sea of glass. All of it is a heavenly scene.

There is another thing that would make me think they are in heaven. The one hundred forty-four thousand are on earth. They are sealed by the Spirit of God; they are protected and kept from harm and death by the sealing of God in their foreheads. But nothing is said about the sealing of this great multitude simply because they do not need it any longer. They are in heaven and need no protection. They are there before the throne of God. They worship the Lord and serve Him in His temple and call upon His name. They look into His face and live. I would suppose many of them have been martyred. In the days of that awful trial, the Great Tribulation, in that time of sorrow and blood, many who have accepted the love of Christ and named the name of Jesus are martyred. John in heaven, as he sees the seals that are broken and the earth that is shaken, and as he sees the one hundred forty-four thousand that are sealed, also sees in heaven that great multitude coming out of the blood and the trials and the tears and the sorrows of that awful hour. He sees them as they come home to God. Oh, what a marvelous thing, what an incomparably glorious thing! In heaven, where the Almighty is, where the Lamb is, where the enthroned elders are, where the angels are. In heaven. That would be a great thing to say about anybody: "He is in heaven." Lazarus in Abraham's bosom is infinitely more blessed than Dives in the most luxurious sumptuousness this earth could ever afford. "These are in heaven."

There is another thing about them: They stand; their acceptance is based upon their trust in Jesus as their Saviour. They stand because their sin-stained garments have been washed white in the blood of the Lamb. That is a peculiar idiosyncrasy of John, describing the forgiveness of sin as the washing of robes in the blood of the Lamb. By describing these as such he means that the basis of their entrance into heaven lies in the completed sacrifice and atonement of Christ. "These are they who are coming out of the Great Tribulation; *therefore,* are they before the throne of God . . ." That "therefore" is very emphatic. *Dia tauto,* "on this basis," "on this account," "because of this," they are before the throne of God. The ground on which they stand and the basis by which they look into God's face and live lies in the atoning sacrifice of Jesus Christ, the washing of their sins away in the blood, in the pouring out of the life of the Son of God.

Three different times in this short passage, their white robes are mentioned, and withal, what a beautiful reference. "In white robes," *tas stolas tas lukas.* What an effective picture that is! You women have a word "stole." If you have a whole lot of money, you can buy a beautiful ermine stole of purest white. It would cost you thousands of dollars. That is just for a stole. If you bought an ermine robe, I do not know what figure the price would reach. The picture here is one of gorgeous beauty. The Greek word *stola* refers to an outer garment, worn for dignity and grace and beauty and distinction. When the words are used *tas stolas tas lukas,* actually it could be paraphrased "dressed in richest wedding garments of purest, dazzling white." Oh, we can just see it! God's blood-bought, who are washed clean and pure, standing without blemish in the presence of the Almighty God Himself. The basis of their standing is found solely in this: they have looked in faith, in repentance, in trust, to the atoning Lamb of God.

They stand there, not only in their robes of purity and dignity and glory and beauty, but they stand there with palm branches in their hands. That is an Old Testament reference to the Feast of the Tabernacle. We read of one of those glad occasions in the Book of Nehemiah where the sentence is written in the passage, ". . . and there was very great gladness" (Nehemiah 8:17). The Feast of Tabernacles, when the people sat in booths and when they carried palm branches called to remembrance the deliverance of God out of the darkness of the servitude of Egypt. Now they are free unto God. In Nehemiah, the people also are rejoicing over the deliverance from Babylonian Captivity. So also, these are rejoicing with palm branches in their hands, delivered from the captivity of the sin and the death of this world. They are triumphant and praise the name of God with palm branches in their hands.

THE PROTECTING PRESENCE OF GOD

"He that sitteth on the throne shall dwell among them." The actual meaning of the Greek words is far richer and stronger. "He that sitteth on the throne shall cast His protecting tabernacle over them." The Greek word for "tent," "tabernacle," is *skene*. The Greek word for "to tent," "to tabernacle," "to cast a tent," is *skenoo*, the word used here. Among them *epi* (on) *outous* (them). What John wrote is, "and God shall tabernacle over them." God's grace and love and mercy and protection will be cast over them. The reference again is to the Old Testament story of the children of Israel coming out of the land of Egypt when the Shekinah glory of God was above them. In the daytime it looked like a cloud. In the nighttime it looked like a pillar of fire. But whether in the day or in the night, they were under the sheltering, shepherdly keeping, protecting, loving care of God. The great God who sits on the throne shall *skenoo epi outous* — "shall tabernacle over them," "the Shekinah glory of God shall cover above them."

The next description is: "They shall hunger no more, they

shall thirst no more, neither shall the sun light on them, nor any heat." These negatives are often used in the Revelation. In the twenty-first chapter, where heaven is described, there is an abundance of negatives. The Greeks, as they wrote things, had an emphatic way of putting them down. In English, double negatives mutually eliminate each other. If you say "I don't not," then you actually do. That is in English. But in Greek, the more negatives are piled up, the more emphatic the meaning. We get the meaning, even in English when we do that. If someone said to you, "I don't know nothing nohow," you would get the idea that he did not know anything. If a man comes up to you and asks for a job, saying, "You don't know nobody nowhere what wants nobody to work for him, don't you?", you know he is asking you for a job. But that is good Greek. It may be bad English, but it is marvelous Greek. That is what God says here. He just piles up these negatives, "no," "not," "neither," "nor," adding one to the other, as He describes God's separate remembrance and provision for His people.

Then the last verse reads: "For the Lamb which is in the midst of the throne shall feed them, and shall lead them unto living fountains of waters." The words bring to mind a familiar scripture. I trust that when you were a small child, just as I was, someone who loved you taught you the Twenty-third Psalm. "The Lord is my shepherd; I shall not want. He maketh me to lie down in green pastures; he leadeth me beside the still waters. He restoreth my soul . . ." I may be all broken up and defeated in spirit; I may be cast into sorrows that overwhelm me like a flood, but "he restoreth my soul." The same thing is true of the Lamb which is in the midst of the throne. He shall feed His own. "He prepareth a table before me in my hunger, in my thirst and in my want and shall lead me unto living fountains of water." "And the Spirit and the Bride say, Come. And let him that heareth say, Come. And let him that is athirst come. And whosoever will, let him take the water of life freely . . . and shall lead them unto living fountains of waters: and God shall wipe away all tears from their eyes" (Revelation 22:17 and Revelation 7:17). There are no sorrows in heaven; no graves on the hillsides of glory; no funeral wreaths on the mansion doors of the New Jerusalem; no sorrowful processions over those golden streets. There are no tears in heaven. God shall wipe them all away.

Yet these multitudes of tribulation saints, as blessed as they are, are not in that blessedness to be compared to us, who in this day of grace have opportunity to accept Jesus now and to become a part of the Bride of Christ. His church is the enthroned elders. We have an opportunity to be among them. As much greater as a king is than a servant; as much greater as it is to be on a throne than to stand before one; as much greater as it is to have a crown than a palm branch; by so much is it greater for us now who have opportunity to come into the enthroned presence of God as an elder, as a member of the church, than to be one of those tribulation saints. This is our present opportunity. They missed it. It was too late for them. They were plunged into the flood and into the fire and into the blood-bath of a great judgment. Out of that sorrow and trial and martyrdom, they were brought up to heaven to stand in the presence of God. They are never a part of the enthroned elders, never a part of the great and true Bride of Christ. They are just standing there, having missed the great, incomparable day of grace and opportunity. That is what we have now. It is now God's time. It is now that accessions are made to the body of Christ. It is now that God makes us a part of His Holy Bride. It is now in this day of grace that we have the incomparable opportunity to be added to Him. Our great Head is in heaven; our Lord is in heaven. We now have opportunity to become part of His body, and some day, with our Lord, to be joined to Him forever in heaven, an elder, enthroned. These missed it. If a man is ever going to be saved, he ought to be saved now. If ever you are going to give your heart to Jesus, give your heart to Him now. If ever you intend to walk in the love and the glory and the presence of God, do it now. If ever you intend to give the preacher your hand and to give your heart to God, give the preacher your hand now and give your heart to God now. If ever you intend to choose Jesus, choose Him now, for the day of grace is now. Make it now, make it now.

Chapter 14

The Seventh Seal

And when he had opened the seventh seal, there was silence in heaven about the space of half an hour. And I saw the seven angels which stood before God; and to them were given seven trumpets. And another angel came and stood at the altar, having a golden censer; and there was given unto him much incense, that he should offer it with the prayers of all saints upon the golden altar which was before the throne. And the smoke of the incense, which came with the prayers of the saints, ascended up before God out of the angel's hand. And the angel took the censer, and filled it with fire of the altar, and cast it into the earth: and there were voices, and thunderings, and lightnings, and an earthquake. — Revelation 8:1-5

When the Lamb of God opened the last and the seventh seal, there was silence in heaven. That is unusual because heaven is never silent. It is filled by day and by night and through all the unending ages with the worship and praise and adoration of the heavenly hosts, offered unto God our Father and unto God our Saviour and unto God our Holy Comforter and Keeper. But at the opening of the seventh seal, all heaven was mute. When the Lamb opened the first seal, there was heard a voice as of thunder saying, "Come." When the Lamb opened the second, third and fourth seals, that same thunderous voice was heard. When the Lamb opened the fifth seal, John heard the cry of those who were martyred for Christ, saw their souls under the altar, beseeching God for vengeance upon their blood shed in the earth. When the Lamb opened the sixth seal, there was a great tremor throughout all the framework of nature, pro-

160

ducing vast, illimitable consternation. But when the Lamb of God opened the seventh and last seal, there was a silence that could be felt. One dared hardly breathe. All motion in heaven stopped. All praise and adoration ceased. There was stillness, a vast calm of silent intensity.

Why this silence in heaven? It is, first, the silence of awe and of intense expectancy. This is the last drama of the ultimate mystery of Almighty God. This is the ultimate seal. We can almost hear the unspoken intensity and expectancy of the hosts of heaven as they say to themselves, "What now will God do and what will be the final disposition of His judicial administration in this rebellious and blaspheming world?" It is an intense silence of expectancy. We are told in the twenty-second chapter of the Book of Acts that Paul stood on the steps of the Tower of Antonio and before a maddening mob clamoring for his life, he raised his hand and spoke unto them in the Hebrew tongue. When he did so, the Bible says, ". . . and there followed a great silence." When Numa was crowned King of Rome, and they came to that august moment when they were to look for the birds by which the gods would foreshow his destiny, the priest put his hand devoutly on the head of the crowned king, and the historian says, "And there reigned among the people an incredible silence." So here, all heaven was mute and motionless with awe.

There is a second reason for the silence in heaven. It is a silence of ominous foreboding. Even the Lord God Almighty pauses before the onward rush of this great, final judicial administration. In the first, second, third, fourth, fifth and sixth seals, by war and by famine, by pestilence and by bloodshed, by violence and by storm, one-fourth of all the inhabitants of the earth have been swept away. Now, as they come to that great, last and final seal, what does it mean for the remainder of the dwellers on this earth? There is a calm before a storm. Have not you seen the clouds gather and the heavens turn black above this fearful and trembling earth? For a moment there is a hush and a quiet and a calm, when a leaf hardly moves. Then there is the crash of a resounding lightning flash, there is a thunderous roar, and the deluge begins. Such is the silence here. Before the awful sounding of the final judgment trumpets of God, there is a pause in heaven by the space of about half an hour. Is that a brief while? No, indeed. It is seemingly interminable, unbearable. It is as if you saw a drowning child, when one minute, and even half a minute, is an eternity. So it is here. The silence, the stillness in heaven is a pause one could never forget. We can feel, we can touch the very intensity. Remember that time is altogether circumstantial and relative. A thousand years sometimes is as a day, and a day sometimes is as a thousand years.

THE SEVEN ANGELS OF THE DIVINE PRESENCE

The silence in heaven at the opening of the seventh and last seal brings to view the drama of the Great Tribulation. After that silence, the first thing the rapt apostle sees is the seven angels who stand in the presence of God and to whom were given seven trumpets. They are a septemvirate of celestial arch-regents described here as "the angels of the Presence." They are designated as the seven angels who stand in the presence of God. In the fifteenth chapter of the Revelation, we are introduced to seven angels to whom are given the seven bowls of the vials of the wrath of the Almighty. But they are just seven angels. The article here in chapter eight, verse two, is distinct and emphatic. "The," "the" seven angels of the Presence. The King James Version translated it "who stand before God." The Greek word is *enopion,* seven angels who stand *enopion,* "in the presence of," the Lord God. There are ranks of angelic preference and administration and creations. Paul names some of those ranks of the angels of the hosts of heaven. Some of them he calls "principalities," others "dominions," and others "powers." The prophet Daniel spoke of princes among the angelic hosts. Paul and Jude refer to archangels in glory. So these seven are a distinct, select, septemvirate of vice-regents, administering the government of God on the earth. We possibly know the name of one of them. In the first chapter of the Book of Luke, it is written that Gabriel, whom Zacharias saw on the right side of the altar of incense, said, "I am Gabriel who stands in the presence of God."

To these seven distinct, highly favored, marvelous, celestial arch-regents of the Almighty there are given seven trumpets, to each one a trumpet. Why a trumpet? Because it is the most used of all of the instruments of the holy Scriptures and portrays the life of the people in the presence of God. If there is a war declared, there is the blowing of the trumpet. In the fourth chapter of the Book of Jeremiah, the prophet cries, "Oh, my soul, the sound of the trumpet, the alarm of war!" In the great convocations of the people, there was the sounding of the trumpet. All of the great festival days of the Lord were introduced by the sound of the trumpet, as at the year of Jubilee. In the crowning of a king, there was the sounding of the trumpet. In the awful descent of the presence of God on Mt. Sinai, there was the voice as of a trumpet; and the people feared because of the awfulness of the sounding of the trumpet. Therefore, it is reasonable to expect, in the judicial administration of God, that those seven angels with those seven trumpets will bring a like meaning in their heralding and in their sounding. If there is a trumpet sound of war, then one would expect war, even in the last great battle of the Almighty. If there is a trumpet that sounds the convocation of the people, then one would expect a great concourse of God's people to gather together unto Him. If there is a sounding of a trumpet for the crowning of a king, then one would expect the crowning of the greater son of David as the Lord God of heaven and earth. If there is a sounding of the trumpet describing the fall of the cities of the ungodly, then one would expect the fall of the great city, Babylon. Such is the meaning of the seven angels in whose hands are placed the seven trumpets of the last and final judgment of God.

THE ANGEL-PRIEST

After the introduction of the seven "Presence-Angels," there follows an interlude, an intermission. Those seven herald angels do not sound their trumpets immediately. There is an interlude in which another angel appears while those seven Presence-Angels stand ready to herald the judgment of God. This other angel came and stood at the altar, having a golden censer in his hand, "and there was given unto him much incense, that he should offer it with the prayers of all saints upon the golden altar which was before the throne. And the smoke of the incense, which came with the prayers of the saints, ascended up before God out of the angel's hand." Who is this angel? "Another angel." At least four times in the Apocalypse that identical designation is used, always with reference to a mighty, indescribably glorious personality in heaven. For example, in the seventh chapter, the second verse: "And I saw another angel [the same language] ascending from the east, having the seal of the living God: and he sealed the one hundred forty-four thousand." In the tenth chapter, the first verse, similarly: "And I saw another mighty angel come down from heaven, clothed with a cloud: and a rainbow was upon his head, and his face was as it were the sun, and his feet as pillars of fire." Once more he is referred to in the eighteenth chapter of the Revelation, verse one: "And after these things I saw another angel come down from heaven, having great power; and the earth was lightened with his glory." Here in Revelation 8:3, this angel stands at the altar and in his hand is the golden censer which alone belongs to the priest. Because of these descriptions and especially because of his priestly ministry, many students of the Book say this is the angel of Jehovah which in the Old Testament is the pre-incarnate Lord Jesus Christ. I have no objection at all to the identification that would make this holy angel none other than Christ Himself. But I have this observation to make: Everywhere in the Apocalypse that our Lord appears He is distinctly designated. In the first chapter He is called the Son of Man, and there follows the description of Him with the keys of life and death in His hand. In the fifth chapter of the Revelation, He is called "the Lion of the Tribe of Judah," "the root of David." Later on in that same chapter, He is described as "a lamb as it had been slain." In the nineteenth chapter of the Revelation when He comes in power and in triumph and in glory, He is called "the Word of God." The Lord Christ is always distinctly designated. But here, and in other like passages in the Revelation, the word is used "another angel." So to me this is an angel-priest and we should call him that, an "angel-priest."

While those seven, select angels of God, with their trumpet-judgments, stand ready to sound, there appears this angel-priest, standing at the great burnt offering of sacrifice. Both altars of the heavenly temple are mentioned here in this verse. The angel-priest, standing in the court, fills his golden censer with fire from the brazen altar, and with incense, offers it at the golden altar before the throne. All of us acquainted with the tabernacle worship are familiar with this scene. Outside in the court was the great brazen altar of sacrifice, the fire upon which never died by day and night, and on which all the sacrifices were offered up unto God. On the inside, in the Holy Place, before the veil, was the golden altar of incense with its four golden horns, one at each corner. Once a year, on the day of atonement, the High Priest, with blood shed by a victim offered on the sacrificial altar, went inside and sprinkled the blood of atonement on the four horns of that golden altar. Twice a day throughout the year, at the time of the morning sacrifice and at the time of the evening sacrifice, the priest went in and offered incense on the golden altar while the people prayed outside. Remember the story of Zacharias in the first chapter of Luke? Each day a priest chosen by lot went into the Holy Place, there to offer incense on the golden altar of prayer while the people outside waited in intercession before God. These are the two altars: the brazen altar of sacrifice mentioned six times in the Apocalypse, the golden altar of prayer mentioned twice.

In the scene here in Revelation 8, the Angel-Priest stands at the brazen altar of sacrifice, filling his censer with the fire from the altar. He then proceeds to the Holy Place, putting incense on the coals of fire. The text explains that he offers the incense with the prayers of all the saints. The imagery and the meaning of this scene is everlastingly celestial, heavenly and blessed. The incense represents the merit and the virtue of the life of Christ. The prayers of all God's people are forwarded, they are perfected, they are made beautiful and acceptable to heaven by the merit and worth and virtue of the sacrifice and the resurrection and the intercession of our glorious High Priest in glory. However we may strive to be perfect in our worship of God, even our prayers have in them imperfection. They are not said right. They are not offered right. There is imperfection in all we do in the presence of God, even in our finest, highest hours of worship and intercession. This angel-priest adds to our prayers the incense, the sweet savor, of the merit of the life of Christ. Do you notice that the Angel-Priest offers the incense with the prayers of *all* God's saints? *All* of them. The prayers of God's saints yesterday and today and until time shall close. No prayer is ever lost. It is kept before God. Whether the prayer was uttered when time was young or whether behind a door so closed nobody could ever know or see, all of them are kept before God, and to them is added the merit and virtue and grace of our blessed Lord Christ.

THE REASON FOR THE APPEARANCE OF THE ANGEL-PRIEST

Why interpose this passage here? For two reasons. First, the great and final judgment of this earth is in answer to the prayers of God's people. What is the high and holy intercession, what is the spiritual appeal of God's saints through all the ages? It is the prayer that Christ placed on the lips and in the hearts of His people, "Thy kingdom come and thy will be done in this earth as it is in heaven." The time has now come for that prayer uttered by God's people through the millenniums to be answered by God. That is why at this point when those prayers are finally to be answered, God has brought before Him the remembrance of those intercessions through the ages. The time has come when God will cast out Satan, will dethrone the usurper, will judge sin. The time has come when iniquity and death and hell and the grave will be destroyed forever. The time has come when God's kingdom shall be established in the earth. At that time God has brought before Him the remembrance of all of the prayers of His saints through the ages. "Thy kingdom come, thy will be done." Some people think meanly of the prayers of God's humble children. They repeat the cry in Job, "What does it profit a man if he prays to the Almighty?" But God says that these prayers move heaven. They bring into action the princes of glory. They are the means by which justice is administered in the earth. Their answer is the astonishment of all creation. Before the final denouement comes, before that final judgment falls, and before the final and ultimate kingdom of God is established, there are brought before the Lord the remembrance of all of the prayers of all of His children. I spoke of that previously in the sermon on the fifth chapter of the Revelation. There John saw the vision of the Lamb and the four cherubim and the four and twenty elders. Each one of the elders had a golden bowl and in the bowl incense which represented the prayers of all God's people. They are all treasured in golden bowls in glory, these precious prayers of His people.

There is a second reason why the interposition of this scene in Revelation 8:3-5 comes before the angels sound their trumpets. It is this: God is revealing to us that judgment, justice, perdition are nothing other than the terrible side of rejected faith and love. Look! "The angel took the censer, and filled it with fire from off the altar, and cast it into

the earth." Then follows that inevitable formula of catastrophe: ". . . and there were voices, and thunderings, and
lightnings, and an earthquake and the scorching of this
earth and the visitation of the judgment of the Lord God
Almighty." What a scene, what a scene! Do you see it?
This angel-priest takes the golden censer and fills it with
fire from off the altar. That brazen altar is the judgment
of God, the righteousness of God, the holiness of God, as it
burns against sin. On that altar the victim is slain and the
sacrifice is offered, making atonement for the sins of the
people. The angel-priest fills the censer with fire from that
altar of brass, of judgment. He takes his censer, filled with
fire from the altar, and goes into the holy place and there
pours on top of that fire, those coals that flame and burn,
the incense, the sweet savour of the merit and the worth
of Christ. There ascends unto God a picture of the devotion and love and hope and prayers and intercession and
longing of God's people. Now look. That same angel-priest
comes back to the same altar of judgment. His now empty
censer that he poured out on the golden altar of prayer he
fills again with fire from the coals off the altar of brass; but
this time he flings the censer into the earth, and there it
scorches and it burns and it consumes. The same censer,
the same fire, the same ingredients, as ascended in the worship at the golden altar! Do you see the meaning? The
figure reveals what is judgment, what is damnation, what
is perdition. On the inside of that golden censer is the
meaning of damnation and judgment and perdition and the
wrath of Almighty God. These terrible visitations are nothing other than all of the graces that ascended unto God on
the golden altar, turned downward and flung outward,
despised, refused, rejected, cast out. As Paul says as he
preached the Gospel of the Son of God, "We are the savour
of Christ, life unto life, to them that believe, death unto
death unto them that reject." This is the meaning of the
passage in the tenth chapter of the Book of Hebrews: "For
if we sin willfully after that we have received the knowledge

of the gospel truth, there remaineth no more sacrifice for sin but a certain fearful looking for of judgment and of fiery indignation that shall devour the adversaries. He that despised Moses' law died without mercy unto two or three witnesses. Of how much sorer a punishment suppose ye shall he be thought worthy who have trodden under foot the Son of God, who have counted the blood of the covenant wherewith he was sanctified an unholy thing and have done despite unto the spirit of Grace; for we know him who hath said, Vengeance belongeth unto me, I will recompense, saith the Lord. And again the Lord shall judge his people. It is a fearful thing to fall into the hands of the living God. For our God is a consuming fire."

"And he took the censer, and filled it with fire from off the altar, and cast it into the earth." Then follows the inevitable judgment of God upon a gainsaying, apostasizing, blaspheming, rejecting, unbelieving earth. O God, my soul trembles. It is life — this Lord Jesus, His death, His Resurrection, His intercession — it is life for those who turn and believe. It is judgment, it is death, it is perdition, it is damnation for those who say "No" to the spirit of Grace and who spurn God's overtures of mercy. "For," said the prophet of old, "why will ye die? Turn ye, turn ye, for why will ye die?" "As I live," saith the Lord, "I have no pleasure in the death of the people. Turn ye, turn ye, for why will ye die?" As the song we sometimes sing asks, "When the cleansing cross, when the fountain of blessing, when the spirit of God, when the loving favor of Jesus, is so nearby, why, Oh, why will ye die?" Why would a man choose to be lost, when God's grace and mercy are his for the taking, when rejection is death now and forever? This is why we preach, why we pray, why we sing, why we make appeal, that you might turn and be saved.

Chapter 15

The Sounding of the Trumpets

And the angel took the censer, and filled it with fire of the altar, and cast it into the earth: and there were voices, and thunderings, and lightnings, and an earthquake. And the seven angels which had the seven trumpets prepared themselves to sound. The first angel sounded, and there followed hail and fire mingled with blood, and they were cast upon the earth: and the third part of trees was burnt up, and all green grass was burnt up. And the second angel sounded, and as it were a great mountain burning with fire was cast into the sea: and the third part of the sea became blood; And the third part of the creatures which were in the sea, and had life, died; and the third part of the ships were destroyed. And the third angel sounded, and there fell a great star from heaven, burning as it were a lamp, and it fell upon the third part of the rivers, and upon the fountains of waters; And the name of the star is called Wormwood: and the third part of the waters became wormwood; and many men died of the waters, because they were made bitter. And the fourth angel sounded, and the third part of the sun was smitten, and the third part of the moon, and the third part of the stars; so as the third part of them was darkened, and the day shone not for a third part of it, and the night likewise. And I beheld, and heard an angel flying through the midst of heaven, saying with a loud voice, Woe, woe, woe, to the inhabiters of the earth by reason of the other voices of the trumpet of the three angels, which are yet to sound! — Revelation 8:5-13

We have come to the point in apocalyptic history where all things are in readiness for the climactic consummation of the age, the coming of our Lord and the establishment of His kingdom in the earth. The seventh and last seal has been opened. There is silence in heaven, one of intensest interest. An awe of expectancy overwhelms the hosts of glory. The prayers of all the saints of all the ages are brought before God in remembrance, "Thy kingdom come, thy will be done." Under the fifth seal, the cry of the saints of God whose blood had been shed in the earth was for vengeance. The day has come for the answer to that cry. The angel-priest fills the golden censer with fire of judgment from the altar and flings it into the earth, a picture of the wrath and the doom and the judgment of God upon this unbelieving and blaspheming world. This is the signal for the seven angels of that judgment, of that visitation, to sound. When the seventh angel has sounded, the final day has come, the day of the great battle of Almighty God that ushers in the visible appearing of Christ and the establishment of His millennial kingdom in the earth.

There are two great events that color all destiny. The first event is the translation of God's people to heaven. The first event is the coming of Christ *for* His saints. The second great event is the return of our Lord *with* His people from heaven. That first great event is spoken of often by the Apostle Paul. "For the Lord himself shall descend from heaven with a shout, with the voice of the archangel, and with the trump of God: and the dead in Christ shall rise first: Then we which are alive and remain shall be caught up together with them in the clouds, to meet the Lord in the air" (I Thessalonians 4:16, 17). This is the first great event of the future and it can happen any day, any hour, any time, any moment. There is nothing separating between us and that coming of the Lord for His people. Then, the second tremendous event that lies ahead is the coming of Christ openly, visibly, with the armies of glory and with His sainted people from heaven. That will be the establishment of His kingdom on this earth, when the kingdoms of this world have become the kingdoms of our Lord and of His Christ and when He reigns forever and ever. Between those two great events, the septenary series of judgments fall, the seven seals, the seven trumpets and the seven vials of the wrath and the judgment of God. When these sevens are finished, then is finished the mystery of God on the earth.

As we face these tremendous events, there are seven things that lead up to the establishment of Christ's kingdom on earth. First, peace. Always, it starts that way. An ambitious leader presents himself as a world-saviour. He claims to have the answers to all of the problems. This has happened time and again and is happening now. He comes on the scene and delivers us, he says, from war, and he promises to solve all of our economic problems. Then inevitably, there follows blood and war and famine and need and want and pestilence. I see this happen all the time. I read it in history. I read it in the present story of Cuba. I read it in the present tragedy of China. I read it in the present dilemma of Eastern Europe. I read it all the time, whether it is written in history past or in history present. Always it follows that pattern. These men come with their schemes and their programs and promise to bring Utopias with them. But beyond them, always is that shedding of blood, the baring of the sword, the execution squad, the want and the famine and the lack and the need and the scarcity that leads to pestilence. Then, of course, follows the persecution of God's people. Always, always, there comes the slaughter of God's people. Then comes the great warning signs of God in heaven and then the final visitation of the wrath and judgment of God from above. Those are the seven seals: First, peace; second, war; third, famine; fourth, pestilence; fifth, the persecution of God's people; sixth, the warning signs of God from heaven; seventh, the final visitation from above.

The seven trumpets describe that day of awful wrath and judgment of Almighty God. No nation, no dictator, no tyrant has ever yet defied God and lived. There is a judgment upon him and there is a judgment upon his people. Every time a nation turns in those directions, there inevitably follows the same events, the same awful judgments.

Iniquity, unbelief, infidelity, atheism, the defiance and rejection of God — these things always bring a certain and inevitable intervention of God. That final intervention of God is seen in the blowing of these seven trumpets. They herald the great, final consummation of the age as God judges a disbelieving, blaspheming and rejecting world.

All of those septenaries, all of those series of seven, are divided exactly alike, four and three. Then those last three are separated, two and one. We have the division here in the blowing of the trumpets. The first four are in a series to themselves. The last three are in a series to themselves. Of these seven trumpets, the first is the judgment of God on the land, the trees, the grass. The second is on the sea and the creatures in the sea and the commerce of the world. The third is upon the fountains of water and of rivers. The fourth is on the stellar sky in the heavens above us. These first four are general judgments upon the earth. The last three judgments are directed pointedly, terrifically, horribly toward mankind. They increase in intensity and severity as they follow through. The fifth trumpet is the breaking of the partition, the opening of the door, between the earth of mankind and the abyss of hell. The sixth trumpet is the loosening of the four restraining angels and the army of two hundred million horsemen and the seven thunders and the testimony and agony of God's two martyr-witnesses. Then the seventh trumpet brings the great battle of the day of God Almighty and the intervention of Christ in human history. This sermon concerns the first four trumpets.

THE FIRST FOUR TRUMPETS

"The first angel sounded, and there followed hail and fire mingled with blood, and they were cast upon the earth: and the third part of trees was burnt up, and all green grass was burnt up. And a third part of the earth was burnt up." There are those, and I respect them greatly, who believe that these things are exactly as they are described and that they are not representative of, they are not symbols of, other things. When the first angel sounds, there follows hail and fire mingled with blood. The trees, a third, the grass, a third, and the earth, a third, are burnt up. I have no quarrel with that interpretation at all. We read, for example, in the ninth chapter of the Book of Exodus: "And Moses stretched forth his rod toward heaven: and the Lord sent thunder and hail, and the fire ran along the ground; and the Lord rained hail upon the land of Egypt. So there was hail, and fire mingled with hail, very grievous, such as there was none like it in all the land of Egypt since it became a nation" (verses 23 and 24). I have no quarrel, none at all, with those who look upon these things as being literally described. But, these things could also be symbols, pictures of the judgments of God. For example, in the second sounding of the trumpet the text says: "And as it were a great mountain burning with fire cast into the sea." Then John will say of the third trumpet which sounds: ". . . there fell a great star from heaven, burning as it were a lamp." What the seer is saying here is that the thing was not a mountain, actually, but *"as it were"* a mountain burning with fire; that it was not a lamp, actually, but *"as it were"* a lamp, falling, burning. So, these things could represent, they could be symbols of the judgments of God in this earth.

Now, herewith are some suggestions concerning the possible meaning of these symbols: "Hail" is a sudden, sharp, interposition of the judgment of God (Isaiah 28:2, 17). "Fire" is an unsparing evidence of the wrath of God in burning judgment, mostly in the form of war (Deuteronomy 32:22; Isaiah 33:14). "Blood" is death, moral death, spiritual death, physical death. "The earth" is the civilized world, constituted as we know it under a regular and established government. "The sea" is restless masses of humanity (Daniel 7:2-3; Isaiah 57:20). "Trees" represent the pride of human greatness, flaunting the presence of God (Daniel 4:10, 20-22; Ezekiel 31:3-18). "Grass" is men generally, people generally (Isaiah 40:6, 7). "The green grass," of course, would be the finest, the flower, the fruit of mankind. When a nation goes to war, whom does it destroy first? Always "the green grass," the flower, the fruit, the finest of the land. When men go down to enlist in the army, the army picks out the finest of the group. It is only the finest of our manhood that fights in a war. Young men go to Annapolis by appointment, they go to West Point by appointment, they go to Colorado Springs to the Air Force Academy by appointment — our finest. When the green grass is destroyed, when the green of the world is burned up, we are to understand the scorching devastation of war. "A mountain" represents a firmly established power or kingdom (Jeremiah 51:25). "A star," as in Revelation 1, is a pastor, a teacher, a man of great authority standing before the people. "A lamp," of course, is the congregation, the church. When the star falls it represents an apostate teacher who fills the earth with terrible, darkening doctrine. There is not anything on earth so tragic as the misleading of people by teaching a wrong evaluation, a wrong revelation, a wrong doctrine. The "rivers" and "the fountains" which are embittered by this fallen star represent the sources of life-giving water, the doctrine, the salvation, the hope which are destroyed by false teaching. The teaching is poison. It darkens the skies above and embitters the sources of life beneath.

The first angel sounded and there occurred dagger-sharp visitations from God. But notice, only a third part is destroyed. Only a third. This means that God still deals with His people in mercy. God still has hope for the people, even though they may be indoctrinated with the most false propaganda mind could imagine. We have that false teaching here in the United States, and we have it by the uncounted, illimitable worlds-full beyond us. Whenever men listen to it and follow it, there inevitably follows tragic loss of life, loss of property, loss of home, loss of true vision, loss of godliness. But God still waits, God is still merciful, God still hopes. There is only a third part of the world that is destroyed.

The second angel sounded and as it were a great mountain, burning, was cast into the sea, that is, into the restless masses of humanity. "And the third part of the sea became blood and the creatures died and a third part of the ships were destroyed." Wherever today there is a seething humanity, I can tell you exactly the burning mountain that will be cast into it: It will be the doctrine of communism and the doctrines of rejection and of disobedience. Wherever there is a restless mass of humanity, there will be that infiltration, that burning; for these subversions cannot live, they cannot survive, other than in the restless masses of humanity. Instead of bringing order out of chaos, and instead of seeking to bring a righteous government out of anarchy, wherever there is restless disillusionment and tragedy, communists feed it for they live only in the wretchednesses of the restless mass. That is where they breed, that is where they are given life. When that burning mountain on fire is cast into that restless sea, there we find the world, the nations, the seas, bathed in blood. The third part of the sea became blood and the third part of the creatures died and a third part of the commerce is destroyed. Never on this earth will there be a prosperous communist. Commerce is destroyed. Never on this earth will there be a prosperous Soviet government. Depression is built into the system. That is what it is to have it, just as it says here in the Book. The system is saturated with blood, the loss of life itself. But God hopes, God waits. It is only a third part destroyed. This earth will never, never altogether be subjected to such devastation. Not as long as God can see that there are people who bow in His presence, who look up in faith to Him. Only a third is destroyed.

"The third angel sounded and there fell a star from heaven burning as it were a lamp and it fell upon the third part of the rivers and upon a third part of the fountains of waters." Here again notice that "third": there will never be a time until the end (and then we come in victory) when wrong doctrines absolutely and positively and fully

cover the earth. It never will be. There will always be
those who give themselves to purity of thinking and purity
of doctrine. But, the tragedy lies in those who poison the
rivers and the fountains of waters, the sources of our hope
and the sources of our lives and the blessedness of our
destiny. These are destroyed by those who teach wrong
doctrines. "And the name of the star is called Wormwood
and the third part of the waters became wormwood and
men died because they were made bitter." The fallen star
pulled a whole world down with him.

When the fourth angel sounded, the third part of the sun
was smitten and the third part of the moon and the third
part of the stars. The miasmic, dismal, darkening clouds
of apostasy, false teaching and false doctrine clouded earth
and heaven. All this shows how God needs His stars to
shine, His lamps to burn, His teachers to teach, His preachers to preach, His people to live in a world that grows
darker and darker. The sun, the great central power; the
moon, the lesser power; the stars, still lesser powers are
darkened by apostate teaching. "And they shone not for a
third part of the day and the night." Apostasy blots out the
truth, but it never is able to cover the whole earth. God
in His mercy still gives us opportunity to live, to turn, to
teach, to preach. God gives it to us if we are given to God
in our dedication to these holy privileges.

THE THREE TRUMPETS OF WOE

"And I beheld (at the end of the fourth sounding) and
heard an eagle flying through the midst of heaven, saying
with a loud voice, Woe, woe, woe, to the inhabitants of the
earth by reason of the other voices of the trumpet of the
three angels, which are yet to sound!" These three following trumpets are so terrible and so horrible, they are so
intensive, that before the angels sound, before those judgments fall, a great warning is made throughout the earth.
In Deuteronomy 28, Jeremiah 48 and Matthew 24, an eagle
like this is a harbinger of judgment. Sin has a voice in

heaven. Execution and judgment upon it may not fall immediately, but it will fall. It will come. The Lord delayed long in the days of Noah, but the judgment fell. Jezebel lived in her villainy many years, but the day came when she was eaten of the dogs, and the horses trampled her body under the rolling wheels of the chariots. Sin has a repercussion in heaven. It may not be just at this moment and at this time and at this minute, but there is coming a day when it will be judged. This eagle, as he crosses in his flight the vast meridian of the earth, sees his prey from afar and he cries, "Woe, woe, woe to the inhabiters of the earth." The warning in itself is a mercy of God. God gives warning that a man might turn, that a people might repent, before these awful judgments of God fall upon them.

Before God ever does anything in the way of judgment, He always warns. He did in the days of Adam. "Adam," warned God, "touch this tree and you die." Again in the days of the antediluvians, for one hundred and twenty years, Noah preached righteousness to the people. God warned in the days of Judah. He did in the days of Samaria. He did in the days of Israel. He did in the days of Jesus. He did in the days of Paul and He does it in our day. God says that if we go a certain way, it leads to damnation, to judgment and to death. One time I heard a preacher say that in the Bible there were six hundred warnings about hell. He added that if a man were going down a road and there were six hundred signs on that road saying, "This road leads to hell," by the time a man got there it would be because of his own choice, his own volition, his own predetermined will. That is exactly the way it is with God and this whole world. God has made His way plain and God has said, "You follow this wrong road and it leads to disaster and to damnation and to judgment and to death and to hell." That is why God warns. "I beheld, and heard this eagle flying through the meridian sky saying look, stop, consider, woe, woe, woe."

Incomprehensible to us is the reluctance with which the

Lord God Almighty gives up His people, His creatures in the earth. Why does not God damn the demons out of His sight? Why does not God destroy them? Why does not God burn them with fire? Why does God let a tyrant live? Why does God let sinful people continue in their terribleness? Why does He do it? Because of the longsuffering of the Almighty. Maybe, maybe they will turn. Maybe they will hear. Maybe they will listen. Maybe they will repent. Maybe they will be saved. "As I live, saith the Lord, I have no pleasure in the death of the wicked, but that the wicked turn from his evil way and live. Turn ye, turn ye, for why will ye die?" There is always an appeal from God, a warning from the Lord, lest we fall into perdition and into damnation and into death. That is why this warning is given here before the sounding of the last three trumpets, beyond which it is forever and forever too late.

The graphic scene depicts an eagle flying through the midst of heaven, saying with a loud voice, "Woe, woe, woe." Woe to whom? There are two words in the Greek language for dwellers, people who live in the earth. One is *paroikeo*, which means to dwell as a sojourner. The other is *katoikeo*, which means to settle down. That is the word used here. It is addressed to those who make this world their home. "Woe to those who have lost their heavenly vision." They are pilgrims no longer. They do not have God in their hearts any more. Their Utopia is down here. They say, "We like it here; this pleases us." Their paradise is down here. Their hopes are down here. Their life is down here. They have lost the heavenly vision. They do not feel any longer the upward pull. The truth of God is not in their hearts. "Woe," says the Lord, "to those *katoikeo*, those who have built every hope and dream down here in this world, who are no longer pilgrims from this world to the world that is yet to come."

> Day of anger, day of wonder,
> When the world is driven asunder,
> Smote with fire and blood and thunder.

King of majesty tremendous,
Who doth free salvation send us,
Well of mercy, Oh, defend us.

As we face death, as we face trials, as we face conflicts, as we face judgment, as we face the inevitable of all the unfolding future, O well of mercy, O God of salvation, remember us, befriend us, save us!

Chapter 16

The Trumpets of Woe

And the fifth angel sounded, and I saw a star fall from heaven unto the earth: and to him was given the key of the bottomless pit. And he opened the bottomless pit; and there arose a smoke out of the pit, as the smoke of a great furnace; and the sun and the air were darkened by reason of the smoke of the pit. And there came out of the smoke locusts upon the earth: and unto them was given power, as the scorpions of the earth have power. And it was commanded them that they should not hurt the grass of the earth, neither any green thing, neither any tree; but only those men which have not the seal of God in their foreheads. And to them it was given that they should not kill them, but that they should be tormented five months: and their torment was as the torment of a scorpion, when he striketh a man. And in those days shall men seek death, and shall not find it; and shall desire to die, and death shall flee from them. And the shapes of the locusts were like unto horses prepared unto battle; and on their heads were as it were crowns like gold, and their faces were as the faces of men. And they had hair as the hair of women and their teeth were as the teeth of lions. And they had breastplates, as it were breastplates of iron; and the sound of their wings was as the sound of chariots of many horses running to battle. And they had tails like unto scorpions, and there were stings in their tails: and their power was to hurt men five months. And they had a king over them, which is the angel of the bottomless pit, whose name in the Hebrew tongue is Abaddon, but in the Greek tongue hath his name Apollyon. One woe is past; and, behold, there comes two woes more hereafter. And the sixth angel sounded, and I heard a voice from the four horns of the golden altar which is before God, Saying to the sixth angel which had the trumpet, Loose the four angels which are bound in the great river Euphrates. And the four angels were loosed, which were prepared for an hour, and a day, and a month, and a year, for to slay the third part of men. And the number of the army of the horsemen were two hundred thousand thousand: and I heard the number of them. And thus I saw the horses in the vision, and them that sat on them, having breastplates of fire, and of jacinth, and brimstone: and the heads of the horses were as the heads of lions; and out of their mouths issued fire and smoke and brimstone. By these three was the third part of men killed, by the fire, and by the smoke, and by the brimstone, which issued out of their mouths. For their power is in their mouth, and in their tails: for their tails were like unto serpents, and had heads, and with them they do hurt. And the rest of the men which were not killed by these plagues yet repented not of the works of their hands, that they should not worship devils, and idols of gold, and silver, and brass, and stone, and of wood: which, neither can see, nor hear, nor walk: Neither repented they of their murders, nor of their sorceries, nor of their fornication, nor of their thefts. — Revelation 9:1-21

Oh, what a horrible vision and what a devastating visitation! We have come in the unfolding of this drama to the final assault of Satan against God, and to the final unfolding of the development of evil in the world. This is the mystery of God's elective purpose as He brings to realization a new kingdom in which Christ will reign and His subjects will love and worship Him forever. These are the last and consummating days as God shall bring to pass in judgment His will in the earth. As the seventh and last seal is broken, the whole revelation of the counsel and purpose of God in the earth is made known through the sounding of the seven trumpets. The sounding trumpets are divided into two parts, into four and three. The first four trumpets are sounded in the eighth chapter of the Revelation. The last three trumpets are so terrible and so horrible that they are set apart. An eagle announces their coming, flying over the meridian of this earth, crying: "Woe, woe, woe to the inhabiters of the earth by reason of the voices of the three trumpets which are yet to sound." As tragic and as terrible as were the four trumpets that have already sounded, they are nothing to compare with the judgment and the visitation of these last three that God calls "the trumpets of woe."

THE TERRIBLE FIFTH TRUMPET

The first trumpet of woe dissolves the demarcation, the wall of separation, between earth and hell. The second trumpet of woe looses the four magnates of evil who are chained over the river Euphrates. The last trumpet of woe is the seven bowls of the wrath, of the final judgment of God, that leads up to the great battle of the day of the Lord Almighty. In this unfolding drama, we are approaching that final hour when God shall cast out evil forever, when the Lord shall take unto Himself His great power, and when the kingdoms of this earth become the kingdoms of our Lord and of His Christ. It pleased God in that vast consummation that evil be destroyed in these days of judgment as they are revealed here in the Word of God. "And the fifth angel sounded, and I saw a star [in the King James Version it is translated *fall*] fall from heaven unto the earth." The Greek word translated "fall" is *peptokota,* perfect tense, "fallen." The Authorized Version translates the word as though John saw the star fall. No, John saw the star "fallen." It had already fallen. We do not know who this angel is. It could be Satan. In any event, when John saw him, he had already fallen. It refers to some great, spiritual, enthroned creation of God who was set as a luminary in God's heaven to uphold God's glory and God's moral government, but now fallen. Whoever this creature is, whether Satan or one of the archangels who serve him, when John saw him, he had fallen from heaven into the earth.

". . . and there was given to him the key of the bottomless pit." The Greek word here is *abyss.* We have taken the Greek word bodily into our language. ". . . and there was given to this principality of darkness and evil, this fallen archangel, the key of the abyss." Not only here, but throughout the Word of God, that abyss is looked upon as the darkness in which are imprisoned those fallen spirits who are reserved unto the day of judgment. For example, in the eighth chapter of the gospel of Luke, when Jesus met the Gadarene demoniac, the demons in him, vile and unclean, cried out lest the Lord come to torment them before their time, before their day of final judgment. Then they cried unto the Lord saying, "Do not command us to go into the [and it is translated in the King James Version "the deep"] into the *abyss*. Seven times in the Book of the Revelation is that "abyss" referred to. The last time it is mentioned is in the twentieth chapter when a mighty angel comes down from heaven and lays hands upon the devil, the dragon, the serpent, and binds him for a thousand years in that abyss. It is not the eternal home of the devil for he will be cast into the lake of fire, with all of the dupes who serve and worship him. In this abyss, in this darkness, are these spirits of evil who are reserved unto the day of judgment. "And there was given to this fallen spirit the key to the abyss."

"And he opened the bottomless pit, and there arose a smoke out of it, like the burning of a great furnace; and the sun and the air were darkened . . . And there came out of the smoke locusts upon the earth." These infernal creatures were vile in body, they were malignant in disposition, they were terrifying in form and they were equipped to afflict and torment mankind. Such a vision, such a vision! When the pit is opened, a great blackness obscures the sun and covers the earth, and out of that blackness and out of the darkness, come these infernal, indescribable creatures to afflict and torment the race of men. When I read this passage, I remembered an experience of my boyhood. When I was a youngster, Carlsbad Cavern was discovered by a cowboy from Texas named Jim White. Soon after its discovery, I went through the Cavern with a lantern. It had just been opened. After we had gone through that miraculous wonderland, we gathered around Jim White and listened to him talk for hours. He said he was riding along on his pony when he saw smoke coming out of the ground. He guided his pony to the place where the smoke was issuing out of the ground and discovered that the smoke was uncounted millions of bats. He said the next day the same thing happened — he saw smoke pour out of the ground. He guided his little pony to the place, and there again were uncounted numbers of bats pouring out of the heart of the earth. I thought of that when I read this vision. When the pit was opened there was a great smoke, a corrupting of social and moral life, the very obscuring of government and of authority and of ordered society. And out of the darkness and out of the smoke, came these infernal creatures. They are not actual locusts, for, it says, they did not eat grass, they did not eat any green thing, nor did they touch any tree. John is telling us here that they are not actual locusts, for locusts eat green things. Where there is an actual visitation of locusts, nothing is left behind but devastation. Again, the wisest man who ever lived, Solomon, as a keen naturalist and observer, said in the thirtieth chapter of the Book of Proverbs that the locusts have no king over them. But John is careful to tell us that these have a king over them, the angel of the bottomless pit whose name in the Hebrew tongue is *Abaddon*, in the Greek tongue *Apollyon*, in the English tongue "Destroyer." That name is the opposite of *Soter*, "Saviour," Jesus our Lord. So, what John sees coming out of the very pit of hell is the darkness, the tragedy, the corruption, the obscuration of the very authority and government of Almighty God. Society is corrupt, life is corrupt, the social order is corrupt, the government is corrupt and the whole earth is as it was before God destroyed it with the flood.

Out of the smoke came these unholy creatures. John is careful to describe the unclean things. The shapes of these

creatures were like unto horses prepared unto battle, capari-
soned for war, panoplied for conflict. They were not horses
but were "like unto horses"; that is, they were swift. On
their heads were, as it were, "crowns like gold"; that is,
they did their work with power. They were successful.
And their faces were "as the faces of men"; that is, they
were intelligent. They obeyed commands and orders and
they discerned between those who had the seal of God and
those who did not. They "had hair as the hair of women";
that is, they were given destructive strength. "They had
breastplates, as it were, of iron"; that is, they were difficult
to confront. The sound of their wings was as the sound of
chariots, of many horses, running to battle; that is, they
were bold in their challenge to the entire, social, moral,
governmental, religious, ecclesiastical world. "They had
tails like unto scorpions." We are to meet that reference
again in the description under the sixth trumpet. In Isaiah
9 the prophet said: ". . . a false prophet, a lying prophet,
a misleading teacher is a tail."

The intensity of this terrible plague of scorpion attack
lasted five months. Two comments are to be made about
this unearthly agony. The first is this: Notice that the
dissolution of the moral, social life of the world happens
under the permissive will of Almighty God. Sometimes one
is tempted to think that since evil is so rampant, false doctrine so dark, the apostasy of those who lead astray in their
teaching so powerful, "Surely God is dead or He cannot
cope with the corrupting situation. God's Gospel must be
emasculated and must have lost its virility and its power.
Surely the Lord must have turned His back and He does
not know, or if He does know, He does not care." But:
"Five months," God said. Five months. There is a stated
limitation. Another limitation God set is this: "And you
are not to kill; you can torment but you cannot kill."

These delineations of the sovereignty of Almighty God
are found throughout Scripture. God does not change, and

the elective purpose carries through whether it is now, yesterday or in the day to come. Consider this torment inflicted by these infernal apostasies. Wherever there is false teaching, the defying of God, the challenging of the spiritual realities of heaven, there are people in misery, tormented, beaten down into the dust of the earth. The principle does not change, whether it is in our generation and we look upon it or here in this final, consummating hour. When we fear that God has abandoned this world and that He does not look upon it, remember, these things come to pass in His permissive will. "Five months," God said, and added, "you are not to kill, you can only torment." Compare the case of Job. Said the Lord God to Satan, "You can take away everything he possesses, you can afflict him with boils from the top of his head to the sole of his foot, but you are not to touch his life." Such is the sovereignty of the Lord God Almighty, and He never abdicates His throne. In days of grossest darkness and in days of the most violent challenge to the spiritual powers of heaven, God still reigns. It is in His permissive will that any dictator dictates or any apostate apostasizes or any evil comes to pass.

What I have just said leads us to the second observation. II Thessalonians, chapter two declares that the mystery of evil was already at work in the days of the Apostle Paul. Paul describes those who give themselves to unclean spirits, to rejection, to blasphemy and to unbelief. Then finally (notice it carefully), the Scripture passage says, "For this cause God shall send them strong delusion that they should believe a lie." The development of evil follows the same course that we see here in the Revelation. These developments are forever the same. The same truth is revealed in the first chapter of the Book of Romans wherein Paul writes an indictment of Roman civilization. After Paul describes the sins of the Roman people, he says in verse twenty-four: "Wherefore God also gave them up . . . [then in verse 26] For this cause God gave them up . . . [then in verse 28] God gave them up . . ." These three judgments in Romans sound like the three woes here in the Revelation. When people persist in iniquity, when people choose to be vile and blasphemous, God lets iniquity run its course. God lets it develop, God lets it continue. If a man chooses the administration of Satan, God lets that man experience what it is to be a servant of the devil. That is what has happened here in the Book of the Revelation. The spirit of iniquity works, and it continues and it goes on, and finally it ends in indescribable torment, hurt, agony and pain. We can always remember this: The man who lives in sin builds his house by the very pit of hell. He is next door. This that we find under the fifth trumpet is nothing other than an outworking of evil when men choose to be servants of Satan and when they wear the livery of the devil. Tormenting judgments inevitably come and inevitably follow.

The Sounding of the Sixth Trumpet

"And the sixth angel sounded, and I heard a voice from the four horns of the golden altar which stands before God. And that united voice of the four horns said to the sixth angel, Loose the four angels which are bound over the great river Euphrates. And those four angels were loosed, which were prepared for an hour, and a day, and a month, and a year." This terrible second woe is the sounding of the sixth trumpet. Heretofore there have been infernalities, creatures diabolical, darkness of corruption, that afflicted and tormented mankind, but now follows this judgment of double woe. Not only are men tormented, but one out of three now are slain. Out of the great population of the earth, there rises the cry and the wail of death and destruction.

I do not know of a more powerful imagery in the Word of God than this described in Revelation 9:13, 14. Remember, there were two altars in the tabernacle. Moses said a pattern for the tabernacle was given to him from heaven.

What he wrought here on earth in building the tabernacle, he wrought after the pattern that was shown to him in heaven. God showed him the pattern there and Moses copied it. In the Revelation, we see that heavenly original which Moses copied. There are those two altars. One is the Great Altar, the Brazen Altar, the Altar of Burnt Sacrifice, located outside the sanctuary in the Court. The other altar was small, made out of gold, and stood before the veil of the Holy Place. This was the altar of worship, of prayer, of mediation, of intercession. The outside, Brazen Altar was the altar of judgment upon sin. It was the altar of sacrifice, of the pouring out of blood, of the slaying of the victim. Now, in the golden censer, fire was taken from the Altar of Sacrifice and carried to the Golden Altar, where incense was burned unto God. Blood was taken from the Altar of Sacrifice on the day of atonement and sprinkled on the four golden horns of the Altar of prayer. All of this ritual was to teach that prayer and worship are based upon sacrifice, the shedding of blood, without which there is no remission of sins, and without which no man can come into the presence of God. Now, it is from the four horns (the combined voice of that Golden Altar) that the awful cry comes to loose those four terrible angels bound over the river Euphrates. What an amazing thing! Heretofore, the blood of the sacrifice and the prayers of intercession have always been for mercy, that God would forgive us, that God would save us. But now the blood that cries and the voice that is raised is no longer for forgiveness, for salvation, for God's mercy, but the voice is for judgment and damnation. Oh, the horror of it! How could such a thing be? For a very plain and simple reason: God's way for a man to be saved is in the blood. This is the way for a man to meet God, through the great mediation of the High Priest, Jesus Christ. This is God's propitiation for our sins. This is the only way that a man can ever see God's face and live. When a man turns the offer down, when a man treads under foot the blood of the covenant wherewith Christ was sanctified as an unholy thing, when a man spurns and rejects the one and only propitiation for sin, the one and only way of salvation, then the very altar cries out against that man's blasphemy and unbelief and rejection. The cry is from the four horns of the golden altar of intercession and propitiation. The Book says again and again that it is a terrible thing to fall into the hands of the living God, "for our God is a consuming fire." When a man rejects God's love, then the very voice that cried out for mercy and for forgiveness cries out for judgment and perdition.

The voice cries, "Loose the four angels which are bound over the great river Euphrates." Twice in the Book of the Revelation that Euphrates is referred to in the same, identical language. The river Euphrates begins in the Armenian Mountains, some of the highest in the earth. Flooded in the springtime with melting snows, it goes through the Taurus Range and through the Mesopotamian Valley down to the Persian Gulf. The Euphrates River, the most important, the longest, the biggest in all western Asia, was the place where sin was first known, where misery first began, where the first lie was told, where the first murder was committed, where the first grave was dug. The Euphrates River was the scene of the two great apostasies before and after the flood. The Euphrates River was the scene of the rise of Israel's greatest and most oppressive enemies. The Euphrates River was the scene of the long years in which the children of Israel dragged out the wearisome days of their captivity. The Euphrates River was the scene of the rise of those great world empires that oppressed civilization in the ancient day, cruel empires like Assyria, like Babylon, like the Persians and the Medes. There in that place, these four angels, these magnates of evil are chained. They have in their hands power of awful destruction and satanic evil. They are prepared for an hour, and a day, and a month, and a year. At the exact second, at the exact moment in God's calendar, their vile judgment is loosed upon this world.

THE INEVITABLE JUDGMENT OF GOD

It is an amazing thing how God chooses, in His elective purpose, to run this universe. Evil continues and God seemingly overlooks it. But, at a certain place, at a certain time, on a certain day, in a certain month, in a certain second, God has ordained a judgment upon it. For example, in the fifteenth chapter of the Book of Genesis, the Lord said to Abraham in a vision: "Abraham, all this land is yours. But for four hundred years your descendants are going to be captives in a strange land. Because," God said, "the iniquity of the Amorites is not yet full." The vile Canaanite worship, the vile social life of the Amorites, the indescribable wickedness and the unnamable depravity of those heathen tribes had not yet run their course. The Canaanites for years and years and for generations and for centuries thought that a righteous God does not see, does not know, that He does not look upon this villainy. But God said to Abraham, "Four hundred years, four hundred years and the iniquity of those Amorites will be filled and then the great avenging sword of the Lord God Almighty will be placed in your hand." That is the identical situation here. Iniquity runs its course, and the Lord lets it develop and continue; but there is an hour, there is a day, there is a month and there is a year when God shall judge it. These terrible evil angels of visitation were prepared for that awful day.

John now describes what he saw. When those four angels were loosed, they in turn loosed an army (actually "armies," for the Greek word is plural) of torment and destruction, and the number of the horsemen in those armies were twice ten thousand times ten thousand, two hundred million. If we had a cavalry a mile wide and eighty-seven miles long, that is the size it would be. John could not count them; no spectator could count them. John says, "I *heard* the number of them." The greatest army that was ever fielded in the ancient empires was that by Xerxes when he invaded Greece. Herodotus, the Greek historian, says they numbered two and one-half million men. But here "two hundred million"! Then John described those horses. They are not actual horses. Their heads are like lions and out of their mouth issued fire and smoke and brimstone, the elements of hell and damnation. They have breastplates of fire and jacinth. He says, "jacinth" because jacinth to them was blue, the color of a livid, burning flame. Their tails were like serpents, to hurt and to destroy. By these a third part of men were slain. Oh, the judgment of the visitation of God!

As a result of these judgments, after men had seen the development of evil and had looked upon the cost they paid in serving Satan, one would expect the next verse to describe a turning to God and a great repentance and a great believing in Jesus. The last two verses, instead, depict just the opposite. "The rest of the men who were not killed repented not." "Repented not." They ceased not to worship these demons and idols of gold and silver. The last verse repeats the same tragic truth: "Neither repented they of their iniquities." One of the strange things about human nature is that a man is not changed because of punishment. We do not change a man through incarceration or imprisonment. He may desist from evil because he is afraid, but his heart is still evil. He would do the evil if he could get by with it. A man is really changed only by the Gospel of the grace of the Son of God. He is a new man only in a new birth, in the creation of a new commitment. That is why our final answer to sin is not to build bigger jails. We are forced sometimes to enlarge our penitentiaries, but that is no answer. We are forced sometimes to have juvenile homes for the delinquent, but that is no answer. The great answer for the changing of men lies in the power of the Gospel of the Son of God. It lies in a new birth, in a new hope, in a new commitment, in a new dedication, in a new love, in a new faith, in a new man. That is the reason we preach and pray and assemble ourselves together, that through us maybe God will mediate the love and mercy that will save our people from death. Our hope lies in the saving power of the Gospel of Christ.

Chapter 17

The Finished Mystery of God

And I saw another mighty angel come down from heaven,
clothed with a cloud: and a rainbow was upon his head, and
his face was as it were the sun, and his feet as pillars of fire:
And he had in his hand a little book open: and he set his
right foot upon the sea, and his left foot on the earth, And
cried with a loud voice, as when a lion roareth: and when
he had cried, seven thunders uttered their voices. And when
the seven thunders had uttered their voices, I was about to
write: and I heard a voice from heaven saying unto me, Seal
up those things which the seven thunders uttered, and write
them not. And the angel which I saw stand upon the sea
and upon the earth lifted up his hand to heaven, And sware
by him that liveth for ever and ever, who created heaven,
and the things that therein are, and the earth, and the things
that therein are, and the sea, and the things which are therein,
that there should be time no longer: But in the days of the
voice of the seventh angel, when he shall begin to sound, the
mystery of God should be finished, as he hath declared to his
servants the prophets. — Revelation 10:1-7

This passage is a part of the longest interlude between the
series of septenary judgments. All three of those series are
framed exactly alike — the series of the seven seals, the
seven trumpets and the seven bowls of the wrath of God.
They are divided into four and three. The last three, which
are always separate and apart from the first four, are divided into two and one. Between the two and the one
(between the sixth and the seventh), there is always an
interlude. Between the sixth and seventh seals, the seventh
chapter of the Book of the Revelation, is an interlude. Between the sixth and seventh bowls, Revelation 16:13-16, is

an interlude. In this series that we are following (the trumpets) between the sixth and the seventh trumpets, chapters ten and through verse fourteen of chapter eleven is an interlude. The briefest interlude is between the sixth and seventh bowls of the wrath of God. The longest interlude by far is this one between the sixth and seventh trumpets. The interludes are written for the encouragement and the comfort of God's people in a dark and burning earth. We would think from the progress and development of evil, that the ultimate king of this earth is Satan and that evil will overflow it like a flood. But these interludes are to remind us that God is still sovereign, that His people are still remembered and that the ultimate victory belongs to us.

THE SUBLIME HERALD-ANGEL

The text in the tenth chapter of the Book of the Revelation begins with a tremendous description: "And I saw another mighty angel come down from heaven, clothed with a cloud: and a rainbow was upon his head and his face was as it were the sun, and his feet as pillars of fire . . . he set his right foot upon the sea, and his left foot on the earth, And cried with a loud voice, as when a lion roareth: and when he had cried, seven thunders uttered their voices . . . And the angel which I saw stand upon the sea and upon the earth lifted up his hand to heaven, And sware by him that liveth forever and ever . . . that there should be delay no longer: But in the days of the voice of the seventh angel, when he shall begin to sound, the mystery of God should be finished, as he evangelized [as he declared] the glad tidings of triumph to his servants the prophets." There is no sublimer apocalyptic vision imaginable, conceivable than this. The grandeur of that description is beyond anything in all literature. For example, I copied out these two reactions as men have read this passage. Here is one: "The description of this angel has been admired by every classical scholar. Abstracted from its spiritual meaning and considered merely as a literary pro-

duction, it stands unrivaled by anything we meet with in all
the pages of Grecian and Roman literature." In majesty
and dignity and glory and celestial wonder, no word description excels the picture of this herald angel in the tenth
chapter of the Revelation. I have copied another most eloquent tribute. This author followed an alliterative description of the angel, and this is what he said: "Be pleased to
observe the *aspect* of this august personage. All the brightness of the sun shines in his countenance and all the rage
of the fire burns in his feet. See his *apparel.* The clouds
compose his robe and the drapery of the sky floats upon
his shoulders. The rainbow forms his diadem and that
which compasses the heaven with a glorious circle is the
adornment of his head. Behold his *attitude.* One foot stands
on the ocean and the other rests on the land. The wide
extended earth and the world of waters serve as pedestals
for those mighty columns. Consider the *action.* His hand
is lifted up to the height of the stars. He speaks and the
regions of the firmament echo with the mighty accents as
the midnight desert resounds with the lion's roar. The artil-
lery of the skies is discharged at the signal. A peal of
seven-fold thunder spreads the alarm and prepares the universe to receive his orders. To finish all and give the highest grandeur as well as the utmost solemnity to the representation, he swares by him that liveth forever and ever."
Is not that magnificent? I do not know who the man was
who said these words. I never heard of the author. But I
would love to hear that man preach. That is real eloquence.

This mighty angel came down from heaven. Heaven here
is not so much a point of departure as a description of his
abode. He is a heavenly creature. He comes down from
heaven clothed with a cloud. It is a picture of the majesty
and the dignity of his person. Around him burns in glory
the Shekinah of God. A rainbow is upon his head, a picture
of the mercy and the remembrance of the covenant-keeping
Lord. His feet are as pillars of fire. That is the picture of
the judgment of God, the brazen, burning, brass pillars of

fire. This representative of the very throne of heaven has the power of judgment in the earth, "his feet as burning pillars of fire," but also the remembrance of mercy in the day of wrath and visitation, "a rainbow upon his head." "His face as it were the sun." How brilliant, how indescribably iridescent, so glorious that a man could not look upon his face with unshaded, unsheltered eyes! "His face as it were the sun." "He set his right foot upon the sea and his left foot upon the earth and sware by him that liveth forever and ever that there should be delay no longer but that now the time has come when God shall take unto Himself His great power and reign over the earth." It is a magnificent portrayal; so much so that almost by unanimous consent scholars say this great angel is none other than a description of the Lord Christ Himself. That may be true.

This may be a description of Jesus. It may be a description of our glorious Lord. Nor would I have any quarrel with those who see in this angel a picture of our Saviour. But I do not think that the angel is Jesus. I think that the description here of this angel is altogether appropriate of a pleni-potentiary, a full, ambassadorial representative of the Lord. It says here that his face shone as the sun. In the eighteenth chapter of the Book of the Revelation in the first verse is a description of a like angel. So brilliant was his countenance that the whole earth shone in the glory of his presence. But very few expositors would say that this angel in the eighteenth chapter of the Book of the Revelation is a picture of the Lord. This text in Revelation 10 says that this mighty angel had a rainbow upon his head, that his feet were pillars of fire, and that in the name of him that liveth forever and ever he takes possession of all creations. That could be the Lord Christ, Himself, doing these things. But, it sounds like a representative of God. He swears by the Lord. In the Book of Genesis, because God could not swear by anybody greater than Himself, He swore by His own name. It could be so here. Maybe when

He swears by Him who lives forever and ever, he swears by Himself. But to me it seems more plausible that this is a description of a heavenly being swearing by the God of the throne.

This angel appears all through the Book of the Revelation. In chapter five, there is a strong angel proclaiming with a loud voice, "Who is worthy to open the book and to loose the seals thereof?" In the seventh chapter of the Revelation, there is that same mighty angel ascending out of the sunrising, having the seal of the living God. In the eighth chapter of the Revelation, there is that angel-priest who ministers at the altar of God and brings before God the remembrance of all the prayers of God's sainted children. The eighteenth chapter describes a brilliant angel who lights the earth with the glory of his presence. Then there is this angel in Revelation 10. I would suppose that they were all the same angel. If he is but an angel (and not the Lord-Christ), he is certainly some glorious creation of God who serves and ministers before the throne of heaven. Michael, the archangel, has a name that means "one like God." If we were to look upon the form and figure and glory of Michael, we would think that we had seen God Himself. The brilliance, the dignity, all of the heavenly gifts that God, Himself, created are in Michael, who looks like God. So, to me, this glorious angel in Revelation 10 is a representative of heaven and one of the most glorious. More than sixty times, besides the reference to the angels of the seven churches, are angels referred to in the Revelation, and every time the reference is to their employment in the service to God. So this angel is a glorious servant of the most High God.

THE POSSESSION OF HEAVEN AND EARTH

God's representative set one foot upon the sea and one foot on the land and sware by his Lord that liveth forever that these things belong to Him. When he set his foot on the land and on the sea, that is a sign that God intends to take these things for Himself. When a man sets his foot on something, that means he is possessing it. For example, in the eleventh chapter of the Book of Deuteronomy God says to His people: "Every place whereon the soles of your feet shall tread that shall be yours. No man shall be able to stand before you. The Lord God shall lay the fear of you upon all of the people round about and every place where you shall tread upon that shall be yours." That same declaration was repeated in the first chapter of Joshua: "As I said to Moses, my servant, every place that the sole of your foot shall tread upon that have I given you." It is thus here in Revelation 10. When the angel set his foot down on the sea and on the earth, it was a sign of his possessing these things for the Lord God.

The angel who is possessing all creation for God swears that the time had come when there would be no longer delay. "But in the days of the voice of the seventh angel, when he shall sound, the mystery of God is intended to be finished." It is God's predetermined, foreordained, elective purpose that in the days of the sounding of the seventh angel the mystery of God shall be finished, "as he evangelized through his servants the prophets," (so reads the Greek text). The "mystery of God" is the long delay of our Lord in taking the kingdom unto Himself and in establishing righteousness in the earth. The mystery of God is seen in these thousands of years in which sin and death run riot. There is no village and there is no hamlet without its raging, and there is no human heart without its dark, black drop. There is no life without its tears and its sorrows. There is no home that ultimately does not break up, and there is no family that does not see the circle of the home dissolve in the depths of the grave. There is no life that does not end in death. The pages of history, from the time of the first murder until this present hour, are written in blood, tears and death. The mystery is the delay of God in taking the Kingdom unto Himself. That is the most inexplicable mystery that mind could dream of, the mystery of the presence of evil. For these thousands of years, God has allowed Satan to wrap his vicious, slimy, filthy, cruel tentacles around human life and around this earth. Does God know it? Is He indifferent to it? Is He not able to cope with it? Oh, the mystery of the delay of God! That mystery has brought more stumbling to the faith of God's people than any other experience in all life. The infidel, the atheist, the agnostic and the unbeliever laugh and mock us, and God lets them mock and laugh. The enemies of righteousness and the enemies of all that we hold dear rise and increase in power and spread blood and darkness over the face of the earth, and we wonder where God is. Our missionaries are slain, our churches are burned to the ground, people in this earth by uncounted millions and millions are oppressed, living in despair, and God just looks. He seemingly does not intervene; He does not say anything, and He does not move. Sin just develops. It goes on and on. Oh, the mystery of the delay of the Lord God!

But somewhere beyond the starry sky, there stands a herald angel with a trumpet in his hand, and by the decree of the Lord God Almighty, there is a day, there is an hour, there is a moment, there is an elected time when that angel shall sound and the kingdoms of this world shall become the kingdoms of our God and of His Christ. "In the days of the voice of the seventh angel the mystery of God shall be finished." The forbearance and longsuffering of God shall end. God shall say to death, "This is your last victim." God shall say to Satan, "This is your last destruction." God shall say to evil, "This is your last effort." God shall say to sin, "This is your last waste and damnation." Evil, broad as the river Euphrates, rolls to a vast, illimitable sea of corruption, and every departure from God is tributary to it. Every generation receives from the generation before it these awful and terrible inheritances of iniquity. We pass its judgment on to our children and to our children's children. Is the flood tide to go on forever? Is sin to reign forever? Is death to reign forever? Is the grave to be filled forever? No. God says that there is a barrier, there is a boundary, there is a dike, beyond which and over which the flood-tides of iniquity shall not roll. Evil ripens to a harvest of inevitable reaping. God says in the days of the sounding of the voice of this seventh angel, Satan and all his works shall be overthrown and the kingdoms of this world shall become the kingdoms of our Lord and of His Christ.

These things that seemingly work so tragically against us, things that we do not understand and seemingly cannot cope with, God says that for His people, in an explicable and mysterious way, these things are for the development of our souls, for the strengthening of our lives. They are intended to grow great spirits and great hearts and great men. In battles and in challenges and in losses that we do not understand, some day God shall say all of these things worked together for good to them that love God, to them who are the called according to His purpose. So God would say we are not to lose heart, we are not to be discouraged, we are not to give up, we are not to think the battle belongs to our enemy and the victory belongs to those who oppose God and blaspheme us. God says behind all the smoke and the darkness and the tragedy and the hurt of these awful hours, there is a sovereign will, an eternal will — God's will. And when God's people give themselves to His holy purpose, God says that even our losses and our tragedies lead to an ultimate, final victory. "The mystery of God." Why God chooses that it be wrought in tears, why God chooses that it be wrought in conflict, why God chooses that it be wrought in death, I cannot understand. It belongs to the mystery of God.

THE DELAYED BUT INEVITABLE VICTORY

This universe was not only created *by* Christ, but this whole, vast world around us was created *for* Christ. The history of the world ultimately moves to that great consummation when God's people shall reign with their Lord in the earth. That is why I say that these interludes are written in the holy Apocalypse lest we be discouraged, lest in the mystery of the impenetrable, permissive will of God, lest in these darknesses and these conflicts, we think we have lost the battle. Even in the war of death, God's sovereign grace is extended in remembrance to us. The Lord is pleased to give the kingdom to His children. Ah, what a blessedness! In the days of the voice of the seventh angel, darkness, death, sorrow, heartache, all shall be cast out. Even Satan shall be bound in the abyss for a thousand years and then cast into the lake of fire forever. There is a great day coming, a grave, a new world coming. There is a marvelous, heavenly, benedictory gift of God in the offing.

According to the text in Revelation 10:7, these are the good tidings that God has "evangelized" to His servants the prophets. The Greek word "evangelized to the prophets" is very meaningful. Always in the message of the prophets the good tidings are announced. Always. The prophet might see storm and furor and battle and blood and conflict. The prophetical writings are filled with woe and lamentations and heartache. But the prophet always saw the glorious day of dawning, his faith saw the flood-light of glory on the everlasting hills. That is why John uses the word "evangelized," "preached the good tidings" to His servants the prophets. Beyond what they might encounter, beyond what they might experience, beyond what they might face in this life, always there was the incomparable victory that lay beyond.

But this final triumph is not now, not yet. We live in the days of the delay. We live in the day of tears and heartache and strife and conflict. These are our days of suffering and sorrow. God says that His delay is to be accepted by us now as a part of the mystery of God. We cannot explain it, but the Scriptures are very faithful to point it out to us, this delay in the ultimate victory of God. Look at these passages. When the Lord closed His Apocalyptic sermon in the twenty-fourth chapter of Matthew, He closed it with

a parable concerning this delay. The parable is about a
servant who said in his evil heart: "My Lord delayeth his
coming. He is not going to come. We are not going to see
him." Again, in the thirty-sixth verse of that same chapter:
"But of that day and hour knoweth no man, no, not the
angels of heaven, but my Father only." Then in the parable
in the twenty-fifth chapter of Matthew, all of those virgins
slumbered and slept. The delay was long. The wise and
the foolish all slumbered and slept. In the nineteenth chapter, the eleventh verse of the Book of Luke reads: "Then
he spake this parable unto them because they thought that
the kingdom of God should immediately appear." They
thought that God was going to intervene immediately, that
the age was to be consummated at once. Then He told
this parable of delay, a parable of a nobleman who went
away into a far country to receive a kingdom for himself.
You find that delay mentioned again in II Peter 3:3:
". . . there shall come in the last days scoffers . . . saying,
Where is the promise of his coming? for since the fathers
fell asleep, all things continue as they were from the beginning of the creation." Here is described a delay so long
that finally even the scoffers have cause to question the
basis of the Christian faith.

Every generation has felt that his generation was a time
when God would intervene. When Eve gave birth to Cain,
practically all expositors will say that she thought the great
promise that the seed of the woman would bruise Satan's
head had come to pass. When John the Baptist preached
the Gospel, he said, "I am introducing you to Christ, the
One following me, who shall lay the axe at the root of the
tree and whose fan shall divide the chaff from the grain."
John thought the judgment would be in his day. Certainly
the apostles thought it would be in their day. In the great
Reformation, those men thought it would be in their day.
We look in expectancy toward heaven and think that it will
be in our day. We do not know. There is a mystery in the
purpose of God that is unfathomable to us in this long de-

lay. But we can be assured of this: first, that God intends a great blessedness for His people; and the trial, the heartache, the tears and even death, God has purposed for the good of His people. Second, do not ever be persuaded that the battle belongs to our enemy. The victory belongs to us. That is why the saints sing unto Him who loved us and washed us from our sins in His own blood and has made us kings and priests unto the Lord our God, for we shall reign on the earth. To Him be glory and dominion and power forever and forever. That is what John said when He "evangelized," when He spake the good tidings to His servants the prophets. Any true minister of the Gospel who preaches today is an echo of that ultimate and final victory. Gird up your loins, lift up your faces, take a new hold of what God hath assigned us to do, for God's Spirit, in triumph, marches before us.

Chapter 18

The Bitter-Sweet Little Book

And the voice which I heard from heaven spake unto me
again, and said, Go and take the little book which is open in
the hand of the angel which standeth upon the sea and upon
the earth. And I went unto the angel, and said unto him,
Give me the little book. And he said unto me, Take it, and
eat it up; and it shall make thy belly bitter, but it shall be
in thy mouth sweet as honey. And I took the little book out
of the angel's hand, and ate it up; and it was in my mouth
sweet as honey: and as soon as I had eaten it, my belly was
bitter. And he said unto me, Thou must prophesy again before many peoples, and nations, and tongues, and kings. —
Revelation 10:8-11

One of the sublimest of all apocalyptic visions is this
one in chapter ten wherein is described the heavenly angel
who comes down to earth as God's representative. He reminds us of Michael. The name Michael means "he is like
God." This angel representative from heaven is as God,
clothed with a cloud, a rainbow upon his head, his face
as the brilliance of the burning sun and his feet like pillars
of fire. He sets one foot upon the sea and one foot upon
the land, and in the name of the Lord God who lives forever, he claims all creation for the Almighty. He lifts his
right hand to heaven and swears by God who lives forever
that the delay of the mystery of God is to be finished in the
days of the sounding of the next trumpet. He has in his
hand a little book. John, who here for the first time becomes
an actor in the drama, is commanded to eat it. When he
does so, it is in his mouth as honey and in his stomach as
gall. The Lord then says that the apostle, having digested

the word of the Apocalypse, is to deliver it to peoples and nations and tongues and kings.

THE SEVEN THUNDERS

When that angel who had in his hand the open little book spoke, it was as a lion roaring. All the ends of God's creation heard his voice and the foundations of the earth reverberated. When he spoke, there were seven thunders that uttered their voices in reply. The narrative continues: "When these seven thunders uttered their voices I was about to write what the first voice said and the second voice said and all seven of them. I was about to write and a voice from heaven said unto me, Seal up those things which are uttered and write them not." True to this interdiction, John carried them to the grave. We do not know what those voices of God said. Now we know the type of thing that was said, for the definite article in the introduction of these seven thunders is very explicit. They are not just seven thunders, they are *the* seven thunders. In each instance, the Greek language with that definite article is very positive and very *emphatic*. "*The* seven thunders." They are not the reverberations of a crash of lightning, but they are the voices of the judgment of God. In the fourth chapter of the Revelation the first vision that John saw was the glorious, heavenly throne and on it the Almighty seated. Then he heard out of the throne the thunderings and the voices; that is, these are the judgment pronouncements of God. Several times in the Apocalypse we find those thunderings referred to, and always with reference to the judgment of the Almighty. They are seven in number because they represent the plenitude, the fulness, the completion of the intervention of God in human history. They are not called seven in the first vision in Revelation chapter four, but they are called seven here in keeping with the characteristic number of the throne. There are seven lamps, there are seven spirits of God, there are seven seals, seven trumpets, seven vials, seven thunders, representing the whole magnitude, the fulness of the pronouncements of God.

When those seven thunders responded to the voice of this mighty, angelic representative from heaven, John was about to write what they said. As he was about to write, there came an interdiction from heaven to write them not, to seal them up. Now what could that mean? Why mention their words if he is not going to reveal them to us? Why leave us in suspense? Why make us wonder what these voices said? To me it had in it a profound lesson. There are great, broad outlines of the future revealed by the Lord. All through the Scriptures, especially in that written by the Apostle Paul and finally, explicitly in the writings of the seer, John, the vast outlines of the future are made known. But there are also principles and agencies and forces that work in history that are unknown to us. They are known but to God. That is why no man can with accuracy predict the future; because he does not know and he does not understand all of the forces that work behind these incidents that make up the annals of humanity. Many of them are revealed, many of them are plainly delineated in the Bible, many of the things that are to come to pass are explicitly said, but there are also things that we do not know and things we cannot understand. We cannot accurately know the future. These things are known but to God. There are literally thousands of questions about these days that are yet to come to which I can find no answer at all. As I have asked for answers to some of them from scholars who have no pastoral duties, who have no administrative responsibilities, who give their lives to no other thing but to study the Word of God, they have no idea how to answer. There are thousands of questions about the dead and the life that is to come that I cannot understand. There are a thousand questions about the millennium that I cannot understand. There are another thousand questions about the eternity that is yet to come that I cannot understand. They are beyond my comprehension. I have no answer to them. But this very unknowing is also in the will of God. Paul said that we see through a glass darkly. We can see the shape of things, the broad outline of things, but there are many things that we do not know, and we shall never know until the day and the hour comes that they are revealed. That is why all of us, however much we may study, should be filled with profound humility. God has kept many things secret in His own wisdom. Some things He has revealed to us in His Word, but many things are kept hidden in His own counsels. Had God willed that we know them, He would have written them. But there are some things God in His wisdom has kept sacred, and for these things we wait till the final day and hour. Thus John writes, "The mandates of heaven I was about to record, the voices of the judgment of God, but the Lord said, Seal them up and write them not." Even Daniel, who was God's beloved prophet, said, "Lord, I hear thy voice and I see the vision, but I do not understand what the words mean and I do not understand the vision. Lord, what does it mean?" And God said to Daniel, "Go thy way, Daniel, for the words are closed up and sealed till the time of the end." Many things that Daniel sealed up in a lack of understanding are revealed to us today; but there are many areas in which, like Daniel, we stand wondering what the vision means, wondering what the words refer to. We can never know ultimately until the day when these things come to pass.

The angel lifted up his hand and swore by God in heaven that there should be *chronos*, "time," no longer. Time is a creation of God, like the world of matter and of light. For God there is no such thing as time. Time is just for us. God looks upon all the ages as a present. He can see it here, He can see it there, He can see the end from the beginning, and all of it is in constant review before His eyes. We who are creatures see things happen a day at a time, as events turn the corner of each successive hour. We divide time into millenniums, thousands of years. We divide years into three hundred and sixty-five days. We divide

days into twenty-four hours. We divide hours into sixty
minutes. We divide time, but God looks upon it as a whole,
a complete creation. This present creation of time is for
man. It refers to a man's day and a man's hour. But there
is coming, says this angel with his hand lifted up to heaven,
an inevitable and final moment when a man's day shall
end, when time shall be no longer, when delay of the
mystery of God shall cease and we shall enter that consummation which leads into the eternity of the infinite ages.
What an amazing thought, that we shall live through those
eons and eternities! It brings a man to his knees. It humbles him as he faces the great day of the Almighty through
which some day we shall live and in which some day we
shall stand.

THE IDENTIFICATION OF THE LITTLE BOOK

"And the voice which I heard from heaven spake unto me
again saying, Go and take the little book . . . eat it . . . then
prophesy [declare its message to the people]." Now we are
going to speak of this bitter-sweet little book. First of all,
as for me, and I must admit that there are very few who
believe like this, but as for me, I recognize that little book.
In the first vision of the Apocalypse, after the days of the
churches, John saw the throne of God and the Almighty
seated. In the hand of God he saw a *biblion*. In the King
James Version the word is translated "a book." When the
reader comes to the tenth chapter and finds that word translated "little book," he would suppose (and practically all
scholars suppose the same thing) that here is a different
book. But I do not think so, for the same Greek word is
used to describe both of them. In the fifth chapter the
word is translated "book" and in the tenth chapter it is
translated "little book." But the word is the same that describes both of them. The Greek word for book is *biblos*.
Our word "Bible" comes from it. The diminutive of *biblos*
is *biblion* or *biblaridion*. In the fifth chapter, the first diminutive, *biblion*, is used. In the tenth chapter both diminu-

tives are used. So to me they are the same book, "a little book." In the hand of the Lord God, in the first vision that John saw, there lay that little book.

Now the difference is that in the fifth chapter of the Revelation, that little book was sealed with seven seals, whereas the book in the angel's hand is open. In the Greek as well as in the English that word "open" is very emphatic. He had in his hand a little book *open*. Look at the eighth verse. The Greek language can certainly emphasize a thing when it is so desired. Here is the way the Greek text reads: *To biblion to eneogmenon,* "the little book, the one which is open." The word is very emphatic. It must have reference to what has gone before. That little book that lay in the hand of God was sealed with seven seals, but now in the tenth chapter of the Revelation, all seven of those seals have been broken, and the whole of the little book is open. It is the same little book. That little book in the hand of God, sealed, represents a forfeited inheritance. The breaking of those seals represents the redemption of that inheritance and the casting out of the interloper, the usurper, that old dragon, Satan. The creation of the world was not for him, but for us, the children of Adam. As each seal is opened, there is revealed the story of how God casts out the intruder and how God redeems the inheritance for man. God has purposed to give it to us, and we shall reign with our Lord, fellow-heirs, kings and priests in the earth. The story of that purpose is presented as each seal is broken, until finally the little book is fully viewed and we can see the whole broad outline of how God is to redeem this lost creation for man. To me that is the meaning of the little book. It is a recounting, it is a revelation, it is an apocalypse, it is an unveiling of how God will redeem this lost creation and give it back to us for whom God made it.

The angel now gives the little book to John, and the angel says to him to take it and eat it up. That refers to a very plain and simple symbol that we often find in the Word of the Lord. To eat it up is to assimilate it, to digest it, to get it in your soul. As Jeremiah said: "Oh, Lord, thou knowest, thy words were found and I did eat them" (Jeremiah 15: 16). Another reference is in Ezekiel, the last of chapter two and the first of chapter three: "Open thy mouth [said the Lord to Ezekiel] and eat that I give thee. And I looked and behold an hand was sent unto me and lo a roll of the book lay thereon and he spread it before me and it was written within and without and there was written lamentations and mourning and woe and the Lord said, Son of man, eat this book, eat this roll, then go speak. I opened my mouth and ate the roll and it was in my mouth sweet as honey, but it was filled with lamentations and mourning and woe." We are to experience, then to testify. We are to study, meditate, learn, and then we are to preach. We are to consume God's Word and then prophesy. John was to eat this book, *then* prophesy before the peoples and the nations and the tongues and the kings of the earth. So John did that. He took the word of God, he took the revelation of the Almighty and he ate it, and it was in his mouth sweet like honey and in his stomach it was bitter like gall.

THE SWEET AND THE BITTER

Herein is one of the most profound truths to be found in the Scriptures. The Apocalypse itself, the unveiling itself is just like that. The sweetness of this little book, this apocalypse, this unveiling, this redemptive program of God, can be easily verified and seen in the great mass of apocalyptic literature that has grown up around it. There are simply libraries, volumes and volumes of writings, elucidations, interpretations, about God's revelation. It is a magnificent thing, and full of interest, and it has stormed the hearts of men ever since it was disclosed. But there is no student of the Word of God and there is no scholar who has ever sought to understand these prophetic messages but that learns in them the terrible violence of the storm that is coming. The Apocalypse describes a bitter future.

I have come to believe that any true preacher who studies

the Scriptures is the kind of man who sees the awful hand of judgment that is written against us. That is the reason for the apocalyptic message — that we might be warned and that we might be saved. To have a word from heaven is sweet like honey; to possess God's Scripture is like sugar. But there are in those heavenly words prophetic warnings of disaster to a people who turn aside from God's message. That is exactly what is written here. All the blessings of God, how sweet they are! But to a people who refuse God's admonitions, the words are as bitter as gall. True prophetic experience is like this, always.

Men of God delineated in the Bible shared this bitter-sweet response to God's Word. For example, the prophet Isaiah saw the Lord high and lifted up. The vision was glorious. But in the glory and the light of that marvelous revelation he began to look at himself and he cried, "Woe is me." Then he listened to the message that God told him to deliver. It was filled with warning and with judgment: "Except these people awake and except they turn they will be destroyed." When God described the destruction, Isaiah said, "How long, O Lord, how long, how long?" And the Lord said, "Until the whole thing be destroyed, until it all be taken away, until the Lord has removed men out of his sight." The vision of God was sweet, but the words were bitter. We find another instance of this bitter-sweet in Second Kings the twenty-second chapter. The scribes found the Book of God in the house of the Lord, and when the King heard the words of the Book and saw the inevitable judgments, he rent his clothes and wept before God, saying, "O how great is thy wrath and the judgment of God that is kindled against us!" These blessings are sweet, but the apocalyptic judgment is bitter. That is the way with our people and our preaching and our nation and our appeal, and our souls today. Every message of hope and of glory, every message of liberty and of God's blessings, every message of salvation and goodness, every promised remembrance from heaven — these things are sweet beyond compare. But the prophet, the true man of God, the man who understands, can always see back of the sweetness and the blessedness and the gloriousness, always that sudden judgment; which, if we forget, if we deny, we fail our Lord. That is why we need the prophet; that is why we need the true preacher; that is why we need the man who can see and who can discern the times. That faithful minister will speak of these things that are sweet and dear that God has given us, but he will also warn us lest we fall into sin and judgment.

That same truth is found in the hope we have in Jesus. The promise we have in our Saviour is as sweet as honey. The assurance of God's triumph is enough to comfort a man in deepest lamentation and mourning. Some day in Christ, Satan is to be defeated; some day in Jesus, the Lord God shall triumph; some day there will be no more darkness, and sin and misery and oppression and death; some day in Jesus, we shall win our ultimate triumph. We love our Lord who forgave our sins. He died for us on the cross, and we seek to reflect the goodness and mercy of God to a lost world. The message is as sweet as honey. But oh, that is why God's children weep when they pray. That is why a sainted family will sometimes lament over the dereliction and prodigality and waywardness of a son or a daughter; and that is why the Church gives itself in prayerful fasting and intercession before God. "O Lord, the blessings of Christ mediated to us are sweet, sweet as sugar, sweet as honey. But, O God, the judgment of its refusal is bitter, bitter as gall." How marvelous to be a Christian, but also how terrible to face an eternity without hope and without God! That is what the Apostle Paul meant when he said, "We are the savor of life unto life to those that believe, but we are also the savor of death unto death to those who refuse." Sweet and bitter. The true prophet of God delivers and experiences both.

If I have one indictment against the modern pulpits, it is this: the preacher so often preaches about the love of God and about the things that are fine, nice, sweet and good. But there has dropped out of the modern pulpit that awful sound of warning. We do not have the prophet and his message any longer. We do not often hear the threatenings of God and the voice of the judgment of God. We need it, for one is as true as the other. How wonderful to be a Christian! How grand to be a Christian! Wonderful it is for the child, wonderful for the home, blessed for the life — God's richest benedictions upon a nation and a country and a people. How wonderful! But oh, how tragic says the true prophet, how tragic when men turn away from the blessings of heaven and give themselves to these things that destroy the soul and destroy the life of the people! Both messages ought to be delivered together. "And the Lord said, Go prophesy unto the people and the nations and the tongues and the kings, speaking the whole counsels of God." Our people ought to be warned. God help us to warn. Our people ought to be encouraged. God help us to encourage. Our people ought to be made conversant with all that God says. God help us to declare the whole counsels of the Lord.

Expository Sermons on Revelation

Volume 4—Revelation 11 through 17

Expository Sermons
on Revelation

VOLUME 4—REVELATION 11 THROUGH 17

by
W. A. CRISWELL, Ph.D.

This volume is affectionately and gratefully dedicated
to
MR. PAT ZONDERVAN
God's publisher of the good news
By whose hand the printed page
Has come to bear the glad tidings
Of Jesus to uncounted thousands
Of hearts and homes around the world.

FOREWORD

There is so much in the Revelation that belongs to the deep, deep things of God. The middle chapters of the Apocalypse are akin to the middle chapters of Paul's letter to the Romans. After wrestling with the profound problem of the sovereign and elective purposes of God for Israel, the apostle finally concluded in Romans 11:33,36, "O the depths of the riches both of the wisdom and knowledge of God! how unsearchable are his judgments, and his ways past finding out. For of him, and through him, and to him, are all things: to whom be glory forever. Amen." This exclamation of adoration and human limitation on the part of Paul before the infinitude of God is especially my own before these chapters in the Revelation. Many of the details that outline the future are still hidden to us. We must wait for their fulfillment before we can know exactly what they mean and to whom they refer.

There has been one profound impression left upon my soul after preparing and delivering the sermons included in this fourth volume in the series on the Revelation. That impression is this: In the vast sweep of God's sovereign purpose through time and eternity, we are so small, so helpless, so infinitely dependent. God must be our strength and refuge or else we are fearfully lost. The universe is so big, eternity is so long, God is so great, until we are but diminishing minutiae in the ultimate consummation of the age. How easy to forget us, overlook us, pass us by, were it not for the love and mercy of Christ! It was this sentiment Henry van Dyke expressed in his oft-quoted and beautiful poem entitled, "Thy Sea Is Great, Our Boats Are

Small." Do you remember its appeal to God for guidance and refuge?

O Maker of the mighty deep
  Whereon our vessels fare,
Above our life's adventure keep
  Thy faithful watch and care.
In Thee we trust, whate'er befall;
Thy sea is great, our boats are small.

We know not where the secret tides
  Will help us or delay,
Nor where the lurking tempest hides,
  Nor where the fogs are gray.
We trust in Thee, whate'er befall;
Thy sea is great, our boats are small.

When outward bound we boldly sail
  And leave the friendly shore,
Let not our hearts of courage fail
  Until the voyage is o'er.
We trust in Thee, what'er befall;
Thy sea is great, our boats are small.

Beyond the circle of the sea,
  When voyaging is past,
We seek our final port in Thee;
  Oh! bring us home at last.
In Thee we trust, whate'er befall;
Thy sea is great, our boats are small.

In preparation of these sermons for publication my sincerest appreciation is herein expressed to Mrs. B. B. Binford and to Mrs. Bailey Forester. The messages were taken from tape recordings as they were delivered in the pulpit of the First Baptist Church in Dallas. They were grammatically corrected by Mrs. Binford, who in her own right is a most gifted author. Her background in Greek and Latin and English poetry is of inestimable value to me. No less so has Mrs. Forester been carefully diligent in following through all the corrections and presenting to the publishers a beautifully prepared manuscript.

Now may the Lord be pleased with what we have tried to do, thus delivering His message of judgment and glory, of warning and triumph, in the sermons published here. May they be as meaningful to you who read them as they were to the dear people of our church who heard them.

W. A. CRISWELL

Pastor's Study
First Baptist Church
Dallas, Texas

CONTENTS

Expository Sermons on Revelation

Volume 4—Revelation 11 through 17

Chapter 1

CRUX INTERPRETATORUM

Revelation 11

1. And there was given me a reed like unto a rod: and the angel stood, saying, Rise, and measure the temple of God, and the altar, and them that worship therein.

2. But the court which is without the temple leave out, and measure it not; for it is given unto the Gentiles: and the holy city shall they tread under foot forty and two months.

3. And I will give power unto my two witnesses, and they shall prophesy a thousand two hundred and threescore days, clothed in sackcloth.

4. These are the two olive trees, and the two candlesticks standing before the God of the earth.

5. And if any man will hurt them, fire proceedeth out of their mouth, and devoureth their enemies: and if any man will hurt them, he must in this manner be killed.

6. These have power to shut heaven, that it rain not in the days of their prophecy: and have power over waters to turn them to blood, and to smite the earth with all plagues, as often as they will.

7. And when they shall have finished their testimony, the beast that ascendeth out of the bottomless pit shall make war against them, and shall overcome them, and kill them.

8. And their dead bodies shall lie in the street of the great city, which spiritually is called Sodom and Egypt, where also our Lord was crucified.

One of the most learned and able of all the expositors of Holy Scriptures is named Dean Alford. Dean Alford said that the eleventh chapter is undoubtedly the most difficult in the Book of Revelation. Indeed, there are many difficult chapters in the Apocalypse and this certainly is one of them. The interpretations of this present passage are confusing and inconclusive. One man says the temple is used here figuratively for the faithful portion of the church of Christ. Another one says the command is given to John to measure the temple of God in order to call attention to the size of the church. Another one believes the altar is the church. Another one thinks the outer court signifies a part of the church. Another one declares that in the Apocalypse the Holy City is always the type of the church. Another one says the two witnesses represent the elect church of God, embracing both the Jew and the Christian, and the witness she bears concerning God in the Old and the New Testament. Another interpreter says the one thousand two hundred sixty days constitute a period during which the church, though trodden underfoot, will not cease to prophesy. Another one thinks the whole vision of the war of the beast against the two witnesses is symbolic and the intention is to convey the idea that the church, in her witness for God, will experience opposition. Another comments that the death of the witnesses is the fate of the church pictured in the life of Christ.

Someone else says that in the ascension of the witnesses to heaven, the church is triumphantly vindicated. Another one holds that the elders who worship God after the sounding of the seventh trumpet are the church. To these interpreters, every diverse expression, every delineation, every symbol, every pattern, every presentation is "the church." To make every diverse expression and delineation and symbol say the same identical thing, whether it means it or not, whether it has any reference to it or not, to force everything to mean the same thing, is to lose all opportunity to listen to the mind of the Holy Spirit. So, what we are going to do is to look at this passage in the light of what God has written already and then to see what the Lord has revealed.

When I look at the text carefully and read it earnestly, the first impression that I have is this: Here we are distinctly and unmistakeably upon Jewish ground. Look at verse 8: "Their dead bodies shall lie in the street of the great city, which spiritually, symbolically, is called Sodom and Egypt." "But," John says in the text, "I am referring to the city where our Lord was crucified." Our Lord was not crucified in Damascus. Our Lord was not crucified in Memphis or in Thebes. Our Lord was not crucified in Gaza or in Ashkelon. Our Lord was not crucified in Philippi or in Antioch or in Rome. Our Lord was crucified in Jerusalem. The apostle describes the sinfulness of that city by saying that spiritually it is Sodom in its sin and spiritually it is Egypt in its worldliness. "But," says John, "I am actually talking about Jerusalem." The symbolic words are *Sodom* and *Egypt*, but he was referring to Jerusalem.

THE HOLY CITY JERUSALEM

Look at the text again. The second verse reads, "But the court which is without the temple leave out, for it is given unto the Gentiles: and the holy city shall they tread under foot forty and two months." "The holy city" is a word, an expression, that is used in the Bible for one city alone. There is no other city on earth that is called "the holy city" except Jerusalem. The only exception is in Revelation 21 where the new Jerusalem is called "the holy city come down from God out of heaven," and certainly it will never be trampled by the armies of the Gentiles. All of the other references (and there are many of them) in the Bible to the holy city refer always to Jerusalem. For example, in Nehemiah 11:1 the prophet says, "One tenth of the people he placed in the holy city [in Jerusalem]." Nine tenths of them were placed out in the cities of Judea. One out of ten was asked to live in "the holy city." Look again at that magnificent expression of praise and glory in Isaiah 52:1: "Awake, arise; put on . . . thy beautiful garments, O Jerusalem, the holy city." Again, when our Lord was tempted, in His second temptation, the Devil took Him to "the holy city" and set Him on top of the pinnacle and asked Him to fall down and let the angels bear Him up as a sign to the world of His deity. Again in

Matthew 27 there is the record, after the resurrection of Jesus, of the saints being raised out of their graves and appearing to many "in the holy city," in Jerusalem. All these references are undoubtedly to Jerusalem.

Jerusalem is a city that dwarfs in importance all other cities in the world. There is none like it. There is none in the elective purpose and economy of God that can even begin to approach it. I once listened to one of our illustrious ministers who avowed: "Take a map or take a globe and put a cross in the Levant, in the Near East, in its heart, in Jerusalem. When you do, you will find that all of the nations to the right of it, to the east of it, read from right to left. Then, keeping your center there, all the nations to the left of it, to the west of it, will read from left to right. Here in the western world we read from the left side of the page to the right side of the page . . . But when you go to all the nations to the right of it, to the east of it, the Chinese, the Arab, and on and on, all of them read from the right to the left side of the page."

As Ezekiel says, God placed Israel in the center of the nations. Three great continents center in that country: Africa, Asia and Europe. It is a line-bridge between those three great land-masses of the earth. The strategic area is also the dividing of time. What happened there in that place divides all the centuries. Before the crucifixion of our Lord in that place, it is B.C. After the crucifixion of our Lord in that place, it is A.D.

There has been an increasing interest through the years in that part of the globe occupied by Israel. A stupendous, immeasurable reservoir of oil is in that great area and will become increasingly prized through the years that unfold. This explains the terrific drive among the nations of the world, and especially among our enemies, for the control and the possession of those riches. That is why this government, under which we, by God's grace, abide, and the other governments of the free world have no other choice but to seek to do our best to preserve those immeasurable riches for the people of the earth to enjoy. However history may turn, there is no escaping what God has decreed: that the center of the nations is found in Jerusalem. History may turn in many directions; we may be interested in Latin America, in the Orient, in many, many other places; but the interest that God has focused upon that area in the Middle East abides forever. When I read of these things in the Bible, they correspond to the things that I read in the daily newspapers, that I read in the books of history and that I see unfolding before my eyes every day.

In Romans 15 Paul is discussing what God has elected for this whole world. He avows in verse 8, "Now I say that Jesus Christ was a minister of the circumcision." Jesus was a preacher of Israel. "Salvation," Christ said, "is of the Jews." Christ is a minister of the circumcision to confirm the promises made unto the fathers, that the Gentiles might glorify God for His mercy. ". . . as it is written, for this cause I will confess to thee among the Gentiles . . . And again . . . Rejoice, ye Gentiles, with his people." Now, do you see the meaning of that passage? There is no such thing as a blessing upon us that does not also call for a blessing upon His people. God said, "Rejoice, ye Gentiles." It is not the elective purpose of God in blessing us so greatly that we forget His covenant promises to Israel. All of us are in the purposes of God to be blessed, and all of us in God's elective program shall be blessed. But that program also includes God's people. The Psalmist said: "Pray for the peace of Jerusalem. They shall prosper that love thee" (Psalm 122:6). We cannot find in the Bible any program of God that in its consummation ultimately leaves out the covenant promises the Lord made to the fathers of Israel.

DANIEL'S SEVENTY WEEKS

We have another tremendous indication of God's purposes in the earth in the time element that is written here in this text. Not only is a particular place designated, namely the city of Jerusalem, but there is also a very definite pointing in the time words used here. ". . . and the holy city shall they tread under foot forty and two months." Forty-two months. In the next verse: "And I will give power unto my two witnesses, and they shall prophesy a thousand two hundred and sixty days [forty-two months]." Then in the next chapter, in Revelation 12:6: "And the woman persecuted shall find refuge and shall be fed of God a thousand two hundred and sixty days." Again, in that same twelfth chapter, verse 14: "She shall be nourished for a time, and times, and half a time." For three and a half years. Time, times, and half a time. Then in Revelation 13:5, "forty and two months."

There are in that little space of writing five references, each one always to the same length of time, forty-two months, one thousand two hundred and sixty days, three and a half years. What of this? Did God conjure up that period meaninglessly? Why did not God write in one place forty-eight months and in the next place why did not He say a thousand two hundred and two days? In the next place why did not He say five and a half years? Why, always, is it that same period of time: one thousand two hundred and sixty days, forty-two months, three and a half years, time, times and a half a time, time, times and a dividing of time? Evidently it means a special thing and something particularly profound.

It is very plain to what that time period refers, for I have met it before. In the Book of Daniel, there are those same expressions and those same time limits. By reading Daniel and the Apocalypse, I can see exactly what it is that God has given to John as He delineates the future of the consummation of this age. Listen to it. In Daniel 9:24, the words "Seventy sevens" are translated in the King James Version "weeks." In the Revised Standard Version they are translated "weeks of years," which is correct. In the Hebrew the words mean "weeks of years." The passage reads: "Seventy sevens [four hundred and ninety years] are determined upon thy people and upon thy holy city, to finish the transgression, and to make an end of sins

. . . to bring in everlasting righteousness, and to seal up the vision and prophecy [to bring it to its final conclusion], and to anoint the most holy" (Revised Version, "to anoint the most holy place").

That is a very plain prophecy. Seventy sevens, four hundred and ninety years are determined to make an end of sin, to make an end of transgression, to bring in everlasting righteousness, to seal up the visions and the prophecies, to bring them all to pass. The prophet takes those seventy sevens and he divides them into two parts. "Know therefore that from the commandment to restore and to build Jerusalem . . . ." That decree was issued in the twentieth year of Artaxerxes in 455 B.C. From the twentieth year of Artaxerxes, "from the commandment to restore and rebuild Jerusalem until Messiah the Prince [until the coming of Jesus] shall be sixty-nine weeks, [seven weeks and threescore and two weeks, sixty and nine weeks] . . . And after threescore and two weeks [after that seven weeks and threescore and two weeks, after sixty-two plus seven, after the sixty-nine weeks] Messiah shall be cut off." So, starting at the twentieth year of Artaxerxes and reading forward four hundred and thirty-four years, sixty-nine sevens, we come to A.D. 30 when Jesus was cut off, when the Messiah was cut off. Then the prophet separates that last week, that seventieth week. That seventieth week is the climax, for that seventieth week brings in the everlasting kingdom of God. It brings in the consummation of the age. It brings in the fulfillment of all God's purposes in the earth. It fulfills all prophecies and all visions. In it the everlasting kingdom comes and Christ reigns forever thereafter as Lord of heaven and earth.

THE CONSUMMATION OF THE AGE

What is told about that seventieth week, that last week, that is set apart here? "He [that prince, that anti-Christ, that one who wars against God] shall confirm the covenant . . . for one week [for that week]: and in the midst of the week he will turn and these with whom he has made a covenant [He is talking to Daniel about God's people], he will break that covenant in the midst of the week and cause the sacrifice and the oblation to cease." Then follows the terrible prophecy here of the Great Tribulation. So Daniel divides that final week into two parts, the first part three and a half years and the second part three and a half years; each part forty-two months, one thousand two hundred and sixty days, time, time and dividing of time, time, times and half a time. For example, in Daniel 7:25: ". . . a time and times and the dividing of time [half a time]." In Daniel 12:7: ". . . and he sware lifting up his hand to God that it shall be for a time, times, and a half a time." That is the source of that number. It comes from Daniel's seventieth week that God divided into three and a half years, half of seven, three and a half years, forty-two months, one thousand two hundred sixty days, time, times and a dividing of times.

This last week, this seventieth week of the prophecy, brings the great consummation of the age. Between those sixty-nine weeks, at the end of which the Lord is cut off, and this seventieth week that brings in the consummation, there is a great interlude, a great intermission. Paul says in Ephesians 3 and elsewhere in his epistles that this great intermission is the time period in which we now live. The great interlude is called a *musterion*, a secret hid in the heart of God. The Old Testament prophets never saw it. They never dreamed of it. But God revealed it to His holy apostles that we might rejoice in our election to the household of faith and in our part in the consummation of the age. This is the reading of the Revelation.

To think that these mortal eyes of mine some day shall see these heavenly things, that this poor weak frame of dust shall some day share in these promises, that God has given to us a fellow-heirship in the celestial coming kingdom of the Lord! We seem so poor, we seem so wretched, we seem so sinful. Made out of the dust of the ground, we are like worms of the earth. But God in His elective purpose has it in His heart to elevate us above the highest angels. Oh, blessed be His name that we should be included in the family of faith and in the household of those who are to possess the eternal riches of glory in Christ Jesus! We do not realize, but oh, that we might realize! God wrote His purpose for us in the Revelation, the uncovering, the Apocalypse, that we might see and rejoice.

CHAPTER 2

MEASURING THE TEMPLE OF GOD

Revelation 11

1. And there was given me a reed like unto a rod: and the angel stood, saying, Rise, and measure the temple of God, and the altar, and them that worship therein.

2. But the court which is without the temple leave out, and measure it not; for it is given unto the Gentiles: and the holy city shall they tread under foot forty and two months.

Almost all expositors refer everything in this passage, as well as everything else in the Revelation, to a picture of the church. For example, one expositor said the temple is here figuratively used as the faithful portion of the church. Then another one wrote: "The command is given to John to measure the temple of God in order to call attention to the size of the church." Then another one: "The altar is the church." Another one commented: "The outer court signifies a part of the church." Still another said: "The Holy City is always, in the Apocalypse, the type of the church." Another one stated: "The two witnesses represent the elect church." Again another wrote: "The one thousand two hundred and sixty days constitute a period when the church will not cease to prophecy." Another expositor said: "The whole vision of the war of the beast against the two witnesses is symbolic of the church." And another one interpreted: "The death of the witnesses is the fate of the church." Another one asserted: "In the ascension of the witnesses to heaven, the church is vindicated." Then another declared:

"The elders who worship God after the seventh trumpet are the church." And so on.

Whatever the diverse expression, whatever the delineation, whatever the vision or whatever the meaning, it is taken to refer to the church, always the church. In that case, we have here just a kaleidoscopic presentation of the church, and the Apocalypse has no particular pertinency at all. However, I believe that when God writes something there is in it a profound and basic meaning. The prophecy bears a message to us of deep significance. Different things mean different things, not same things. There are some truths that are distinctly and pertinently evident in these words of prophecy.

THE PLACE AND TIME OF THE VISION

Here is one. In this chapter we are manifestly, openly, on Jewish ground. Verse 8 of the text out of which I read says this great city that John is describing is spiritually, symbolically, Sodom and Egypt. "But the city I am talking about," says the seer, "is where our Lord was crucified." The symbol of it, he says, is Sodom because of its sin. It is Egypt because of its worldliness. But it is actually where our Lord was crucified. He was crucified outside of the gate of Jerusalem. Here we are on Jewish ground; we are in Palestine; we are in the Holy City, Jerusalem. Out of all of the cities that are mentioned in the Bible, there is only one that is ever called "the Holy City" and that is Jerusalem. Jerusalem dwarfs in importance all the other cities of the world. There is none like it. It is the city of the great king. Out of Zion proceed the words and the revelation of God. Jesus steadfastly set His face to go toward Jerusalem, the Holy City. We know where we are in this passage: we are in Palestine, we are in Jerusalem.

And we know where we are in the prophetic chronology of God's revelation. "It shall be trodden down [this Holy City] forty and two months and my two witnesses shall prophesy a thousand two hundred and threescore days." When we look at chapter

12 and chapter 13 and elsewhere, again and again we find that
same identical time period: forty-two months; a thousand two
hundred and sixty days; three and a half years; time, times and
half a time; a time, times and a dividing of time. All of those
designations are the same time period. Did John use it adventitiously, accidentally? No. That time period has a tremendous,
prophetic meaning in the Word of God. To understand it, we
must turn to the Book of Daniel. There this period of time is
used again and again. It refers to the last of the seventy sevens,
the seventy weeks of years.

In the vision in Daniel 9, for example, Daniel divided all
of the time by which God works with His elect people, Israel,
into seventy sevens. The translation in King James Version
says "seventy weeks." "Seventy weeks of years" would be an
actual translation. In chapter 9, Daniel said that between the
decree to rebuild Jerusalem (which decree went forth in the
twentieth year of Artaxerxes, the king) until the cutting off of
the Messiah (until His rejection), should be sixty-nine sevens
(sixty-nine times seven years). After describing the first sixty-
nine sevens, the prophet then set apart that last, that seventieth
week. Between the sixty-ninth week and the last seventieth
week is our present vast interlude, this great intermission.

The Apostle Paul in the Ephesian letter and in the Roman
letter said that this great intermission in which we now live
is a *musterion*, a secret hid in the heart of God. It is a thing
no man could learn by ferreting it out, by studying. It had to
be revealed by God. That vast intermission is the age of the
Holy Spirit, the age of the church, in which there is neither
bond nor free, male nor female, Greek nor barbarian, Roman
nor provincial, alien nor indigenous. We are all alike in the
great brotherhood of the body of Christ. But the Jew never
saw that truth. The prophet never saw it. It was a secret hid
in the heart of God. Between that sixty-ninth week and this
seventieth week is this vast interlude in which we now live.

But there is coming a great consummation. There shall be

an interdiction of God in the work of sin and death, the grave, and Satan. God shall intervene some day in history. And when that intervention is made, when that judgment day comes, when history reaches toward its final and ultimate consummation, that will be the seventieth week of Daniel described here in the Apocalypse.

The Apocalypse is not the unveiling of human history. It is not a recounting of the story of the church on earth, for the church is not mentioned in it after the third chapter, after it is taken up into heaven. But the Apocalypse is the unveiling of Jesus Christ when He comes on clouds descending, with ten thousands of His saints; when history and time and all God's creation reaches up to its grand and ultimate climax. That event is Daniel's seventieth week and that is the Apocalypse. When we read the Revelation, we read the account of God's unfolding, unveiling of the great and final judgment, the consummation, the end of the age, toward which all history moves. The prophet Daniel divides that seventieth week into two parts — three and one-half years on one side, and three and one-half years on the other side. He divides it exactly in the middle. The first part in the New Testament is called "the Tribulation" and the second part is called "the Great Tribulation" — *he thlipsis he meagale* — "the tribulation the great."

This time period in the Book of Revelation, these forty-two months, or one thousand two hundred sixty days, or time, times and half a time, a time, times and the dividing of time, these three and one-half years, is spoken of by the prophet Daniel. The Book of Revelation is the unveiling of what was sealed in the Book of Daniel. Therefore, when I turn to chapter 11 of the Book of the Revelation and see these things, I know that we are standing in the great and final judgment day of God. We are in the seventieth and last week of Daniel. We are in the heart of the Great Tribulation, and this is the elective purpose of God in purging the earth and bringing in a kingdom in which the Lord Christ shall reign forever and we shall be fellow-princes and fellow-heirs at His side.

The Great Interlude

As we interpret the vision we must be aware of one other thing. In each of these septenary series there is an interlude. There is an interlude between the sixth and the seventh seals. There is an interlude between the sixth and the seventh bowls, the vials of judgment. There is an interlude between the sixth and the seventh trumpets. The longest interlude is here between the sixth and the seventh trumpets. It begins with verse 1 of chapter 10 and continues to verse 13 of chapter 11. In that interlude this passage we have read is included. In our Bibles there is a chapter division in the middle of the passage, but when John wrote it he did not put a chapter division here. It is all one great vision and what we read in chapter 11 of the Book is a continuation of what we have read in chapter 10 of the Book.

Chapter 10 is the vision of the great and mighty angel that came down from heaven. He placed his right foot on the sea, he planted his left foot on the land, he raised his hand and swore by God that there should be delay no longer (time should be no longer) but that the hour had come when God shall take to Himself His great power and reign. The angel-representative of Christ had in his left hand a little book open, the same little book that was sealed. When the seals were broken, the forfeiture of this earth to Satan was redeemed, the mortgage lifted, and God, in Christ, took back to Himself that which was lost in our sin and transgression. As he held in his hand the title-deed to this universe, the angel swore by God, with his hand raised to heaven, not only that there would be no longer delay, but that the mystery of God should now be finished, the mystery of why God delays, why sin reigns, why the grave is never filled, why God delays His ultimate triumph. But God delays no longer, for at the time of the sounding of that one other trumpet the great mystery of God is finished and the title-deed to this universe that the mighty angel held in his hand is executed.

The glorious angel-representative then gave two commandments. First, he said to John: "You come and take this book and eat it. The inheritance is yours." And John, as a representative of all of us who look to God in faith, took the inheritance. It was sweet. It is indeed sweet to us, what God has purposed for us, giving us life everlasting, raising us from the dead, giving us an inheritance in heaven. The Book, indeed, is sweet.

This dramatic act on the part of John is typical of the prophets. The prophets acted out their prophecies. In Jeremiah 12, Jeremiah is described as going around Jerusalem with a yoke on his neck. He was prophesying that Judah should go into Babylonian captivity, and he carried a yoke on his neck. Hosea was commanded to marry a harlot, showing the harlotry, the idolatry, of the nation Judah.

Isaiah, for example, was commanded of God to name his little boy (who was not yet born) Mahershalalhashbaz (Isaiah 8:1-3). What a name! Mahershalalhashbaz. This was to depict an enemy coming for the prey. That is what his name means.

Thus the prophet John here begins to act out for the first time the prophecy that is made. He took the inheritance, he took what God intends for us, and he ate it. It was as sweet as honey. But it made his stomach as bitter as gall for, said the angel, "thou must prophesy before peoples and nations and tongues and kings" and "the things that you are to reveal are bitter." What God has in store for us is sweet, but between us and that inheritance is a dark, deep stream, and the things that are revealed are as bitter as death.

Then a chapter division separates this eleventh chapter. But it is a part of the same prophecy. That bitterness, what lies ahead, dark and tragic, is described in the first verses of this chapter eleven: "There was given me a reed like unto a rod: and the angel stood, saying, Rise, and measure the temple of God, and the altar, and them that worship therein."

THE REBUILT TEMPLE IN JERUSALEM

What temple is that, this temple of God? There are five temples in the Bible. First, Solomon's temple which was destroyed by Nebuchadnezzar in 587 B.C. Second, Zerubbabel's temple which was built after the captivity, and which was desecrated and pillaged and consecrated to Jupiter by Antiochus Ephiphenes in 168 B.C. Third, Herod's temple, rebuilt in lavish and gorgeous splendor, destroyed by Titus in A.D. 70. The fourth temple is this one we are discussing. The fifth temple (and one that I cannot understand) is a millennial temple described by Ezekiel in chapters 40 through 43 in his prophecy.

Concerning this fourth temple described in Revelation 11, John is commanded to ". . . Rise, and measure the temple of God, and the altar, and them that worship therein." This temple, the fourth in the above series, is the temple referred to in Daniel 9 when "that Prince," that Man of Sin, that ultimate anti-Christ, makes a covenant with the Jewish people, and Israel rebuilds the city and the temple. In the midst of that covenant, in the midst of the seventieth week, the terrible Prince breaks his promise; and even those who befriended Israel turn to wreak their vengeance upon the city, and it is trampled down for forty-two months, the Great Tribulation. It is the same temple Paul refers to in the second Thessalonian letter, chapter 2. He says there will come this ultimate time, after the apostasy, when that Man of Sin is revealed, the Son of Damnation, the Son of Perdition, the great and final anti-Christ, "who opposeth and exalteth himself above all that is called God or that is worshipped, so that he as God sitteth in the temple of God, shewing himself that he is God." ". . . Rise, and measure the temple of God, and the altar, and them that worship therein." That passage refers to the rebuilt temple of the Jew in Jerusalem.

The Return of the Jew to Palestine in Unbelief

God says the Jew is going back in unbelief (Ezekiel 36: 24, 25). The prophecies about the return are many. For two thousand years, there were practically no Jews in Palestine. Yet God's prophets had said thousands of years before that the Jews will go back. The Jew will rebuild Jerusalem and the same Jew will rebuild the temple. You may have been there and stood and looked on the Mosque of Omar, the Dome of the rock, the Mohammedan edifice of worship; remember that every stone of it, every piece of it, every mosaic of it, every part of it, will be cast down. In its place, on that sacred spot where Solomon built his temple, where Abraham offered up Isaac on Mt. Moriah, the Jew will rebuild a glorious temple unto God. The Lord called that reprobate temple (Herod's) "my Father's house," even the building by that Edomite, that Esau-man, Herod. In that same place will be a temple erected in the name of Jehovah God, and the institutions of Moses will be re-enacted, reinstituted.

It is hard for us to realize the deep, undying devotion of the Orthodox Jew to the Mosaic institutions through thousands of years. I was in Jerusalem a year after the Jews had captured a little spur of Mt. Zion, which they possess today, the only part of the old city in Jewish hands. They had turned that little space on Mt. Zion that contains David's tomb into a synagogue. I stood for a long time in that synagogue and watched those Orthodox Jews worship. Their devotion to the Torah, the Word of God, is beyond imagination. Those colorful old patriarchs with their long beards, their headdress, their robes, were deeply devout in their reverence for the Word of God. After the worship was over, they took the scroll, the Torah, the Law of Moses, and rolled it up. They kissed the pages as they rolled it up, and when the scroll was rolled, they kissed the clasps. When they had kissed the clasps in their places, they kissed the tassels. Then they kissed the container that held the scroll. Then they kissed all of it again. Then reverently and tenderly they laid it all in the sacred ark.

Those people have never been able to be engulfed by all of the Gentile nations in which they had lived. One of the great proofs that God is and that what the prophets said is true, is the Jew in the world today. God says that the Jew will go back to Palestine and God says he will rebuild that temple. In his rejection of Christ, in his unbelief, and in the rebuilding of that temple, the Jewish nation shall make friends with the political ruler of the world, the great and ultimate Man of Sin. But the supposed friend is to reveal his true self in the midst of that final week, when he shall break his covenant and when the Jewish people are to be trampled underfoot for three and one-half years. That portent is a part of the bitterness that John felt when he took the inheritance, the title-deed, which at first tasted sweet like honey, precious like heaven itself; then as he looked upon his people crushed in blood, in tears and in death and the whole Gentile world a sea of blasphemy, the vision became bitter.

"And there was given me a reed like unto a rod . . . saying . . . measure the temple of God." In Revelation 21:15, John sees the heavenly city measured with a golden reed, a golden measuring stick. But, ah, "There was given me a reed like unto a *rod*." Wherever in the Revelation that word "rod" is used, it refers to chastisement, to correction, to judgment. "There was given me a reed like unto a rod." And with that rod, John was commanded to measure the temple and the people. Let us turn to the Old Testament to see the significance of this command.

Many times you will find "a measuring" commanded of God. Such a commandment refers to one of two altogether different things. First, to measure was to claim for God. "Measure this; this belongs to God." "God acknowledges this." "Measure it; this is mine." Then again, to measure for God meant to devote things measured to correction, to judgment, to destruction.

In II Samuel 8, for example, God said, "Measure Joab for destruction." In Lamentations 2, God says, "Measure Jerusalem for destruction." Then in Amos the prophet saw a plumb line and was commanded: "Measure Judah and Israel for destruction." Both of those ideas of possession and of destruction are signified in this passage in the Revelation: "And there was given me a reed like unto a rod . . . and the angel stood, saying, Rise and measure . . . ." This measurement concerns the people of God who are to be measured for judgment and for correction. When the Jew turns his face toward the homeland and rebuilds his great city Jerusalem, when he rebuilds his temple and he reinstitutes the Mosaic institutions and rituals, he does so with great hope and anticipation. But John, in his vision, saw beyond those days of gladness and happiness. John saw the rod of the anger of God because of their unbelief, because of their rejection, because of their blasphemy against Christ, their Lord and Messiah, our Saviour and King. "There was given me a reed like unto a rod . . . and the city shall be trampled down forty and two months — the holy city."

THE CHASTISEMENT OF ALMIGHTY GOD

I conclude with a word concerning the chastisement of God. I am not speaking now of the fierce judgment of God upon the alien and the heathen. I am speaking from the Book, of the fierce chastisement of God upon His people, of that rod that lies in His hand by which He measures His own. In his day and time, Isaiah, the incomparable prophet, the poet-preacher, saw Ashurbanipal, Sargon, Sennacherib, Tiglath-pileser sweep down in turn from the north, from Assyria, from Nineveh and destroy Israel as a man would wipe a dish and turn it upside down. Isaiah witnessed the fall of Samaria and saw the wasting of the northern ten tribes.

Isaiah also saw the bitterness, the merciless cruelty, the heathenism and the blasphemy of those awful winged bulls of Ashur. He cried to the Lord God: "Lord, how is it? However thy inheritance may be in Israel and however they may have blasphemed, yet they are not as vile and as villainous, they are not as wicked and as wayward as these from Assyria. Lord, why is Israel destroyed at their wicked hands?" Then the Lord said to Isaiah: "Assyria is the rod of mine anger and the staff of mine indignation. They may be vile, and they are; they may be heathen, and they are; they may be blasphemous, and they are; but I have raised them up as the rod of mine anger and the staff of mine indignation for the correction and the judgment of my people Israel."

Nor is that instance unique. Long after the death of Isaiah, there stood up another prophet by the name of Habakkuk. Habakkuk described in the first chapter of his prophecy the coming of the Babylonian, that bitter and hasty Chaldean, whose countenance was terrible and dreadful. Under his besieging hand, the whole nation of Judah was destroyed. God's temple was razed to the ground and God's holy city was plowed under. Habakkuk, when he saw it by prophecy, cried unto the Lord and said: "Oh, God, thou art of purer eyes than to look upon evil and thou canst not bear iniquity; wherefore lookest thou upon them that deal treacherously and holdest thy tongue when the wicked devoureth a man that is more righteous than he?"

"We may be sinful," Habakkuk was saying in effect, "and Judah and Israel and Jerusalem and Thy holy temple may have been profaned; but O God, are we as vile and are we as evil as those Chaldeans who come to destroy us and to carry us into captivity and waste our people? Lord! Lord!"

When the Lord answered Habakkuk, the answer was this: "I have ordained them for judgment and I have established them for correction." The Babylonian may be more vile than the Judean, and the Babylonian temples may be dedicated to a thousand unnamable, unspeakable gods while this temple in Jerusalem is dedicated to the Lord Himself. "But I have raised them up because of the iniquities of my people," said God.

"They are ordained for judgment; I have established them for correction."

All this makes a man tremble in the presence of the mighty God. The Lord of the Revelation, of the Apocalypse, the Lord of Isaiah, the Lord of Habakkuk, the Lord of yesterday is the Lord of today. However God may have blessed and favored our beautiful land, yet if America does not turn to God and if there is not among our people a spirit of repentance and faith and prayer and holy worship, God can raise out of the heart of the vast expanse of Siberia, God can raise out of the five hundred millions of Red China a rod of correction and a staff of indignation. Out of the very skies so beautiful above us can fall lurid death.

It was after God had spoken that Habakkuk cried: "O Lord, I have heard thy speech and was afraid. O Lord, revive thy work in the midst of the years. In the midst of the years make it known, in wrath remember mercy." The beginning of wisdom is the fear of the Lord, to tremble before the imponderables in His mighty hand. If there was any salvation for Habakkuk's people it lay in a great turning back to God.

That was also the preaching of Jeremiah the prophet. "Return," said Jeremiah, "return, return." They did not turn and Nebuchadnezzar came in 605 B.C. Jeremiah cried again, saying, "Oh, return, repent." They did not repent. Nebuchadnezzar came in 598 B.C. Still Jeremiah preached, "Oh, let us turn back to God." They did not turn. Nebuchadnezzar came in 587 B.C. and he did not need to come back any more, for Judah was wasted. Her women were ravished. Her children were sold into captivity. Her holy city was destroyed and the temple lay in ruins. "O Lord, I have heard thy speech and was afraid. O Lord, revive thy work in the midst of the years. In the midst of the years make it known. In wrath remember mercy." If there is a destiny for our people, it lies in the imponderables of the Lord God.

God will not keep His anger forever. Forty-two months,

God says, but just forty-two months. "In wrath remember mercy." God is the salvation of His people. God is the hope of those who trust in Him according to the Book; dark days lie ahead, tears lie ahead, sorrows lie ahead. But beyond them is the glorious sunrising of the presence of our coming and living and reigning Lord. Blessed are they who place their trust in Him. Not only do we save ourselves when we turn to God, but we save the nation. It is God's people who save the families of the earth, whose arms are shielding the homes of this beautiful land. Why would a man debate within his heart whether or not to give himself to Jesus? Why would a man even enter into discussion as to whether or not he would lead his family to God? Infinitely blessed it is, through the hallowed holiness of the open door, to come, to bow, to look up into the face of the great God, our Saviour, and to ask His blessings upon house and home and child and family and nation.

CHAPTER 3

GOD'S TWO WITNESSES

Revelation 11

3. And I will give power unto my two witnesses, and they shall prophesy a thousand two hundred and threescore days, clothed in sackcloth.

4. These are the two olive trees, and the two candlesticks standing before the God of the earth.

5. And if any man will hurt them, fire proceedeth out of their mouth, and devoureth their enemies: and if any man will hurt them, he must in this manner be killed.

6. These have power to shut heaven, that it rain not in the days of their prophecy: and have power over waters to turn them to blood, and to smite the earth with all plagues, as often as they will.

7. And when they shall have finished their testimony, the beast that ascendeth out of the bottomless pit shall make war against them, and shall overcome them, and kill them.

8. And their dead bodies shall lie in the street of the great city, which spiritually is called Sodom and Egypt, where also our Lord was crucified.

9. And they of the people and kindreds and tongues and nations shall see their dead bodies three days and an half, and shall not suffer their dead bodies to be put in graves.

10. And they that dwell upon the earth shall rejoice over them, and make merry, and shall send gifts one to another; because these two prophets tormented them that dwelt on the earth.

11. And after three days and an half the Spirit of life from God entered into them, and they stood upon their feet; and great fear fell upon them which saw them.

12. And they heard a great voice from heaven saying unto them, Come up hither. And they ascended up to heaven in a cloud; and their enemies beheld them.

13. And the same hour was there a great earthquake, and the tenth part of the city fell, and in the earthquake were slain of

men seven thousand: and the remnant were affrighted, and gave glory to the God of heaven.

The first part of this sermon concerns the amazing delineation of these two witnesses. There is nothing like them in recorded history, secular or profane. Never were there two witnesses like these two. They have a capacity and a power beyond anything the world has ever seen, and God does with them what He has never done with any other prophet or speaker or preacher in the vast chronicles of time. They only are able (until their witness is finished and until the time comes for them to be martyred) to withstand the terrible inroads and persecutions and violent waste of the beast. They alone have that unusual gift and power to confront their enemies and to do it in triumph and victory. Of all the prophets and apostles and witnesses in recorded history, there are none like these — none.

Another extraordinary thing about this passage is that John does not see the two witnesses. Unlike the visions which John saw and of which he wrote in the Revelation, telling what he saw and heard, the two witnesses are described to John by the mighty angel who came down from heaven (Revelation 10) who lifted up his hand and in the name of the Lord Christ claimed all creation for God. It is that mighty angel-representative of Christ who describes these two witnesses. John does not see them.

THE AGES OF GRACE AND JUDGMENT

Another strange thing is that the witnesses lived in an altogether different age (era, time, or dispensation) from our own. There is nothing in their attitude and in their ministry congruent with this present Christian age of grace and mercy and love and forgiveness. Look at the text carefully. It says if any man (and the Greek word is *thello* — "wishes," "desires," "wants") — if any man *thello* to hurt them, "fire proceedeth out of their mouth and devoureth their enemies." And if any man (*thello* —again), if any man has a desire or even a will or a wish to hurt them, he must in that fiery manner be destroyed. These witnesses, says verse ten, torment the Christ-rejectors of the earth. How amazingly different from the example that our Lord gave and taught us in this age, in this dispensation! How astonishingly divergent from the example followed by His apostles and disciples!

Look at the Sermon on the Mount. From the fifth chapter of that message our Lord said: "If a man smite you on one cheek, turn the other. If a man compel you to go a mile, go with him twain. If he at law sues you for your coat, give him your cloak also. Bless those that curse you, do good to those that hate you and minister to those who despitefully use you." And the Apostle Paul reiterated that same spirit of love and grace toward our enemies. "My brethren beloved," he says, "avenge not yourselves but give place unto wrath. If thine enemy hunger, feed him. If he thirst, give him to drink."

That holy admonition was acted out in the ministry of our Lord and of His apostles. Our Saviour said, "I have seventy legions of angels at my command," but He refused to use them. Without resistance, He bowed His head before the awful blows of those who destroyed Him. He said, "I came not to destroy men's lives but to save them." When Stephen was stoned to death, he prayed for his enemies. James was beheaded by the sword; Paul and Silas were placed in the innermost dungeon; Polycarp was burned at the stake; Antipas was destroyed in death as a martyr of Christ. Not one of them resisted. But this eleventh chapter of the Revelation is a different world. Concerning these two witnesses of God, if an antagonist even desires to hurt them, wishes to harm or molest them, "fire proceedeth out of their mouth and devoureth their enemies."

This is as it was in the days of the old theocracy when Jereboam I built his golden idol-calf at Bethel. There came from Judah an unnamed prophet of God who denounced the idolatry, and as he was denouncing it, Jeroboam, the king, put forth his right hand to seize the prophet and when he did so his right hand withered. He could not draw it back.

A like thing happened in the days of Elijah the Tishbite. Ahaziah, the son of Ahab and Jezebel, succeeded to the kingdom and proposed to arrest Elijah, the man of God. When they sent the captain of a band of fifty to take Elijah, Elijah commanded fire to fall down from heaven, and it burned up the captain and his fifty soldiers. The eleventh chapter of Revelation describes that kind of a world. It is that kind of an age. It is that kind of a dispensation in which these two witnesses represent God.

When we carefully study the Holy Scriptures, we find both judgment and mercy emphasized in the ministry of Christ. We find them as inevitable corollaries, concomitants, repercussions of the work of Jesus. The two great chapters in the Book of the Psalms that describe the passion and suffering of Christ are Psalms 22 and 69. Both of those psalms are framed exactly alike. The first part of both of them describes the suffering of Jesus. Then beginning at verse 22 in both psalms, there are described the results of the suffering of our Saviour, but the results are diametrically opposite. In Psalm 22, from which psalm the gospel writers quote as they describe the crucifixion of our Lord, after the description of the sufferings of Jesus there follows, beginning at verse 22, verse after verse after verse describing the goodness and grace and mercy and forgiveness and blessing and the praise that flow from the wounds of our Lord. People are saved, people praise God, people are preaching the Gospel to the ends of the earth, "And they shall declare his righteousness to a people that shall yet be born that Jesus hath done this." What a marvelous and beautiful and precious thing, these gifts that flow from the wounds and tears and blood of Jesus!

But in Psalm 69 beginning at verse 22, oh, the judgment and the vengeance and the reckoning of the wrath of God against those who spurn His Son and who wounded the Lord's anointed and who destroyed Christ, God's Messiah! There is a decided contrast. Psalm 69:21, "They gave me gall for my meat; and in my thirst they gave me vinegar to drink." The first part of the psalm describes the suffering of Christ and is quoted in the gospels. Now, look at verse 22: "Let their table become a snare before them . . ."; verse 23, "Let their eyes be darkened, that they see not . . ."; verse 24, "Pour out thine indignation upon them, and let thy wrathful anger take hold of them . . ."; verse 27, "Add iniquity unto their iniquity: and let them not come into thy righteousness . . ."; verse 28, "Let them be blotted out of the book of the living, and not be written with the righteous." And on and on and on.

These two psalms represent the double corollary that follows the preaching of the Gospel of the Son of God and that follows what Christ has done in this earth. This day and this age in which we now live is full of invitation and mercy and forgiveness. "Come, come to Jesus," says the Holy Spirit of grace. If a man says, "No, I despise the Lord," and "No, I'll not give Him the devotion of my heart and the love of my soul," he can walk out the door with impunity. There will be no judgment upon him. There will be no wrath. There will be no fire to burn and consume. He can walk right out the door and down the street, unmolested and unharmed. That is now. That is the day of grace in which we live. This is the hour of the Lord's love and mercy.

But, oh, my soul, there is coming another day, there is coming another hour, there is coming another age, there is coming another dispensation and in that day and that hour and that dispensation, the wrath and the judgment of Almighty God will confront every Christ-rejecting sinner. That is what is described here in the days of these two witnesses. Theirs is the hour of judgment. Theirs is the hour of God's cleansing and purging His earth. Theirs is an hour when men shall face the day of the awful wrath of Almighty God. Oh, how our souls tremble when we read such things! Ah, Lord, for these who say "No" to the preacher, "No" to the invitation, "No" to the spirit of grace, who tread underfoot the blood of the covenant wherewith He was sanctified as though it were an unholy thing, who despise all God has done to reach our sinful and lost souls — oh, the judgment that lies ahead! Our souls tremble in the presence of the Lord. That day is the day of the wrath and the judgment of Almighty God.

THE IDENTIFICATION OF THE TWO WITNESSES

Another startling thing about these two witnesses: With all that is said about them, unlike any other that God has raised up in the annals of history, they are unnamed. We do not know who they are. And how the expositors and interpreters of the Book have tried to identify them! Many times interpreters will say these two witnesses are Enoch and Elijah. They base that identification upon one verse in Hebrews 9:27. It begins with these words: "And as it is appointed unto men once to die, but after this the judgment." So these interpreters look through the Bible and find two men who never died, Enoch and Elijah. They were translated to heaven without death. Since these two witnesses in Revelation 11 are slain by the beast, these expositors conclude that these two witnesses are Enoch and Elijah, sent back to earth, who are slain and therefore fulfill that Scripture in Hebrews 9:27 that all men must die. That is a very weak identification because, to begin with, all men are not going to die. The passage in Hebrews 9:27 is a generalization. All mankind, as they live their lives, fall into the grave. That is true. But, there is going to be one generation that will never taste death. We who are alive and remain until the coming of the Lord shall be caught up together in the clouds along with those resurrected to be ever with the Lord. Or, as Paul said again in I Corinthians 15:51 and 52: ". . . We shall not all sleep [we shall not all fall into death], but we shall all be changed. In a moment, in the twinkling of an eye, at the last trump." So we are not all going to die. To base an interpretation upon that Scripture as identifying these witnesses with Enoch and Elijah is not quite according to the Word of the Lord.

Notice another thing about the witnesses: Their miracles are according to the power of Moses and Elijah. "These have power to shut heaven, that it rain not in the days of their prophecy." That sounds like Elijah. ". . . and they have power over waters to turn them to blood, and to smite the earth with all plagues . . . ." That sounds like Moses.

Beyond the suggested identification of Enoch and Elijah or Moses and Elijah, oh, the maze of the suggestions and hypotheses and theories and endless identifications! For example, if you are a spiritualizer, you will read that passage and you will say those two great witnesses are the Old Testament and the New Testament. If you are a historical interpreter of this Revelation, you will try to say those two witnesses were the Waldenses and the Albigenses. Or, you might say they are John Huss and Jerome of Prague. So imagination goes on and identification runs riot. The simple truth is, there is no man who knows who those two witnesses are. We do not know and we shall never know until we see them, until they come into this earth.

I have only one suggestion to make about their identification and it is this: from every syllable that is written here in the Word, I would think they are men, they are persons. For example: "I will give power unto my two witnesses." The word for witness is "martyr," in Greek *martus*. Those who witnessed for God so often sealed their witness with their blood that finally the word came to mean in English "one who is martyred for God," "a martyr." The Greek word *martus* (martyr) referred to one who witnesses for God, who stands up to testify for the Lord. Now, that word is used ten times in the New Testament, and the corollary Hebrew word is used fifty times in the Old Testament; and in every instance it refers to a person. He is a martyr, a *martus*, a witness. Without exception, every time it is used it is personal.

The same thing is true of *prophetuo*. "And they shall *prophetuo* a thousand two hundred and threescore days." They shall prophesy. That word is used more than a hundred times in the Bible, and without exception every time (except one, in metonomy), it refers to a person. Somebody prophesies. Again in that same verse, the witnesses are described as clothed in sackcloth. To be clothed in sackcloth is often mentioned in the Bible, and always the reference is to a person. It would be hard to see an impersonal object or instrument, like a Bible, clothed in sackcloth. Undoubtedly the two witnesses are people. They are the witnesses of God. We do not know who they are. We shall have to wait and see.

THEIR ASCENSION INTO HEAVEN

Another peculiarity about them is that their resurrection and their ascension are beheld by the people of this earth. Now, it is not an extraordinary thing that they should be raised from the dead. Our Lord was raised from the dead. The saints of the Old Testament who were buried around Jerusalem were raised from the dead after Christ's resurrection. One of these days all of us shall be raised from the dead. That is not strange — not according to the Word of God. But what is unusual is this: this is the only instance where such a thing is ever wrought before mortal, human eye, where enemies and people looked upon it.

When our Lord was raised from the dead, no mortal eye saw Him. There is no hint that this world will see the saints in our translation. When we are caught up into glory, when we are raptured to heaven, there is no other presentation in the Bible but that it is secretly done. The Lord comes like a thief to steal away His pearl of price, His jewels in the earth, those who are to shine in the diadem of His crown. Two working in a mill, one taken and the other left. Two sleeping in a bed, one taken and the other left. Two working in a field, one taken and the other left. In a moment, in the twinkling of an eye, at the last trump, it is done suddenly, furtively, secretly, quietly. It is done immediately, faster than the recognition of an eye. But here in the case of these two witnesses, the resurrection and ascension occur openly and boldly and emphatically. The eleventh verse says that they saw them when they were raised from the dead. This twelfth verse says: "And when they ascended up to heaven . . . their enemies beheld them."

There is another unusual thing here. The King James Version reads: ". . . they ascended up to heaven in a cloud." The Greek is very emphatic concerning that cloud. "They ascended up to heaven [*en te nephele*] in the cloud [a designated vehicle of God]." The Lord sent His golden chariot down for them, the Shekinah glory of heaven, and they were caught up before the gaze of men, an astonishing and amazing thing.

Then another and a last observation: all of this narrative is proleptic, it is anticipative. It is before the time. "And when they shall have finished their testimony, the beast that ariseth out of the bottomless pit shall . . . overcome them, and slay them." The beast does not appear until the thirteenth chapter of the Revelation and we are here at the beginning of the eleventh. This points to the importance with which the Lord surrounds the story of the testimony of these two unnamed servants of God. Their witness covers the entire great tribulation period, the last three and a half years; yet in the unfolding of the Revelation we have not even come to that time period. The Lord took out of the great and final judgment of this earth the story of the witness of those two servants and He wrote it beforehand. The Lord set them beforehand. The Lord set them forth in an amazing description of glory and unction and power before the gaze of the world.

What does it mean? The answer is the message of the next chapter. May the Lord bless it to us as we search the Holy Word, as we read these sacred Scriptures, and as God shall speak to our hearts His message for our day, for our time, and what we are to expect when He pulls aside the veil of the future. Ah, Lord, that we might be ready, our souls prepared whether it is today or this evening, whether in the morning's dawn or at the end of the night, whether now or a thousand years from now. As God knows my heart, Lord so come, so come. Amen.

CHAPTER 4

THE TWO OLIVE TREES AND THE TWO LAMPSTANDS

Revelation 11

3. And I will give power unto my two witnesses, and they shall prophesy a thousand two hundred and threescore days, clothed in sackcloth.

4. These are the two olive trees, and the two candlesticks standing before the God of the earth.

5. And if any man will hurt them, fire proceedeth out of their mouth, and devoureth their enemies: and if any man will hurt them, he must in this manner be killed.

6. These have power to shut heaven, that it rain not in the days of their prophecy: and have power over waters to turn them to blood, and to smite the earth with all plagues, as often as they will.

7. And when they shall have finished their testimony, the beast that ascendeth out of the bottomless pit shall make war against them, and shall overcome them, and kill them.

8. And their dead bodies shall lie in the street of the great city, which spiritually is called Sodom and Egypt, where also our Lord was crucified.

9. And they of the people and kindreds and tongues and nations shall see their dead bodies three days and an half, and shall not suffer their dead bodies to be put in graves.

10. And they that dwell upon the earth shall rejoice over them, and make merry, and shall send gifts one to another; because these two prophets tormented them that dwelt on the earth.

11. And after three days and an half the Spirit of life from God entered into them, and they stood upon their feet; and great fear fell upon them which saw them.

12. And they heard a great voice from heaven saying unto them, Come up hither. And they ascended up to heaven in a cloud; and their enemies beheld them.

13. And the same hour was there a great earthquake, and the

tenth part of the city fell, and in the earthquake were slain of men seven thousand: and the remnant were affrighted, and gave glory to the God of heaven.

This message is the second part, the conclusion, of the sermon begun in the previous chapter. It concerns one of the most difficult passages in the Bible and certainly one of the most difficult in the Apocalypse. These two witnesses are unlike anything to be found in the record of mankind. Not in all the pages of history is there anything like them. The invincible, impregnable power by which they testify to the truth of God is astonishing. What happened to them is no less amazing. Now we come to speak of what they represent.

First of all, as they stand to speak, to witness, to testify, to *prophetuo*, to prophesy, they are clothed in sackcloth. Sackcloth, as you know, is a heavy, coarse garment woven out of camel's hair or mohair. It was worn by the ancients as a sign of sorrow and great mourning. When these two witnesses, therefore, stand clothed in sackcloth, they become a symbol of national, worldwide, personal mourning. The day is evil and the times are filled with sorrow. Sackcloth.

Jacob put on sackcloth when his sons came and said that their brother, Joseph, had been slain by wild beasts. "For," they asked, "is not this his coat of many colors?" They had dipped it in goat's blood. When Israel looked upon the beautiful coat, stained with blood, he rent his own garments and put on sackcloth in personal sorrow and mourning over what supposedly was the death of his boy.

When David heard of the cruel murder of Abner, the captain of the host, he rent his garments and put on sackcloth, mourning over Abner.

In the terrible famine in Samaria, two mothers had agreed that on one day the first mother would boil her son and they would eat him; then when that child was devoured, they would boil the other woman's son and eat him. But one of the mothers hid her son when the first baby was eaten, and in their altercation they had brought their quarrel to the king of Samaria. In desperation, in the terrible famine, the king was seen walking along on the top of the wall; and as he rent his clothes in unspeakable sorrow, the people looked and saw that he wore a garment of sackcloth underneath.

When Sennacherib, the astute and able military genius of the winged Bull of Asher, swept down and carried away Northern Israel, he then placed his armies around Jerusalem as a man would hold a piece of iron in a vice. In blasphemous language the Assyrian called upon Hezekiah to capitulate. Hezekiah with heavy heart went up into the house of the Lord clothed in sackcloth to beseech the help of God. When Daniel came to confess the sins of Judah, he came clothed in sackcloth. So in this passage in Revelation, chapter 11, the days are filled with sorrow, the times are evil and the nations are blaspheming God; and these two witnesses stand in sackcloth to declare the judgment of the Almighty.

THE LIGHT IN A DARK PLACE

This would be an indescribable scene of misery, agony and despair were it not for the elective purpose of God in human history. The next verse speaks of the sovereign will of the Lord revealed to us who ask for hope in our sorrow and in our tears. "These," says the Holy Scriptures, "are the two olive trees and the two lampstands standing before the God of the whole earth."

Let us turn back to see what the two olive trees and the two lampstands were. We read of them in the vision of the prophet Zechariah. Zechariah is the prophet of the restoration, of the new hope, of the new world, of the new day. In his vision in chapter three, he sees Joshua, the high priest, standing before the angel of the Lord, and Satan standing at his right hand to resist him. Joshua is clothed with filthy garments, signifying that although a high priest, he is still mortal, still sinful, still depraved. Satan is there to point out to the Almighty the

depravity in the High Priest's heart, the sin in his life, emphasizing the filthy garments with which he is clothed as he feigns
to serve God. But the Lord said to His angel, "Take away
the filthy garments from him and give him a change of raiment,
pure and spotless." So God elects Joshua, the high priest, to stand
before Him as the cleansed and forgiven minister in a new
temple that is to be built, with a new Israel that is coming back
home and with a new Judah, out of whose loins Christ shall
be born. In the vision of Zechariah, he is one of the lampstands,
representing spiritual worship.

In the next chapter of Zechariah is outlined the second
lampstand, that of national, civil obedience. The angel said,
"What do you see?" Zechaiah said, "I see a candelabra, a seven-
branched lampstand, with all of its conduits and its multitudinous burners and by their side, one on the other, I see olive
trees." An olive tree on one side and an olive tree on the other
side. The oil pours from the olive trees into the lampstands,
into the candelabra. The prophet said, "Lord, what does that
mean?" And the Lord said, "This is the word of God to Zerubbabel, Not by power nor by might, but by my burning Spirit,
saith the Lord of hosts." For further clarification, the prophet
asked, "Then, Lord, what are the two olive trees on either side?"
And the Lord answered him and said: "These are the two
anointed ones that stand by the Lord of the whole earth. This
one is Joshua and this one is Zerubbabel. They are my ministers and my witnesses in the day of the great restoration."

When I read, therefore, in the Revelation that these two
witnesses are the two olive trees and the two lampstands, immediately I know what God is doing. God is in the midst of the
great, final restoration, as illustrated by the restoration of Judah
in the days of the two witnesses, Joshua and Zerubbabel. Notice
here in the Revelation that the candelabra is gone, the multitudinous burners are gone. Only two lampstands remain. Notice that these two witnesses are not "stars." "Stars" are the
preachers of Christ, the ministers in His churches. The can-

delabra is gone, the seven-branched golden lampstand is gone, the churches are gone, the pastors are gone; but these two, the olive trees of God and the two lampstands of the Lord, are the remaining messengers of God in the great, ultimate restoration pictured in the prophecy of Zechariah. God has purposed for His people a great inheritance. He is preparing a better thing for us, a new heaven, a new earth, a new and holy city. Even in these days of terrible judgment, the Lord is preparing for that final victory; and its announcement, its harbinger, are these two lampstands, these two lights from God. They are hailed with holy anointing from above as they testify to the work and truth of the Lord among mankind. All the earth hears their voice as they deliver God's message to the whole human race.

What a merciful, providential kindness God has shown here once more! The two witnesses are called "my two martyrs." The Greek word, as you know, for witness is *martus*. So often did the witness lay down his life rather than recant, and so often did he seal his testimony with his blood, that the English language took the Greek word for witness, *martus,* and made it mean someone who laid down his life in defense of the faith. God sent these two witnesses to warn the earth of the judgments by which He shall clear this whole planet of unrighteousness and wrong and sin. These two witnesses stand to declare the judgment purposes of God to Christ-rejecting sinners.

In His mercy, God always warns before He destroys. Before the Lord destroyed this earth by water, He raised up Enoch and He raised up Noah, preachers of righteousness, to warn the people of judgments to come. Before the Lord destroyed Pharaoh and his armies, He sent Moses to witness, to testify. Before God would destroy Nineveh, He sent Jonah. Thank God, Nineveh in that day turned and repented, but the message of Jonah was one of judgment. John the Baptist was sent to warn Judah that the Lord then stood to lay the axe at the root of the tree. The Lord Himself warned of the impending destruction of Jerusalem. The apostles spoke to the

Roman Empire lest it come under the avenging hand of Almighty God. So it is here, in the mercy of the Lord. God always sends the prophet, the witness, the preacher, lest a man fall into perdition and damnation without first being warned from heaven. The mercy of God is seen in these two witnesses.

God set them there, the two lampstands and the two olive trees, that they might confirm one another in the faith of the Lord. There were two angels who testified to the resurrection of our Saviour, the Lord Jesus. There were two men in white who testified of His ascension into heaven. By the law, and referred to in the eighteenth chapter of Matthew in the gospel, there must always be two witnesses to confirm the truth. Thus the Lord often sends His messengers of truth two by two. There are Moses and Aaron; Joshua and Caleb: Zerubbabel and Joshua; Peter and John; Paul and Silas; and Timothy and Titus. When the Lord sent out His twelve apostles, He did it two by two. When the Lord sent out the Seventy, He sent them out two by two. So God confirms the testimony of His truth by declaring it through His two witnesses.

The Invincible Servants of God

Notice that they are invincible until they have finished their testimony. I believe that in the purposes and in the sovereignty of God every man is invincible until his testimony is finished. I do not mean by that that every man shall live to be as old as Abraham or even as old as Moses. But I do say, according to the Word of the Lord, that our lives are kept in the secure, omnipotent hands of God until our work is done and our task is finished. Some of the mightiest of all of the ministries that have blessed mankind have been very brief. John the Baptist ministered, at the most, three years. Our Lord Jesus ministered, at the most, three and a half years. David Brainerd died when he was twenty-nine years old. Robert Murray McCheyne died when he was twenty-nine years old. Henry Martin died when he was thirty-one. F. W. Robertson, the incomparable preacher of Brighton, died when he was thirty-seven. The promise of God does not mean that the ministry be long and extended. But it does mean that we are invincible and immortal until our testimony is finished. When a man is in the will of God and when he is doing God's work, when he is delivering God's message, God stands by him to strengthen him and to uphold him. God's man does not need to worry about tragic accidents; he does not need to think about death. He does not need to worry or be anxious about himself. God takes care of His servants while His Spirit burns in their hearts as true and faithful witnesses. So these, even in the days of the terrible Beast, these alone in the earth were invincible to harm until their testimony was finished. Then they laid down their lives.

Oh, this evil world! When the Beast slew these two witnesses, he suffered not their bodies to be buried. The whole earth looked upon their corpses for three and a half days. A corpse decomposes quickly in a tropical climate. Central American nations have laws that on the day that one dies he must be buried. Can you imagine the insult, can you imagine the ignominy, can you imagine the indescribable shame as these two mighty prophets of God lay in the streets of the great city, as they turned to corruption and decay? According to the law in Deuteronomy, even the worst of criminals must be buried the day he is executed. When the Lord Jesus was nailed to the cross and bowed His head and died, friends went to Pontius Pilate, the Roman procurator, and asked that His body might be taken down that very hour and buried out of sight lest the land be defiled.

So evil is this time that the murderers send gifts to one another because these two prophets, warning of the judgment to come, are dead. Not long ago I was reading the life of John Huss, the great preacher of the Reformation. In the little town of Constance, the Roman Church burned him at the stake. That night the Council met in a jubilee celebration as over the defeat of mortal enemies because one of God's great witnesses, one of God's mighty preachers, had been burned at the stake. What evil days! Thus here in the Apocalypse these Christ-rejecters made merry and rejoiced and gave gifts to one another because God's two prophets lay out in the street, dead and unburied. But there is always a second chapter, there is always another sentence — always. However apparent the triumph of evil in this world, above and over and beyond there is a sovereign God who reigns; and the issues of life and of death are in His hands, and the imponderables of national destiny pertain to Him.

The Lord God looked down from heaven and saw the rejoicing of that evil world over the slaughter of His two witnesses; and the Lord breathed life into their dead and decaying bodies and they stood on their feet, "and their enemies saw them." These same enemies also heard the voice from heaven saying, "Come up hither." They saw the witnesses ascend into glory in the cloud, in the Shekinah brilliance and burning of the presence of Almighty God. There is in that scene a pattern that runs throughout the Word of the Lord: "Every eye shall see him and they also who pierced him." "And all the families of the earth shall wail because of him." "For the day shall come," says Paul, "when every tongue shall confess and every knee shall bow before Christ, the Lord God of this universe." "And their enemies beheld them."

False and True Repentance

The story continues with these words in verse 13: "And the same hour was there a great earthquake, and the tenth part of the city fell, and in the earthquake were slain of men seven thousand: and the remnant were affrighted, and gave glory to the God of heaven." In that terrible earthquake judgment, seven thousand *onomata anthropon*, "men of name," seven thousand "men of distinction" were slain. I do not know what that ultimately refers to, but seven thousand of the mightiest men of this earth, fleeing when God took this planet and shook it from center to circumference, were killed. The same verse says that in that awful hour of judgment, men gave glory to the God of heaven. In their fears, in their affright, in their terror, they gave glory to the God of heaven, but at a distance, out of temporary fear, not out of conversion. How different from the man who feels the regenerating spirit of the Lord Christ in his soul, when he repents and changes! In the next chapter these same men are blaspheming the Lord again. There they are persecuting and murdering God's servants again. But here in fear they are giving glory to God during this transient moment. After the terror passes, they return to the old life of rejection.

This is one of the most sorrowful experiences that I have in my ministry. I will go see a man who has been through a great fear. The doctor says to him that he is going to die. "I'll give you two more days or maybe a week," he says, "but you are going to die. You have had a severe coronary and you are going to die." I will then go to see him and talk with him and pray with him. He will say to me: "I'll give my life to God. Oh, I have wasted my life. I'm going to be a different man when I get up." In the providence of God, in the goodness of the Lord, I have seen the man get up and be strong again. Then, when I expect him down the aisle to give his life to God, why, he is as far away as he was before. He has forgotten his vow. When I say words of remembrance to him, he extenuates and excuses.

This kind of religion will not save. Just to be afraid of God will not do. Just to be terrified before the judgment will not avail for salvation. The change has to be in your soul, a love for the Lord. True, personal devotion to Christ will last forever. It will make a new man, it will make a new woman, it will make a new home, it will create a new destiny, it will create a new life. It has to be in the soul, in the heart, serving

God for the love of Him, for the grace of Him, for the mercy of Him, for the kind remembrance of our loving Lord, serving Jesus for Jesus' sake. Not because I am fearful or terrified, but because I have love for God in my soul. That is what it is to be saved, to be a Christian.

Chapter 5

THE SOUNDING OF THE LAST TRUMPET

Revelation 11

14. The second woe is past, and, behold, the third woe cometh quickly.

15. And the seventh angel sounded; and there were great voices in heaven, saying, The kingdoms of this world are become the kingdoms of our Lord, and of his Christ; and he shall reign for ever and ever.

16. And the four and twenty elders, which sat before God on their seats, fell upon their faces, and worshipped God,

17. Saying, We give thee thanks, O Lord God Almighty, which art, and wast, and art to come; because thou hast taken to thee thy great power, and hast reigned.

18. And the nations were angry and thy wrath is come, and the time of the dead, that they should be judged, and that thou shouldest give reward unto thy servants the prophets and to the saints, and them that fear thy name, small and great; and shouldest destroy them which destroy the earth.

19. And the temple of God was opened in heaven, and there was seen in his temple the ark of his testament; and there were lightnings, and voices, and thunderings, and an earthquake, and great hail.

In the last message we left off at verse 13 of the eleventh chapter of the Book of the Revelation. In this sermon we begin with verse 14 and follow the passage to the end of the chapter. The verses present a proleptic synopsis of the ultimate work of God in the earth. This is the great climacteric toward which all the elective purposes of God inevitably and inexorably move. In the tenth chapter of the Revelation, John

54

saw the vision of a cloud-robed angel coming down from heaven; and as he stood with one foot on the sea and one foot on the earth, he raised his hand toward heaven and swore by God that liveth forever and ever, that there should be delay no longer. "In the days of the voice of the seventh angel, when he shall begin to sound, the mystery of God shall be finished in the earth." We know from this verse in Revelation 10:7 that the sounding of the seventh trumpet is not one shrill blast, over in a moment, but rather "in the days of the voice of the seventh angel, when he shall begin to sound, the mystery shall be finished." So, this occurrence comprises a period of time: "the days of the voice of the seventh angel." The seventh angel and his sounding and all of the repercussions that follow thereafter constitute the entire program and judgment of God until the final, completed redemption, until the creation of the new heaven and the new earth.

Chapters 12-22, the second half of the Book of the Revelation, are, therefore, a delineation of what has taken place in synoptic form here in the passage we have just read. Chapters 12-22 are but an *exergasia,* a further explanation, of Revelation 11:13-18. The passage embraces everything involved in the completion of the whole mystery of God. It overspans everything this side of the completed redemption. The vintage and the harvest of the earth: the pouring out of the seven last bowls of the wrath and the judgment of God; the great final battle of Armageddon; the personal appearing of the Lord Christ and the establishment of His kingdom in the earth; the great final white throne judgment of the dead; the re-creation of heaven and earth and the descent of the new Jerusalem, our final and ultimate home, into this re-created earth: all of these things in their wonders and in their stupendous, miraculous, marvelous proportions, are encompassed in the days of the voice of this seventh and last angel.

THE MIGHTY VOICES OF JUDGMENT

We shall follow the text as it is written here in the Book: "And the seventh angel sounded; and there were great voices in heaven . . . ." As we turn through the following chapters how many times is that reference to the voices reiterated — ". . . and there was a great voice out of the heavens which said . . ."; ". . . and a great voice out of the temple which announced . . ." ". . . and there were voices . . ." For example, in the fourteenth chapter, in the second verse; "And I heard a voice from heaven, as the voice of many waters . . . and I heard the voice of harpers harping with their harps . . . ." They then sang a glorious song of victory and triumph unto God.

In that same chapter, there is a voice of a great angel flying through the midst of heaven with the everlasting gospel to preach to those that dwell on the earth. Also, in the chapter there is the voice of a mighty angel crying the fall of Babylon, great Babylon. Again in that chapter there is the voice of an angel out of the temple crying to the Lord of the harvest saying, "Thrust in thy sickle, and reap . . . for the earth is ripe to the gathering." When we turn to the sixteenth chapter, for example, there is heard a great voice out of the temple saying to the seven angels, "Go forth and pour out the vials of the wrath and judgment of God upon the earth." In that same chapter there is heard the voice of those who cry, "It is done, it is done. And there were voices, and thunders, and lightnings and a great mighty earthquake."

So we are entering here the final agony of the earth, its travail, its pain, its suffering and its judgment in the hands of a furious and wrathful God. When I read or listen to soft, easy sermons concerning the Judgment Day, I do not understand whence the preacher derives the message. The revelation of God in this Book from beginning to end is always the announcement that there is a final day coming in which God shall deal with this world in wrath, when His judgment shall fall upon sin, unbelief, rejection and unrighteousness. "For," as the eloquent preacher of the Book of Hebrews said, "It is a fearful thing to fall into the hands of the living God . . . for our God is a consuming fire." "He shall burn up the chaff with unquenchable fire," said John the Baptist. Oh, these men in soft clothing and in philosophers' chairs and in polished pulpits, who speak in easy delectable sentences when God says that there are thunderings and lightnings and judgments and unquenchable fire! Oh, that we might be warned and listen to the whole counsels of God!

"And the seventh angel sounded, and there were mighty voices from heaven announcing judgment and triumph for the Almighty and these great voices said, The kingdom of this world [singular, as John wrote it — *he hasileia*, 'the kingdom,' 'the sovereignty' of this world] is become [singular, *egeneto*] the kingdom of our Lord and of his Christ, and he shall reign for ever and ever." Is not that a remarkable conception? When we think of this world, we multiply the kingdoms, here, here, here, and there, there, there, on the map and on the globe, all the way around. But when God looks at it from the standpoint of eternity, there is one kingdom in this world, and it is presided over by a prince-ruler.

You meet that conception of Satan's sovereignty again and again in the Scriptures. It is not just a unique, solitary idea here; it is found throughout the whole Word of God. When Satan took Jesus to the top of the great, high mountain and showed Him all the kingdoms of the world and their glory, he said, "All this will I give thee if thou wilt bow down and worship me." All the glory of all the kingdoms of the world, Satan offered Christ. If Satan did not possess it to offer, it was no temptation. How could it be a temptation to Jesus if it were not Satan's to command? Satan said, "It is mine, it is mine, and all of it will I give unto thee if thou wilt bow down and worship me."

In the second letter to the Corinthians, chapter 4 verse 4,

Paul refers to the god of this world as Satan. When we read the Bible, we find that the portrayal of the governments of this world are in terms of vicious, savage, wild beasts.

That imagery is uniform through the whole Scripture. Take one instance in the seventh chapter of the prophecy of Daniel. Daniel sees four great beasts come out of the seething, restless mass of humanity. The first is like a lion with eagle's wings. "And he beheld another beast like a bear and as it raised itself on its side, there were three ribs in his mouth between his teeth. And the third beast was like a leopard which had four wings and four heads. The last, the fourth beast, was dreadful and terrible, and it had great iron teeth and it devoured and brake in pieces."

As God in His righteousness, from the third heaven, from the heaven of heavens, looks down into this earth, there is a sovereignty here, there is a kingdom here, and it is a kingdom of death and of darkness. As God looks down into this earth, He sees endless cemeteries. This whole planet is none other thing than a place in which to bury people, people created in the image of the Lord God Almighty, made in the likeness of the Lord. This earth is full of death and the dead. There are iniquity, darkness, unrighteousness, violence and savagery everywhere. If a kingdom revolts, after the revolution, it is not greatly changed. The revolutionary regime in Soviet Russia today is as vile and as wicked as it was in the days of the Czars. The revolutionary regime in Red China today is as bloody and as terrible as it was in the days of any of the dynasties before. However the sick man may turn in his bed, he is in the same agony.

That is God's delineation of this earth and of this world. There is here a kingdom and it is presided over by the prince of the power of the air and by the powers of darkness. But God says not forever will sin rule in this earth; not forever will Satan reign unchallenged; not forever will the grave open its arms to receive God's people; and not forever will they dig in the earth to plant His children in the heart of the ground.

There is coming a day, says the Lord God, when death will be no more and sin will be no more and Satan will be no more. There will be a day when these are cast out, for, says this great voice from heaven, the kingdom, the sovereignty, the authority of the kingdom of this world is become the kingdom of our Lord and of His Christ and He shall reign for ever and ever, world without end. What an announcement! What an amazing announcement!

THE PRAISE OF THE FOUR AND TWENTY ELDERS

The scenes that follow this announcement are in keeping with that glorious, triumphant promise. The immediate verses describe the response of the twenty-four elders. The four and twenty elders represent God's resurrected, immortalized, raptured, taken away, transfigured saints in heaven. The four and twenty elders fell down upon their faces and worshiped God. It is the only place in the Bible where we will find that clause, "and they fell on their faces." In the fifth chapter of the Revelation, for example, these four and twenty elders, God's sainted, resurrected children, fall down and worship Him. But at the announcement of this amazing and heavenly promise, "they fall upon their faces." Then is heard their prayer of thanksgiving. ". . . we give thanks unto thee, O Lord God [*pontokrator*] Almighty, who art and wast . . . ."

Look closely at this Greek text. Some scribe came along as he copied the Bible and remembering that in Revelation 1:4 and Revelation 1:8, it was "the Lord who was and is and is to come [*ho erchomenos,* 'the one coming']," and thinking that John did not know what he was talking about, thinking that John left out the last part, the scribe put in here "[*ho erchomenos*] the one that is coming." Herein is a little instance of the inspiration of every syllable and every word of God, for in this passage the Lord has already come, He is here at the sounding of the voice of the seventh trumpet. "O Lord God who art and wast . . . ." Not the One who is coming, but rather the One who is already here.

The Lord here! Is not that an amazing thing that you and I shall live to see a day when the Lord God in presence, in personal appearance, in actuality, will be here and we shall look upon Him? It is beyond human power to comprehend that these mortal eyes should ever see God, and that this dull, squalid world should ever vibrate to the bright glory of the presence of the Almighty. Such has been the faith taught in the Book from the beginning; it is not just an opinion voiced by someone. "Yea," said Job, "though worms through my skin destroy this body, yet in my flesh shall I see God, whom mine eyes shall behold." We, creatures of the dust, worms of this earth, moving toward the grave, shall live in that hour, and in that day see God, "Who is," who is present, the Lord God Almighty.

The words of praise of the four and twenty elders continue: "Thou hast taken to thee thy great power and hast reigned. And the nations of the earth were angry . . . ." The nations are described as being savage and full of iniquity and sin, full of violence and wars. If they are not in war, then they are getting ready for war, beating their ploughshares into swords, sharpening their implements for destruction. The text continues: "Thy judgment is come and the time of the dead that they should be judged." When a man dies, that is not the end. Even the wicked dead shall be raised at the great, final white throne judgment, and God shall judge them according to their works and send them away into darkness and everlasting perdition. ". . . and the time of the dead, that they should be judged [the wicked at that great white throne judgment], and that thou shouldest give reward unto thy servants the prophets, and to the saints, and them that tremble before thy name."

Notice those meaningful words, "And them that fear thy name." Here is another conception all through the Word of God; namely, that the beginning of wisdom is the trembling before God, the fear of the Lord, the awesome reverence with which a man stands in the presence of the Almighty. That is why I do not like to hear in a song or prayer or sermon any presumptuous expressions of man's familiarity with God. As the heavens are higher than the earth, so is God above man. The place of a mortal man, who is dying and made out of the dust of the earth, is always to be one of reverential awe and fear and trembling.

"Behold," said Abraham, "I have taken upon myself to speak unto thee, I who am dust and ashes." Who am I, O Lord God, to come into Thy presence and to call upon Thy great name? Awe and reverence befit God's children who call upon His name. We do not take His name in vain, do we? We do not curse by it, do we? It is God's holy name and "thou shalt not take the name of the Lord thy God in vain, for God will not hold him guiltless who taketh his name in vain."

"They who fear thy name."

THE REWARDS OF GOD FOR HIS PEOPLE

Following the text, we learn that when the seventh angel sounds, God will reward His servants, the prophets, the saints and those who tremble before His presence. There may be no reward for God's people here. Read the eleventh chapter of the Book of Hebrews. The heroes of faith were severely persecuted. God says that down here we do not have our reward, and the books of history say the same thing. How the world has treated God's people! Some of them were burned at the stake; some of them were crucified upside down; some of them were thrown into boiling cauldrons of oil; some of them were made to rot in dungeons. It is so today, even as the Apostle Paul says, "all who will live godly in Christ Jesus shall suffer persecution."

In the last few days I have met two young men. One from the army says: "I have given up my Christian separateness for I cannot rise in the army and not drink. So I am going to drink, and we serve the stuff in my home." A man, he says, cannot rise in the army, he cannot be an officer in the army, without drinking and serving liquor. Can God be pleased with such practice? As He looks down upon our beloved America to see whether or not we live or die, why should God spare America?

The second young man I came across is in the State Department. The young fellow said to me that one cannot rise in the State Department, one cannot rise in the ambassadorial consular services of the American government unless one serves liquor and drinks. When the Lord sees that, can He delight to favor America? In the imponderables of our destiny, what will God do?

Before God all things are either wrong or right. The Lord looks down from heaven and says: "I have a day of reckoning. Some things are right and some things are wrong, and all the extenuating circumstances that a man can conceive do not make wrong right or right wrong." In our sight things may be gray, but not in God's sight. To God they are either black or white, either right or wrong. God judges according to rightness and wrongness. The destiny of our country does not lie in our armies or our navies or our air forces or our atomic achievements, but it lies in the hands of the Almighty God who judges the nations.

That day is coming when God shall reward His servants and prophets and saints and "them that fear thy name." Not now, not here, but there and then. The inequalities in this life are endless. The final adjustment is over there. The Lord says, "When I come, I have my reward with me." Paul says, "We shall all stand at the *bema* of Christ, at the judgment bar of the Lord, and there we receive our rewards." When that time comes, then Paul shall receive his crown of righteousness which he says God has in store for all those who love His appearing.

At that time Moses shall receive the recompense to which he had respect when he chose to suffer affliction with the people of God rather than to enjoy the pleasures of sin for a season. At that time shall Daniel stand in his lot and at that time shall the apostles be seated upon their twelve everlasting thrones. At that time shall all who have loved the Lord, who have forsaken houses or land or brethren, receive not only an hundredfold but also everlasting life. Not here, but there.

In this world we suffer tribulation, we have conflicts and agony and war in our souls. The world is much opposed to the devout, the holy and pious life. But there shall God own His own and shall crown and reward those who have walked in His way and have loved His name and done humble, menial service to our blessed Lord.

The text closes with the words, ". . . and shall destroy them which destroy the earth." The final destruction of the wicked is another concept all through the Word of God. For example, our Lord said in the parable of the tares, "The son of man shall send forth his angels and they shall gather out of his kingdom all them that hurt and do iniquity and shall cast them into a furnace of fire." And we find the same prophecy in II Peter, the last chapter, where he says, "This world now is reserved for that hour when it shall be swept by fire in the judgment day and the perdition of ungodly men." In these chapters that follow, there are described the Beast and the False Prophet and the Dragon, Satan himself, who are cast into the lake of eternal, burning fire. This is a picture of God's purging of the world to destroy them that destroy the earth.

Lest the people of the Lord be discouraged in the violence and horror of those terrible days, there is a vision described in the next verse for us: "And the temple of God was opened in heaven, and there was seen in his temple the ark of his covenant." In the midst of the lightnings, voices, thunderings, earthquakes and great hails, there appears the ark of the promises of God. In that golden ark are all the promises of God. Not a one of those covenants will fail. Every word God has said and every promise the Lord has made will He faithfully keep. In the midst of His judgments and the outpouring of His wrath, there was seen the temple in heaven and in the temple, the ark of His promises, the ark of His covenant.

God says: "I will keep you forever; I will never leave thee nor forsake thee. If I go away, I will come again and receive you unto myself." If we sin, we know we have an advocate with the Father. If we confess our sins, He is faithful and just to forgive us our sins and to cleanse us from all unrighteousness. If the earthly house of this tabernacle be dissolved, we have a house, a new home, made without hands, eternal in the heavens. "And the temple of God was opened in heaven, and there was in his temple the ark of his covenant." His promises to us never fail.

CHAPTER 6

THE RADIANT WOMAN

Revelation 12

1. And there appeared a great wonder in heaven; a woman clothed with the sun, and the moon under her feet, and upon her head a crown of twelve stars:

2. And she being with child cried, travailing in birth, and pained to be delivered.

3. And there appeared another wonder in heaven; and behold a great red dragon, having seven heads and ten horns, and seven crowns upon his heads.

4. And his tail drew the third part of the stars of heaven, and did cast them to the earth: and the dragon stood before the woman which was ready to be delivered, for to devour her child as soon as it was born.

5. And she brought forth a man child, who was to rule all nations with a rod of iron: and her child was caught up unto God, and to his throne.

6. And the woman fled into the wilderness, where she hath a place prepared of God, that they should feed her there a thousand two hundred and threescore days.

This passage represents a great division in the Apocalypse. The first eleven chapters, concluding with the sounding of the seventh trumpet, bring the consummation of this age, when the kingdom of this world, the sovereignty of this world, becomes the kingdom of our Lord and of His Christ. In the days of the voice of the seventh trumpet (described in chapter eleven), the mystery of God is finished. Thereupon the Lord gives us a preview, a prophetic outline, of the final days of this present world. Then in the twelfth chapter immediately following, in the exact middle of the Apocalypse, the Lord begins a delineation of the details, filling in the great, broad, prophetic preview that is stated at the end of chapter eleven. In Revelation 12 we are introduced to some of the personages who are to figure so largely in these last days of God's purposes in the earth. These key characters will move across the pages of history in this final time.

In this passage in Revelation 12, these five personages are introduced in this order: first, the woman clothed with the sun, the radiant woman; second, the great red Dragon; third, the Man-Child destined to rule the nations of the world; fourth, Michael, the remnant of the seed of the woman. Now let us identify these five in their order, starting with the second and coming finally to the first, because this chapter concerns that personage, the radiant woman, primarily. The second figure, the Dragon, is specifically pinpointed. The great red Dragon is that ancient serpent called the Devil and Satan. Third, the Man-Child: "And the woman brought forth a male child who was to rule all nations with a rod of iron." That is an exact quotation from the Septuagint version, the Greek version, of the great Messianic Second Psalm. The Man-Child is the Messiah, the Lord Christ, destined to rule all the nations and families of the earth and to preside as Lord God over all creation. That is Jesus, the Messiah, the Christ of God. Michael, the fourth in the series, appears several times in the Old Testament. He is called the great prince who stands for the nation Israel. He is the archangel, the only one named as such in the Word of God. We shall speak of him at length in the next chapter. The fifth reference concerns the remnant of the seed of the woman. The children of God to whom this passage refers depend upon our identification of the radiant woman. We turn, therefore, to the glorious mother, who brought forth the man child into the world. Who is she?

THE IDENTIFICATION OF THE RADIANT WOMAN

There have been many identifications of this radiant woman. There are many who say that she is the Virgin Mary. But the identification of this radiant woman with the human mother of Jesus is impossible. Look at the whole passage. In verse 6 we read: "And the woman after she gave birth to the child fled into the wilderness, where she hath a place prepared of God, and there she is cared for a thousand two hundred and sixty days." And again, in verse 14 of this twelfth chapter: "And to the woman were given two wings of a great eagle, that she might fly into the wilderness, into her place, where she is nourished for a time, and times, and half a time [three and a half years] . . . . And the dragon was wroth with the woman, and went to make war with the remnant of her seed, which keep the commandments of God, and have the testimony of Jesus Christ." To apply those Scriptures to the Virgin Mary would be unspeakable. No such thing ever was or ever will be. It is inconceivable.

Then there are those who say this radiant woman represents the church. But when they do that, they reverse the apocalyptic vision recorded here in the twelfth chapter, for this woman, whoever she is, gives birth to the Messiah. To say that the church gave birth to Jesus is to speak diametrically opposite the actual truth. It is Christ who gave birth to the church. The church is taken out of the side of Christ. We are born out of His flesh and His blood and His bones. In His sobs and tears and cries and agonies the church was born. When Eve was taken out of the side of Adam, Adam said, "This is now bone of my bones and flesh of my flesh." Paul, in commenting on the passage in Genesis 2:21-24, said, "This is a great mystery, but I speak concerning Christ and the church" (Ephesians 5:25-32). As Eve was taken out of the side of Adam, so the church was born out of the riven, open, bleeding side of our Lord. These who say that the church gave birth to Christ obviate the contradiction by saying that they mean the birth, the forming of Christ in the life of the believer. Others say they mean the travail of the church in the coming of Christ in judgment. But any interpretation that makes the church the mother of Christ is a wrenching, a violation of the plain, simple vision here in the Apocalypse.

Who is this radiant woman? She is plainly identified in the Holy Scriptures. In the ninth chapter of the Book of Romans, Paul describes the "Israelites to whom pertaineth the adoption and the glory and the covenants and the giving of the law and the service of God and the promises, whose are the Fathers and of whom concerning the flesh Christ came, who is over all, God blessed forever. Amen."

The inspired apostle says that the one who gave birth to the Messiah is the nation and the family and the people of Israel. It is Israel who produced Christ. That nation is likened unto the woman who bore in her womb the great Saviour of the world, the Lord who is destined to rule over all men in earth and all the hosts in heaven. Christ is the fruit of the womb of Israel.

When you thus interpret the passage, everything in the Bible will beautifully and marvelously fit together. Israel is called a married woman again and again. Israel is referred to as a mother again and again (Isaiah 54:1). Israel, in her rejection and in her captivity, is referred to as a widow and as a divorced woman (Isaiah 47:7-9; 50:1). But always the church is referred to as a chaste virgin, a bride who is some day to be presented to Christ. As Paul says in II Corinthians 11:2: ". . . for I have espoused you . . . as a chaste virgin bride unto Christ." For the bride of Christ is to be found in this condition, travailing to give birth to a child, would be of all things inconceivable and vastly, indescribably inappropriate. In the Scriptures the church is never referred to as a mother. She is always the bride. As John the Baptist said of the Lord, "He that hath the bride is the bridegroom and I stand, a friend of the bridegroom, rejoicing in his voice." It is Christ who has the bride.

At the great, ultimate consummation of the age, when the Lord shall appear, the marriage supper of the Lamb is come because the bride has made herself ready. This is the background for the idea Paul so beautifully delineates in the fifth chapter of Ephesians. Israel always is a mother, giving birth to children. Through Zion's travail, children are born unto God. But the church, the bride of Christ, is unmarried until the great marriage supper of the Lamb. So this woman, a mother, giving birth to the Messiah refers to the nation Israel.

That identification can also be seen in her description. She is clothed with the sun, and the moon is under her feet, and upon her head is a crown of twelve stars. That is a description that is taken from the thirty-seventh chapter of Genesis, verse 9: "And Joseph dreamed a dream . . . behold, the sun and the moon and the eleven stars made obeisance to me." It refers to Israel and the family of Jacob. The twelfth star is Joseph, himself, the sun and the moon and the eleven stars, and he the twelfth star. So this glorious, radiant woman is prefigured in the life of Joseph. Sold to the Gentiles, sold into captivity, buried among the nations of the world, yet in the promise and purpose and election of God, she is raised to an exalted position with her son, the Messiah, who is destined to rule the earth. The woman, then, is Israel, the chosen family and people of God and the Man-Child is the Messiah, our Lord Christ.

THE CHRONOLOGY OF GOD'S PROPHECIES

We have, also, a chronological note here that tells the whole story and meaning of this revelation: "And the woman fled into the wilderness, where she hath a place prepared of God, that they should feed her there a thousand two hundred and threescore days." Then in the fourteenth verse: "And to the woman were given two wings of a great eagle, that she might fly into the wilderness, into her place, where she is nourished for a time, and times, and half a time [for three and a half years]." That period of time is repeated again and again in the Apocalypse. In chapter 11, verse 2: ". . . and the holy city [Jerusalem. No other city in the Bible is called the holy city. In verse 8 it is distinguished as the place where our Lord was crucified, and our Lord was crucified in Jerusalem] shall the Gentiles tread under foot forty and two months." There is that same time period. In the third verse of Revelation 11 there is that same reference again: "I will give power unto my two witnesses, and they shall prophesy a thousand two hundred and threescore days." In Revelation 13, verse 5, here it is again: ". . . and power was given unto the beast to continue forty and two months." Over and over and over again that time period, an identical time period, is referred to: three and a half years; forty-two months; a thousand two hundred sixty days; a time, times, and a dividing of time; a time, times and half a time. Always that same, identical period of time.

It is in this period that the woman flees into the wilderness where she is separately cared for of the Lord God. We can know exactly where that time period is, for this is the revelation that God made to Daniel. The Lord said to Daniel, and it is re-corded in the ninth chapter of his prophecy, that seventy weeks of years are determined upon Israel until the great and final consummation. "Seventy weeks of years" — that is the way the Revised Standard Version translates the passage, which is an exact translation. Seventy weeks of years are determined upon Israel until that final, millennial consummation. In the vision God divided those seventy weeks of years into two parts, sixty-nine weeks of years and one week of years. From the time of the decree for the building of Jerusalem until the time when Messiah shall be cut off is sixty-nine weeks of years. Then the seventieth and final week in which God deals with the Jewish nation is separated by itself. That last week is divided in two, "in the midst of the week," as Daniel says in verse 27, chapter

9. That final week is divided in two: three and a half on this side and three and a half on that side; a thousand two hundred sixty days on this side and a thousand two hundred sixty days on that side: forty-two months on this side and forty-two months on that side; a time, times and dividing of time on this side and a time, times and dividing of time on that side. That is the source of that period of time.

It is the last prophetic week at the end of which God will bring in the kingdom, at the end of which the great denouement of this world will find its ultimate consummation. Therefore, when we turn to the Book of the Revelation and read of this woman, fleeing into the wilderness where God cares for her three and a half years, half a week of years, a thousand two hundred sixty days, forty-two months, we know immediately the period described. We have come to the great and final end time of this world. This is the day of Jacob's trouble; this is the day of the last, terrible, indescribable persecution of God's elect. But this is also the day in which God will exalt His people as they turn in repentance and in faith to accept their rightful Lord, their King Messiah, destined to rule the nations of the earth.

In this prophecy, all of the vast period in which we live is left out. No reference is made to it. "She brought forth a man child, who was to rule all nations with a rod of iron: and her child was caught up unto God, and to his throne . . . . And the woman fled into the wilderness." In that gap between verse 5 and verse 6, all of this period of grace in which we now live intervenes. Is that the way that God writes prophecy? Is that the way, as we read the Book, that we find God outlining His great purposes of history? Leaving out vast periods and vast millenniums inside a chapter, inside a verse, inside the same sentence? Yes, that is the method we find all through the Word of God. You see, you and I live in time, which is a creation of God, just like matter. We see things happen a day at a time. To us, events come around a corner a day at a time. But they do not appear like that to God. The great sovereign God who stands above this earth, king above the floods, the great sovereign God looks upon all of time as though it were present. He sees it here, here, there, there. It is all present to Him. God sees the end from the beginning.

There is no such thing as events coming as a surprise to the Lord God as they happen to us, for He sees the whole story, from the day of its beginning to the day of its consummation. When God makes a prophecy, He does not write out as we do the annals of history, the chronological events, as they happen day after day. God will follow an event through from beginning to end in one sentence, picking out just those things that are pertinent to the prophecy. One of those recorded events may happen here, another one may happen there, and sometimes there is a whole millennium of time between the things that God is saying are going to come to pass.

Until we see that fact, prophecy has no meaning whatsoever; what God says is an unintelligible jumble. But if we can see as we read the Bible how God plans and how He previews and how He looks at history, suddenly His prophecies will have a vast and infinite meaning. Look at time here in the fifth verse: "And she brought forth a man child, who was to rule all nations with a rod of iron: and her child was caught up unto God, and to his throne." Reading this, one could think Christ had no life at all. One might think He never lived at all, that He was born a child and was caught up to the throne immediately. His ministry is not referred to, His life is not referred to, His death is not referred to, His atoning sacrifice is not referred to. His life is skipped over, all in one breath. "And she gave birth to the child and the child was caught up to God in heaven." What of the great ministry of the Lord? What of the great atonement of the Lord? What has God done?

God here is talking about something else. He is not chronologizing the life of Christ. The Lord has another intent and purpose, and He is speaking of those things that are pertinent to what He is talking about, which in this instance is the great prophetic preview now before us. Compare the Apostle's Creed: ". . . Born of the Virgin Mary, crucified under Pontius Pilate." According to that ancient summary, you would think the Lord had no life or ministry. But the idea of the Apostle's Creed was doctrinal statement emphasizing the virgin birth of the Lord and the blood atonement of Christ. The rest was not under review. So it is with the way the Lord prophesies, the way He writes things in His Book. He leaves out great gaps and great periods of time, centering on those things that are pertinent to the particular prophecy.

This method of prophecy is found throughout the Word of God. Look, for example, at the ways Jesus used a certain passage in the sixty-first chapter of Isaiah: "The Spirit of the Lord God is upon me; because the Lord hath anointed me to preach good tidings unto the poor . . . To proclaim the acceptable year of the Lord, and the day of vengeance of our God . . . ." All in one breath the prophet says, "To proclaim the acceptable year of the Lord, and the day of vengeance of our God." That is the way the passage reads in Isaiah. Now look at it in Luke as Jesus reads the passage: "And he found the place where it was written, The Spirit of the Lord is upon me because he hath anointed me to preach the gospel to the poor; . . . to preach the acceptable year of the Lord" — a period (Luke 4:19). Right in the middle of a phrase, right in the middle of a clause, right in the middle of a sentence, right in the middle of a great prophecy the Lord cuts it off. But the prophecy said, "to proclaim the acceptable year of the Lord and the day of vengeance of our God." Between those two statements two thousand years have already passed. The great day of the vengeance of our God and of the judgment of the Lord God upon this earth is yet future, even at this late hour. After the Lord said that the first part of this passage was fulfilled in Him (which happened two thousand years ago), there follows that enormous gap of now over two thousand years never seen by the prophets, never revealed to the Old Testament seers. Paul says in the third chapter of the Book of Ephesians that this age of grace and the body of Christ, the church, are a *musterion*, hidden in the heart of God and unknown until the Lord revealed it to His apostles. In these prophecies we find the outline of ages in one sentence, with millenniums omitted between the clauses.

Let us take one other instance of the unusual method by which God outlines the future. In the eleventh chapter of the Book of Isaiah: "And there shall come forth a rod out of the stem of Jesse, and a Branch shall grow out of its roots: And the spirit of the Lord shall rest upon him . . . . The wolf also shall dwell with the lamb, and the leopard shall lie down with the kid . . . . They shall not hurt nor destroy in all my holy mountain: for the earth shall be full of the knowledge of the Lord, as the waters cover the sea." Here is that method again: "There shall come forth a rod out of the stem of Jesse, and a Branch shall grow out of his roots." That refers to the birth of the Lord Jesus, the Messiah, coming out of the loins of Israel, coming out of the loins of David. Though cut down, the branch sprouts up in Jesus. "And the wolf shall dwell with the lamb, and the leopard shall lie down with the kid." That prophecy has not come to pass yet. The first part of it was fulfilled two thousand years ago in the birth of Jesus. Yet, the last part of the prophecy does not come to pass until the millennial kingdom of Christ is established in this earth. But the prophets did not see the time separation as they looked at those two vast mountain peaks side by side — the coming of our Lord and the establishment of the millennial kingdom on earth. It was only as we drew near to the peaks that we saw that there was a distance in between. One of them is in front of the other. The whole Bible, in its prophetic message is so written.

THE PRESENT BLINDNESS AND ULTIMATE CONVERSION
OF ISRAEL

In this passage, in chapter 12 of the Revelation, this man-child is born and is caught up to God in heaven. There is no reference to His life, nor any reference to His death; He is just caught up to the throne of God in heaven. Nor is there in between verses 5 and 6 in Revelation 12 any reference to this whole period of grace, the whole story of the church. Why? Because God is dealing with Israel here, with this woman who gave birth to the Messiah, and Israel has no Scriptural history in this day of grace. The clock stopped for Israel when she rejected her Messiah and the sixty-nine weeks were closed. In this present day, the Israelites, like any other people, are lost without Jesus. They have to repent. They have to turn. They have to accept Christ as their Saviour. They have to be born into the kingdom of God. They have to be regenerated just as we are. There is no difference today between a Jew and a Greek or a Barbarian or a Roman or a Scythian or anyone else.

We are all alike before God today. We become members of the household of faith by trusting in Jesus as our Saviour. The Jew, the Gentile, the foreigner, the alien, the indigenous, the fellow-citizen — all of us without Jesus are alike lost today. But God says there is coming a time when this age shall be finished and when the purposes of God for His church shall be accomplished; there is coming a time when the church is to be taken out of this earth. There is coming a time when the clock will start again with Israel. That will be the seventieth week, the last week of Daniel that is separated by itself. This Revelation has to do with that last climactic week. This is the day, here in the Apocalypse, of Jacob's trouble. This is the day of his agony. This is the day of his great indescribable sorrow. But this also is the day when God is dealing with him, and when the Lord is bringing to focus the great elective purposes of the Almighty in this earth. This is the day, as in that final week, when God will purge His nation as He purged the Gentiles at the beginning; when God will purge His people and when they, at the revelation of their Lord, shall look upon Him whom they have pierced and a nation shall be born in a day and Israel shall be converted and become, with her Messiah, the blessing of the whole earth.

That is what Israel, today, cannot see. That is what John the Baptist, in his day, could not see. For when John the Baptist came, he announced the coming of the kingdom, and he said the axe is laid at the root of the tree, and the Lord is going to winnow the chaff from the wheat with His winnowing fan. But there was no axe laid at the root of the tree, and there was no winnowing fan, and the kingdom did not come. John in his despair and in his discouragement, sent word to Jesus and said: "Lord, I do not understand. Are you the One that was to come or do we look for another? I can see the suffering servant and minister in you, but where is that Messiah who is to rule with a rod of iron, who is to cut down the tree of iniquity and separate the chaff from the wheat? Where is that Messiah that I announced when I preached the gospel of the kingdom?" John the Baptist fell into that error. John never saw the great gap between the first and the second comings, the dying of our Lord and the reigning of our Lord. John never saw it.

Paul said the reason he did not see it was that it was not revealed until it was made known to the apostles. The prophets never saw it and that is the veil that covers Israel's heart today. In Panama City I spoke to one of the ablest, finest Jewish merchant-women I ever met in my life. I said to her, "Why don't you accept Christ? Why don't you believe in your Messiah? Why don't you?" She replied to me, "Well, I have a very plain and simple answer and reason for that." She said: "When Messiah comes, all things will be different. There will be no more war. There will be no more hate. Everything will be perfect when Messiah comes. I know He has not come because everything is just as it was. There is bitterness and hatred and persecution and violence. Therefore, I know the Messiah has not come." You see, the veil is over her heart. She has not been able to see that in the purposes and the providences of God and in the elective choices of the Lord, the Lord was coming one time to die for our sins according to the Scriptures, and that He is coming the second time to rule with a rod of iron, personally, visibly.

This dull and stolid earth shall look up and see the coming King. The Book of Revelation describes the days of that unveiling, that returning, that coronation of Jesus Christ. And in that triumphant day, according to the purposes of God that never change, Israel, the mother of the Messiah, shall have a worthy, noble, and glorious part.

If I could be bold enough thus to pass a human judgment upon this purpose of God, I would say that I rejoice in it. For example, I could not conceive of a more tragic thing than for the Lord to have gone back to heaven and for His brethren, James and Joseph and Jude and Simeon, to have been here in unbelief. But the Lord appeared to His brethren before He returned to heaven and won them to Himself. Likewise, I could not imagine a greater tragedy in the face of the false religions (Islam, Buddhism, Romanism, Hinduism, Shintoism) than that the people of God who gave us this Book, every syllable of it, and who gave us our Messiah, should have no part in that ultimate consummation. I am glad if I can pass a human judgment upon the purposes of God; I am glad that the Lord will remember them. And with them and with all who now will associate themselves in the body of Christ, we shall be members together of the household of faith, fellow-heirs with the patriarchs. We shall sit down in the kingdom with Abraham, Isaac and Jacob. The blessedness of what God has in store for His people, for Israel and for us, is beyond word to say or heart to imagine.

Chapter 7

AND THERE WAS WAR IN HEAVEN

Revelation 12

1. And there appeared a great wonder in heaven; a woman clothed with the sun, and the moon under her feet, and upon her head a crown of twelve stars:

2. And she being with child cried, travailing in birth, and pained to be delivered.

3. And there appeared another wonder in heaven; and behold a great red dragon, having seven heads and ten horns, and seven crowns upon his heads.

4. And his tail drew the third part of the stars of heaven, and did cast them to the earth: and the dragon stood before the woman which was ready to be delivered, for to devour her child as soon as it was born.

5. And she brought forth a man child, who was to rule all nations with a rod of iron: and her child was caught up unto God, and to his throne.

6. And the woman fled into the wilderness, where she hath a place prepared of God, that they should feed her there a thousand two hundred and threescore days.

7. And there was war in heaven: Michael and his angels fought against the dragon; and the dragon fought and his angels,

8. And prevailed not; neither was their place found any more in heaven.

9. And the great dragon was cast out, that old serpent, called the Devil, and Satan, which deceiveth the whole world: he was cast out into the earth, and his angels were cast out with him.

In the next chapter we shall speak of the expulsion of Satan from heaven. In this chapter we speak of the violent war between Michael and Lucifer and their cohorts, the angels of glory. This war precipitates the last Great Tribulation period, the last three and a half years, the forty-two months, the one thousand two hundred sixty days, the time, times and the dividing of time, the last half of the seventieth week of Daniel. The violent conflict between good and evil, between God and Satan, rises to its final issue in these concluding days. These forces that have warred in this divided universe from the beginning of God's creation come to a final head. There is war in heaven. Satan knows, as the text says in the twelfth verse, that he has but a short time. When this war is fought, it is the beginning of the end. It is remarkable that this Great Tribulation period begins with a war in heaven and at Armageddon, a war on earth in which God intervenes in human history and Christ comes in glory and power. "And there was war in heaven; Michael and his angels fought against Lucifer [the Dragon, the Devil, Satan] and his angels."

This violent conflict between these two celestial, august, heavenly personalities has been a strife renewed and repeated through the millenniums past. Those two have known one another and have faced each other since the beginning of the untold ages when God created the heavenly hosts. For example, in the ninth verse of the little epistle of Jude, we have these same two antagonists: "Yet Michael, the archangel, when contending with the devil . . . durst not bring against him a railing accusation, but said, The Lord rebuke thee." These are the identical participants, antagonists, that are named here in this final war in heaven. Michael and his angels warred against the Dragon, against Lucifer and his angels.

In the fourteenth chapter of Isaiah, Satan is called Lucifer, Son of the morning. In the twenty-eighth chapter of the Book of Ezekiel, he is described as "the anointed cherub that covereth"; that is, he was assigned, as the highest created angel of God, the guardianship of the throne of glory itself. In that holy mountain of God in the city of heaven, he walked up and down in the midst of the stones of fire, perfect in all of his ways until his heart was lifted up because of his beauty. Satan,

Lucifer, is God's highest creation, and in those days before time was born, presumptuous arrogance filled his heart to assume possession of the reins of the universe and of the throne of God itself. Even Michael, the archangel of God, could not stand in his own strength and in his own power before the tremendous might and glory of Lucifer. Even Michael, the archangel, was forced to say, "The Lord rebuke thee."

THE APPARENT SUCCESSES OF SATAN

In that passage in Jude there is a marvelous insight into the mystery of God in this universe. First, the boundless, indescribably glorious power of Lucifer, when even Michael dare not bring against him a railing accusation. We have also an insight into the unbounded arrogance of Satan, which is supported by unbelievable success. Why would Satan war against Michael, and what hope would he entertain for victory against God? Because, in his past arrogance and unchecked ambition, he has been pre-eminently and immeasurably successful. In Genesis 1:1 the Book states: "God created the heaven and the earth." In Genesis 1:2, the next verse: "And the earth became waste and void and darkness covered the deep." Between those two verses, verse one and verse two in Genesis, lies this inconceivable, rebellious, blasphemous attack of Satan in heaven when he sought to assume the sovereignty of God's universe. He plunged all God's creation into waste and void. Anything God created would be perfect, without spot and without blemish, but Satan in his sin and in his rebellion, blasted God's whole creation.

Success? Incomprehensible was his success. When God re-created this world in the days of the Garden of Eden, Satan again intruded and through blasphemy and lying, he destroyed God's Eden and with it our first parents. Through illimitable, indescribable heartaches during the millenniums since, Satan has ruled this world with tears, sorrow, distress, war, murder, blight, and finally has made of God's world, itself, one vast burying-ground. That is why Satan, in his arrogance and in his pride because of his past successes, lifts himself up even now against the very throne of our God and His Christ.

We have another strange matter here. These antagonists, Michael, the archangel, and Lucifer, the Son of the morning, the daystar of heaven, find their antagonism in a purpose that God has revealed for His people from the beginning. Michael stands for the people of God and their destiny. Satan, Lucifer, seeks to interdict and to destroy the elective purpose of God for His people. That conflict between the two over the fulfillment of the purpose of God for His people is the same conflict described here in Jude, verse 9: "Yet Michael, the archangel, when contending with the devil he disputed about the body of Moses . . . ."

What did the Devil want with the body of Moses? I have two answers to that question. My first observation is this: I think Satan wanted the body of Moses to use it as an instrument of idolatry. Even the brazen serpent that Moses raised in the wilderness was kept and used as an instrument of idolatry until it was destroyed by good King Hezekiah. That same kind of idolatry has existed through all the ages unto this day. In the Red Square in Moscow there is a vast mausoleum. Inside it, behind a glass casket, is the body of Lenin. By the thousands and the hundreds of thousands every year, the Moscovites and the Soviets and the Russians and the strangers from afar pay worshipful obeisance to the memory and the system of Lenin. That is what Satan wanted with the body of Moses. He wanted to destroy the great monotheistic devotions of the people of the Lord and to make them idolaters.

The second answer is the revelation which I think the Bible presents as to the reason Satan wanted the body of Moses. Moses here is a representative of all of the elect children of God, and it is the purpose of God to exalt and to glorify His saints even though it necessitates a resurrection from the dead. It is the purpose of God that His people shall inherit the earth

and that His people shall reign in heaven. If Satan can contro-
vert the purposes of God, keeping in his possession these that
sleep in the dust of the ground, then all of the purposes of
God for us are brought to nought. For not only in our spirits
have we been regenerated and redeemed, but God has promised
us a redemption of the whole purchased possession, and that
includes our bodies. It was the purpose of God that the body
of Moses be raised and exalted and glorified. He represented
that purpose in his appearance at the transfiguration of our Lord
Jesus. Against that purpose Lucifer contended. That conten-
tion precipitates this war in heaven. We have come to the time
of the end, and it is the purpose of God to raise out of the dust
of the ground these that sleep in the earth and these whose
names are written in the Book of Life. It is God's purpose to
exalt them up to heaven and to glorify them in the beatific life
God has prepared for us. Against that purpose Lucifer contends
in his last battle.

How do we know this? In the twelfth chapter of the Book
of Daniel we read that God said when Michael shall stand up
(or as Paul would say it, when the last trump of the archangel
sounds), the time has come when those who sleep in the dust
of the earth shall be resurrected. It is the time when those whose
names are found written in the Book of Life shall be rewarded.
It is the time when God's sainted children shall shine as the
brightness of the firmament and as the stars forever and forever. It is the end-time, when Michael stands up. This is the
time of the sounding of the trumpet. This is the time, these
last concluding days, when God has purposed to exalt and to
glorify His saints. Therefore Lucifer opposes God in this last
stand. If Satan fails here, he fails everywhere, for this is the
dissolution of his kingdom of darkness. This is the emptying of
all graves. This is the destruction of the sovereignty of death.
The end of death means the end of the kingdom of Satan.
This is the reason for this great and final war, the war in heaven.
Michael and his angels fought against the dragon, and the dragon

fought and his angels. If Satan loses here, if he delivers up the saints whose bodies sleep in the dust of the earth, his kingdom is forever destroyed. Paul said that the last enemy that shall be destroyed is death. This is the time of the end.

The Archangel Michael and the Mighty Prince Lucifer

For a moment let us look closely at these two participants. Michael's name means "one like God." Is that not a beautiful name? We are introduced to him in the Book of Daniel, where he is described as one who stands for the people of the prophet. Michael, one of God's great princes, stands for the nation Israel. He defends the destiny of God's elect. At the end of time, God will bring to pass, according to His gracious sovereignty, all the prophecies written in the old Bible concerning His chosen people, who are now outcasts, fugitives, wanderers, sojourners in the earth. But some day, that day when Michael shall stand up, God will bring to pass for His people a great and marvelous thing. "For the gifts and calling of God are without repentance" (Romans 11:29). A man may make a promise and the next day forget it. Not so, God. God may have made a promise thousands and thousands of years ago, but it is today just as vibrant and alive in the memory of the Almighty as it was the day God made it. He does not change. Michael will carry out the promises made to the people of God.

Now let us look at Lucifer. In the third verse of this twelfth chapter of Revelation, the text says: "There appeared another *semeion* [translated here 'wonder' — there appeared another *semeion*, 'sign'] in heaven . . . ." Then John describes the sign. Now a sign is not the thing itself, just as the sign on a storefront is not the store. It is altogether different. A sign on a road may point the way, but the thing to which it points is altogether different. The description here of Satan is not a picture photograph of him as he actually is. This is God's symbolic representation of the Devil. If you would like to know what God thinks about him and how God considers him, this passage reveals it, for this is God's symbolic outline of Lucifer.

Actually, Lucifer is bright like the sun and glorious like God Himself. Paul one time referred to the fact that the Devil transforms himself into an angel of light. This text in Revelation is a symbolic representation of the Devil. "And there appeared another [*semeion*] sign in heaven." Now, what is he like? He is like a dragon, a serpent, vicious, vile, ferocious, terrible. His color is red. The Greek word is *purros*. The Greek word for fire is *pur*, red, *purros*. So he is fiery red, like fire. He is a murderer from the beginning. His whole trail is steeped in blood and in death — a fiery, red dragon. He has seven heads. The number seven refers to fulness; here, to the fulness of evil. On each one of his heads is a diadem. This symbolism of Lucifer is constant throughout all of the Word of God. He is always presented as a crowned monarch. In the twelfth chapter of the Book of Matthew, our Lord referred to Satan as a king with a kingdom. Three times in the Book of John, our Lord referred to Satan as "the prince of this world." In II Corinthians 4:4, Paul referred to Satan as the god of this world. In Ephesians 2, Paul refers to him as "the prince of the power of the air." In the temptation of our Lord, Satan took Jesus up on a high mountain and showed Him all of the kingdoms of this earth and their glory and said, "This will I give you if you will fall down and worship me." In the last chapter, the fifth chapter of I John, John says this whole world lies in the hands of the wicked one.

The kingdom of this world, the sovereignty of this world, does not become the sovereignty of our Lord and of His Christ until the sounding of the seventh trumpet, described in the eleventh chapter of the Book of the Revelation. Without exception, all the way through the Word of God, Lucifer is presented as the god of this world. He has made of it a world of tears, death, graves and sorrow. He has seven heads, each one crowned with a diadem. He is a king of remarkable fulness and power.

"And his tail drew the third part of the stars of heaven and did cast them to the earth." Lucifer is a star, himself. The

word "Lucifer" means "star of the morning." God's angelic
hosts are called "stars" when they sing together in the thirty-eighth
chapter of Job. When Lucifer fell, when iniquity was found
in him, when pride lifted up his heart and in arrogance he
assayed to seize the sovereignty of God's creation, when Lucifer
did that, he drew with him one-third of God's angelic host.
What happened is graphically depicted in the difference in
Greek tenses used here to describe Satan's remarkable achievements. "And his tail *surei* [drags, draws, present indicative active, draws now — and his tail draws, drags,] the third part of the
stars of heaven." The next verb is a second aorist indicative,
ebalen, one referring to action past, "and did cast them down
[threw them down]." The latter event happened in one terrible
moment in the ages past. It is remarkable how these Greek
verbs will describe a situation exactly.

Satan fell in the long ago, and with him one-third of the
angels. It happened in one awesome decision in days past as
described in that Greek verb *surei,* but the horrible results have
continued as one-third of those angels are dragged in the trail
of Satan ever since. In Jude and in the second chapter of
II Peter, evil angels are spoken of as being imprisoned, chained,
until the great day of judgment. Some of those angels are
imprisoned, awaiting a reckoning with Almighty God. But
Lucifer was not thus imprisoned. Nor were these angels described here. Lucifer had permission and liberty to enter into
the Garden of Eden. In the Book of Job he has access to
the very presence of God Himself. Here he is in heaven,
warring against Michael and his angels. Why some are imprisoned and some are at liberty is a mystery God has not revealed.

The Purpose of Satan to Destroy the Promised Seed

The passage continues: ". . . and the dragon stood before
the woman which was ready to be delivered, for to devour her
child as soon as it was born." In the beginning, Satan was

present listening when God said, "And the seed of the woman shall crush thy head." From that faraway hour in the unknown ages of the past in the Garden of Eden, Satan has been seeking to destroy the promised seed. He moved Cain to slay Abel. He sowed wickedness in the earth so that the antediluvians were destroyed in the terrible flood. But as Seth was raised up to Adam and Eve, so Noah found grace in the sight of the Lord. Satan did that same murderous thing in the household of Isaac when he stirred up Esau to say, "I will slay my brother Jacob." But God delivered Jacob. In that same attempt of Satan to destroy the promised seed, he moved Pharaoh in the land of Egypt, when Moses was born, to destroy all the male children of Hebrew families. He nourished that same blood-red purpose during Israel's kingdom days to destroy the chosen seed. He sowed treachery and murder and slaughter among the sons of David. When Jehoshophat died, Jehoram, his son, slew all of the seed-royal; but Jehoram had children.

When the Arabians came and in their attack destroyed all of the children of Jehoram, one of them survived, Ahaziah. When Jehu slew Ahaziah, Athaliah, the queen-mother, usurping the crown (she was the daughter of Ahab and Jezebel), slew all of the seed-royal. But Jehoiada's wife (the aunt of this little child and wife of the high priest) took Prince Joash, an infant-baby, and hid him away. For those six years in which he was hid, the whole purpose of God in the promised seed rested in the life of that tiny infant. In the days of Esther, Satan moved King Ahasuerus to exterminate all of the seed of the elect people of God. But a king's sleepless night spared them in the providence of the Lord.

At last when the child was born and the dragon stood before the woman who was ready to be delivered for to devour her child, Satan moved Herod to slay all of the babes in Bethlehem, hoping to destroy the life of that infant, the promised child. After he failed in that, he sought the destruction of the Lord when he tempted him to cast Himself down from the pinnacle of the temple. The same Satan sought the destruction of the Lord when he moved the people at Nazareth to cast Him off the brow of the hill on which their city was built. He sought the destruction of the Lord in the enmity of the scribes and the Pharisees, who took up stones to slay Him when He walked unharmed through their midst. He sought the destruction of that promised seed when, in the Garden of Gethsemane, he almost slew the Lord in that terrible agony of prayer. And finally, on a Friday afternoon at three o'clock on the day before the high day, the Sabbath Day of the Passover, he slew the Son of God, the promised seed, and saw Him raised on a bloody cross in death between the earth and the sky. What a triumph, what a triumph, when Satan saw the mangled body of the Son of God, wrapped in linen, embalmed in spices and sealed in a sepulchre where no man, no mortal, could touch Him! But God never changes His purposes. He purposed for this Man-Child to rule the nations with a rod of iron, and God caught Him up to His throne in glory, waiting until His enemies be made His footstool.

When Satan saw the resurrection and the enthronement of Christ and the purpose of God thus to raise all of His people, he was wrathful and angry beyond description. Satan had those who preached the Gospel of the Son of God, Christ's emissaries, apostles, missionaries and evangelists, crucified, sawn asunder, slain by the sword, fed to wild beasts while emperors watched and made sport. Edict after edict by the imperial government of Rome was sent out to exterminate the people from the face of the earth. When paganism was supplanted by papal authority, and the robe of the heathen priest was exchanged for the robe of the prelate with the insignia of the Christian, it was the same story — the story of the rock and of the fagot and of the inquisition and of excommunication, of damnation. It has been estimated that more than fifty million of God's confessors laid down their lives in fire and in blood before the awful inquisition of Papal Rome. Such is the wrath of the dragon against the people of the Lord.

And today that same murderous wrath of Satan is manifested. Sometimes it is in the suave, intellectual fragmentation of the Word of God from the pulpits of the land when men empty the Holy Scriptures of their meaning and message, denying the very presence and personality and reality of Lucifer himself, and make sport of the miraculous, supernatural providences of God. Sometimes the attack is in that most subtle and fearful of all ways, when men are taught to believe a lie and to deny the very inspiration of the Word. Then, finally, in our day and time has come the most darksome, fearful, and indescribably terrible of all of the attacks that have ever been made against the people of the Lord. Even the ancient Greek inquired at the Delphian Oracle before he made a vital decision, and no Roman general would go to war until first he had propitiated the gods. But today for the first time in the history of the world, there are nations of this earth who avowedly are blasphemous and atheistic, who denounce God to His face. This is the wrath of the Dragon. We face a holocaust some terrible day with the forces of atheism and communism. And at their choosing it will come. "And there was war in heaven: Michael and his angels fought against the dragon; and the dragon fought and his angels."

But thank God, thank God, whether the story is in Eden or in the household of Noah; whether the story is in Israel or in the dark servitude of Egypt; whether the story is in the slaughter of the household of David or in the dark days of the kings of Persia; whether it is the story of bloody Bethlehem or the story of the laying down of the lives of the apostles; whether it is the story of God's saints who died in the inquisition; or whether it is the story of our missionaries who perish today facing an implacable foe: it is the same word and promise of God, ". . . they prevailed not . . . ." Fire cannot burn up God's elective purpose, and blood and death and persecution cannot destroy God's choices, made from the beginning of creation, that these who trust in Him shall reign with Him. God shall yet share His throne with His saints. They shall be His people and God shall be their God. We shall be fellow-heirs with the Son of Glory when He shall come to reign in the earth. These things do not change. ". . . And Satan prevailed not . . . ." The Lord bless our people as we find our refuge, our strength and our trust in Him.

CHAPTER 8

THE EXPULSION OF SATAN FROM HEAVEN

Revelation 12

7. And there was war in heaven: Michael and his angels fought against the dragon; and the dragon fought and his angels,

8. And prevailed not; neither was their place found any more in heaven.

9. And the great dragon was cast out, that old serpent, called the Devil, and Satan, which deceiveth the whole world: he was cast out into the earth, and his angels were cast out with him.

10. And I heard a loud voice saying in heaven, Now is come salvation, and strength, and the kingdom of our God, and the power of his Christ: for the accuser of our brethren is cast down, which accused them before our God day and night.

11. And they overcame him by the blood of the Lamb, and by the word of their testimony; and they loved not their lives unto the death.

12. Therefore rejoice, ye heavens, and ye that dwell in them. Woe to the inhabiters of the earth and of the sea! for the devil is come down unto you, having great wrath, because he knoweth that he hath but a short time.

13. And when the dragon saw that he was cast unto the earth, he persecuted the woman which brought forth the man child.

14. And to the woman were given two wings of a great eagle, that she might fly into the wilderness, into her place, where she is nourished for a time, and times, and half a time, from the face of the serpent.

15. And the serpent cast out of his mouth water as a flood after the woman, that he might cause her to be carried away of the flood.

16. And the earth helped the woman, and the earth opened her mouth, and swallowed up the flood which the dragon cast out of his mouth.

17. And the dragon was wroth with the woman, and went to make war with the remnant of her seed, which keep the commandments of God, and have the testimony of Jesus Christ.

This passage sets the stage for the final consummation of the age. After the war in heaven and the expulsion of Satan, in a very brief time (forty-two months), he is chained in the bottomless pit for a thousand years; then after the last judgment he is cast into the lake of fire forever.

"And there was war in heaven." These battles in the spiritual world, unseen and above us, from the time of the beginning of the human race, have enthralled the imagination of our greatest poets, who, in vivid and celestial language, have described the wars between the gods. Such unearthly conflicts are rooted in the primeval memory of the race. It is the same kind of ethnic tradition that is found in mythology and in legend among other races and in other languages, concerning the stories of the Garden of Eden and the Fall and the Flood and the tower of Babel. These events made an indelible impression upon the human mind, and beyond the true and recorded Word of God in the Bible, they linger in tradition and in mythology among other peoples and in other languages. That same theme is found in the intuition of our great poets, who have sensed that this conflict of good and evil goes beyond our human frailty and enters into the very spiritual world of the gods above us. I suppose the most dramatic of all of the epochal delineations of this violent conflict in heaven is that written by the immortal poet John Milton in *Paradise Lost*. There is no vividness of language nor majesty of sentence to compare with that incomparable poet's description of this war in heaven. He begins by introducing Satan:

> Aspiring
> To set himself in glory, above his peers,
> He trusted to have equalled the Most High,
> And, with ambitious aim
> Against the throne and monarchy of God
> Raised impious war in heaven and battle proud.

Then, in the great epic, John Milton describes that awesome battle between the archangels:

> Michael bid sound
> The archangel trumpet; through the vast of heaven
> It sounded, and the faithful armies rung
> Hosannah to the Highest: nor stood at gaze
> The adverse legions, nor less hideous joined
> The horrid shock: now storming fury rose,
> And clamour such as heard in heaven till now
> Was never; arms on armour clashing brayed
> Horrible discord, and the maddening wheels
> Of brazen chariots raged; dire was the noise
> Of conflict; overhead the dismal hiss
> Of fiery darts in flaming volleys flew,
> And flying vaulted either host with fire.
> So under fiery cope together rushed
> Both battles main, with ruinous assault
> And inextinguishable rage; . . .

Then in the epic, Milton speaks of the expulsion of Satan:

> . . . him the Almighty
> Hurled headlong flaming from the ethereal sky,
> With hideous ruin and combustion down.

Was there ever such a language in the earth? "Him the Almighty hurled headlong flaming from the ethereal sky." What majesty of expression! Then he closes with a magnificent tribute to the Son of God:

> Hail, Son of the Most High, heir of both worlds,
> Queller of Satan, on Thy glorious reign now enter,
> Hasting complete redemption!
> Thou didst defeat and down from heaven cast
> The false attempter of thy Father's throne,
> And frustrated the conquest fraudulent . . . .

That is the language of John Milton.

"And there was war in heaven . . . ." After the expulsion of Satan, after the celestial victory, the hosts of glory shout, ". . . rejoice, ye heavens, and ye that dwell in them . . . ." Until that hour, Satan had recourse to the presence of God, to walk in and out with the very Sons of Glory. He had ingress into the Garden of Eden and has been our tempter and destroyer ever since. But — ". . . rejoice, ye heavens, and ye that dwell in them . . . ." This is the beginning of the purging and the cleansing of the whole of God's creation.

THE WRATH OF SATAN AGAINST THE EARTH

But there is a dark side to this heavenly victory. The angelic hosts also warn, ". . . Woe to the inhabiters of the earth . . . ." What we read here in the delineation of the great consummation of the age is illustrated in the story of the whole human family. ". . . Woe to the inhabiters of the earth . . . for the devil is come down unto you, having great wrath . . . ." That seven-headed python is red with anger and incrimsoned with wrath and malice. As though one Satanic head were not enough, he has seven, thus picturing the fulness and plentitude of his iniquitous, villainous, wicked ingenuity. He loves the pomp, the ostentation, the display of his evil power, for he is crowned with seven diadems. He has ten horns that set him apart as being the ruling prince of this earth, the ruler of all God's destroyed creation. That has been his role and his character from the first verse of Genesis. Our Lord said he was a liar and a murderer from the beginning. Every tear that falls, every heart that is broken, every vision that is crushed, and every life that is ruined is the work of that Satanic spirit.

In the days of Job, in the permissive will of God, Satan destroyed Job's family, slew his children and sent Job in despair and ruin to the ash heap. He is the ever-present and unplacated enemy of God's people, the great Adversary. In the third chapter of Zechariah the prophet says: "I saw Joshua standing before the angel of the Lord, and Satan standing at his right hand to resist him." In Matthew 3, Satan sought to destroy the Son of God, Himself, through vicious and ingenious, subtle temptations. In Matthew 13, our Lord says: "The evil one steals away the Word of God that is sown in the human heart." He said in that same chapter 13 of Matthew that the evil over-sowing of the tares was the work of the enemy, the Devil.

In the description of the ministry of our Lord, the Book of

Acts says: "He was anointed with power, he went about doing good and healing all that were oppressed of the devil." In Luke 13, our Lord referred to a broken woman, saying: "Lo, these eighteen years she hath been bowed down by Satan." John said Satan put it in the heart of Judas to betray the Lord. Acts 5 says that Satan induced Ananias and Sapphira to lie to the Holy Spirit. In I Peter 5, that great apostle says that the Devil, Satan, "as a roaring lion walketh through the earth seeking whom he may devour." Satan was cast out — ". . . Woe to the inhabiters of the earth . . . for the devil is come down unto you, having great wrath . . . ."

And yet the saints overwhelmed Satan and were victoriously triumphant over him. How? It is an astonishing and incomprehensible revelation that men made out of dust should triumph over that seven-headed python, crowned with his seven diadems. How? It is not because the saints were numerous. The fact is, they were very few in number. It was not because they were men of prestige and wealth and social standing. They had none. Nor was it because they were people of great influence. They never had enough influence to stay out of the dungeons and out of the jails. Nor was it because they were sheltered and protected by the omnipotent arm of the Almighty God. In fact, from reading the story of the lives of the saints both in the Bible and in secular history, my impression is that God feeds them to the lions and that they are the outcasts and the offscouring of the world. As God's sainted children enter the gates of glory, they are covered with scars, victims of the claw and the fang of the Dragon. There is a crying and a moaning that has come from all God's children in all generations: "Oh, wretched man that I am, who shall deliver me from the body of this death?" And yet these feeble folk, these men made out of dust and ashes, these sinners in the earth, even they are victorious over this seven-headed Serpent, this ten-horned Devil, this seven-crowned Dragon.

How? The method is amazing. "They overcame him by

the blood of the Lamb and by the word of their testimony and they loved not their lives unto the death." What an astonishing text and truly one of the most meaningful and significant of all the words in the Bible! They overcame him — this great red Dragon, this reptile of evil, this seven-crowned Satan, this embodiment of evil — they overcame him by the blood of the Lamb and by the word of their testimony and by the devotion of their lives unto death.

THE POWER OF THE BLOOD OF THE LAMB

"And they overcame him by the blood of the lamb . . . ." The power to overcome and overwhelm the kingdom of Satan is found in the blood of the sacrifice of the Son of God. Listen! With your soul, listen! This is the truth and the revelation of the Lord. "They overcame him by the blood of the Lamb." How could this be? First, because atonement gives the saints access to the throne of Almighty God. With courage, with assurance, with boldness, they could approach the very throne of the Omnipotent, Himself. "Yes," said Paul, "ye that were sometimes afar off, interdicted, cast out, shut out, ye who sometimes were afar off are now made nigh by the blood of Christ."

In the blood of the Lamb, we have perfect access to the throne of grace. We can tell the Lord all about this conflict that rages around us. We can speak to Him about the inequality of our battle status. Was ever a battle so unequal as this between us, creatures of dust, and the Prince of the power of the air? So mighty is that battle that even Michael, the archangel, himself, durst not accuse Satan, but said, "The Lord rebuke thee." Yet Satan is our antagonist and we war against him. But in the power of the Son of God and in our right of access by the blood to the throne of omnipotence, covered by the blood, we are invincible and invulnerable.

> The soul that on Jesus hath leaned for repose,
> I will not, I will not, desert to its foes.
> That soul tho' all hell should endeavor to shake,
> I'll never, no never, no never forsake.

This is the word and the promise of God. Through the blood we draw nigh, we have access to the throne of omnipotence. "They overcame him by the blood of the lamb."

This text carries with it, in the next place, a marvelous blessing of God concerning our acceptance in glory, concerning the standing of saved sinners in the heaven of heavenlies. Look at the verse that precedes: ". . . for the accuser of our brethren is cast down, which accused them before our God day and night." Satan stands in the presence of God and says of God's saints: "Look at them! Vile sinners. Listen to them! The very imaginations of their hearts are evil. The dreams of their lives are wicked. Look at them!" Satan accuses God's people day and night.

Where is the man who stands up to say these accusations are wrong? Where is the man who can say, "I am pure in all of my thoughts; these things that Satan says against me are not true; I am perfect in all my life"? There never lived a man who could stand up and avow that perfection, not since God created him in the earth. When Satan says, "Look at him! He is a vile sinner," every man bows his head in shame and says, "O God, that is true." Every man is lost in his wickedness and sin, and Satan accuses him both day and night. "But they overcame him by the blood of the Lamb." The Scriptures answer: "The blood of Jesus Christ, God's Son, cleanses us from all sin." "These are they who have washed their robes and made them white in the blood of the Lamb." "They overcame him by the blood of the Lamb."

We have acceptance and standing in heaven because of the blood of the sacrifice of the Son of God. An old Talmudic tradition among the Jewish people says that Satan, the arch enemy of God's people, accuses the saints day and night except on the day of atonement. Every day and every night for the Christian who looks to the blood of Jesus is a day of atonement.

"And they overcame him by the blood of the Lamb." For another thing, that atonement secured for us an eternal sal-

vation, an everlasting deliverance. Israel was not saved out of
the bondage of Egypt except by blood of atonement, by the
blood of the lamb sprinkled in the form of a cross on the lintels
and on each side of the doorposts. Under the red banner of
the Son of God, in the symbolism of the blood of the paschal
lamb, they marched out of slavery into God's promised land. It
is thus with us. Washed by the blood of the crucified One,
we are saved to an eternal inheritance in Christ our Lord who
says, "I give unto them eternal life and they shall never perish."
"They overcame him by the blood of the Lamb." That sacrifice secures for us our eternal inheritance. Our Lord said, "This
is my blood of the new covenant [of the new promise, of the
new contract, of the new testament], shed for the remission
of sins." All of the covenant gifts of God are vouchsafed to those
who trust in Him through the atoning love of Jesus Christ, our
Lord.

THE TESTIMONY OF GOD'S MARTYR-SAINTS

"And they overcame him by the blood of the Lamb, *and
by the word of their testimony* . . . ." The last phrase of the
text is one of the strongest and most meaningful phrases to be
found in the Greek testament: *"dia ton logon tes marturias,"*
"they overcame him by reason of the word of their martyrdom,
of their witness, of their testimony." "They overcame him by
the blood of the Lamb, and by the word of their devotion." That
speaks of the martyrdom of Stephen whose face shone like the
face of an angel when, in his great defense of his faith, he saw
the Lord high and lifted up, standing by the throne of God.

That is the witness of the faith of Paul and Silas who,
when they were beaten, thrust into the innermost dungeon,
bound down in stocks and in chains, prayed and sang praises to
God. Who could stop a man like that? What could be done
with a prisoner like that? When he is beaten and thrust into
the innermost dungeon and bound down in stocks and in chains,
he prays and he sings praises unto God.

"They overcame him by the blood of the Lamb, and by the word of their testimony . . . ." That is the testimony of the martyr, John Huss, who, when the flames began to rise around the stake to which he was bound, sang praises unto God. That is the martyrdom, that is the witness, that is the testimony of Jerome, his fellow-martyr who, when the fagot was placed at his back to spare him the agony of watching it, said, "Bring it around to the front, set the fire before my eyes; if I had been afraid I wouldn't be in this place."

That is the testimony of Felix Mantz, who was marched in scorn and contempt through the streets of Zurich, Switzerland, his mother walking by his side urging her brilliant, young Baptist preacher-son to be faithful unto death. They took him into the middle of the Limmont River, the river that flows through the great city of Zurich, saying, "He likes water, let's give him lots of water"; and they drowned him in the beautiful Limmont River that flows out of Zurich Lake.

"And they overcame him by the blood of the Lamb, and by the word of their testimony . . ." That is the word of witness when John Bunyan, incarcerated for twelve years because he was a Baptist preacher, pleaded with the people, through the bars that imprisoned him, to turn in repentance and in faith to the Saviour of the world. "By the word of their testimony." That is the same kind of martyr-witness beheld in this seething world today. Some weeks ago I was in a prayer meeting composed of evangelical missionaries in Latin America. When request for remembrance in prayer was made, one missionary stood up and said, "Where I labor for Christ, seven of our Christian converts were murdered." This has been within the last few weeks. "They overcame him by the blood of the Lamb, and by the word of their testimony [*marturias* — by the word of their martyrdom] . . . ."

Then, lest we might have missed the secret of the source of the saints' great power, the Holy Spirit said to John, adding the third clause: ". . . and [they devoted their lives unto the death] they loved not their lives unto death." What a magnificent delineation! "And they overcame him by the blood of the Lamb [access to the omnipotent power and promise of God] . . . and by the word of their martyrdom [sealing their testimony with their blood] . . . for they loved not their lives unto death." When the life of the saint was placed in the balance, he never questioned, he never hesitated, he never feared.

> I saw the martyr at the stake,
> The flames could not his courage shake,
>   Nor death his soul appall.
> I asked him whence his strength was given,
> He looked triumphantly to heaven
>   And answered, "Christ is all."

"And they overcame him by the blood of the Lamb, and by the word of their testimony; and they loved not their lives unto the death." The martyr-witnesses felt, they taught, they believed that they were bought with a price and that their bodies as well as their spirits belonged to God. I marvel at us today. I wonder of what kind of stuff our people who profess to love Jesus are made? Many of our people will give a dime where they ought to give a thousand dollars; will give a nickel, when they ought to give a hundred. Any little discouragement can move us off-base, any little difficulty can send us to the dust of the ground, and any little reverse can defeat us.

"And they overcame him by the blood of the Lamb, and by the word of their testimony; and by the devotion of their lives unto death." There is an enemy of the saints of God across the sea, merciless and cruel and fierce. There is an enemy of the saints of God in the homeland, no less cruel, subtle and ruthless than the enemy across the sea. There are enemies of Christ in our own churches and in our own pulpits: ministers who, purporting to be emissaries of the courts of heaven, lust after the latest sophistry, pant after the new theology, spend their time spinning words and inventing theories and delivering inventions and machinations of men, as though they were the doctrines of the true God. O Lord, where, today in this hour of crisis and need and desperation, where are the men of God and the saints in the house of the Lord who devoted unto our great Saviour their lives unto death? Who seal the doctrines with the words of their martyrdom and who have no other trust and no other assurance but to lean on the everlasting arms, looking to the cross of Jesus, trusting in the blood of the crucified One?

O Lord, if you count your saints today, if you number your soldiers now, and if you call the roll in your Book, O God, grant that my name may be there. Number me, Lord, among those who are true to the faith, who are trusting in the blood of Jesus. Let me be with my brethren who are willing to pour into this ministry the soul and heart and life of all they possess or shall ever possess.

> Am I a soldier of the cross,
> A follower of the Lamb?
> And shall I fear to own His cause,
> Or blush to speak His name?
>
> Must I be carried to the skies,
> On flow'ry beds of ease,
> While others fought to win the prize,
> And sailed through bloody seas?
>
> Are there no foes for me to face?
> Must I not stem the flood?
> Is this vile world a friend to grace,
> To help me on to God?
>
> Sure I must fight, if I would reign:
> Increase my courage, Lord:
> I'll bear the toil, endure the pain,
> Supported by Thy word.

"And they overcame him by the blood of the Lamb, and by the word of their testimony; and they loved not their lives unto the death." This is the victory of the people of God.

CHAPTER 9

THE BEAST FROM THE RAGING SEA

Revelation 13

1. And I stood upon the sand of the sea, and saw a beast rise up out of the sea, having seven heads and ten horns, and upon his horns ten crowns, and upon his heads the name of blasphemy.

2. And the beast which I saw was like unto a leopard, and his feet were as the feet of a bear, and his mouth as the mouth of a lion: and the dragon gave him his power, and his seat, and great authority.

3. And I saw one of his heads as it were wounded to death; and his deadly wound was healed: and all the world wondered after the beast.

4. And they worshipped the dragon which gave power unto the beast: and they worshipped the beast, saying, Who is like unto the beast? who is able to make war with him?

5. And there was given unto him a mouth speaking great things and blasphemies; and power was given unto him to continue forty and two months.

6. And he opened his mouth in blasphemy against God, to blaspheme his name, and his tabernacle, and them that dwell in heaven.

7. And it was given unto him to make war with the saints, and to overcome them: and power was given him over all kindreds, and tongues, and nations.

8. And all that dwell upon the earth shall worship him, whose names are not written in the book of life of the Lamb slain from the foundation of the world.

9. If any man have an ear, let him hear.

10. He that leadeth into captivity shall go into captivity: he that killeth with the sword must be killed with the sword. Here is the patience and the faith of the saints.

In chapter 12 of the Apocalypse, John described the war in heaven between Michael and his angels and the Dragon, that ancient Serpent, the Devil and Satan, and his angels. And Michael prevailed and Satan was cast out and down to the earth. No longer does he have access to the Lord or to the throne of glory. No longer can he enter in with the Sons of God. He is cast out of the heavenlies and in wrath he comes down into this earth, knowing that he has but a short time. Revelation 12:12: ". . . Woe to the inhabiters of the earth . . . for the devil is come down unto you, having great wrath, because he knoweth that he hath but a short time." In Revelation 13:5, the "short time" is described as forty-two months, three and a half years, a thousand two hundred sixty days, a time, times and a dividing of time. In this last stand, earth enters its final and greatest crisis, and this wrathful dragon, this red seven-headed enemy of God, works his final malice and rage through two of his ministers on earth. One is described in these first ten verses of the Revelation 13. He is the political leader of this world, the final and ultimate anti-Christ. The other, the second beast, is described in the same chapter, beginning at verse 11 to the end. He is the final religious leader of this world, the false prophet. The Dragon, warring against God and the saints of the Most High, through these two ministers, finally leads on his dupes until they declare war against Christ and the heavenly armies and are forever and completely destroyed in the intervention of our Lord at the great battle of Armageddon, which is described in Revelation 19.

The Apostle John, "in the spirit," at first stood on the Isle of Patmos; then he was later taken up into heaven; he was later taken out into the wilderness; and finally he was taken to a high mountain to see these differing visions. Here, in the spirit, John stands on the shore of a raging sea. That sea is described in Daniel 7. As John stands on the sands of that turbulent and fearful sea, he sees rising out of it (*anabainon*, present participle of *anabino*, "to rise," "to ascend") this monster. It is a graphic vision. As he watches the storm and fury of that raging sea, out of its deep, he sees a beast emerging. There appear ten horns, each one wearing a diadem. There appear seven heads supporting those ten horns. Then finally emerges the whole terrible creature, himself. His body looks like a panther, a leopard. His feet are like the feet of a bear. His mouth is like the mouth of a lion. His heads have (*onomata*, plural) "names of blasphemy," and he speaks blasphemous things against God and against God's dwelling place and against those who tabernacle in heaven. He wars with those who trust Jesus. This is the vision. Now may God lead in the interpretation thereof.

THE FINAL POLITICAL RULER OF THIS WORLD

God has given us in this vision of the monstrous beast, a symbol of the last world political power that shall hold sway in this earth and over all the nations at the time of the end. I deduce that because, when this beast is destroyed in Revelation 19, there is none succeeding. That is the end of world government and the sovereignty of the nations and the kingdoms and the kings and rulers of this earth. So when I see this vision, I am looking at the final form of political dominion and sovereignty. I would know also that the vision refers to political government from Daniel 7. There a like vision is seen and each separate part represents a political kingdom.

I would know it also as I read the interpretation of that vision in Revelation 17. Chapter 17 describes the great scarlet whore, a picture of the decadence, debauchery and prostitution of God's faith and religion in the earth. That scarlet woman rides this beast. There, in chapter 17, the seven heads are seven mountains, describing the capital city. The seven heads are also seven kings, "five are fallen, one is and the other is yet to come." This is my personal persuasion of those five fallen, of the one that was in the days when John wrote, and of the one that is yet to come: The five fallen are the five ancient empires that preceded the day of the apostle; that is, the Egyptian, the Assyrian, the Babylonian, the Persian and the Greek. They are the five fallen. "And one is." The one that was in John's day, the one "that is" when he wrote, is the Roman Empire. The one that is yet to come is this great, final political dominion, presided over by this anti-Christ, which is world government in its ultimate form. Revelation 17:2 continues concerning the beast, "the ten horns which thou sawest are ten kings which have yet received no kingdom." They are in the future.

The one ultimate form of the government of this world will be divided into nations, into ten kingdoms, and "these ten kings have one mind and shall give their power and strength unto the beast." They will willingly yield their sovereignty and their dominion to this great arch-regent, who will preside in authority and in power over this entire earth, who is here described as a beast, who is here described as the last anti-Christ. This is God's symbol of the last political government in this world.

Again, this beast is God's symbol of a man, of a particular person, of that final anti-Christ. This is God's delineation of him. All of these beast-images are symbols that describe him. The monster is a man, not just a government. He is a particular person, the ultimate ruler and sovereign of this world-system. That is clear to me because Revelation 19:21 (describing their eventual overthrow) says, "And the beast was taken, and with him the false prophet . . . . Those both were cast alive into a lake of fire burning with brimstone." All the nomenclature of the Bible refers to the beast (the political ruler) and the false prophet (the religious leader) as being persons. They are people. They are individuals, and as such they are cast alive into the burning pit, where they go into perdition, everlasting damnation and horror.

There is no such thing as a kingdom without a king. There is no such thing as an empire without an emperor. There is no such thing as dominion and sovereignty and power without somebody to wield them. So it is in this chapter 13 of the Book of the Revelation. The depiction of final sovereignty and world government implies, necessitates, a leader — one person. There cannot be two presidents of the United States. There cannot be two ministers who head the government of the Soviet Empire. The very fact of a kingdom demands a king. The very fact of sovereignty and dominion demands someone to wield it. So it is here in chapter 13 of the Apocalypse. This beast is not only a figure of (God's symbol of; God's description of) a final world government, but it is also a description of a man, that ultimate anti-Christ. I deduce that also from what Paul says about him. In II Thessalonians 2:2, Paul describes that anti-Christ as "that *man* of sin."

I would know that he is a person, that he is a man, from another of many such passages in the Bible. One of the most remarkable statements in all the Word of God is written by this same Apostle John in a general epistle, a letter to all of the churches. He said in I John 2:18: "Little children . . . ye have heard that anti-Christ shall come . . . ." When did they hear that anti-Christ was to come? They heard that anti-Christ was to come because all of the teaching and testimony of the Word of God spoke of that coming, final antagonist of the Lord Christ. It was common doctrine, it was common revelation, it was common knowledge; and wherever the Word of God was preached, wherever the Bible was taught, wherever the message of Christ was delivered, a part of the very framework of the holy revelation of God was that there is an ultimate and final anti-Christ who is coming.

Through all of the prophets, through all of the gospels of Christ and through all of the apostles, that same revelation was made to God's people. In the beginning when the promise was made of an ultimate deliverer, there was also that dark adumbration of an antagonist that would bruise His heel, the brood of the viper that would assail and war against the seed of the woman. The story of conflict has continued through all the centuries since. There has never been an Abel without a Cain; there has never been a Jerusalem without a Babylon;

there has never been a John the Baptist without a Herod Antipas; there has never been an Apostle Paul without a Nero. When Christ seeks to reign in this earth, there is anti-Christ who is His antagonist and who lifts himself up, speaking blasphemous things against God, against the throne of the Lord, against the dwelling place of the Almighty and against those who tabernacle, who rest, in Jesus. So, from the Word of the Lord itself, this delineation is of a definite person, a final and ultimate anti-Christ.

THE PERSONAL ATTRACTIVENESS OF THE ULTIMATE ANTI-CHRIST

Another thing here in the Word of the Lord is that this man, this anti-Christ, this last world-ruler is superlatively fascinating, and intriguing and bewitching in his personal power and prowess. When the Lord, here in the Revelation, describes Satan as a dragon, fiery red, with seven heads and ten horns and seven diadems upon his head, the language is symbolical of Satan's character. Actually Satan is like an angel of light, Lucifer, the morning-star, the summation of God's glorious creation.

So it is in this delineation of this beast. We have here a symbol of him. When you see him, you will not see a creature like a panther, like a leopard, his feet like a bear, with a mouth like a lion. When he appears, you will see the most fascinating, the most scintillating, the most magnetic mortal man that has ever walked across the stage of human history. I know that because the delineation here says: "And the dragon, Satan, gave unto him his power and his throne and his authority and the whole world wondered after the beast, and worshipped him saying, Who is like the beast and who can make war against him?" In all time and tide and history, there will never have appeared a human being with the glory, the personality, the intriguing, bewitching, ingratiating manner of this man, a veritable god of wisdom, insight, accomplishment and achievement.

Satan gave him his power and his throne and his authority.

This man accepts the gift that Jesus spurned when Satan offered him all of the glories of the kingdoms of this world; and the whole earth acclaims the man as the very incarnation of glory and wisdom and might and power and honor. Had I read this passage when I was a youth, I would have thought: "Not in our enlightened age. Such a thing is impossible." But later I stood day after day at radios, listening to hundreds of thousands of Italians crying, "Il Duce! Il Duce!" I stood before those same radios, listening to hundreds of thousands of Germans crying, "Der Führer! Der Führer!" These Italians and Germans who cried thus belonged to the most cultured, enlightened, civilized and literate of all of the nations that have ever existed; and yet they looked upon their hero and their leader as though he were their God.

This final anti-Christ will be received in gladness and the kings of the earth will peaceably yield their authority to him, "for there is none like him." How will that come to pass? Here is another instance of how, if we interpret the Revelation correctly, every little detail will fit in precisely. John says he stood upon the sand of a raging sea. That raging sea, pictured also in Daniel, is a symbol of the violent, chaotic masses of humanity in a day of crisis and revolution. Out of these horrible, chaotic revolutions, arise these tyrannical leaders. Out of the chaos of the blood and mass of the French revolution, Napoleon was born. Out of the vast chaotic revolution of the labor movement, Lenin was born. Out of the chaos and mass of revolution, Hitler was born. Always out of the raging turmoil of social chaos, these anti-Christs come.

It is so with this one. In a day of revolution, in a day of chaos, in a day of storm and fury, comes this great and final ruler. That is the meaning of the opening of the first seal in Revelation 6. In keeping with the opening of the first seal, chapter 17 of the Apocalypse says that those ten kings willingly, with one mind, gave to him their power, their strength and their authority. When the first seal is opened, this final anti-

Christ appears. He comes riding a white horse, with a bow and no arrows. He comes conquering and to conquer, but he is a bloodless conqueror. There is no war, there is no battle, there is no resistance. In the midst of their chaos and despair, these kings of the earth, the rulers of the earth, gladly yield to him the authority and dominion of the governments of all the world, and they hail him as the savior of the race. They say: "This is the man who can lead us out, this is the man who has the answer to our questions, this is the man who can bring peace and prosperity to all mankind. All hail!" The people will be attracted to him and they will wonder after him and wonder will turn into worship. This is the great and final ruler of the earth.

In another place (Revelation 17:8) John beholds the beast arise out of the abyss. When he sees him rise out of a raging sea, John is describing his political origin. He arises out of social turmoil and trouble. When he sees him arise out of the abyss, John is describing his actual origin. The monster is diabolical, a son of damnation and perdition. He is like a leopard; he is like a bear; he is like a lion; he is a terrible, nondescript beast. Now let us see what God means by these descriptions.

In Daniel 7, the prophet looks ahead and describes the coming great kingdoms and their glory. First, he sees the lion; second, he sees the bear; third, he sees the lion; and finally, the nondescript. When Daniel saw them, they succeeded each other, but when John looks upon this great and final anti-Christ, he is a conglomerate of all of them, the summation of all of them. What John is saying to us, in the symbolism of God about this final anti-Christ, is that he will sum up in himself, in that one sovereignty and in that one dominion, the honor and glory of the entire world in its magnificent past. All of it will be summed up in him whom the world wonders after and finally worships, saying, "Who is like him, who is like him, or who could stand in his presence?" When we consider the honor and the glory of this ancient earth, we cannot help but somewhat share in the wonder and the marvel of it. All of the classics were produced in that ancient world. The seven great architectural triumphs of the world were in the seven wonders of the world of that ancient day.

Think of the golden majesty of Babylon. Of the mighty, ponderous massiveness of Cyrus and Persia. Think of the beauty and elegance and intellect of the ancient Greek world. Think of the Roman with his laws and his order and his idea of justice. All of these glories will be summed up in the majesty of this one eventual anti-Christ, who will be like a Nebuchadnezzar, a Cyrus, a Tiglath-Pilezer, a Shalmanezer, a Julius Caesar, a Caesar Augustus, an Alexander the Great, a Napoleon Bonaparte, a Frederick the Great, and a Charlemagne, all bound up in one. Impressive it is to read what God has written in His book of that final captivating, spell-binding, be-witching, resplendent ruler of this world system. He is Satan's masterpiece. This is the best that Satan can do. "And Satan gave to him his glory and his power and his throne and his authority." All the things that Christ spurned are bestowed upon him.

This monster is the arch-persecutor of all time. Upon his heads are names (pural) of blasphemy and "there was given unto him a mouth speaking great things and blasphemies"; and he blasphemed against God and against His name and against His dwelling place and against His tabernacle in heaven, "and it was given unto him to make war with the saints." And all who did not receive his mark in their right hands and on their foreheads were put to death, and no one stood before him to resist him save those whose names were written in the book of the Lamb, slain from the foundation of the world.

This beast is the great arch-enemy of God. He comes in glory and in peace, but in the midst of that last week of Daniel 9, the vile serpent breaks his covenant with Daniel's people, and his true character immediately is seen. In a blood-bath, he wars against God and God's people. In Revelation 11, it is this beast that slays God's two great witnesses in the earth. In chapter 12, he is used by the Dragon to persecute the woman and the remnant of her seed. Here in chapter 13 is a third picture of that violent and vile persecution; here he is slaying the saints and those who oppose him, those who name the name of the true God. Those who dare to worship Jesus seal their testimony with their blood in martyrdom.

GOD'S ENCOURAGEMENT FOR HIS PEOPLE

God closes this passage: "If any man have an ear, let him hear." That is an expression found many times in the Word of the Lord. In the Book of Matthew and in the Book of Luke, when the Lord Christ said something that He wished to impress upon His followers, He emphasized it by saying, "He that hath an ear, let him hear." That same passage occurs in the Book of the Revelation, in chapters 2 and 3. Seven times do we read it, each time that the Lord speaks to one of the churches of Asia: "He that hath an ear, let him hear."

Here again is an example of the fact that if we interpret this book correctly, every little piece and detail will fall into place. "If a man have an ear, let him hear what the spirit saith to the churches"—this is the word of the Lord seven times in chapters 2 and 3. But we do not have that last phrase here—". . . what the spirit saith to the churches," for they are gone. God has taken them out of this awful trial and tribulation. But to the saints who turn to God in that fearful and bloody hour, He says, "If any man have an ear, let him hear."

God has a message in His prophecy, in the lessons He seeks to teach us by these outlines and symbols. What is that message? "He that leadeth into captivity shall go into captivity; he that killeth with the sword must be killed with the sword. Here is the patience and the faith of the saints." As terribly as the saints suffered under Selucius when they were fried on iron pans; as terribly as they suffered in the days of the bloody Caesars; as terribly as they suffered in the days of the awful

Inquisition under the Papal leaders; their suffering is as nothing compared to the agony of these tribulation saints.

But God has a message for His people. The first concerns judgment: "He that leadeth into captivity shall go into captivity, he that killeth with the sword must be killed with the sword." That is according to the moral government by which God has framed this universe. When Simon Peter pulled out his sword and struck off the right ear of Malchus, when Jesus was being arrested, the Lord said: "Peter, put that sword back in the sheath. They that take the sword must perish by the sword. I have twelve legions of angels at my command (seventy-two thousand of them, and only one of them was necessary to slay one hundred eighty-five thousand of the soldiers of Sennacherib). Put the sword back, for the weapons of the people of God are not blood and violence and war. They are faith and trust in God."

"He that leadeth into captivity must go into captivity and he that killeth with the sword must be killed with the sword." Inherent in every system of tyranny and war is destruction. God so ordained.

The text continues, ". . . here is the endurance and the patience and the faith of the saints." God is not forgetful of our trials. These are limited. "And there was given unto him to continue forty and two months." The Lord limits the extent of this persecution. The Lord Christ said, "Except those days should be shortened, not even the elect would be saved: but for the elect's sake those days shall be shortened." No tyrant can endure but according to the permissive will of God. Then he is cut off by the judgment of God Almighty. "He that leadeth into captivity shall go into captivity; he that killeth with the sword must be killed with the sword." "And there was given unto him power to continue forty and two months" — just forty and two months, in the permissive will of God.

In Revelation 13, describing this beast, six times these words occur: "it was given unto him." Even Satan has no authority, no might and no destiny in himself. Why the permissive will of God allows the purging of this world in blood, I do not understand. The Book of Revelation calls it "the mystery of God that shall be finished in the days of the voice of the seventh trumpet." It is not for us to understand why God permits the persecution and martyrdom of His children. There is no answer from heaven. But all of these things that come to pass, come to pass in the permissive will of the Almighty.

"It was given unto him." God holds the world, God holds the creation, and God holds all destiny in His hand. Here is the *hupomone*, the patience, the endurance, the steadfastness and the faith of the saints; namely, that God watches over His own. The same principles that govern here in the last Book, govern through all of the rest. The same Lord God who reigns here, reigns through all of the rest. He is the same Lord God who presides above the circle of the heavens in our day and in our generation. To look up in faith and in trust is the patience, the steadfastness, the endurance of the saints. The future belongs to God.

Chapter 10

THE VILE FALSE PROPHET

Revelation 13

11. And I beheld another beast coming up out of the earth; and he had two horns like a lamb, and he spake as a dragon.

12. And he exerciseth all the power of the first beast before him, and causeth the earth and them which dwell therein to worship the first beast, whose deadly wound was healed.

13. And he doeth great wonders, so that he maketh fire come down from heaven on the earth in the sight of men.

14. And deceiveth them that dwell on the earth, by the means of those miracles which he had power to do in the sight of the beast; saying to them that dwell on the earth, that they should make an image to the beast, which had the wound by a sword, and did live.

15. And he had power to give life unto the image of the beast, that the image of the beast should both speak, and cause that as many as would not worship the image of the beast should be killed.

16. And he causeth all, both small and great, rich and poor, free and bond, to receive a mark in their right hand, or in their foreheads:

17. And that no man might buy or sell, save he that had the mark, or the name of the beast, or the number of his name.

18. Here is wisdom. Let him that hath understanding count the number of the beast: for it is the number of a man, and his number is Six hundred threescore and six.

The first ten verses of Revelation 13 describe a political and ultimate anti-Christ. Beginning at verse 11, the Seer describes for us the false prophet in one of the most instructive of all of the visions to be found in the Apocalypse. Chapter 13 begins with the description of a beast that John beheld rising out of a raging sea. The terrible creature is a composite of the four vicious, wild animals that Daniel saw coming out of that same sea. As a political leader, the creature combines in his sovereignty and in his kingdom all of the characteristics of the great empire rulers that Daniel saw in prophecy.

But in the Revelation we learn that this political anti-Christ is not alone. John saw something that Daniel was not privileged to behold. Not only does this final anti-Christ have the ten kings who yield to him the power and strength of their kingdoms, but this political beast has a coadjutor by his side. This coadjutor is described in the second vision which John beholds. He sees a second beast arising out of the earth. In chapters 16, 19 and 20, he is called "the false prophet." He looks like a lamb. He has two horns like a little lamb, but when he speaks, his dragonic voice betrays him, for he has the heart of a serpent and the voice of a dragon; and he exercises authority and military power in the name of the anti-Christ. He does miraculous things as he uses the power of the state to coerce the whole world to bow down and conform to the program and the will of the first beast. He is a remarkable genius, this second beast, this false prophet. He is one of the most unusual figures to be found in all of the Word of God, and without him, the political anti-Christ could never be what he is or achieve the world-wide program that he does. For a moment let us contrast these two beasts.

THE CONTRAST BETWEEN THE FIRST AND SECOND BEASTS

The first beast rises out of the sea. The second one rises out of the earth. I think the figure means that the first one arises out of social chaos and revolution. In the turmoil, strife and raging conflict of races and nations and economic orders, this great, final tyrant rises to preside over the might and strength of the whole earth. All tyrants and all dictators arise out of that raging sea, out of the social disruption of civil power and authority. The second beast arises out of the land, out of the earth. Now, to me, that symbolism means that he comes out of an established civil order. He does not come, like the first one, out of chaos and revolution. Rather, he is a product of an ordered society; he comes out of the development and growth of civilization.

The first beast is definitely political. He is crowned, he is a king, he is a military sovereign over the world. The second one is religious. He is like a lamb, and he exercises his power to deceive the whole earth in accepting the authority, the program, and ultimately the self-chosen deity of this final antiChrist. It is instructive to pause here and think for a moment. I do not suppose that in the history of mankind, it has ever been possible to rule without religious approbation and devotion, neither today nor in any of the centuries and millenniums past.

In the days of Pharaoh, when Moses and Aaron stood before the sovereign of Egypt, he called in Jannis and Jambres, the magicians, the religionists of his day, to oppose Jehovah. When Balak, the king of Moab, sought to destroy Israel, he hired the services of Baalim to curse Israel. In the days of Dan, when that marauding, avaricious tribe conquered Laish, they stole a priest and an ephod in order that they might worship some kind of a deity in the far north. When Absalom entered his revolutionary scheme to destroy his own father, David, he did so by the wisdom and the advice of Ahithophel. When Jeroboam revolted against Judah, he felt compelled to build gods of gold at Bethel and at Dan. Ahab and Jezebel were able to do what they did in Israel, in the debauchery of the kingdom, because they were abetted and assisted by the prophets of Baal.

The French revolution had a goddess of blasphemy, of infidelity, of atheism, and poured into their fraternity of equality and liberty the devotion of fanatical religionists. Anyone who has studied Communism would be blind not to see in it the same fanatical devotion to materialism that we have in our devotion to the spiritual meaning of the Lord God. Without that ability to bring into his cause the devotion of the religious life of the people, no national tyrant, no supreme dictator could survive. Thus it is to be in the consummation of the age. As this anti-Christ builds for himself, through the yielded sovereignty of the ten kings, this great, final, world rule, he has by his side a coadjutor who is the false prophet.

Let us compare these two beasts in yet another way. It is a remarkable development to see how these two stay together, the first beast and the second beast, the political anti-Christ and the religious prophet. They abet one another, they support one another, and that is unusual because in the kingdom of evil mostly the leaders war and destroy one another. For example, in Acts 19 there were some vagabond Jews who sought to be exorcists, to cast out devils, in the name of Paul and of Christ. When they sought to cast out a demon from a poor wretch, the demon said, "Paul I know, Christ I know, but who are you?" The demon almost ripped apart those seven sons of Sceva, those seven evil deceivers.

When Mohammed was reigning at Medina, there was another like prophet in another town who pretended to the same prophetic order of Mohammed. The second one proposed to Mohammed that they divide the world between them and make common cause. So this fellow, Moseilma, wrote a letter to Mohammed and this is what he said: "From Moseilma, the prophet of Allah, to Mohammed, the prophet of Allah, Come now, let us make a partition of the world and let half be thine and half be mine." Mohammed replied: "From Mohammed, the prophet of God, to Moseilma, the liar and prophet of the devil . . . ." And from then on, there was nothing but war between them.

Thus the kingdom of evil rages against itself through all time. When Napoleon arrogated to himself all of the sovereignty of Europe, from then on, he and the Pope did nothing but damn and excommunicate each other. Such is the kingdom of darkness and evil, tearing itself apart. It always is that way. If you follow your newspaper, you see dark headlines again and again of gang warfares fought over the attempt to divide up the gambling racket, to partition out the bootlegging, to divide up the prostitution. The vile underworld lives in blood, in hatred, in greed and avarice. That is the kingdom of Satan. That is why this is such an astonishing prophecy here in the Revelation. These two, the political anti-Christ and the false prophet, are blood-brothers. One gives authority, financial support and military power to the other; and the other takes it and uses it for the tremendous, unbelievable, immeasurable support of the first one.

The Apocalypse says that the whole world moves toward one vast political unit. That would demand that the world also move in the same direction toward one great, common religion. He would be a blind reader of history, of present-day newspaper headlines, who did not see that inevitable development. And as the Devil looks upon it he says: "I like that. They want one great supra-government. I will give it to them. They want one great supra-religion; I'll give it to them." History moves in that direction, every day, just as we see it outlined here in the Word of God.

THE LAMB-LIKE FALSE PROPHET

Let us look at this false prophet a little more closely. Let us get acquainted with him more intimately. You will not find in the earth a creature, a monster, a character like this one. "And I beheld another beast coming up out of the earth; and he had two horns like a lamb, and he spake as a dragon. And he exerciseth all the power of the first beast . . . and he uses it to compel men to bow down and obey the mandates and orders and commands of the political tyrant."

There is a mixed-up group of metaphors here. The beast is like a lamb. There is a gentle domesticity about him. There is a softness about him, an easiness about him. What could be more sweet or tender or precious than someone who counsels people and who seeks to make them conscious of God and happy in their lives and to solve all of the problems they face in this world and to give them a program by which they can be at peace with themselves and with God? "Like a lamb." There is a gentleness about him, a softness about him that is deceiving, for, of these two beasts, *he* is the far more dangerous. Why? Because any man who proposes to guide and command the consciences and minds and hearts and souls of men, has in his power an unbelievable authority over mankind. He is indescribably the more dangerous of the two. "Like a lamb," but his voice betrays him, and his manner of speech and actions reveal him.

One of the most ironic things I have ever read in history and one of the most hypocritical deceptions I have ever come across in human life is this: the terrible persecuting church says it has never destroyed any heretic, never. It solemnly avows: "We never burned any heretic at the stake. We never drowned any antagonist. We never destroyed anyone." But if representatives of that church would read the Bible, they might change some of the explanations they make. They are described exactly in what God says about the lamb who acts like a dragon. He is soft, easy, spiritual. He counsels his people, he seeks to guide their consciences and their souls and their lives. But the authority by which he does this is the authority of the state. The state supports him and in return he supports the state.

Let us look more closely at this fellow. He is an interesting character. He is a hybrid if there ever was one. He has two horns, the text says, like a lamb. But he is not a real lamb; he just says he is. The real lamb of God has seven horns, the plentitude of the fulness and power of the Almighty. But this one is an imitation lamb. He just *says* that he is a lamb, that he is an icon of Christ in the earth. He is like a lamb. From this description, we can know that he is a product of an apostate and perverted Christianity. It is astonishing that out of the development of Christian civilization and Christian history this false prophet should come.

A second remarkable thing about him is that he imitates

all of the things that are of the Lord. For example, Paul says, "I bear in my body the *stigmata* of the Lord Jesus [the brandmarks of the Lord Jesus]." And in Revelation 7, we find those *stigmata*, the markings of God, upon Israel. In chapter 14, we find them again upon the one hundred forty-four thousand. We find them upon God's saints in heaven, the mark of Christ, the mark of God. But this fellow has a mark, too, which he places on the hand and on the forehead of his dupes. He also has a mark. Another amazing thing about him is that he is able to perform miracles. He is able to do miracles just as they are done at Lourdes, France, just as they are wrought at the shrine of the Virgin of Guadalupe. It has not been many weeks since I stood at Cartago in Costa Rica. Gathered there by the thousands and thousands from the ends of the nation, were the superstitious addicts of the shrine of the Virgin of the Angels, waiting for miracles.

IDOLATRY IN THE CHURCHES

But the strangest thing of all, and the most astonishing development in Christianity, is the use by the false prophet of his authority and power to promote an idolatrous worship. Is it possible that out of the rigid monotheism of Judah and out of the preaching of the Gospel of Jesus, the Christian churches have given themselves to an unbelievable idolatry? History is more astonishing than fiction. Somehow there is a weakness in humanity which demands that we must have some kind of visible representation to help us to worship. It was true in ancient Israel when Aaron made gods of gold. It has been true in the story of religion ever since.

There is a witchery in idolatry that is vastly appealing. There is a fascination about images, about idols, that is almost incredible. God says image worship is the bane and the abomination and the scourge of the earth. Yet it is the churches that lead in this world of images and idolatry. Mohammedanism arose as a violent reaction to idolatry in the churches. Mohammed and his prophets and the Caliphs who followed them felt called of God to destroy idolatry, and the idolatry they attacked was the idolatry in the churches. What God says here of the development of religion in the future is just what John saw in the Revelation. The great religion of the future will not be the rigid monotheism of the Mohammedans nor will it be the rigid monotheism of the Jew; the religion of the future is going to be the idolatry of the so-called Christian churches. When finally this evil thing works out and this development comes to pass, we shall not have a universal religion that is Jewish or Mohammedan, but it will be this unbelievable Christian idolatry. What astonishing things God writes in His Book!

There is another strange prophecy in Revelation 13 concerning the ultimate development of civilization. As the first great world kingdom was represented by a tremendous image, an instrument of idolatry, so is the last. The first world empire was the golden sovereignty of Nebuchadnezzar. "And Nebuchadnezzar the king made an image of gold whose height was sixty cubits and whose breadth was six cubits and he set it up in the plain of Dura. And he compelled all of his subjects to bow down and worship it." Nebuchadnezzar reasoned that as long as his empire was cluttered up with divers and diverse religions, he was weakened in his sovereignty; so in order to make one tremendous kingdom, he had the decree sent out that all must bow down before his god of gold.

When we turn to the last kingdom of the age, humanity repeats that same weakness. Revelation 13:14-17 describes the terrible mandate by the false prophet. There is an idolatrous program to follow and an image to adore, and if one does not obey, he is violently coerced by the financial, political and military authority given to this false prophet. All must bow down or they cannot sell. I was surprised listening to the president of a college in Istanbul, a man who had married a Bulgarian and who for the years of his life had lived in Bulgaria. He said to me: "You cannot understand and you cannot know that the

most terrible instrument of persecution ever devised is an innocent ration card. You cannot buy and you cannot sell except
according to that little, innocent card. If they please, you can
be starved to death, and if they please, you can be dispossessed
of everything you have; for you cannot trade, and you cannot
buy and you cannot sell, without permission." Oh, the coer-
civeness that lies so easily in the hands of a dictatorial tyrant!
Bow down or else! The whole story of humanity ends in that
same dictatorial authority.

THE AMAZING NUMBER, 666

John now writes a verse, closing chapter 13, that in itself
is enigmatical. He says, "Here is wisdom. Let him that hath
understanding count the number of the beast: for it is the number of a man; it is 666." That is the most famous of all of the
apocalyptic figures in history and in literature — 666. What
does it mean? The righteous will understand what that means
when the time comes. God's saints will understand what that
refers to when the hour arrives. We do not know. There may
be a thousand speculations, and there are. There may be another thousand speculations, and there will be. But no man
knows that 666, which is the number and mark of the beast,
that final anti-Christ; no man knows until the day and the
hour comes. But God's children will know when the time arrives. It will be revealed unto them and the saints will understand.

There is only one thing about it that we know and that
is this: six is the number of a man; six — falling short of the
perfect seven. Man was created on the sixth day. He is to work
six of the seven days. A Hebrew slave could not be a slave
more than six years. The fields were to be sown not more than
six years and then they were to be allowed to rest on a Sabbath. Six is the number of a man. There is a trinity of sixes,
666. Six raised through three decimal points, six units, six tens
and six hundreds. All that I can say in the present light is

this: This beast, in his number, represents the ultimate of all human ingenuity and competence. The most mankind will ever be able to attain to is beneath the perfect seven, always a six. With himself a six, with his national government a six, with his laws a six, with the whole program by which he seeks to make an Eden in this world and a millennium among mankind, always that deafening, defeating, discouraging six. When we come to the end of the way, the Book says here, it is still a six. The height of a man's arrogance and the height of a man's folly and the ultimate of a man's self-will is still one short — a six, a six, and another six. This is the number of man, 666. Age, discouragement, death failure, sin, war, destruction, hatred — the Book says we never get beyond them.

Had the Apocalypse closed with the thirteenth chapter, of all things known and prophesied, our lives would be most discouraging and full of despair. But, beyond, as we turn the pages of the prophecy, here is the perfect seven, the seven-horned Lamb of God. Here is the perfect Holy Spirit, the seven spirits of God. Yonder is the holy, blessed next world, the seven times blessing that God has poured out upon His new creation. There is the glorious Lord, and the saints sing the seven-fold doxology of dominion and glory and power and honor unto Him that liveth forever and ever. Our perfection, our victory, our new world, our ultimate and final government and our marvelous salvation, these are in the Lamb of God, the perfect seven.

COUNTERFEIT RELIGION

Revelation 13

11. And I beheld another beast coming up out of the earth; and he had two horns like a lamb, and he spake as a dragon.

12. And he exerciseth all the power of the first beast before him, and causeth the earth and them which dwell therein to worship the first beast, whose deadly wound was healed.

13. And he doeth great wonders, so that he maketh fire come down from heaven on the earth in the sight of men,

14. And deceiveth them that dwell on the earth, by the means of those miracles which he had power to do in the sight of the beast; saying to them that dwell on the earth, that they should make an image to the beast, which had the wound by a sword, and did live.

15. And he had power to give life unto the image of the beast, that the image of the beast should both speak and cause that as many as would not worship the image of the beast should be killed.

16. And he causeth all, both small and great, rich and poor, free and bond, to receive a mark in their right hand, or in their foreheads:

17. And that no man might buy or sell, save he that had the mark, or the name of the beast, or the number of his name.

This message concerns the religion of the false prophet, a religion expressed in an instiution which I have called the counterfeit church. In chapter 16, in chapter 19 and in chapter 20 of the Revelation, the second beast of Revelation 13:11 is called the false prophet. Chapter 13 begins with John standing on the sand of the sea, and out of the raging waters he sees a monster rise from the deep; that is, out of the social, chaotic turmoil of nations, out of boiling social revolutions, out of the volcanic eruptions of national and political life, he sees this monster rise. This first beast is a picture of the last political government on this earth, headed up in an ultimate anti-Christ.

Then John saw another beast rising out of the earth. As the first one rose out of anarchy, chaos and social revolution (the raging waters of the sea of humanity), the second rises out of the earth; that is, out of civilized, ordered, social government. This second beast is the sovereign head of the ultimate, final religious system of this world. The Bible everywhere, and especially in the Revelation, reveals (and all of these things are corroborated in human history) that the nations will move toward political unity. In the last days, even the ten kingdoms into which this whole earth is divided in its national life — even those ten kingdoms will give their sovereignty and their power to an ultimate ruler, the final anti-Christ. Civilization, the Bible says, moves toward one political unit, and the same Bible says that this earth moves also toward one religious unit. The trend of religious life in the world will be more and more to get together, to combine, to unite, until eventually, in the ultimate consummation, all religious systems of the world will be headed up in one beast, one monster, one false prophet.

John describes this false prophet: "And I beheld another beast coming up out of the earth; and he looked like a lamb, but he spoke like a dragon." He looked like a lamb, but actually he was the mouthpiece and spokesman for the Dragon. Now, there cannot be government without religious devotion. That is true of even a Communistic government. The Communists make a religion out of their devotion to materialism, blasphemy and atheism. Without that religious, fanatical devotion, the system could not live. There must be religious fervor back of any system that endures. So this false governmental leader must have a religion, and the false prophet supplies it. He does it through a counterfeit church, through counterfeit religion.

We propose to look closely at this counterfeit church, the religion of this false prophet.

THE COUNTERFEIT CHURCH SAYS WHAT THE WORLD DESIRES TO HEAR SAID

There are several things that characterize the counterfeit church and its counterfeit religion. The first is that it says what the world wants to hear said. It pleases the itching ears of the people. I could not think of a better illustration of that than the story of Micaiah. When Ahab said to Jehoshaphat, "Let us go up against Ramoth-Gilead; it belongs to us; let us take it out of the hands of the Syrians," Jehoshaphat said, "Before we go, let us call the prophets together and ask them whether it is wise, whether God will bless the war or not." So Ahab gathered together four hundred of his prophets and they all said: "Go up to Ramoth-Gilead. The Lord will deliver it into your hands." But when Jehoshaphat looked at those four hundred, he said, "Is there not yet another prophet of the Lord before whom we might inquire?" Ahab replied: "Why, yes, there is another, but I hate him. He always speaks evil of me and never good." Jehoshaphat replied: "Oh, let not the king say so. Call him." So Ahab sent an officer of the government to Micaiah the prophet of God to bid him to come before the king. The officer said to Micaiah: "Micaiah, four hundred prophets are now standing before the king and they are all prophesying good. Now Micaiah, you prophesy what will please the king. You prophesy what is good." But Micaiah, the man of God, answered, "As the Lord liveth, what God says, that will I say."

When Micaiah stood before Ahab, he said, "I saw Israel like sheep scattered over the mountains because their leader was dead." Ahab turned to Jehoshaphat and said: "Isn't that what I told you? I hate him. He blasphemes." Ahab said, "Take this fellow and put him in a dungeon and feed him bread of affliction and water of affliction until I come back in peace and in triumph." So, Ahab went out to war. Remember the story? A man drew back his bow at a venture (he did not aim it) and let fly the arrow. But God guided that arrow through a joint in the harness of Ahab, in the armor of Ahab, where it pierced his heart. Blood flowed out of the wound, covering the floor of the chariot and, when it was washed, dogs licked up the blood, according to the saying of Elijah the prophet years before. Yet the officer said to Micaiah: "Tell Ahab something good. Say it beautifully. Say what he wants to hear said." Such is counterfeit religion; such is the false prophet.

It is a rare thing that a prophet of God, a true prophet of God, will ever say what the world wants to hear said. Zedekiah was king in Jerusalem when Nebuchadnezzar and his Chaldean army surrounded him as a man would hold iron in a vice. Zedekiah said to Jeremiah, "Is there any word from the Lord?" Jeremiah said, "There is." Zedekiah asked, "What does God say?" Jeremiah then replied, "If I tell you you will slay me; you will put me to death." Zedekiah answered, "Your life will be precious in my sight. I swear. What does God say?" Jeremiah said, "God said this city shall be burned with fire and the Chaldeans shall take the people into captivity." It is a rare thing that a man of God will deliver to the world a message that the world likes to hear. When a preacher is suave, sweet, pacifying and placating in what he says, the chances are that he is a counterfeit, a representative of the religion of the false prophet. So the first characteristic of counterfeit religion is that it says what the world wants to hear said, not what God says.

THE COUNTERFEIT CHURCH TEACHES WHAT THE WORLD WANTS TAUGHT

A second characteristic of the counterfeit church, of the religion of the false prophet, is that it teaches what the world wants to hear taught. The false prophet believes what the world wants to believe. The religion of the false prophet and of the counterfeit church is one that looks upon Scriptural doctrine as being outmoded. It avows that we have outlived the usefulness of the old-time faith. It asserts that we have so progressed in this enlightened, scientific era that we need a new theology, a new sophistry of enlightenment. The exponents of the new faith say that no man in this scientific and enlightened age can believe in the miracles of the Bible.

They look upon the Scriptures as an antiquarian would look upon any other antique document. In ancient times, Aesop wrote his *Fables*. In centuries past, Homer wrote his *Iliad* and his *Odyssey*, examples of Greek mythology and legend. The counterfeit preacher picks up the Bible and uses it also as an example of myth and legend. He reads the Bible as he would read about Jason and the Golden Fleece. He empties the Bible of all of its supernatural, miraculous context. He thinks religion evolved along with supposed evolution of the whole human race. He believes the theory that we have all come from tadpoles and green scum, that we have gradually evolved until our orboreal ancestors quit hanging by their tails and began walking upright. That is the way the counterfeit church looks upon religion; that the myth and the legend of God in those primitive, stone ages gradually evolved until finally we arrived at this present, enlightened age in which we are to believe nothing.

Counterfeit pulpiteers have the same evolutionary persuasion concerning old-fashioned piety and the reverential awe and fear in which a man ought to walk humbly before his Maker. They say all of the old rules of conduct are passé; that now we have new rules for our new day. They say we have been freed from the bondage of the morality and piety of that old medieval superstition found in the Bible. This is a new day and we have new rules to live by.

Recently a broken-hearted mother (the family does not belong to our church) came to see me. Her daughter, who is but a child, is going to be an unwed mother. The mother, in her distress and agony, said to me: "I took my girl and I took the boy and brought them to his church and to his minister. This man of the cloth turned to the two children, and he said to the girl: 'You — this is your fault. You should have protected yourself. This is not the boy's fault. He was just indulging in permissible, pre-marital experience, and the reason you are in the condition you are, is because you did not protect yourself. The boy is not to blame at all.'"

This is the new day. This is the new theology. This is the new morality. Only by taking God out of the Bible, thereby nullifying its supernatural, moral character, could that minister be right; for the rules of morality, fundamentally, are anchored in the character of Almighty God. A changed God means changed rules. According to the new sophistry, the new enlightenment with the new rules, that minister of the cloth is correct: it *is her* fault. She should have protected herself, for this boy was just engaging in legitimate, natural pre-marital experience. That is the religion of the false prophet. That is the religion of the counterfeit church. That is the religion of the Dragon.

The same modern attitude is expressed toward the great doctrines of the faith. In this enlightened age, whose cultivated ears, whose cultural tastes, whose aesthetic nature would respond to a religion of blood — blood atonement? The counterfeit religionists refer to it as a religion of the slaughterhouse, a religion of the shambles, a religion of the packing plant, of the butcher shop. I have preached in churches where every hymn on the blood has been purged out. They say, "It is offensive to our aesthetic natures, and it violates our cultural consciences, this religion of blood." But all through the Word of God, the story of blood atonement follows like a scarlet thread. The difference between religions ultimately is this difference made by the blood. As God said in the land of Egypt, "Sprinkle the blood on the lintels and on the doorpost in the form of a cross, above and on either side, that there may be a distinction between my people and the world."

We can classify all religions in two categories: the religion of works, Mohammedanism, Romanism, Humanism, Shintoism, or Buddhism, all religions that are based upon works; then that one separate and unique Gospel of the Son of God, the religion of the blood. "When I see the blood, I will pass over you." "And they washed their robes and made them white in the blood of the lamb." The humanists and the counterfeiters hate the religion of the blood. Their attitude is the same toward the revelation of the Scriptures concerning damnation, perdition and the judgment of Almighty God: "There is no such thing." To the counterfeits, to the false prophet, there is no such thing as the judgment of God; there is no such thing as the perdition and the fire of hell and eternal damnation. They say such things are negatives, that they are vestiges from a primitive and superstitious past. They say we must be positive in our approach today. They say if we do not teach our children about sin, they will never sin; "Let us be positive about it." But significantly, every one of the Ten Commandments is negative. "Thou shalt not," says the Lord God. He has not endorsed this new sophistry of a positive approach which says: "Do not ever mention sin and they won't sin. Don't ever teach our children about the judgment of God, and they will never fall into aberrations." God's Book says that we are born in sin and conceived in iniquity and the black drop of depravity is in all of our veins. We are born into that kind of a judgment. But this scriptural doctrine is unacceptable to sophisticated and modern ears. To the counterfeit church and counterfeit religion, God is man, whom they worship; their doctrine is humanism; their paradise and Eden is the socialistic welfare state.

THE COUNTERFEIT CHURCH ENJOYS WHAT THE WORLD ENJOYS

Not only does the counterfeit church say what the world wants to hear said, not only does it teach what the world wants to hear taught, but the counterfeit church enjoys what the world enjoys. There are great cities in America where the elected councilmen are helpless before the rising tide and scourge of gambling because "the Church" finds its greatest lucrative source of revenue from gambling. The city is powerless before the racketeers and all of the dark underworld that inevitably follow the gambling syndicate. This nation of America is being plunged into the depths of alchoholism that is worse than the tragedy of France because of the approval of the counterfeit church and counterfeit religion. More and more, our beloved America is dragged by liquor and gambling on a toboggan road down and down and down. The family is destroyed by it; homes are broken by it; wedding bands are snapped by it; children are orphaned by it; men's lives are destroyed by it; the weakness of a whole nation is laid bare by it! All with the approval and approbation of a counterfeit church!

Recently I was in a funeral home, waiting for the service to begin. A big man, filled up with deep emotion, came to me and said: "I just want to thank you for the sermon last Sunday night. I listened to it on the radio and it gave me hope. You see," he said, "my son and my daughter-in-law both are alcoholics." He was referring to my mention of a man who sat beside me on an airplane, traveling to a distant city. When I asked him where he was going, I learned that we both were going to the same destination. When I asked him why he was going there, he told me he was going to hear me preach. I was going there to preach for the State Evangelistic Conference. I asked him why he was going down there to hear me preach. He said that one time he had a chain of stores and a beautiful home, but that he lost his stores and his home because of liquor. He said that in those sorrowful days when he was cast out, he went to a service and heard me preach, and there gave his heart to God. He went back and his wife took him into the home again. God took him back into His loving grace again. The man said that now he has more stores than he ever had before, a bigger chain than he ever had. He said he is a deacon, the treasurer, and the head usher in his church and God has blessed him. "So," he said, "whenever you are in my part of the world, if I can get there, I always go to hear you preach." That was the incident, briefly, that I had told the previous Sunday night; and that father at the funeral said: "I just want to thank you. You gave me hope, you gave me hope for my boy and for my daughter." Any man on earth who stands up and says that it is a legitimate business to break up homes, to wreck lives, to orphan children and to destroy the souls of men, is a counterfeit; I do not care who he is or what his name.

Before one of our legislative committees appointed to listen to discussions of a liquor bill, a Bishop stood up and spoke of the liberty and right of a man to drink. When the Bishop got through speaking his piece before the legislative committee, a humble, unnamed man stood up and said: "My wife and I had an only son, an only child, and he fell into the terrible throes of the alcoholic. In love and tenderness, we won our boy back to life again. As our boy was ascending and God's favor was upon him, he was invited to a social gathering where a minister of the cloth, with a liquor glass in his hand, said, 'This is the right of any man.' He drank and encouraged all the others to drink. My boy was there, and, seeing the man of the cloth lead the way, he followed after. Our boy was soon again on the toboggan road, down and down. Our boy died of delirium tremens. And, Gentlemen," the broken-hearted man said, "the man of the cloth who set that example that night before our boy is the Bishop who has just addressed you."

When the Eighteenth Amendment was destroyed, William E. Borah of the Senate of the United States said, "God will punish America for bringing back the legalized liquor traffic." From that day until this, America has stumbled into one tragic crisis after another.

The God Almighty who judges America is the same Lord

God Almighty who shall judge the counterfeit church. Someone once asked me, "Preacher, is there any word in the Bible against liquor?" My soul! in all the language and literature of the earth, there was never written as scathing, as terrible a castigation as you find in the Word of God against liquor. Listen to the words of the wisest man who ever lived: "Who hath woe? who hath sorrow? who hath contentions? who hath babbling? who hath wounds without cause? who hath redness of eyes? They that tarry long at the wine; they that go to seek mixed wine. Look not thou upon the wine when it is red, when it sparkles in the cup . . . . At the last it biteth like a serpent, and stingeth like an adder" (Proverbs 23:29-32).

Whoever fools with liquor, fools with death. He is destined to ruin the lives of his children and of other children. Do not ever persuade yourself that the example of the bum in the gutter, down and out, is a temptation to a fine, upstanding young boy. When he sees that fellow in his vomit and filth, ragged, in the gutter, he is offended in him and he passes by. Do not suppose that he is the one who destroys the boy. The man who destroys the boy is the big executive, in his swivel chair, in a beautiful office. He drinks and that fine, upstanding young fellow coming up sees the big executive and he follows after him. Then the boy is destroyed. One out of every nine becomes a problem drinker and cannot help himself. The man who leads the boy into that debauchery, ruin and damnation is accountable unto God. The church that approves it is a derelict and a counterfeit church. This is the religion of the false prophet, He urges us to enjoy what the world enjoys. At numerous social gatherings in this city, whatever the riotous, drunken, debauched world is doing, there will be some minister and there will be some communicant, enjoying it alike, drunken alike, in the orgy alike. Such is the counterfeit church and such is counterfeit religion. It is unspeakable to the true child and to the true prophet of God.

THE COUNTERFEIT CHURCH OFFERS INSTITUTIONAL SALVATION

We are speaking of the false prophet who looks like a lamb. He is soft, sweet and easy. He counsels people, and he professes to care for their consciences and their souls; but he is the more dangerous monster of the two beasts, for his heart and his leadership is of the Dragon. The counterfeit church says what the people want to hear said; it indeed teaches what the world wants to hear taught; it enjoys what the world enjoys. I have a last characterization of the counterfeit church. It offers an institutional salvation. That is, it avows the false doctrine, "You go with us, and we will take you to heaven by virtue of the fact that we are *the* church of God." I speak of that doctrine briefly in two ways. Its adherents offer a national salvation by their institutional organizations. The world likes to have one religion so it can write concordats with it, so it can make treaties with it, so it can use it. It pleases the world to have *a* church and *a* religion. However the truth of God may be, however obedience to the Almighty may be, if the nations can just have *a* religion and *a* counterfeit church, life is simplified for the world. Then people do not have to worry about what God says; they do not have to worry about the will of the Almighty. Here is a religion that they can handle, use, tinker with, mold, cast, compromise with, make laws concerning, write treaties with, do anything that they want to. They say let us forget about God, forget about the will of heaven, forget about the Bible. Religion is this packaged organization. Thus national life is framed according to the organized expression of religion in a counterfeit church and in a false prophet.

The counterfeit church and the counterfeit religion offer institutional salvation to the individual heart. "Belong to mother church and mother church will take you to heaven." But outside of mother church is damnation and hell. This is the awful, fearful thing held over the heads of the people. They live in panic and fear at the very thought of being separated from the church, for outside of that institution there is no salvation — nothing but damnation and hell. They live in fearsome torment.

The awful power that lies in the minister of the cloth among people who believe in his institution and in his church is indescribable. What he says is the rule of life and of soul. For instance, he says that all of us married outside his organization live in adultery — all of us, all of us. We were married by a Baptist minister; so we live in adultery. We were married according to the laws of the State of Texas, but we are living in adultery. All of our children are illegitimate, all of them, for we were married by a Baptist minister. Even today, we have committed a mortal sin, for we are *in* a Baptist church, listening to a Baptist minister. That awesome fear by which they govern their people makes it almost impossible to deliver anyone from it because to them to leave it is to be damned. Outside of that church is to live in adultery and to bring up children illegitimately. I could go on for hours and hours about the counterfeit church, a counterfeit religion, the doctrine of the false prophet. It pleases the world to have it so.

Last night, I pleaded with a sweet, precious young girl who is just beginning to build her home. I said: "Listen, young lady, listen! Go to God for yourself, for *yourself*. Pray to God for yourself, for *yourself*. Do not confess your sins to a man. Confess them to God. Our Saviour is a great High Priest who can be touched with the feeling of our infirmities. In all points was He tried as we are, though without sin. Wherefore come boldly before the throne of grace and find grace to help in time of need. Come for yourself. Ask for yourself. Pray for yourself. Confess your need to God for yourself and listen to the voice of the Lord who will answer by fire, who will answer by words, who will answer by strength and by might and by power, who will answer from heaven. Go to God for yourself. Ask for yourself. Pray unto Him for yourself. Look to God for yourself."

"Come," saith the Lord, "Come." This is the true religion, this is the true church and this is the true prophet of God. "And the Spirit and the Bride say come. And let him that heareth say, Come. And let him that is athirst come. And whosoever will, let him take the water of life freely." Come. Come for yourself. Let God speak to you heart to heart, face to face. Find life and assurance and salvation and truth in the blessedness of the name of our glorious and incomparable Redeemer. Come. Come. God bids us find help from His gracious and precious hand.

CHAPTER 12

THE ONE HUNDRED FORTY-FOUR THOUSAND ON MOUNT ZION

Revelation 14

1. And I looked, and, lo, a Lamb stood on the mount Sion, and with him an hundred forty and four thousand, having his Father's name written in their foreheads.

2. And I heard a voice from heaven, as the voice of many waters, and as the voice of a great thunder: and I heard the voice of harpers harping with their harps:

3. And they sung as it were a new song before the throne, and before the four beasts, and the elders: and no man could learn that song but the hundred and forty and four thousand, which were redeemed from the earth.

4. These are they which were not defiled with women; for they are virgins. These are they which follow the Lamb whithersoever he goeth. These were redeemed from among men, being the firstfruits unto God and to the Lamb.

5. And in their mouth was found no guile: for they are without fault before the throne of God.

As often in the Apocalypse when tragic days are delineated, there will be inserted a vision of the light of the glory and beauty of God, so it is in this vision of Revelation 14, containing this wondrous scene with the Lamb on Mt. Zion and the one hundred and forty-four thousand. Revelation 12 delineates the malice of Satan and the rage of the evil one who is cast down into the earth. Revelation 13 describes the terrific and sickening horror of the beast. It depicts those two terrible monsters, who are God's symbols of the ministers of Satan, the ultimate anti-Christ and the false prophet, who delude and deceive the people of the earth and lead them into perdition and damnation. This beautiful chapter 14 immediately follows the horror of those darkening days. It reminds us that, after the storm and rage of the tempest is over, then, in the quiet beauty of the calm, God over-arches the heavens with a rainbow of promise. The clouds have emptied themselves, the raging tempest has spent itself; and the thunders no longer roar, the lightning no longer flashes. Beyond and back of the clouds, break the beautiful rays of a golden light.

That is the situation here in the Revelation. In those terrible, trying times the Lord says: "For the elect's sake those days are going to be shortened. They cannot last. I will come to you." And before the time of the destruction of those two terrible monstrous instruments of Satan (the detail of their destruction is presented in Revelation 17 and 18), God gives us this beautiful picture of the Lamb on Mt. Zion and these one hundred and forty-four thousand who stand before Him and sing a new song in the land of the new and glorious beginning again.

Chapter 14 is simply the other side of chapter 13. They are contemporaneous in history. These things all happen at once, and chapter 14 is but the counterpart of chapter 13. One side is the dark description of the beast and of Satan and of the judgment of God upon those who worship the vile image. At the same time, in contrast, is this beautiful scene of these glorious ones who serve God and Him alone. In chapter 13 is the beast; in chapter 14 is the Lamb, gentle and precious, on Mt. Zion. In chapter 13 are the spurious, the counterfeit and the false. In chapter 14 are the true, the genuine and the lovely. In chapter 13 is the mark of the beast, and in chapter 14, the mark of God. In chapter 13 is the work of idolatry and the corruption of the earth. In chapter 14 is the worship of the true Lamb of God and the saint's dissociation from the corruption of the world. In chapter 13 are those who go with the beast and the idolators down into damnation and perdition. In chapter 14 are those who are redeemed from the earth and who are taken up into heaven. In chapter 13 are those that follow the beast in all of his ways. In chapter 14 are those who follow the Lamb wherever he goes. In chapter 13 is the number of the beast, 666, six hundred, three score and six. In chapter 14 are the one hundred and forty-four thousand, the fulness and the plenitude of the glory, the grace and beauty of God. The two chapters are side by side.

Who are these one hundred and forty-four thousand who stand with the Lamb on Mt. Zion? There are some who say the figure *one hundred and forty-four thousand* is simply a symbol of all of the sanctified hosts of God through all generations and all time. They say the one hundred and forty-four thousand represent the great, ultimate gathering together of the congregation of the Lord. They say this vision symbolizes that congregation. Then there are those who say the one hundred and forty-four thousand represent preeminent Christians. Among the common, ordinary Christians these are the outstanding witnesses, preachers, servants, missionaries and evangelists of God. We could continue these interpretations on and on almost without end. As many interpreters as there are, so many identifications are there of the one hundred and forty-four thousand. Let us follow the text in the Book and see if we can find the identification of the one hundred and forty-four thousand who sing a new song with the Lamb on Mt. Zion.

First of all, I notice here that these one hundred and forty-four thousand sing their new song in the presence of the elders. So, there is a difference between the elders, whoever they represent, and the one hundred and forty-four thousand, for they are together. In the presence of the elders the one hundred and forty-four thousand worship God and sing their new song.

Notice a second thing in the text: just the number, itself, is unique. "I saw and behold, a Lamb stood on mount Sion, and with him an hundred and forty and four thousand." That is not the first time we have met this throng, this number. We have been introduced to it in Revelation 7. Here in chapter 14, the number is presented just as though we had met it before, and there is nothing about it to distinguish it from the one hundred and forty-four thousand that we have met heretofore in the Revelation. The number is so unusual and the whole situation is so remarkable that we could suppose the reference in both chapters is the same. So, when we turn back to Revelation 7, we see that before the raging storm broke and the terrible tribulation began, the Lord God said to the four angels that held the four mighty winds of the judgments of God: "Wait, wait, until you seal the servants, the ministers of God in their foreheads. And I heard the number of them which were sealed: and there were sealed an hundred and forty and four thousand." Twelve thousand from the tribe of Judah, twelve thousand from the tribe of Gad, of Asher, of Simeon, all the way through, twelve thousand sealed from each of the twelve tribes of Israel, make up the one hundred and forty-four thousand.

Another thing I notice here in the Apocalypse is that all of these people, these separate groups, are together in the same vision. Here are the elders and here are the one hundred forty-four thousand sealed by God. And here in the same vision, at the same time, are the great throngs of Gentiles who stand before God and the Lamb clothed with white robes, out of every kindred and nation and people and tongue and tribe under the sun. They are all here together. Here are the elders, and here are the one hundred and forty-four thousand, and here are the great multitudes of the Gentiles, who are coming out of the Great Tribulation with their robes white in the blood of the Lamb, and here are the four living creatures, all here together. Now, to me, to identify all of those as being the same thing makes the vision a jumbled, impossible, unacceptable revelation. It has no meaning at all. If the elders represent the church; if the one hundred and forty-four thousand represent the church; if the multitude coming out of the Great Tribulation represent the church; if the altar represents the church; and if the angels represent the church: then, according to that interpretation, it is impossible to me to understand why God set these things in such contrast and described them as being different.

So, seeking to find what God means by these marvelous revelations, I have arrived at a very simple explanation: First, the elders, twenty-four in number, represent the resurrected, glorified saints of God in the Old Testament and the New Testament. The twelve patriarchs, the twelve apostles, stand before God. The same symbolism is in the beautiful city of Jerusalem: There are twelve gates, and each one of those gates represents one of the twelve patriarchs, one of the twelve tribes of Israel. The city has twelve foundations, and each one of those foundations, the Apocalypse says, represents the name of an apostle. The city represents the old and the new, all the saints of God, the old dispensation and the new dispensation. It includes the old era, those who were saved by looking to the cross. It includes the new dispensation, the new era, the age of grace in which we live, those who are saved by looking back to the cross. The elders represent all of the saved of God, twelve for the old and twelve for the new, twenty-four of them, the four and twenty elders in the presence of the Lord.

The great multitude coming out of every nation and language and tribe are those who have been won to Christ by these one hundred and forty-four thousand sealed messengers of God. There never has been, nor will there ever be again, any revival meeting comparable to that which is coming to pass in those dark days when men will lay down their lives as martyrs in the confession of Christ. "The blood of the martyrs is the seed of the church." In those days of terrible and indescribable martyrdom, in those days of blood and sickening horror, the earth will witness its greatest revival. It will be led by these messengers of God, sealed by the Holy Spirit of God, the one hundred and forty-four thousand. They are a select, elect, separate, unique group who pour out, in those dark and terrible days, their testimony to the saving grace of the blessed Lord Jesus.

The text presents these as the firstfruits unto God and

to the Lamb — "the firstfruits." We must pause here because the elders, after Christ, also represent the firstfruits. But they are already in heaven. They have already been translated. The Lord has already come for them. They have been resurrected and glorified, and they sit in the presence of God on their thrones, gold-crowned, victorious. After Christ, "Christ, the firstfruits, and afterwards, they that are Christ's at his coming" — these are represented by the elders. Yet the one hundred and forty-four thousand also are called the firstfruits unto God and to the Lamb. This one hundred and forty-four thousand must be the firstfruits unto God of this new era, of this new time, of this new period, after the translation of the church, after the rapture of the people of God, represented by the elders, crowned and enthroned in heaven. Before those last days of tribulation begin, God says, "First seal out for me these one hundred and forty-four thousand." They are the first set aside, called here the "firstfruits unto God and to the Lamb." Then, after that, John saw the great multitude of the Gentiles that no man could number coming out of that Great Tribulation, having their robes washed and made white in the blood of the Lamb. So this one hundred and forty-four thousand are the firstfruits unto God of the new beginning, of the time after the days of the Gentiles. When our present history has run its course; when the church service is done, and the age of grace has passed; when God has taken His people out of the earth, and we are raptured and translated; then comes this final day described here in the Apocalypse. In the days of the judgment of God and the ultimate appearing of Christ, when God intervenes in human history, in that period, in that day, these are the firstfruits unto God.

We have adumbrations of this sealing of God among the people of Israel many times in the Bible. One example is in I Corinthians 15, where Paul is describing our blessed Lord Jesus crucified, buried, and raised again. Then Paul says: "He appeared to Cephas, then to the twelve. After that, he was seen of about five hundred brethren at once . . . . After that, he was seen of James; then of all the apostles. And last of all he was seen of me, he appeared unto me." How did He appear to the Apostle Paul? The Greek text says, *"hosperei to ektromati."* What an unusual phrase! "And last of all he appeared to me before the time for me to be born, as an abortion, as of one born out of due time." What does that mean? Paul is referring to the fact that there is coming a time when our Lord will appear to His brethren, to Israel, for, "There shall come a Deliverer out of Sion, and shall turn away ungodliness from Jacob . . . . And so Israel shall be saved . . ." (Romans 11:25). "And a nation will be born in a day" (Isaiah 66:8). ". . . And Israel," said the prophet Zechariah, "shall look upon him whom they have pierced . . . . And they shall mourn in bitterness . . ." (Zechariah 12:10). "And so all Israel shall be saved," Paul says. But before that time, which is at the end of this tribulation period, Paul says "he appeared to me as one in an abortion, before the time, before that great and ultimate hour, he appeared unto me." These firstfruits are those of a new era and a new dispensation, when God deals with apostate and unbelieving Israel. God will remember the promises He had made to Abraham, to Isaac and to Jacob, and then Christ will win back to Himself His brethren, just as He appeared to James and to Joseph and to Jude and to Simeon. Before He went back to heaven the first time after His crucifixion, He won His brethren to Himself. He is going to do that for Israel some day. But now there is a veil over their hearts, and when they read Moses and the prophets, they do not see Jesus and they do not accept their Messiah. But some day that veil will be taken away, the Lord will appear to Israel, and they are going to be saved in accepting their Lord. These are the firstfruits of that new dispensation and that new era. This is the mercy, the grace and the goodness of God to the lost sheep of the house of Jacob.

Let us look at the passage again. The text says: "I looked, and, lo, a Lamb stood on mount Sion, and with him an hundred forty and four thousand." What is Mount Zion? Just to name it is to call to mind the many promises of God that on Mount Zion His king shall reign as Lord forever and ever. I do not know of a more rewarding study of the Word of God than to take a commentary and look up all the passages on "Mount Zion." One of the great Messianic Psalms is Psalm 2.

2. The kings of the earth set themselves, and the rulers take counsel together, against the Lord, and against his anointed, saying,

3. Let us break their bands asunder, and cast away their cords from us.

4. He that sitteth in the heavens shall laugh: the Lord shall have them in derision.

5. Then shall he speak unto them in his wrath, and vex them in his sore displeasure.

6. Yet have I set my king upon my holy hill of Zion.

7. I will declare the decree: the Lord hath said unto me, Thou art my Son: this day have I begotten thee.

8. Ask of me, and I shall give thee the heathen for thine inheritance, and the uttermost parts of the earth for thy possession.

Then, of course, that glorious anthem:

Psalm 48

1. Great is the Lord, and greatly to be praised in the city of our God, in the mountain of his holiness.

2. Beautiful for situation, the joy of the whole earth, is mount Zion, on the sides of the north, the city of the great King.

3. God is known in her palaces for a refuge . . . .

8. As we have heard, so have we seen in the city of the Lord of hosts, in the city of our God: God will establish it for ever . . . .

11. Let mount Zion rejoice, let the daughters of Judah be glad, because of thy judgments.

12. Walk about Zion, and go round about her: tell the towers thereof.

13. Mark ye well her bulwarks, consider her palaces; that ye may tell it to the generation following.

14. For this God is our God for ever and ever; he will be our guide even unto death.

Another beautiful Psalm is Psalm 132:

11. The Lord hath sworn in truth unto David; he will not turn from it; Of the fruit of thy body will I set upon thy throne.

13. For the Lord hath chosen Zion; he hath desired it for his habitation.

14. This is my rest for ever: here will I dwell; for I have desired it.

17. There will I make the horn of David to bud: I have ordained a lamp for mine anointed.

And this beautiful passage in Isaiah 2, which describes the millennial earth with its capital in Mount Zion: "And it shall come to pass in the last days, that the mountain of the Lord's house shall be established in the top of the mountains, and . . . all nations shall flow unto it. And many people shall say, Come . . . let us go up to the mountain of the Lord. . . and he will teach us his ways . . . for out of Zion shall go forth . . . the word of the Lord. And he shall judge among the nations, and . . . they shall beat their swords into plowshares, and their spears into pruninghooks: nation shall not lift up sword against nation, neither shall they learn war any more. O house of Jacob, come ye, and let us walk in the light of the Lord."

Mount Zion was the capital city of David. It was the home of the royal palace and king. It was the place chosen of God that there should He reign for ever and ever. This passage in Revelation describes a scene in that heavenly, millennial day when the Lord Christ shall reign on Mount Zion; and to be with Him is the reward of the one hundred and forty-four thousand, when their task is finished and their assignment is done. In chapter 7, therefore, we see the one hundred and forty-four thousand in their ministry upon earth. They are preaching the Gospel. They are calling men to repentance and faith; and men, by the myriads and millions are coming out of those heavy, dark days of the tribulation, having washed their robes and made them white in the blood of the Lamb. There the one hundred and forty-four thousand are seen in their work upon earth. Here in chapter 14 of the Revelation, the one hundred and forty-four thousand are seen on Mount Zion. Their task is finished, their work is done, and they are being rewarded by the Lord God for their devoted faithfulness.

Let us notice the attributes of these unusual preachers of Christ, the one hundred and forty-four thousand. First of all, in a day when it was death to have the mark of God and to confess Christ as Lord, these evangelists are preserved from martyrdom by the Spirit of God. Any man is like that who preaches the Gospel of the Son of God. His life is invincible and immortal until his task is done. He may be flying through the air in a plane; he may be going down the Amazon River on a boat; or he may be crossing the ocean; or he may be where the vile and vicious enemies of Christ are seen on every hand; but if he is in the will of God and if he is doing the work of God, until his task is finished his life is invulnerable and invincible. So with these one hundred and forty-four thousand.

Observe also their completed number. We read in chapter 7 of the Revelation that God seals one hundred and forty-four thousand. Here at the end, when they finish their ministry and are numbered before God, there are not one hundred thirty-nine thousand, nine hundred and ninety-nine. No. There are still one hundred forty-four thousand. Not a one is lost — not one. As Christ said, "I give unto them eternal life; and they shall never perish" (John 12:28). As the Lord said in His high priestly prayer, in John 17: "Of all those thou hast given me . . . there is not one lost, except the son of perdition; that the scripture might be fulfilled." When our names are written in the Lamb's Book of Life, they are there forever. When a man is saved, he is saved forever. He is kept by the power of God forever and forever. Of the one hundred and forty-four thousand whom God sealed at the beginning of this terrible tribulation, when the roll is called in heaven and they are assembled on Mount Zion to receive the reward of their faithfulness, there are one hundred and forty-four thousand in the presence of the Lord. Not a one has been lost. The man who puts his destiny, his life and his soul in the hands of God is kept forever and ever. When the roll is called up yonder, you will be there. God will see you through. Such is the guarding, keeping care of the Almighty.

Another thing that I read about them is that they sing a new song no one else on earth can sing. That is, they have a separate ministry, they are unique. It is foolish for all of us to try to be alike in our separate ministries. God does not want us to be alike. He did not want even our noses alike. He did not want even our ears alike. God likes differences; He likes ramifications. He does not make any two leaves alike. He does not make any two snowflakes alike. And so in His churches, God calls one to be a preacher; He calls another to be a singer; another to be a pastoral helper, a shepherd of the sheep, an assistant pastor; another to be a business administrator. God calls you and God calls others; and for all of us to do God's work, each in his own place, is to glorify the Lord. For us to be jealous or envious of one another and for us not to be happy where God has placed us, is unchristian. Once in a while I meet a girl who wishes that she were a boy. She is foolish. It is the Lord who has made us different, and let us exalt Him in it. If you are a businessman, be a successful businessman for God. If you are an organist, be an accomplished organist for God. If you are a teacher, be a dedicated teacher for God. If you are a physician, be a Christian doctor for the Lord. God made us different. These one hundred and forty-four thousand comprised a unique ministry unto the Lord. No one could sing that song but the one hundred and forty-four thousand.

The unique exaltation of these one hundred and forty-four thousand does not mean, however, that anyone else is denied. Look at the scene in heaven. The elders are there, and they are separate and different from the one hundred and forty-four thousand. There are degrees in heaven, just as there are degrees in angelic orders. There are some angels that are archangels. There are some that are seraphim, some that are cherubim, and some that are judgment angels. I do not know how many orders God has in heaven, but I know there are many. These elders are crowned, enthroned and seated. These one hundred and forty-four thousand are not crowned, they are not enthroned and they are not seated. They are in different orders. I do not know to what extent the one hundred and forty-four thousand are exalted, but they are not exalted like the elders nor as you are going to be. There are different governments and different orders in heaven. And just as it is down here (we differ here in this earth), so we are going to differ up there. You are going to be you, with your reward and your assignment, and I am going to be myself, with my reward and my assignment. That is what heaven is like.

Then, the text also says that the one hundred and forty-four thousand are virgins and that they "follow the lamb whithersoever he goeth." Many commentators think that means that they never were married. Marriage has nothing to do with it whatsoever. Consider, for example, II Corinthians 11:2, where Paul says to the church at Corinth: " . . . for I have espoused you to Christ, that I may present you as a chaste virgin to our Lord." Now, does that mean that all those folks in the church at Corinth were unmarried, that all the men were bachelors and all the women were spinsters? Would not that be a tragic thing? What on earth would you do for the generations that were following, as Psalm 48 says? The idea is impossible. But we know what Paul means. He says to the Corinthians that the church is going to be presented to Christ as a chaste virgin. Likewise, when the text describes these men in Revelation as virgins, it refers to the fact that they separated themselves from the pollutions and the corruptions of the earth. They were virgins unto God. They had given themselves in pure devotion to the Lord.

The text also says: ". . . In their mouth was found no guile: for they are without fault." This reminds us of when Jesus first looked upon Nathaniel. When Philip brought him to the Lord, Jesus said: "Look for here is an Israelite in whom is no guile." That describes God's people. You do not have to have a Christian put his hand on the Bible to swear that what he says is true. No! If he is a man of God and a true Christian, when he tells you something, you may believe it. His word is better than his bond. You do not have to have him sign. When he says a thing is so, it is. "An Israelite in whom is no guile," and "in their mouth is no guile." God's people are singlehearted, simple, plain, humble. They are so described on earth. They are no less gloriously presented in heaven.

CHAPTER 13

THE ANGEL MESSENGERS

Revelation 14

6. And I saw another angel fly in the midst of heaven, having the everlasting gospel to preach unto them that dwell on the earth, and to every nation, and kindred, and tongue, and people.

7. Saying with a loud voice, Fear God, and give glory to him; for the hour of his judgment is come: and worship him that made heaven, and earth, and the sea, and the fountains of waters.

8. And there followed another angel, saying, Babylon is fallen, is fallen, that great city, because she made all nations drink of the wine of the wrath of her fornication.

9. And the third angel followed them, saying with a loud voice, If any man worship the beast and his image, and receive his mark in his forehead, or in his hand,

10. The same shall drink of the wine of the wrath of God, which is poured out without mixture into the cup of his indignation; and he shall be tormented with fire and brimstone in the presence of the holy angels, and in the presence of the Lamb:

11. And the smoke of their torment ascendeth up for ever and ever: and they have no rest day nor night, who worship the beast and his image, and whosoever receiveth the mark of his name.

12. Here is the patience of the saints: here are they that keep the commandments of God, and the faith of Jesus.

13. And I heard a voice from heaven saying unto me, Write, Blessed are the dead which die in the Lord from henceforth: Yes, saith the Spirit, that they may rest from their labours; and their works do follow them.

In ancient Greek drama, messengers announced the development of some parts of the story, describing scenes that could not be enacted on the stage or that so greatly complicated the de-

149

velopment of the story that it would have otherwise become tedious. For example, if a great battle had been fought, or if a city had been burned, or if there had been a fierce engagement between navies at sea, these events were not attempted on the Greek dramatic stage, but they were announced rather by messengers. A like dramatic presentation is found here in chapter 14 of the Apocalypse. There are seven angel-messengers who come and make tremendous announcements regarding consummation of the age under the last and seventh trumpet. The first angel-messenger is a preacher, announcing the Gospel of the Son of God and calling men everywhere to repentance and to faith in the Lord. The second angel-messenger announces the fall of Babylon. The third announces the eternal torment of those who worship and follow the beast. The next angel-messenger announces the blessedness of the sainted dead. The next angel-messenger announces the reaping of the harvest of the earth, and the last two announce the battle of Armageddon on the great and final day of the Lord.

THE MESSAGE OF THE THREE ANGELS

The first angel-messenger is a preacher. He stands with his pulpit in the firmament of the sky, and his voice reaches the extremities of the earth, as he announces the great judgment of God and calls men to reverential fear and worship of the Lord. God raises up His witnesses when human lips are silent. At the triumphal entry of our Saviour into Jerusalem, when the Pharisees and the Scribes objected to the praise of the people, our Lord replied, "Verily, if these were silent the very stones would cry out." So in the days of the Apocalypse, when the witness of God's servants is drowned in blood, there is an angel-messenger that stands in the sky, who thunders to the ends of the earth the almighty and eternal gospel message of the Son of God. Chains and blood, martyrdom and death, bars and prisons, cannot stop the testimony of the Word of God. As the Apostle Paul wrote in the Mamertine dungeon in his last letter to Timothy, his son in the ministry, "I may be in chains, I may be bound, but the Word of God is not bound." "The grass withereth, the flower fadeth, but the Word of our God endureth forever." "And I saw another angel fly in the midst of heaven, having the everlasting gospel to preach unto them that dwell on the earth . . ."

The second angel-messenger announces the fall of Babylon. *"Epesen, epesen,"* John wrote, using an aoristic Greek verb that describes as one great climactic act the destruction of this evil world system. "Babylon is fallen, is fallen . . . because she made all nations drink of the wine of the wrath of her fornication." In one vast intervention of God, the whole vile system that debauches this earth is taken away in order that God may create a new world in which righteousness shall prevail.

The third angel-messenger announces the torment of those who give themselves to the worship of the beast and his image. This torment is to last forever. Their suffering is in deepest contrast to the martyrdom of God's servants who, for example, are burned at the stake. For just a moment the Christian suffers agony; then there is the glory when God gives him the crown of life. But these who worship the beast and his image and give their hearts to the defilement of this earth are tormented forever and ever, with no final reward but damnation.

THE MARVELOUS MESSAGE CONCERNING THOSE WHO DIE IN THE LORD

The marvelous verses (14:12, 13) immediately following the description of the fate of the beast-worshippers are written for the comfort and the assurance of God's servants who paid with their lives for their witness to the grace of Christ. "Here is the patience of the saints: Here are they that keep the commandments of God, and the faith of Jesus . . . . Write, Blessed are the dead which die in the Lord. Yea, saith the Spirit, that they may rest from their labours; and their works do follow them." This is not an observation of the sainted Apostle John.

Rather, it is a commandment, it is a mandate, it is a decree by God the Father in heaven. "And I heard a voice from heaven saying unto me, Write . . . ." This is the verdict of God concerning His children who die in the earth; namely, that they are blessed of the Lord. The text is a golden phrase. Every syllable is sweet like honey and the honey-comb. The New Testament message begins with the sayings of Jesus, His beautiful beatitudes for the living. The New Testament message closes with this last, final beatitude for God's sainted dead. The words are written, of course, for those who were martyred and perished in that day of awful trial and tribulation. But the comfort, and the assurance and the strength of it is for all God's saints in all generations. "I heard a voice from heaven saying unto me, Write, Blessed are the dead which die in the Lord."

God says death is an enemy. God calls death the king of terrors. Death is an interloper; it is an intruder. It was never planned in the purposive, elective goodness and grace of God. It wastes, it destroys God's creation. The aspirations of a man, the dreams of his heart, the tenderest ties that bind him to those whom he loves, are severed by the cruel and merciless hand of this pale horseman. But God in Christ has taken the sting out of death and has taken away the victory from the grave. The Lord has made even death and the grave to minister to the good and to the blessedness of His children.

"Blessed are the dead which die in the Lord." The Bible, without exception, avows the comforting truth that upon death, immediately we are blessed; not at some other time, not at some other day, not in some other eon, not in some other era, not in some faraway epochal period, but in the moment of death, the child of God is blessed in being received into the presence of the Lord. There is no exception to this truth in the Holy Scriptures. When we die, we are with the Lord. "Absent from the body, present with the Lord." In chapter 7 of this Apocalypse we read: ". . . These are they who . . . have washed their robes, and made them white in the blood of the Lamb.

Therefore are they before the throne of God, and serve him day and night in his temple . . . and God shall dwell among them. They shall hunger no more; they shall thirst no more; neither shall the sun light on them, nor any heat. For the Lamb . . . shall feed them, and shall shepherd them and lead them into living fountains of waters: and God shall wipe all tears away from their eyes."

Immediately are these saved of the Lord in His presence when they are taken from the earth. The Lord avows the same precious truth in the last chapter of the Apocalypse, "Blessed are they whose garments are washed that they may have right to the tree of life." In like manner our Lord said to the church at Ephesus, "To him that overcometh will I give the right to eat of the tree of life which is in the midst of the paradise of God" (Revelation 2:7). Again He said to the church at Smyrna, "Be thou faithful unto death and I will give thee the crown of life" (Revelation 2:10). The Lord said to the thief who died on the cross, "Today [not in some future eon, but today] shalt thou be with me in paradise." Paul avowed: "I am in a strait betwixt two, for to depart and to be with Christ is far better. For to me to live is Christ and to die is gain." Blessed, blessed are the dead who die in the Lord. Upon death, they are immediately with their Saviour.

How opposite are the judgments of God from our own human persuasions. We say, "Blessed are the living." But God says, "Blessed are the dead." We look on appearances, we look on the outside, we look upon the fading flower and the withering grass, we look upon the open grave, we see the head bowed in sorrow and the tears falling like rain to the ground; but God sees the eternity that is yet to come, God sees the rewards of His people, God sees the crown of life, God sees the holy fellowship of His children who are gathered home. The Lord admonished us to look, not at the things which are seen, but at the things which are not seen; for the things which are seen are temporal, but the things which are not seen are eternal. If

it is happiness to have the smiling favor of God here, how infinitely more so in glory! If it is good that we can see even
darkly here, how much infinitely more precious when we can
see face to face! If we are comforted by what we now know
in part here, think of the fullness of the revelation when we
shall know, even as God knows us. If it is an assurance here
that we have an anchor within the veil, how much more glorious
will be the reality when we are there ourselves! "Blessed,"
says God, "blessed are the dead who die in the Lord."

OUR REST AND OUR WORK IN HEAVEN

But the Lord has yet other comfort for His people. "Yea,
saith the spirit, that they may rest from their labours." There
is a magnificent picture in the Greek word for "rest," *anapauo*. It
is a picture of a mariner who spends his life at sea, and after
the battle of tempest and wave, he comes into the port of home.
It is a picture of a soldier who is scarred with battle strife, and
after the miseries of war and carnage and conflict, he turns his
face toward home. It is the sentiment of Robert Louis Stevenson,
who wrote the verses carved on his tomb:

> Under the wide and starry sky,
> Dig the grave and let me lie,
> Glad did I live and gladly die,
> And I lay me down with a will.

> This be the verse ye grave for me:
> Here he lies where he longed to be,
> Home is the sailor, home from the sea,
> And the hunter home from the hill.

"Yea, saith the Spirit, that they may rest [*anapauo*] from their
labours."

It is a remarkable interpretation, this dramatic Christian
description of what it is to die. They called the place where
they laid their beloved dead a *koimeterion*. When we spell that
Greek word in English, it becomes in our language and pronun-
ciation "cemetery." The Greek *koimeterion* is an ordinary word

for "a sleeping place," "a cemetery." That is why the early Christians so carefully laid their dead away. They believed, according to the Word and promise of God, that these who sleep in the dust of the ground will rise again, will live in the sight of God. A visitor to Rome, therefore, will find in those vast, almost endless catacombs, places where the Christians laid to rest their beloved dead. The pagan and the heathen burned the body. To them it was the end of all life; it was the end of the way; it was the end of every hope and aspiration. But to the Christians, death was just a falling asleep. With tender and loving care, they laid their dead away, awaiting the final voice of the archangel and the sound of the trumpet, when these they loved and had lost for awhile should be raised to live in His sight.

The figure of death as a sleep is used consistently throughout the New Testament. When our Lord went to the home of the synagogue leader named Jairus, whose little girl had died, He said, "The girl is not dead; she is sleeping." When Lazarus had been dead four days, Jesus said to His disciples, "I go to wake our friend out of sleep." The great revelation of comfort given the Apostle Paul in I Thessalonians 4, beginning at verse 13, reads like this: "But I would not have you to be ignorant, brethren, concerning them which are asleep, that ye sorrow not, even as others which have no hope. For if we believe that Jesus died and rose again, even so them also which sleep in Jesus will God bring with him." Death is a falling asleep in the arms of Jesus. It is this to the Christian.

The passage in Revelation 14:13 continues, "Yea, saith the Spirit, that they may rest from their labours." Those two words "rest" and "labour" describe a life in heaven very different from the conception of the popular artists of our day. They conceive of the life to come as of a fellow sitting on some cloud, flapping his wings and strumming his harp. But such is not God's portrayal of our eternal life in glory. Far from it. There is no intimation, there is no hint anywhere in the Bible of such a thing as sterile inactivity in heaven. The revelation of God to us is this, that the life that is yet to come is to be filled with an intensive activity. Said our Lord in the famous parable of the talents, "Because thou hast been faithful over a few things, I will make thee ruler over many things" (Matthew 25:21). And again in the parable of the pounds, He said to another: "Be thou also ruler over ten cities"; and to yet another, "Be thou over five cities" (Luke 19:17, 18). In the great economy of God in the world that is yet to come, in that holy society, there is heavenly work to be done to the praise and glory of God, world without end.

What is meant then, here by "rest," *anapauo,* and "labour," *kopos?* Sometimes it is difficult to transfer into one language the meaning of words in another language. That word *anapauo,* translated here "rest," does not mean inactivity. It means "refreshment," "rejuvenation." The word *kopos,* translated "labour," means "weariness," "the fatigue and toil of laborious effort." When we serve God in the glory that is yet to come, every activity will be with new refreshment. I have heard of birds that rest upon the wing. It will be thus with our service and ministry to God in the heavenly places that He has prepared for us. The labor we do for the Lord in heaven will bring rejuvenation. The fatigue and weariness, the toil and effort, the laborious tedium of this life will be taken away, and our service to God will be one of perpetual strength, youth and uplifting vigor. Like a bird out of a cage, we shall be liberated from the drag of this mortal life. Freed, resurrected, glorified, immortalized, we shall serve God forever in the beauty and power of a new life, of a new day, of a new gift, of a new creation. This is the "rest" of God from the weariness of our pilgrimage here.

OUR WORKS DO NOT PRECEDE BUT FOLLOW OUR COMMITMENT OF FAITH

The passage continues, ". . . and their works do follow them." Notice that the text is true to all the rest of the teaching of the Holy Scriptures. The Book is always true to the doctrine and teaching of the Holy Spirit. Here again is that marvelous consistency. For example, consider the meticulously true doctrine of the Twenty-third Psalm, "The Lord is my shepherd; I shall not want. He maketh me to lie down in green pastures: he leadeth me beside the still waters. He restoreth my soul: he leadeth me in the paths of righteousness for his name's sake." Observe the doctrine. First, God restores the soul; *then* He leads us in the paths of righteousness for His name's sake. That is the faithful teaching here, ". . . and their works do follow them." Preceding us is the grace and love of Jesus; not our works first, but our works last. Jesus comes first, always. To Him be the glory and the honor and the dominion and the gratitude forever and forever, for He saved us and washed us from our sins in His own blood. He preceded us, preparing a place for us in heaven. Then our works follow after.

What a blessedness, what a comfort is the remembrance of God! ". . . and their works do follow them." It would seem that the man still in death, silent in the grave has lost all, every hope, every ambition, every dream, every aspiration, every reward. He lies so still. But God says, all of those assignments, all of those tasks, and all of those works become an eternal reward for these who fall asleep in Jesus. God saw the tears that no one else saw fall. God heard the prayer that no one else heard. No one else noticed that penny, the small gift that the poor could afford, placed in the treasury of the church; but the Lord noticed it. The gracious gesture of the hand, the word, the letter written for encouragement — God put them all in His Holy Book, and it is our reward forever and ever. ". . . and their works do follow them."

It would be an incomparable assurance if all men could thus receive in faith this precious beatitude. But sadly it is not true, for the text says: "Blessed are the dead which die in the Lord." Thus would God say to us, not that all who die are blessed, for some die without God, without hope, without Christ. Some die in unforgiven sin, some die spurning the overtures of grace, saying "No" to the Holy Spirit. For them, living unpardoned and dying in unforgiven sin, there is no blessedness.

But in contrast, how infinitely precious is the reward for the soul that looks in faith and in trust to Jesus! "Lord, in thy blood wash my sins away, in thy love and sobs and tears, in thy cross and atonement, O God, wash me and make me whiter than snow. O God, write my name in the Lamb's Book of Life. O Lord, when I stand before the judgment bar of God, be thou my Advocate, my Saviour. O Christ, I cast my soul, my life, my destiny into Thy care and into Thy keeping hands. So, Lord, humbly and reverently, I bow at thy blessed feet. O God, remember me." Those are blessed who turn in faith to the precious Lord Jesus.

If we are to be saved there, we must be Christians here. If God is to remember us there, we must remember Him here. If the Lord is to receive us with hands of welcome in the glory that is yet to come, we must open our hearts to receive the blessed Lord Jesus here. For the Christian, there are no terrors, there are no ultimate wasting, destructive enemies. Whether we live or whether we die, we are the Lord's. "I heard a voice from heaven saying unto me, Write, Blessed are the dead which die in the Lord . . . Yea, saith the Spirit, that they may rest from their labours; and their works do follow them." To the one who believes in Jesus on the weary pilgrimage through this world, the future is one of joy and triumph on heights of glory in a world that is yet to come.

CHAPTER 14

THE HARVEST OF THE EARTH

Revelation 14

14. And I looked, and behold a white cloud, and upon the cloud one sat like unto the Son of man, having on his head a golden crown, and in his hand a sharp sickle.

15. And another angel came out of the temple, crying with a loud voice to him that sat on the cloud, Thrust in thy sickle, and reap: for the time is come for thee to reap; for the harvest of the earth is ripe.

16. And he that sat on the cloud thrust in his sickle on the earth; and the earth was reaped.

17. And another angel came out of the temple which is in heaven, he also having a sharp sickle.

18. And another angel came out from the altar, which had power over fire; and cried with a loud cry to him that had the sharp sickle, saying, Thrust in thy sharp sickle, and gather the clusters of the vine of the earth; for her grapes are fully ripe.

19. And the angel thrust in his sickle into the earth, and gathered the vine of the earth, and cast it into the great winepress of the wrath of God.

20. And the winepress was trodden without the city, and blood came out of the winepress, even unto the horse bridles, by the space of a thousand and six hundred furlongs.

Not in this book of wonders are there more striking visions than these two, closing chapter 14 of the Apocalypse. The expressive imagery and the awesome administration of God that they unfold would strike terror to a heart that is not given in trust to Christ. In Revelation 14:7 there is the announcement of the hour of the judgment of God. This proclamation is followed by another announcement, that the great city Babylon is

159

on the brink of destruction. Verses 9 through 11 declare that those who follow the beast, who give themselves to blasphemy and rejection, are now to be judged; and their judgment is an everlasting, unending torment. Then after precious words of encouragement to God's people, the remaining verses record two visions that depict the final administrations of God in this earth. They are the vision of the harvest of the earth and the vision of the gathering of the grapes of wrath.

There are many who, when they read these two visions, are persuaded that they depict the same thing, that there is no difference between them, that they reveal the same, final end of this earth; the one under the imagery of a harvest and the other under the imagery of a winepress. Now, I can see why readers would be thus persuaded. There is a sharp sickle in both and there is a reaping in both. But there are also differences in the two visions that, to me, are remarkably meaningful and significant. The visions, after all, are not alike. They are different in many details. Another point: if they refer to the same and identical thing, why record them both? One would have been sufficient. We would not need two. They are alike only in this, that a harvest and a vintage describe the end time. But they are greatly unlike in the reference that each vision bears. To me, that difference of reference lies in this: The harvest is superintended by the Son of God, who always carefully separates the chaff from the wheat; the vintage is gathered by an angel without regard or distinction. The harvest is a discriminating reaping. It is not all the same. There is a harvest of wheat and at the same time there is a harvest of tares. The Son of God is taking care of his own. There is a discrimination in the first vision, in the visions of the harvest of the earth. In the second vision, presided over by an emissary of God, an angel, there is no discrimination, for it is the harvest of the grapes of wickedness. It is the winepress of the unmitigated, unadulterated wrath and fury of Almighty God. Now, let us look at these differences and their meaning for us who live in the earth.

"I looked, and behold," *kai eidon kai idou.* I suppose that phrase was a very common, idiomatic expression among the Greek-speaking people — *kai eidon kai idou* — "I looked, and behold," but wherever it is found in the Word of God, it introduces a remarkable and significant revelation. "I looked, and behold a white cloud, and upon the cloud one sat like unto the Son of man, having on his head a golden crown, and in his hand a sharp sickle. And an angel came out of the temple, crying . . . to him that sat on the cloud, Thrust in thy sickle, and reap: for the time is come . . . the harvest of the earth is [*exeranthe,* dried up, dead] ripe. And he that sat on the cloud thrust in his sickle . . . and the earth was reaped." Notice and remember that even in this day of the last Tribulation, God has His own in the earth. They are so many that they cannot be numbered. In chapter 7 of the Revelation, John saw their multitude. After the one hundred forty-four thousand were sealed (these twelve thousand out of the twelve different tribes of Israel, who are evangelists and preachers of power) then John saw their converts, the multitude who had come out of the wickedness and blasphemy of this world, who had washed their robes and made them white in the blood of the Lamb. God has His own in this earth, even in those terrible, last dark days. In this reaping there are both: there are God's children, the wheat, and there are the children of the evil one, the tares. For in a harvest you have both. As there is a harvest of good, so there is a harvest of evil. Wickedness has its harvest, its woes and its miseries, its judgments and its damnations. When the Son of man sends forth His reapers and with His sharp sickle He cuts down the harvest of the earth, both are reaped, the harvest of good and the harvest of evil.

These two reapings, the reaping of the wheat into the garner and the gathering of the tares to be burned with unquenchable fire, are presented faithfully in the Word of God. For example, in chapter 13 of the first gospel, which contains the parables of the mysteries of the kingdom of heaven, the disciples came to Jesus and said: "Declare unto us the parable of the tares." Jesus then answered and said unto them: "He that soweth the good seed is the Son of Man: the field is the world; the good seed are the children of the kingdom; but the tares are the children of the evil one; the enemy that oversowed them is the devil; the harvest is the end of the world; and the reapers are the angels. As therefore the tares are gathered and burned in the fire; so shall it be in the end of this world. The Son of man shall send forth his angels, and they shall gather out of his kingdom all things that offend, and them which do iniquity; And shall cast them into a furnace of fire; there shall be wailing and gnashing of teeth. Then shall the righteous shine forth (the wheat in the garner of heaven) as the sun in the kingdom of their Father. Who hath ears to hear, let him hear." That last admonition sounds like the Revelation, doesn't it? "He that hath ears to hear, let him hear."

In the harvest there is both the reaping of the good and the bad. This same truth is repeated in another parable of the mysteries of the kingdom (Matthew 13:47-50): ". . . the kingdom of heaven is likened unto a net, that was cast into the sea, and gathered of every kind: Which, when it was full, they drew to shore, and set down and gathered the good into vessels, but cast the bad away. So shall it be at the end of the world: the angels shall come forth, and sever the wicked from among the just, And shall cast them into the furnace of fire: there shall be wailing and gnashing of teeth." This parable reveals the same truth that is presented in the vision of the harvest of the earth. There is a discriminating harvest that is carefully superintended, watched over, by the Son of man, Himself. Not the least one who has placed his trust in Jesus shall fall into the fire. An angel may superintend the execution of the wrath of the judgment of Almighty God, but when the Lord harvests this earth He, Himself, carefully watches over lest one of His least, humblest saints be forgotten or overlooked. There is everything in the Bible to comfort and to give assurance to those who lean on the strong arm of our Lord.

THE CHILDREN OF THE LORD LIKENED UNTO WHEAT

Let us pause here for a moment and discuss the difference between that harvest of wheat and that harvest of tares. Wheat is a beautiful, magnificently meaningful representation and symbol of God's children. When it ripens, the full, rich heads are bowed to the earth. When the tares ripen, they stand up erect, but when the wheat ripens, it bends its face to the ground. As God's children grow in grace, as they are made heavy with the knowledge, the presence and the goodness of God, they bow lower toward the ground. A church member who is proud of himself, proud of his goodness, proud of his personal excellence, walking in his self-sufficiency and adequacy, is, in God's sight, a tare. But a church member who is lowly and humble, in honor preferring others before himself, and whose life is given to intercession and to prayer in behalf of those who do not know God, belongs, you may be sure, in the garner of heaven. The more we grow in grace and in the knowledge of the Lord, the more our faces will bow to the earth, weighted down with the presence and the grace of God.

For example: When Isaiah saw the Lord, he cried of the woe of his life for he was a sinful man. When Simon Peter recognized the deity of Jesus, he fell at His feet and begged the Lord to depart from him, "for I am a sinful man." When the proud Saul of Tarsus, who became an apostle, was journeying from Jerusalem to Damascus with a high hand, met the Lord, he had to be led by the hand into the city. It is always so. The finer and nobler the children of God are, the more they bow in humility and lowliness.

Another thing about wheat, the harvest of God, is that as

the wheat ripens upward, it dies downward. As the grain ripens unto God, the stalk and the roots that hold onto this earth die earthward. In my study of this passage in preparing this sermon, I read one of the most spiritually significant sentences that I have ever read. Referring to the ripening upward and the dying downward, the sentence read: "This is the sanctity of the relaxing grasp." As we grow Godward and heavenward and as we draw near the end of our pilgrimage, more and more there will be the relaxing of our hold upon this earth and this life, until finally, when we near the gates of heaven, the things of this present earth fade away. "The sanctity of the relaxing grasp."

One other observation about wheat, the symbol of God's child, is that wheat is an annual that is reaped in succesive harvests. As the sun beats down upon it, it turns sear, brown, and ripens to death, to the harvest. So it is with God's children of the earth. In the trials of life, in the heat of the sun, under the burning, blazing sky, God's children ripen toward God. As the wheat is helpless before the storm, so the saints are helpless before the storms of the tempest that sweep over this life. In these trials, God is preparing us for the celestial garner in heaven. Two or three times recently, I have been asked to pray for homes in sorrow. One family told me: "We have met an insoluble problem. We know not where to turn. Pastor, pray for us. There is nothing you can do, we know, but just call our names. Remember us." I do not seek to parade our tears and our sorrows, but God's children always go through these valleys. I suppose there would be no mountaintops without them. I suppose if it were all daylight and sunshine, we would never know the sweetness and blessedness of the presence and grace of God. It takes the sorrows to make us conscious of the joys. It takes age and death to make us conscious of the celestial promises of heaven. That is God's way of leading His dear children along.

We are under the burning sun, ripening toward God. We are the harvest of the earth.

THE GRAPES OF WRATH

The second vision (Revelation 14:18-20) is one of carnage. "And another angel came out from the altar who had power over fire and he said to him that had the sharp sickle, Thrust in thy sickle, and gather the clusters of the vine of the earth; for her grapes are fully ripe. And the angel thrust in his sickle into the earth, and gathered the vine of the earth, and cast it into the great winepress of the wrath of God. And the winepress was trodden without the city, and blood came out of the winepress, even unto the bridles of the horses, by the space of a thousand and six hundred furlongs."

That vision has reference to a very definite and horrible holocaust that is prophesied through all of the Word of God. From the altar there came an angel who had power over fire. Notice where this fire-angel came from. In Revelation 6:9-11 we read: "And when he had opened the fifth seal, I saw under the altar the souls of them that were beheaded for the witness and for the testimony of Jesus. And they cried unto him that liveth forever and ever, How long, O Lord, dost thou not judge and avenge our blood on them that dwell on the earth?" That is the altar from which comes this angel of fire with wrathful indignation and burning fury because of the evil in this earth, the wickedness of men, the injustice of mankind. He comes to answer that cry, a cry like the cry of Abel's blood unto God; like the cry of the wickedness of Sodom and Gomorrah unto heaven; like the cry of that sinful Babylon described here in the Revelation, a cry that reached the very throne of God; the cry of judgment and of wrath and of indignation. This fire-angel comes in fury from that altar, and he says to the angel with the sharp sickle, ". . . gather the clusters of the vine of the earth; for her grapes are fully ripe."

This vision describes the last day of God's permissive will for wickedness and rejection. The last hour of evil has finally come. "And the angel thrust in his sickle unto the earth, and gathered the vine of the earth." "The vine of the earth" is a reference used in contradistinction to the vine of heaven, which is our blessed Lord, with us the branches. "The vine of the. earth" is the vine of rejection, of unbelief, of blasphemy and of unrepentance.

". . . and he cast it into the great winepress of the wrath of God. And the winepress was trodden without the city, and blood came out." Notice that it was grapes that were cast into the winepress, but when they were ground under the heel of the omnipotent Almighty, blood ran out. And it was such a flow of the crimson of life that to the bridles of the horses it flowed by the space of a thousand and six hundred furlongs. That word "furlongs" is *stadia* in Greek. It is the measurement of an eighth of a mile. Divide eight into a thousand six hundred and you get two hundred. For two hundred miles, there was a river of blood in this final holocaust of the great day of the Almighty. That is the first reference in the Apocalypse to the indescribably awesome, terrible and final battle of the great day of the Lord, called the battle of Armageddon. It is the judgment of God upon unbelieving and blasphemous men. The gainsaying world said in Revelation 13 that the anti-Christ, the first beast, is invincible. It said: "Who can make war against him? Look at the power he has. Look at his ingenuity. Look at his forces. He is invincible. Who can make war against him?" He is not invincible now, crushed under the heel of Almighty God. And the world said of the false prophet: "Look at his power to work miracles. He can even make fire fall down from heaven." He cannot make fire fall down from heaven now, for he is under the judging hand of the Lord God.

THE FINAL BATTLE OF BLOOD AND JUDGMENT

What an imagery is here! This chapter opens with the gathering of God's children to the Lamb on Mount Zion and records the beautiful song that they sing. But it closes with the gathering of the rejecting and unbelieving, the kings and the mighty men, into the harvest of the earth. It closes with the gathering of those vast hosts in the land of Palestine that measures from Bozra, which Isaiah describes, to the valley of Jehoshaphat, that Joel describes, to the hill of Megiddo, that John describes exactly a thousand and six hundred furlongs. This great end time has been before the mind of the prophets since the world began. How this age shall close and how this earth shall come to its final historical consummation in the intervention of God is the burden of the prophetic message throughout the centuries. Listen to Isaiah as he speaks in the chapter 63 of his book: "Who is this that cometh from Edom, with dyed garments from Bozrah? he that is glorious in his apparel, travelling in the greatness of his strength? . . . Wherefore art thou red in thine apparel, and thy garments like him that treadeth in the winepress? I have trodden the winepress alone; and of the people there was none with me: for I will tread them in mine anger, and trample them in my fury; and their blood shall be sprinkled upon my garments, and I will stain all my garments. For the day of vengeance is in mine heart, and the year of my redeemed is come. And I looked, and there was none to help; and I wondered that there was none to uphold: therefore mine own arm shall intervene in human history and bring salvation unto me; and my fury, it upheld me. And I will tread down the people in mine anger, and make them drunk in my fury, and I will bring down their strength to the earth." These garments that the King of kings and the Lord of lords wore were red; they were red with the blood of His enemies.

Now turn to chapter 19 in the Book of the Revelation. In the description of that great, final battle of the Lord, we read: "And he was clothed with a vesture dipped in blood . . . . And out of his mouth goeth a sharp sword, that with it he should smite the nations . . . with a rod of iron; and he treadeth the winepress of the fierceness and wrath of Almighty God. And he hath on his vesture and on his thigh a name written, KING OF KINGS, AND LORD OF LORDS." Blood! His vesture is dipped in blood. That is the blood of His enemies. That is the destruction of this unbelieving world in the great and awful day of the judgment of Almighty God.

In Joel we read: "Proclaim ye this among the Gentiles; Prepare war, wake up the mighty men, let all the men of war draw near; let them come up: Beat your plowshares into swords, and your pruninghooks into spears: let the weak say, I am strong. Assemble yourselves, and come, all ye heathen, and gather yourselves together round about: thither cause thy mighty ones to come . . . . Let the nations be wakened, and come up to the valley of Jehoshaphat: for there will I sit to judge all the heathen round about. Put ye in the sickle, for the harvest is ripe: come, get you down; for the press is full, the winepresses overflow; for their wickedness is great. Multitudes, multitudes in the valley of decision: for the day of the Lord is near in the valley of decision. The sun and the moon shall be darkened, and the stars shall withdraw their shining. The Lord shall roar out of Zion, and utter his voice from Jerusalem; and the heavens and the earth shall shake in that great vintage of the Lord God Almighty."

The Apostle John describes this same event in chapter 16 of the Revelation. The question could be rightly asked: How do all those kings come together, how do all those assemblies of armies converge? John answered: "And I saw three unclean spirits . . . come out of the mouth of the dragon, and out of the mouth of the beast, and out of the mouth of the false prophet. For they are the spirits of evil men, evil workings, working miracles, which go forth unto the kings of the earth and of the whole world, to gather them to the battle of that great day of God Almighty . . . . And he gathered them together into a place called in the Hebrew tongue Armageddon." Armageddon is the hill of Megiddo, the vale of Esdraelon. "And the winepress was trodden . . . and blood came out of it up to the horses bridles by the space of two hundred miles." There never has been in the history of mankind, there never has been recorded on the pages of the chronicles of man, such a deluge of blood and war as shall end this earth, in which great battle the Lord Christ intervenes. This is the judgment of the earth, the day of the wrath of God.

Do not ever persuade yourself that evil will be here forever. Do not ever be persuaded that death will reign king forever. Do not be persuaded that violence, wickedness, lying, greed, murder and war shall be rampant in this earth forever. According to the Word of God, evil rises to an ultimate climax, and when it comes to its worst, God shall judge it and in that intervention, the kingdom of our Lord shall come.

In the closing vision of Joel (Joel 3:16), in that awful day, the Lord shall be the hope of His people. "Judah shall dwell forever, and Jerusalem from generation to generation. For I will cleanse their land." The poet-prophet-preacher Isaiah describes the beautiful millennium after the battle of Armageddon and after the cleansing of the land. "The wolf shall dwell with the lamb, and the leopard shall lie down with the kid . . . . They shall not hurt nor destroy in all my holy mountain: for the earth shall be full of the knowledge of the Lord, as the waters cover the sea." What a glorious day, when armies shall beat their swords into plowshares and their spears into pruninghooks, when nation shall not lift up sword against nation, neither shall they learn war any more, when God is the hope of His people! That is the interpretation of the discriminating harvest: the Lord is taking care of His own.

CHAPTER 15

THE SEVEN LAST PLAGUES

Revelation 15

1. And I saw another sign in heaven, great and marvellous, seven angels having the seven last plagues; for in them is filled up the wrath of God.

Revelation 16

1. And I heard a great voice out of the temple saying to the seven angels, Go your ways, and pour out the vials of the wrath of God upon the earth.

Fast and furious is this ultimate denouement of time and history. Chapter 11 of the Revelation brought us to the end of the world, chapter 14 brought us again to the end of the world. But before the millennium and the descent of the new Jerusalem, and before the planting of the tabernacle of God in this earth, in that awesome period before the final intervention of God Almighty, He draws aside the curtain that we might see some of the details of that final consummation. God would have us know, for example, what is the end of the trinity of evil, the Dragon and the Beast and the False Prophet. God would have us know what is the end of that great city called in the Revelation "Mystery and Babylon." Before the blessing of this earth there is to be a purging. Sin, death, unrighteousness, blasphemy and rejection are to be swept from it. In that place of the curse that we now see, the briars, thorns, brambles, hate, greed, war and bloodshed, God shall establish a kingdom of holiness and of righteousness. In that supreme, celestial dominion of Christ, we shall be fellow-citizens and fellow-heirs.

170

Chapters 15 and 16 of the Revelation go together. They are a part of the same vision, describing the seven last plagues, in what is called in the last part of chapter 8 of the Revelation "the last woe," the third of the three terrible woes. This section, chapters 15 and 16, is also the judgment of the last trumpet, the seventh trumpet that is sounded in the last part of chapter 11. In chapter 11 a temple of God was opened in heaven, and that temple appears now in chapters 15 and 16. In chapter 11 the elders announce that the great day of the judgment of Almighty God is come "and the nations are angry and the time is come that they who would destroy the world should be destroyed." That delineation is found in chapters 15 and 16. In the last of chapter 11, the sounding of the seventh trumpet, the kingdom of this world is become the kingdom of our Lord and of His Christ. The final preparation for the establishment of that kingdom is found in this vision of the seven last plagues.

The text reads in Revelation 15:1, "And I saw another sign in heaven, great and marvellous, seven angels having the seven last plagues; for in them is filled up the wrath of God." There are three signs referred to in the Apocalypse: In chapter 12, "There appeared a great sign in heaven, a woman clothed with the sun"; in verse 3, "And there appeared another great sign in heaven, and behold a red dragon"; then this third sign, "And I saw another sign in heaven, great and marvellous, the seven angels having the seven last plagues." The emphasis is upon the word "last," *eschatas*. The word "eschatology," the doctrine of last things, comes from that word *eschatas*. ". . . having the seven last plagues; for in them is filled up the wrath of God." After the seals, were the trumpets; after the trumpets, are these bowls of wrath; and after the bowls of wrath, there is finished the judgment of God in the earth, and the kingdom has come.

THE SONG OF MOSES AND OF THE LAMB

But before God describes for us those great and final days of the visitation of His judgment, He gives us a wonderful vision of the immortality, safety, and salvation of His people who are standing on the fiery sea. "And I saw as it were a sea of glass mingled with fire: and them that had gotten the victory over the beast, and over his image, and over his mark, and over the number of his name, stand on the sea of glass, having the harps of God. And they sing the song of Moses the servant of God, and the song of the Lamb, saying, Great and marvellous are thy works, Lord God Almighty; just and true are thy ways, thou King of saints." In chapter 4 of the Revelation, when God has taken His saints up into heaven, John saw before the great throne of the Almighty, a crystal sea, a sea of glass, calm and beautiful. Those elders enthroned by the side of that quiet, beautiful, crystal sea are we, God's sainted children of this day and of this age. But when John sees this sea before the throne of God and these saints standing by its shore, he says this sea is a sea of glass, *mingled with fire*. The added words "mingled with fire" refer to the fact that these saints have come out of great trial and tribulation. "And they sing the song of Moses the servant of God, and the song of the Lamb."

In Exodus 15, on the further shore of the Red Sea, delivered from the enemies that oppressed them, the children of Israel sang the song of Moses. And on that final shore beyond the fiery sea, there shall gather in immortality and glory, in heavenly salvation, God's tribulation saints. They are singing the songs of infinite and glorious redemption, the song of Moses and the song of the Lamb. The song of the Lamb is the song of the victory He won for us over sin, death and the grave, like the triumphant song that Moses sang over the destruction of the enemies of Jehovah. It is a strange coincidence that the first recorded song in the Word of God is in chapter 15 of Exodus, the song of Moses, and that the last recorded song in the Bible is in chapter 15 of the Revelation, the song of Moses, the servant of God, and the song of the Lamb.

The vision further states that "To these were given the harps of God." There are three groups in glory to whom God gives the harps of heaven. In chapter 5 of the Revelation, those who were raptured and taken up to glory have harps from God. In chapter 14 of the Revelation, the one hundred and forty-four thousand gathered to the Lamb on Mount Zion possess the harps of God. This third company is standing on the shores of the fiery sea, having the harps of God and singing the song of Moses and of the Lamb, a song of triumph and heavenly deliverance.

Next in the vision John sees the opening of the temple in heaven: "I beheld, and the temple of the tabernacle of the testimony in heaven was opened." John looked into the very innermost shrine of deity itself, into the very heart of the sanctuary, into the center of the holy of holies. What he saw coming out of the very heart of the temple of God was not the great Mediator, our High Priest, not the ministering servants of mediation, grace and mercy; but what he saw was this amazing vision of seven angels, priest angels, dressed like priests, the seven angels of the seven last plagues.

One of the four cherubim gave unto these seven angels seven golden censers. The King James Version uses the term "vials" as though they were bottles. The Greek word is *phiale,* which denotes a shallow pan. We call them censers. In them the coals were placed from off the altar, and on top of the coals, incense was poured to burn unto God. Notice that these golden censers are given to the angels of judgment by one of the cherubim. Remember that in chapter 6 of the Revelation, the cherubim are instruments of judgment. One of them said to the first horseman, "Come," and the rider of the white horse burst upon the scene. Then another said to the next horseman, "Come," and the rider of the red horse came. Then the black horse and the pale horse. It is one of these cherubim who gives to these seven angels the seven censers. When the seven angels received those censers, the temple was filled with smoke from the glorious power of God, and no man was able to enter into the temple until the seven plagues of the seven angels were fulfilled. The meaning is that the great and final interdiction of God has come. As God has set a boundary to the restless sea that thus far can those tides arise and no further, thus can those waves beat and no more, so God has set a boundary to the evil days of the nations of the earth. When that time comes, known to God, all mediation ceases. The great and final unpardonable sin has been committed, and no man can enter the temple of prayer and supplication. The door is shut and the temple has become a house of indignation, of wrath and of judgment until these seven plagues have been poured out into the earth.

THE SEVEN TERRIBLE VISITATIONS

Chapter 16 presents a description of those seven visitations: "And I heard a great voice out of the temple saying to the seven angels, Go your ways, and pour out the censers of the wrath of God upon the earth." In chapter 8 of the Revelation, before the sounding of the seven trumpets, an angel who came out of that same temple and took coals of fire from off the altar, and after placing them in the censer, he flung it upward, to God. The smoke of the incense of that censer, according to Revelation 8, is the prayers of the saints ascending up to heaven. The same angel then turned and flung the censer down into the earth, and the fire, the fury and the judgment of God burned in the earth. The same figure occurs here. The holiness and the fragrance of the prayers and intercessions of God's saints ascend up before the throne of grace. But to a people who will not turn and will not repent and will not believe in the Lord Jesus, every one of those censers with every element of its fragrance, every prayer of its intercession, every facet of its appeal, becomes one of damnation and judgment.

It is the judgment of God upon those who tread underfoot the grace of the Son of God, who despise the blood of the covenant wherewith He was sanctified, who say "no" to the wooings of the Holy Spirit and the call of the Almighty. All of those holy intercessions turn into condemnation and judgment.

That is one of the laws of God that is fearful to contemplate. When God, in grace and mercy, sends His Son to die for us, and raises up a preacher to preach to us, to open the Holy Scriptures and to plead for men to come in repentance and faith to Jesus; and a wicked, rejecting, blaspheming unbeliever says, "No, I will not turn, I will not believe, I will not accept," then every gracious deed that God has done turns into fury and judgment upon that Christ-rejecter. Such is the imagery in this passage. These censers are holy instruments used in the service of God in the temple; but now, spurned and rejected, the grace of God which they represent becomes fire, indignation, judgment and fury. These seven angels take the seven censers and pour out the contents of wrath into the earth.

Heretofore, these successions of sevens have moved with deliberation. As the seals were broken, there was deliberation. When the trumpets were blown, there was deliberation. But as the Apocalypse moves toward its final climax, it moves furiously and fast. Immediately these things come to pass. In the authorized King James Version, the seven angels are introduced with the words, "and the second angel," "and the third angel," "and the fourth angel," etc. But not so in the Greek. Only the ordinals are used, one after the other, in rapid succession. *Ho Protos*, the first. *Ho Deuteros*, the second. *Ho Tritos*, the third. *Ho Tetaros*, the fourth. *Ho Pempros*, the fifth. *Ho Ektos*, the sixth. *Ho Hebdomos*, the seventh. Just like that, in rapid succession. When the judgment finally comes, it comes in a fury.

Let us pause before one of those judgments. "And the sixth angel poured out his vial upon the great river Euphrates; and the water thereof was dried up, that the way of the kings of the east might be prepared. And I saw three unclean spirits like frogs [creatures of filth and dirt and slime and of the night] come out of the mouth of the dragon, and out of the mouth of the beast, and out of the mouth of the false prophet. For they are the spirits of evil ones, working . . . going forth unto the kings of the earth and of the whole world, to gather them to the battle of that great day of God Almighty . . . And he gathered them together into a place called in the Hebrew tongue Armageddon." Notice that the great sections of the Apocalypse always end in that final day of the Lord God Almighty, the battle of Armageddon. The visions in chapter 14 of the Revelation ended in that great battle of the day of the Lord. And here in chapters 15 and 16 the visions do the same thing again, they end in the great battle of the day of the Lord; and so in the next section, chapters 17 and 18 and 19. Chapter 19 ends in that great battle of the day of the Lord. God's Book says that time, history and government inevitably move toward a final, indescribable conflict in this earth.

THE GATHERING OF THE HOSTS FOR THE
BATTLE OF ARMAGEDDON

The strange thing about that war, as revealed in the Bible, is that all armies and leaders are gathered in Palestine. They are all there. How do they come to be there? The sixth seal says one of those armies numbers two hundred million men, a fantastic astronomical number. In the battle of Armageddon are the armies of the earth, with the leaders and the chiefs of staff of the earth. How is it that they are all there? No strategy on the part of government and rulers would ever bring such a thing about. That is why the Apocalypse explains the situation. The vision says in Revelation 16:13: "I saw three unclean spirits out of the mouth of the dragon and out of the mouth of the beast and out of the mouth of the false prophet . . . and they went forth unto kings of the whole earth . . . to gather them to the battle of that great day of God Almighty." Evil deception brought them to the battle; otherwise, they would never have come. There is an illustration of that same deception in the story of Ahab in I Kings 22. God said: "Ahab is going up to Ramoth-Gilead and die there, be slain there." How is he going? An evil spirit said, "I will put a lying testimony in the mouth of all his prophets . . . . And they will persuade him to go up." So Ahab was persuaded to go up to Ramoth-Gilead by the spirit of evil and of lying where he was slain. That kind of thing is going to happen, God says, in this last, great battle. That trinity of evil spirits is going to persuade those armies and those leaders to gather in Palestine where final Armageddon is to be fought.

There is a strategy in this mighty battle of Armageddon that is unusual. I asked about it one time. It happened like this. I was changed from the airliner I was to go on from Los Angeles to Detroit to another flight. I ran out to the exit and came up the ramp just in time to go through the door before the airplane took off. I looked around hastily, but could find no seat except one toward the front. I dashed up there, sat down and fastened my safety belt. When I got my breath and the plane had taken off, I looked around. Over here was a Colonel, over there was a Brigadier General, over there was another one, and in front of me were a couple more. I looked at the man with whom I was seated and to my amazement discovered he had five stars on each shoulder — five of them! I looked into his face and immediately recognized our Chief of Staff from the Pentagon. No wonder he was seated there by himself! No one would be sitting by him, either, but a Baptist preacher!

I never had a more blessed visit with a man in my life. We fought the Korean War all the way through, from top to bottom, back and forth, on sheets of paper. We ran the Pentagon. Finally, we talked about his family. I asked him if he had any children and he said that he had a boy, and through that son, several little grandchildren. His boy was a test pilot flying jets, but, tragedy of tragedies, his boy had been killed not too long before. The General was rearing those little grandchildren. Tears filled his eyes when he told me about it. For a long time he looked out of the window in silence. Then he looked back at me and said, "You know, I am an old man to start over again with those little children." That great man has a great heart in him.

Anyway, this is what I wanted to know. We live in a day of jet planes, atomic fission, thermo-nuclear warfare, and hydrogen bombs that can blot out the earth. Yet the Bible speaks about armies, armies. So I asked the General: "Do you think that the foot-soldier, the infantry, the army is archaic, antiquated, will never be used again?" He replied: "No, indeed, Listen. However we may develop instruments of destruction, and however we may progress in the art of atomic warfare, there will never come a time, ever, in any development forseeable, when we do not have to have the foot-soldier, the infantryman." He added: "I'll give you two reasons for it. Whenever we conquer a country, someone has to be there to possess it, to control it, to guide it. That means you must have soldiers. If we are ever victorious, we must have someone to occupy the land. Second," he said, "and the biggest reason we shall always have an army is this." He then took out a piece of paper and, emphasizing his words with diagrams, he said: "We have to have an army to push our enemies together. For," he said, "atomic weapons and hydrogen bombs are of no use whatsoever if the enemy is deployed over the face of a continent. For if we explode it here [pointing to a spot], we might kill ten soldiers. If we explode it there [pointing to another spot], we might kill fifty. The only way that an atomic bomb is ever useful and profitable is when we have a concentration of the enemy so you can drop it on them. But in order to push those enemies together we must have an army to compress them so you can drop your bomb effectively."

And that is what Armageddon is about. Why are these vast armies in Palestine? How does it happen that these great leaders of the world are in Palestine where this awesome thing can happen, with blood two hundred miles long, flowing, a river of blood? The answer is plain. "I saw three unclean spirits and they went forth unto the kings of the whole world to gather them together to the battle of the great day of God Almighty."

THE APPEAL OF CHRIST TO LISTEN

Finally in the middle of these terrible descriptions, are the words from Christ: "Behold, I come as a thief" (Revelation 16:15). If a man will not hear the voice of God, he lays his heart open to listen to the voice of destruction, evil and damnation. When the kings and the people and the armies of the earth will not listen to God, then they lay themselves open to listening to the persuasive voice of the spirits of darkness and evil. That is the explanation for the little verse: "Behold, I come as a thief. Blessed is he that is ready." Oh, listen to the voice of God! Listen to the voice of God! There is salvation in none other.

The chapter closes: ". . . and men blasphemed God because the plague was great." Would not you think they would turn? Hear their agonizing cries: "O God, the galling government! O God, the oppression! O God, the darkness! O God, the judgment, O God, save us!" But, no, they just blasphemed God the more. Is not that a picture of the world today? Oppressed in chains and in slavery, do the peoples turn to God and follow the Lord? No! There is no sign of revival, no sign of appeal, no sign of repentance, no sign of turning. Such is the spirit of depravity in the world. Oh, that the Lord would bless our people with an open heart for God! Remember us, have mercy upon us, Lord, and upon thy people. Save us, Lord, now, in this day of opportunity, golden and precious, and in the world that is to come. That is why we are preaching the Gospel, that is why we extend this invitation. God be good to us, be merciful to us and save us; and in that great salvation, may we all be numbered among those who stand by the sea, singing the song of Moses and of the Lamb.

CHAPTER 16

THE REIGN OF THE SCARLET WOMAN

Revelation 17

1. And there came one of the seven angels which had the seven vials, and talked with me, saying unto me, Come hither; I will shew unto thee the judgment of the great whore that sitteth upon many waters:

2. With whom the kings of the earth have committed fornication, and the inhabitants of the earth have been made drunk with the wine of her fornication.

3. So he carried me away in the spirit into the wilderness: and I saw a woman sit upon a scarlet coloured beast, full of names of blasphemy, having seven heads and ten horns.

4. And the woman was arrayed in purple and scarlet colour, and decked with gold and precious stones and pearls, having a golden cup in her hand full of abominations and filthiness of her fornication:

5. And upon her forehead was a name written, MYSTERY, BABYLON THE GREAT, THE MOTHER OF HARLOTS AND ABOMINATIONS OF THE EARTH.

6. And I saw the woman drunken with the blood of the saints, and with the blood of the martyrs of Jesus: and when I saw her, I wondered with great admiration.

Chapter 17 of the Revelation is one of the most astounding of all of the prophecies to be found in the Word of God. It is one that cannot only be verified in history but that can also be followed closely in the daily newspapers of this present hour.

This section in the Revelation, chapters 17 and 18, is an interlude. The passage begins: "And there came one of the seven angels which had the seven bowls of the wrath and the final judgment of Almighty God." Those seven angels were introduced to us in chapters 15 and 16. At the end of chapter

16, the seventh angel poured out his bowl of the wrath and judgment of God upon this Christ-rejecting and sinful world. Immediately thereafter, we would have expected the personal appearance of Christ upon this earth. But the Lord does not come from heaven until chapter 19. Before the final coming of Jesus, there is this interlude, this intermission. In this parenthesis one of those seven-vialed angels of the judgment and wrath of God comes to the seer and says, "God would reveal to you, God would make known to you, the future of religion in the earth." So this intermission between chapters 16 and 19 (which latter chapter brings the personal appearing of our Lord) reveals to us Mystery Babylon, the course of religion in this world (chapter 18) and the City Babylon, the course of culture and commerce in this world. The vial angel (the bowl angel) says to John, "Come hither, I will show thee the judgment of the great whore that sitteth upon many waters with whom the kings of the earth have committed fornication and the inhabitants of the earth have been made drunk with the wine of her adultery." He then carries John away in the spirit into the wilderness. When the Lord showed the Apostle John the bride of Christ, the new Jerusalem, the city and the people of the Lord, He took him to a mountain, great and high. But when the Lord shows to John the course and development of religion in this world, He carries him into the wilderness. Wherever there is spiritual harlotry, there is desolation and a desert of dreary, weary waste. So He carries John into a wilderness, and there John says, "I saw a woman sit upon a scarlet beast, full of names of blasphemy. . . . And the woman was arrayed in purple and scarlet colour, and decked with gold and precious stones and pearls, having in her hand a golden cup full of abominations and filthiness of her fornication."

THE GREAT AMAZEMENT OF THE APOSTLE JOHN

In the first part of this vision, John sees this woman with her name on her forehead, "MYSTERY, BABYLON THE GREAT,

THE MOTHER OF HARLOTS AND ABOMINATIONS OF THE EARTH."
In the interpretation which follows in the remainder of the chapter, John writes his own personal reaction in language that is
extremely strong: "And when I saw that woman drunken with
the blood of the saints, and with the blood of the martyrs of
Jesus . . .*ethaumasa thauma mega* — [looking upon her and
understanding what she meant, *I was amazed with a great amazement*, I was filled with the wonder of a great wonder, I was
astonished with a great astonishment]." He did not write those
words of amazement when he saw the Beast, the course of the
political empire and governments of this world. He did not write
of that astonishment when he saw any other thing that God
revealed to him concerning the future. But when John saw this
scarlet woman, and came to understand what she represented,
as he saw the development of the course of religion in this
earth, *ethaumasa thauma mega* [I wondered with a great
wonder]."

It is apparent why John's reaction should have been one
of amazement. The background of the development of this
religious idolatry, this scarlet whore, is seen in the very name
written on her forehead: "And upon her forehead was a name
written, MYSTERY, BABYLON THE GREAT, THE MOTHER OF
HARLOTS AND ABOMINATIONS OF THE EARTH." Idolatry began
in the city of Babel, or Babylon. Contrary to the interdiction of
God, men began the raising of a tower toward heaven, an attempt by their own works to obtain salvation. From the lives
of the people we know, this attempt also included the use of
images and rituals, contrary to the Word of God. The Bible
calls the use of images and sensualities in worship contrary to
the revealed Word of God, harlotry. The Bible calls it whore-
dom. The Bible calls it spiritual adultery and fornication. That
is a nomenclature used throughout the whole Word of God.
This idolatry, this use of images in approaching the great God
of heaven, began in the city of Babel (or Babylon) as it was
established by Nimrod.

One of the most amazing of all of the books that have ever come into my hands is the one entitled *The Two Babylons*, by the great British author, Alexander Hislop. He traces the development of this Mystery Babylon, the idolatry of Babylon, through the years and the centuries to this present day. Nimrod's wife (Nimrod who founded Babel and the kingdom of Babylon) was named Semiramis. In Assyria and Nineveh she was called Ishtar. In the Phoenician pantheon she was called Ashteroth or Astarte. In Egypt she was called Isis. Among the Greeks she was called Aphrodite. Among the Latins, the Romans, she was called Venus. She became the first high priestess of an idolatrous system. In answer to the promise made to Eve that the seed of the woman would deliver the race, Semiramis, when she gave birth to a son, said he was miraculously conceived by a sunbeam, and she offered her son as the promised deliverer of the earth. His name was Tammuz. When he was grown, a wild boar slew him; but after forty days of the mother's weeping, he was raised from the dead. In this story of Semiramis and Tammuz, began the cult of worship of the mother and child that spread throughout the whole world. In Assyria she is called Ishtar and her son, still Tammuz. In Phoenicia she was called Astarte or Ashteroth, and her son, Baal or Tammuz. In Egypt she was called Isis, and her son was called Osiris or Horus. In Greece she was called Aphrodite, and her son was called Eros. Among the Romans she was called Venus, and her son was called Cupid.

The cult of the worship of mother and child spread throughout the whole earth. She was worshiped by the offering of a wafer (a little cake) to her as the queen of heaven. And there were always forty days of Lent, of weeping over the destruction of Tammuz, before the feast of Ishtar, at which time his resurrection was celebrated. The sign of Tammuz was an Ishtar egg, a symbol of his resurrection to life. The secret of the Babylonian mystery was to be found in priestly ablutions and in sacramental rites and rituals, in the dedication of virgins to the gods, in purgatorial fires, and in a thousand other things that are familiar to us today.

The prophets bitterly inveigh against that mother and child cult. In chapter 44 of Jeremiah, Jeremiah describes the idol worshipers among the children of Israel, who burn incense to the queen of heaven and who offer cakes (little wafers) in her name. In chapter 8 of Ezekiel, God takes the prophet and shows him the inner life of the people of the Lord who are not idolatrous: "He said also to me, Turn thee yet again, and thou shalt see greater abominations than these. Then he brought me to the door of the gate of the Lord's house which was toward the north; and, behold there sat women weeping for Tammuz." Ezekiel was beholding the forty days of Lent in which they afflicted themselves and wept for Tammuz, the child that was slain by the wild boar. But after those forty days, in commemoration of the story of his being raised from the dead, the end of weeping was celebrated with the feast of Ishtar, in which the people exchanged Ishtar eggs.

As we have observed, that cult of the worship of mother and child spread throughout the whole world, from Babylon to Assyria, to Phoenicia, to Pergamos, and finally, to Rome itself. There the Roman Emperor was elected Pontifex Maximus, the high priest of all of the idolatrous systems of the Roman Empire. And when the Roman Emperor passed away, that title of high priest of the rites and mysteries of the cult of mother and child, the Bablyonian mystery of idolatry, was assumed by the Bishop of Rome.

There is no such thing in the Bible as the exaltation of a female deity, and least of all is there any hint or suggestion that Mary was other than what she is presented to be in the New Testament. The last time she is seen she is a humble, fellow-suppliant in the prayer meeting described in the first chapter of the Book of Acts. After that she is never mentioned again, she is never seen again, she is never referred to again. This cult of the idolatrous worship of the mother and child is, purely and simply, Babylonian idolatry. "And upon her fore-head was a name written, MYSTERY, BABYLON THE GREAT, THE MOTHER OF HARLOTS [or idolatries] AND ABOMINATIONS OF THE EARTH." How amazing that out of Babylon, according to the Word of God, should arise those idolatrous systems that would spread over the entire face of the civilized world! And when John saw it, he said: "*Ethaumasa thauma mega,*" that is, "and I wondered with a great wonder."

THE SCARLET WOMAN RIDING THE BEAST

The woman is portrayed as riding the Beast. The Beast is the symbol in the Word of God for government, for political power. ". . . and I saw a woman sit upon a scarlet beast . . . . And the woman was arrayed in purple and scarlet, decked with gold and having precious stones and pearls for embellishment, and a golden cup in her hand." She is arrayed in royal, luxurious, haughty power. She is rich, and she rides, she controls, the political turn of the government. When John looked upon that woman, "*ethaumasa thauma mega,*" for to John the only church he knew was despised, poor, hunted, hounded and hated. For a man to name the name of Christ, was to be brought before a Roman provincial judge and there to be sentenced to be burned at the stake, or to have his head cut off (if he were a Roman citizen), or to be crucified (if he were an ordinary peasant as most of them were). The church John knew was poor and per-secuted. But this thing, this organization, is rich, she controls government, she is dressed in scarlet and purple, and her em-bellishments are precious stones and pearls; she rides the beast, she snaps the whip, she crowns and uncrowns kings, she says "yea" and "nay" to legislation. And when John looks upon her, "*ethaumasa thauma mega,*" he is astonished with an indescrib-able astonishment.

But further on, as the angel interprets this scarlet whore to the sacred seer, he writes: "And I saw the woman drunken [*methuousan*, a present active linear participle, meaning 'continuously drunk'; not that just one time she made a mistake and slew God's servants, but 'continuously drunken']." "I saw that scarlet whore drunken with the blood of saints, and with the blood of the martyrs of Jesus." John could not believe his eyes, for in his day it was pagan Rome that was persecuting the Christians. When the Christian in John's day was martyred with the sword or was crucified or was thrown into a boiling cauldron of oil or was fed to the wild beasts, it was pagan Rome that crucified him or slew him or fed him to the wild and ferocious animals. But in this vision that God gave to John, the blood of the saints and the blood of the martyrs of Jesus is shed by that rich and scarlet idolatrous church. John *"ethaumasa thauma mega"* he wondered with a great wonder.

Who invented the Inquisition? Who invented the torture chamber and the rack? Who burned at the stake uncounted thousands and millions of God's servants in the earth? This scarlet whore, dressed in purple, decked with gold and precious stone and pearls, riding in control of the governments of the world. John "wondered with a great wonder." Who would ever have dreamed that those humble, persecuted, outcast, little *ecclesias,* those little communities of Jesus, would ever rise to be so rich, so bedecked, so merciless and cruel, and so filled with the blood of the martyrs of the Lord? It has been estimated that she has slain more than fifty millions of the servants of Jesus Christ.

Then the angel reveals to the Apostle John the end of this scarlet whore. How will she fare, so rich? How will she fare, so bedecked? How will she fare, with her skirts so filled with the blood of God's people? How will she fare, riding the beast, controlling the governments, saying "yea" and "nay" to legislation — how will she fare? The answer, in itself, is astonishing. "And the ten horns which thou sawest upon the beast are the ten kingdoms." Remember the great image of Daniel? The gold, the silver, the brass, the iron, and the ten toes? The end of the world, the Bible says, shall come with governments being separated into different kingdoms. The Apocalypse reveals that those kingdoms shall willingly, yieldingly, give their authority to the great so-called emancipator and final deliverer, the anti-Christ. Those kingdoms shall hate the whore and make her desolate and naked, and shall eat her flesh and burn her with fire.

I want you to see a remarkable thing here. In chapter 18 of Revelation, it is God who destroys the city of Babylon. In chapter 19 of Revelation, it is God who destroys the Beast and the False Prophet. But do you notice here that it is not God who destroys the scarlet whore? It is man who destroys her. That is an astonishing thing.

THE DESTRUCTION OF THE IDOLATROUS SYSTEMS OF THE WORLD

When we read history and watch the course of this world, that is exactly what God has said and what God has done. We are not to think that God is peculiarly different here in the Revelation. The great, eternal, spiritual principles by which God directs history and destiny are no different in the Revelation from what they were yesterday, or will be tomorrow, or are today. We can follow these things in history books. We can read these things in the daily newspapers. God is ever true to the great principles by which He governs the world. We can herein follow the work of God as it is projected out to the end of time. The Apocalypse says it is not the intervention of Christ, it is no appearing from God that destroys this scarlet whore. Men do it. "The ten horns which thou sawest upon the beast, those kingdoms of the earth, they hate the whore, and they make her desolate and naked, and they eat her flesh, and they burn her with fire."

Let us see if this prophecy made two thousand years ago is demonstrated in history. God has said in the text that men shall destroy this whore, this idolatrous system. Men do it. Do you remember reading in history of the ferocious onslaught of the terrible Moslem, Mohammedan, Islamic movement and its conquest with the scimitar? That terrible, bloody conquest began in the seventh century and continued through the centuries. Against what was Mohammedanism a reaction, and against what was the fierce onslaught of Mohammedanism thrust? It was against idolatry. In the fierce conquest of the Caliphs of Mohammed who overran the world as they destroyed idolatry, could you imagine someone standing before those great armies of Mohammed and saying: "Remember, remember, this is an idol of Mary, and not of Minerva. The image is not to be touched. This is an idol of Joseph, and not of Jove. This idol is not to be touched. Remember, this is an idol of Christ, and not of Krishna." Could you explain that to a Mohammedan Caliph who felt called of God, with a sword in his hand, to destroy idolatry in the earth? The change of the name of that idol does not change idolatry. Whether that idol is named Krishna or Christ, whether that idol is named Minerva or Mary, whether that idol is named Jove or Joseph, it is an idol; and when the Mohammedan Caliph came with his sword in hand, he destroyed the idol temples, the churches of all Africa, of all Palestine, of all Asia Minor and Turkey and of Istanbul, and thrust himself to the Philippine Islands on the east. It was against idolatry that the Mohammedan religion arose as a fierce and a terrible antagonist. The sweep of the Mohammedan was the sweep of the fierceness of the wrath and the judgment of Almighty God. Men destroyed the idolatrous whore in Africa and Asia.

And the prophecy is that the kingdoms of the world, some day, are going to get weary of the same idolatrous church. They are going to get tired of being told by a Nuncio or a legate or an emissary what they shall do and what they shall not do. The prophecy is that the kingdoms of the world shall hate the whore, make her desolate, rob her of all of her riches and make her naked, stripping her of her beautiful scarlet robe and her purple gowns and her bedecking pearls and precious stones.

The world, these kingdoms, shall "eat her flesh," that is, they shall appropriate all of her riches. The richest institution in the earth, outside of the United States of America, is this scarlet whore. These kingdoms shall eat her flesh, appropriate all of her wealth, and burn her with fire, making her a social, a political, an economic outcast. That, God says, shall be a development in human history. It is not to be of the Lord at His coming again. It will not be of God's judgment, as upon Babylon. But it will come at the hands of men. And when he saw it, this vast, illimitable, immeasurable system of idolatry that grew and grew to cover the earth, rich and powerful, and saw its tragic and despicable end John says: *"ethaumasa thauma mega,"* "and I wondered with a great wonder."

Now, pick up your Bible and turn to I John, a letter written by the same author who wrote the Revelation. I John 5:21: This is the earnest, last admonition of the seer. He has said nothing about idolatry in this entire little book, but look at this last verse: "Little children, keep yourselves from idols." Amen, amen. For the worship of God is spiritual. God desires that those who worship Him shall worship Him in spirit and in truth. It is between you and your soul with no mediating priest in between. It is between you and God for yourself. Talk to Him for yourself, confess to Him your sin. He alone can forgive us. Give your heart and life to the blessed Jesus. Walk by His side. Be filled with the glory of His presence. Love our Lord in spirit and in truth, for God seeks such to worship Him. "Little children, keep yourselves from idols." Amen. This is the Word and the Revelation of God to our souls.

Expository Sermons on Revelation

Volume 5—Revelation 18 through 22

Expository Sermons
on Revelation

VOLUME FIVE

VOLUME 5—REVELATION 18 THROUGH 22

by
W. A. CRISWELL, Ph.D., D.D.

Dedication
to
DR. AND MRS. W. R. WHITE
He a prince among preachers
She a paragon among teachers
They both so greatly loved
By us in earth
And by God in heaven above

FOREWORD

After years and years of study, preparation and preaching, this fifth and last volume of *Expository Sermons on Revelation* is offered to the reading world. It is difficult to describe how I feel after so long and so sustained an effort. I have learned so much, so very much, in the preparation and delivery of these messages. God has blessed my soul no less in the private hours of searching and meditation than in the living experience of preaching from the pulpit to the thousands of people who listened to the results of my endeavor. Preaching through the Bible and finally through the Revelation has been the mountain peak of transfiguration in my life. I can almost sing with Mary the mother of Jesus:

> My soul doth magnify the Lord,
> And my spirit hath rejoiced in God my Saviour,
> For he that is mighty hath done to me great things
> And holy is his name.
> His mercy is unto generations and generations
> On them that fear him.
> He hath showed strength with his arm,
> The hungry he hath filled with good things.
> He hath given help to [me] his servant
> That he might remember mercy
> Toward us [his people] for ever.

The Revelation is a summation of all the past, all the present, all the future. It is the celestial capstone to all God's handiwork. What the Book of Genesis is to the story of God's redemptive grace, the Book of the Revelation is to the fruition of our Lord's atoning mercy. The first is meaningless without the last. Almost literally, in preaching through the Revelation, I preached again through the Bible itself. Every promise, every theme, every hope, every dream of the Holy Scriptures finds its fulfillment and consummation in the glorious pages of the Apocalypse.

But if I have learned much, so much, in these years of study and preaching through the Revelation, I must also confess that I have come to sense even more deeply and poignantly the multitudinous areas of God's grace and program into which I see as through a shaded glass, darkly. There is so much I do not understand, so much that God will have to make plain by and by. We have to wait until the time of fulfillment, until we see face to face, to know the fullness of God's elective purpose for us. There are a myriad of details that the Almighty has not chosen to reveal. I feel like the Apostle Paul in Romans 11:33-36, after he had discussed the sovereign choices of God concerning Israel in the three chapters of Romans 9, 10 and 11:

> O the depth of the riches
> Both of the wisdom and the knowledge of God!
> How unsearchable are his judgments,
> And his ways past finding out!
> For who hath known the mind of the Lord?
> Or who hath been his counsellor?
> Or who hath first given to him
> And it shall be recompensed unto him again?
> For of him, and through him, and to him,
> Are all things, to him be glory for ever. Amen.

Thank you, Mrs. Bailey Forester, for typing these pages and thank you, Miss Olive Carter, for checking the manuscript. And thank you, dear reader, for taking time out of a busy world to follow the messages I have sought to deliver. As there is a beatitude promised those "who read and who hear the words of this prophecy," so may God grant a special blessing to you who follow the exposition of the visions through these concluding sermons.

And now, as in these years past, so in these years to come, "The grace of our Lord Jesus Christ be with you all, Amen." Till we see Him who saith, "Surely, surely, I come quickly."

W. A. CRISWELL

Pastor's Study
First Baptist Church
Dallas, Texas

CONTENTS

Foreword

Expository Sermons on Revelation

Volume 5—Revelation 18 through 22

THE JUDGMENT OF GOD UPON BABYLON

Revelation 18

1 And after these things I saw another angel come down from heaven, having great power; and the earth was lightened with his glory.

2 And he cried mightily with a strong voice, saying, Babylon the great is fallen, is fallen, and is become the habitation of devils, and the hold of every foul spirit, and a cage of every unclean and hateful bird.

3 For all nations have drunk of the wine of the wrath of her fornication, and the kings of the earth have committed fornication with her, and the merchants of the earth are waxed rich through the abundance of her delicacies.

4 And I heard another voice from heaven, saying, Come out of her, my people, that ye be not partakers of her sins, and that ye receive not of her plagues.

5 For her sins have reached unto heaven, and God hath remembered her iniquities.

6 Reward her even as she rewarded you, and double unto her double according to her works: in the cup which she hath filled, fill to her double.

7 How much she hath glorified herself, and lived deliciously, so much torment and sorrow give her: for she saith in her heart, I sit a queen, and am no widow, and shall see no sorrow.

8 Therefore shall her plagues come in one day, death and mourning, and famine; and she shall be utterly burned with fire: for strong is the Lord God who judgeth her.

9 And the kings of the earth, who have committed fornication and lived deliciously with her, shall bewail her, and lament for her, when they shall see the smoke of her burning.

10 Standing afar off for the fear of her torment, saying, Alas, alas that great city Babylon, that mighty city! for in one hour is thy judgment come.

11 And the merchants of the earth shall weep and mourn over her; for no man buyeth their merchandise any more:

12 The merchandise of gold, and silver, and precious stones, and of pearls, and fine linen, and purple, and silk, and scarlet, and all thyine wood, and all manner vessels of ivory, and all manner vessels of most precious wood, and of brass, and iron, and marble.

13 And cinnamon, and odours, and ointments, and frankincense, and wine, and oil, and fine flour, and wheat, and beasts, and sheep, and horses, and chariots, and slaves, and souls of men.

14 And the fruits that thy soul lusted after are departed from thee, and

all things which were dainty and goodly are departed from thee, and thou shalt find them no more at all.

15 The merchants of these things, which were made rich by her, shall stand afar off for the fear of her torment, weeping and wailing,

16 And saying, Alas, alas that great city, that was clothed in fine linen, and purple, and scarlet, and decked with gold, and precious stones, and pearls!

17 For in one hour so great riches is come to nought. And every ship-master, and all the company in ships, and sailors, and as many as trade by sea, stood afar off,

18 And cried when they saw the smoke of her burning, saying, What city is like unto this great city!

19 And they cast dust on their heads, and cried, weeping and wailing, saying, Alas, alas that great city, wherein were made rich all that had ships in the sea by reason of her costliness! for in one hour is she made desolate.

20 Rejoice over her, thou heaven, and ye holy apostles and prophets; for God hath avenged you on her.

21 And a mighty angel took up a stone like a great millstone, and cast it into the sea, saying, Thus with violence shall that great city Babylon be thrown down, and shall be found no more at all.

22 And the voice of harpers, and musicians, and of pipers, and trumpeters, shall be heard no more at all in thee; and no craftsman, of whatsoever craft he be, shall be found any more in thee; and the sound of a millstone shall be heard no more at all in thee;

23 And the light of a candle shall shine no more at all in thee; and the voice of the bridegroom and of the bride shall be heard no more at all in thee: for thy merchants were the great men of the earth; for by thy sorceries were all nations deceived.

24 And in her was found the blood of prophets, and of saints, and of all that were slain upon the earth.

When the heavens open as a scroll rolled back and when the Lord is revealed in personal triumph, how shall these things be? What is the sign of Christ's coming and of the end of the world? The Apocalypse, the unveiling of Christ, is the presentation of our Lord when God intervenes in human history.

Chapter 19 of the Revelation records the Second Coming of Christ. Chapter 20 is the binding of Satan and the introduction of the long-prayed-for Millennium. Chapters 21 and 22 describe the new heaven, the new earth, the New Jerusalem, the new home of the soul. As the Revelation develops, as these events fall into consecutive, chronological order, chapter 19 (describing the coming of Christ) should have immediately followed chapter 16, which depicts the pouring out of the seven bowls of wrath in which are filled up the judgments of God. But, between chapter 16 and chapter 19 there is an interlude, a parenthesis, an intermission. In these two intervening chapters of 17 and 18, one of the seven angels, in whose hands are the bowls of the wrath of God, took John and said: "Come hither; I will shew unto thee the judgment of the great whore that sitteth upon many waters." The angel would also show John the judgment of the city Babylon, which epitomizes the life of a godless and Christ-rejecting world. So, in this interlude, in this parenthesis, there is uncovered to John in chapter 17 the judgment of God upon mystery Babylon, the ecclesiastical system that is described as a great whore. Then in chapter 18 the angel reveals to the seer the judgment of the Lord upon the city Babylon, upon the great center of the social, political, cultural and commercial life of this globe.

BABYLON IN PROPHECY

We have already twice been introduced to the ultimate destruction of Babylon. In Revelation 14:8 there came a great announcement from heaven, carried by the voice of an angel messenger, crying, "Babylon *epesen, epesen* [Babylon is fallen, is fallen] . . ." In Revelation 16:19, when the seventh bowl of the judgment and the wrath of God is poured out upon the earth, are written these words, ". . . great Babylon came in remembrance before God, to give unto her the cup of the wine of the fierceness of his wrath." Then in the present chapter 18, this announcement by anticipation is made: "And after these things I saw another angel come down from heaven, having great power; and the earth was lighted with his glory. And he cried mightily with a strong voice, saying, Babylon the great [*epesen, epesen*] is fallen, is fallen." We have heard that before. *Epesen,* "is fallen," is an aoristic verb. When God destroys this great city, it will not be over a period of time, it will not be by continuous assault that lasts through weeks or months or years. Rather, its destruction will come suddenly, as lightning cleaves the bosom of the livid sky. It will come instantaneously, *"mia hora"* (which phrase is repeated again and again in chapter 18), "in one hour." "In *mia hora,"* and the thing is done. The judgment is poured out. It sounds like an atomic explosion, this description of the destruction of this great city at the hand of God.

The city of Babylon is mentioned more times in the Bible

than any other city except Jerusalem. More than 260 times Babylon is referred to in the Holy Scriptures. For example, in chapters 50 and 51 of Jeremiah, Babylon is called by name thirty-seven times. It was the city of the first great monarch of the earth, the capital of the golden kingdom of Nebuchad-nezzar. It was the city of the king who destroyed Judea, that destroyed Jerusalem, that destroyed the Solomonic temple of God. It was the city of the great Babylonian captivity, located among "the rivers (canals) of Babylon." "By the rivers of Babylon, there we sat down, yea, we wept, when we remem-bered Zion. We hanged our harps upon the willow trees in the midst thereof" (Psalm 137:1, 2). Babylon — the great avenger of the sins of God's people. Babylon — more vile, wicked, ruth-less, merciless than those whom God judged at her hand. "The sins of Babylon came into remembrance before God." It was the city of Nimrod, the grandson of Ham, who, on the vast plain of Shinar built Babel in order that by man's strength and ingenuity he could reach up to heaven.

The city has a great part in prophecy. For example, in chapter 5 of the Book of Zechariah, beginning with verse 5 and reading to the end of the chapter, there is the vision of the ephah, and in the ephah (when a talent of lead covering it was lifted up by the angel) he saw a woman. The angel said this woman is "wickedness." In the vision the prophet also saw two women who had wings like a stork and the wind was in their wings and they lifted up that ephah between the earth and the sky. The prophet then said to the angel, "Whither do these bear the ephah?" And the angel replied, "To build it an house in the land of Shinar: and it shall be established, and set there upon its own base" (Zechariah 5:10, 11). In Babylon in the land of Shinar is set the wicked center of the social, com-mercial life of this world and there it is to be judged by Al-mighty God.

Did you notice the reference in Revelation 18 that Baby-lon is to be judged *by God Himself*? As you look at chapters 17 and 18, there is a vast difference between the judgment that falls upon the "scarlet whore" and the judgment that falls upon the social, commercial, political, cultural life of this earth, epito-mized by the great city of Babylon. It is the hand of man that destroys the whore. It is the political power and governments of the world who hate her, destroy her flesh, burn her with fire, make her naked, confiscate all of her wealth and property. That is done by man. That is what God says will happen to this great, ecclesiastical system who has the golden cup in her hand. The kings of the earth (Revelation 17 says) will become weary of her pretenses, of her superstitions, of her arrogance, of her parading in gold and scarlet and purple. They will become weary of her financial burden, of supporting her endless institutions. Finally, God's Book says, the nations of the earth, the people of the earth (not God, not by the intervention of heaven; rather, it is something that man does), the political leaders of the earth grow so weary of her they destroy her. Now look at chapter 17 again. When her destruction comes to pass, everyone is glad. They are tired of the system. They are weary of it, burdened by it. Its monstrous, indescribable superstitions and inanities are more than the political governments are able to endure. When she is destroyed, the earth is glad to be rid of the last vestige of the scarlet whore.

But the destruction of the city of Babylon is in an altogether different category. It is God who destroys Babylon. The beast is not mentioned, the ten kings are not mentioned, the governments of the earth are not mentioned. This is an intervention of God. This is something God does. When Babylon is destroyed, there is lamentation all over the world. The kings of the earth lament, the virgins of the earth lament, the seamen of the merchant marines lament. The lamentation over the destruction of the city of Babylon is world-wide. There is a reason why. We can see it exactly. If I, as a messenger of God, were to announce over the radio (and the radio were to carry it through networks over the entire face of the earth) that within thirty minutes the heavens would roll apart and Christ would descend and the end of the age would come, the reaction would be just as it is here in chapter 18 of the Book of Revelation. It would be a twofold reaction. One is described in chapter 18, verse 19: "And they cast dust on their heads, and cried, weeping and wailing, saying, Alas, alas that great city, wherein were made rich all that had ships in the sea by reason of her costliness! for in one hour is she made desolate." The other is described in chapter 18, verse 20: "Rejoice over her, thou heaven, and ye holy apostles and prophets; for God hath avenged you on her." You would find that double reaction this very day if I were to make the great announcement that within thirty minutes this world system would be destroyed. God's children would be so glad, they would be so happy because our Lord is coming!

> Oh, joy! oh, delight! should we go without dying,
> No sickness, no sadness, no dread and no crying.
> Caught up thro' the clouds with our Lord into glory,
> When Jesus receives "His own."

There would be rejoicing. But, the great mass of this world would lament and wail because their hearts and their lives, their visions, their hopes are all in this world. "What about my mortgages? What about my stocks? What about my bonds? What about my treasures? What about my wealth? What about my possessions? What about all these accumulations?" they would say. When God intervenes in history, it will be as we find it here in chapter 18 of the Revelation. There was lamentation on the part of those who had everything they had in Babylon. But there was rejoicing on the part of the saints and the hosts of heaven.

We cannot but ask the question, What does Babylon represent? Many answers are offered. There are scholars who believe that this Babylon is to be an actual, rebuilt city on the banks of the Euphrates River, on the great plain of Shinar, at the head of the Persian Gulf. They believe that India, Asia, Malaya, Indonesia and all of the vast East will rise to stupendous power. They believe that the great possibilities of irrigation in damming up the Tigris and Euphrates Rivers will make the Mesopotamian Valley like the garden of God east of Eden. They believe that there in the very center of the continents of the earth with Europe to the north and west, with Africa due west, with the vast multitudes of Asia east and with the Australian continent south, and the Americas beyond, they believe that there is going to be rebuilt in that place a vast world center of commerce, social life and political government. There are many scholars who believe this will come to pass and that this Babylon refers to a rebuilt city in the heart of the earth.

Then, there are other scholars who believe that this Babylon represents a system of life and culture whose basic, essential principle is alienated from God. They are persuaded that this secular system is epitomized and symbolized by this great world-city. It could be a great world-city in America, a great world-city in England, a great world-city in Europe. Again, there are those who believe that this Babylon represents the social, cultural, political and commercial life of the end times and that this entire system is summarized in one great world-city called Babylon. Now, as I have studied, I have come to the conclusion that all three of these interpretations can be true. This Babylon may be an ultimate, great world-city built at the head of the Persian Gulf where most of the oil of the world is found, where the teeming masses of the continents live to the right and to the left, to the north and to the south. That could be. It certainly represents that system of commerce, social life and culture that alienates the soul from God, whether in that age or today, whether then or now, epitomized by these vast, godless, urban centers. And, of course, it certainly represents the age when Christ shall come, for it is the direct intervention and appearing of Christ Himself that destroys this vast-world-city.

THE REASONS FOR THE DESTRUCTION OF BABYLON

Let us now consider another perinent question. Why is it that God's judgment so terribly falls upon this city? Whether it is a city in our country or abroad, whether it is a particular city built on the plain of Shinar or the commercial capital of another land, why is God's judgment so severely to fall upon it? The text (Revelation 18:5) says, first, "For her sins have reached unto heaven, and God hath remembered her iniquities." In the first Babel, their infamous tower was built block by block, brick by brick, up and up and up and up until Nimrod proposed to reach heaven with it. That evil, God says, has come before His remembrance. The like sin of wicked Babylon, building up, building up, building up, has stored for herself as waters behind a mighty dam the judgment of God upon her godlessness, materialism, secularism and denial of Christ. Babylon's sins have reached unto heaven like the tower of Babel. "God hath remembered her iniquities."

The second reason for the judgment of God is described in Revelation 18:7: "How much she hath glorified herself, and lived deliciously . . . for she saith in her heart, I sit a queen, and am no widow, and shall see no sorrow." "I am immortal and invincible," she says, and in her arrogance, self-conceit and self-glorification she boasts of her atheism, blasphemy, infidelity and Christ-rejection. To her there is not any God, there is not any Christ, there is not any Holy Spirit. She proposes for herself a dominance in history and in the future that will last forever. "I sit as a queen and I have glorified myself." This false, self-glorification, in a boasting that defies God, is another reason for Babylon's judgment.

There is a third reason for the destruction of this great city. Look closely at verses 12 and 13. In them are listed twenty-eight articles of merchandise. The enumeration starts off with gold and after the list is completed it closes with "the souls of men." Think of that! Souls used just as one would pack freight. Crate them up, ship them out, drop them from a boom! So here in Babylon, the lives and the souls of men are matters of commerce. Would not you have thought, after the philosophers have philosophized and the teachers have taught and the preachers have preached and the people have spoken and the books have been written, that by now we would have reached that great apex when men look upon the value of human life as being the most supremely appointed of all of the precious gifts in the earth? Wouldn't you? God says it is just the opposite. As we increase in our culture, as we go further into scientific achievements, as civilization and culture grow, God says our culture becomes more merciless, more cruel, more ruthless, more blasphemous and God-dishonoring. Is this not corroborated in the newspapers and in the magazines of our day?

The majority of the millions of the populations of this earth live under governments that believe the human soul and human life nothing but merchandise. "Destroy them, waste them, bury them, shoot them down, feed them into the maw of cannons," they say. As Lenin avowed, "What would it matter if two-thirds of this earth were destroyed if the one-third that remains be Communist?" Did you ever think what that saying might mean? How many people are in this earth? The total population is beyond three billion. What would it matter, the godless says, if they were to destroy two billion people? Just think of that! The population of the United States of America is about two hundred million. The population of Canada may be thirty million. The population of Mexico may be thirty million. If altogether on this entire North American continent there be three hundred million and if with all of South America we might number one-half billion, yet that man whom the Communist world so glorifies that he is looked upon as very God and his writing as the very Bible, yet that man says it would not matter if they were to destroy two billion of the people of this earth if those who remained were Communist! Trafficking in the souls of men! To them it is as nothing for a man if he is slain; it is nothing for a nation if it is destroyed; it is nothing for a family if they are tortured on the rack, starved to death, shot by the firing squad, thrown into the incinerator.

When a people lose the concept of God, no longer is a man anything but an animal. Where do we get the idea that a man is worth something, anyhow? Where were you persuaded that a man's soul is worth something? I know exactly where we learned that idea. We received it not from Hitler. Nor from Karl Marx. Nor from a philosopher. We learned that idea from our Lord who told the story of the one lost sheep and the one lost coin and the one lost boy. From our Lord we learned that the life of a man was worth something; that there is a dignity, that there is an innate, God-given, congenital endowment that belongs to every creature into whose face God has placed the light of intelligence and whose soul He has made in the image of God and whose very body is the temple of the Holy Spirit from heaven. We learned that from the Lord. When we depart from the Lord, and when we depart from those teachings, when we say "no" to those things, there is nothing left but the emptiness of the persuasion that a man's life is like that of any animal. He is a dog. He is a beast. Woe to a nation that can slay a man and think no more about it than the destruction of an animal. God brings upon this arrogance, this conceit, this blasphemy His terrible judgment.

There is a prediction which to me is plain from the Word

of God. We are not going to be able to purge the earth of this debasing doctrine of the worthlessness of the human soul. The idea is here for us to contend with, to batttle with and to war against to the end of the age. That is why I think our people ought to prepare themselves for the long assault. These sweet little dilettante words, "sugar and spice and everything nice," "getting better and better," "just wait awhile and everything will be all rosy and good," will not suffice. We are in a spiritual war of ideas to the death. God says the evil is here and will grow and grow. We are going to have to contend with this challenge to the end of the age. This is modern Babylon.

The fourth reason for God's judgment upon Babylon is stated in verse 24, "And in her was found the blood of prophets, and of saints, and of all that were slain upon the earth." In this one city of Babylon! That is an amazing indictment: "In her was found the blood of prophets and of saints, and of all that were slain upon the earth." Personal accountability for sin is one of those great principles by which God governs our destiny and yet we hardly realize it at all. Let me pause to expatiate on that for a minute. Do you remember in chapter 23 of the Book of Matthew where the Lord is condemning the scribes and the Pharisees? He says that upon the city of Jerusalem will come all the blood shed since the blood of Abel to the blood of Zacharias, the son of Barachias, "whom you slew between the altar and the holy place." Upon *that* generation, upon *that* city, will come all the blood of the prophets and of all of the saints that was ever shed from the days of Abel to the death of Zacharias, the prophet of God, whom they slew by the side of the altar. How could this be? How could that one generation be guilty of murders they never actually committed? The answer is found in one of God's principles illustrated here, "for in Babylon was found the blood of the prophets, and of saints, and of all that were slain upon this earth." The truth is simple and it applies to us as it applies to them. You do not need to murder all of the prophets to be guilty of all the prophets' blood. You do not have to kill all the saints in order to be guilty of all of the blood of the saints. You do not have to commit every sin in the decalogue in order to be judged by God. You do not have to commit every sin — just one — for it is the tendency toward sin that God judges.

In the courts of the earth a man is judged for his acts — what he does. One man is judged because he slew another man. But, in heaven, God judges that man for the sin of murder that was in his heart. God looks at the tendency of his sin. God looks at the spirit of his act of murder. It may be just one overt act of murder in the earth that human courts will judge, but in heaven it is the tendency of the man to destroy that God's court will judge. James says, "He that breaks the law in one part is guilty of all." It is like a chain; you do not have to break every link in order for the chandelier to fall. Break one link and the whole thing falls. So it is with our sins. When a man sins in one transgression, God sees the tendency of that sin. God knows that the man will do it again and he will do it again, and if he lives a thousand years he would still be doing it. So the Lord calls this city in judgment for all the blood of the prophets, though they slew just some of them; and for the blood of all the saints, though they slew just some of them; and for all that were slain upon the earth, though they slew just some of them. Sin is sin and the tendency of it violates everything in God's nature. When a city slays a prophet of God, though they may not have slain but that one prophet, God judges that city as though they had slain every prophet because the tendency of that sin is to destroy all God's messengers. It is the evil in a man's heart that condemns him. It is the evil in the city that would destroy the prophet of God that God judges. Just think of the judgment of some of the nations and cities of this world who have slain God's people and who have exiled God's witnesses! Just think of the sins in our own lives. Oh, Lord, all these transgressions in my life are but typical of other transgressions in my life, and all the sins in my life are but typical of other sins in my life, and Lord, they heap up and they mount up until, O God, could even the blood of Jesus wash away such stains and such sin?

THE CALL FOR SEPARATION

The judgment of God upon Babylon is seen in verse 1 of chapter 18: "And after these things I saw another angel come down from heaven, having great power; and the earth was lightened with his glory." And Babylon in the light of that glory looked like a habitation of demons, a prison of every foul spirit and a cage of every unclean and hateful bird. In the light of the glory of God from heaven the city looked cheap and tawdry. What seemed to be so glorious was nothing but the depths of iniquity, the scum, the corruption, the sewer of every vile and unclean thing. In the cities that we think are so glorious today, when the light of the judgment of God falls upon them, how ugly and how bestial they are going to appear! That is the judgment of God upon Babylon. We share the deep conviction of John Ackerson when he wrote:

> My hand now scoops up Babylon,
> Her walls and all that city fair,
> Her jewels, arms, and heart of stone
> I toss into the careless air.
>
> She ruled, bent nations to her ire,
> Nor hosts of slain could slake her lust,
> Until a Vengeful Hand of fire
> Gripped hard, reduced her to this dust.
>
> I turn, struck numb with fear and shame:
> Is it mere fancy that a Hand
> Throttles with fingertips of flame
> The towers of my own proud land?

Look again. "For in one hour [in *mia hora*] is thy judgment come" (Revelation 18:10). This phrase is repeated again and again in chapter 18, "in *mia hora*," "in *mia hora*," "in *mia hora*," "in one hour" God judges it. Verse 21 is a recapitulation of the great prophecy of Jeremiah 51. "And a mighty angel took up a stone like a great millstone, and cast it into the sea, saying, Thus with violence shall that great city Babylon be thrown down." Look again. The phrase "no more," "*ou me*," "not not" is used more than six times in verses 21, 22 and 23. It is the strongest way the Greek language could say "not at all" and it is repeated six times closing this chapter. It sounds like the tolling of a funeral bell, a death knell. I took at the final cry of verse 4: "And I heard another voice from heaven, saying, Come out of her, my people, that ye be not partakers of her sins, and that ye receive not of her plagues." God says, "I am going to judge this world, and if you put your

life in the world, when it is destroyed, then you are destroyed."
God says, "I judge Satan, and if you link your life with Satan,
when God destroys Satan, you are destroyed." God says, "I
judge sin and unbelief and, when these are judged, judgment
falls upon you." God says, "I judge Babylon," and if we are
in the city of Babylon and link our lives with Babylon, God
judges us. That is the reason for the call to "come out from
among them, my people." This is the appeal of the Apostle
Paul in II Corinthians 6:14-18: "Be ye not unequally yoked
together with unbelievers: for what fellowship hath righteousness with unrighteousness? and what communion hath light
with darkness? And what concord hath Christ with Belial? or
what part hath he that believeth with an infidel? And what
agreement hath the temple of God with idols? for ye are the
temple of the living God; as God hath said, I will dwell in
them, and walk in them; and I will be their God, and they
shall be my people. Wherefore come out from among them,
and be ye separate, saith the Lord, and touch not the unclean
thing; and I will receive you. And will be a Father unto you,
and ye shall be my sons and daughters, saith the Lord Almighty."

If we refuse the salvation offered in Christ, we are not
going to escape death. Do not think we shall. We are not
going to escape the judgment of God. Do not think we shall.
We have an appearance to make before God some day. In that
hour what of our sins? What of our depravities? Lord, what?
We need God. We need an Advocate. We need Jesus. Without Him we are not equal to the awesome Day of Judgment.
That is why this sermon and that is why this appeal.

CHAPTER 2

THE MARRIAGE OF THE LAMB

Revelation 19

1 And after these things I heard a great voice of much people in heaven, saying, Alleluia; Salvation, and glory, and honour, and power, unto the Lord our God:

2 For true and righteous are his judgments: for he hath judged the great whore, which did corrupt the earth with her fornication, and hath avenged the blood of his servants at her hand.

3 And again they said, Alleluia. And her smoke rose up for ever and ever.

4 And the four and twenty elders and the four beasts fell down and worshipped God that sat on the throne, saying, Amen; Alleluia.

5 And a voice came out of the throne, saying, Praise our God, all ye his servants, and ye that fear him, both small and great.

6 And I heard as it were the voice of a great multitude, and as the voice of many waters, and as the voice of mighty thunderings, saying, Alleluia: for the Lord God omnipotent reigneth.

7 Let us be glad and rejoice, and give honour to him: for the marriage of the Lamb is come, and his wife hath made herself ready.

8 And to her was granted that she should be arrayed in fine linen, clean and white: for the fine linen is the righteousness of saints.

9 And he saith unto me, Write, Blessed are they which are called unto the marriage supper of the Lamb. And he saith unto me, These are the true sayings of God.

Notice the four "Hallelujahs" (Alleluias). The first Hallelujah is over the destruction of the great whore, mystery Babylon, the scarlet woman with a golden cup in her hand. When she is destroyed, all heaven says, "Hallelujah!"

The second Hallelujah is over the destruction of the city Babylon. The iniquity of Babylon lies heavy on the heart of God's holy universe, and when she is annihilated, when the final apostasy of evil, depraved and Christ-rejecting men is destroyed, all heaven feels the triumph of the glory and grace of God. "And again they said, Alleluia. And her smoke rose up for ever and ever."

The next Hallelujah is uttered by the exalted and glorified creation of our Lord in heaven: "And the four and twenty elders and the four beasts fell down and worshipped God that sat on the throne, saying, Amen; Alleluia." Notice the word "Amen." We first come to that word "Amen" in Numbers 5:22. It is the special word of sacred ratification, of holy acquiescence. It continues as the sealing word of the gospels and the epistles. It is the heavenly word of avowal, of committal to truth. It seals, it affirms, it binds. It is the highest word of praise that human speech can utter. In Psalm 72 we read, "He" (talking about our Saviour), "shall have dominion also from sea to sea, and from the river unto the ends of the earth . . . His name shall endure for ever . . . blessed be his glorious name . . . and let the whole earth be filled with his glory: Amen, and Amen. The prayers of David the son of Jesse are ended" (Psalm 72:8, 17, 19, 20). The "Amen" is the highest word of sealing affirmation. Human utterance could go no higher. It is thus with the twenty-four elders and the four cherubim, who are most intimately connected with the Throne of God. They express their utmost consent to the razing of wicked Babylon.

The fourth Hallelujah is uttered in answer to a call from the Throne itself. "And a voice came out of the throne, saying, Praise our God [that is, 'hallelujah'], all ye his servants . . . small and great." The mighty answering voice of the vast, innumerable multitude surrounding the throne sounded like the roar and the thunder of many waters. The throng cried in thunderous exaltation, "Hallelujah: for the Lord God omnipotent [*pontokrator*] reigneth." Then the tremendous ovation continues with the sublime and exalted announcement: "Let us be glad and rejoice, and give honour to him: for the marriage of the Lamb is come, and his wife hath made herself ready. And to her was granted that she should be arrayed in fine linen, clean and white." The fine linen is the *dikaiomata*, "the righteousnesses" (plural) of the saints. What a day! What a prospect! What a consummation! What a victory! What a triumph! "For the marriage of the Lamb is come, and his wife [his bride] hath made herself ready. And to her was granted that she be arrayed in fine linen," lustrous, iridescent, white like the light of the glory of God. That fine linen is the righteous acts and deeds of the saints.

THE BRIDEGROOM AND THE BRIDE

At the marriage of the Lamb we are first introduced to the bridegroom. The bridegroom is Christ, referred to as "the Lamb," a description of His blood-bought, redemptive relationship with us who have been saved by His grace. The bridegroom is Christ, the Lamb of God, our Saviour. Many times will you read from His own blessed lips the reference to Christ as the bridegroom. For example in Matthew 9:15, when the Pharisees and others were finding fault with His disciples because they did not fast, the Lord replied (paraphrased), "How could the disciples fast when the bridegroom is with them? But the days will come when the bridegroom will be taken away; then shall my disciples fast." In Matthew 22:1-13, He tells the story of the marriage of the king's son and of the wedding garment. He is the Son who is being married. In Matthew 25:1-10, our Lord tells the parable of the ten maidens (the ten virgins), and of their going out to meet the bridegroom when he cometh. John the Baptist referred to Jesus as the bridegroom. In John 3:29, 30 the Baptist says: "He that hath the bride is the bridegroom . . . He must increase, but I must decrease." The Apostle Paul, in II Corinthians 11:2 and in Ephesians 5:23-32, refers to Jesus as the bridegroom, the husband of the bride God is preparing for Him.

Who is the bride? The bride is the Church of our Christ. The bride is not the Old Testament Israel. Old Testament Israel in Isaiah, in Ezekiel and in Hosea is described as the wife of Jehovah who is now a put-away wife. Israel is a forsaken wife, she is a repudiated wife. Because of her idolatries and her adulteries and because of her rejection of her great Maker to whom God married her, she is a divorced wife. The prophets say that some day she will be restored. But when she is restored, when she comes back, even then she will not be a bride. No restored wife is ever referred to as a virgin. But this bride in Revelation is a virgin. For example, in II Corinthians 11:2, Paul says: ". . . I have espoused you to one husband, that I may present you as a chaste virgin to Christ." And in Ephesians 5:

30-32, Paul says: "For we are members of his body, of his flesh, and of his bones. For this cause shall a man leave his father and mother, and shall be joined unto his wife, and they two shall be one flesh. This is a great mystery [*musterion*]: but I speak concerning Christ and the church." The bride married to our Lord is the Church, the household of the Christian faith. Out of all of the languages, tribes, peoples and families of the earth, among the Jews, from the Gentiles, among the barbarians and the Scythians and the provincials over this earth, God is now calling out a people for His name that He might present them unto the Lord at the great marriage day of the Lamb. That bride is His Church. God is preparing her now for that celestial presentation. "And to her was granted that she should be arrayed in fine linen, clean and white: for the fine linen is the righteousness of saints." What a holiness, what a gladness, what a triumph, what a prospect, what a victory for the Lord's own people!

"And to her was granted that she should be arrayed in fine linen . . . for the fine linen is the righteousness of saints." There are two robes that the bride of Christ, that the Christian, will wear. As was the custom of the Roman world, our Lord wore an inner garment called a tunic. He also wore an outer garment, a loose-fitting outer garment that the Romans called a toga. Both of those garments, the inner garment that Christ gives us, and the outer garment, the weaving of our own works, we shall wear in that beautiful, consummating day of our Lord. There is an inner garment of justification by faith which is the gift of God. There is also an outer garment of our own obedience to the mandates and commandments of our Lord. There is an inner garment of imputation, the righteousness that comes to a child of faith. There is also an outer garment, the deeds by which we have sought to adorn the doctrine and to glorify the name of our Saviour. There is a positional righteousness that a Christian has that is given him by our Lord. There is also a practical righteousness that we have in doing good deeds for our Lord. So the inner garment is something that Christ bestows upon us when He washes our sins away, when we wash our robes, our souls, and make them white in the blood of the Lamb. But there is also an outer garment that we shall wear which is woven by our own hands and is made up of all of those things we have sought to do and pray to do for our blessed Jesus. "And to her was granted that she should be arrayed in fine linen, clean and white," and the fine linen is the righteousness of the saints.

The text also says: ". . . his wife hath made herself ready." She has her garments beautiful and white, ready to go to her marriage with her Lord. When did she make herself ready? When were all of those rewards given to her? How was that beautiful robe so arrayed and adorned? We are told that very plainly. Paul says in II Corinthians 5:10: "For we must all appear before the judgment seat of Christ." That is not the Great White Throne Judgment, where God assigns to perdition and damnation all of those who have rejected Him. This is the Judgment Seat, the Bema, of our Lord, before which all of His people shall stand that we may receive the things done in the body, whether they be good or bad. That is the great reward judgment. So Paul writes again in I Corinthians 3:11-16 that we shall stand before our Christ when we are taken up into heaven and there shall our works be tried as if by fire. If our works are wood, hay and stubble, they are burned, they are destroyed. If our works are gold, silver and precious stones, they abide as an adornment for the beautiful wedding garment we shall wear when we are presented to the Lamb, ". . . for his wife hath made herself ready."

Some of our people will have beautiful garments. All the good things they have done and the works by which they have dedicated a holy life to the Saviour will make up their garments that sparkle like the jewels of heaven, their rewards at the precious hand of Jesus. Some of our people are going to be practically naked, "saved as if by fire." All their works burned up, all of them. Some of the things our people do issue in nothing but loss. Their deeds are going to be burned up by fire. Their souls are going to be saved as if by fire, as if they ran out of a house naked. What a day! What a day! O Lord, that in that awesome hour when God shall give us of the fruit of our hands, of the reward of our deeds, that we may be found worthy! "Therefore, my beloved brethren," (how often did Paul thus plead with us) "therefore, my beloved brethren, be

ye stedfast, unmoveable, always abounding in the work of the
Lord, forasmuch as ye know that your labour is not in vain
in the Lord" (I Corinthians 15:58). That garment will belong to you forever and forever, God's eternal reward. The
beautiful robe is of our weaving "when the wife hath made
herself ready."

THE MARRIAGE CEREMONY

Concerning the marriage itself, is it not a strange narrative
that God should omit to describe it? Nothing is said about it,
no word is used to describe it. The Greek word here says,
"*elthen* [aorist], the marriage is come . . ." and that is all. Just
the fact of it. John just hears the Hallelujah chorus announcing
it. He has a word to say about the wife, the bride of Christ,
who has made herself ready. He describes the robe of our
righteousnesses that shall be our reward at the Bema of Christ.
But He never recounts the actual wedding itself. The event
just happens and all heaven bursts into Hallelujahs concerning
it, but there is no word about the ceremony itself.

For a moment let me speculate. What kind of ceremony
do you suppose it will be, when the bride is presented to our
Lord? What will happen? Now, this is an imaginative specu-
lation. There is nothing in the Bible about it. This is just a
possibility. In Revelation 21:9, 10 we read: "And there came
unto me one of the seven angels which had the seven vials full
of the seven last plagues, and talked with me, saying, Come
hither; I will shew thee the bride, the Lamb's wife. And he
carried me away in the spirit to a great and high mountain,
and shewed me that great city, the holy Jerusalem, descending
out of heaven from God [and Revelation 21:2 adds, 'prepared
as a bride adorned for her husband']." Maybe our wedding
day is the day that the Lord will place us in the beautiful city
of God, the New Jerusalem. And maybe the investiture will be
accompanied with all the rites and ceremonies described in
the dedication of the Old Testament tabernacle and temple.
Do you remember, when the tabernacle was completed and all
things were ready? Do you remember the beautiful ceremony,
how God came down and how the people worshiped and how
their hearts were filled with wonder, amazement and glory?

Do you also remember when the Solomonic temple was completed? The priests could not even enter in because of the presence of the glory of God. Do you remember those ceremonies and feasts and all of those marvelous things that attended the dedication of Solomon's temple and the dedication of the tabernacle? Remember those things in the Bible? Now, this is my thought: When God claims His people, when He sets us in that holy and beautiful city, there are going to be many rituals and ceremonies of investiture, and those glorious rites will be our marriage to the Lamb. We can well imagine many things that could happen and many things our Lord could do in a plenitude of beautiful, marvelous, meaningful ceremonies when He takes His resurrected people and places them in that holy city, the New Jerusalem, our heavenly and eternal home. But in any event, we shall be married to the Lamb, and we shall live in the beautiful city of God.

THE GUESTS AND THE MARRIAGE SUPPER

Now let us notice the marriage supper. "And he saith unto me [this is after the marriage], Write, Blessed are they which are called unto the marriage supper of the Lamb . . . These are the true sayings of God." The wedding is one thing, the marriage is one thing, but the supper, the feast, the refreshments, the banqueting is something altogether different. The bride is wed, the guests sup, and the angels are the spectators — three different groups. Had all of the saved of all time been the bride, then the angel would have commanded John to write, saying, "Blessed are they who are the wife, who are the bride, of the Lamb." But he did not do any such thing. After he announces the wedding of the Lamb and after it is over, then he says, ". . . Blessed are they which are called unto the marriage supper of the Lamb." The supper is something altogether different from the marriage. You will find that difference expressly stated in the Word of God. For example, in Matthew 25:1-13, we read about the ten virgins, five wise and five foolish. The ten virgins go out to meet the bridegroom. Where is the bride? She is in the father's house. These friends of the bridegroom and of the bride are there to meet them and to rejoice with them and to enter with them into the festivities, the gladnesses of the nuptials. They are there to share in the feast, the marriage supper of the Lamb. It would have been no thought of those ten virgins that they were going in to be the bride. They are the friends, they are the guests, and they are waiting until the couple come out and they can enter in with them to the feast, to the supper, to the bridal refreshments. It is thus in Revelation 21:9, 10. The city includes the bride and all her friends. "Come hither, I will shew thee the bride, the Lamb's wife. And he carried me away in the spirit . . . and he shewed me that great city, the holy Jerusalem, descending out of heaven from God." In that city I think you will find all of God's children. But there is a bride there as well as her attendants, her companions and her friends. The whole city is called the bride because they do honor and glory to her. But the bride in the city is one thing and all of the friends, companions and attendants are another. The city is made up of the bride and the guests.

The blessedness in this beatitude of Revelation 19:9 covers a greater, broader group than is represented by the bride. "Blessed are they which are called unto the marriage supper of the Lamb." Let us take, for example, one of those honor guests, John the Baptist. John the Baptist died before the cross. He was never a part of the visible Church of Jesus Christ. He belonged to and he died in the "old dispensation." That is why the great Baptist says in the third chapter of the fourth gospel: "He that hath the bride is the bridegroom: but the friend of the bridegroom, which standeth and heareth him, rejoiceth greatly . . . this my joy therefore is fulfilled." John the Baptist is not a part of the bride. He is not a part of the Church. John is a guest. John is a friend who stands and rejoices in the favor of God upon the couple who are married. That is why I think in Matthew 11:11, speaking of John the Baptist, our Lord says: "Verily I say unto you, Among them that are born of women there hath not risen a greater than John the Baptist: [but] he that is least in the kingdom of heaven [in the dispensation and age of our Lord's Church] is greater than he." Why? Because the least of us who has been saved, the humblest, belongs to the bride of our Lord. We belong to His Church. These others are the guests who are invited to the marriage supper of the

Lamb, but they do not belong to that body God is now calling out in this age of grace. But, lest someone think that they are less honored and less blessed, these guests of the "old dispensation," the commandment was given to John to write down a special blessing for them. "Blessed are they [the guests] who are called to the marriage supper of the Lamb." This is a special blessing for the saved of the Old Covenant. With holy imagination we can see the guests come in to the marriage supper of the Lamb. I suppose John the Baptist will be the most honored of all. He comes in and is seated at the great banquet of our Lord. Then, maybe, Abraham is next, who saw the day of our Lord and rejoiced in seeing it. Then think of the others who come, all the prophets, all God's children who lived in the old days and under the Old Covenant. They sit down and break bread with the bride in that glorious day of our blessed Lord.

THE BANQUET WE SHALL ENJOY

Let us now write of that feast of Christ, the marriage supper of the Lamb. It is often mentioned in the Bible. For example, in Isaiah 25:6-10: "And in this mountain shall the Lord of hosts make unto all people a feast of fat things . . . And he will destroy in this mountain the face of the covering cast over all people, and the veil which is spread over all nations. He will swallow up death in victory; and the Lord will wipe away tears from off all faces; and the rebuke of his people shall he take away from off all the earth . . . And it shall be said in that day, Lo, this is our God; we have waited for him, and he will save us: this is the Lord; we have waited for him, we will be glad and rejoice in his salvation. For in this mountain shall the hand of the Lord rest." In the next chapter there is the song: "In that day shall this song be sung in the land of Judah; We have a strong city; salvation will God appoint for walls and bulwarks. Open ye the gates, that the righteous nation which keepeth the truth may enter in. Thou wilt keep him in perfect peace, whose mind is stayed on thee; because he trusteth in thee. Trust ye in the Lord for ever: for the Lord JEHOVAH is everlasting strength. Thy dead men shall live, together with my dead body shall they arise. Awake and sing, ye that dwell in dust: for thy dew is as the dew of herbs, and the earth shall cast out the dead" (Isaiah 26:1-4, 19). We read again in Luke 22:15, 16 as the Lord sat down with His disciples at the Passover: "With desire I have desired to eat this passover with you . . . For I say unto you, I will not any more eat thereof, until it be fulfilled in the kingdom of God." Remember again at the feast when He instituted the Lord's Supper: "I say unto you, I will not drink henceforth of this fruit of the vine, until that day when I drink it new with you in my Father's kingdom" (Matthew 26:29). These passages look forward to the marriage supper of the Lamb. ". . . till I drink it new with you," a new kind of drink.

You know, people sometimes are so disturbed about Jesus changing the water into wine. They suppose (notice, it is all supposition) that when Jesus turned water into wine He did something by which He could make people drunk. But read the story closely. The narrative in John 2:7-10 goes like this: When they brought the wine that our Lord had made out of water, and when the governor of the feast tasted it, he said: "I have never tasted fruit of the vine, grape juice, wine, I never tasted it like this. It is a new kind." How was it different? It is the kind we shall drink at the marriage supper of the Lamb. A delicious, heavenly wine prepared by the hand of God. When Melchizedek brought those celestial elements and spread them out before Abraham, he broke bread and drank of the fruit of the vine. Thus it will be when we gather around the table of the Lord and we break bread and drink the fruit of the vine. The story is a prophecy and a foretaste of that beautiful, heavenly banquet when we sit down with our Lord at the marriage supper of the Lamb. That final and glorious feast is described so beautifully in this quaint old hymn:

> There be prudent prophets all,
> The Apostles six and six,
> The glorious martyrs in a row,
> And confessors in betwixt.
>
> And though the glory of each one,
> Doth differ in degree,
> Yet is the joy of all alike
> And common certainly.

There David stands with harp in hand,
As master of the choir.
A thousand times that man were blest,
That might his music hear.

There Mary sings "Magnificat,"
With tune surpassing sweet,
And all the maidens bear their part,
Singing at her feet.

"Te Deum," doth saintly Ambrose sing,
And Augustine the same,
Old Simeon and Zacharias,
Anew their songs inflame.

There Magdalene hath left her tears
And tearfully doth sing
With all those saints, whose harmony
Through every street doth ring.

And in that holy company,
May you and I find place,
Through worth of Him who died for us,
And through His glorious grace;

With cherubim and seraphim,
And hosts of ransomed men,
To sing our praises to the Lamb,
And add our glad Amen.

Remember again the glorious Psalm 72:8, 19, 20: "He shall have dominion also from sea to sea, and from the river unto the ends of the earth . . . let the whole earth be filled with his glory; Amen, and Amen. The prayers of David the son of Jesse are ended." What a glory, what a blessedness, what a heavenly prospect God has given to us!

CHAPTER 3

THE BATTLE OF ARMAGEDDON

Revelation 19

11 And I saw heaven opened, and behold a white horse; and he that sat upon him was called Faithful and True; and in righteousness he doth judge and make war.

12 His eyes were as a flame of fire, and on his head were many crowns; and he had a name written, that no man knew, but he himself.

13 And he was clothed with a vesture dipped in blood: and his name is called The Word of God.

14 And the armies which were in heaven followed him upon white horses, clothed in fine linen, white and clean.

15 And out of his mouth goeth a sharp sword, that with it he should smite the nations: and he shall rule them with a rod of iron: and he treadeth the winepress of the fierceness and wrath of Almighty God.

16 And he hath on his vesture and on his thigh a name written, KING OF KINGS, AND LORD OF LORDS.

17 And I saw an angel standing in the sun; and he cried with a loud voice, saying to all the fowls that fly in the midst of heaven, Come and gather yourselves together unto the supper of the great God;

18 That ye may eat the flesh of kings, and the flesh of captains, and the flesh of mighty men, and the flesh of horses, and of them that sit on them, and the flesh of all men, both free and bond, both small and great.

19 And I saw the beast, and the kings of the earth, and their armies, gathered together to make war against him that sat on the horse, and against his army.

20 And the beast was taken, and with him the false prophet that wrought miracles before him, with which he deceived them that had received the mark of the beast, and them that worshipped his image. These both were cast alive into a lake of fire burning with brimstone.

21 And the remnant were slain with the sword of him that sat upon the horse, which sword proceeded out of his mouth: and all the fowls were filled with their flesh.

What an unimaginable catastrophe! What death and carnage! This vast holocaust closes human history.

The Battle of Armageddon, the War of Megiddo, is the scene in which the great God and Saviour Jesus Christ appears, intervening in human history. The first verses of chapter 19 of the Revelation recount the marriage supper of the Lamb, which supper is preceded by the marriage of the Son of God to His bride, who has made herself ready. Speedily and immediately after the marriage of the Lamb and after the nuptial supper, the gates of heaven burst open in the triumph of the hosts of glory. As Jude said in verses 14 and 15, "Behold, the Lord cometh with ten thousands of his saints, To execute judgment upon all." Immediately after the wedding supper, our Lord appears in glory with His angelic hosts and with His saints. He intervenes in this awesome, catastrophic holocaust that God calls the Battle of Armageddon. Notice that history does not quietly and gradually merge into the kingdom of our Messiah. The end comes violently; it comes in fury. The whole earth is bathed in blood, in the judgment of the great day of God Almighty.

THE FINAL BATTLE DESCRIBED THROUGHOUT THE BIBLE

The mighty conflict described here in chapter 19 of the Revelation is one that has been foretold all through the Bible. The Book of the Revelation is the unveiling, the presentation of Jesus Christ at the consummation of the age. And prophecy, in the Old Testament and in the New Testament, without exception, says that the end of this world comes in a vast, mighty, indescribable conflict. World history ends in war and desolation.

This great battle called Armageddon has been described several times previously in the Book of the Revelation. For example, in Revelation 11:15 we read, at the sounding of the seventh trumpet: "And the seventh angel sounded; and there were great voices in heaven, saying, The kingdoms of this world are become the kingdoms of our Lord, and of his Christ; and he shall reign for ever and ever." Then follows a description of His reign: "And the four and twenty elders, which sat before God on their seats, fell upon their faces, and worshipped God, Saying, We give thee thanks, O Lord God Almighty . . . because thou hast taken to thee thy great power, and hast reigned. And the nations were angry . . . [because the time has come when God] shouldest destroy them which destroy the earth." These last words refer to that great and final battle. The conflict is mentioned again in Revelation 14:17-20: "And another angel came out of the temple . . . And another angel came out from the altar, which had power over fire; and cried with a loud cry to him that had the sharp sickle, saying, Thrust in thy sharp sickle, and gather the clusters of the vine of the earth; for her grapes are fully ripe. And the angel thrust in his sickle into the earth, and gathered the vine of the earth, and cast it into the great winepress of the wrath of God. And the winepress was trodden without the city, and blood came out." (Notice that grapes cast into a winepress is the figure, but when the grapes are trodden in the wrath and judgment of God, blood pours out.) "And the winepress was trodden . . . and blood came out of the winepress, even unto the horse bridles, by the space of a thousand and six hundred furlongs." A furlong is an eighth of a mile. Divide eight into sixteen hundred and the result is two hundred miles. Blood up to the bridles of the horses for two hundred miles! It is unimaginable. The world has never read of, it has never conceived, it has never seen anything comparable to this last, great battle that will destroy apostate humanity. There is another reference to this last conflict in Revelation 16:12-16. "And the sixth angel poured out his vial upon the great river Euphrates; and the water thereof was dried up, that the way of the kings of the east might be prepared." They are coming from the north, the south, the east, and the west by the millions. "And I saw three unclean spirits like frogs come out of the mouth of the dragon, and out of the mouth of the beast, and out of the mouth of the false prophet. For they are the spirits of devils, working miracles, which go forth unto the kings of the earth and of the whole world, to gather them to the battle of that great day of God Almighty . . . And he gathered them together into a place called in the Hebrew tongue Armageddon." Revelation 9:16 describes the army of one of the kings: "And the number of the army of the horsemen were two hundred thousand thousand: and I heard the number of them." Two hundred million. It is unbelievable, it is unimaginable. "He gathered them together in a place called in the Hebrew tongue *har megiddo* — 'the mountain of Megiddo,' " which is before the valley of Esdraelon. These passages in the Revelation add vivid details to the account of the battle described in the text here in chapter 19.

This Battle of Armageddon, the final conflict that dissolves human history and at which time Christ comes from heaven in glory and in great power, is referred to time and again in Old Testament prophecies. For example, Isaiah 63:1: "Who is this that cometh from Edom, with dyed garments from Bozrah? this that is glorious in his apparel, travelling in the greatness of his strength?" Then Isaiah, looking at him, notices that he is stained with blood. "Wherefore art thou red in thine apparel, and thy garments like him that treadeth in the winefat?" Dyed red. The Almighty Warrior replies: "I have trodden the winepress alone . . . and their blood shall be sprinkled upon my garments, and I will stain all my raiment . . . And I will tread down the people in mine anger, and make them drunk in my fury, and I will bring down their strength to the earth." Crush it into the dust of the ground. This is the battle of the great day of God Almighty. In Ezekiel 38 and 39 we read of that same, vast destruction. In Daniel 2, 7, 9 and 11 are references to the same great holocaust. We meet it again in the third chapter of the Book of Joel: "Proclaim ye this among the Gentiles; Prepare war, wake up the mighty men, let all the men of war draw near; let them come up: Beat your plowshares into swords, and your pruninghooks into spears; let the weak say, I am strong. Assemble yourselves . . . . Let the heathen be wakened, and come up to the valley of Jehoshaphat . . . . The sun and the moon shall be darkened, and the stars shall withdraw their shining . . . and the heavens and the earth shall shake: but the Lord will be the hope of his people." Then, of course, in Zechariah 14:1, 2, 4, 5: "Behold, the day of the Lord cometh . . . . For I will gather all nations against Jerusalem to battle . . . . And his feet shall stand in that day upon the mount of Olives . . . . and the Lord my God shall come, and all the saints with thee."

The prophets with one accord say that the armies of the earth will be assembled in Palestine. They will gather from one end of the globe to the other. The king of the north is coming down; that is Russia. The king of the west is coming over; that is the leadership of the nations of the confederated European states of which we are a part. The United States belongs to the federation of the west. We shall always be identified with Europe, always. We belong to it. And the kings of the east shall come. One of those armies (Revelation 9:16) numbers two hundred million. The king of the south is coming; that is Africa and all of the nations of that vast continent. These armies will be converging on Palestine. Enemies will gather from every side. It will be a war to exterminate Israel; it will be a war of nation against nation; and it will be a war against God.

The great rendezvous, the great assembly of those hosts will be at Megiddo. That is the battlefield of the world, Megiddo. There Barak and Deborah fought against Sisera. There Gideon fought against the Midianites. There Saul was slain at the hand of the Philistines. There Ahaziah was slain by the arrows of Jehu. There Pharaoh Necho slew good King Josiah. There Jeremiah lamented the slain of the armies of Josiah. And through the ages since, each battle fought there, whether by the Druses or the Turks or the armies of Napoleon, is a harbinger of the great day of the battle of God Almighty.

In the King James Version, the Greek word *polemos* in Revelation 16:14 is translated "battle." We are apt to think of that translation in terms of one isolated skirmish. The word, rather, is actually "war." The whole earth is plunged into a vast militarism. There is the spirit and the march of slaughter, murder, bloodshed and violence among all mankind. This is the *polemos*, the war of the great day of God Almighty. It has many phases and many parts and the whole earth is involved in it. That is why a man who reads the Bible and looks out over the world today and sees the immeasurable preparation for war is not taken by surprise. It is the development of history according to the prophets. And America is in it to the hilt. Why do you think we are spending billions of dollars to get a man to the moon? Just for the sake of a joy ride up there? No! We are spending billions of dollars in order to place a man on the moon simply because, if we do not, we lie a prey to those who are able to explore space and thereby able to send enemy craft over our nation to pinpoint a bomb on any city or installation in our land. It is a matter of self-defense; it is a matter of survival. This whole earth is getting ready for war. That is why we are forced to spend money on space exploration. That is why France is trying to build an independent nuclear deterent. It is national defense.

Always remember, there is no such thing as having instruments of war and not using them. Whenever you build a tank, you are going to use it some day. Whenever you invent a gun, you are going to shoot it some day. When the scientists were trying to split the atom and thus discover nuclear power, the prophecy was made that if it was ever achieved it would first be used in an atomic bomb. Was atomic fission first used in order to manufacture electricity? Was atomic power first used for peaceful purposes? No. It was used in war. Thus, the whole earth is getting ready for a final holocaust. When we read the Word of the Lord, then look at the newspapers, we tremble in the presence of the prophets who describe this coming day.

THE VICTORIOUS WARRIOR CHRIST

Now, let us look at the text more closely. First, in the midst of that terrible and indescribable conflict, there is the bursting open of heaven and the appearing of the Son of God. He is thus described: "His eyes were like a flame of fire [burning fire, probing into the darkest recesses of the human soul], and on his head were many crowns." One could preach a sermon on the diadems that rest so marvelously and appropriately upon the brow of the Son of God.

Next we read, ". . . and he had a name written, that no man knew, but he himself." That refers to His essential deity, the uncommunicable, unpronounceable, unknowable name of God. No man can know God. Finite as we are, restricted as we are, the essential deity of God is something a man cannot enter into. It is the very Lord God who is coming, for Christ Jesus is God of this universe. We are not going to see three Gods in heaven. Never persuade yourself that in glory we are going to look at God No. 1 and God No. 2 and God No. 3. No! There is one great Lord God. We know Him as our Father, we know Him as our Saviour, we know Him as the Holy Spirit in our hearts. There is one God and this is the great God, called in the Old Testament, Jehovah, and, incarnate, called in the New Testament Jesus, the Prince of heaven, who is coming.

"And he was clothed with a vesture dipped in blood [that is the blood of His enemies] . . . and he treadeth the winepress of the fierceness and wrath of Almighty God [against His enemies]."

We read again, ". . . and his name is called The Word of God." This is His pronouncable name; this is His communicable name; this is the name by which *we* who are mortal know Him. "In the beginning was the Word and the Word was with God and the Word was God" (John 1:1). He became incarnate and we saw His glory as the glory of the only begotten of the Father, full of grace and truth. This is "The Word of God," the Lord Jesus Christ.

We read again: "And out of his mouth goeth a sharp sword, that with it he should smite the nations." He does not need to strike. He speaks and the thing is done. There is illimitable power even in His voice. For example, in the days of His humility, in the days when He was condemned and rejected of men, evil men came to arrest Him. The Lord asked, "Whom do ye seek?" And they said, "Jesus of Nazareth." He said, "I am he." And they all fell to the ground. Even in the days of His humility, the armed guard of the Romans and of the Sanhedrin and of the temple could not stand in His presence. If it was thus in the days of His sorrow, think what it will be when He comes in glory with the hosts of heaven! What power! What strength! The scene is indescribable.

We read again, ". . . and he shall rule them with a rod of iron: and he treadeth the winepress of the fierceness and wrath of Almighty God." This is the day of judgment. "And he hath on his vesture and on his thigh a name written, KING OF KINGS, AND LORD OF LORDS." King of kings and Lord of lords. When the Magi came from the East, they said, "Where is he that is born king?" When Pilate crucified Him and nailed Him to a tree, they put an inscription above Him, saying, "This is Jesus of Nazareth, a *king*." Whether He is born in a manger or whether He is nailed to a cross or whether He is coming in power with the clouds of heaven, He is a King. *He is a King!*

The Revelation also describes the saints that come with Him: "And the armies which were in heaven followed him upon white horses clothed in fine linen, white and clean." We have already been introduced to these saints in Revelation 19:8. The white linen in which they are clothed is the right-eousness of the saints. God's tried, chosen, and faithful people follow their Lord out of heaven. But how did these saints get up there in heaven? Here is another illustration of the fact that, when you interpret this Bible correctly, every little incident or detail will fit. You see, in the fourth chapter of the Revelation, the Church, God's sainted people, are all taken up to glory. Here in chapter 19 when the Lord Jesus comes, these glorious ones, these shining ones, come with Him, hav-ing already been up there with Him. Here they come with Him out of the bursting gates of heaven.

The Seer now describes the armies that are warring against the Lord Christ. This is the most unbelievable development in the earth. These who oppose God and oppose His Christ and oppose His Church and oppose His truth, who are they? "And I saw the beast, and the kings of the earth . . . and the false prophet." This trio is leading the blasphemous opposi-tion to the Lord God. In Revelation 13, listen to the boast of the unbelieving as they speak of the invincibility and the im-mortality of the beast: "And his deadly wound was healed: and all the world wondered after the beast. And they wor-shipped the dragon which gave power unto the beast: and they worshipped the beast, saying, Who is like unto the beast? who is able to make war with him?" They boast: "We have an invincible and an immortal leader. Look at him! Our great Fuhrer. Our great Il Duce. Our great Commander-in-chief. Look at him, look at him!" And the whole world will wonder after him and worship him. We get a little inkling of that in history. Think of a people adoring a murderer like Hitler. Think of a people adoring a reprobate like Mussolini! Think of a people who have to go through a revolution just to de-throne the memory of a bloodthirsty tyrant like Stalin! All of these things are earnests, types, harbingers, portents, pic-tures of that awful, ultimate, final tyrant who will come and say: "I can deliver the world. Look at me! Look at me!" And the world follows him.

By the side of the beast is the false prophet. He knows

everything. He has all of the answers. He is infallible. There they are, the beast and the false prophet and the dupes who follow them. They are the product of godless government and godless religion. There they stand, all together. You just put this down as an axiom in human history: When a people, when a nation turns aside from the truth and from obedience to the mandates of God, they turn to the most unimaginable oppressions that mind can think of. They do not turn from God and the Word of God and the blessed Christ into other great truths and into other great revelations and into other great moral and spiritual obediences. They turn to slavery, to oppression and to all things evil, sordid, damning and terrible. There is no exception to that axiom in history. Look at it today. Anywhere you find a government that repudiates God, and a people who say "No" to our Lord, they are in the morass and the miasma of misery. That is where revolution and war come from. We are not going to have any trouble with a great Christian nation or a godly people. These terrible things come out of the evil spirits that find lodgment in the hearts of men who repudiate God. This is the beast and the false prophet.

THE GATHERING OF THE ARMIES IN PALESTINE

It is astonishing that all of these vast multitudes of armies are in Palestine. How were they brought together? You would not ordinarily find that great concourse of people in any one country. How do they get there? The answer is found in Revelation 16: 13, 14, 16: "I saw three unclean spirits like frogs come out of the mouth of the dragon, and out of the mouth of the beast, and out of the mouth of the false prophet. For they are the spirits of devils, working miracles, which go forth unto the kings of the earth and of the whole world, to gather them to the battle of that great day of God Almighty. And he gathered them together in a place called in the Hebrew tongue Armageddon [*har megiddo*]." That gathering would not ordinarily happen. But when men give themselves to vile rejection, blasphemy and atheism, when men give themselves to that, then they open their hearts to the spirits of evil and to malicious lies of demons. This is the illustration of the truth in II Thessalonians 2:11: "God shall send them strong delusion [these that reject God] that they should believe a lie." To them a lie is more truth than truth itself and atheism is more real than God Himself. These evil spirits gather these millions and millions together at this great Judgment Day of Almighty God.

Now, let us look upon the invincible warrior, Christ, and His triumphant victory. The war is over instantly. Is not that a strange thing? You would think, "What power these men have, and these great nations, what power they have!" Against God, they have no might at all. One angel from the Lord, just one, brought to the vast camp of the Assyrians destruction and death when Sennacherib came against the people of Jehovah. Before the terrible power of the Assyrians, Hezekiah the king went down on his face, crying to God for help. The Lord listened and said, "I see your tears falling on the pavement of the temple and I hear your prayers." Then God sent just one angel, one. When Sennacherib woke up the next morning, as far as his eyes could see there were thousands and thousands and thousands of corpses that once comprised his proud army. Just one angel! Do not ever be persuaded that God who lives in heaven and who looks down upon this earth is about to be overcome. "He that sitteth in the heavens shall laugh: the Lord shall have them in derision." These little Napoleonic crackpots saying big things against God. . . . "He that sitteth in the heavens shall laugh: the Lord shall have them in derision" (Psalm 2:4).

Look how the battle is fought. The beast was taken. God just went down there and snatched him; He just grabbed him! The Almighty, like a big cat with a mouse, just shook the living daylights out of him! The Lord just grabbed him. It says here: "And the beast was taken, and with him the false prophet." With all of his infallibility, he was taken. The Lord just took him and cast him into the lake burning with fire and brimstone. (Notice that a thousand years later, in Revelation 20, they are still in the lake of fire and brimstone.) That is the way the Lord does. He works quickly, instantly, suddenly, with blasphemers and unbelievers. He has always done that. In the Garden of Eden when the woman fell, God talked to her. He turned to the man and talked to him. But notice that He never asked the serpent anything. He never said anything to him. He just cursed him. There are no extenuating circumstances and there are no mitigating details. It is always thus with God-haters and Christ-rejectors. When an apostate who rejects God stands in the presence of the Lord God Almighty, there is nothing to be said. The judgment is over just like that. It is decisive and final.

John does not see the battle. As he did not see the marriage of the Lamb, so he does not see the battle here. He just sees the angel who stands in the sun, stationed in glory, calling for the fowls and the birds of the heavens to come. That is all John sees. The actual war itself and the way it is fought he does not see. But he sees that angel with that awful, awesome announcement. The vultures of the earth come when the earth is bathed in blood. There are only three places in the Bible where that word translated here "fowl" or "bird" is used — in Revelation 18:2 and twice here, once in verse 17 and once in verse 21. These are the only places you will find that word *arnin*. I suppose it refers to "vultures." The angel calls the carrion-eating birds of the earth to come to eat the great men who thought they were bigger than God. They are the wise ones who thought they knew more than God and they are the apostates who rejected the very idea of God. There they are, food for the buzzards, carrion for the vultures. This is the end of those who refuse our great Lord.

We close with Psalm 2, which is a picture of what we have been speaking about today: "Why do the heathen rage, and the people imagine a vain thing? The kings of the earth set themselves, and the rulers take counsel together, against the Lord, and against his anointed." The word in Hebrew for "anointed" is "Messiah." When translated into Greek, it is "Christ." These apostates gather themselves together against the Lord and against His Christ, saying, "Let us do away with them." I once saw a cartoon taken out of one of the newspapers in Russia. At the bottom of the cartoon were pictures of the churches all broken up. Beyond the rubble of the ruined churches was a ladder leaning against the clouds and there was a workman with a big hammer climbing that ladder to heaven. In heaven was pictured God the Father, God the Son, and God the Holy Spirit. The Soviet workman was taking that hammer and getting ready to bash their brains out. The caption below the cartoon said, "Having destroyed this God business down here in the earth, we are going to destroy it in heaven." What does the Psalm say? "The kings of the earth and the rulers take counsel against his anointed saying, Let us cast them out." But, "He that sitteth in the heavens shall laugh; the Lord shall have them in derision." Oh, the humor of God, the laughter of God! "Then shall he speak unto them in his wrath, and vex them in his sore displeasure . . . I have set my king upon my holy hill of Zion." An irrefutable, invincible,, immovable, unchangeable decree of God is this: Christ shall reign over this whole earth and over all the hosts of heaven. "Thou shalt break them with a rod of iron; thou shalt dash them in pieces like a potter's vessel." The psalmist then makes appeal: "Be wise now therefore, O ye kings: be instructed, ye judges of the earth. Serve the Lord with fear, and rejoice with trembling. Kiss the Son, lest he be angry, and ye perish from the way, when his wrath is kindled but a little. Blessed are all they that put their trust in him." It is no light thing when a man says "No" to God. It is no triviality, it is no minutia when a man faces the judgment of the Lord God Almighty. All ye judges and ye kings and ye souls in the earth, kiss the Son, bow down before Him, love the Lord Jesus, trust in Him. Blessed are all they that commit their souls' destiny to the Lord Christ.

CHAPTER 4

THE BINDING OF SATAN

Revelation 20

1 And I saw an angel come down from heaven, having the key of the bottomless pit and a great chain in his hand.

2 And he laid hold on the dragon, that old serpent, which is the Devil, and Satan, and bound him a thousand years,

3 And cast him into the bottomless pit, and shut him up, and set a seal upon him, that he should deceive the nations no more, till the thousand years should be fulfilled: and after that he must be loosed a little season.

7 And when the thousand years are expired, Satan shall be loosed out of his prison,

8 And shall go out to deceive the nations which are in the four quarters of the earth, Gog and Magog, to gather them together to battle: the number of whom is as the sand of the sea.

9 And they went up on the breadth of the earth, and compassed the camp of the saints about, and the beloved city: and fire came down from God out of heaven, and devoured them.

10 And the devil that deceived them was cast into the lake of fire and brimstone, where the beast and the false prophet are, and shall be tormented day and night for ever and ever.

Chapter 19 of the Revelation closed with the Battle of Armageddon, at which battle the Lord God intervened openly, publicly, in human history through the coming of Christ. In that war in which the beast and the false prophet lead the kings and the armies of the earth, there is indescribable bloodshed. These enemies of God are destroyed and the beast and the false prophet are cast into the hell of fire and brimstone. That is the awesome destruction at Armageddon. But beyond that beast and false prophet and beyond those kings and armies and nations of the earth there is a sinister, cunning personality who has led them into the winepress of the wrath and judgment of the Almighty. It is due to his luring cunning and to his suave deception that these have been brought to that ulti-

49

mate and final rejection of God and their open warfare against heaven. What about that sinister personality? What about that unusual, gifted, and subtle deceiver? His dupes have been judged, they have been slain, they have been cast into perdition. Does he escape? The answer is found in Revelation 20. God has singled him out. God has marked him out for a special judgment and damnation. This is the binding of Satan, the enemy of the people of the Lord.

"And I saw an angel come down from heaven, having the key of the bottomless pit and a great chain in his hand. And he laid hold on that dragon, the old serpent, called the Devil, and Satan, and bound him . . . And cast him into the bottomless pit [abyss], and shut him up, and set a seal upon him that he should deceive the nations no more till the thousand years be fulfilled." The angel came down with the key of the "abyss." *Abyss* is the actual Greek word; we took the word bodily into our English language. The angel came down with the key to lock him up in the bottomless pit. In Revelation 9 a fallen angel appears with a key to open the abyss and out of it came the terrible plague of locusts that waged war on the earth. This angel came down from heaven with a key to lock Satan up. The angel had in his hand a great chain. Now that chain is not like a blacksmith's chain. That chain is of the Lord's making. In verse 6 of his book, Jude writes: "And the angels which kept not their first estate, but left their own habitation, he [God] hath reserved in everlasting chains under darkness unto the judgment of the great day." Whatever kind of a chain it is that God welds by which He holds these evil, black, foul demons in the abyss, it is that kind of a chain that the angel comes to lay upon Satan. Satan is the ultimate cause and fountainhead of all the misery in the world. He has many agents, but he is the root of this dark work. God finally, ultimately comes to deal personally with this great enemy in whose cunning lies all of the tears, heartache, death, destruction and waste in the earth.

THE MEANING OF SATAN'S FOUR NAMES

Satan is described here by four names, the same identical names in the same order by which he is described in chapter

12 of the Revelation. The first two names reflect his personality and the second two are his actual, personal names. As most of us have two names, so Satan has two personal names. The first two of the four employed here described his character, his personality: "And he laid hold on that dragon." The designation "dragon" refers to his bestial leadership of the beast governments of the world. The second designation "that old serpent" refers to his subtle nature. In the beginning, in the Garden of Eden, it was as a serpent that he insinuated himself into the confidence of our first parents and deflected them away from God. The next two designations comprise his personal names. That ancient serpent is "the devil." The Authorized Version, the King James Version, several times in the New Testament uses the term "devils," plural. That is never correct. There is only one "diabolos," a term always used in the singular. There is only one devil. There are many demons. Sometimes the Authorized Version translates the Greek word, *daemon,* as "devil." This is not accurate. The Greek word, *daemon,* should always be translated "demon" and never "devil." There are many "demons," the agents of Satan. There is only one devil and the word is always used in the Scripture in the singular and always refers to Satan. *Diabolos,* devil, refers to his character as a liar and as a murderer. Jesus said he was a liar and a murderer from the beginning. He is Diabolos, an archfiend.

His first name is the same in Hebrew as it is in Greek and as it is in English. The Hebrew name is transliterated into Greek which in turn is transliterated into English, "Satan." "Satan" means "accuser." He is the one who deceived our first parents. He is the one who brought death into our world. Satan is the enemy of God's people and of God Himself. He opposed God in the beginning. He is the one who would have destroyed Job had it not been for the intervention and the kindness of God. He is the one who assailed our Lord Jesus. He is the one who lies back of all of the evil in this world. God sent a mighty angel from heaven with a key and a great chain in his hand. True to that assignment, the angel laid hold on that old dragon, that ancient serpent, called the devil and Satan, and cast him into the abyss. He set a seal upon him. He shut him up in the bottomless pit.

THE DIFFERENCE BETWEEN "THE ABYSS" AND "HELL"

Now, where is that abyss? In answering that question we come to a discussion of the whole nether world, the world beyond our sight, the world beyond this present life. The devil is cast into the abyss where he is bound for a thousand years. But after the thousand years, he is loosed for a season after which he is cast into the lake of fire and brimstone where the beast and the false prophet are. There he is tormented day and night, world without end and forever. What is the difference between "the abyss" and "the lake of fire"? The difference is plainly stated in the revealed Word of God. The lake of fire is hell. The abyss is something else. The word "abyss" is used nine times in the New Testament. It is a Greek word meaning "bottomless pit." Seven of the nine times it is used are in the Revelation. One time it is used in Luke 8:31 and one time it is used in Romans 10:7. We get a good idea of what it refers to in Luke 8:31. The passage recounts the story of the Gadarene demoniac who had in him a legion of demons (not devils, but demons). He was filled with every vile and unclean thing, as men today are filled with all manner of concupiscence, iniquity, vile lust and immoral filth. A like condition is seen today when one is filled with unclean spirits. There was a legion of them that lived in that man and drove him into violence. When the Lord came, those demons recognizing Jesus said, "Lord, don't send us into the abyss before the time." There is that word "abyss." It is a horrible place. It is an imprisonment, it is a place where demons, foul and wicked, are chained by the Lord God. Another time the word is used is in Romans 10:7. We are there warned not to say that the Lord Jesus is to come up from the abyss as if He were one of those demons. All seven times the word is used in the Book of the Revelation it has the same meaning; it always refers to a place where fallen angels and where foul and evil spirits are imprisoned by God. That is the abyss. That is the only way that the word is used, to refer to that prison where these evil spirits are imprisoned. That is where Satan is going to be cast, chained, locked and sealed for these thousand years.

But there are other places beyond this life and grave beside the abyss. We read in Revelation 19:20: "The beast was taken, and with him the false prophet that wrought miracles before him . . . both were cast alive into a lake of fire and burning brimstone." That is the ultimate place where the devil is cast (Revelation 20:10), "And the devil that deceived them was cast into the lake of fire and brimstone, where the beast and the false prophet are." That is also the place where the wicked dead are cast (Revelation 20:13, 14): "And the sea gave up the dead . . . and death and hell were cast into the lake of fire." Then in the next chapter, Revelation 21:8: "But the fearful, and unbelieving, and the abominable, and murderers, and whoremongers, and sorcerers, and idolaters, and all liars, shall have their part in the lake which burneth with fire and brimstone." Now what is that? Our continuous confusion lies in the translation. It lies in the King James Version, the Authorized Version. They take the word "Sheol" and translate it "hell." They take the word "Hades" and translate it "hell." In these mistranslations we come to the position where we have no idea of what God has revealed to us of that other world.

Let us discuss those words briefly. First, the word "abyss" we have already defined. The abyss, the bottomless pit, is a place where God has imprisoned against the day of judgment, evil, vile, fallen angels and demons, spirits of evil. That is the abyss. Now, the word "Sheol." The word "Sheol" is used in the Old Testament sixty-five times. Thirty-one times in the Authorized Version it is translated "hell." Thirty-one times it is translated "the grave." Three times it is translated "the pit." The Greek word "Hades" in the New Testament is the exact equivalent to "Sheol" in the Old Testament. They are identical words. One is the same as the other. The word "Hades" in the New Testament is used eleven times. Ten times it is translated "hell." One time it is translated "the grave." But there is nothing in the words "Sheol" or "Hades" that refers to hell, nothing. All that Sheol means and all that Hades means is the departed, unseen world beyond this life. When we die, we enter into Sheol, we enter into Hades. Now, there are those who, in reading the Scriptures, say that Sheol or Hades has two parts in it. One part is "torment" and one part is "paradise." There are those who think that when Christ died, He entered into Hades, into paradise, and brought those Old Testament saints who were in paradise into heaven. "Wherefore he saith, When he ascended up on high, he led captivity captive, and gave gifts unto men" (Ephesians 4:8). However these things may be, the word "Sheol" and the word "Hades" refer to nothing other than that unseen world beyond which we live.

But "hell" is something altogether different. In the Old Testament the word "hell" is "Tophet," in the New Testament it is "Gehenna." "Gehenna" is used twelve times in the New Testament and each time it is properly translated "hell" in the Authorized Version. For example, here is one of them. Our Lord said in Matthew 5:29, 30 that if your right hand offends you, cut it off. Cast it from you. It is better for you to enter into life everlasting with one hand rather than having two hands to be cast into hell, into Gehenna, into the burning fire of damnation. If your eye offends you, He continued, cut it out, cast it off. Better to have one eye and enter into everlasting life than to have two eyes and to be cast into hellfire. That is true hell. The word "Tophet" in the Hebrew is exactly "Gehenna" in the Greek. Gehenna is the valley of Hinnom, outside Jerusalem. In that valley idolaters once burned their children to Moloch, a thing that God despised. God cursed the place. The Jewish people used the valley of Hinnom for the refuse of the city. For centuries and centuries filth, garbage, even the carcasses of animals were thrown into that valley. The fire never died and the worm was never killed and the jackals fought and gnashed one another with their teeth as they ate the refuse cast into the horrible place. From this background the word Gehenna was used to describe the everlasting damnation of hell where there is weeping and wailing and gnashing of teeth, where the worm never dies, and the fire is never quenched. That is hell.

Up to this present moment no soul has ever entered hell. Not yet. The first ones to be cast into hell are the beast and the false prophet. They are first. The second to be cast into hell is the devil. The third to be cast into hell are those whose names are not written in the Lamb's Book of Life. That is why the urgency of the preaching of the Gospel of the cross. This is the imperative that brought our Lord down into this world.

He never came just to preach us better ethics or a finer way to pronounce holy words. Because we are in danger of hellfire and damnation, our Lord was incarnate. He came into this vile world; He died on the cross; He gave His life for us that we might be saved from the judgment and penalty of our sins. To those who turn in repentance and in faith to Him, God writes their names in the everlasting Book of Life. They are saved. But those who spurn the overtures of mercy and whose names are not written in the Lamb's Book of Life, they are forever and forever consigned to this everlasting, unending damnation. This is the revealed Word of God. It makes the soul to tremble. "The beginning of wisdom," says God, "is the fear of the Lord." Do not be afraid of him, says the Lord Jesus, who can take away this life and after that has no further power; rather be afraid of Him who not only can destroy this life, but can cast the soul into everlasting hell. There is that word "hell." Fear Him who can cast the soul into hell, says our God. Tremble before God. That is the beginning of wisdom. As I face the grave and as I face the judgment, O God, I pray that I might find an Advocate and a Friend and a Saviour in the crucified One who gave His life for me. That is the immediacy and the urgency of the preaching of the Gospel of the Son of God. That is why we press upon every heart the ultimate decision. Either we look in faith to Jesus for salvation or we live in unforgiven sin.

WHY SATAN IS LOOSED AFTER THE MILLENNIUM

We now come to a revelation in the Word of God that I cannot understand. I do not think any man can understand it. There is something here that lies beyond human comprehension. After Satan is bound for a thousand years, he must be loosed for a little season. "When the thousand years are expired, Satan shall be loosed out of his prison. He shall go out to deceive the nations in the four quarters of the earth, Gog and Magog." Gog and Magog (words you find describing the great nations to the north in Ezekiel 38, 39) apparently typify the mass of humanity in this world. The purpose of Satan's deception is ". . . to gather them together to battle: the number of whom is as the sand of the sea." They violently war against the camp of the saints and the beloved city. For this grievous rebellion they are destroyed by fire from heaven. Why is Satan loosed?

The Millennium is marked off from eternity by this loosing of Satan. The word "Millennium" refers to this period of time when Satan is bound for a thousand years. It is built from the Latin words *mille* (thousand) and *annum* (year), a thousand years. The demarcation that separates the thousand years from the eternity of the eternities is this loosing of Satan for a little while, for a season. Why does God loose Satan, having him bound and imprisoned and under a key and a seal and in chains? Why does God loose Satan? It is a part of the inexplicable problem that no man can enter into. Why did God create Satan in the first place? When evil was found in him and he sinned against heaven, why did not God obliterate him? Why did God allow him to come into the Garden of Eden? The problem of the presence of sin is inexplicable to the human mind. We cannot fathom it. It belongs to the secret counsels of heaven. The close of this Millennium lies in a necessity in the economy and government of God that I cannot understand. There is a necessity why Satan must be loosed for this season after his being bound a thousand years.

Men speculate upon the reasons why Satan is loosed. Practically all of them say this: Satan is loosed in order that those who grow up under the Millennium, under the perfect and righteous reign of Christ, may have the chance to choose between good and evil, between God and Satan. They have never been tempted. They have never been tried. At the close of the thousand years Satan is going to be loosed and everyone who has grown up in the Millennium is going to have an opportunity to choose between God and Satan, between righteousness and unrighteousness, like everyone else who has ever been born into this world and who has had that same choice. Satan is to be loosed to try them and to tempt them. Whether that is true or not, the thesis is plausible. Wherever man is placed, in the Millennium or out of it, before it or after it, in the Garden of Eden or today, whether he is young or old, wherever man is, he is a sinner. Satan deceives him and his story is one of utter depravity. Satan is always Satan. Though he is bound in prison for a thousand years, yet still he is as vile and as subtle, as merciless and as ruthless, as diabolical and as evil as he was in the beginning. He has not changed. And mankind has not changed. Here after the Millennium, after the thousand years, Satan goes out and he finds the hearts of men by the uncounted millions open to his deception. Their number is as the sand of the sea.

What an indictment against man and what an attestation to the depravity of human nature! This evil of human nature! How in the world did all of those kings and all of those armies find themselves in Armageddon as we read in chapter 19 of this book? How? The book says because three unclean spirits were sent out from the dragon and the beast and the false prophet and they deceived the nations of the earth and brought them together for that awful holocaust called Armageddon. The evil work is a deception. It is the same working in this chapter 20 of the Book of the Revelation. It is the machination, it is the cunning, it is the evil, it is the deceiving of that vile, false, fallen Lucifer. So mighty is he, so great and powerful is he, that Michael himself, the Archangel, dared not rebuke him, but said, "The Lord rebuke thee." How much more a man, an ordinary man, a man made out of the dust of the ground, is unable to stand before him! Oh, the weakness to fall, to err, to stray, to be deceived by this sinister and tragic spirit!

But this is the last confederation against God. This is the last deception. This is the last death. This is the last sin. When Satan has been loosed out of his prison for that little while, God comes down and seizes him and casts him — where? Back into the abyss? No. The abyss is a prison where the vile, evil spirits are chained against the final day of Judgment. The Lord God comes down and takes that diabolos, that Satan, and He casts him into hell, into the lake of fire and brimstone, where the beast and the false prophet are, and there does God judge him, in torment, day and night, forever and ever. Oh, the unending, the unending, the unending forever and ever and ever! What it is to be lost in that place of fire and brimstone, that hell a-burning! Hell was not made for man. It was not created for human souls. Christ said hell was prepared for the devil and his demons, his angels. Not for us. The lost man goes there by choice, by volition. He says, "I had rather serve evil, I had rather be a disciple of Satan, I had rather follow the devil than to look in faith to the Lord Jesus." He chooses his eternal home in hell by refusing heaven. Oh, how could a man choose to spurn the overtures of the Son of God and cast his life into the perdition of the duped, of the deceived, of the lured, of the damned, who follow after Satan? O Lord, open our eyes that we can see. Open our ears, Lord, that we can hear. Open our hearts, Lord, that we can believe and accept. Open our souls, Lord, that we can dedicate to Thee the love, the devotion, the confession, the repentance, the dedication that leads into life everlasting. O God, save me! Remember me! O God, save our people, remember our people! These things bring us to our knees. Oh, the trembling, the searching! O God, how we need Thy grace, Thy care and Thy forgiving mercy! That is why the message and that is why the sermon and that is why the Revelation and that is why the praying and that is why the preaching and that is why the invitation and that is why the appeal. Oh, that all of us may come to Jesus! May we look in faith to the blessed Lord. That is our invitation to you. Come and be saved.

CHAPTER 5

THE FIRST AND THE SECOND RESURRECTIONS

Revelation 20

5 But the rest of the dead lived not again until the thousand years were finished. This is the first resurrection.

6 Blessed and holy is he that hath part in the first resurrection: on such the second death hath no power, but they shall be priests of God and of Christ, and shall reign with him a thousand years.

13 And the sea gave up the dead which were in it; and death and hell delivered up the dead which were in them: and they were judged every man according to their works.

This message meant as much to me in its preparation as any I have ever tried to deliver in the more than thirty-five years I have been a pastor. It is a message that concerns every one of us. Some day, somewhere, sometime, all of us shall experience the power of God when He raises us up from the dead. As surely as we die (and we are a dying people), we shall be raised again. As surely as we are raised, we shall stand before God. We have our assignments in destiny. We have an ultimate rendezvous with the Lord.

Revelation 20:4, 5 says: "And I saw thrones, and they sat upon them, and judgment was given unto them: and I saw the souls of them that were beheaded for the witness of Jesus, and for the word of God, and which had not worshipped the beast, neither his image, neither had received his mark upon their foreheads, or in their hands; and they lived and reigned with Christ a thousand years. But the rest of the dead lived not again until the thousand years were finished. This is the first resurrection." The Greek text is most emphatically expressed, *"he anastasis he prote."* The translation literally is, "This is the resurrection, *the first.*" Wherever in the Bible (and more than forty times the word is found in the New Testament) that word *anastasis* is used, it refers to the raising again of a fallen body. Our text comprises no exception in the use of the term. The word *anastasis*, translated "resurrection," refers to the raising up of a body that has fallen upon death. Let us first look at this promised resurrection minutely. Then let us look at what God says in other Scriptures about the life in the world to come.

The vision begins: "And I saw thrones and them that sat upon them, and judgment was given unto them." This is the occasion for the ultimate, final reward God has in store for His sainted and believing people. "I saw all of them in glory," says John. When Satan is cast into the abyss and when God inaugurates the millennial age, the first vision that John sees is the glorious panorama of all of God's people rewarded and enthroned. A Christian does not get his crown of reward until the end time. The reason for this is simple. A man does not die when he dies. His influence lives on and on. Therefore it is only at the end of the age that a reward can be given to him. Thus, at the consummation of the age John sees all of these gloriously resurrected, sainted children of God enthroned, rewarded. This is the fulfillment of the promise the Lord made to His disciples in Matthew 19:28 that they would sit upon thrones judging the twelve tribes of Israel. This is the word of the Apostle Paul in I Corinthians 6:2 that God's saints will judge the world. But the apostle goes even further in the next verse to say that God's saints will judge the angels. This is the promise of our Lord in Revelation 3:21, that we who overcome shall share His throne in heaven. This vision brings that promise to pass. "I saw thrones, and they sat upon them, and judgment was given unto them." This is the millennial, triumphant age of the enthronement, the exaltation, the glorification, the rewarding of God's resurrected people.

In that vast panorama, looking upon all God's saved people, John sees a special and a particular group. He singles them out: ". . . and I saw the souls of them that were beheaded for the witness of Jesus . . . and they lived and reigned with Christ a thousand years." There are two reasons why the apostle marks out this special group of martyrs among all of those who have been resurrected and enthroned. First, a martyr has offered to

Jesus the highest fidelity of which life is capable. A man can surrender no more to Jesus than the surrender of his life. When the laws takes a man's life, the law lays upon him the heaviest penalty known to the state. When a man offers his life to Jesus and lays down his life for the witness of the Gospel of the Son of God, he has offered to his Lord his highest testimony. These martyrs, therefore, are especially designated. They are not all of that great company of God's resurrected and redeemed saints. They are a special group. The marking out of these martyrs is the same kind of a designation as you find in Revelation 1:7: "Behold, Christ cometh . . . and every eye shall see him, and they also which pierced him." They who pierced Him are not a separate group from the whole group who shall see Him, but John especially points them out at the coming of our Lord, when the whole earth shall see Him. These murderers of Jesus will especially and particularly be forced to confront the living Lord. But they also belong to the great group that will look upon Him. So these martyrs here are a part of that vast host of God's children who are resurrected, redeemed, rewarded and enthroned.

There is another reason these martyrs are especially marked out. It is found in Revelation 6:9, 10. When the fifth seal was opened, John saw "under the altar the souls of them that were slain for the word of God . . . and they cried . . . saying, How long, O Lord, holy and true?" That cry necessitates some kind of an answer. What is God to do about these martyrs who have laid down their lives for the testimony of Jesus, who have been slain by murderous and blasphemous men? Their appeal to God necessitates an answer and a part of that answer is found here at the consummation of the age. God raised them up from the dead and they lived again. The rest of the answer will be found in the Great White Throne Judgment.

Some are troubled by the Scripture reference to these martyrs as "souls," *ta psukas*. But the Bible uses the word "souls" in the sense of referring to people. Acts 2:41 says: "And there were added unto them about three thousand souls." In Acts 7:14 Stephen speaks about Jacob going down into the land of Egypt at the invitation of Joseph, making the observation that there went down of Jacob's household seventy-five *souls*. Acts

27:37, describing the shipwreck of Paul on his way to Rome, says that there were in the ship two hundred seventy-six *souls*. I Peter 3:20 counts those who were saved in the ark in the days of Noah, saying, "Eight *souls* were saved." Our modern language uses the word "souls" to refer to people.

These martyrs, beheaded, were dead as to their bodies. A soul, a spirit, cannot be decapitated. A soul does not die; it is the body that dies. In the fifth seal (Revelation 6:9), John saw those souls disembodied. They were dead as to their bodies. But here at the resurrection day, in the millennial triumph of our Lord, John sees those same disembodied souls raised again, as to their bodies. These souls are resurrected in their bodies and they live again with our Lord in triumph and in glory. The living again refers to the dead body. There is a resurrection of the bodies of dead men, but no such thing as the resurrection of the spirits of dead men. The soul (the spirit) never dies. Only the body dies and only the body is resurrected.

It is a strange thing that there is no place in the Word of God where the entire vision of the resurrection from the dead is presented. The truth is always revealed in parts, in pieces. It is found here, there, yonder, throughout the Word of God. We shall now attempt to put together these references to the resurrection of the dead and see what God says to us about these who shall live again who have fallen upon death.

First, God says there is such a thing as the resurrection. In Matthew 22:23-31 our Lord discussed the doctrine with the Sadducees, who avowed that there is no such thing as a resurrection. Our Lord, in answering a question the Sadducees brought to Him, began with the words, "But as touching the resurrection of the dead . . ." Speaking of the resurrection, He avowed that in that perfected state we do not marry nor are we given in marriage. We are as the angels in heaven. But the point of the discussion centered around the fact that there is a resurrection. Again, in John 11:23, Jesus tells Martha that her brother, Lazarus, shall live again. Martha replied, "I know, Lord, that he shall live again in the resurrection, at the last day." In this statement Jesus acquiesced. He did not deny it. There is a resurrection. Again, in Acts 26:8 the Apostle Paul, in the defense of his life before King Agrippa, said to that Jewish monarch: "Why should it be thought a thing incredible with you, that God should raise the dead?" So, to begin with, we have in the Bible an avowal of the resurrection of the dead.

The Scriptures go further to reveal a second truth about the dead. In the resurrection there is a select, elect group "out from among" the dead. There is an elect resurrection of the just. For example, in Luke 14:14, our Lord, commending certain people for doing a certain thing, says: "Thou shalt be recompensed at the resurrection of the just." There is a resurrection of God's saved people, a select, elect group. "Thou shalt be recompensed [we shall have a reward for doing good things] at the resurrection of the just." Again, in John 6:40, our Lord, in speaking to His disciples about those who trust in Him, says: "This is the will of him that sent me, that every one which . . . believeth upon [the Son] may have everlasting life: and I will raise him up at the last day." An elect group. Our Lord makes the same avowal again in verse 44: "No man can come to me, except the Father which hath sent me draw him: and I will raise him up at the last day." An elect group. Jesus repeats the truth in verse 54: "Whoso eateth my flesh and drinketh my blood, hath eternal life; and I will raise him up at the last day." Among the dead there is an election, there is a select group God will raise up, namely, those who trust in Him. That same truth is expressed by the Apostle Paul in Philippians 3: 7-11, "But what things were gain to me, those I counted loss for Christ . . . . That I may know him, and the power of his resurrection, and the fellowship of his sufferings . . . . If by any means I might attain unto the resurrection of the dead." The last phrase Paul uses in this passage is most descriptive in the Greek language. It is "*exanastasis ek ton nekron*," which literally translated would be "the resurrection out from among the dead." In the great cemetery that is this earth there is going to be a selection "out from among." God is going to raise up those who believe in Him and who trust in Him. That is an elect, select resurrection.

From the Scriptures we learn yet another thing about the raising of the body. There is also to be a resurrection of the lost, of the damned. Daniel 12:2 says, "And many of them that sleep in the dust of the earth shall awake, some to ever-

lasting life, and some to shame and everlasting contempt."
Again, in John 5:28, 29, our Lord said: "Marvel not at this:
for the hour is coming, in the which all that are in the graves
shall hear his voice, And shall come forth; they that have done
good, unto the resurrection of life; and they that have done
evil, unto the resurrection of damnation." Read also Acts 24:
15, which avows the same doctrine. There is not only an elect
group that is going to be raised in the resurrection of life, but
there is also for those left behind a resurrection of damnation,
a resurrection into hell, a resurrection to the terrible judgment
of Almighty God.

The Bible reveals another truth to us. There is a period
of time between the first resurrection of the elect of God's
people and the second resurrection of damnation and condemnation. There is a time between them. The dead are not all
raised together. They are raised one group at one time and
one group at another time. In I Thessalonians 4:16 we read,
"For the Lord himself shall descend from heaven with a shout,
with the voice of the archangel, and with the trump of God:
and the dead in Christ shall rise first." The word "first" is used
with reference to us who are living at the time of our Lord's
coming, but it also means "first" with regard to the resurrection
of these others who will remain in their graves. Here in Revelation 20:5 I learn that there is a thousand-year period between
the raising of those who have trusted in Jesus and those who
die lost. Revelation 20 teaches us that, after the first resurrection of the saved, "the rest of the dead live not again until the
thousand years were finished." After the first resurrection,
those who are still in the grave will be raised at the second
resurrection. When the two are mentioned together, the saved
are always named first. The second are altogether different, for
those who are raised in the first resurrection are saved. The
text says, "Blessed and holy is he that hath part in the first
resurrection." But those who are raised in the second resurrection are under the judgment of God. They belong to a resurrection of damnation, of condemnation, a resurrection into hell
and torment.

Having looked at what God has to say about the fact of the
resurrections, let us look at what the Lord has to say about the

first resurrection, the resurrection of His sainted people. We learn from God's Book that the resurrection of God's people is not all at the same time, but comprises in itself a series. The raising of God's elect is in a succession. In I Corinthians 15:20-24 Paul outlines the succession, the series, the companies, the troops, that appear before God in resurrection glory. "But now is Christ risen from the dead, and become the firstfruits of them that slept. For since by man came death, by man came also the resurrection of the dead. For as in Adam all die, even so in Christ shall all be made alive. But every man [everyone, every soul] in his own order [*tagma*]: Christ the firstfruits; afterward they that are Christ's at his coming." There are four groups in that *tagma*, order. *Tagma* is a Greek word for "a series," or "a succession," or "a troop," or "a company." Paul says that every one is to be raised in his own succession, in his own order, in his own time, in his own troop, in his own company. Paul names those companies: One, Christ; two, the firstfruits; three, they that are Christ's at His coming; four, those at the end. Paul is following here a pictorial typology found in the feast of the Firstfruits.

In Leviticus 23 God names the great convocations of Israel. All of them have a profound spiritual meaning. They are tremendous prophecies. They harbinger sublime events in the life of our Lord. For example, the first feast is the Passover and that represents the death of our Lord. The second one is the feast of Unleavened Bread and that represents the burial of our Lord, the taking of unleavened bread and hiding it away. The third is the feast of the Firstfruits. That is the resurrection of our Lord. The next, the fourth one, is the feast of Pentecost. That is the coming of the Holy Spirit. The fifth one is the feast of Blowing of the Trumpets. That is the harbinger of the return of Christ, the triumphant descent of our Lord. The next feast (the Jews later turned it into a fast) is that of Atonement and that pictures the tribulation and the mourning of the Jewish people when they come back to the Lord and accept their Messiah. The last is the feast of Tabernacles which is a pictorial representation of the glory and happiness of God's ultimate and final millennial age.

In those seven feasts the Apostle Paul takes the feast of

Firstfruits to depict the resurrection of our Lord. The feast of Firstfruits began on Sunday, on the first day after the Sabbath. It began on the first of the week after the Passover. Our Lord was crucified during the Passover. After His death and burial, on the first day of the week He was raised from the grave. Every time we meet on Sunday, we celebrate the feast of the Firstfruits. Every time we gather in God's house on the first day of the week, we are celebrating an Easter, the resurrection of our Lord. We are under no commandment to meet on Sunday. We are under no commandment to meet on any other day. We gather together out of the love of our hearts, out of the rejoicing of our souls that Jesus is living again, that God raised Him from the dead. This is our Sunday, this is our first day of the week, this is our feast of Firstfruits.

The feast of Firstfruits had three parts. First, on that day, the first day after the Sabbath, on the Sunday after the Passover, the faithful Israelite went out into the barley field and there he plucked a handful of the ripe heads of grain. He took that handful of the firstfruits of the coming harvest to the priest and dedicated it to the Lord. The priest took the offering into the Tabernacle and waved it before the Lord. It was a sign, it was a harbinger, of the dedication of the whole harvest promised by the Lord. The firstfruits offered unto God were just a handful of the ears of barley. The second part of the harvest came in the summertime. It was then that the whole crop was gathered. Finally, at the end of the season the harvesters gathered the gleanings. So in the dedication of the harvest unto God there was first, the handful of the firstfruits, then there was the harvest itself, and finally the gleanings, the picking up of the heads that had been crushed and trampled down in the gathering. Paul uses that imagery and follows it precisely here in the resurrection of the just, in the resurrection of God's people, in the resurrection of those who are saved. The harvest has a *tagma*, it has a succession, it has a series. We come before the Lord by troops and in different companies.

The first is Christ. He was the first one raised from the dead. In the Scriptures we read of several resuscitations. For example, the dead man who in his burial touched the bones of Elisha and came to life again was resuscitated. Remember the story of Elisha raising from the dead the son of the Shunammite. Remember the story of the resuscitation of Lazarus. Remember the story of the daughter of Jairus. But in all of those instances the body was merely revived. The body later and ultimately went back into the dust of the ground. It died. It was not immortalized. It was not resurrected. The first to be resurrected from the dead is the Second Adam. "Since by the first Adam came death, so by the Second Adam came the resurrection from the dead." The first one to be raised from the dead is our Lord Jesus Christ. Paul said *He* is first.

Paul says next in order is the firstfruits, the little handful, the little company who are brought before the Lord as an earnest of the great harvest that is yet to be dedicated, to be raised. Let us see if Paul is right in describing this succession. We are to look for a little harvest, a little firstfruits, the earnest of a few heads of grain to be waved before the Lord. Matthew 27:51-53 tells us: "Behold, the veil of the temple was rent in twain . . . and the earth did quake, and the rocks rent; And the graves were opened; and many bodies of the saints which slept arose, And came out of the graves after his resurrection, and went into the holy city, and appeared unto many." Paul said Christ first, then the firstfruits, the little handful. When the Lord entered into heaven, raised from the dead, He did not go by Himself. He had a little company with Him. He had a little troop with Him. He had a few souls with Him. They were the firstfruits, the firstfruits that were brought before the Lord. They are a harbinger, they are an earnest, they are a guarantee, they are a promise of the great harvest that is yet to come. Paul speaks of that. He says, "every man in his *tagma*." Christ is first, the first one raised from the dead. "Then the firstfruits," that little handful of saints who were raised after Christ was raised, who went up into glory with our blessed Lord.

Then Paul names the third group, "Afterward they that are Christ's at his coming." That is the rapture, the taking out of God's people from the world when the Lord comes. "For the Lord himself shall descend from heaven with a shout, with the voice of the archangel, and with the trump of God: and the dead in Christ shall rise first" (I Thessalonians 4:16). That is the great harvest, when the Lord comes for His own. Christ, then the little group of firstfruits, then all of us. We shall comprise the great, main body of the harvest of the resurrection. Paul further says, "Then the end." The King James Version translates "then cometh the end." But the word "cometh" is not a part of the original text. Paul wrote, "Then the end." So we have some "end" ones, just as it was after the harvest; there were the gleanings. The first head, then the great harvest, then the gleanings. We have some gleanings, some "end ones." After the great harvest, the sublime rapture, Revelation 7 pictures some gleanings. Remember, the twenty-four elders (twelve representing the saints of the Old Testament, twelve representing the saints of the New Testament) represent all of God's saints resurrected at the rapture, at the great harvest. There they are enthroned just as you see them in Revelation 4 and in Revelation 7. They represent God's people, but they are not all of them. There are some gleanings, for here in the presence of the elders is a great group. John asked: "Where do they come from and who are they? I never saw them before. I do not recognize a one of them." Had they been those who had been saved in John's day he would have recognized some of them. Why, you would recognize your mother, you would recognize your father, if they had preceded you. You would recognize some of your friends. But when John looked upon that group, he did not recognize one of them, not one of them. He said: "I never saw these before. Where do they come from?" One of the elders said, "These are they who have come out of the great tribulation." They are a part of the gleanings, saved after all the rest of us are in glory. Down here in the earth during those awful days of the terrible tribulation God saves some and these are some of the gleanings, after the rest of the harvest has already been reaped.

When we turn to Revelation 11:11, we read about God's two witnesses, those two marvelous servants of the Lord who served Him in the dark day of tribulation and oppression. They were slain by wicked men, but after three and a half days the spirit of life entered into them and they ascended up into heaven. They are some of the gleanings. Here are two more that the Lord has saved after the rapture. They have been

raised from the dead. Now let us turn to Revelation 14:1 and
we read, "And I looked, and, lo, a Lamb stood on the mount
Sion, and with him an hundred forty and four thousand" redeemed from the earth. There are more gleanings. One hundred and forty-four thousand of them. The gleanings of the
Lord. Then we turn to the passage of the text in Revelation 20
and read: "Here are the souls of them that were beheaded for
the witness of Jesus." They have been raised from the dead.
They live again. These are the gleanings that God hath raised
up and enthroned with all of His sainted children.

Is it not a wonderful thing? Not one is going to be lost.
Every one of God's saved will, in God's time and in God's ableness and power, be raised up. When the mighty Resurrection
of Christ is told, we have not told it all. Wait a minute. There
is something else. There is another story yet. There is the story
of the resurrection of that handful who were raised after Christ's
Resurrection and who went with Him up into glory. But wait
a minute. That is not all. There is something more. Those few
are just a harbinger, an earnest, a guarantee of the great host,
the main harvest of those who have fallen asleep in Jesus and
who shall be raised at the coming of the Lord, at the sound
of the trumpet. But wait a minute. That is not all. There are
still some who are left behind. There are some who have gone
through that terrible tribulation. There are some who are going
to be cut down by the beast and the false prophet. They have
not been forgotten. The Lord goes through this earth and
gathers His gleanings. Finally, when the Lord calls the roll in
glory, every one whose name is in the Lamb's Book of Life,
every one of them is present without loss of one. Oh, the elective keeping of God! Without loss of one. There were a hundred and forty-four thousand in Revelation 7 who were sealed,
and in Revelation 14, when they are counted on mount Sion,
there are not a hundred forty-three thousand, nine hundred
ninety-nine of them, but there are the full one hundred forty-
four thousand of them. Every one of them arrived safely. And
oh, what a blessedness that the Lord remembers us and that
the Lord keeps us!

Recently, I was reading some sermons of ministers who
preached long ago. Someone had confronted one of them and

had said to him: "Now this doctrine of the election of God and the purpose of God, why, that is a terrible teaching. That means that some are not going to be saved." The preacher replied: "That may be correct. In the elective purpose of God there may be some who will say 'No' to Jesus and 'No' to the Lord, who will not repent and be saved. But," he added, "I have the assurance every time I stand up to preach, every time I deliver God's message, that the elective purpose of God says to me there are some who are going to be saved." That assurance is always with the Lord's people. Of those He has chosen, not the least is going to be left behind. There are to be the resurrections of those whom God has written in His Book. I have never seen that Book of God. I do not know whose names are in it. But every one of those whose names are in the Lamb's Book of Life is going to take Jesus as his Saviour; and he is going to be at that great and final rendezvous. And if one of those whose name is written in the Lamb's Book of Life falls into the dust of the ground, the Lord is going to raise him up. The Lord marks the place; the Lord sees the dust and it is a separate and precious dust to Him. In God's day and in God's time the Lord is going to raise them up, each in his own *tagma*, each in his own time, each in his own order, each in his own succession, but all of us will be remembered before the Lord. It is a comfort to know, just as John wrote it, "Blessed and holy is he that hath part in the first resurrection; . . . and [they] shall reign with Christ a thousand years."

CHAPTER 6

THE TRIUMPHANT AND GLORIOUS MILLENNIUM

Revelation 20

4 And I saw thrones, and they sat upon them, and judgment was given unto them: and I saw the souls of them that were beheaded for the witness of Jesus, and for the word of God, and which had not worshipped the beast, neither his image, neither had received his mark upon their foreheads, or in their hands; and they lived and reigned with Christ a thousand years.

5 But the rest of the dead lived not again until the thousand years were finished. This is the first resurrection.

6 Blessed and holy is he that hath part in the first resurrection: on such the second death hath no power, but they shall be priests of God and of Christ, and shall reign with him a thousand years.

Revelation 20:4 reads, "And I saw thrones, and they sat upon them, and judgment was given unto them." This refers to the glorified, resurrected host of God's sainted people. Then John continues in the verse as he describes another group he sees: "I saw the souls of them that were beheaded for the witness of Jesus, and for the word of God, and which had not worshipped the beast, neither his image, neither had received his mark upon their foreheads, or in their hands; and they lived and reigned with Christ a thousand years. But the rest of the dead lived not again until the thousand years were finished. This is the first resurrection. Blessed and holy is he that hath part in the first resurrection: on such the second death hath no power, but they shall be priests of God and of Christ, and shall reign with him a thousand years." The verses that immediately follow describe the deception by Satan with the announcement that, "When the thousand years are expired, Satan shall be loosed out of his prison." The result of this loosing is seen in the gathering together of Satan's dupes against the Lord God. But they are immediately destroyed by fire from

71

heaven, and the devil that deceived them is cast into the lake of fire, where the beast and the false prophet are, to be tormented day and night for ever and ever. Then follows the revelation of the Great White Throne Judgment. This is followed by the ultimate and eternal kingdom of our Lord and the new city in which His people will dwell in blessedness, in holiness, in righteousness, forever. Our discussion concerns the millennial age of our Lord. The fullness of the riches of the revelation of God in what He has prepared for His children is immeasurable, unfathomable, illimitable. We touch just the hem of the garment in the few pages assigned in this book. So, as briefly as we can, we shall speak of this glorious day that God has promised for His Son and for us in this earth.

THE DREAM OF A GOLDEN AGE

As long as the human race has lived, just so long has there been a dream of a "golden age." It is found in the literature of all of the families of the world. The beginning of that vision is lost in the dim antiquities of the past. We find it recurring again and again in the literature of the ancient Egyptians, of the ancient Babylonians and Chaldeans, of the ancient Persians and Medes, of the Greeks and of the Romans. Time and again do we find it in the Word of God. Prophet after prophet, apostle after apostle, book after book records that blessed hope. There is more said in the prophetic Scriptures regarding this millennial age than of any other one thing in the prophecies themselves. For example, in the Book of Daniel, when Daniel saw the course of world history in the likeness of an image, he saw last of all a stone cut without hands that broke in pieces that vast image and grew to fill the whole earth. Then he interprets it: "In the days of those kings shall the God of heaven set up a kingdom, which shall never be destroyed . . . . forasmuch as thou sawest that the stone was cut out of the mountain without hands, and that it brake in pieces the iron, the brass, the clay, the silver, and the gold; the great God hath made known to the king what shall come to pass hereafter" (Daniel 2:44, 45). There is a kingdom coming that will be established by the intervention of the Lord God Himself. In chapter 7 of the Book of Daniel we read: "I saw in the night visions, and, behold, one like the Son of man came with the clouds of heaven, and came to the Ancient of days . . . . And there was given him dominion, and glory, and a kingdom, that all people, nations, and languages, should serve him: his dominion is an everlasting dominion, which shall not pass away, and his kingdom that which shall not be destroyed" (verses 13, 14).

The preaching of the apostles is not different from the visions of the prophets. Simon Peter, in his sermon in the third chapter of the Book of Acts, said: "Repent ye therefore, and be converted, that your sins may be blotted out, when the times of refreshing shall come from the presence of the Lord; And he shall send Jesus Christ, which before was preached unto you: Whom the heaven must receive until the times of restitution of all things" (Acts 3:19-21). In that one Greek word, *apokatastasis,* translated "restitution" is the great Jubilee described in Leviticus 25:27: "Whom the heaven must receive until the times of restitution [earth's great Jubilee] of all things, which God hath spoken by the mouth of all his holy prophets since the world began." There has never been a time, says Simon Peter, when this great Jubilee of God's Edenic re-creation has not been spoken of through the inspiration of the Holy Ghost. Again, in chapter 11 of the Book of the Revelation, the seventh angel sounded and by anticipation he announces the coming of the kingdom: "There were great voices in heaven, saying, The kingdoms of this world are become the kingdoms of our Lord, and of his Christ; and he shall reign for ever and ever" (Revelation 11:15). There has never been a time when God has not purposed this for us; namely, that we, with our Lord, shall reign in holiness, in glory and in triumph on this earth. In chapter 20 of the Book of the Revelation, that glorious millennial kingdom has come to pass. This is its reality.

For three hundred years in the dark centuries of persecution by the Roman Empire the hope of a millennial kingdom was the one luminous light to comfort the souls of the Christian believers. Every one of the Ante-Nicene Fathers, every preacher of Christ who lived in the first three hundred years after Jesus, spoke of the hope of the personal reign of our Lord in the earth. Papias and Justin Martyr and Ignatius and Irenaeus and Tertullian, all of them with one accord, without exception, spoke of that glorious hope of a Millennium. They delivered this message, not only as a doctrine of the Holy Scriptures, but they said that they had also received it as a tradition from the Lord and the apostles themselves.

The Millennium is a time period. Several of the time words in our language come from the Latin. "Millennium" is just another one of those several time words. The Greek word for "hour" is *hora*. The Latin word is *hora*, and when it comes into our language we pronounce it "hour." The Latin word for "year" is *annus*. Our "annual" is derived from that Latin word referring to a year. The Latin word for one hundred is *centum;* our word "century" comes from the word "hundred." The English word "millennium" comes from two Latin words *mille,* which is a thousand, and *annum,* which is a year. So, "millennium" is a thousand-year period. It is a time period just as an hour is a time period, a year is a time period, a century is a time period. But so pre-eminent and so celestially glorious is the prophesied Millennium that we have come to refer to it as "The Millennium." It begins when Satan is bound after the great Battle of Armageddon, and it ends after a thousand years when Satan is loosed for a little season. It is a new age, it is a new order. There are many things concerning it that we cannot understand and there is no need to try. We cannot conceive of a world without sin, where Satan is bound, where righteousness reigns. These things to us are beyond experience because we have never known a world that was not oversown with sin. Our lives have never known a time when we did not battle against iniquity. Weeping, crying, bereavement, separation, despair — these are the common lot of every life. But in the Golden Age these shall be taken away. We can hardly conceive of what it will be like. We have thousands of questions concerning it. But whether we can answer all the questions or not, we know that it will be glorious even as the Lord God has written on the pages of His holy Word.

ONLY THE SAVED ENTER THE MILLENNIUM

No one will enter that millennial age who is a sinner. All who enter that holy and heavenly era will be saved, washed by the blood of the Lamb. No one who is not converted can enter. The saints alone inherit the kingdom. For example, Daniel 7:18 says: "But the saints of the most High shall take the kingdom, and possess the kingdom for ever, even for ever and ever." The prophet repeats for emphasis. Daniel says again in verse 22: "The time came that the saints possessed the kingdom." And he repeats in verse 27: "And the kingdom . . . shall be given to the people of the saints of the most High." All who enter that millennial kingdom are saved. They are regenerated by the blood of the Crucified One and no rejector, no blasphemer, no unbeliever will have any part in the glorious, coming kingdom of our Lord.

THE JUDGMENTS PRECEDING THE MILLENNIUM

In preparation for that Golden Age, there are two great judgments the people in this earth will go through. First, Israel will go through a judgment. God's chosen people who now live in unbelief and who gather in their services in rejection of Christ, will go through a judgment. No Israelite who refused the Lord Christ will ever enter that Millennium. In chapter 20 of the Book of Ezekiel, there is described the judgment that Israel will go through: "As I live, saith the Lord God, with a mighty hand, and with a stretched out arm, and with fury poured out, I will rule over you: And I will bring you out from the people, and will gather you out of the countries wherein ye are scattered, with a mighty hand, and with a stretched out arm, and with fury poured out. And I will bring you into the wilderness of the people, and there will I plead with you face to face. Like as I pleaded with your fathers in the wilderness of the land of Egypt, so will I plead with you, saith the Lord God. And I will cause you to pass under the rod, and I will bring you into the bond of the covenant: And I will purge out from among you the rebels, and them that transgress against me: I will bring them forth out of the country . . . and they shall not enter into the land of Israel: and ye shall know that I am the Lord" (verses 33-38). As a shepherd places his rod, his staff, over the door of the sheepfold and as the sheep go through, one by one, he calls their names, so the Lord says that He will bring all of Israel into the wilderness and plead with them there in the wilderness, causing them to pass under the rod, judging them one by one. There will be no rebel spared and there will be none left that transgress against the Lord. There will be no rejecter or unbeliever who will enter into the land. This is the great judgment of Israel before the days of the Millennium.

There is also a judgment of the Gentiles. No Gentile will enter the millennial kingdom of God who is not saved, born again, converted. The judgment of the Gentiles is described in Matthew 25:31-46, "When the Son of man shall come in his glory, and all the holy angels with him, then shall he sit upon the throne of his glory: And before him shall be gathered all Gentiles" (translated in the Authorized King James Version, "nations"). "And [God] shall separate them one from another, as a shepherd divides the sheep from the goats." Some will enter the glorious kingdom of our Lord and some will be shut out forever. No one will enter that kingdom who is not saved, washed clean and white in the blood of the Crucified One.

The Millennial kingdom is not temporary. It is finally merged into the great, final kingdom of the Lord God Almighty in the eternities of the eternities. There is a perpetuity of that kingdom that lasts forever and forever. Daniel even multiplies the forevers. We are not to think that Christ comes into this world to establish a kingdom only for Satan to destroy it. Not so. I cannot fully explain why God allows the loosing again of Satan, having placed him in the abyss. Why does not God keep him there? I cannot understand the purposes of God in the creation of Lucifer, nor can I understand the presence of iniquity in God's creation. I just know that there is something in the economy and in the government of heaven that necessitates this trial by fire through which we go as we wrestle against the dissimulations and deceptions of the Evil One. I cannot explain the loosing of Satan for a season, but I know from reading the Bible that when Christ establishes His kingdom it will never be destroyed. It is an everlasting kingdom and our Lord has in it an everlasting dominion. That avowal is confirmed by the Apostle Paul in I Corinthians 15:14-28. At the end time Christ "shall have delivered up the kingdom to God, even the Father; when he shall have put down all rule and all authority and power. For he must reign, till he hath put all enemies under his feet." When the kingdom is established and in the purposes of God has run its magnificent and triumphant course, then Christ will offer it unto God, beautiful, holy, perfect, even as God Himself could re-create us and this world.

THE BLESSINGS OF THE MILLENNIAL KINGDOM

Now, let us speak of the blessings of the millennial kingdom. First of all, we shall speak of the blessings of God for Israel, God's chosen people. Then we shall speak of the blessings of God for us who are Gentiles. Then we shall speak of the blessings of God for the whole creation when God remakes it. Then we shall speak of the blessings of the kingdom as they are dedicated to the honor and the glory of our living Lord who reigns personally, in presence, over the people who have placed their trust in Him.

First of all, let us consider the elect of God, the children of Jehovah, the people of Israel. They are to be restored to their home and to their land. Amos 9:14, 15 says: "And I will bring again the captivity of my people of Israel . . . . And I will plant them upon their land, and they shall no more be pulled up out of their land which I have given them, saith the Lord thy God." This is just one out of a multitude of passages (compare Isaiah 43:1-7; Jeremiah 24:6,7; Ezekiel 28:25,26; Zephaniah 3:20) where God says His people are going to be given Palestine for an inheritance forever and no one shall ever take it from them. Not only is Israel to be restored to the land, but they are to be regenerated, they are to be converted, they are to accept the Lord Christ as their Saviour and their Messiah. Listen to the word of God in Jeremiah 23:3-8: "And I will gather the remnant of my flock out of all countries whither I have driven them, and will bring them again to their folds; and they shall be fruitful and increase. And I will set up shepherds over them which shall feed them: and they shall fear no more, nor be dismayed, neither shall they be lacking, saith the Lord. Behold, the days come, saith the Lord, that I will raise unto David a righteous Branch, and a King shall reign and prosper, and shall execute judgment and justice in the earth. In his days Judah shall be saved, and Israel shall dwell safely: and this is his name whereby he shall be called, THE LORD OUR RIGHTEOUSNESS. Therefore, behold, the days come, saith the Lord, that they shall no more say, The Lord liveth, which brought up the children of Israel out of the land of Egypt; But, The Lord liveth, which brought up and which led the seed of the house of Israel out of the north country, and from all countries whither I had driven them; and they shall dwell in their own land." The number of passages that could be read are legion (Isaiah 4:3-6; Jeremiah 31:31-34; 32:36-41; Ezekiel 11: 18-20; 12:10-14; 13:1, 8, 9; 16:60-63; 21:40-44; 36:24-28; 37: 26). Beside all these there is another tremendous passage from Paul in Romans 11:26-29. After stating that, "Blindness in part is happened to Israel, until the fulness of the Gentiles be come in," the apostle continues: But there is a time when "all Israel shall be saved: as it is written, There shall come out of Sion the Deliverer, and shall turn away ungodliness from Jacob: For this is my covenant unto them, when I shall take away their sins. As concerning the gospel, they are enemies for your sakes: but as touching the election [the divine sovereign purpose of God], they are beloved for the fathers' sakes. For the gifts and calling of God are without [turning, without changing, without] repentance." God made some great promises to Abraham, to Isaac, to Jacob, to David, through His holy prophets. God made some great promises to His people. He made an Abrahamic covenant with them; He made a Davidic covenant with them; He made a Palestinian covenant with them; He made a covenant of a "new heart" with them, and God does not change. Man may change. Man can forget what he has promised. But not the Lord. Every promise that God has made to Israel God will faithfully keep. Some of these days in that millennial kingdom Israel will have a praiseworthy and a believing part. The day is coming, said the prophet Zechariah, and the day is coming, said the Apostle Paul, when Israel will turn in faith and accept the Lord Christ as their Messiah. At that time the Jews will mourn over their rejection of their Saviour, and God will provide a healing fountain for their sins in which they will be forgiven and will be saved. It is then that they will have a part in the millennial kingdom of our Lord.

As there are blessings for Israel, so there are blessings for the Gentiles, for us. "It shall come to pass in the last days, that the mountain of the Lord's house shall be established in the top of the mountains, and shall be exalted above the hills; and all the nations [Gentiles] shall flow into it." This is the prophecy of Isaiah 2:2-4. "And many people shall go and say, Come ye, and let us go up to the mountain of the Lord, to the house of the God of Jacob. . . . And he shall judge among the nations, and shall rebuke many people: and they shall beat their swords into plowshares, and their spears into pruninghooks: nation shall not lift up sword against nation, neither shall they learn war any more." These are a few of God's blessings upon the Gentiles, upon us, in the millennial kingdom. Let us take time to read how God has included us Gentiles in the kingdom and especially do we read this because of the terrible bitterness that is likely to ignite war any moment, any day, any hour in Palestine. Look at Isaiah 19:23-25: "In that day shall there be a highway out of Egypt to Assyria, and the Assyrian shall come into Egypt, and the Egyptian into Assyria, and the Egyptians shall serve the Lord with the Assyrians. In that day shall Israel be the third with Egypt and with Assyria, even a blessing in the midst of the land: Whom the Lord of hosts shall bless, saying, Blessed be Egypt my people, and Assyria the work of my hands, and Israel mine inheritance." Can you imagine a thing like that? Think of the bitterness among those Palestinian people. Think of the years of hatred ever since Ishmael and Isaac grew to despise one another. From that day until this has there been war between Israel and the Arabs. But there is coming a time, says the Lord, when the Lord of hosts will bless them all, saying, "Blessed be Egypt my people, and blessed be Assyria the work of my hands, and blessed be Israel mine inheritance." All of us, saved Jews, and saved Gentiles, are to be together in the glorious and ultimate kingdom of our Lord.

ALL CREATION BLEST IN THE MILLENNIUM

In that millennial kingdom there is to be a new creation. There are blessings for the whole universe. One of the most sublime and meaningful of all of the passages in the Word of God is in Romans 8. (Many think this is the greatest chapter in the Bible.) Listen to Paul as he describes what God is going to do: "For the earnest expectation of the creature waiteth for the manifestation of the sons of God. For the creature was made subject to vanity, not willingly, but by reason of him who hath subjected the same in hope, Because the creature itself also shall be delivered from the bondage of corruption into glorious liberty of the children of God. For we know that the whole creation groaneth and travaileth in pain together until now. And not only they, but ourselves also, which have the firstfruits of the Spirit, even we ourselves groan within ourselves, waiting for the adoption, to wit, the redemption of our body" (Romans 8:19-23). The prophecies of the Old Testament confirm this passage from Paul. Isaiah 11:6-9 speaks of the change in the animal kingdom. "The wolf shall dwell with the lamb, and the leopard shall lie down with the kid; . . . and the lion shall eat straw like an ox." God never intended "balance of nature" such as we have it in this world. God never intended for animals to eat one another, to lie in wait, to destroy, to drink blood. This is a mark of sin in the world. God never intended for one man to kill another man, much less for one nation to go to war and slay millions of his fellow men. The Lord made this creation to be filled with light, goodness, glory, holiness, love and happiness. But all that we lost in Eden, God will give us back again in the new creation. Think of a day when the wolf and the lamb, the leopard and the kid, the lion and the fatling will lie down together! When that vicious, ferocious, carnivorous lion is a vegetarian! He will eat straw like an ox. Oh, what God has prepared in that millennial day!

But we are not done. In that millennial day all of the disease, futility and despair, whereby our bodies are afflicted and laid low, will be taken away. Isaiah 35:5, 6 says: "Then the eyes of the blind shall be opened, and the ears of the deaf shall be unstopped. Then shall the lame man leap as an hart, and the tongue of the dumb shall sing . . . in the wilderness shall waters break out, and streams in the desert." This is the glorious day of our Lord. The curse of Genesis 3:17-19 is removed. (Compare Isaiah 35:1, 2; 55:13.) Sickness, sorrow, sighing and crying are no more. God Himself will wipe away the tears from our eyes.

As there are blessings in the Millennium for God's chosen people, Israel, and as there are blessings in the millennial kingdom abounding for us who are Gentiles, and as there are blessings in the Millennium for all God's creation (even the animal world will be remade), so there will be blessings in the millennial kingdom for our glorious and reigning Lord. Zechariah 14:4-9 promises: "And his feet shall stand in that day upon the mount of Olives, which is before Jerusalem on the east . . . . And the Lord my God shall come, and all the saints with thee. But it shall come to pass, that at evening time it shall be light. And it shall be in that day, that living waters shall go out . . . And the Lord shall be king over all the earth." This is what God has promised for His Son. "He shall be king over all the earth." In Luke 1:32 the angel Gabriel said to Mary: "[This son whom you are to call Jesus] He shall be great, and shall be called the Son of the Highest: and the Lord God shall give unto him the throne of his father David: And he shall reign over the house of Jacob for ever and of his kingdom there shall be no end." That is the prophecy that Gabriel brought from the courts of heaven. The Lord God shall give Him the throne of His father, David, and He shall reign over the house of Jacob forever and of His kingdom there shall be no end. This is the ultimate and final glory that Paul describes for our Lord in Philippians 2:6-11. Because Christ bowed Himself under the weight of our sins and became obedient unto the death of the cross, "therefore God also hath highly exalted him, and given him a name which is above every name: That at the name of Jesus every knee should bow, of things in heaven, and things in earth, and things under the earth; And that every tongue should confess that Jesus Christ is Lord, to the glory of God the Father." And that glorious consummation is seen in the Revelation, the unveiling of Jesus the Christ, the rightful Ruler of the Universe. "And the seventh angel sounded; and there were great voices in heaven, saying, The kingdoms of this world are become the kingdoms of our Lord, and of his Christ; and he shall reign for ever and ever" (Revelation 11:15). In II Corinthians 4:4 Paul says that Satan is "the god of this world." Surely the devil is a usurper. God never intended it to be like that. But Satan shall be cast out and the rightful

King, our living Lord, shall ascend the throne of His father, David, and amidst the chorus of the angels and the adoration of the saints shall he reign over all the works of God's hands. There is a triumph, there is a glory, there is a hallelujah in the message of the Son of God beyond anything that heart could imagine or tongue could describe.

> All hail the pow'r of Jesus' name!
> Let angels prostrate fall:
> Bring forth the royal diadem,
> And crown Him Lord of all.
>
> Ye chosen seed of Israel's race,
> Ye ransomed from the fall,
> Hail Him who saves you by His grace,
> And crown Him Lord of all.

Dear people, this is just a little introduction into what the Lord has prepared for those who place their trust in Him.

CHAPTER 7

THE GREAT WHITE THRONE JUDGMENT

Revelation 20

11 And I saw a great white throne, and him that sat on it, from whose face the earth and the heaven fled away; and there was found no place for them.

12 And I saw the dead, small and great, stand before God; and the books were opened: and another book was opened, which is the book of life: and the dead were judged out of those things which were written in the books, according to their works.

13 And the sea gave up the dead which were in it; and death and hell delivered up the dead which were in them: and they were judged every man according to their works.

14 And death and hell were cast into the lake of fire. This is the second death.

15 And whosoever was not found written in the book of life was cast into the lake of fire.

There is no more somber or solemn passage to be read in all of God's Word than this description of the final Judgment Day of God. "And I saw a great white throne, and him that sat on it . . ." In Revelation 4:2 (a vision that begins the tribulation judgments before the Millennium) the first thing that John saw when he was taken up into heaven was "a throne . . . and one sat on the throne." We would suppose the two thrones to be the same. This is not the case, however. There are some significant differences between that throne and this final judgment throne of Almighty God. Let us consider some of these differences.

First, when John saw the throne set in heaven at the beginning of the judgments of the tribulation, he saw around the throne a rainbow. That rainbow is a sign of the covenant-keeping God who remembers His promises to those who repent, to those who are His righteous believers. But there is no rainbow around the judgment throne. There is nothing but the nakedness of almighty justice and retribution. There are no covenant promises of good to remember in that awesome hour.

Another thing, from the throne that John saw in Revelation 4 there proceeded lightnings, thunderings and voices. These are the threatenings of God. They are the warnings of heaven, warnings like the flashing of a red light back and forth when one drives across a railroad track in the path of an oncoming train. At the beginning of the tribulation, there proceeded out of God's throne lightnings, thunderings and voices, the warnings of Jehovah. But there are no voices, no lightnings and no thunderings that proceed out of this final throne. There is nothing but retributive and final justice, nothing but the silence of almightiness in that day of doom and damnation. There are no more warnings, no more threatenings, nothing but the final perdition and doom of the lost.

Another thing, in Revelation 4 John saw seven lamps of fire burning before the throne, which seven lamps are the seven Spirits of God. At that throne of grace John saw the intercessions, the groanings, the prayings and the pleadings of the Holy Spirit of God. But not here. There is no longer any intercession, there is no longer any pleading of the Holy Spirit, for the day of God's grace has forever and finally ended. The lamps of the grace and the blessing of the Spirit of God that glorified the first throne are in this final throne forever taken away.

Another thing, before that first throne that John saw in heaven there was a sea of glass like unto crystal. There was a vast pavement before that first throne, a sign of the refuge of the people of God, a celestial pavement upon which God's people could stand. But there is no pavement of righteousness and there is no sea of refuge before the final throne. There is no longer a platform on which the people can find shelter from the day of wrath and judgment of Almighty God.

A final difference is this: In Revelation 4, from the throne that John saw in heaven, he also heard the singing and the praising of those who look in grace and salvation to their Lord. There are songs and praises unto God. But at this final Great White Throne, set at the end of time and at the end of history, there are no longer any voices of praise, there are no songs sung, there are no exaltations. There is nothing but the silence of the doomed, the damned and the judged in this ultimate day of the wrath and justice of Almighty God. I repeat, what a sober thing is this passage, looking upon the burning of God against the unbelieving and the wicked in this earth!

THE LAST OVERSOWING OF SATAN

The text continues, after it describes the Great White Throne, "And [I saw] him that sat on it, from whose face the earth and the heaven fled away; and there was found no place for them." Three times in the story of our world has Satan over-sown God's creation, turning it into desolation and despair. Satan did that when God created the heaven and the earth. Genesis 1:1 declares, "In the beginning God created the heaven and the earth." The work of God's hand is always pure, holy, beautiful and perfect. Therefore, we know that when God made this vast creation, He did it in beauty and in perfection. But the next verse, Genesis 1:2, says: "And the earth was [became] *tohu wa bohu* [translated here] without form, and void." The prophet Isaiah says (Isaiah 45:18) God did not create this great universe and this earth *tohu wa bohu*, but rather that God made it beautiful, made it to be lived in, made it a glory to His excellent majesty. Therefore, I know that something happened between that first and second verse of Genesis, for God, at the first, created the universe in beauty and in glory. God's beautiful creation became waste, void and uninhabitable. The terrible tragedy that happened was the entrance of sin into the world. Out of Satan's rebellion was born the waste of God's whole creation. That was the first time that Satan destroyed God's excellent work.

Then Satan brought woe again into the re-creation when God remade this planet Earth. After God saw that His work was good, He made for divine fellowship an order of beings who could think His thoughts after Him, who could call His name in prayer, and who could love the Lord God. He made a man and a woman in His own image that they might walk with Him, talk with Him, live with Him, respond in love and adoration. But for the second time there came into God's beautiful creation this subtle and destroying angel. He led our first parents into deception and sin and thus wasted God's creation. The Lord God said to the sinning parents of our fallen race, "Cursed is the ground for thy sake; in sorrow shalt thou eat of it all the days of thy life." Because of the transgression by which Satan destroyed our first parents, this whole earth was cursed. That was the second time that Satan destroyed God's world.

Here in Revelation 20 we read of the third time Satan oversows God's work. When the Lord comes from heaven with His saints, when their bodies are raised from the dead, when the blessed of the Lord enter the Millennium, God's world again is beautiful and glorious. Then, for the third time, we read that Satan, who deceives men and wastes God's inheritance, is let loose after a thousand years. This evil one goes before the nations of the earth (whose number is as the sand of the sea) and he gathers them in war against God's people and against God Himself. But that is the last and the final time that Satan is ever allowed to waste God's creation. For, the text says, this time fire comes down from God out of heaven and the devil that deceived the nations is cast into the hellfire of damnation and brimstone. He stays there forever. This is the final judgment whereby the Lord condemns Satan and those who are gullibly enticed by his deceptions.

We read of this judgment by fire in II Peter 3:7: "But the heavens and the earth, which are now, by the same word are kept in store, reserved unto fire against the day of judgment and perdition of ungodly men." When that final day of the judgment and damnation of ungodly men arrives, that is the day in which Simon Peter says that God is going to purge this whole creation. He is going to cleanse it, make it anew. Peter further describes that day: "[It is a day] in which the heavens shall pass away with a great noise, and the elements shall melt with fervent heat, the earth also and the works that are therein shall be burned up . . . these things shall be dissolved . . . wherein the heavens being on fire shall be dissolved, and the elements shall melt with fervent heat . . . [we] look for new heavens and a new earth." Thus Simon Peter writes in II Peter 3:10, 13. There is a day coming when God will say to Satan: "You have come thus far, but no further. Judgment day is now." This whole creation will be purged with fire; God will establish a new heaven and a new earth for His redeemed people. Satan will be no more. The time of this purging mentioned by Peter is the time of this passage in the Revelation. Simon Peter says this comes to pass in that day of the judgment and perdition of ungodly men. The exact thing is also said in this text in the Revelation: "And I saw the dead, small and great, stand before God; and the books were opened: and another book was opened, which is the book of life: and the dead were judged out of those things which were written in the books . . . And the sea gave up the dead which were in it; and death and hell delivered up the dead which were in them: and they were judged every man according to their works." This is the great, ultimate, final Judgment Day of Almighty God. This is the congregation of the unblessed, of the doomed, of the damned. There is no blowing of the trumpet here as there is when God's righteous are called out of the dust of the ground. There is no voice of an archangel here as when God's sleeping saints are called to meet Jesus in the air. There are no white robes here, there is no linen here, the pure, clean righteousnesses of the saints. There is no mention here but of damnation, of doom and of judgment.

THE RESURRECTION UNTO DAMNATION

Who are these who are sentenced at the Great White Throne Judgment? In the earlier part of Revelation 20 we read: "Blessed and holy is he that hath part in the first resurrection: on such the second death hath no power, but they shall be priests of God and of Christ, and shall reign with him a thousand years." But the rest of the dead — the unblessed, the unholy, the unrighteous, the lost and the rejecting — do not live again until after the thousand years is done. There are two resurrections. Wherever the word "resurrection," *anastasis*, is used in the Bible, it always refers to a corporeal, bodily resurrection. It does not refer to a man being saved or a man being regenerated in his heart. The word *anastasis* always refers to one thing, namely, the raising of a dead body out of the dust of the ground, out of the depths of the sea, out of the heart of the earth. So, the first *anastasis*, the first corporeal, bodily resurrection concerns those who have trusted in the Lord Jesus and have been saved. They are the blessed and the holy. But the rest of the dead, those who are not raised at the coming of Christ, are raised at this terrible time of the judgment of God at the Great White Throne day. Oh, what a trembling and what a fearsome thing!

We must understand that there are two resurrections. The Bible speaks of them again and again. There is the resurrection of the just and of the unjust. There is a resurrection of the righteous and of the unrighteous. Always the resurrection of the righteous, the resurrection unto life, is mentioned first. There is the resurrection of the sainted people of God who place their trust in Him and then there is the resurrection of the lost, the doomed, the damned, the rejecting, the unbelieving. The two are always placed in that order. That is why the Bible says those who fall asleep in Christ shall rise first, always first. There is a resurrection unto incorruption. There is also a resurrection to corruption. There is a resurrection to honor and to a glorified body. There is also a resurrection to shame and to contempt. There is a resurrection unto eternal life. There is also a resurrection into eternal damnation and the fire of perdition. These things make the soul to tremble as we face the ultimate destiny of the lost.

"And the books were opened: and another book was opened, which is the book of life: and the dead were judged out of those . . . books [plural]" which were written recounting the deeds of those who reject our Lord and who are lost. Then, lest any say God is not fair and righteous, the great Book of Life is opened and its pages are scanned to see if perchance and by any means those who had rejected our Lord might have their names written in the Book of Life. But their names are not there. Everyone whose name is not written in the Book of Life is cast into the lake of fire. All of the deeds that men do in this world are written down in God's Books and to those who trust in Jesus, whose sins are washed away in the blood of the Lamb, who have looked in repentance to Him, to those who are saved, the things that are written in the Book are things that are blessed. They become our reward at the Bema of Christ. There are also books that are filled with the deeds of those whose sins are not covered. At the end of time, at this final judgment, their reward is according to the things that are written in those books.

It is most evident why these judgments are at the end of time. A man does not die when He dies. His life continues. His influence continues. The deeds of this life continue. God only is able to unravel out of all of the skeins of human history the influences of a life. For those whose sins are covered and who are saved, God unravels the good of their lives and the record becomes our crowning reward at the final Bema of Christ when we stand before the Lord. But those who refuse the Lord, who reject His overtures of grace and mercy, all of their deeds are written in the Book of Judgment. At the end of time, at the final judgment day of God, the Lord unravels the skein of their influence and life, and these iniquitous records become the basis of their eternal reward of damnation. It cannot be done until the end of time.

I remember, in the little town where I grew up, a father who had his little boy stand on a table. He was teaching the little fellow to curse. He filled the mind of the little boy with every foul, dirty and filthy thing. That man, the father of the boy, is now dead, but his son, my age, is still living. The ruined life of the boy is the result of the wickedness of the father. That father did not get his reward when he died, for he lives in the wretchedness and the filth of the boy he taught to blaspheme. The evil goes on and on and on. When the lost, the damned, the doomed, the unbelieving, the Christ-rejecting get to the end of the way, to that White Throne Judgment, Oh, what an appalling thing when God sums up the wickedness of a man's life! What a somber, what a fearful summation!

The Opening of the Book of Life

When the books recording the deeds of men are opened and each man has received his reward according to the influence of his life through all of the generations and the ages, then another book is opened, the Book of Life. How many times in this Bible is that Book of Life referred to! Lest any mistake be made and any man be unjustly damned, the Book of Life is thoroughly searched. "Is this man's name in the Book of Life, Sir?" The recording angel replies, "It is not in the Book of Life." This one? This one? This one? "And whosoever was not found written in the book of life was cast into the lake of fire," into the brimstone and torment that lasts forever. The one unfathomable, un-understandable, inexplicable thing to me in life, above all others, is this: Why would a man refuse to be counted among the children of the saved? I cannot understand it. It is just as if an angel entered into Sodom and Gomorrah and stood in the gate and said, "All who will turn to God, I will write their names in this Book and they will be saved." But the citizens of Sodom and Gomorrah say: "No, we had rather be damned and be burned with eternal fire." And the fire came and burned up Sodom and Gomorrah. It is the same kind of thing as if a representative from God had stood in the gate of Jericho and said: "God is going to judge this city. God is going to destroy this city. But all who will turn and look to the Lord in faith, I will write their names in this Book." But the citizens of Jericho say: "No, we had rather be damned than have our names written in the Book of Life. We had rather be lost. We had rather be put to the edge of the sword and sent into eternal darkness and perdition." That is what men say today. "I do not want my name written in the Book of Life. I do not want to be saved. Do not put my name in that Book. I do not want to turn in repentance and faith and look to Jesus for salvation. Do not write my name in that Book. I had rather be damned, I had rather spend eternity in burning torment." I cannot understand such an awesome decision.

Out of all of the assignments of the preacher, there is none like that of going to a home and trying to comfort a family where death has entered and the people are not Christians. What do you say? When a man is lost, he is lost. When a family is unsaved, it is not saved. When a man dies outside of the grace of God, he dies forever. This is the second death.

There is nothing you can say. There is nothing you can read. All you can do is lament, weep and cry. Why would a man choose to die like that? Why would a family choose to be that way? I cannot understand it. There is a deception, there is a blindness that Satan thrusts over the minds and hearts of people. I cannot understand it. He is able to place a veil over our very souls. That is why we preach and sing and pray and visit. We are trying to remove that darkness from the hearts and souls of those who reject our Lord.

Oh, the swiftness and the immediacy of the execution of God's judgment! There is no delay when the hour for sentencing comes. For centuries and for eternities, it seems, God has been patient and longsuffering. He has waited, He has pled. Preachers have preached, singers have sung, people have prayed, invited, asked, begged, interceded. The lost have been cried over, wept for; but all to no avail. When that final day comes, it comes quickly. Peter tells us it comes like a thief in the night, suddenly, immediately. And the sentence is executed forthwith. Read again Revelation 19:20: "And the beast was taken, and with him the false prophet . . . These both were cast alive into a lake of fire." Read again Revelation 20:10: "And the devil that deceived them was cast into the lake of fire and brimstone." And read again Revelation 20:15: "And whosoever was not found written in the book of life was cast into the lake of fire." The unrepentant and the unbelieving are sent away into an everlasting, eternal damnation.

Oh, Lord! Oh, God! Oh, Christ! This terrible tragedy brought the Saviour from glory. He did not come just to teach us another ethic. He did not come just to tell us shopworn, moralizing aphorisms. He came to save our souls from an eternal damnation. That is why God had to do it. No angel could save us. No man could save us. Only God could save us. Our tragic condition brought Him down in incarnation, in humility and finally into the crucifixion of death that we might be saved. Remember the chorus:

> O, my loving brother,
> When the world's on fire,
> Don't you want God's bosom
> For to be your pillow;

> O hide me over
> In the Rock of Ages,
> Rock of Ages,
> Cleft for me.

Let me hide, O God, myself in Thee. That is our appeal to your soul today.

CHAPTER 8

THE FIRE OF HELL

Revelation 20

14 And death and hell were cast into the lake of fire. This is the second death.

15 And whosoever was not found written in the book of life was cast into the lake of fire.

We speak first of the solemnity of this subject. Against the background of this awesome and final torment the entire Word of God is written. Its warnings, its appeals, its threatenings are all delivered against this solemn background of the great Judgment Day of Almighty God. I could not think of a more recurring refrain than that written by the author of the epistle to the Hebrews when he said: "It is a fearful thing to fall into the hands of the living God. For our God is a consuming fire." Against that background the prophets preached. Listen to Ezekiel as he says: "As I live, saith the Lord God, I have no pleasure in the death of the wicked; but that the wicked turn from his way and live: turn ye, turn ye from your evil ways; for why will ye die?" (Ezekiel 33:11). Listen to the Apostle Paul as he pleads: "Knowing therefore the terror of the Lord, we persuade men . . . We . . . beseech you also that ye receive not the grace of God in vain. (For he saith, I have heard thee in a time accepted, and in the day of salvation have I succoured thee: behold, now is the accepted time; behold, now is the day of salvation)" (II Corinthians 5:11; 6:1, 2). But of all of them who spoke of this great and solemn judgment, it is our Lord Christ, Himself, who spoke of it most solemnly. "Yea," said our Lord, "if thy hand offend thee, cut it off and cast it from thee. It is better to enter into eternal life maimed than to be cast into Gehenna [hell] where the fire is never quenched,

93

where the worm never dies, amidst the wailing and the gnashing of teeth. If thy foot offend thee," He said, "cut it off, cast it from thee. It is better to enter into eternal life with one foot than having two feet and to be cast into the Gehenna of hell. Or if thy eye offend thee, pluck it out. It is better to enter into eternal life with one eye than to have both eyes and to be cast into the Gehenna of hellfire." (See Matthew 5:29, 30.) This is the Word of our living Lord. Truly, against the solemn background of terror the entire Bible is delivered from the warning hand of God.

THE AWESOME JUDGMENT OF GOD UPON SIN

It was the curse upon the sin of lost humanity that brought down our Lord from heaven. Paul says that Christ was made a curse for us that we might be redeemed from the damnation pronounced by the law. Our Lord became a man, was given a body, that He might be sacrificed for our sins, that He might pour out His holy blood for our salvation. Never let anyone persuade you that our Lord came down from heaven in order to teach us a better example. We had all the fine examples we needed. What drew our Lord down from heaven was the tragic plight of our souls, facing eternal damnation in the presence of a holy God. He came to deliver us from evil, to offer us remission of sins in His blood. The awful tragedy we faced as lost sinners brought our Lord down from heaven.

Let me say another word about the solemnity of this message. Against that background of damnation a true minister preaches. With the hope of a soul's salvation he delivers his message from God. It matters not the service, it matters not the song, it matters not the worship, if the soul is lost. Always and always over every service there is that shadow of what it means to be damned. Always before the faithful worker is the tragedy involved in the rejection of a man who says "No" to God and "No" to Christ and "No" to the wooing appeal of the Holy Spirit of grace and intercession. It is a fearful thing to fall into the hands of the living God.

> I dreamed that the great judgment morning
> Had dawned, and the trumpet had blown;
> I dreamed that the nations had gathered
> To judgment before the white throne;

From the throne came a bright, shining angel
And stood on the land and the sea,
And swore with his hand raised to heaven,
That time was no longer to be.

The rich man was there, but his money
Had melted and vanished away;
A pauper he stood in the judgment,
His debts were too heavy to pay;
The great man was there, but his greatness,
When death came, was left far behind!
The angel that opened the records,
Not a trace of his greatness could find.

. . . .

The gambler was there and the drunkard,
And the man that had sold them the drink,
With the people who sold them the license —
Together in hell they did sink.

The moral man came to the judgment,
But his self-righteous rags would not do;
The men who had crucified Jesus
Had passed off as moral men, too;
The soul that had put off salvation —
"Not tonight; I'll get saved by and by;
No time now to think of religion!"
At last, he had found time to die.

And oh, what a weeping and wailing,
As the lost were told of their fate;
They cried for the rocks and the mountains,
They prayed, but their prayer was too late.

"And whosoever was not found written in the book of life was cast into the lake of fire." The solemnity, oh, the solemnity of this word from the Lord!

THE SEPARATION BETWEEN THE SAVED AND THE LOST

Let us turn now to the revelations of God concerning the doomed and the damned. Time and again, over and over again, page after page, God says in this Holy Book that there will someday be a separation between the lost and the saved, between those whose sins are forgiven and those who die in unforgiven sin. There is an example of this in the parable of the tares. "Let them grow together," said our Lord, "the wheat and the tares." But at the end of the age God will send forth His angels and burn the tares with a fire that is never quenched, after He has gathered His saints, His children, His wheat into the garner of Paradise. (See Matthew 13:24-30.) In Matthew 13 is the parable of the fish caught in the net. The good fish are kept and the bad fish are thrown away. "So shall it be," said our Lord, "at the time of the great separation between the good and the bad, between those whose sins are forgiven and those who die in unforgiven sin." I turn the pages: "As it was in the days of Noah when Noah was taken out and the judgment of God fell upon this earth, so shall it be at the time of the coming of Christ. Two shall be sleeping in a bed, one shall be taken and the other left. Two shall be grinding at a mill, one shall be taken and the other left. Two shall be working in a field, one shall be taken and the other left." (See Matthew 24:37-41.) This is the great separation. I turn the page and read the story of the five wise virgins (maidens) who enter into the kingdom of heaven and the five foolish maidens who were left out "and the door was shut." (See Matthew 25:1-13.) I turn the page and read the story of the great Judgment Day when Christ comes and, as a Shepherd, divides His sheep from the goats (Matthew 25:31-46). So shall God divide His saved from the lost. As we turn the pages of the Bible, this great separation is everywhere evident. Finally we come to the Great White Throne Judgment where the records are searched "and whosoever was not found written in the Book of Life was cast into the lake of fire." This tragic sentence is made the more awesome with the words of Revelation 21:7, 8: "He that overcometh shall inherit all things . . . But the fearful, and unbelieving, and the abominable . . . shall have their part in the lake which burneth with fire . . . which is the second death." Over and over and over God reveals that tragic, final separation between the saved and the lost.

Another awesome thing God reveals in His Book: As there is an eternal abode for the saved, so there is an everlasting habitat for the damned. The Scriptures say that angels came and carried Lazarus to Abraham's bosom, to paradise, to the presence of God, where the people of the Lord dwell with their Saviour. The same Scriptures also say that when Dives died he lifted up his eyes in torment, in the flame and the fire of his sins, unforgiven. He died without God. And those two states in which Lazarus and Dives found themselves are eternal and fixed. There is a great gulf fixed in between. The residents cannot pass from one side to the other. There is an eternal abode for those who are saved and there is an eternal abode for those who are lost. The abode of the saved is heaven. When God has washed away the sins of His children, they stand in His presence, perfect, without spot and without blemish, their names written in the Lamb's Book of Life. These are the children of God. But there is also an eternal abode for those who reject the mercies, the overtures and the intercession of the Spirit of grace.

In the Greek language Jesus called that place of torment "Gehenna" or "hell." "Gehenna" means "the valley of Hinnom." It was located outside of Jerusalem and was the place where the heathen had burned their children to the fiery god Moloch. God cursed the place and it became the dumping ground for the filth of Jerusalem through the centuries. In that refuse of Gehenna the worm never died as it ate into the putrid mass; the fire was never quenched as it burned the endless waste; and the gnashing of teeth never ceased as the jackals fought with one another over the dead carcasses that were cast into that horrible place. This is the Gehenna of hell. It is our Lord who speaks of it, even Jesus.

And oh, the fixedness of those eternal states! No lost man is ever saved beyond death. No lost man is ever saved beyond the grave. No lost man is ever saved in that eternity when the great separation is made and he falls into hell. That is the end forever and forever. There is no other chance. There is nothing left but damnation. In the terrible blitzkreig of London in World War II, after one of the worst raids, a fire was raging uncontrolled and the cries of the dying were drowned only by the buildings toppling to the ground. In the midst of this agony an evangelist of Christ was standing in the streets of London preaching the Gospel of the Son of God. While he was preaching, a skeptic broke into his sermon and said, "Listen, preacher, this is hell, the bombing of London." But the preacher replied: "Sir, this is not hell. And I will give you three reasons why. One, I am a Christian and there are no Christians in hell. Second, there is a church house right around the corner and there are no church houses in hell. Third, I am preaching the Gospel of the Son of God and there is no preaching of the Gospel in hell." About three weeks later the same evangelist was standing in an open-air service in Hyde Park, preaching the Gospel of Jesus. When he gave the invitation, the first to come forward was the skeptic. When he took the preacher's hand, he said: "Preacher, I am the man who said of the bombing of London that this is hell. You answered so well and so truly. Your words convicted my heart. I have come forward to turn to Jesus as my Saviour and I accept Him now." There is no goodness and no hope for any man in torment. Oh, the barren eternity of that place where God separates the sinners who refuse His overtures of grace from the saints who trust in Jesus. And that separation is forever and forever. Our Lord said that those on His right hand, His sheep, His saved, will go away into life eternal, but those on His left hand who refuse the overtures of the grace of God go away into everlasting punishment.

In the King James Version, the Greek word *aionion* is translated in Matthew 25:46 in the first clause "everlasting" and in the second clause "eternal." But in the Greek language it is the same word, *aionion*. That word *aionion* is used sixty-nine times in the New Testament. Sixty-two times it refers to the enduring life of the blessed. For example, John 3:16 reads: "For God so loved the world, that he gave his only begotten Son, that whosoever believeth in him should not perish, but have *aionion* life, everlasting life, eternal life." But seven times that same word *aionion* is used to refer to the life of the lost, the doomed, the damned. If the word used to describe the duration of the life of the damned means to be brief, then the word used to describe the duration of the life of the blessed refers to a brief period, also. If one is shortened, the other is shortened. It is the same word. If the saved live forever, the damned live forever. If there is an everlasting life in heaven, there is an everlasting damnation in the fires of hell. The Scriptures say, "These [lost] shall go away into everlasting [*aionion*]

punishment and these [saved] shall go away into everlasting
[*aionion*] life." It is the same duration.

THE CHOICE THAT CONFRONTS EVERY HUMAN SOUL

Now let us speak of the choice God gives us concerning
our eternal destiny. No man can ever say that God sent him
to perdition. No man can ever say that God damned his soul.
No man can ever say that he is tormented in the flame because
of the injustice and cruelty of Almighty God. Look: "Then
shall he say unto them on the left hand, Depart from me ye
cursed into [*aionion* fire] eternal fire, prepared [not for us, but
prepared] for the devil and his angels." The fire is not made
for us; it is not made for any man; it is not made for a soul; it
is not made for you. It is prepared, that flame of fire, that torment in hell, for the devil and his angels. The only people who
are there are those who *choose* to cast their lot, life and destiny
with the devil and his angels. There is no one there except
those who choose to go. For a man to fall into hell with the
devil and his angels is for a man to choose to go there. It is
not made for you; it is made for the evil one. It is prepared
for the devil and his angels. In it is cast the false prophet and
in it is cast the beast and in it is cast Satan and then, lastly, are
cast Satan's dupes, who would rather have that lot than the
lot of the people of Christ.

How certain and obvious is this judgment! I cannot think
of a plainer separation. God says this world shall pass away,
the very fashion of it shall perish. And if your life is in this
world, when the world is lost, you are lost, too. The judgment
is the obvious result of an investment of your life. God says
there is a judgment upon sin. When you give your life to
iniquity and to unbelief, when the judgment of God comes
upon righteous rejection, then the judgment falls upon you.
I wonder how many will say in the fires of the torment of hell,
"Oh, I felt the tug of the Holy Spirit of God, I felt the call of
my conscience turning me to Jesus, I felt the call of the
preacher when he made an appeal for Christ; but I gave up
Christ for the bottle; I gave up Christ for a lewd and a leacher-
ous life; I gave up Christ for the pleasures of the world; I gave

up Christ for easy money; I gave up Christ for my profession and my job; I gave up Christ for the cheap, tawdry rewards of the world." When the judgment of God falls upon this world, if we are in it, if it is our love, our life, our lot, then the judgment falls upon us. No man ever goes to damnation except when he chooses to be lost and damned.

There is a choice for every man in this word "whosoever" in our text in Revelation 20:15. In my reading through exegetical studies where men strive to understand the meaning of the Apocalypse, I have found one explanation of why Satan is loosed in Revelation 20:7 after the Millennium. The explanation is most worthy of consideration. It is this: Every man who ever lived will have a choice as to whether he worships God or Satan, whether he chooses heaven or hell, whether he will give his life to Christ or invest it down here in the cheap, tawdry rewards of this world. In the period of that thousand year Millennium many think that there are those born who will never have been tempted and who will never have been tried by evil. But at the end of that period of time called the Millennium, Satan is loosed to go out to tempt the nations of the earth who number, the chapter says, "as the sands of the sea." These nations of people must decide for or against the Lord. God has purposed in His heart to people heaven with those who choose God, with those who love Christ, with those who bow in His presence and ask for the forgiveness of sin. And the man who does not bow, and the man who is too proud to kneel, and the man who is too self-righteous to confess his sins, and the man who thinks he is sufficient for death, and the man who thinks he is sufficient for the judgment, is going to have his choice. God says he will have his choice to become one of the "whosoevers" who believes and is saved or to become one of the "whosoevers" who refuses and is lost.

This "whosoever" in Revelation 20:15 is the same kind of a "whosoever" as is found in Revelation 22:17, "And whosoever will, let him [come]." It is the same "whosoever" found in John 3:16: ". . . that whosoever believeth in him should not perish, but have everlasting life." Oh, that men would turn to Christ and be saved! "It is appointed unto men once to die, and after this the judgment" (Hebrews 9:27). But Christ was once offered to bear the sins of many; and to us who look to him in hope, in forgiveness, in salvation, to us shall He appear the second time apart from sin, without sin, unto salvation. The "whosoevers" who reject are lost forever. "And whosoever was not found written in the Book of Life was cast into the lake of fire." "But whosoever will, let him come." "Let him be saved; let him choose me," saith the Lord. "Let him stand by me."

THE PLEA TO CONFESS CHRIST AS SAVIOUR

We must close. I point out one other thing in that choice for or against God. In this next chapter, Revelation 21:7, 8 it is written: "He that overcometh shall inherit all things; and I will be his God, and he shall be my son. But the fearful . . ." Is not that a strange word to be used here? "But the fearful . . . shall have their part in the lake which burneth with fire . . . which is the second death." What does God mean by that designation, "the fearful"? There are three Greek words that the Lord could use for "fear." One is *phobos*. Our English word "phobia" comes from it. It refers to fear in general, whether good or bad. There is another Greek word, *eulabeia*. It is always used in a good sense, as when a man fears the Lord. It refers to godly and pious fear. But the word used here is *deilia*, a word which is always used in a bad sense. It is used with reference to a cringing coward who refuses to take his stand. He will not come out for God. He will not stand up for Christ. God says that the *deilia*, the fearful, the cowardly who will not take a stand for Jesus will be cast into the judgment of the fires of condemnation.

The Holy Spirit pleads with lost men to look in saving faith to Jesus! Man, standing in the way of judgment, look to Jesus. Man, look to Jesus, give your heart and your life to Jesus. Bow in the presence of the Lord; ask Him to forgive your sins; ask Him to write your name in the Lamb's Book of Life; ask Him to save you in the day of judgment. Ask Him. Christ says that if we confess Him before men, He will confess us before God in heaven. Confess Him openly, confess Him publicly, where every man can see. When I baptize a convert, among other words I always say one thing and it is this: "Upon an open, unashamed confession of your faith in Jesus, I baptize you, my brother [sister], in the name of the Father and of the Son and of the Holy Spirit." God calls for an open confession of faith in Him, where everyone can see, where everyone can know. "Publicly and openly I confess my faith in Jesus, my Lord." Do it and you are saved. Whosoever will, let him come.

CHAPTER 9

THE NEW HEAVEN AND THE NEW EARTH

Revelation 21

1 And I saw a new heaven and a new earth: for the first heaven and the first earth were passed away; and there was no more sea.

2 And I John saw the holy city, new Jerusalem, coming down from God out of heaven, prepared as a bride adorned for her husband.

3 And I heard a great voice out of heaven saying, Behold, the tabernacle of God is with men, and he will dwell with them, and they shall be his people, and God himself shall be with them, and be their God.

4 And God shall wipe away all tears from their eyes; and there shall be no more death, neither sorrow, nor crying, neither shall there be any more pain: for the former things are passed away.

5 And he that sat upon the throne said, Behold, I make all things new. And he said unto me, Write: for these words are true and faithful.

6 And he said unto me, It is done. I am Alpha and Omega, the beginning and the end. I will give unto him that is athirst of the fountain of the water of life freely.

7 He that overcometh shall inherit all things; and I will be his God, and he shall be my son.

8 But the fearful, and unbelieving, and the abominable, and murderers, and whoremongers, and sorcerers, and idolaters, and all liars, shall have their part in the lake which burneth with fire and brimstone: which is the second death.

In our preaching through the Revelation we come to the last and the climactic vision, recorded in chapters 21 and 22. Revelation 21:1-8 describes the new heaven and the new earth. Revelation 21:9-22:5 describes the holy city of God, the New Jerusalem. Revelation 22:6-21 is the epilogue to the Apocalypse.

These passages in the Bible are so rich in meaning. The Word is illimitable. The wisdom and truth of God are unfathomable. I am like a diver who goes down into the depths of a southern sea to find pearls and gems on the floor of the ocean. And when I get down there I am overwhelmed by the profuse, vast treasures scattered all around me. Which jewel shall I take and which jewel shall I leave behind? What shall I place in this sermon, and what of those thousands of other things that I wish I had time even to mention? The riches of God in Christ Jesus are past finding out, much less capable of being exhausted by being exegeted, homiletized and preached on. Oh, this rich, incomparably glorious Word of God!

The text speaks of the re-creation: "And I saw a new heaven and a new earth: for the first heaven and the first earth were passed away; and there was no more sea. And I John saw the holy city, new Jerusalem, coming down from God out of heaven, prepared as a bride adorned for her husband. And I heard a great voice out of heaven saying, Behold, [Greek original — the *skene*, the dwelling-place] the tabernacle of God is with men, and he will [Greek original — *skenoo*, cast his tent] dwell with us and they shall be his people, and God himself shall be with them and be their God." This is the new, redeemed creation.

THREE NEW THINGS MADE BY THE HAND OF GOD

The passage presents three new things made by the hand of God: "I saw a new heaven and I saw a new earth . . . And I John saw the holy city, new Jerusalem." The first new thing is a new heaven. The Bible speaks of three heavens. The first heaven is the atmospheric world around us, the heaven through which the birds fly and the clouds float. The second heaven described in the Bible is the heaven of the starry spheres, the milky way, the sidereal universes, all that you see when you stand at night under the blue firmament of the sky. The third heaven is the heaven of heavens. It is the throne and the dwelling place of God.

When the Bible says there is to be a new heaven, it refers, certainly, to the heaven immediately above us, the heaven of the atmosphere, the heaven that bring storms and fury, the heaven of lightning and thunder, the heaven of the lowering, swarming clouds. There is to be a new atmospheric heaven above us. I think the new heaven also includes the heaven of the starry skies, for in that universe beyond us there are stars that have turned to cinders and solar systems that have become ashes. In the re-creation of God, the whole universe above us will be remade in primeval, primordial and pristine glory. I have not the mind that could imagine what God will do in the firmament in the remaking under His hand. To me now, as with the psalmist, when I stand and look at the workmanship of God,every piece and part of that infinite chalice declares the glory of our great Creator. What shall it be when God redeems it, renovates it and makes it new? Its supernal splendor will be beyond what mind could imagine or tongue could describe. That is the promise of God. John, therefore, begins the chapter by saying, "I saw a new heaven."

The Apostle continues the description: "And I saw a new earth." The miseries of this present earth in its deep and dark apostasy from God are seen and felt everywhere. This earth is blighted and cursed. The desert places that are burned and seared, the floods that wash our villages and cities away, the earthquakes that tear down the handiwork of man, the diseases and death that waste the very life of the race, these are but evidences of the wages of sin. But this earth is to experience a redemption and a rejuvenation. No longer will it be torn by hooks and irons in order that it yield its increase and its fruit. No longer will it be infested with thistles and thorns and briars. No longer will it be cut into graves and plotted into cemeteries. No longer will its soil be moistened by showers of human tears. No longer will it be stained with the crimson of human blood. No longer will its highways bear the processions of those who are brokenhearted and bereaved. There is to be a new, redeemed world. It is to be a paradise regained, an Eden restored, the whole beautiful creation of God remade and rebuilt. "And I saw a new earth . . ."

"And I John saw the holy city, new Jerusalem." John saw a capital city made by the glorious workmanship of our infinite Lord. In the new creation God is to build a new heavenly city as a center for God's government and God's people and God's dwelling place. In Revelation 18:1-24, there was described for us the city Babylon, the ultimate work of the hands of men, built in defiance and in blasphemy against God. But this city will reflect the glory of the Lamb, a new, heavenly, capital city for God.

Oh, what marvelous wonders God purposes for His people! In the nature of the fall in Eden, man was dispossessed of all God intended for him. It was the purpose of God that he should have dominion over the height above and the depth below and the vast world around him. But sin cursed this dream and damned the life of the man . By the laborious sweat of his brow in a world of death and misery, he lives his life until he goes back to the dust of the ground out of which he was made. This is the curse of sin in the earth. But as far as sin destroyed, just that far does redemption go. Because of sin man has been dispossessed from his rightful dominion, but in grace God will restore to man the lost creation. Whatever sin has touched and destroyed, God will redeem and cleanse. If redemption does not go as far as the curse of the sin, then God has failed. But whatever the extent of the consequences of our fall, just so shall be the extensiveness of our redemption. However sin has wasted, God's grace will abound in glorious regeneration and renovation. There will be a new heaven, a new earth and a new city.

Not Annihilation but Renovation

When John says, "I saw a new heaven and a new earth: for the [old] first heaven and the [old] first earth were passed away," does John mean that the old, first heaven and the old, first earth were annihilated, that they entered into extinction and nothingness, that they were swept into non-existence? Is that what he means? Does John mean that the heaven above us is destroyed and this planet on which we live is swept away and God creates another heaven and another earth? Is that what John means? Or, does he mean that it is the same heaven renovated and redeemed and that it is the same earth purified and regenerated? What does he mean? I have a very definite persuasion from the Word of God and it is this: I think this earth is our home forever and forever into the ages of the ages. I think the heavens and the earth are everlasting, I think they were here before sin entered in. I think the heavens above us and the earth beneath us will be here after they are swept clean of the curse that has wasted them. I think this new heaven and this new earth is a redeemed and regenerated heaven and a redeemed and a regenerated earth, the one I see above me and the one I see below and around me. This "new" of which John speaks is a redemption, a regeneration.

Now, why do I think that? First, because of the meaning of certain Greek verbs in describing these great revelations. Turn to the last verse of the Book of Matthew: "And, lo, I am with you alway, even unto the end of the world." What does that mean, "the end of the world"? There are three Greek words translated in our English Bible "world." One is *ge*. *Ge* is the Greek word for "earth," "ground," this terrestrial globe. That Greek word appears in the first syllable of our word "geography," "geophysics." A second Greek word translated "world" is *kosmos*. The primary meaning of *kosmos* is "adornment," "embellishment." The word "cosmetics" comes from that word *kosmos*. When the ancient Greeks looked at the well-ordered universe, they began to apply the word "adornment," "embellishment," to God's beautiful creation and they began to call it the *kosmos*. Eventually they used the word to refer to the well-ordered, cultured civilization of man, the world of man's civilized life. The third Greek word that is translated "world" is *aion*. The word has been taken wholly into English and comes out in our language "aeon." *Aion* in the Greek language first was used to refer to an indefinite period of time. Then it began to be used to refer to an era, to a dispensation, to an order of things. This is the word used when you find in the Bible the expression "the end of the world." Never is the word *ge* used, "the end of the ground, the earth, the terrestrial planet on which we live." Always the word used is *aion*, "the end of the age," "the end of the dispensation," "the end of this order of things." The Lord said, for example, in the passage in Matthew 28:20: "Lo, I am with you alway, even to the consummation of the age." When history finally reaches its ultimate denouement, Christ will still be with us, even "to the end of time and history." So the expression, "end of the world," used in the Bible does not connotate the end of this terrestrial globe.

There is another Greek word we must consider. Revelation 21:1 says: "For the first heaven and the first earth were *parerchomai* [translated here 'passed away']." That word is often used in the New Testament. In Mark 13:31, for example, the Lord said: "Heaven and earth shall *parerchomai*." What does the Lord mean when He says: "Heaven and earth shall *parerchomai*"? The first, original, primary meaning of the word is not extinction and annihilation. Rather it referred to a change from one place or kind or situation to another. For example, a ship would *parerchomai* through the sea; that is, pass through the sea over the horizon. But it does not refer to the extinction and annihilation of the ship. The ship just passes over the horizon. It is not seen any more. Or, as a man *parerchomai* through the door, he goes outside and I cannot see him anymore. But it does not refer to his extinction, to his annihilation. So it is with this word in its primary meaning. When John says the first heaven and the first earth *parerchomai*, "passed away," the apostle does not mean that they became extinct, but rather that they changed from one condition to another. The word *erchomai* means to pass from this place, in location from here to there, in condition from this to that. So when John says, "I saw a new heaven and a new earth: for the first heaven and the first earth *parerchomai*," the apostle means it underwent a tremendous change, a vast renovation. The heaven is still here and the earth is still here, but they are changed, redeemed and regenerated under the hand of Almighty God.

Let us look at this interpretation from the viewpoint of what God's Word says concerning the end time. Turn to II Peter 3:6: "Whereby the world that then was, being overflowed with water, perished." Peter is talking about, possibly, Noah's flood. In the days of the terrible flood, the *kosmos*, the civilized order of man, overflowing with waters, perished. The cities were destroyed, the villages were wiped away, everything that had breath in nostrils died. The whole fashion of that civilized order and culture in the days of Noah ceased to exist. "Whereby the world that then was, being overflowed with water, perished." But the earth did not perish, the planet did not cease to exist, this world did not undergo annihilation. Yet Peter says, "The world overflowing with water, perished." The *kosmos*, the order of civilized mankind perished, but not the terrestrial earth.

Let us look at the next thing Peter says. The apostle is going to speak of this ultimate judgment of God described in our text in the Revelation: "But the heavens and the earth, which are now, by the same word [of Almighty God] are kept in store, reserved unto fire [the cleansing fire, the rejuvenating fire, the purging fire] against the day of judgment and perdition of ungodly men." When is that cleansing to take place? Peter here says that that great, final renovation and purging by fire will be in the day of the judgment and perdition of ungodly men. In Revelation 20:11 we read: "And I saw a great white throne, and him that sat on it, from whose face the earth and the heaven fled away; and there was found no place for them. And I saw the dead, small and great, stand before God; . . . and [they] were judged . . . and whosoever was not found written in the book of life was cast into the lake of fire." That is the day of Judgment of ungodly men. "And in that day," John says, "I saw the [old] heaven and the [old] earth flee away." The day of fire, the day of purging, the day of renovation is the day of the judgment of ungodly men. In the language of Simon Peter, the first world perished, but not the terrestrial earth. So the same judgment described by the Apostle John will be no different. The judgment will be a rejuvenation, not the annihilation of this earth. The two passages in Peter and in John refer to the same event.

THE GLORIOUS PALINGENESIS, THE REGENERATION

Let us look again. In Matthew 19:28 we read: "Jesus said unto them, Verily I say unto you, That ye which have followed me, in the regeneration [*palig genesia*] when the Son of man shall sit in the throne of his glory, . . ." We have taken that Greek word *palig genesia*, "the remaking," "the rebirth," "the regeneration," syllable by syllable, into the English language. It becomes our word — "palingenesis." A "palingenesis" is a rebirth, a re-creation, a renovation, a remaking. Jesus referred to the regeneration, the *palig genesia*, the palingenesis of this earth, in Matthew 19:28.

In Romans 8:19 Paul describes that *palig genesia*, that palingenesis, that renovation of the earth, in one of the grandest passages of all literature and one of the most meaningful promises to be found in the Word of God. "For the earnest expectation of the creation waiteth for the manifestation of the sons of God. For the creature was made subject [to futility and to emptiness] to vanity." The earth was cursed, wasted, destroyed. All of God's creation was ruined in sin. This earth — look at it! Our humanity — look at it! Childhood, youth, manhood, age — look at them! Even the stars burn out. The vegetable world is cursed, the animal world is cursed, the whole creation is made subject to futility and despair. "Not willingly" — the creation did not choose to fall into ruin, "but because of him" — because the Lord God allowed the creation to fall in preparation for a greater redemption yet to come, "in hope." "Because the creature itself also shall be delivered from the bondage of corruption into the glorious liberty of the children of God. For we know that the whole creation groaneth and travaileth in pain together until now." When the animal world gives birth, it gives birth in suffering and many times in death. Cursed, it groans and travails in pain even until now. The animal world is also so largely carnivorous. It lives off blood and the tearing of fang and claw. The animal world is a cursed world that groans and travails in pain. And not only the animal world, but "we ourselves also, which have the firstfruits of the Spirit, even we ourselves groan within ourselves, waiting for the adoption, namely, the redemption of our body." Our human world is filled with disappointment, bereavement, death, pain and tears. But in the regeneration, in the *palig genesia,* there is to be a remaking of the whole creation of God, the animal world, the vegetable world, the planetary world, the astronomical world, everything that God has created, that sin has cursed, God will remake. It is hard for us to realize that. Some day the lamb will lie down with the wolf; the leopard and the kid will dwell together; the child will put his hand on the cockatrice's den and play by the hole of an asp. No one will hurt or destroy in all God's holy mountain. Think of it! It is beyond imagination, what God shall do in the *palig genesia.*

But we are not done yet. Let us look at another thing. We are speaking of the fact that God is to rejuvenate this present creation. He is not going to destroy it, annihilate it, sweep it into nothingness and extinction, but God is going to re-create this present world in which we live. Our eternal home will be here. Turn to II Corinthians 5:1: "For we know [we who are saved and believe in Jesus] that if our earthly house of this tabernacle were dissolved [if this house in which I live turns back to the dust of the ground and it is dissolved], we have a building of God, an house not made with hands, eternal in the heavens. For in this we groan [in illness, senility, age and finally death], earnestly desiring to be clothed upon with our house which is from heaven." Now, what is that? Paul is speaking of the resurrection of the body, "this house." But if there is no identity and continuity between this body and that house God will make for me, then the resurrection has no meaning whatsoever. It is no resurrection if this house in which I now live turns back to the dust and God raises up something else. A resurrection refers to the raising up of *this* body. That is what resurrection is. The power of God that raised Jesus from the dead is to raise us also.

When the Lord was raised, He was the same Lord Jesus. Jesus said to Thomas: "Look at these scars in my hands, look at them. Put your finger in them. Put forth your hand and thrust it into the great, gaping scar in my side and be not faithless but believing that it is I myself." (See John 20:27.) That is resurrection. It is the raising out of the dust of the ground, out of the depths of the sea, this body that is planted in the heart of the earth. That is the very heart of the Christian faith and the Christian hope. Let us read again and with new appreciation and understanding I Corinthians 15:50-52: "This I say, brethren, that flesh and blood cannot inherit the kingdom of God . . . Behold, I show you a mystery; we shall not all sleep [we may not all die], but we shall all be changed, In a moment, in the twinkling of an eye, at the last trump: for the trumpet shall sound, and the dead in Christ shall be raised incorruptible, and we shall all be changed." Changed, resurrected, rejuvenated, the *palig genesia*. Not I, someone else, raised from the dead; not I, someone different, brought to life; but I, me, myself, made like unto the image of my glorious Lord. Now, I am marking by comparison that if God does that for this house, this body in which I live, the same body and the same house, remade and regenerated, if God does that for this body, that is exactly what God means when He refers to a *palig genesia* for His creation. It will be the same earth and the same heaven, only remade, washed, cleansed, purified, redeemed. However deep the curse has gone, just so mighty will God's able power regenerate and remake.

THIS EARTH OUR HEAVENLY HOME

As for me, I like the prospect of our home being forever on this earth. I would not look forward to God's sentencing me out on some planet a hundred million miles away that I know nothing about. I like almost everything here. The only things I do not like are the tears, the separation of bereavement in the funerals and the graves so ever open and empty and the heartache and despair they bring. Just think how it will be when there are no more funerals, no more telephones ringing, saying "Our little boy has just died," or "Our little girl has been run over by a car," or "I have just been told that my husband has leukemia." No more agonizing pleas asking God to give us strength for the trials that lie ahead. There will be no more of that. The new world will be filled with gladness and glory, with strength and health.

We shall break bread together in that new and happy land; we shall dine together world without end. You say that is material? Well, who invented eating? God must like it! God invented it and He says we are going to eat in heaven. The resurrected Jesus said, "Do you have anything here to eat?" They gave Him a broiled fish and a honeycomb and He did eat before them. (Read Luke 24:36-43.) This is the same blessed Lord Jesus. He is the One who said we are going to eat in the kingdom of God, at the banquet of the marriage supper of the Lamb. I like everything about it. That is what God is going to do for us. Oh, the goodness of God!

May I make one other observation? You will find in the promises of the Book that God says we are to inherit this earth. Out of a group of Scriptures I choose the passage in Psalm 37:9: "They that wait upon the Lord, they shall inherit the earth." Then verse 11: "But the meek shall inherit the earth." Jesus was repeating that promise in Matthew 5:5: "Blessed are

the meek, for they shall inherit the earth." Then verse 29 in
Psalm 37: "The righteous shall inherit the land, and dwell
therein for ever." These are just typical of the promises of
God regarding this world. The righteous people of God are to
inherit the earth, this very terrestrial globe on which we now
stand, a world regenerated, renewed.

CHAPTER 10

WHEN GOD WIPES AWAY OUR TEARS

Revelation 21

> 4 And God shall wipe away all tears from their eyes; and there shall be no more death, neither sorrow, nor crying, neither shall there be any more pain: for the former things are passed away.
> 5 And he that sat upon the throne said, Behold, I make all things new. And he said unto me, Write: for these words are true and faithful.
> 6 And he said unto me, It is done. I am Alpha and Omega, the beginning and the end. I will give unto him that is athirst of the fountain of the water of life freely.
> 7 He that overcometh shall inherit all things; and I will be his God, and he shall be my son.

Just to read the text is a benediction to our souls. It is a comfort to God's saints in our pilgrimage through this weary world.

Contrary to everything I had thought, I had supposed that when I came to prepare these sermons on heaven they would be the easiest of all of the discourses I would deliver. I have found it just the opposite. In my studying for this message, I came across this sentence from a world-famed expositor: "Out of all of the subjects in the Bible, the most difficult to speak on is the subject of heaven." That is so different from anything I had supposed. I thought the middle chapters in the Revelation would be hard, but when I came to the last chapters and the subject of heaven, I thought the sermons would be easy to prepare. This is not so. Heaven is a most difficult subject to preach about.

The vast difficulty in describing heaven is illustrated in the utterances of the men of God who have written the Bible. For example, the Apostle Paul says, as he describes his celestial experience in II Corinthians 12:1-4, that he was taken up into Paradise, into the third heaven, the heaven of heavens where God dwells. Can Paul describe his experience? Does he say what he heard and what he saw? No. All the apostle says is this: That having been taken up into the paradise of God, into the third heaven, he heard words that are unspeakable and that are not lawful for a man to utter. Weak language could not bear the weight of the glory he experiences, nor could sentence and syllable say the words that he heard. We have another like illustration of this inability to describe the glory of the Lord in the experience of Moses who asked of Jehovah that he might behold His glory. And the Lord said to Moses: "You come and stand by me on this rock and in the cleft of the rock I will hide you and cover you with my hand until my glory shall pass by. Then I shall take away my hand and you can see my backpart but no man can see my face and live." How would a mortal describe the presence of God and how could he enter into the glory of the great Jehovah? For no man can look upon God's face and live. We have another human inability to enter into the glories of the other world in I Corinthians 2:9: "Eye hath not seen, nor ear heard, neither have entered into the heart of man, the things which God hath prepared for them that love him." We cannot enter into it. Our spirits, our very minds and souls, cannot imagine it, this creation that God calls our heavenly and eternal home. But in the next verse, in I Corinthians 2:10, Paul says: "But God hath revealed them unto us by his Spirit." These things that eye cannot see and ear cannot hear and heart cannot imagine, God has revealed to us by His Spirit. Paul is saying that there is a language of the soul, there are eyes of faith, and we can feel these things, we can sense these things and we can experience these things, even though we cannot describe them in language, much less adequately present them in a sermon.

We find that difficulty of describing the glories of heaven (and preparing a sermon commensurate with what God has prepared for us) illustrated here in what John has written in the text: "And I heard a great voice out of heaven saying, Behold, the tabernacle [Greek, *skene*, 'dwelling place'] of God is with men, and he will dwell [Greek, *skenoo*, 'tabernacle'] with them." The dwelling place, the pavilion, the house of the Lord will be visibly with us. How can we imagine that? By what language can we describe the very pavilion of the Lord, the tabernacle, the tent of God, set up among men? In days past the Lord tabernacled with us. The Lord dwelt with our parents in the Garden of Eden. He walked with them, talked with them, visited them. God tabernacled with the patriarchs. He spoke to Abraham as a man would talk to his friend, face to face. The Lord cast His tabernacle among the children of Israel and His presence was seen among them, a pillar of fire by night and a cloud by day. In the days of the temple, the Lord dwelt in the darkness of the Holy of Holies. In the gospel of John (John 1:14), the author of this Revelation says: "And the Word was made flesh and dwelt among us [*skenoo*, 'tabernacled,' the same and identical word used in our text here in Revelation 21:3], (and we beheld his glory, the glory as of the only begotten of the Father)." The Lord tabernacles today in His Church and lives in our hearts by the Holy Spirit. But how shall it be and with what words could we describe it, when God Himself shall live in our midst and our eyes shall see Him, our ears shall hear Him and we shall behold the glory and beauty of the Lord God Jehovah? We cannot say those words; we cannot describe those realities. There is a sensitivity of the soul that can enter in by faith, but a man cannot preach about it in the reality that it is. The assignment is beyond him, whatever poetry he might quote or whatever song he might sing or however eloquent perorations by which he might seek to describe the infinite, celestial, unimaginable glories of the dwelling of God among us.

We find that struggle to describe the indescribable in the passage beginning here in Revelation 21:1 of the re-establishment, the redemption, the rebirth, the regeneration of this universe. "I saw a new heaven and a new earth, for the first heaven and the first earth were passed away; and there was no more sea." "And there was no more sea." What does that mean in this new creation of God, "and there was no more sea"? A spiritualizer would say that the text refers to the tearing down of all political, national, social barriers; that it is a prophecy of the common brotherhood of all the families and nations of the world. A symbolizer would say that the text refers to the fact that John is trying to say for us that in heaven there is no more separation. There is a basis for this interpretation. The symbolizer, a man who sees in the Revelation symbols of great spiritual truth, has a place in our midst. For example, when the Revelation speaks of "the Lamb of God," we know that is a symbol of our blessed Redeemer, the Lord Jesus. A man who sees in the language of the Revelation symbols of spiritual realities could easily understand the verse, "and there was no more sea," to be a symbol of the fact that there will be no more separation. John was on a lonely isle in exile, sent there to die of starvation and exposure. Across the waste of the sea were those he loved, the church at Ephesus, all the friends and the saints of the household of faith. The dark sea rolled in between. I can see how, as a symbol, John could say that in glory there will be no more exile and no more separation. There is certainly a dark sea that rolls between time and eternity. There is a dark river of death, a flood that rolls between us and our loved ones gone before. But in heaven "there will be no more sea." I can see how, symbolically, John might mean that there is no more separation between us and our loved friends and family. We shall be together in the other world, world without end, in God's holy and heavenly tomorrow. I can understand that.

What do I think it means, "And there shall be no more sea"? One of two things. The lesser possibility of the two, I think is this: The passage could refer to the annihilation of the seas. There will be no more bodies of water in heaven, in the new creation. That is possible. However, I am persuaded (and this is just something of intuitive response) that what that verse actually means is the same kind of a thing that is meant when John refers to the new heaven and the new earth. John is not saying, in my understanding, that there is going to be an annihilation of what God has already done in His creative majesty. The glorious firmament and the paradise of the Lord in the earth were here before sin and the curse came. God says they will still be here when the curse is taken away. They are to be a redeemed earth, a redeemed heaven. There will be a regenerated creation with sin, Satan and the curse cast out. God promises to make the world new, beautiful and lovely for us.

Now, I have the same feeling about the great sea. One of the reasons I feel that way is because to an ancient (those who lived in John's day) the sea was a frightful, a fearsome and an awesome monster. They had no compasses, for example, and when the cloudy day came, their ships were absolutely lost on the vast bosom of the deep. Their frail barks were subject to destruction before the face of those fearful storms that did suddenly arise. The loss of life in the sea was beyond measure, innumerable. To the ancient the sea was a horrible monster, a fearsome and an awesome enemy. But when God makes the new heaven and the new earth, life will be as the psalmist said: "He maketh me to lie down in green pastures [in the paradise of God], and leadeth me beside the still waters." No more angry, turbulent, fearsome disasters on the surface of the deep — "still waters." God has made it new, and the sea as we know it, with its tempestuous, raging, mountainous and destructive waves, is no more. In its place are the still waters beside which God will shepherd His holy and heavenly flock. Those are just some things I feel in my heart as I read the Book. I have already told you I cannot describe it nor can I enter into it fully. We will just have to wait and see in God's time.

John now writes a beautiful thing. "And God shall wipe away all tears from their eyes; and there shall be no more death, neither sorrow, nor crying, neither shall there be any more pain: for the former things are passed away." I can know from this passage, then, that as long as we are in this life, tears will be in our eyes. Until we come to the gate of heaven itself, God's people will know how to cry. We may forget how to laugh, but we will never forget how to cry. Not until we enter the New Jerusalem will God wipe away the tears from our eyes. Our pilgrimage in this world is like the pilgrimage of the children of Israel to the Promised Land. We are delivered in the grace of God from so much of the hurt and trial of the journey, but we are not delivered from the heartaches, diseases and afflictions of this life. Suffering is a common denominator and the experience of all of God's people. Even Jesus wept. He bowed His head in sorrow, in strong crying and tears. He poured out His soul unto God. Several times Paul speaks of his tears. As long as we are in this pilgrimage and until we come to the gates of glory, God's people will know how to cry. It is only there, beyond the pearly gates and the jasper walls, that the Lord will wipe away our tears.

There is another encouraging thing to be said about this passage before we look at the actual words themselves. We are not to forget, in our earthly pilgrimage with its burdens and trials, its losses and its crosses, that our crying and bereavement yield for God's people a marvelous and heavenly reward on the other side of the river. For example, Paul says in II Corinthians 4:17: "For our light affliction [the sorrow and the burden of our life in this world Paul calls a light affliction], which is but for a moment, worketh for us a far more exceeding and eternal weight of glory." Paul says the things we suffer down here, the agony, the tears, the burden, the heartache and the disappointment of our lives, work for us a far more and exceeding weight of glory. Here again, how do we put the reality in language? The more we suffer, the more heaven will mean to us.

Spurgeon once said a most unusual thing. I recall it when I think of our innate desire to escape suffering and death. Spurgeon said: "If I had my choice between being raptured at the coming of the Lord and taken up into glory and changed in a moment, in the twinkling of an eye, at the last trump; if I had my choice between being raptured to the Lord and dying and being resurrected, I would choose to die in the agonies of death, for," said the great preacher, "my Saviour suffered and died and only through this did He experience the power of God in His resurrection." He continued: "I would like to experience the suffering of my Lord, the pangs of death, to die and to be buried that I also might experience the power of the resurrection of God as He raises me up unto glory." That is a tremendous thing to say and so different from anything I had ever thought. I have always thought, "O Lord, to be raptured! to be here when Jesus comes!" As the song sings:

Oh, joy! oh, delight! should we go without dying,
No sickness, no sadness, no dread and no crying,
Caught up thro' the clouds with our Lord into glory,
When Jesus receives His own.

I have always felt like that. I never had thought about the experience Spurgeon describes, to suffer as the Lord suffered, to die as the Lord died, to be buried as the Lord was buried, that I might know the power of His resurrection. If we are to be like our Lord, we must suffer. Our Lord suffered. He was called a man of sorrows and acquainted with grief. Our Lord suffered and if we also suffer we are that much like Him. Paul said in II Corinthians 1:5: "For as the sufferings of Christ abound in us, so our consolation also aboundeth by Christ."

True consolation is like this: God says that heaven is a place where there are no more tears. What would that mean to someone who had never cried? What would the promise, "God shall wipe away our tears," mean to someone who had never wept? God says there shall be no more death. What would that mean to someone who had never stood by an open grave, had never seen someone he loved like his own soul laid beneath the sod? "And there shall be no more sorrow." What would that mean to someone who had never bowed under the weight of care? "Nor crying, nor pain . . ." It is because we have known these things in this life that heaven is sweet. So "our light affliction," says Paul, "which is but for a moment, worketh for us a far more exceeding and eternal weight of glory." That is what heaven is. Having suffered here, wept here, cried in agony here and died here, we shall find heaven God's release from this bondage of tears and death.

Let us follow the text word by word. "And God shall wipe away all tears from their eyes." The story of this world is a story of bereavement. Jesus wept with Mary and Martha at the tomb of their brother. Here in this earth is misfortune and poverty, as Lazarus was laid at the door of Dives. Here in this world of woe is lamentation like the cry of Jeremiah, "Oh that my head were waters, and mine eyes a fountain of tears, that I might weep day and night for the slain of the daughter of my people" (9:1). Here are despair, agony and disappointment. But God purposes some better thing for His people. All our tears will be wiped away.

"And there shall be no more death." Can you conceive of a world without the scythe and the stroke, without the dreadsome visit of the pale horseman? A world in which "there shall be no more death"? There is no home without its shadow. In the circle of every family, a mother or a wife or a husband or a daughter or a son or a friend is gone.

> There is no flock, however watched and tended,
> But one dead lamb is there!
> There is no fireside, howsoe'er defended,
> But has one vacant chair.
> —Henry W. Longfellow, "Resignation"

In a cemetery plot in another state there is a little grave with a little inscription on the headstone. It is the grave of my baby sister, who died before I was born. I suppose this is the first time I have ever referred to it in my life. I have wondered what she will be like in heaven? That little baby girl. Does she grow? Is she still a child? There is so much that is not revealed to us, so much of which we are not told. But God has revealed this much, that there are no stonecutters chiseling epitaphs in glory. There are no wreaths on the mansion doors in the sky. There are no graves on the hillsides of heaven. There are no obituary columns in the newspapers. There are no funeral processions over the streets of gold. The whole creation echoes with the glad and triumphant refrain of God's holy redeemed when they sing, "Death is swallowed up in victory." "And there shall be no more death." Death, an enemy, the last and the final one, is cast with the false prophet and Satan into the lake of fire.

"And there shall be no . . . sorrow, nor crying, neither shall there be any more pain." Sorrow follows us like a shadow. Every heart knows its bitterness. How many pillows at night are wet with the teardrops that this world never sees and never knows, known and seen only by our Lord. Sorrow, sorrow! We had a great preacher in this pulpit. He held a revival meeting here. From the days of my teen-age boyhood I loved that marvelous, wonderful man. While here in the revival, he began telling me about the days of his childhood. He was a mountain boy. His father was killed when he was a little boy. His stepfather was vile and vicious. One day at the breakfast table the stepfather picked up, in anger, the plate of biscuits that displeased him and threw the plate into the face of his mother. He cursed her. He doubled up his fist and beat her. He then strode away from their mountain cabin. The little boy went over to the side of his mother and said, "Mother, let's leave, let's leave. I don't know how, but I'll make a living for you. Mother, let's leave." The mother replied: "Son, not so. There has never been a separation in our family, never. And son, I shall not live long. Soon I'll be with the Lord Jesus. God take care of you, my boy." And according to this intuitive knowing that God revealed to her, she died soon after. The little boy went to live in the city and according to the prayers of his mother, he was saved in the city and became the preacher that I loved and admired so much. Sorrow, sorrow. Grief and disappointment, sorrow and crying. These shall be no more. God shall wipe away all tears from our eyes.

"And he that sat upon the throne said, Behold, I make all things new." New, perfect, all things "new." A new heaven, a new earth, a new city. We shall dwell in a Jerusalem that shall never be stormed; we shall bask in a sun that shall never go down; we shall swim in a tide that shall never ebb; we shall eat from a tree that shall never wither; we shall drink at a river that shall never go dry. "I make all things new."

> I will sing you a song of that beautiful land,
> The far away home of the soul,
> Where no storms ever beat on the glittering strand,
> While the years of eternity roll.

The author of that hymn believed that there would be a new creation by the still waters, where God's people dwell together in glory world without end. He continued with these words:

> Oh, how sweet it will be in that beautiful land,
> So free from all sorrow and pain.
> With songs on our lips and with harps in our hands,
> To greet one another again.

"And God shall wipe away all tears from their eyes; and there shall be no more death, neither sorrow, nor crying, neither shall there be any more pain: for the former things are passed away. And he that sat upon the throne said, Behold, I make all things new." Oh, blessed be God for His goodness, immeasurable, indescribable, unfathomable. We praise His name forever.

CHAPTER 11

THE HEAVENLY CITY OF GOD

Revelation 21:9 - 22:5

There should be no chapter division between Revelation 21:27 and 22:1. Revelation 22:1-5 are the concluding verses of chapter 21. Beginning at verse 6 in chapter 22, John writes an epilogue to the book. The visions, however, close at Revelation 22:5. This message is an exposition of the concluding vision of the Apocalypse, Revelation 21:9 - 22:5. In this vision John sees the holy city, the New Jerusalem. He describes it first from the outside as he saw it descend out of heaven; then he describes it from the inside as though he entered within the gate of the city.

This is the description of the outside, recorded in verse 9 to the first half of verse 21: "And there came unto me one of the seven angels . . . and talked with me, saying, Come hither, I will shew the the bride, the Lamb's wife. And he carried me away in the spirit to a great and high mountain, and shewed me that great city, the holy Jerusalem, descending out of heaven from God, Having the glory of God: and her light was like unto a stone most precious, even like a jasper [*iaspis*] stone, clear as crystal." I think the *iaspis* stone (A.V. "jasper") is a diamond. All of these stones named here in the Revelation are Greek words spelled out in the English language. We just suppose that they are this and this and this. But I think that "*iaspis* stone" (when translated into English it is pronounced "jasper") is a diamond. Every description I find of it in the Revelation is like that of a diamond. Our modern "jasper" is not clear as crystal. But a diamond is, and it has the glory of the fire of God in its heart.

124

The description continues, "And had a wall great and high, and had twelve gates, and at the gates twelve angels, and names written thereon, which are the names of the twelve tribes of the children of Israel: On the east three gates; on the north three gates; on the south three gates; and on the west three gates. And the wall of the city had twelve foundations, and in them the names of the twelve apostles of the Lamb. And he that talked with me had a golden reed to measure the city, and the gates thereof, and the wall thereof. And the city lieth foursquare, and the length is as large as the breadth: and he measured the city with the reed, twelve thousand furlongs. The length and the breadth and the height of it are equal. And he measured the wall thereof, an hundred and forty and four cubits, according to the measure of a man, that is of the angel." The angel used man's measure even though the reed was in his own hand. The measure is true for men and true for angels, true for the redeemed of earth and true for the hosts of heaven. "And the building of the wall of it was of jasper [diamond]: and the city was pure gold, like unto clear glass. And the foundations of the wall of the city were garnished with all manner of precious stones. The first foundation was jasper; the second, sapphire; the third, a chalcedony; the fourth, an emerald; the fifth, sardonyx; the sixth, sardius; the seventh, chrysolyte; the eighth, beryl; the ninth, a topaz; the tenth, a chrysoprasus; the eleventh, a jacinth; the twelfth, an amethyst. And the twelve gates were twelve pearls; every several gate was of one pearl."

We are now going inside the city. John has described it from the outside as he saw it descending from God out of heaven, an amazing array of light, beauty and wonder. Now he comes to the gate, enters into the city, and describes what is inside. "And the street of the city was pure gold, as it were transparent glass. And I saw no temple therein; for the Lord God Almighty and the Lamb are the temple of it. And the city had no need of the sun, neither of the moon, to shine in it: for the glory of God did lighten it, and the Lamb is the light thereof. And the nations of them who are saved shall walk in the light of it: and the kings of the earth do bring their glory and honour into it. And the gates of it shall not be shut at all by day: for there shall be no night there. And they shall bring the glory and honour of the nations into it. And there shall in no wise enter into it any thing that defileth, neither whatsoever worketh abomination, or maketh a lie: but they which are written in the Lamb's book of life. And he shewed me a pure river of water of life, clear as crystal, proceeding out of the throne of God and of the Lamb. In the midst of the street of it, and on either side of the river, was there the tree of life, which bare twelve manner of fruits, and yielded her fruit every month: and the leaves of the tree were for the healing of the nations. And there shall be no more curse: but the throne of God and of the Lamb shall be in it; and his servants shall serve him: And they shall see his face; and his name shall be in their foreheads. And there shall be no night there; and they need no candle, neither light of the sun; for the Lord God giveth them light; and they shall reign for ever and ever." Thus the vision ends. In the remaining verses of chapter 22, John writes an epilogue, a benediction, an affirmation, an authentication. Thus God's Holy Word is closed.

The beautiful, heavenly, holy city of God — what a delightful, glad, glorious prospect! What a precious revelation is this wonder John saw when he looked upon the city descending out of heaven. "And there came unto one of the angels . . . and talked with me, saying, Come hither, I will shew thee the bride, the Lamb's wife." And when he looked upon the bride, he saw a city, a New Jerusalem in contrast to the old. So our eternal home is a city, real and actual. It is called the bride, the Lamb's wife, because of those who inhabit it. The Lamb's wife is to live in a golden city whose builder and maker is God.

The bride is the Church of our Lord. But the city is also the home of the redeemed of all time. In the city are not only the saved in the fellowship of Christ's Church, but also her attendants, her friends and those who are invited to the marriage supper of the Lamb. Remember Revelation 19:7-9: "Be glad and rejoice . . . for the marriage of the Lamb is come, and his wife hath made herself ready." The wife is the Church, the bride of the blessed Lord Jesus. But not only is she there — the Church taken out of His side, born out of the suffering and the crimson of our Saviour — not only is she there, but other guests are present. We read in Revelation 19:9: "Blessed are they which are called unto the marriage supper of the Lamb." Not only is there a wedding when the bride of Christ is presented to Jesus, but there is also a marriage supper to which guests are invited. Some of the friends of the bridegroom are men like John the Baptist, a saint who never lived to be a part of Christ's Church, a prophet, who was in no sense a part of the bride of Christ. Men like John the Baptist died in the old dispensation. But, lest someone think they might be less blessed, there is a special beatitude for them: "Blessed are they also [those beside the bride who is being married to the Lamb], who are called to the wedding supper, the marriage supper of the Lamb." So in that beautiful city there is not only the bride of Christ, but there are also her attendants and her friends, the guests called to the marriage feast, all of the saints of the old dispensation. Even our Lord said, "Many shall come from the east and west, and shall sit down with Abraham, and Isaac, and Jacob, in the kingdom of heaven" (Matthew 8:11). So when we come to live in that beautiful city of God, we shall see not only those who have been saved in this age and in this dispensation, the bride of the Lamb, but we shall see also those who have been converted and saved from the days of Abel to the last martyr slain by Antichrist. All of God's redeemed saints will live in that beautiful and holy city.

We find an affirmation of this truth, that the city is the home of all the redeemed of the Lord, in the names that are written on the gates. We read in Revelation 21:12: "And had a wall great and high, and had twelve gates, and at the gates twelve angels, and names written thereon, which are the names of the twelve tribes of the children of Israel." Jesus said, "Salvation is of the Jews" (John 4:22). God gave to them the oracles of divine grace, and the names of the twelve tribes, representing all of the saved of the Old Covenant, are on the twelve gates of the heavenly city. But there is more. We read in Revelation 21:14: "And the wall of the city had twelve foundations, and in them the names of the twelve apostles of the Lamb." In that city are those who are saved in this age and in this dispensation. That is the reason I think the elders, so singularly referred to in the Apocalypse, are numbered twenty-

four, twice twelve. They represent the twelve patriarchs of the
Old Covenant; they represent the twelve apostles of the New
Covenant. The total twenty-four elders represent all of God's
redeemed of all of the ages, resurrected from the dead, raptured
and changed at the Lord's coming, all of them living in the
beautiful city of God. We shall be blest with a new heaven
above us and a new earth beneath us and a new eternal home
around us.

John saw the city coming "from God [*apo tou theou*]" and
"out of heaven [*ek tou ouranou*]." These little Greek preposi-
tions mean so much. It is not coming "from" heaven as though
the city might be nearby, but it is coming "out of" heaven.
When we go to heaven, we enter that beautiful city. That is
where we go when we die. That is where the marriage supper
of the Lamb is going to be, in heaven. That is where the wedding feast is going to be, in heaven. And in God's providence,
at the end of these climactic days, out of heaven will descend
this incomparable home, the city where we have been living.

John now describes the New Jerusalem by color and by
proportion. He says it is a perfect cube. It is foursquare. Its
size, oh, how tremendous and how vast! There is room for us
all. Our Lord Jesus is preparing that celestial home for us now.
When our Saviour went away, He went away to do two things.
One, to pray for us. He intercedes for us as our high priest
who enters into the veil to plead for the saints. Because of His
prayers, we shall not fail to reach the heavenly portal. "Wherefore he is able also to save them to the uttermost that come
unto God by him, seeing he ever liveth to make intercession
for them" (Hebrews 7:25). We are not equal to Satan, the
diabolos, who controls and runs this world. Quicker than the
eye could recognize, quicker than a man could take a breath,
would Satan destroy us, were it not for the keeping intercession
of our great advocate and mediator in glory.

But Jesus went inside the veil not only to intercede for us,
but He went also to heaven to prepare a place for us. Through
these years, and now through these centuries, the hands of our
dear Saviour have been fashioning what no architect in this
life could ever dream of. He is building a city and a home for
us in glory. And, as the Revelation outlines, its size is tremen-

dous, a vast cube. "And the angel measured it and it measured twelve thousand *stadia*." To the Englishman the cube measured twelve thousand "furlongs"; to the American the cube measured one thousand five hundred miles. It is a city as though it began in Maine and went all the way down to Florida. It is so vast in its length, its breadth and its height that the city would cover all of Ireland, all of Great Britain, all of France, all of Spain, all of Germany, all of Austria, all of Italy, all of European Turkey and half of European Russia. One thousand five hundred miles one way, one thousand five hundred miles the other way and one thousand five hundred miles upward. Street upon street and story upon story, the beautiful, golden municipality of God.

Now the wall and foundation are measured. The angel measured with the measure of a man. He measured the wall and found it to be an hundred and forty-four cubits high. About two hundred fifty feet high. The city is placed upon a vast, solid foundation. The description of this foundation leads us to notice its variegated, multiplied, glorious colors. God must like color. For example, do you ever see the sunset in the evening when the clouds are burning with fire and there is gold, crimson, orange, blue, all the riot of rainbows in the sky? Is there a man who ever lived who could tell us any earthly, utilitarian use for a sunset? Do you buy them, can you plow them, can you water with them? What good are the colors of the sunset? Just this, that God loves color and things beautiful. So it is with His holy city. Beyond imagination is the flooding of color in that incomparable city. All of these stones named here are exquisite in color: the diamond and the sapphire, the chalcedony and the emerald, the sardonyx and the sardius, the chrysolyte and the beryl, the topaz and the chrysoprasus, the jacinth and the amethyst. God took the azure blue of the chalice of His sky, the surf of the raging sea, the emerald of the verdant meadow, the glory of the autumnal fall, the fire of an August sunset, and He crystalized them all into the living color of His holy city. Oh, what color, what beauty!

Behold the symmetry of our celestial home. God loves form and proportion just as He loves color and beauty. We also love excellence of arrangement, although we sometimes are not aware of it. Can you imagine a man making a crooked column, one that leaned this way or leaned that way? Could you imagine that? Would it not violate something on the inside of you if you were to see a column twisted around like that? A column has to be symmetrical and straight. Where did you get that conception? That is God. That is just a little piece of the Lord's image in you. God loves things beautiful, symmetrical and proportionate. That is why the life of our Lord is so incomparably precious. He was symmetrical and proportionate, without flaw, in all of His life and personality: His mind and His heart, His soul and His affections, His will, His desires, His physical manhood. So our home in heaven is like our Lord — beautiful, proportionate and symmetrical. We shall live in a metropolis where there is harmony, not monotony; variety, not sameness; unity, not uniformity.

We now enter the marvelous city. We go inside, through one of its gates, made out of solid pearl. There is a sermon in the fact that the gates are pearl. Heaven is entered through suffering and travail, through redemption and blood, through the agony of a cross. A pearl is a jewel made by a little animal that is wounded. Without the wound the pearl is never formed. We enter heaven through gates of pearl.

As John looked down one of the wide avenues of the city, he writes, "And the street of the city was pure gold, as it were transparent glass" (Revelation 21:21). There is nothing of defilement in heaven. Even the thoroughfares are pictures of the purity of the place. The pure gold is unstained and unclouded, looking like transparent glass.

The Seer continues in Revelation 21:22, "And I saw no temple therein: for the Lord God Almighty and the Lamb are the temple of it." There is no need for a temple in heaven. The city itself is a sanctuary. God's presence is there. No need of veils, curtains, ceremonies, rites, altars. No need for expiation, atonement, covenants, arks and intermediaries. We shall live in the presence of God and shall worship immediately and directly. The place could be called *Jehovah Shammah.* "God is here." God is present as He was in the Garden of Eden. This is paradise restored and regained. The Lord God is there and we do not need a temple. We shall see Him face to face.

John continues in Revelation 21:23, "And the city had no need of the sun, neither of the moon . . . for the glory of God did lighten it, and the Lamb is the light thereof." The garments of God reflect the glory, the iridescence, the incomparable effusion of beauty, color, splendor and light that stream from His Person. When Moses talked with the Lord and came down the mountainside, his face shone. He had been with God. On the Mount of Transfiguration the face of our Lord became bright above the glory of the sun. When Paul on the road to Damascus met the Lord, above the splendor of that Syrian orb that shined in the sky he saw the light of the glory of God in the face of Jesus Christ. There is an inherent light and glory in the city because Jesus is there, "and the Lamb is the light thereof." All light, hope and blessing stream from His blessed face. From the first promised blessing in Genesis to the last benediction in the Revelation, it is Jesus as He was then, is now, and ever shall be, world without end. Amen.

John now presents a remarkable parallel between what he sees in the paradise of God, in the beautiful city, and what is described in the first and the second chapters of the Book of Genesis. Revelation 22:1, 2: "And he shewed me a pure river of water of life, clear as crystal . . . In the midst of the street of it, and on either side of the river, was there the tree of life, which bare twelve manner of fruits." John sees "a pure river of the water of life." In Eden there was a beautiful river with four branches that watered the garden. The heavenly Paradise also is glorified with a beautiful river. As the psalmist said, "There is a river, the streams whereof make glad the city of God." There is nothing so refreshing as cool, clear water. There is a beautiful stream in the city of God, where the redeemed may drink and live forever.

But there is more. John says in Revelation 22:2 that the fruit of the trees are for the nourishment of God's immortal saints. That means that we are going to eat in heaven. We have spoken of that with delight and anticipation. Who could object to that? The angels ate when they were entertained by Abraham. Our Lord Jesus ate when He was raised from the dead. At the solemn institution of the Lord's Supper, He said that He would not drink henceforth of the fruit of the vine until that day when He would drink it new with us in the kingdom of our Father (Matthew 26:29). We are going to be at the marriage supper of the Lamb. We are going to eat the twelve manner of fruits that mature every month on those marvelous trees. I wonder what it will taste like, this ambrosia of God? Oh, the fellowship and the gladness of such a thing as God has prepared for us!

John avows further in Revelation 22:3, "The throne of God and of the Lamb shall be in it; and his servants shall serve him." How many times do you hear people say as someone said to me last week, "I cannot imagine heaven being interesting; we shall just sit and sit and do nothing." There is no intimation that heaven is such a vacuum as that. In the Garden of Eden before the man was made, God said He needed someone to till the ground. When He made the man He placed him in the Garden that he might dress it and keep it. The man was to have dominion over things above and things around and things below. There was tremendous assignment and responsibility for the first man in the Garden of Eden. In like manner every indication points to our increasing responsibilities in a New Jerusalem. For example, in the parable of the pounds, when the Lord blessed the man that had gained ten pounds, He said, "You shall have authority over ten cities." And to the man who had gained five pounds He said, "You shall have authority over five cities." There is intricate administration in the future kingdom of God. There are nations mentioned. There is government, there are responsibilities. In that celestial civilization each man shall have his place according to his faithfulness in this world and in this life. "His servants shall serve him."

Now John speaks of the most climactic and meaningful blessing of all, "And they shall see his face; and his name shall be in their foreheads" (Revelation 22:4). This is what it is to be in heaven, to look upon the face of God, our Lord, and to be with one another and live. That is heaven. Incidentally, gates of pearl; incidentally, streets of gold; incidentally, walls of jasper. But mostly and foremost, our Lord and one another. I can hear the Lord as He will say to you, "On what street would you like to live in glory and what mansion would you like to call your home?" And I can hear a true saint reply, "Dear Lord, any street, any mansion, just so the windows open on the palace of the great King that I might see Him come and go." Does it strike a chord in your heart? "Any street, Lord, any house, Lord, just so I can see Thy blessed and precious face and that we might be together in heaven." Blind Fanny Crosby wrote a song like that and it is found in our hymnbook. She entitled it, "My Saviour First of All." We seldom sing it any more. But when I was a boy we sang it so often. It goes like this:

When my life work is ended, and I cross the swelling tide,
When the bright and glorious morning I shall see;
I shall know my Redeemer when I reach the other side,
And His smile will be the first to welcome me.

Thro' the gates to the city in a robe of spotless white,
He will lead me where no tears shall ever fall;
In the glad song of ages I shall mingle with delight,
But I long to meet my Saviour first of all.

"And they shall see his face; and his name shall be in their foreheads and they shall reign for ever and ever." Think of stepping on shore and finding it heaven. Think of taking hold of a hand and finding it God's. Think of breathing new air and finding it celestial. Think of feeling invigorated and finding it immortality. Think of passing through tempest to a new and unknown calm. Think of waking up well and finding it home. This and more is what God will do for us who place our trust in Him.

Chapter 12

THE ALPHA AND THE OMEGA

Revelation 22

12 And, behold, I come quickly; and my reward is with me, to give to every man according as his work shall be.
13 I am Alpha and Omega, the beginning and the end, the first and the last.
16 I Jesus have sent mine angel to testify unto you these things in the churches. I am the root and the offspring of David, and the bright and morning star.

Four times in the Revelation do we read the words: "I am the Alpha and the Omega." The first time is in Revelation 1:8: "I am Alpha and Omega, the beginning and the ending, saith the Lord, which is, and which was, and which is to come, the Almighty [Greek, the *Pontokrator*]." This is an avowal of the omnipotence of the Lord Christ. The Alpha is the beginning letter of the Greek alphabet as the Omega is the concluding letter. Our Lord Christ is the beginning and the ending, the first and the last, the all-inclusive revelation of the reality, the being, the existence of God Himself. He is all of God. "I am Alpha and Omega, the Lord God which was and which is to come, the *Pontokrator*, the Almighty."

The second time that expression is used is in this same first chapter, Revelation 1:10, 11: "I was in the Spirit on the Lord's day, and heard behind me a great voice, as of a trumpet, Saying, I am Alpha and Omega, the first and the last: and, What thou seest, write in a book, and send it unto the seven churches which are in Asia." Here Christ avows that He is the Lord of time and of history. All of the unfolding ages are in His hands. John is commanded to write the future as Christ reveals it and to send the revelations to the churches.

Revelation 21:5, 6 is the third time that expression is used: "And he that sat upon the throne said, Behold, I make all things new [a new heaven, a new earth and a new capital city, the holy Jerusalem] . . . . I am Alpha and Omega, the beginning and the end." Here it is affirmed that He is the Lord God of the new order and the new creation.

The last, the fourth time the expression is used is in this epilogue, Revelation 22:12, 13: "And, behold, I come quickly; and my reward is with me, to give every man according as his work shall be. I am Alpha and Omega, the beginning and the end, the first and the last." Here it is affirmed of our Lord Christ that He is the Judge of all men: "My reward is with me, to give every man according as his work shall be." He is the great Judge of the earth, sitting in jurisdiction upon time, history and creation. All four of these passages are affirmations of the deity of our Lord Christ.

An affirmation of the deity of our Lord is also found in this epilogue in Revelation 22:16, "I am the root and the off-spring of David." The phrase, "the offspring of David," would be a reference to his genealogical descent from the great king of Israel. His descent according to the flesh of His human body came from David. But do you notice that the text says first, "I am the root of David"? That identical expression is used in Revelation 5:5: "And one of the elders saith unto me, Weep not: behold, the Lion of the tribe of Juda, the Root of David, hath prevailed to open the book, and to loose the seven seals thereof." "The root of David." A tree grows from its root. The root is first, then afterward the sprout and the trunk. This saying, therefore, is an avowal that our Lord Christ was anterior to David. In Isaiah 11:10 He is called "the root of Jesse." He existed before them both; their spiritual life was derived from Him. Before Abraham was, before Jesse was, before David was, this great God *Pontokrator* existed, who created them and gave them their spiritual and heavenly assignment.

This expression is also an avowal of the eternal existence and being of our Lord, "the root of David." We see that marvelously prefigured in the glorious prophecies of Isaiah. "For," the prophet said of that matchless Prince of Glory, "unto us a child is born . . . [a virgin shall conceive, and bear a son, and shall call his name Immanuel, with us is God] . . . For unto us a child is born, unto us a son is given: and the government shall be upon his shoulder: and his name shall be called Wonderful, Counsellor, The mighty God, The everlasting Father, The Prince of Peace" (Isaiah 9:6). That child born is the eternal Word in the flesh. This son that is given is the everlasting Father in the person and presence of a child, the offspring of the womb of Mary. "And his name shall be called Counsellor." He was in the counsels of God from the beginning. "And his name shall be called The mighty God, or God the Almighty, the everlasting Father, the Father of eternity." The beginning of all time and of all creation is found in Him. He is "the Prince of Peace," the King of the saints making reconciliation for the sins of the world. The Son is not just another man sent here to teach us a new ethic, as some super-Socrates, nor was His death that of a distinguished martyr. In the providence of God, in the fullness of time, the Lord God descended from heaven, wrapped Himself in human flesh in the womb of a virgin girl, offered Himself as a sacrifice for our sins in the body God prepared for Him, in whose blood and atonement our iniquities and transgressions are washed away. Afterward he was exalted up to glory, King forever of all the saved of mankind and of all God's creation. He is truly "the Alpha and the Omega," "the root and the offspring of David."

But we have not touched the hem of the garment of the exalted deity, being and existence of our Lord Christ. All of the qualities, attributes and perfections of the Lord Jehovah are also the qualities, attributes and perfections of the Son, our Saviour. Whatever can be said of the holiness and glory of Jehovah God can also be said of the manifestation of God in the flesh in the person of His Son, Jesus Christ. For example, in the incomparable reference of John to Jesus in John 12:37-41 he quotes a passage from chapter 6 of the Book of Isaiah. After he quotes that passage in Isaiah 6, John adds, "These things said Esaias [Isaiah] when he saw his glory and spake of him." What is this reference when John says: "These things said Isaiah when he saw the glory of Jesus and spake of him"?

Turn back to chapter 6 of Isaiah and this is the vision: "In the year that king Uzziah died I saw also the Lord sitting upon a throne, high and lifted up, and his train filled the temple. Above it stood the seraphims: each one had six wings; with twain he covered his face, and with twain he covered his feet, and with twain he did fly. And one cried unto another, and said, Holy, holy, holy, is the Lord of hosts: the whole earth is full of his glory. And the posts of the door moved at the voice of him that cried, and the house was filled with smoke." Whose is this glory that Isaiah saw? Who is this exalted Person high and lifted up? John the apostle says Isaiah saw the glory of the Lord Jesus and spake of Him. This is confirmed in the words of Jesus Himself, who said, "I and my Father are one." The Father and the Son are one in the mystery of the Trinity. There are not two or three immutable, eternal, infinite, omniscient, omnipotent Gods. When we arrive in glory and mingle with the saints on those golden streets we shall not see three Gods. That would be basic paganism and idolatry. When we get to heaven and walk the streets of that celestial city we shall see the one Lord God, Jesus, Jehovah Christ. The only God there is the Lord God our Father. The only God we shall ever see is the Lord God Christ our Saviour. The only God we shall ever feel is the Lord God the Holy Spirit, who lives in our hearts and in whose power we shall be raised from among the dead.

But we continue. There are no attributes, there are no perfections of the Lord God Jehovah but that they are also the attributes and perfections of the Lord Christ Himself. Let us speak of His immutability. The immutability, the unchangingness of the Lord God is also ascribed to our Lord Christ. We read in Hebrews 1:10-12: "Thou, Lord [Christ], in the beginning hast laid the foundation of the earth; and the heavens are the works of thine hands: They shall perish; but thou remainest; and they all shall wax old as doth a garment; And as a vesture shalt thou fold them up, and they shall be changed: but thou art the same, and thy years shall not fail."

We speak of His eternity. Christ is from eternity in the same unending life as that of the Lord God Himself. Notice the last part of the prophecy in Micah 5:2: "But thou, Bethlehem [over there just beyond the hills], though thou be little among the thousands of Judah, yet out of thee shall he come forth . . . that is to be ruler in Israel; *whose goings forth have been from of old, from everlasting.*" There was no time, not in the eternity of the eternities, when He did not live, though born of a virgin in that little town of Bethlehem. In John 8:58 Jesus says, "Verily, verily, I say uno you, Before Abraham was, I am." Read Colossians 1:17: "And he is before all things, and by him all things consist." All things hold together in Him. Look at Hebrews 1:3: ". . . upholding all things by the word of his power." Look at John 1:1,3: "In the beginning was the Word [Christ], and the Word [Christ] was with God, and the Word [Christ] was God . . . All things were made by him; and without him was not any thing made that was made." Every quality and attribute of the Lord God is the perfection and glory of our Lord Christ. I could conceive of these worlds and God's starry universes passing away like the moats that dance in a sunbeam, like the sparks that fly up from an anvil, like the bubbles that rise and fall on the crest of an ocean wave, but I could never conceive of the oblivion of our living Lord. After the very substance of the creation has passed into nothingness, our Lord Christ will still be "God over all, blessed for ever. Amen." "The same yesterday, and to day, and for ever." "Thou, Lord, in the beginning hast laid the foundation of the earth; and the heavens are the works of thine hands: They shall perish; but thou remainest; and they all shall wax old as doth a garment; And as a vesture shalt thou fold them up, and they shall be changed; but thou art the same, and thy years shall not fail" (Hebrews 1:10,11). The immutability and the eternity of our Lord Christ is a basic revelation set in the very heart of the Holy Scriptures.

Christ is also the One who forgives our sins. He said to the paralytic, "Thy sins be forgiven thee" (Mark 2:5). But the scribes who specialized in carping criticism said that no man can forgive sins but God; therefore they concluded, "This man blasphemes!" But the Lord said, "But that you may know that the Son of man hath power on earth to forgive sins, (he said to the sick of the palsy,) . . . Arise, and take up thy bed, and go thy way." And before the astonished amazement of these who looked, the man sick with the palsy stood up, carried his bed and walked. The Son of man has power in the earth to forgive sin.

The Lord Christ accepted divine worship, as it is written, "And they fell down and worshipped him." (Matthew 2:11; 8:2; 9:18; 14:33; 15:25; 28:9; Luke 24:52; John 9:38, etc.) One of the characteristics of the Apocalypse is found in the worshipful refrain heard from the beginning to the ending. "Saying with a loud voice, Worthy is the Lamb that was slain to receive power, and riches, and wisdom, and strength, and honour, and glory, and blessing. And every creature which is in heaven, and on the earth, and under the earth, and such as are in the sea, and all that are in them, heard I saying, Blessing, and honour, and glory, and power, be unto him that sitteth upon the throne, and unto the Lamb for ever and ever. And the four beasts said, Amen. And the four and twenty elders fell down and worshipped him that liveth for ever and ever" (Revelation 5:12-14).

Christ is the foundation of His Church. He said in Matthew 16:18, "On this rock [the rock of the deity of the Son of God avowed in the great confession, 'Thou art Christ, the Son of the living God'] I will build my church." Paul the apostle added, "Other foundation can no man lay than that is laid, which is Jesus Christ" (I Corinthians 3:11).

Our Lord Christ is not only the Alpha and the Omega, the beginning and the end, the revelation of the existence, the being and person of deity, but He is also the Alpha and the Omega of the Holy Scriptures. All the Bible is a revelation of our blessed Saviour. From the first verse of the Book of Genesis, when by Him all things created were flung into orbit, until the last benediction, when the grace of our Lord Jesus Christ is bestowed upon us all, He is the great alphabet of the entire story, the Alpha and Omega. In Genesis 1:26 it is written, "Let *us* make man." Christ was in the counsels of eternity. When our parents fell, they were promised that the seed of the woman should crush the serpent's head, a protevangelium of the coming of our Lord into the world. The rest of the Book is the unfolding of His story. If there is an ark in which the family of the earth is saved, that one door into the ark is a type of the hope we have in our blessed Lord. If there is a Lamb slain at the Passover, it is a prefiguration of His atoning blood, spread over the houses in which we live, covering our hearts and our lives that the angel of judgment and death might pass over us. If Israel [Jacob] dies and says to Judah, "The sceptre shall never depart from thy hand nor a lawgiver from between thy feet until Shiloh come," the promise is of our coming Saviour. If there is a Levitical law of sacrifice and if there is a temple with altar, veil, propitiation and atonement, all prefigure a gospel message of blessed hope and forgiveness in our great High Priest, the Lord Jesus. And if there are prophecies that are spoken and if there are messages of God that are delivered, they all point toward the coming of the great King, our God and Saviour, whose name is Wonderful, Counsellor, the Everlasting Father.

The New Testament also is nothing but the story of our blessed Lord Jesus. Take Him out of the Gospel and there is nothing left. Take Him out of the epistles and they become a fabric shorn of meaning and substance. Take Him out of the epistle to Hebrews, take Him out of the letters of Peter and John and Jude, take Him out of the Apocalypse, and there is nothing left. The books of the Bible are the golden garments of our blessed Lord. They are the chariots of fire in which He rides. Unwrap the swaddling bands of the Scriptures and you will find the Babe of Bethlehem, God manifest in the flesh. The quintescence of the Holy Word of God is Jesus of Nazareth. The very essence of the holy narration is of Him the Lord Christ, who came to die for our sins in the world.

Christ is always the Alpha and the Omega of honor and exaltation. If there is any reference to any high and holy majesty in the Bible, it is of Him. If there is any description of a prophetic office or any delineation of a priestly character, its sublimest counterpart is found in Him. Is there a prophet? Then all of the other prophets follow at a humble distance from Him. Is there a priest? Then He is the great High Priest, making atonement for the souls of the people. Is there a king?

Then He is King of kings and of His dominion there is no end. Other empires may fall, but His kingdom is an everlasting kingdom. Is there a shepherd? Then He is the good and the great Shepherd of His sheep. Is there a stone? Then He is the chief cornerstone of the building of God. All worship, adoration and glory belong unto Him.

And did He die? Then His death is an atonement for the sins of the whole world and an occasion for His exaltation above the heaven of heavens.

> Were you there when they crucified my Lord?
> Were you there?
> Oh, sometimes it makes me to tremble, tremble, tremble.
> Were you there when they crucified my Lord?

Such misery, such shame and disgrace! Surely, that is the end of Christ. Surely, having thus descended into the likeness of a man and into the fashion of a felon, crucified and dead, like a common criminal, oh, surely this is the end of Him. But:

> Were you there when God raised Him from the dead?
> Were you there?
> Were you there when He burst the bonds of death?
> Were you there?
> Were you there when He came forth from the tomb?
> Were you there?

"Wherefore God also hath highly exalted him, and given him a name which is above every name: That at the name of Jesus every knee should bow, of things in heaven, and things in earth, and things under the earth; And that every tongue should confess that Jesus Christ is Lord, to the glory of God the Father" (Philippians 2:9-11). He is truly the Alpha and the Omega, the beginning and the end, of all worship and devotion, of all exaltation and glory.

And last, Christ is the Alpha and Omega of our salvation, the beginning and the end, the all-in-all. What it is to be saved is to be saved by the Lord Jesus. What it is to be a Christian is to be a follower of the Lord Jesus. What it is to have hope is to have hope in the Lord Jesus. What it is to be forgiven is to be forgiven in the love and mercy of the Lord Jesus. What it is to go to heaven is to see His dear and blessed face. He is the Alpha and the Omega of our salvation. "Unto him that loved us, and washed us from our sins in his own blood, And hath made us kings and priests unto God and his Father, to him be glory and dominion for ever and ever. Amen" (Revelation 1:5, 6).

"And he said unto me . . . I am Alpha and Omega, the beginning and the end. I will give unto him that is athirst of the fountain of the water of life freely" (Revelation 21:6). Do our hearts hunger for God? Then we must come to Jesus. Do our souls seek forgiveness of sins? Then we must go to the blessed Lord Jesus. Is there to be stain washed away from our souls? Then we are to carry the burden of our wrong and our transgressions to the blessed Lord Jesus. He is the Alpha and the Omega of our salvation.

The first breath we breathe comes from Him. The first light of our newborn, born-again life comes from Him. And the last shout of these who die in the Lord, as they come to the streets of celestial glory, are to the praise and honor of Him. If we are kept in the way, He has kept us. If we have been blessed in these years of our pilgrimage, it is by His gracious nail-pierced hands. If we know ought of God, it is in His revelation. If we someday arrive, without fault or blemish, before the throne of His glory in that celestial city, it is in His mercy and His grace. He is the Alpha and Omega of our salvation.

The Atonement of Christ is the basis upon which God forgives our sins. To become a Christian, we must confess our faith in the Lord Jesus. "And [falling] down before Paul and Silas . . . [he] said, Sirs, what must I do to be saved? And they said, Believe on the Lord Jesus Christ, and thou shalt be saved" (Acts 16:29-31). "If thou shalt confess with thy mouth the Lord Jesus, and shalt believe in thine heart [that He liveth] that God hath raised him from the dead, thou shalt be saved" (Romans 10:9). "There is none other name under heaven given among men, whereby we must be saved" (Acts 4:12). The Alpha and the Omega of our salvation is the blessed, eternal, atoning Lord Jesus. We are to come to Him in a public, unashamed, open, unreserved confession of faith. "Whosoever therefore shall confess me before men, him will I confess also before my Father which is in heaven" (Matthew 10:32). And that is the substance, prayer and purpose of this holy hour this day. Maybe *you* will humbly bow at the feet of our blessed Lord, confessing the sin and unrighteousness of your life, and in His love and mercy ask for forgiveness and be saved.

CHAPTER 13

THE RIGHT TO THE TREE OF LIFE

Revelation 22

14 Blessed are they that do his commandments, that they may have right to the tree of life, and may enter in through the gates into the city.

Revelation 22:14 is the last beatitude in the Bible. It is written in the King James Version, the Authorized Version, in these words: "Blessed are they that do his commandments, that they may have right to the tree of life, and many enter in through the gates into the city." That is the way the verse reads in the Textus Receptus, the Greek text that was used as the basis for the translation of the King James Version. But that is not the way John wrote it. When John wrote the verse, be said: "Blessed are they that wash their robes, that they may have right to the tree of life, and may enter in through the gates into the city." Hundreds of years before printing was invented, a scribe copying the Bible saw that passage in the Revelation, "Blessed are they who wash their robes [*plunontes tas stolas*] . . ." But he said to himself: "No man can be saved just by trusting Jesus. One cannot go to heaven and enter through those beautiful gates just by washing his robes in the blood of the Lamb. A man has to earn heaven." Said that scribe to himself, "A man has to obey the laws of God in order to be saved." So the scribe took upon himself the authority to change that "*plunontes tas stolas auton*" (washing their robes) into "*poiountes tas entolas autou*" (doing his commandments).

The Textus Receptus is the Greek text that Erasmus, the famous Renaissance scholar, published in A.D. 1516. It was the first New Testament Greek text ever published. The basis for the Textus Receptus was three minuscules, three cursive manuscripts that Erasmus had before him. One was copied in the tenth century, the second was copied in the twelfth century, and the third, the one he mainly relied upon, was copied in the fifteenth century. The Textus Receptus became the standard Greek text for over three hundred years. It contained this changed reading in Revelation 22:14, "Blessed are they that do his commandments."

Since 1516 the world of scholarship and archeology has discovered thousands of earlier Greek texts. The great uncials that were copied from the very beginning when the books of the New Testament were first gathered into one have been discovered since Erasmus. An uncial is a Greek text written in large, square capital letters. We have thirty-two uncials written on papyri and one hundred seventy written on parchment. We also now have two thousand three hundred and twenty Greek manuscripts written cursively. They are called minuscules. The writing of uncials with big, square letters, was slow and difficult. In the seventh century, a way was invented to write cursively, as you write longhand in English, writing in a running hand. After the seventh century all of the manuscripts were written in that cursive style. There are two thousand, three hundred twenty Greek minuscules. There are one thousand five hundred sixty-one Greek lectionaries, that is, sections of the New Testament from which a man would teach a lesson or preach a sermon. We have, then, four thousand eighty-three Greek manuscripts of this New Testament, each manuscript containing all the books of the New Testament or portions of the books.

Beside this overwhelming collection in Greek, scholars have discovered more than eight thousand Latin versions and more than one thousand other versions of the New Testament. Added up, all this means that there are more than thirteen thousand manuscripts from which a man can study to find the true and original text written by the apostle. This is an astonishing and an amazing total when you remember there is only one manuscript of the annals of Tacitus, the great Roman historian. There is only one manuscript of the Greek anthology. So much of the literature of the ancient world of Plato, Sophocles and Euripedes will depend upon one or two manuscripts. But there are thousands and thousands and thousands of manuscripts of the Greek New Testament and its versions into Latin, Syrian, Coptic and other languages. By comparing those thousands and thousands of manuscripts, the scholars can easily find the original text the apostle wrote; for, as you compare those thousands of manuscripts, you can see where a scribe emended the text here, where he wrote a little explanation of the text there, where he changed a word here. Essentially, practically, doctrinally, for all worship purposes, for our own reading and edification, the King James Version, the Authorized Version, the Textus Receptus, is superlative. But once in a while you will see where a scribe has made a change, has interpolated, has emended, has (what he thought) corrected. These emendations are most apparent and are not a part of the Word of God.

An emendation of a copyist is found in our text in Revelation 22:14. Why did that scribe change that gospel message from one of faith and trust to one of obedience and works? For the plain and simple reason that there is the everlasting tendency in a man to try to merit, to try to achieve, to try by self-advancement to find his way into heaven. That is a weakness of human nature and it is seen everywhere in religion.

This system of merit represents the great religions of the world. It represents much of Christianity. Many churches in Christendom believe that we are saved by works, that a man toils his way into the kingdom of heaven, that he deserves heaven as a reward after he has done certain things that he thinks are acceptable unto God. Certainly the great religions, like the Hindu, the Confucian, the Buddhist, are religions of works. A Hindu will keep his hand raised up toward heaven until it becomes stiff, or he will lie on a bed of hot coals or spikes, or he will crawl on his knees from one city to a shrine miles away, seeking to deserve the pardon of God. This same kind of merit system is seen in the Christian religion. So much of Christianity is built around the doctrine of trying to deserve the favor of heaven. A man is saved, says one preacher, by trusting in Jesus *and* by being baptized. Another preacher says a man is saved by trusting Jesus *and* doing all kinds of good works. Another says a man is saved by believing in Jesus *and* taking the Lord's Supper. Another says a man is saved

by trusting in the Lord Jesus *and* becoming a member of the
church *and* by being obedient to all of the commandments of
the church.

The doctrine of merit is a reflection of human pride. The
falsely proud, conceited man says: "*I* can do this assignment
myself. I can merit heaven myself. I can work out this problem of sin by myself. And when I am saved it is because *I*
have done it. Look at me. Here I am walking golden streets,
going through gates of pearl, mingling with the saints of God
because *I* did good, *I* obeyed commandments, *I* kept laws and
I did great things. Therefore am I here in the presence of
God." That is the religion of the flesh; that is the religion of
human pride; and that was the religion of the scribe who, when
he found this passage in Revelation, changed the text from one
of washing robes to one of doing commandments.

Let us read the Word of God to learn how our sins are
forgiven, how God saves a lost soul and how it is that a sinner
can one day stand in the presence of the Almighty and live.
Let us read of this first in the Old Testament. Turn with me
to Psalm 51. This is the Psalm David wrote after his great sin.
What does David do? He casts himself upon the mercies of
God: "Have mercy upon me, O God, according to thy loving-
kindness: according to the multitude of thy tender mercies
blot out my transgressions. Wash me throughly from mine
iniquity, and cleanse me from my sin . . . For thou desirest not
sacrifice; else would I give it [I would buy the cattle on a thousand hills and sacrifice them if it would wash my sin away]:
thou delightest not in burnt-offering [I would buy the sheep of
the whole nation and offer them unto Thee if that would blot
out my transgression]" (Psalm 51:1, 2, 16). How do we come
to God? Listen! "The sacrifices of God are a broken spirit:
a broken and a contrite heart, O God, thou wilt not despise"
(Psalm 51:17). The forgiveness of sin lies in the mercy, goodness, love, compassion and forbearance of God. All the burnt
offerings in the world and all the commandments that a man
could keep could never suffice to blot out the stain of the sin
in his soul. In Isaiah 55:1, 3 listen to the invitation of our Lord:
"Ho, every one that thirsteth, come ye to the waters, and he
that hath no money; come ye, buy, and eat; yea, come, buy

wine and milk without money and without price . . . Incline
your ear, and come unto me; hear, and your soul shall live . . ."
Come, come, come just as you are, penniless, poverty-stricken,
naked, unworthy, sinful, come; come, buy without money and
without price. "Incline your ear . . . hear, and your soul shall
live."

Turn with me in the New Testament to Romans 4:2. How
was Abraham justified? "If Abraham were justified [if Abraham were declared righteous] by works [by the things that he
did and by commandments he obeyed], he hath whereof to
glory [to boast]." In that event the patriarch could say: "Look
what I have done. I have merited salvation and I deserve
heaven." But Paul avows that Abraham could not thus boast
before God, for God knew his heart as He knows our hearts.
I can take the sweetest, purest, finest girl in the world, put
on a screen all the secrets of her heart and of her life, and
she will blush with indescribable shame. Abraham could boast,
if he were justified by works; but he could not do it before God.
God knew him as He knows us. Well, then, how was Abraham
justified? Look at the next verse, Romans 4:3: "What saith
the scripture? Abraham believed God, and it was counted unto
him for righteousness." Then Paul writes the inevitable conclusion in Romans 4:5: "But to him that worketh not, but believeth on him that justifieth the ungodly, his faith is counted
for righteousness." Turn again to Ephesians 2:8, 9: "For by
grace are ye saved through faith; and that not of yourselves;
it is the gift of God; Not of works, lest any man should boast
[Lest he say: 'Look what I did. I earned heaven.']." No, salvation is the gift of God. We are delivered by the grace and
mercy of heaven. Turn to Titus 3:5: "Not by works of righteousness which we have done, but according to his mercy he
saved us, by the washing [Greek, by the laver] of regeneration."
Emphatically Paul avows we are not saved by works of righteousness which we have done. Our works of righteousness,
in God's sight, are as filthy rags (Isaiah 64:6). "Not by works
of righteousness which we have done, but according to his
mercy he saved us, by the washing of regeneration."

Let us turn back to the Revelation. Turn to Revelation 7:
13, 14: "And one of the elders answered, saying unto me, What

are these which are arrayed in white robes? and whence came they? And I said unto him, Sir, thou knowest. [That vast throng I have never seen.] And he said to me, These are they which are coming out of the great tribulation [the Greek reading], and have washed their robes, and made them white in the blood of the Lamb." These are they, in the presence of God, saved and redeemed, who have washed their robes and made them white in the blood of the Lamb. This exactly corresponds to our text in Revelation 22:14: "Blessed are they that wash their robes, that they may have the right to the tree of life, and may enter in through the gates into the city." Blessed are they that wash and are clean, who look to Jesus and live, who believe in Him and are saved. But, oh, when that scribe read it he said: "Not so, not so; for a man cannot be saved by trusting Jesus. He has to work, he has to keep the commandments."

This altercation over faith and works occasioned the first Jerusalem conference described in Acts 15. In Antioch Paul and Barnabas were preaching to idolaters, heathen, pagans, to trust in Jesus, to turn and be saved, to look and live, to wash and be clean. That is what Paul and Barnabas were preaching in Antioch. But the Pharisaical, the legalistic segment of the Church came down and, listening to Paul and Barnabas as they preached, said: "One cannot be saved by trusting Jesus. One must also keep the law of Moses. To faith must be added the keeping of the commandments."

The mighty Protestant Reformation occurred over that same doctrinal difference. There was a monk by the name of Martin Luther, who in Rome attended the services of St. John Lateran's church. In front of the church of St. John Lateran is a building housing what is called Scala Santa, the Holy Stairs. It is supposed to be the stairway up which the Lord Jesus walked into the judgment hall of Pontius Pilate. On the stairway are supposed to be the blood drops of the Lord Jesus. In order to preserve the stairs and the blood drops lest they wear out with countless devotees climbing over them, the stairs are covered with wood with little glass holes to exhibit the blood drops. As people climb the stairway on their knees, they kiss those little glass holes where the blood drops of Jesus are supposed to be. If they do that they get a great reward for it. Indulgences and reprieves are granted. So the people, in order to achieve those rewards, climb up those steps, hour after hour, trying to work their way into the kingdom of God by penance, by saying prayers and kissing spots. Martin Luther was doing that. He was climbing up the Scala Santa on his knees, kissing all those spots, when, as he was half-way up, like the sounding of a bell, like the booming of a cannon, like a declaration of war, there came into his soul the great text of Habakkuk 2:4, which is the basis of the Book of Romans and which is the basis of the Book of Galatians and which is quoted in Hebrews. There came to his soul that resounding text: "The just [God's forgiven] shall live by his faith." Martin Luther stood up, turned around, walked down those steps. He went to Wittenburg, Germany, and there on the door of the church he nailed his ninety-five theses and the Reformation had begun. "Not by works of righteousness which we have done, but according to his mercy he saved us, by the washing [*plumontes tas stolas*] of our robes [by the forgiveness of our sins] in the blood of the Lamb."

This great doctrine of salvation by faith is illustrated so clearly from a story in the Old Testament. Naaman was a great, mighty man. He was the captain of the host of the king of Syria. He never lost a battle, not in all his life. By him the Lord God gave deliverance on every side against his enemies. He was a mighty warrior, a noble general. But he was a leper. He lived to himself. Wherever he walked he put his hand over his mouth, crying, "Unclean, unclean, unclean." The word came that there was a prophet in Samaria able to heal a man of his leprosy. The king of Syria called for the captain of his hosts and, enriching him with gold, silver, horses, chariots and raiment, sent him down to the prophet of Samaria to *buy* his cleansing with the wealth of these presents. The Bible describes Naaman as he came down to the house of Elisha with his changes of raiment and with his gold and silver and horses and chariots. He stood there in the grandeur of the great military Napoleon of that age. But Elisha never even bothered to go out to look at him. He sent Gehazi, his servant, to say to the mighty and proud Naaman, "Go down to the Jordan River

and wash seven times and your flesh will come again like the
flesh of a little child and you will be clean."

But Naaman was insulted. "Here I am, the greatest military leader of the age; here I am, the mighty deliverer of my
people; here I am, with my horses and my chariots and my
gold and my silver; here I am. Some miraculous, some wonderful thing ought to be done commensurate with my position
and my dignity." The Bible says that he got in his chariot and
rode away in a rage. But he rode away a leper, still a leper.
While he was driving back, his pride so wounded and his spirit
so insulted by what Elisha said, while he was driving back to
Damascus still a leper, one of his servants riding in the chariot
with the proud captain of the host of Syria put his hand on his
arm and said, "My father, if the prophet had bid thee do some
great and mighty thing, wouldst thou not have done it? If he
had said for you to crawl on your knees a thousand miles to
a certain shrine, or if he had said to overcome the entire kingdom of the Midianites, or if he had said to bring him a hundred
thousand talents of gold, or if he had bid thee do some other
great and mighty thing, wouldst thou not have done it? How
much rather then when he said to thee, Wash and be clean,
look and live, trust and be saved." It was then that Naaman
drew up those mighty steeds, turned them around and went
down to the waters of the Jordan River. When he came up
the seventh time from the water of the river, the Book says,
his flesh came again like unto the flesh of a little child and he
was clean. He was clean!

"Not by works of righteousness which we have done, but
according to his mercy he saved us, by the washing [by the
cleansing] of regeneration." "These are they which . . . washed
their robes, and made them white in the blood of the Lamb."
That is the great text, the theme and the song of the hosts in
glory with which we began the preaching of the Revelation:
"Unto him that loved us, and washed us from our sins in his
own blood . . . to him be glory and dominion for ever and ever."
Not by works of righteousness which we have done but (thanksgiving and glory to Jesus) in the blood of His cross and in the
sacrifice of His life and in the atonement of His blood are our
sins washed away. This is the Gospel and this is the Book.

"Blessed are they [*plumontes tas stolas* — just as John wrote it] who wash their robes [who look in faith, who open their hearts to the grace of the blessed Jesus and are forgiven and saved] . . . blessed are they who wash their robes, that they may have right to the tree of life, and may enter in through the gates into the [God's holy] city."

Herein we ought to be most grateful and thankful. Were our salvation dependent upon us we might have missed it, we might yet fail in it. But Jesus never fails. Trust in Him, for He will see us through and keep us forever. Those nail-pierced hands that open for us the doors of grace will some day open for us the gates of glory. Blessed be His name.

CHAPTER 14

THE LAST INVITATION

Revelation 22

17 And the Spirit and the bride say, Come. And let him that heareth say, Come. And let him that is athirst come. And whosoever will, let him take the water of life freely.

This sermon is a message from one of the most meaningful and beautiful of all of the texts in the Word of God. We could entitle it "The Heavenward and Earthward Cry of Come." The visions of the Revelation closed at Revelation 22:5. Beginning at Revelation 22:6 John, by the Holy Spirit, writes an epilogue, a final, concluding passage, not only to the Revelation but (in the providence of God) to the entire Canon of Holy Scripture. The verses of this epilogue are like the final moment of a great concerto in which the instruments of the orchestra all join in one vast flood of triumph. The different voices in this epilogue are all heard alternately. Sometimes it will be the voice of the Seer who is speaking, the Apostle John. Sometimes it will be the voice of the angel. Sometimes it will be a deeper voice from the throne, the Lord Christ Himself speaking. Sometimes it is difficult amidst the swift transitions to tell which one is speaking, they so blend the one into the other. It is thus with this text: "And the Spirit and the bride say, Come. And let him that heareth say, Come. And let him that is athirst come. And whosoever will, let him take the water of life freely."

The first three "comes" are an answering cry to the tremendously significant and triumphant messages of our Lord, who announced in verse 12 above: "Behold, I come quickly." The first voices of the text, the voice of the Spirit, the voice of the bride of Christ, the voice of him that heareth (each in-

153

dividual member of the congregation who has listened to the prophecy) are those that reply to the sublime announcement of our Lord, "Behold, I come quickly." They say, "Come, Lord, come." Then the Lord's voice is heard again, remembering the lost and the thirsty of this weary world. Jesus' invitation to come is to him that is athirst: "And whosoever will, let him come, let him take the water of life freely." So we shall speak of the text in that twofold manner. First, the reply of the Spirit, of the Church and of the individual hearer to the sublime announcement of the living Christ, "Behold, I come quickly." Then we shall speak of the pathos in the voice of our blessed Lord as He encourages the thirsty and the willing to come and to drink of the water of life.

"And the Spirit [says], Come." When the Lord announced: "Behold, I come quickly," the Spirit of Jesus, the Vice-regent of our Lord in the earth, answered with deep-seated longing: "Come, Lord, come." Our Saviour said it was expedient that He go away, for if He went away He would send as His Vice-regent on earth the Spirit of truth, the Paraclete, who would teach us the way of truth and who would be our Comforter, our Guide, and our Keeper. But for the years of this dispensation how the rejection and wickedness of the world has grieved and quenched the Holy Spirit of God! The forty years of wandering in the wilderness when Israel provoked the Spirit of God are as nothing compared with the centuries and the generations of these nineteen hundred years that have known no other thing than the rejection of Christ and the grieving and the provoking of the Holy Spirit. When the Lord announced: "Behold, I come quickly," a grieving, agonizing Spirit replied: "Come, Lord, come, blessed Jesus." It is the desire, the longing, the assignment of the Holy Spirit to glorify the Lord Jesus. The last time this unbelieving world ever saw our Master was at Calvary, when He was raised between the earth and the sky on a cross. The world saw Him die in shame, between two felons. The longing and the desire of the Holy Spirit of God is to exalt the Lord Jesus, to reveal Him in beauty and in glory, in splendor and in triumph. When the Lord announced, "Behold, I come quickly," the Spirit replied, "Come, Lord, do come," for the day of Christ's glory is at hand.

"And the bride [says], Come." "The Spirit and the bride say, Come." The bride of Christ repeats the invitation, "Lord, come quickly." The bride of Christ, His Church, through all of these ages and centuries and now these two millenniums, has been in prayer, waiting for her coming Lord. However the different groups may interpret the manner of His coming, the true Church of Christ is ever moved by that prayer of appeal: "Thy kingdom come, yea, come, Lord Jesus." Do you notice with reference to the Spirit and the bride that there is just one "Come"? "The Spirit and the bride say, Come." Not two. Not "The Spirit says, Come, and the bride says, Come," but one "Come." The Spirit and the bride say, Come." They are identified in that longing. If the Church is filled with the Holy Spirit and if the Holy Spirit speaks through His Church, they have a common prayer, "Come, blessed Lord Jesus." The Church cries in the Spirit and the Spirit prays and cries in the Church, "Come, Lord, come, blessed Jesus." The true Church is espoused to the Lord, but the marriage is not yet. It is not until the return of our Lord that the wedding supper of the Lamb is celebrated. The Church now looks up to her espoused husband, waiting for that final consummating day when she shall belong to her Lord and the Lord shall possess His own. "And the Spirit and the bride say, Come."

"And let him that heareth say, Come." At the sublime announcement of our Lord, "Behold, I come quickly," let every individual member of the congregation, let every member of the household of faith, when he hears the word that is read and the revelation that is delivered, let him say in his heart, "Yes, Lord, come, blessed Jesus." That is the token and the sign of a born-again Christian, a true child of the Lord. No unsaved man, no worldling longs for the return of the Saviour. To him the day of the return of the Lord is a day of foreboding, it is a day of judgment, it is a day of perdition and damnation, it is a day of loss and terror. That is why the unsaved man says, "Where is the promise of his coming? for since the fathers fell asleep, all things continue as they were" (II Peter 3:4). To the unbeliever the coming of the Lord is a dreadful thing. But not so with the true child of God. The Lord announces, "Behold, I come quickly," and when the true child of God reads of the blessed promise in the Bible, he says: "By revelation I am taught that Jesus shall surely come. Amen. It is a blessedness and a happiness to my soul. Even so, Come, Lord Jesus." That is the sign of a true, devout, God-fearing Christian. "Let him that heareth [each individual saved member of the household of faith]," let him answer, "Come, Lord, yea, come."

In the midst of the answering cry of the Spirit and of the bride and of the individual church member, the Lord speaks. Do you see the difference between those two "comes"? "The Spirit and the bride say, Come. And let him that heareth say, Come." Then the text turns in its grammatical construction: "And let him that is athirst come. And whosoever will, let him take the water of life freely." There are two different "comes" in the invitation. One is voiced by the Spirit and the individual hearer. The other is the message of our Lord to the sinner, to the unbeliever who is not prepared for that triumphant day. It is as though the Lord remembered you who are lost, especially *you*. It is as though He took up the pen and before the last, final benediction was written, before the Canon was closed, before the last prophet and the last apostle had concluded, He says: "Let me make one last appeal to the lost that they might be saved, that they might come." The Lord appeals: "Come. Let him that is athirst come. And whosoever will [whosoever would desire] let him take the water of life freely. To him that is athirst, come. To him that desires, come. To him that wills, come."

The word "Come" is a favorite of the Lord God in this Holy Book. In the face of the terrible judgment of the flood, the Lord commanded Noah to build an ark, and when it was built He said to Noah: "Come, Noah, come, you and your family, into the ark of safety, Come." The great lawgiver, Moses, standing in the midst of the camp among his people in idolatry and in an orgy of sin, said, "Let him who is on the Lord's side, let him come and stand by me." It is the message of the Gospel of the Old Testament in Isaiah 1:18: "Come now, and let us reason together, saith the Lord: though your sins be as scarlet, they shall be as white as snow; though they be red like crimson, they shall be as wool." "Come now, saith the Lord." Or in Isaiah 55:1: "Ho, every one that thirsteth, come ye to the waters . . . come ye, buy . . . without money and without price."

The word "Come" was the constant word of invitation on the lips of our blessed Lord. Passing by the sea, He saw the first disciples fishing and He said, "Come, follow me and I will make you fishers of men." The Lord said, "Suffer little children to come unto me, and forbid them not, for of such is the kingdom of heaven." The Lord said to the rich young ruler with the world in his heart, loving the wrong world, "Get rid of it, give it away, and come, follow me." And the Lord said to Zaccheus, "This day, Zaccheus, is salvation come to thy house; come, make haste and come down." And our Lord says to those who are weary and heavy laden, "Come unto me, come unto me, and I will give you rest." And the Lord said in the great parable of His gospel message, "Go out into the highways and the hedges and compel them, constrain them to come in." This is the great climactic purpose of every worship service, every gospel sermon and every true message of the Lord. "Come, ye who have never been saved, come to Jesus. And ye who have already come, come closer, draw nigh, come still closer." The preacher does not need to be clever, he does not need to be oratorical, he does not need to be profound or theological, he does not need to be forensic or argumentative. He needs but the simple text with the simple sermon: "Come, come to the Lord Jesus. Come and be saved. Come with us in this pilgrimage to heaven. Come."

But also, the entire passage with all the voices of "come" can share in this last invitation to the lost: "The Spirit and the bride say, Come. Let him that heareth say, Come. And let him that is athirst come. And any one who will, let him come." They all invite the lost to be saved. This is no violation of the text. They all join in this appeal to the sinner, that he come to Jesus. "The Spirit says come." When a preacher stands in a pulpit with an open Bible and raises his hand in appeal, he can be assured of the wooing of the Holy Spirit, encouraging the sinner to come to Jesus. "And the bride says, Come." This is the deep desire and prayer of any true Church of Jesus, to see lost people come and be saved. With all of the abuse and criticism of the true Church of Jesus, His bride in the earth, would you like to know whether the church really loves a lost city and a lost world? Then, at any service, any hour, let any sinner come down the aisle and take the pastor by the hand and say: "Pastor, I want to be saved. I want to be born again. I want to be a child of God. Men and brethren, pray for me. I want to go to heaven and see the face of God some day." Thus let a sinner come and throughout a faithful congregation there will be hearts lifted heavenward, saying: "Bless the name of God. Here is another sinner who has turned in repentance and faith to the saving Lord Jesus." Such a spirit represents the true Church of the Lord. It is in her heart to sing, "Rescue the perishing." The true bride of Christ stands with her Bibles, her altars, her prayers, and her tears of concern flowing to the earth. She sends out her missionaries and ministers to help in shepherdly care those who need the Lord. She worships with her songs of praise and gladness, with her face lifted up to the glory of God. That is the Church. The bride, the blessed Church of Jesus, invites the lost sinner to come.

"And let him that heareth say, Come." Have you heard there is a Saviour? Have you heard there is a God in heaven? Have you heard there is a way to be reconciled to the Almighty, who judges the earth? Have you heard the grand and glad invitation, "Come, come to the Lord, come and be saved"? When I think of this invitation, "Let him that heareth say, Come," I think of the woman in Samaria who listened to the blessed words of Jesus and who, leaving her pitcher, her water-pot, hastened to the city and said, "Come, come, come and see that Saviour of the world, the Messiah of God." "Let him that heareth say, Come." Possibly I speak today in the name of a sainted father or mother who heard the gospel message and believed and, now in glory, repeats the glad refrain and invitation to your heart, "Come, come."

"And let him that is athirst come." What a simile! What a metaphor! What a figure, how intense! The most agonizing longing known to the human frame is that of thirst. Every tissue, every atom of the body seems to sympathize with that agonizing cry for water. To know the intensity of true desire, look upon the fevered eyes, the parched lips, the thick tongue

and the dry, broken skin of a stranger lost in the burning desert
and hear him cry for water. It is a picture of the longing of
the soul after God. Our Lord said, "Whosoever drinks of the
water of this life shall thirst again." Pleasure, fame, riches and
success do not feed the soul. As Bobby Burns said:

> Pleasures are like poppies spread:
> You seize the flow'r, its bloom is shed;
> Or like the snow falls in the river,
> A moment white, then melts forever.
> Or like the Borealis race
> That flit 'ere you can point their place;
> Or like the rainbow's lovely form,
> Evanishing amid the storm.

Truly Christ said, "Whosoever drinks of the water of this life
shall thirst again, but whosoever drinks of the water that I
give him shall never thirst." Oh, that cup of immortality, that
fountain of life and of youth! Oh, God, where can we drink
and be satisfied? Where can we find immortality and happiness, Lord, but in Thee?

The gospel of John records of the Saviour that in the great
day of the feast Jesus stood up and said, "Let him that is athirst
come unto me and drink." This invitation is poignantly illustrated in a beautiful hymn. For so many years I have been
quoting for comfort and assurance the first stanza of saintly
Horatius Bonar's song:

> I heard the voice of Jesus say,
> "Come unto Me and rest.
> Lay down, thou weary one, lay down
> Thy head upon My breast."

I love that stanza. But it was only in preparing this sermon
that I noticed the second stanza, so rewarding and so satisfying:

> I heard the voice of Jesus say,
> "Behold, I freely give
> The living water, thirsty one,
> Stoop down and drink, and live."
> I came to Jesus and I drank
> Of that life-giving stream.
> My thirst was quenched, my soul revived,
> And now I live in Him.

"Let him that is athirst come, come."

We have now arrived at the last, the most inclusive, the summation of all of the invitations of God in all of the Word: "And whosoever will, let him take the water of life freely." "And whosoever will" — that must include us all, every soul that ever lived, every soul that now lives, every soul that shall ever live. The invitation includes us all. "And whosoever will, let him take the water of life freely." "Whosoever will." If I elect, God elects. If I will, God wills. The elect are the whosoever wills; the non-elects are the whosoever won'ts. It is that simple. "And whosoever will" — the condition is not with God, it is not in Christ; the condition lies in me. God says, "Whosoever will." The invitation is as broad as the race is broad, as time is broad, as life is broad. God does not coerce or force. All who enter in do so of their own choice. I must answer "Yes" to Christ's invitation.

Notice that little word "let." "Whosoever will, let him." Oh, the significant meaning in that word "let." When God says, "Let him," where is the power that can interdict God's mandate? "Let him." When God said "Fiat lux," "Let there be light," who could deny the light that burst into this darkened world? When God says, "Let him," who can deny the humblest, feeblest, most timid of sinners coming to the Lord to be saved? Who could interdict, who could intervene? Could all the power of hell? Could Satan, could the devil, could evil angels so black and dark, could doubt and fear, could anything stand between us and God? When God says, "Let him come," the Almighty Sovereign of heaven and earth means, "Let him come."

"Whosoever will, let him *take* the water of life freely." Let him *take*, let him *take*. Oh, what a simple Gospel and what a simple message! Let him *take*. Does a man desire Christ? Let him *take* Christ. Does a man desire life? Let him *take* life. Does a man desire heaven? Let him *take* heaven. Does a man desire reconciliation? Let him *take* reconciliation. Does a man desire forgiveness? Let him *take* forgiveness. Does a man desire Jesus? Let him *take* the blessed Lord Jesus. "And whosoever will, let him take . . ." No word about feelings, no word about carrying a load of righteousness and good works. God says just let him come and let him take.

Is it not a marvelous invitation? God says grace, abounding grace, will provide the repentance, the faith and the gifts that bring us nigh unto God. It is enough on our part that there is a willingness to come and to take. "Let him come and take the water of life freely." There is only one condition, namely, that you take the offer freely. Do not bring a price. Do not seek to buy at a cost. Do not bring good works and commendations. Do not bring recommendations. Just come as you are. "Let him that heareth say, Come. And let him that is athirst come. And whosoever will, let him take the water of life freely." It is God's good pleasure to give us our salvation. It is a gift of God. It is the Lord's love and desire to bestow it upon us without money and without price.

> Could my tears forever flow,
> Could my zeal no languor know,
> These for sin could not atone;
> Thou must save, and Thou alone:
> In my hand no price I bring;
> Simply to Thy cross I cling.

Let the lost sinner take the gift of salvation freely. Let him drink at the fountain of the river of life and live forever. Drink full and deep. It is yours without price. I heard one time of a little, emaciated boy from a large family, being taken to a hospital, there to be ministered to because of his starvation. The sweet nurse came to the starved lad with a big glass of milk in her hand. She gave it to the little fellow and said, "Drink." With eager hands the lad took the glass of milk and asked, "Nurse, how deep can I drink?" What a picture of poverty, want and need in that question! For, you see, every glass of milk that little fellow had ever seen had to be divided with the children of a large family. Each one could drink just so much, just so far down the glass. There was not enough to spare. So the little fellow, holding the glass in his hand, said, "Nurse, how deep can I drink?"! The nurse replied: "Dear child, drink to the bottom. Drink to the full." We shall never exhaust the goodness, the grace and the mercy of our Lord God. Come, drink to the full. These things are ever and forever ours. "And the Spirit and the bride say, Come. And let him that heareth say, Come. And let him that is athirst come.

And whosoever will, let him take the water of life freely." Christ is manna from heaven to eat. He is water of life to drink. Come and be fed. Come, draw nigh to the blessed Lord Jesus. Come, give your heart in trust to Him. Come, look into His blessed face in faith, in expectancy. He will keep every promise that He made. Come, join yourselves to the household of faith. Come, be one with us in the pilgrimage in this earth to the glory of a world that is yet to come. Come now. Come, bow before the Lord, our great High God. Give your life anew to Him. Come!

CHAPTER 15

THE WORDS OF THIS PROPHECY

Revelation 22

18 For I testify unto every man that heareth the words of the prophecy of this book, If any man shall add unto these things, God shall add unto him the plagues that are written in this book:

19 And if any man shall take away from the words of the book of this prophecy, God shall take away his part out of the book of life, and out of the holy city, and from the things which are written in this book.

This message is a summation of the whole Book of the Revelation. This sermon is a preparation for the closing, final sermon in the next chapter of this book.

Before I begin, may I say a word regarding a theological problem raised by the text in its dire warning and somber threat? Is it possible for God's people to be blotted out of the Book of Life? Having been saved and regenerated, can they fall away from the grace and keeping of our Lord? The answer is very plain to me. This passage is not discussing the possibility of the saved being ultimately lost. The text is but a warning from God, solemn and serious, that His Word is immutable, eternal, unchangeable. "For ever, O God, thy word is fixed in heaven." God's Word is like Himself, the same yesterday and today and forever. This is God's serious, solemn mandate that His Word is not to be changed or mutilated or impaired; it is not to be added to and it is not to be taken away from. But what, then, is the meaning of this dire threat that if any man take away from the Book, God will take away his name out of the Book of Life and his part out of the holy city?

Does the threat imply that a man who is regenerated, saved, born again, could fall away and finally be lost? Im-

possible! It is as impossible as is the suggestion that a regenerated man would mutilate God's Holy Word. He would
not do it! It does not belong to the elect of God to change
God's Word, nor would it enter the heart of a man who was
regenerated to do ought else but to reverence God's Holy Book.
I may not be able to understand all that is written in the Bible;
I may not be able to explain it; I may not be able to enter into
the depths of its riches and its mysteries; but to emasculate,
to interdict, to change, to mutilate, to add to, to take away
from God's Word is something no sincere child of God would
ever do. One of the signs to me of a born-again Christian is
his reverence for and devotion to the Word of God. A preacher
may be an intellectually trained minister of Christ, and he may
stand in a great pulpit, and he may have a vast following, but
if he does not honor God's Word, to me he exhibits a sign that
he does not know the Lord as personal Saviour. He is not born
again. Those who love Jesus, who are elect, who belong to
His kingdom, would never mutilate or change God's Holy
revelation.

Having spoken of this problem of "falling from grace," let
us turn to the announced subject and text, "the words of this
prophecy." In these few brief pages we shall seek to do what
a man would do on a lofty mountain as he looked over the
broad expanse of a forest or as a man would do climbing up
into a high building, surveying the vast panorama of the city.
Thus we shall take an exalted place by the side of our Lord
and with Him look over the extensive vista of the Apocalypse.

First of all, let us say a word about the book itself. Without the Apocalypse the Bible would be incomplete. However
great and broad the base, without the capstone the rising pyra-
mid is forever unfinished and incomplete. So with this Book
called the Bible. Without this final, climactic vision the great
issues raised in the Scriptures are forever unresolved and un-
answered. The Apocalypse is God's revelation of the denouement of history.

The vision was given to a man named John. Three times
He calls his name, "John." He says in Revelation 1:4, "John
to the seven churches which are in Asia." Then in Revelation
1:9: "I John, who also am your brother, and companion in trib-

ulation, and in the kingdom and patience of Jesus Christ, was in the isle that is called Patmos, for the word of God, and for the testimony of Jesus Christ." In Revelation 22:8, in the epilogue, he says, "I John saw these things, and heard them."

Who is this John? He is a man of such authority in the churches that his word is immediately accepted as the Word of God Himself. Who is this John who has such an unusual place and prominence among those early Christians? The answer is simple and plain. He is the Apostle John. When the Judean War broke out against Rome in the latter part of the A.D. 60's, John left the city of Jerusalem and finally came to the Roman province of Asia in A.D. 69. He became pastor of the church at Ephesus and the spiritual leader for all of God's people in that part of the Eastern Roman Empire. Irenaeus, a disciple of that Polycarp who was pastor of the church at Smyrna and a disciple of the Apostle John, repeating Polycarp, said that in the latter part of the reign of Domitian John saw the Revelation. Domitian reigned as emperor of the Roman Empire from A.D. 81 until A.D. 96. Thus, the Revelation was seen on the Isle of Patmos about A.D. 96. Clement of Alexandria, another Father of the Early Church, said that after the death of the Roman Emperor Domitian, John left his exile in Patmos and returned to Ephesus. So the vision was seen and written down about A.D. 96, toward the latter part of the reign of the Emperor Domitian.

The beginning word of the first sentence in the Revelation is a startling word. In the Greek document it is *Apocalypsis*. There is no article; there is just that beginning word *Apocalypsis*. Another fact is astonishing. It is the only time John ever employs the word. John has other writings, such as the gospel of John and the three epistles of John, but nowhere does he use that meaningful, significant, startling word except right here, as though he had reserved it for this one place. "*Apocalypsis Iesou Christou*," which translated literally means the unveiling, the uncovering of Jesus Christ. The vision describes the exaltation of our Lord which God accorded Him because He became obedient unto death in atonement for our sins. Because of this sacrifice, God has highly exalted His Son and given Him a name which is above every name, that at the name of Jesus every knee shall bow and every tongue shall confess that He is Lord over all. That confession is made by the hosts in heaven and by every tribe and nation and family in earth, and even by those under the earth, the beings of the nether-world. God has ordained that all shall praise Jesus our Lord. That uncovering of the glory of Christ is the *Apocalypsis*, the unveiling of things God has given unto Him. This unveiling is both of His deity and of His humanity. Twenty-eight times He is called "The Lamb of God," a reference to His humanity, but many times He is worshiped in heaven as God.

The Apocalypse is a book of prophecy. Four times it is called that (Revelation 1:3; 22:10, 18, 19). In Revelation 1:3, it is written: "Blessed is he that readeth, and they that hear the words of this prophecy." There are seven beatitudes in the Book of the Revelation and this is the first one: "Blessed is he that readeth and they that hear the words." The book was written to be read publicly in the churches of the Lord. "Blessed is he that readeth." There is a blessing for the minister who reads it aloud before the congregation. There is also a blessing for those who hear the words of the prophecy. In the Old Testament there are many books of prophecy. The New Testament has one volume of prophecy and that is the Revelation. It comprises God's answer to the questions of the ages. For two millenniums God's people have prayed, "Thy kingdom come, thy will be done, on earth as it is in heaven." Is that prayer never to be answered? We petition, "Thy kingdom come," but there is no kingdom coming yet. We ask, "Thy will be done" but God's will is not done on this earth as yet. Consider the great promise of our Lord, "And if I go away I will come again." Is that promise never to be fulfilled? This book of prophecy is God's answer to that tremendous prayer of His people, "Thy kingdom come," and to the great promise of our Lord, "And if I go away I will come again." The book is the unveiling, the open vision of the coming of our incomparable and triumphant Christ.

The vision follows an outline given to us in the book itself. There are many effective, manmade outlines of the Revelation, but God's outline under three great Roman numerals is stated in Revelation 1:19. "Write," said the Lord to John, "write [Roman numeral one] the things which thou hast seen, and [Roman numeral two] the things which are, and [Roman numeral three] the things which shall be [*meta tauta*] after these things." John then took his pen and wrote according to the inspiration of the Holy Spirit. Roman numeral one, "Write the things which thou hast seen," and he wrote down the vision that he had seen, the vision of our glorified Lord recorded in the first chapter of the Revelation. Then, Roman numeral two, "and the things which are." John belonged to the same dispensation of grace in which we live, the era of the churches. "The things which are" are the things of the churches. So John wrote down under Roman numeral two the things which are, the course of the churches. There is an Ephesian period in the Church, the days of the apostles. There is a Smyrnan period in the life of the Church, the days of the martyrs when they laid down their lives under the iron heel of the Roman Empire. There are Pergamian days in the Church when the Church was married to the State. There is a Thyatirian period in the Church when the Church was dressed in purple with a gold chain around her neck, bedecked as the woman Jezebel. Notice that the Church is always referred to as a "she." You never refer to a Church as a "he." A Church is a "she" because in the symbolism of the Bible she is the bride of Christ. But in Thyatira there is a harlot named Jezebel ruling the apostate church. She is dressed in purple, living in luxury, supported by the political systems of the world. There is a Sardian period of the Church wherein are such great names as Martin Luther, John Wesley, John Knox, John Calvin, Balthazar Hubmaier, Felix Mantz, calling the people back to the true faith. There is the Philadelphian period in the Church, the Church of the wide open door, the Church of the great missionary movements seeking to bring the name of Jesus to the whole earth. Then, finally, there is the Laodicean period of the Church when the doors have been closed.

The reason I think we are entering the Laodicean period of the Church is this: the Philadelphian era of the open door is beginning to close. When I was a boy we could send missionaries anywhere on this earth. We could send them to China, to Russia, to Yugoslavia, to Poland, to Cuba. But now a vast portion of the population of this earth is apparently shut out forever, unless there is an intervention of God. Nation after nation is closed to the preaching of the Gospel and to the sending out of missionaries. The Philadelphian era is beginning to close and the Laodicean period of the Church is beginning.

There is apostasy everywhere: in the chairs of theology, in the pulpits, in the unconcern and indifference of the people. The Lord's Day is become like any other day. The great commandments and teachings of our Saviour are beginning to be looked upon as those of any other philosopher, his mind being the product of his own times. To most of the world today religion is altogether optional. If a man wants to go to church, it is his business. If a man wants to join the country club, that is his business. If he wants to be a member of a civic club, that is his business. The conception of the Church being the very fountain of life and the difference between hell and heaven is impossible to the average man of today. The very ideas of damnation are offensive to the modern, intellectual mind. There is no God of wrath, there is no God of judgment, there is no damnation, there is no fire of hell. The traditions of the Christian Church are looked upon as being part of the cultural life of a people and therefore still evolving. This is the Laodicean era of the Church. This is the day in which we live. The Apocalypse is a book of prophecy, outlining these great eras in the history of the Church. As described in Revelation 3:20, in the Laodicean era the Lord is standing on the outside. Our Lord says, "I stand at the door and knock; if any man hear my voice . . ."

But God has His own in every age. There are people devout and holy and there are churches who preach the truth in any age, in every age, in this age. May God bless this congregation and every congregation that seeks to be faithful to the true message of the Revelation of our Lord.

We come now to Roman numeral three. "Write," said the Lord, "what thou hast seen [and John wrote down the vision of the blessed Jesus], the things which are [and he wrote of the church age] and the things which shall be [*meta tauta*] after these things." When we come to Revelation 4:1, we find that "*meta tauta*": "After this I looked, and behold, a door was opened in heaven: and the first voice which I heard was as it were of a trumpet talking with me; which said, Come up hither, and I will shew thee things which must be hereafter [*meta tauta*]." Revelation 3 closes the Church era. Revelation 4 marks the opening of the vista that lies beyond the rapture of God's people. Roman numeral three, "*meta tauta*," "after these things," describes events after the churches disappear. They are seen no longer here in the earth. The bride of Christ is in heaven.

In Revelation 19 the bride of Christ, after her marriage to the Lamb and after the marriage supper of the Lamb, is seen coming in glory with her triumphant Lord. How did the people of the Church get up there? They were taken up. The old Anglo-Saxon word is "raptured." They were "snatched away" up into glory. "I will shew you a mystery. We shall not all sleep," said Paul, "but we shall all be changed. In a moment, in the twinkling of an eye, at the last trump. For the trumpet shall sound and the dead shall be raised incorruptible, and we shall all be changed. For the Lord himself shall descend from heaven with a shout, with the voice of the archangel, with the trumpet of God. And the dead in Christ shall rise first and we who are alive and remain shall be caught up together with him in the clouds to meet the Lord in the air and we shall be forever then with our Lord." (See I Corinthians 15:31-52; I Thessalonians 4:16, 17.) The symbol and the sign of that rapture in the Revelation is the transporting of John in Revelation 4:2. John is taken up into heaven and there he sees the raptured Church of our blessed Lord. He sees the throne and around the throne the four and twenty-elders, twelve patriarchal elders representing the Old Covenant and twelve apostolic elders representing the saved of the New Covenant. They are all there with their Lord in glory.

After the removal (the rapture) of the Church, what of this earth and what of those left here? These chapters that follow in the third great division of the Revelation (chapters 4-19) are by the Spirit of God a revelation, a disclosure of the days spoken of by our Lord in the apocalyptic discourse in Matthew 24:21: "For then," said our Lord, "shall be great tribulation, such as was not since the beginning of the world . . .

or ever shall be." Immediately after the Tribulation, said our Lord, shall appear the sign of the Son of Man in heaven, coming in clouds of heaven with power and great glory (Matthew 28:29, 30). In keeping with these disclosures of our Saviour, Revelation 4:19 is the depiction of that terrible time called Jacob's trouble, the Day of the Lord, or the wrath of the Almighty. This is the day of Tribulation. God's people are taken out, and the Lord deals with this earth in its blasphemy, rejection and unbelief. Chapter 4 to chapter 19 of the Revelation is the vision of those awesome days before Christ comes. The text of the whole book is truly Revelation 1:7, "Behold, he cometh with clouds; and every eye shall see him, and they also which pierced him: and all kindreds of the earth shall wail because of him." Oh, these days of judgment when God deals with a gainsaying and rejecting earth!

Chapters 4 and 5 of the Apocalypse prepare us for the Book of Redemption placed in the blessed hands of our Lord. Chapter 6 describes the first six seals. Chapter 7 recounts the sealing of God's witnesses, twelve thousand from each one of the tribes of Israel. Chapter 8 records the opening of the seventh seal and the blowing of the first four trumpets. Chapter 9 describes the sounding of the fifth and sixth trumpets. Chapter 10 follows the story of the Little Book given to John that he might understand the bitter judgments of God upon the unbelieving. Chapter 11 records the two great witnesses of the Lord and, finally, the blowing of the last, the seventh trumpet. This takes us up to the great climax of the age when Jesus comes and the kingdom of this world is become the kingdom of our Lord and of His Christ and He reigns forever and ever. The great climax of the coming of our Lord and the establishment of the kingdom is seen in chapter 11 of the Book of the Revelation.

But God has much more to reveal to His people. Beginning with chapter 12, God gives us a review of the great personages in that final denouement. There is the woman who gave birth to the man child who is to rule the earth with a rod of iron. The woman is Israel who gave birth to the Saviour, the Christ, the Son of God. And there is the devil, that old dragon, ready to destroy the Lord and His people. There is

Michael, who stands up for God's people against Satan. After Michael's victorious war in heaven, Satan is flung down to earth like that golden censer with its fire blazing and burning. Thus in thunder and lightning the judgments of God fall in the final days of the earth. In chapter 13 of the Revelation there is the disclosure of the two final earth systems, the political system headed up by one beast and the religious system headed up in a false prophet, a second beast.

Chapter 14 brings to view God's people who are saved in those awesome days of tribulation. Is not that an amazing disclosure, that in the days of severest judgment, this earth witnesses the greatest revival the world has ever seen? That is always true. When things are dark and when God's people seem to be cursed, then God does something great and we call it revival. In the beginning days of the Tribulation God sealed a hundred and forty-four thousand, and in chapter 14 of the Revelation there are saved, not a hundred and forty-three thousand nine hundred and ninety-nine, but one hundred and forty-four thousand. None of God's elect is lost. Not one. Then in the same chapter 14 is the great revelation of the harvest of the earth and the vintage of the earth.

Chapters 15 and 16 are the pouring out of the last vials of wrath. Chapter 17 describes the judgment upon that false religious system called Jezebel, called that old whore, who lives in a city of seven hills. Is not that revelation a remarkable thing? Notice that God does not destroy her. The political powers of the earth destroy her. The kings and the princes, the presidents and the rulers of the earth say, "We have borne that whore these years and these centuries and we are tired of her pretenses." They destroy her with her gold and her purple robe and her chains around her neck encrusted with all kinds of precious stones. Is it not a strange thing how the political life of the day destroys that final system of religion?

Chapter 18 is the judgment of God upon men who worship mammon. Chapter 19 of the Revelation is the coming of Christ. In the midst of a fearful battle called the Battle of Armageddon, when it looks as though men will destroy one another in their blasphemy, hatred and unbelief, in the midst of those horrible wars, the heavens open and the Lord comes with His people, openly and publicly. "Behold, the Lord cometh with ten thousands of his saints" (Jude 14). "Behold, he cometh with clouds; and every eye shall see him, and they also which pierced him" (Revelation 1:7). Even those who crucified the Saviour will be forced to confront the Lord in His day of triumph. Is not that an amazing thing? John saw Jesus die. John saw the hard looks of those who crucified Him and John says that when He comes those who nailed Him to the tree and those who delivered Him to death will be forced to see Him face to face, and the unbelievers in this earth will wail and cry because of Him. But oh, the triumph of God's people! Chapter 20 of the Revelation is the binding of Satan and the millennium days. Satan is loosed for a season, after which finally arrives the judgment of the wicked dead.

We now look upon the new creation. There is a new heaven and a new earth. There is no more sadness, no more crying, no more tears, no more sorrow and no more death. The Lord comes and reigns with His own, with us, forever and ever and ever.

> I hear the sob of the parted,
> The wail of the broken-hearted,
> The sigh for the loved departed
> In the surging roar of a town.
>
> But it is, oh, for the joy of the morning,
> The light and the song of the morning,
> There'll be joy in the glorious morning,
> When the King comes for His own.
>
> Now let our hearts be true, brothers,
> To suffer and to do, brothers,
> There'll be a song for you, brothers,
> When the battle is fought and won.
>
> It won't seem long in the morning,
> In the light and song of the morning.
> There'll be joy in the triumphant morning,
> When the King comes for His own.
>
> Arise and be of good cheer, brothers,
> The day will soon be here, brothers,
> The victory is near, brothers,
> And the sound of the glad, "Well done."
>
> There'll be no sad hearts in the morning,
> No tears will start in the morning,
> There'll be joy in the victorious morning,
> When the King comes for His own.

And that leads us to the last, the glorious and the incomparable message of the next chapter. "He which testifieth these things saith, Surely I come quickly." The answering prayer of the true child of God is always, "Even so, let it be. Amen. Come, Lord Jesus." If I know my heart, if I know my soul, I am ready. Come, precious Saviour. It is a day of terror and trembling for those who spurn His mercy. It is a day of triumph and glory to those who lift up their faces in love and adoration, in reverence and expectation for the return of our blessed Lord.

CHAPTER 16

THE LAST PROMISE

Revelation 22

20 He which testifieth these things saith, Surely I come quickly. Amen. Even so, come, Lord Jesus.
21 The grace of our Lord Jesus Christ be with you all. Amen.

This is a day that means more to me as a preacher than any I have ever known. Eighteen years ago when I began preaching through the Bible the prophecy was made that I would lose my congregation. Many said that people will not come to hear just the Bible; their ears must be tickled with fancies of the passing fashion and scene. They said that to commit oneself to preach just the Bible, the whole Word of God, the Old Testament, the minor prophets, the small and general epistles, would be to lose the interest of the congregation. But this series of sermons has been sustained for almost two decades. The joy that has come to my heart in standing here this Lord's Day is inexpressible. This is one of the largest church auditoriums in America and for years our people have filled it three times every Sunday. Coming to hear what? The latest fancy, fad, notion, theory? Not at all nor ever at all, but coming to listen to a man open the Bible and expound the words of the living God. The personal joy that I feel in this hour is beyond description, nor could I say in sentence and in word the depth of the riches I have discovered in the holy Word of God during these last and several years. We have been in the ocean of God's unfathomable, illimitable depths, finding pearls and jewels. And for all of the few that we have found and discussed, there are ten thousand others equally as glorious and great lying there waiting to be seen by the eyes of men and to be enjoyed by the hearts and souls of His people.

We have now come to the end of the Revelation and to the end of the Bible. Our text, these last and closing verses, closes the canon of the Holy Scriptures. Revelation 22:20, 21: "He which testifieth these things saith, Surely I come quickly. Amen. Even so, come, Lord Jesus. The grace of our Lord Jesus Christ be with you all. Amen." And the Book is closed. There are no more prophets to proclaim the mind of God. There are no more apostles to write with infallible authority. There are no more instructions and mandates from heaven. The visions recorded here reach to the end of time and into the eternity of eternities. They encompass all history, all ages and all dispensations. There is one great remaining event and that is the *parousia*, the presence, the descent, the coming, the return of our Lord God from heaven.

In this text is the last time Christ's voice is heard on earth. The next time we hear the voice of the Son of Man it will be when He descends in glory with a shout, with a voice of the archangel and with the trump of God. This last and concluding sentence, these last verses that close the Canon of the Holy Scriptures, are so full of the truth of God, as though the Holy Spirit did sum up in these few words the whole revelation and testimony of the Lord through the ages. First, the certainty of His coming. Second, the last words of a man, the affirmation, the last prayer that fell from the lips of a human being. And third and last, the last benedictory remembrance of the love and grace of the Lord Jesus upon His people.

"He which testifieth these things saith, Surely I come quickly." This is an avowal of the certainty of our Lord's return. This has been the text and the theme of the Apocalypse, as seen in Revelation 1:7: "Behold, he cometh with clouds; and every eye shall see him." In the epilogue that closes the Apocalypse, three times does the Lord Himself make that sublime and exalted announcement. In Revelation 22:7: "Behold, I come quickly." In Revelation 22:12: "Behold, I come quickly." And in verse 20: "He which testifieth these things saith, Surely I come quickly."

The Bible opens with a promise of a coming Lord. The Holy Spirit closes the Scriptures with a promise of the coming again of our Lord. In the Book of Genesis, in 3:15, God said to the serpent, the devil, the dragon that has brought heartache and tears, that sowed this earth with death and sorrow, the Lord said to that serpent, "And I will put enmity between thee and the woman, and between thy seed and her seed; it shall bruise thy head, and thou shalt bruise his heel." In this mighty prophecy, according to Romans 16:20, there are two comings promised by the Lord God. The first coming of our Lord saw Satan bruise our Saviour, "Thou shalt bruise his heel." The Lord was crucified in ignominy, in shame, in sorrow, in tears and agony. His life and blood were poured out because of our sins. "Thou shalt bruise his heel." But there is another part to that first promise. There is a day coming, the Lord avows, when the Christ of heaven shall crush Satan's head, when God shall reign over His people in triumph, when righteousness shall fill the earth as the waters cover the sea. The Lord in His personal glory shall reign over His own redeemed people. There are two comings in that first Genesis promise. The Bible opens with that prophecy and the Bible closes with that same promise.

First, the Saviour is to come that He might be crushed, bruised, crucified and made an offering for sin. He is to come to die as the Redeemer for the souls of men. After God made that promise in Eden, hundreds of years passed, millenniums passed, and the Lord did not come. When finally He did arrive He came unto His own and His own received Him not. He was in the world and the world was made by Him and the world knew Him not. The thousands of humanity had forgotten the promise or else they scoffed at its fulfillment. When finally announcement came that He had arrived, the learned scribes pointed out the place where He was to be born but never took the time to journey the five miles from Jerusalem to Bethlehem to welcome this promised Saviour of the world. But however long he delayed and however men forgot and scoffed and however few of a faithful band waited for the consolation of Israel, as old Simeon, yet He came. In keeping with the holy, faithful promise of God, the Lord Jesus came. It is thus in the text that God speaks in closing His Bible, "Surely I come quickly." Here a second time, however infidels may scoff and however others may reject and however the centuries may grow into the millenniums, this is the immutable Word and promise of the Lord God, "Surely, I come."

It is interesting to see the first time God uses that word "surely." In chapter 2 of the Book of Genesis, the Lord said to Adam and to Eve, "That tree, interdicted and forbidden, thou shalt not eat of it for in the day that thou eatest thereof thou shalt *surely* die." This is the first time God uses that word "surely." It is also interesting to see the second time that word "surely" is used: "And the serpent [the subtle Satan] said unto the woman, Yea, did God say thou shalt *surely* die?" Then Satan tells the first lie, "Ye shall *not surely* die." The denial of the Word of God is always the beginning of a fall. "Surely, surely, thou shalt die," says the Lord God. But Satan says, "Yea, did God say such a thing?" "Ye shall *not* surely die," answered Satan. Whatever that "surely" meant, when God first said it, is what that "surely" means when God last uses it. "In the day that thou eatest thereof, thou shalt *surely* die." And when Adam partook of that forbidden fruit, that day his soul died. And in a day of the Lord's calendar (II Peter 3:8), which is a thousand years, Adam's body died. Did you ever notice that in these long records of the longevity of men, there has never been a man yet that outlived that thousand-year day of the Lord? Adam died when he was 930 years of age. "In the day that thou eatest thereof thou shalt surely die." Every grave cut into this earth, every tear unbidden that falls on the ground, every heartache, every pain, every sorrow, every despair is an exclamation point after God's "surely, surely thou shalt die."

But there is a second "surely." There is another part to that promise. There is another side to that awful curse of death and despair. The Saviour is coming. He is coming. He shall come who shall bruise Satan's head and crush out his life of evil forever. There is a Redeemer coming, there is a Saviour coming. One of the most interesting of all the passages in the Hebrew text of the Old Testament is this one: "And Adam knew Eve his wife; and she conceived, and bare Cain, and said, I have gotten a man from the Lord." That is the way it is translated in the King James Version, out of which I always preach. But in the Hebrew text there is revealed a startling and an amazing thing on the part of Eve as she remembered

God's promise of a coming Redeemer. When she bare Cain she said: "Cainithi ish eth-Jehovah," which literally means: "I have gotten a man even the Lord Jehovah." When that child was placed in the bosom of Eve she thought he was the answer to the promise from the Lord. She thought the Deliverer had come. She thought Christ had come, the final, the ultimate, the glorious Redeemer. She thought Him to be Cain. She was mistaken, we know, but the promise, the hope and the expectancy of that coming Lord never died in the earth or in the hearts of men.

In Jude 14, Jude says: "And Enoch also, the seventh from Adam, prophesied . . . Behold, the Lord cometh with ten thousands of his saints." In later years Job, sitting on an ash heap in despair and in agony with sores covering his body, cried, "I know that my Redeemer liveth, and that he shall stand at the latter day upon the earth. And though after my skin worms destroy this body, yet in my flesh shall I see God: Whom I shall see for myself, and mine eyes shall behold" (Job 19:25-27). Still later, David lifted up his voice and sang in Psalm 24: "Lift up your heads, O ye gates; and be ye lift up, ye everlasting doors; and the King of glory shall come in." Centuries later, Isaiah prophesied: "There shall come forth a rod out of the stem of Jesse, and a Branch shall go forth out of his roots. And with his mouth shall he smite the earth, and with the breath of his lips shall he slay the wicked. And the wolf shall lie down with the lamb, and the leopard shall lie down with the kid, and the earth shall be filled with the knowledge of the Lord, when he cometh." (See Isaiah 11:1-9.) Many, many years later Daniel prophesied: "I saw in the night visions, and, behold, one like the Son of man came with the clouds of heaven . . . . And there was given him dominion and glory" (Daniel 7:13, 14). And Zechariah prophesied: "And his feet shall stand in that day upon the Mount of Olives . . . but it shall come to pass, that at evening time it shall be light" (Zechariah 14:4, 7). And Malachi closed the Canon of the Old Covenant with the promise: "But unto you that fear my name shall the Sun of righteousness arise with healing in his wings" (Malachi 4:2).

That same holy expectancy is found throughout the pages and the books and the letters and the gospels of the New Covenant. Our Lord said, "If I go . . . I will come again" (John 14:3). The angels in heaven said, "This same Jesus, which is taken up from you into heaven, shall so come in like manner" (Acts 1:11). The Apostle Paul wrote, saying, "Our conversation, our citizenship, is in heaven from whence we expect, we look for the great God our glorious Saviour, the Lord Jesus Christ." (See Philippians 3:20.) The author of the Book of Hebrews said, "And unto them that look for him shall he appear the second time without sin unto salvation" (Hebrews 9:28). And the great Seer, the Apostle John wrote the Revelation around this text, "Behold, he cometh with clouds; and every eye shall see him" (Revelation 1:7). The receding ages echo the glorious promise, "He is coming! He is coming!" The surging billows of the restless seas cry, "He is coming! He is coming!" The riverlets and the water-brooks down a thousand hillsides sing, "He is coming! He is coming!" The angels in glory and the Church of the redeemed, shout and say, "He is coming! He is coming!" And the saints of the ages and the voice of the Church with whom we mingle our words of love and adoration repeat the same refrain, "He is coming! He is coming!" "Surely, surely, I come quickly."

Who is this "I" in the text, "Surely, *I* come quickly"? Whom are we to expect? Who is descending from heaven? Many of the spiritualizers and commentators who read this book say the Lord came in A.D. 70 at the destruction of Jerusalem. That is the coming of the Lord. Some say the Lord came at the conversion of Constantine. That is identified as the coming of the Lord. Some say the Lord comes in the diffusion of the gospel message of Christ over the earth. That is the coming of the Lord. Some say the Lord comes in culture and in civilization. Some say the Lord is coming in these fantastic, scientific breakthroughs that we achieve today. These things that are said and these identifications which are made make all the more pertinent the question, Who is this "I" in "Surely *I* come quickly"?

In John 14 Jesus said, "I go to prepare a place for you. And if I go and prepare a place for you, I will come again, and receive you unto myself; that where I am, there ye may be also." Who is that "I"? What did the Lord mean when He told the disciples that if He went away He would come again? Did He mean He would return at the conversion of the Emperor Constantine? Did He mean He would come again in the diffusion of the gospel message in the earth? Did He mean He would come again in the advancement of civilization and in scientific breakthroughs? Is that the "I" we are expecting? Oh, no! "Surely *I* come quickly." Who is that "*I*" we are expecting? For whom are we looking? Let the angel answer: "Ye men of Galilee, why stand ye gazing up into heaven? this same Jesus, which is taken up from you into heaven, shall so come in like manner." We are looking for the same Lord Jesus. Let the Apostle Paul answer: "For the Lord *himself* shall descend from heaven." "Surely *I* come quickly." Who is that "*I*"? It is the blessed, blessed appearance and presence of our Saviour, the Lord Jesus. It is Jesus Himself we long to see. So wrote the blind poet Fanny Crosby:

> When my life work is ended, and I cross the swelling tide,
> When the bright and glorious morning I shall see;
> I shall know my Redeemer when I reach the other side,
> And His smile will be the first to welcome me.
>
> Oh, the soul-thrilling rapture when I view His blessed face,
> And the luster of His kindly, beaming eye;
> How my full heart will praise Him for the mercy, love and grace,
> That prepares for me a mansion in the sky.
>
> Thro' the gates to the city in a robe of spotless white,
> He will lead me where no tears will ever fall;
> In the glad song of ages I shall mingle with delight;
> But I long to meet my Saviour first of all.

"Surely, I come quickly." Quickly, quickly. Ah, Lord, two thousand years have passed and there has been no answer to that promise, "Surely, I come quickly." *Tachu* is the word in Greek and it means in English, "quickly." Lord, what is "quickly"? The Lord answers in II Peter 3:8: "With the Lord . . . a thousand years [is] as a day." By God's calendar our Lord went away day before yesterday. And before the third day He may come, any moment, any time. "Surely, I come quickly."

It is hard for us finite creatures of the dust and of time to realize that there is no such thing as "time" with God. The past, the present, the future are all alike to God. He sees the beginning, He sees the end, He sees the present; all are alike to Him. Time is a creation like matter, and to the timeless One these days are as nothing. Even to us the coming of the Lord is near, as near as the length of our life away. In Cairo I saw a mummy embalmed three thousand years before Christ. That long ago they wrapped him in those clothes. If he were to awaken now, those centuries would be as a watch in the night. There is no time in eternity or with God. We are as near to it in our own personal selves as between now and the time our eyes close in death.

We must remember that God's prophecies are seldom given with a notation of time. God's prophecies are like our seeing a mountain range. To us at a vast distance the peaks are all side by side. Actually there may be vast distances between them. It is as our looking up into the firmament of the sky. The stars all seem equidistant in the blue chalice of the sky, but actually they are billions of light years apart. So it is with God's prophecies. There is no time with our Lord. He has been away almost two days. He may come back at the dawning of a third. "Surely, I come."

God intends a spiritual discipline in this uncertainty of the time of our Lord returning. There is a reason. God would have His people know the *certainty* of His coming, but the *uncertainty* of the time creates in every generation, in every household of faith, in every church that names the name of Jesus, a spiritual watchfulness and preparedness. He may come today, He may come at twilight, He may come at the midnight watch, He may come at the dawning of the morning. Watch, remember, and pray, for "Surely, I come quickly."

The answering prayer and benediction of the holy apostle who listened to this last promise spoken by our Saviour, was, "Amen, even so, come, Lord Jesus." These are the last words of a man recorded in the Bible. Do you remember the first words spoken of a man recorded in the Bible. The record states that when the Lord came into the garden in the cool of the day and could not find the man, that He raised His voice and asked: "Adam, Adam, where art thou?" And Adam replied, "Lord, I heard Thy voice and I was afraid for I am naked and I hid myself in the trees of the garden." The first time the man's voice is heard is to express fear and shame. When is the last time the voice of a man is heard? It is the precious expectancy. "Even so, come, Lord Jesus." Our nakedness is covered with the blood of the Lamb. Our sins are washed away in the Atonement of the crucified One. Our names are written in the Lamb's Book of Life. Waiting, we expectantly cry with the great Seer, "Even so, come, Lord Jesus." There are no more fears, no more dread, no more crying. "Even so, come, Lord Jesus."

And now the final benediction: "The grace of our Lord Jesus Christ be with you all. Amen." Do you remember the last verse of the Old Covenant, of the Old Testament Scriptures? The last verse of chapter 4 of Malachi reads: "Lest I come and smite the earth with a curse." The Old Covenant never gets beyond that curse. "Cursed," it says, "is every one that keepeth not the words of this law." The Old Testament closes with the dreadful words, "Lest I come and smite the earth with a curse." But there is another Covenant, there is another Testament, there is another Word. It is the sweet grace of our blessed Lord. John writes, "The favor and the remembrance of the precious Lord Jesus be with you all, Amen, Amen." As the Book of Hebrews so eloquently describes: "For ye are not come unto the mount that might be touched, and that burned with fire, nor unto blackness, and darkness, and tempest, And the sound of a trumpet, and the voice of words; which voice they that heard intreated that the word should not be spoken to them any more: (For they could not endure that which was commanded, And if so much as a beast touch the mountain, it shall be stoned, or thrust through with a dart: And so terrible was the sight, that Moses said, I exceedingly fear and quake:) But ye are come unto mount Sion, and unto the city of the living God, the heavenly Jerusalem, and to an innumerable company of angels, To the general assembly and church of the firstborn, which are written in heaven, and to God the Judge of all, and to the spirits of just men made perfect, And to Jesus the mediator of the new covenant, and to the blood of sprinkling, that speaketh better things than that of Abel" (Hebrews 12:18-24).

"The grace of our Lord Jesus be with you all. Amen."

"For I am persuaded, that neither death, nor life, nor angels, nor principalities, nor powers, nor things present, nor things to come, Nor height, nor depth, nor any other creature, shall be able to separate us from the love of God, which is in Christ Jesus our Lord" (Romans 8:38, 39). Thus the Canon is closed and the Apocalypse is finished and God's people gathered in His churches lift up their faces awaiting the day of their final triumph and ultimate redemption. "Even so, come, Lord Jesus." We rejoice in the words of the unknown poet who wrote:

> My soul crieth out for a jubilee song!
> There is joy in my heart, let me praise with my tongue.
> For I know, though the darkness of Egypt still lowers,
> That the time ere release is not ages but hours.
>
> As sailors not yet within sight of the strand
> Know well their approach by the "loom of the land."
> So they who will bend but a listening ear
> Can now catch the whisper that tells He is near.
>
> He is near — the stars in their courses prepare
> To utter the sign He hath bid them declare.
> The world in its guilt is haggard and grim,
> And its cup of iniquity fills to the brim.
>
> And thither to gather the tribes have begun;
> From the east and the west, from the climes of the sun,
> In a land, still despised, but preparing e'er now
> For the feet that shall stand upon Olivet's brow.
>
> The world as of yore, naught of all doth divine —
> Saith again that believers are filled with new wine —
> Suffers warning to pass all unseen and unheard,
> And, like Herod, fulfills while opposing God's Word.
>
> Then welcome, thrice welcome, ye tokens of God!
> What else but His coming can comfort afford?
> What presence but His set this prisoned earth free?
> O Star of the morning, our hope is in Thee!

Even so, come, Lord Jesus!